THE NEW
SOUTHERN POLITICS

THE NEW

SOUTHERN

POLITICS

J. DAVID WOODARD

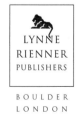

LYNNE
RIENNER
PUBLISHERS

BOULDER
LONDON

Published in the United States of America in 2006 by
Lynne Rienner Publishers, Inc.
1800 30th Street, Boulder, Colorado 80301
www.rienner.com

and in the United Kingdom by
Lynne Rienner Publishers, Inc.
3 Henrietta Street, Covent Garden, London WC2E 8LU

Library of Congress Cataloging-in-Publication Data
Woodard, J. David.
   The new southern politics / J. David Woodard.
   Includes bibliographical references.
   ISBN 1-58826-373-8 (hardcover: alk. paper)
   ISBN 1-58826-397-5 (pbk.: alk. paper)
   1. Southern States—Politics and government—1951– 2. Southern
States—Politics and government—21st century. 3. Political
culture—Southern States. I. Title.
JK2683.W66 2006
320.975—dc22

                                                  2005031030

British Cataloguing in Publication Data
A Cataloguing in Publication record for this book
is available from the British Library.

Printed and bound in the United States of America

      The paper used in this publication meets the requirements
 ∞   of the American National Standard for Permanence of
      Paper for Printed Library Materials Z39.48-1992.

   5   4   3   2   1

Contents

Illustrations

Tables

Preface

This book had its beginnings in the weeks before the South Carolina GOP presidential primary in March of 2000. A number of reporters called to ask questions about the patterns of partisanship in the state. I wished at the time that there was a book showing county allegiance in a state-by-state analysis, as well as the general electoral trends across the South. In 2002 I attended the biennial Citadel Symposium of Southern Politics, where Don Fowler of the Democratic National Committee gave a down-to-earth explanation of southern voting trends. On the way home from the conference I concluded it would be a good time to write a book that answered many of the questions asked about southern politics in the years around the millennial election.

This work has a distinct historical and cultural flavor. Present-day politics are best understood as a play acted out on a stage decades in the making. The approach owes much to work in the field of comparative politics on the effects of political culture, the original analysis by V. O. Key, and subsequent insights provided by Earl and Merle Black. The chapters here are thematic, and include state and county-by-county analysis when appropriate. The examination of county loyalty is the familiar "targeting" for partisanship used by political consultants prior to any election.

The Ranney Index of party competition was expanded to include federal elections and give a summary measure of political partisanship in each state. I confess that much of the inspiration for this book came from my experience as a political consultant examining county election data showing urbanization and partisanship in congressional districts in South Carolina. I thank Bob Inglis, Lindsey Graham, Jim DeMint, and Gresham Barrett for allowing me to learn at their expense. The original election methodology was expanded to include all eleven southern states. My colleague at Clemson University, Bruce Ransom, provided expertise on racial politics and state legislatures to assist my writing of those chapters. Ideas in Chapter 1 of this book were first presented at the Citadel Symposium on Southern

Politics in 2002. The original effort owes much to the work of graduate student Rob Carey, who worked tirelessly on the maps in this book. Portions of the first chapter were published in a volume after the 2002 Citadel Conference.

Jerry Trapnell, dean of the College of Business and Behavioral Sciences at Clemson University, and Robert Becker, director of the Strom Thurmond Institute at Clemson, provided financial support for travel and research on the project. Priscilla Munson, of the Clemson University Library, was especially helpful. A number of undergraduate students—Cindy Pettitt Barrios, Nathan Ilderton, Andrew Mathias, Megan Barnes, Amy Bruce, Rebecca Steadings, April Sutton, and Jenny Dunaway—assisted in the research. My class on southern politics at Clemson University in the spring of 2001 helped on the original version of the manuscript. Our secretary in the Department of Political Science at Clemson University, Angie Guido, worked on the production of various tables and other data.

I profited from the resources in the Special Collections Room of the Jean and Alexander Heard Library at Vanderbilt University. The experience of reading Alexander Heard's notes more than fifty-five years after the fact is something only a lover of southern politics can appreciate.[1] Anonymous reviewers greatly improved the manuscript. One draft was finished with the assistance of my mother, June Woodard, and in-laws, Jim and Mildred Wyatt, who read and critiqued various chapters. My debts to these people go far beyond this book, but I would like to thank them for yet another kindness. Despite this assistance, all errors and omissions in this work are mine alone.

I dedicate this book to Gary Thompson, a teacher at Abilene Christian University, who opened Clifton McCleskey's book on Texas politics thirty years ago and began to explain the relationship between the oil depletion allowance and the Texas Railroad Commission as an introduction to how politics worked. I've been fascinated ever since.

In 2003–2004 I benefited from a sabbatical year at Vanderbilt University, where I conducted interviews and used valuable library resources to enhance the manuscript. Larry Romans, Paula Covington, and Gretchen Dodge, along with a host of other research librarians, were helpful in ready reference at the Heard Library, the law school, and Owen Graduate School facilities on campus. The staff of the Department of Political Science at Vanderbilt patiently answered questions and assisted me during my year's visit. Brad Palmquist opened his seminar on southern politics to me, and his students were diligent in their critiques of chapters in this book. I enjoyed discussing politics with Neal Tate, the department head, who—like myself—is a former Texan, full of stories.

Lynne Rienner Publishers was a gracious host for this project. I especially appreciate Leanne Anderson and Steve Barr, who together patiently endured endless questions and assisted with suggestions on how to improve the book. Lynne Rienner herself was a patient leader, and her unrelenting push for perfection did much to inspire me.

The greatest debt goes as always to my wife, Judy, who was a tireless editor, patient listener, and assistant in producing this book.

—*J. David Woodard*

Note

1. The Heard family required that names and titles be omitted from any citations in the interviews used as a basis for Key's *Southern Politics*. The only reference to these interviews in this book is by state.

Memory believes before knowing remembers.
— *William Faulkner,* Light in August

1

Southern Politics in the Twenty-First Century

The South remains the most distinctive part of the nation because in so many ways life there has always been a contradiction of American values and ideals. When John Winthrop wrote in 1630 that settlers in New England should see themselves as a "modell (sic) of Christian charity . . . a City set upon a Hill," Virginia had been importing Africans and enslaving them for eleven years.[1] When Abraham Lincoln asked for national unity after his election in 1860, he was met by the secession of southern states. When Franklin Roosevelt said he saw one-third of the nation, "ill-housed, ill-clad, ill-nourished," in 1936, he was describing every state south of the Mason-Dixon Line.[2] Finally, when Martin Luther King Jr. spoke of his dream of racial equality, that one day "the rough places will be made plain, and the crooked places will be made straight" he named the states of Georgia, Alabama, and Mississippi in his speech.[3]

Today the South remains as much a contradiction as at any time in its past. Southerners know the best and worst of human qualities; their native land is a place where legend is history, and sometimes history is legend. The southern record is notorious for slavery, class consciousness, white supremacy, segregation, poverty, and isolation. Yet the region is also known for charity, family, manners, humor, religion, and some of the best political oratory ever to touch a voter's ear. "History, like God and nature," wrote the poet Donald Davidson, "has been both generous and unkind to . . . the South."[4]

At the beginning of the twenty-first century, despite dramatic economic growth, increased political power, and cultural acceptance, the region is as much an enigma as at any time in its past. The South has more churches per capita, and more of its residents attend church services regularly, than anywhere else in the country. It also leads the nation in annual surveys of gun violence, murder, and racial antipathy.[5] The South has a history of the best writers. Mark Twain once wrote that "Southerners talk music," but the region also has some of the worst public schools, and the lowest SAT scores in the nation.[6] Southern landowners were among the

1

wealthiest in the original colonies, but the region also has a history of dirt-grinding, enervating poverty. More than one hundred and forty years after General Robert E. Lee's surrender to end the Civil War, the public display of a Confederate flag still sparks political controversy, complete with sidewalk demonstrations and acrimonious debate in state legislatures. "I am the grandchild," wrote Texas novelist Katherine Porter who died in 1980, "of a lost war."[7]

US history was once synonymous with southern history. The founding of the United States was the vision of southern aristocrats; men like Madison, Jefferson, and Washington left their imprint on the character of the country's institutions. The aristocracy of the Old South was the embodiment of Aristotle's political animal, with an education auspicious for political leadership and a record of effective administration when called upon. Not surprisingly, Virginia spearheaded the American Revolution and gave the infant republic its early leadership.

As the southern aristocracy grew richer and more secure in the antebellum years, it found itself removed from the mainstream of citizens in the rest of the country. Elite leadership insulated the region from egalitarian ideals. The small farmer republic model of yeoman agrarians stood opposite genteel planters who defended slavery. Conflict was inevitable. The South reached the eve of the Civil War opposed to the secular spirit of science and the leveling spirit of democracy.

From the end of the Civil War in 1865 to 1976, the legacy of the South was a liability in political races outside the region. The record of white supremacy and slavery checked political ambition such that no southern politician could seriously challenge for the national office of president. Politicians who won the office, like Andrew Johnson and Lyndon Johnson, used the vice presidency as a stepping stone. "Southerners were the junior partners . . . not until 1912 did a southern politician . . . seriously attempt to win the Democratic presidential nomination."[8]

After Jimmy Carter won the White House in 1976, the southern past was rehabilitated for voters, and forgiven by the mainstream press. Televised softball games between the administration and the White House Press Corps in Plains, Georgia, made good public relations; the contests washed out the blemish of inferiority from one hundred years earlier. At the end of the twentieth century the memory of second-class political citizenship was receding when politicians from the South were the standard-bearers of both major political parties in the 2000 presidential election. In 2004 the presence of North Carolina senator John Edwards on the Democratic presidential ticket hinged in part on his ability to deliver electoral votes from his native South, something he failed to do.

Political Science and Political Culture

The irony of the millennial presidential elections was that a part of the country, historically outside the mainstream experience of US life, found itself critical in selecting leaders for the nation as a whole. The best way to understand this change of status in the South is to liken the region to a subset of the larger political culture.

The influence of culture in terms of ethnic identity, urbanization, and religion has been a guiding principle in political science since the time of the ancient Greeks and Hebrews. Aristotle looked not only to the culture of the state, but also to its potential of being directed to some end.[9] The idea of the "just regime" implied public action that was in agreement with the values and habits of its citizens. Similarly, Moses ruled the Israelites in accordance with divine law and instructed the citizens as to its precepts. The ancients regarded the formation of character and development of civic virtue as the fundamental responsibility of government.

The classical tradition was challenged in the sixteenth century when Niccolo Machiavelli abandoned culture and focused on the passions and behavior of egotistical human beings.[10] The new political science focused on changing circumstances to achieve peace and prosperity, as well as individual freedom and equality. Thomas Hobbes suggested that the fear of violent death was basic to all cultures. The social contract conceptualization of Hobbes, Locke, and Rousseau rendered culture and character superfluous, because the contracting humans were not political animals, but natural, precultural beasts. Later, Marxists damned culture and character as byproducts of the economic substructure. Their arguments were that political culture was the dead hand of the past that ignored the primary role economics played in political life.

In the 1950s scholars like Gabriel Almond and Bingham Powell responded that "political culture" was a better way of understanding political action than the mechanistic concepts of some Marxian material consciousness. Almond defined political culture as a "particular pattern of orientation to political action." The approach regarded politics as the "cognitions, preferences and evaluations or choices through the application of standards or values to the cognitive and effective components."[11] In other words, the orientation people collectively had to politics was based on transmitted patterns of conduct and their attachment to group symbols. This cultural orientation of a people determined their political orientation.

The concept of political culture explains a wide range of systematic differences in political behavior and structure in the southern states. For example, political culture research contends that people do not enter social contracts as separate individuals, but as culture-bearing beings and members of groups seeking to accommodate their interests with others. The persistence of traditional values in the South is an understood part of the cultural legacy. Political party realignment and economic development cannot be explained apart from the culture and ideology of the region. Again, in Aristotle's words, the principles of justice are to be tailored to the character and circumstances of a region's inhabitants.[12]

Political culture is the summation of ethnic settlement patterns, historical episodes, and persistent patterns of political attitudes and values. V. O. Key opened his book on southern politics by saying, "The South remains the region with the most distinctive character and tradition."[13] Elements of life such as heritage, religion, regional ethnicity, the timing and size of migrations to a place, and the settlement patterns once there, are all part of the character of the region. Another term for this is the political culture of the area. Contemporary US political culture reflects the values of the European people who settled the country hundreds of years ago. Settlers did not come with a blank cultural slate; they brought with them elements of life from their native lands. Gabriel Almond and Bingham Powell describe this development when they "refer to these special propensities located in particular groups as *subcultures* [my emphasis]," with different roles, substructures, and subsystems within a nation. "There may be traditions and attitudes, current in the different roles, structures and subsystems of the political system" but the area as a whole remains distinct.[14]

The history and values of the South make it a discrete subculture to the US experience. It is distinct in language, as when native president Jimmy Carter referred to Italians as "Eye-talians." It is distinct in race, having the nation's highest percentage black population. Southerners relate to each other the way Martin Luther King Jr. did to Lyndon Johnson when he addressed him as, "my fellow southerner." It is distinct in religion, and *Time* magazine recognized this when it said, "southerners are the most church-going people in the nation."[15] It is distinct in history, attitudes, and a host of other ways that make it a subculture of the larger national whole.

The southern political culture is a product of the land itself. The geography of the South is very different from Europe and the rest of the United States. The challenge of confronting the Appalachian wildness, the forests of the alluvial plain, and the starkness of the frontier made different demands on the political system than had been the case in civilized Europe. Settlers did not have the luxury of a social support system and had to face challenges alone. The verdant undergrowth of the South flourished in relentless summer heat and there was enough rainfall to sustain any crop. A dominant characteristic of southern political culture is a "rugged individualism" that emphasizes self-reliance as applied to economic and social relations.

Today, waves of change have washed over the South, smoothing off its hard edges while keeping the traditions of certain manners, emotions, and interests intact. A lost war, decades of poverty, a history of individualism and the systematic segregation of a major part of its population created a distinct subset of the national political culture. Certain values, cherished in the South, persisted over time, and their legacy is the subject of this book. The belief systems formed the meanings of cultural values and life patterns, and were transmitted, learned, and shared over time.[16]

Political culture refers to the attitudes and evaluations people have toward gov-

ernment. Here, too, the South remains unique. One-party politics, legislative governance, a distinct Christian rhetoric about values, colorful executives with flamboyant leadership styles, a preference for an elitist social system, and a popular resistance to centralized authority made southern politics extraordinary. These attitudes
and patterns of life are transmitted from generation to generation through political
socialization and participation.

A political subculture is not necessarily contained by geographic boundaries or
state borders. The South shares a unique culture, but within that whole are differen-
tiated parts that have a separate and more specific experience. Almond and Powell
say these "regional groups, or ethnic groups, or social classes which make up the
population of a political system may have special propensities or tendencies."[17]
There are differences within the South, and these dissimilar elements determine
political competition.

When V. O. Key compares two southern states by saying that, "The political distance from Virginia to Alabama must be measured in light years," he is talking about
subcultural values without using the word.[18] Another example of this subculture
analysis is illustrated by Key's detection of a pattern of party cleavage in western
North Carolina and eastern Tennessee of Republican strength in the mountain areas
of these otherwise Democratic states. The influence of culture, particularly ethnic
identity, migration, and heritage from the time of the Civil War reflecting different
sources of settlement explain these political differences. Today subcultural values
are primarily divided between urban and rural areas. What new patterns are in evidence with the migration to city living, with new minority groups, and with an interstate highway system that allows someone to commute from fifty miles away?

In a continuation of Key's analysis, patterns of rural land settlement influenced
rates of urbanization and economic growth. The strength and activity of local governments, the extent and quality of education, and the amount of voter participation
all make for a patchwork political culture across the South. Although all southern
states share a geohistorical past, they adapted to the twentieth century in different
ways. A variety of subcultures meant that the rates of economic, social, and political change varied from state to state, and within states as well. The "Byrd" machine
in Virginia produced a different political leader than the "Barnwell Ring" of South
Carolina, or the network of county judges in Alabama.

The concept of political culture has come under criticism, for including too
much and excluding too little.[19] While it does have some shortcomings, the term is
useful for explaining a wide range of differences in political behavior and the political structure of southern states. Political culture is a concept broad enough to
encompass a dispute over the Confederate symbol on the Georgia state flag, and at
the same time allow for specific measurement of the change in partisanship of a
single Georgia county. The political culture exerts its greatest influence by establishing a framework wherein individuals and groups may orient themselves for
political action.

The term "political culture" has several components, three of which are: (1) the appropriate role of government in the society, (2) the role of the individual in relation to the state, and (3) the evaluation of existing institutions and officeholders.[20] The pattern in the South was that tradition, habit, and elite leadership gave stability to society. As a result individual liberty was seen as more important than centralized government authority. While recent urbanization and a more uniform US culture weakened many of these distinctions, they remain in force when it comes to politics. There was some overlap of these values with other regions of the country, but the minimalist views on the role of government and rampant individualism remain as relevant attitudes of the South that make it different from northern and western states.

Daniel Elazar offers a comprehensive theory of political culture that addresses the how and why of US development, and describes the boundaries of major subcultural cleavages within the nation. His analysis is very useful for confirming southern political distinctiveness, and showing subcultural differences within the South. Elazar argues that three political subcultures—individualistic, moralistic, and traditionalistic—have been the primary influence in the historical development of the United States. By researching the social and historical immigration patterns within each state, the roots of a particular social and geographic culture are defined.[21]

The traditionalistic culture is appropriate for most of the South. It is rooted in the elitist agricultural social order that once characterized the region. Government's principle function in the traditionalistic culture is to preserve the social order relative to the position of various social and economic classes. Politics is dominated by representatives of the social and economic elite, who benefit from their position at the top of the social order. Elazar contends that the traditionalistic culture developed most fully in South Carolina and Virginia, but dominated every southern state, as well as a few in the Midwest and southwestern areas. Texas and Florida were a mixture of traditionalistic and individualistic cultures, but even there the older social order dominated politics. The individualistic political culture emphasizes politics as a marketplace where government is a business proposition that depends on professional politicians for stability.[22]

Elazar's conception of US culture is as a dynamic system, one that assumes the patterns of belief and behavior will evolve over time. As a result, cultural values are subject to modification and mixing of subcultural components. In the traditionalistic political culture mass participation is not encouraged since individuals see themselves as subservient to the ruling elites. Political participation is discouraged, voter turnout is low, and leadership is entrusted to a governing elite, a body like a state senate or a group of legislative leaders. Urbanization or a population shift can change these belief patterns, but they remain strong in defiance of replacement.

The central idea of the cultural basis of politics is that any explanation of political change in the South involves the interaction of numerous factors. To focus on a single aspect of cultural development is inadequate when it comes to explaining the political behavior of diverse southern states. These states are defined as the ones of rebellion in the Civil War: Alabama, Arkansas, Georgia, Florida, Louisiana, Mississippi, North Carolina, South Carolina, Tennessee, Texas, and Virginia. They are the same ones V. O. Key used in his midcentury analysis, despite compelling evidence that the political culture is similar in states like Oklahoma, Kentucky, and West Virginia.[23] Fifty years ago they had much in common; today because of urbanization, in-migration, and economic growth the differences among them are significant.

While a host of factors separate the South from the rest of the nation, six are identified for the current analysis as being components of the political culture. These six aspects of southern politics help explain the historical differences between the region and the rest of the nation, and are useful in analyzing the present distinctions within and among the states. These cultural legacies are: (1) the geographic legacy, (2) the agricultural economy and the inheritance of economic underachievement, (3) the racial tradition, (4) religious sentiment, (5) one-party political competition, and (6) political leadership in legislatures and executive offices.

These six persistent and significant aspects of the southern political culture, acting in different combinations, have a commanding influence on the political behavior in each of the eleven states. History is a significant part of culture, so is ethnic makeup and settlement patterns. Present-day politics emerged from the past, and is a prologue for understanding behavior at the start of the twenty-first century.

The Traditional Southern Political Culture

The political culture exerts its greatest influence when it establishes the means by which people relate to one another and to those who make its decisions. In the South, the **physical geography** and climate promoted a society of rulers who had land. Land has been a resource over which disputes have historically centered because the natural topography of an area often dictates political divisions. Natural resources in the South supported the agricultural economy, but later the land and waterways became havens for tourism and recreation.

Societies are shaped by the land from which they emerge. Soil and climate play a role in any political history, but the weather and terrain in the South created a distinctive rustic culture that flourished with short winters and hot, humid, windless days. "Summers are powdery hot; the white ball sun . . . rolling around and around in the sky," describes five months of the southern calendar, and the hot seasons slow the pace of life and allow residents to indulge themselves in outdoor recreational living.[24]

The South is many geographical regions: a coastal plain along the Atlantic Ocean and the Gulf of Mexico, the red-soiled Piedmont, the high mountains of

North Carolina and Tennessee, and a variety of bluffs, flood plains, and delta river basins. If there is a pattern here, it is that flat plains fall away to a coast or river that accommodated an "Old South" plantation culture in Black Belt counties of agriculture and slavery, while elevated interior regions were home to poorer farming practices, manufacturing ventures, "Cracker" whites, urban centers, and the "New South." Birmingham, Atlanta, and Charlotte are "New South" urban areas along interstate highways with green grass suburbs, while Montgomery, Charleston, and New Orleans are rich in the rural, plantation life of the "Old South" tradition.

The geography created an **agrarian economy**, which was labor intensive. Productive agricultural lands, tropical summer temperatures, and the right amount of rainfall during the growing season defined the boundaries of southern life. In his *Notes on Virginia,* Thomas Jefferson wrote that agricultural workers were "the chosen people of God."[25] "Among the farm laborers," he said, "God was able to keep alive that sacred fire which otherwise might escape the face of the earth." For white Southerners the farm was the native habitat of the family that allowed independence from corporations and government. The suspicion in the South among whites was that northern capitalists would undermine farmers and small traders, effectively ending the "Southern Way of Life."

The primacy of land ownership became part of the southern mindset that kept residents from living under the economic rainbow enjoyed by the rest of the nation. Relatively few Southerners lived in cities, and the South had no way of developing a complex economy. Ben Robertson's record of life on a cotton farm in upstate South Carolina is typical. He describes his grandfather's belief, "that eventually the United States would come back to the South for the key to its culture . . . [and] that was why he always pleaded with us never to mortgage the land . . . We could hold on as long as we owned our land."[26] An agricultural miracle never came, and the economy of the region had to change to other endeavors.

African Americans were locked in racial segregation in counties ruled by white elites, but they had a similar affinity for the land. Ralph David Abernathy, who would become a lion in the civil rights movement, grew up as the son of a landowning farmer in Depression Alabama. "My father," he wrote in his biography *And the Walls Came Tumbling Down,* "was, after all, a respected farmer in a part of the country where farming was the most respected of all vocations . . . we never wanted for life's necessities."[27] A social structure once dominated by white landowners and planters supervising a subservient black race later became, in the words of Janice Holt Giles, "Forty Acres and No Mule."[28]

Defiance of national trends and support for the farming life was evident in the 1930 manifesto, *I'll Take My Stand: The South and the Agrarian Tradition.*[29] In the book, twelve southern sectionalists questioned the benefits of industrialism imposed on the region, and saw virtue in a return to the traditional agrarian practices that made the South distinctive. Their creed was that an agricultural environment produced good men and women as well as crops, and the resulting rural civilization was the essence of the South. The agrarian manifesto critiqued centralized industry because it reduced man to a functional cog in a manufacturing and production assembly line. At the same time the whites defended the region's traditional culture with its virtues of religious humanism and simplicity. For the southern agrarians the true South was rural, conservative, stable, and devout.

Unfortunately, the agrarian life was better in theory than in practice. Slow job growth and a suspicion of centralized government kept the South at the bottom of the economic ladder. The political culture stressed democratic participation by elites with an emphasis on self-reliance. After the Civil War the region's economy collapsed. C. Vann Woodward's *The Burden of Southern History* recalls that the South was the only part of the nation to experience the pain of a military defeat, occupation by a victorious external foe, and subsequent domination by its former servants.[30] A memory burdened by anguish, despair, and cruelty was in the blood of southern whites, but, it also pulsed with a reminiscence of rare courage, honor, and sacrifice. Black Southerners endured decades of economic despair and racial separation.

Minimal expectations and doing without were a part of life in the South. White Southerners felt cheated by the past in the same way as African Americans. The South experienced disappointments in politics, economics, industry, agriculture, and a permanent national suspicion about the races in the early decades of the twentieth century. A magazine editor interviewed in 1947 said that the South was behind the rest of the country, and likely to stay there, but "Franklin Roosevelt did much to destroy the importance of [the personal followings of disreputable politicians] by awakening the lower economic classes . . . the poor farmers, to real issues and the possibilities of their economic improvement."[31] Still, life below the Potomac lagged behind the standards and expectations of the rest of the nation. Rick Bragg, a Pulitzer Prize–winning journalist from Alabama, captured his native, regional inferiority when he described his time with the Nieman fellows at Harvard in 1992 as, "perfume on a hog."[32]

The physical geography and agrarian economy were based on an abiding **racial legacy** that began with an inherited white slave owner and planter class. From the colonial period to the 1850s the South was home to a diverse population, but after the Civil War the lack of economic opportunity forced homogenization. A lack of diversity in the white population came when European immigrants flowed into other areas of the country, avoiding the South. The resultant "Caucasian culture" was set in the middle of a huge number of enslaved Africans. Slavery was common in the early days of the nation, but only in the South was the institution the foundation of the economy. The feudal life of the plantation mirrored the structure of the southern social world, with slaves forming the working element in the society. As Gavin Wright has noted, "slavery generated a weaker and looser connection between property holders and the land they occupied."[33] The logic of slavery meant that southern slave owners had their investment in labor, not land, and had little to gain from improvements in roads and marketing facilities in a particular area.

Much of the life history of slaves and slavery is lost because virtually none of the African Americans could read and write. A black activist lawyer in a 1970 Nashville newspaper interview concluded, "Whites make their own history, and they write the Negro out of American history."[34] Those who had the ability and foresight to put their thoughts on paper were few, and the historical record of life in the slave quarters, written in a black hand, is largely nonexistent.

Race was the constant preoccupation of southern white politicians, and almost an obsession in the society structured along superordinate and subordinate lines. Among the elites the declaration of racial segregation was an unspoken necessity after the abolition of slavery in 1865. Miscegenation, the dread of "race-mixing" between dominant whites and subordinate blacks, defined the culture of the region. In its worst form, the idolatry of southern white women was used to justify the subjugation of black men. White women were "ladies" in the South because they bore the racial purity of the dominant society. W. J. Cash writes in *The Mind of the South* that during the Civil War, "there was hardly a sermon that did not begin and end with tributes in her honor, hardly a brave speech that did not open and close for her glory."[35] Praise for women was an endorsement of the established caste system, and a warning about the danger of new ideas.

The hegemony of white supremacy after the Civil War retarded economic development in the region. While the rest of the nation rushed into the industrial revolution at the turn of the twentieth century by accepting immigration, social diversity, and economic innovation, the South stuck to its communal traditions reluctant to change. The advocates of a "New South" believed that economic regeneration was possible without a change in the racial social structure. The businessman hero replaced the planter, and across the South self-made men from the middle class became prominent in lumber, tobacco, textiles, furniture, and manufacturing. Ambitious young Southerners were now allied with northern businessmen, not fighting them as their fathers had. In politics, the lawyer-politician replaced the agrarian elites that once dominated courthouse rings and monopolized state legislatures.

The conservative Redeemer governments that came to power in the 1870s were composed of elites that disenfranchised virtually all blacks and poor whites as well. The South shared fully in the national railroad building boom (1865–1880), the growth of small interior towns, and the expansion of manufacturing. The spread of cotton mills in the 1880s resulted in a public-spirited rhetoric of boosterism across the region.[36] All this growth, while laudatory, could not change the racial scar that was the daily reality in every southern state.

The president of Fisk University declared in 1947 that, "like the white people, the Negro 'votes' in middle and eastern Tennessee, but 'is voted' by the Crump machine in Memphis."[37] Black voters in west Tennessee, and other places across the South, had an inbred fear of ever standing up to the white man. Life for black Southerners remained at the back door of the store, the separate facility, and the rear of the bus. Their subsistence reached a nadir between the end of Reconstruction (1877) and the beginning of World War I (1914). Why was resistance to racial integration so fierce in the face of economic development? "It was based upon fear," writes C. Vann Woodward of the politics in Georgia during the time of populist Tom Watson's crusade (1891–1896), "fear of the Negro menace, the scalawag menace, the Federal menace, menaces real and imaginary."[38] The white South justified the caste system as crucial to the economy, but it was also rooted in a belief that blacks were a diseased and debauched population that could not survive without the paternalism of the tenant farm. In a region settled by whites, be they English, Scotch-Irish, or German, the fate of their economy rested inextricably on the question of race. While there were pockets of diversity, tolerance, and pluralism, the theme of white dominance and black inferiority was pervasive in southern political history.

The agrarian economic system of slavery and elite rule accommodated a growth in fundamental **religious values** that emphasized a reliance on supernatural explanations at the expense of secular and scientific ones. The South has always been sensitive to the fervor of the fundamental Christian faith. The enthusiasm was intense, heartfelt, emotional, and not subject to academic study or interpretation. Southern Baptists, Presbyterians, and Methodists all broke with their northern neighbors before the Civil War. The subsequent defeat at the hands of a freethinking "Yankee" culture was a double tragedy because Southerners saw the sacred virtues of their homeland corrupted by those with no appreciation of morality or the fundamental Christian faith. "The people had believed so absolutely in the support of a just God for a just cause that when this cause went down to defeat, it became plain to all that they had sinned."[39]

The fervor of religious attitudes of Southerners was exposed by the 1925 Scopes Trial on the merits of teaching evolution in the schools in Dayton, Tennessee, and the attendant subjection of Southerners to national ridicule. The "Baltimore Barb," H. L. Mencken, abrasively declared the South of the 1920s to be a "cesspool of Baptists, a miasma of Methodism, snake charmers, and syphilitic evangelists."[40] Seventy-five years later Mencken could still be carping, because the regional attitudes are little changed. Today the "Bible Belt" of the southeast comprises the largest block of Protestant Christian evangelicals found anywhere in the world. In the majority of counties, Baptists and Methodists, along with some independent Bible churches, account for nearly all church affiliation.[41]

The Christian religion was a focus of life for both whites and blacks. For African Americans the comfort of the next life was the route from personal salvation to group deliverance. Faith and religious rhetoric were central to the civil rights movement. Martin Luther King Sr., the father of the more famous son, wrote that words for racial reconciliation "were spiritual, not political . . . I told folks that I never believed in political action that did not come out of a set of ethics, a sense of fair play, a high regard for the humanity and rights of all people."[42] Jimmy Carter, a Southerner converted to racial equality, echoed this sentiment when he discussed a "second conversion" after losing his first race for governor. "I formed a much more intimate relationship with Christ, and, since then, I've had just about a new life."[43] Though whites and blacks worship separately, the same religious sentiment guides their reconciliation behavior.

Regardless of political subculture values, political parties exist to accommodate division, conflict, and opposition within the body politic. In the South this function was mitigated by **one-party politics**. Before the Civil War the South had two active political parties, the Democrats and the Whigs. War and Reconstruction led to domination by a single political party, the Democrats. Political participation was modest when it was restricted to just one party. A more liberal stance by the national Democratic Party, the Voting Rights Act of 1965, and economic development, all altered the social fabric of the South and changed the participation and allegiance of voters in every southern state.

When Jimmy Carter took the oath of office as president in 1977, the fabled southern landscape remained one-party Democratic even though it was as lacquered with plastic, Styrofoam, and processed fast food as the rest of the country. The expanded social base for politics and elections in the region gradually came to reflect a political struggle between traditional conservatives with their states' rights proponents, more moderate forces composed of voters who moved to the region, and black voters who embrace an activist role for the federal government. The latter group saw states' rights rhetoric as a mask for discrimination and racism.

The political subculture research has suggested that citizens can acquire new social attitudes and values and then mobilize their interests in a new way (political socialization) to form coalitions and make demands on the political system (political aggregation.)[44] This happened in the South, and two-party politics began to emerge in the last decades of the twentieth century. The legacy of one-party politics, however, remains in rural pockets at the county and at the state level of many southern states.

Perhaps because of this legacy of one-party politics, the South has an unusual history of **political leadership.** Allegiance to a single political party meant that elections were decided by factions who knew each other well. The southern states engendered a casual familiarity, usually with one state law school and experience with several previous campaigns. In interviews for the book *Southern Politics,* V. O. Key and his associates were struck by the personal and regional divisions in virtually every state. Sometimes the conflicts were more geographic, as in Tennessee (east, middle, and west), South Carolina (upcountry and low country), and Mississippi (delta and hills). At other times the disagreements were more personal, as in Georgia (pro- and anti-Talmadge) and Louisiana (pro- and anti-Long).

Sometimes politics was both; in a 1947 interview a Tennessee newspaper editor opined, "Mr. Crump represents the same white supremacy sentiment in Tennessee that Mr. Bilbo represents in Mississippi."[45] The political goal was protection of the "Southern Way of Life," which involved a belief in homespun values, racial rhetoric, the outdoor life, faith in the Ten Commandments, and the superiority of southern womanhood.

The term "demagogue" means an unscrupulous politician who gains power by pleasing the baser nature of the electorate; the term was appropriately applied to politicians as diverse as: Benjamin Tillman and Coleman Blease of South Carolina, Eugene Talmadge of Georgia, James K. Vardeman and Theodore Bilbo of Mississippi, and W. Lee "Pappy" O'Daniel and James "Pa" and Marian "Ma" Ferguson of Texas. These politicians were known for their white supremacy rhetoric, criticism of northern capitalism, and suspicion of federal initiatives. A more populist element was seen in politicians like "Big" Jim Folsom of Alabama and Tom Watson of Georgia. They viewed politics as a class movement of the poor against the rich, and even sought black support. Such appeals left them vulnerable to Democratic race baiting, and the charge of allowing "Negro domination." By 1904 Tom Watson changed his stance to endorse the disenfranchisement of African American voters and by 1908 he ceased to define populism in racially inclusive terms and ran for president as a white supremacist.

The most notorious southern politician of the populist line was undoubtedly Huey P. Long of Louisiana, whose nationwide appeal in the years of the Roosevelt administration almost brought an end to two-party politics in the US democracy. These politicians from the past have modern, though less radical, imitators: men like Herman Talmadge of Georgia, Strom Thurmond of South Carolina, and George Wallace of Alabama. Their political antics and rhetoric mark the South as a region of political distinctiveness. Protest movements, like Huey Long's "Every Man a King" crusade, the Dixiecrat revolt of 1948, and Wallace's American Independent Party, repeatedly reinforced the South's sense of political alienation and impotence. The rhetorical appeals of southern leaders found fertile ground in an environment of poverty, illiteracy, racism, political defeat, agrarian decline, and rural bareness.

Congressmen and senators from the region characteristically compiled a record of influence based on the security of reelection at home, and legislative seniority in Washington. The South survived for decades in the twentieth century by reelecting senators and representatives who chaired powerful committees in Congress committed to an agenda of racial segregation, national defense, state autonomy, and the second amendment. These same legislators voted for generous federal resources for the construction of highways, disaster relief, recreation facilities, sewer plants, and an expanding defense industry. When threatened, Southerners used the menace of filibuster and the inability of their opponents to impose cloture as a protection for their values. After one civil rights vote a senator wrote, "with less than 25 percent of the membership of the Senate, the Southerners have won one of the most notable victories in our history."[46] Today, as much as any time in the past, incumbency has a powerful advantage in southern politics.

Walker Percy summed up the influence of southern leadership when he said, "The South has entered the mainstream of American life for the first time in perhaps 150 years, that is, in a sense that has not been the case since the 1870s or 1830s."[47] The region can be captured in many different images, and these six legacies are as fragile as an old photograph. The burden of the past, and the isolation of the region, would be ultimately plowed under by suburban shopping malls, homogenized by television, and made to follow the directives of the federal government. Yet something still endures. "The past is never dead," wrote William Faulkner, "it's not even past."[48] Politically, the transfiguration of the party system reflects new partisan allegiances shaped by the infusion of political newcomers and insurgents into the South's traditional conservative political milieu. The emergence of a new cultural matrix is anchored by a changing economic structure, a more inclusive social topography, conflicting perceptions, and attitudes about the role of government and political leadership.

The six aspects of political culture can only be seen in interaction with each other. For example, the racial legacy influenced one-party politics, and the agrarian heritage produced unique populist political campaigns and leaders. While these traditional legacies may have originally defined the South, today the region is far different from what it once was. During the Great Depression it was the nation's greatest economic problem. Franklin Roosevelt said as much in 1936, yet the South grew faster economically during the last decade of the twentieth century than the rest of the country. By 2000, if the eleven southern states were a separate country, they would combine to have the world's fourth largest economy.[49]

Times change, and Daniel Elazar's theory of political culture helps to explain the transformation of southern life. He believed the key component in any change was the concept of migration.[50] While many of his fifteen migration streams influenced settlement patterns elsewhere and had little effect on the South, some—like the African American influence—left a stamp on southern culture that is still felt today. Undoubtedly, the most important migratory trend in recent southern history is urbanization. The compact settlement in southern cities has restructured society.

In 2003 Daniel Elazar changed his analysis of political culture to accommodate the high rate of mobility and extensive individualism in contemporary urban life. Communities in the old sense, with the same families occupying the same space under the same political jurisdictions for generations, have disappeared. They have been replaced by metropolitan statistical areas (MSAs) located near the city for which they are named. "We can understand the American urban place as a community only when we view it as a 'civil community'—a term . . . to better describe the way an urbanized area . . . frequently extends beyond the formal city limits of most central cities or occupies less than the area of formal jurisdiction [and is] bound together as a meaningful political system."[51]

These civil communities now dominate the southern urban political landscape. "In the 1980 Census, the South had only 10 metropolitan areas of one million people or more . . . now the region has twenty-two."[52] The settling of cities after World War II, and especially in the last two decades of the twentieth century, is as much a migration as any covered wagon experience mentioned by Elazar in his original work. The urban South ended agrarianism, changed rural religious patterns of worship, provided a multicultural mix of Hispanic, black, and Asian neighbors in new suburbs, and led to a two-party political system and a new style of televised political leadership.

Classification of the Southern States

Political culture has been defined broadly, yet it can be seen in different aspects across the South. Each of the eleven states has unique patterns and structures in its political culture, which dictate that it be viewed independent of its neighbors. How do these states relate to the larger American political culture? Some classification scheme is needed to examine the effect of the six aspects, which have produced varying rates of party competition and economic growth among the states, and their influence on politics and culture.

The southern states share a similar past, but the very structuring of politics and government is different in each. For example, the manner and rate in which states opened their voting rolls to blacks varied. Citizen access to government through political reforms like the constitutional initiative, political party competition, and voting rates are measures of subcultural differences. As V. O. Key noted more than fifty years ago, Virginia is clearly different from Alabama, Texas is almost the opposite of Mississippi, and Florida is a populous upstart. Given the abysmal economic past of the southern states, the recent surge to financial respectability may be the most important measure of southern state differences. The South has been divided into the "Rim South" (or "Border South") and the "Deep South." Florida and Texas have been excluded in some studies, and others have included states omitted by Key.[53]

To examine the states independent of each other, the eleven states are classified into three different groups, based on an analysis of their economic and social standing, which helped to rank them as to their political importance. The rankings in Table 1.1 are based on a composite of indicators associated with several social, political, and economic indicators in each state. Some of the criteria are drawn from government statistics; others are based on the size and importance of the state in national politics. The entries are the rankings of the eleven southern states on various issues. In Key's midcentury study, Florida was a backwater anachronism in US

Table 1.1   Composite Ranking of Southern States, 2000

	Population	Per Capita Income	Diversity: Non-Southern Born Population	Registered Voters	Education: Percent with 4-year Degree	Gross State Product	Infant Mortality Rate[a]	Unemployment Rate	Composite Average
National States									
Texas	1	4	2	8	2	1	1	7	3.25
Florida	2	2	1	2	3	2	2	2	2.00
Georgia	3	3	5	3	4	3	5	4	3.75
Virginia	5	1	3	1	1	5	3	1	2.50
Emergent States									
North Carolina	4	5	6	10	6	4	8	2	5.63
Tennessee	6	6	7	7	7	6	4	5	6.00
Traditional States									
South Carolina	9	9	8	6	5	9	9	5	7.50
Alabama	8	7	9	4	8	8	11	9	8.00
Arkansas	11	10	4	9	11	10	6	8	8.63
Louisiana	7	8	10	5	9	7	7	10	7.88
Mississippi	10	11	11	11	10	11	10	11	10.63

Source: Statistical Abstract of the United States, Bureau of Economic Analysis.
Notes: State Rankings are among the eleven southern states.
a. Infant mortality rankings based on statistics for 1998.

politics; today it is the nation's fourth most populous state and presidential candidates covet its electoral results.

The first category consists of what I call **national** states, that is, those states that have a measure of economic and social development approaching that of the rest of the country. These states are at, or above, the national median in per capita income. They have a substantial, professional, and urbanized labor force. They are key states in the calculus of any presidential election, and prominent politicians from these states are listed as potential party nominees. Two or three cities in these states, and, in one case, a single city, can determine the outcome of any statewide political race. In sum, they are larger and more prosperous than their southern cousins and in some ways have more in common with the rest of the country than their neighbors. Four states make up this category: Virginia, Florida, Georgia, and Texas.

These states have gained congressional seats after every census since 1980, and are also bellwether states for registering national trends. Their size makes them targets in any presidential campaign, and the four of them together contain over 57 percent of the total southern population. Texas has produced two recent presidents, and Florida decided the 2000 election. Both Texas and Florida have a sizable Hispanic population to complement a relatively low proportion of blacks. Georgia's economy is carried by the city of Atlanta, while Virginia lives on federal dollars and technology-based industries in an urban crescent that stretches from the Washington, D.C., suburbs, through Richmond to the military installations in the Hampton Roads/Norfolk/Virginia Beach area. Subregions in these states differ. The noncoast part of the Florida panhandle and south Georgia are far from national, and rural Texas is a throwback to the frontier. Yet these states are national because they have dominant cities, are more similar to each other, and collectively are quite different from other states in the South.

The second category contains two states that have moved from the economic backwaters, and are well on their way to achieving national status. They have produced presidential candidates, and attract national media attention, but are still below the national average in per capita income and have pockets of poverty that are more reminiscent of Great Depression poverty than twenty-first century affluence.

On a host of these criteria these states consistently rank behind the achievements of the national states. They are classified as **emergent** states because they are below their national cousins in terms of economic development and political importance, but are more important than their smaller and more destitute Deep South cousins. Two states, North Carolina and Tennessee, are classified as emergent states. North Carolina was predicted by V. O. Key to be a state with the possibility of breaking out of the southern mold of one-party political competition and stagnant economic growth. Tennessee has a border state history of racial moderation and two-party political competition. Each state has several dynamic and growing urban sectors, and a national reputation for innovation and progress. Both these states are destined for national importance in the decades to come, but for the present they constitute a separate category.

The final group is composed of states that still lag behind the national average when it comes to income, and retain some of the rural poverty so typical of the South fifty years ago. Vestiges of the racial, economic, and demographic divisions so familiar to those who know the South are in these states. Despite five decades of change, and efforts by government and the private sector, the national rankings of these states are not substantially changed. The **traditional** southern states are: South Carolina, Alabama, Mississippi, Louisiana, and Arkansas. They are often classified as the "Deep South." They are five of the last ten states in the United States in terms of per capita income. Each has a historically high proportion of blacks and a strong agricultural tradition. The tripartite division of the South, as set forth in Table 1.1 is based on all of the criteria mentioned in this section, and is used as a categorical scheme throughout the book.

A Political Culture Approach

The change in allegiance from the one-party Democratic South to two-party competition is one of the great transformations in US political history. A problem with the study of this alteration in allegiance is that there is no agreed upon approach to the subject. Most studies take social and economic variables to explain subsequent voting behavior. These thematic studies are very helpful, but they do not allow for much of a state-by-state analysis. Also these studies cannot explain the persistence of an issue like the flying of the Confederate flag or the removal of the Ten Commandments from the lawn of a courthouse square.

The political culture approach of this book broadens the analysis, but comes with a price; it is a concept that excludes very little from consideration. The six cultural factors introduced earlier are a compromise between narrow specificity on the one hand, and overly broad inclusiveness on the other. An understanding of the cultural basis of politics depends on analyzing the mix of these six cultural aspects (geography, agrarian past, race, religion, one-party politics, and political leadership) and explaining how they relate to the changing politics of each state as well as the region. The analysis in this book will take into account change and continuity with previous studies and current trends. The book will deliberately delve into historical explanations when appropriate. At the same time a consistent methodology will analyze voting trends and patterns in the various states, with a county-by-county explanation of allegiance. A state-by-state analysis under the classification scheme introduced in Table 1.1 and discussed above will reflect urbanization and partisanship. Historical voting trends will be combined with present-oriented research.

The approach here is deliberately eclectic. It is painted with a broad brush to give a full picture of the personalities and events of southern politics. Vignettes of important personalities and events are included to deepen the analysis. Some of the presentation is visual with county maps of the various states. The subsequent investigation raises some straightforward questions: How different are the subcultures of the states when it comes to elections? How do Republicans and Democrats approach a campaign for statewide office? What effect has urbanization had on the strategies of the two parties?

The chapters that follow are arranged in a way that examines each of the six aspects of political culture in order. Chapter 2 presents a background history on the traditional South. Readers unfamiliar with the historical legacy will see that it stimulated the patterns of migration, and racial incidents that made the South unique. Chapter 3 examines the geographic legacy of the South, and the individual urbanization patterns in each state. Chapter 4 explains the racial legacy of white supremacy that dominated the region for much of its history. The racial past is related to the civil rights movement, busing for school integration, and the election of African American officials. Chapter 5 explains the religious legacy of the South, showing its effect in both the black and white community. Chapter 6 examines the one-party legacy in the South by showing the demise of one-party politics in both federal and state offices, and introduces a measure to summarize this change. Chapter 7 examines the rise of Republican voting in presidential elections and shows how the GOP has emerged to win a variety of offices in southern races. Chapter 8 considers the Democratic Party's response to rising Republican success in the South during the 1990s, showing Democratic successes in appropriate states. Chapter 9 analyzes the uniqueness of southern legislators and governors. Chapter 10 places conflicts in the South in a national context, by looking at the cultural legacy of the South in national politics. The final chapter, 11, examines the future of the political culture in the South.

Poet and novelist James Dickey wrote that the South was a promised land, and he uses the biblical story of Jericho as the first city of conquest as a metaphor to talk about it. Behind the political science analysis is the poetry of the region, with its localness, sense of history, and fierce independence. Modern culture has changed this, but it has not disappeared. A cultural analysis presupposes something besides facts and statistical rankings; there is a feeling about the place, a mystery, and the political life is a part of that. As Dickey said, "you never *just* pass through the South. The South not only grows on you; it grows *around* you. Once there, you will come back, or you will stay in it long enough to die there."[54]

Notes

    1. John Winthrop, "A Modell of Christian Charity," in Michael B. Levy (ed.), *Political Thought in America*, 2d ed. Prospect Heights, Ill.: Waveland Press, Inc., 1992, p. 12.

2. Franklin D. Roosevelt, "Second Inaugural Address," in David Newton Lott, *The Presidents Speak*. New York: Henry Holt, 1994, p. 285.

3. Stephen B. Oakes, *Let the Trumpet Sound*. New York: Harper & Row, 1982, pp. 260–262.

4. Donald Davidson, "Still Rebels, Still Yankees," in Thomas Daniel Young, Floyd C. Watkins, and Richmond Croom Beatty, *The Literature of the South*. Atlanta, Ga.: Scott Foresman and Co., 1968, p. 744.

5. "Religious Regions," in Charles Reagan Wilson and William Ferris (eds.), *Encyclopedia of Southern Culture*. Chapel Hill: University of North Carolina Press, p. 557. "Violent Crime Rate, 1997," in Kendra A. Hovey and Harold A. Hovey, *C.Q.'s State Fact Finder*. Washington, D.C.: C.Q. Press, 1994, p. 285.

6. Deidre A. Gaquin and Katherine A. DeBrandt (eds.), *Education Statistics*. Lanham, Md.: Bernan Press, 2000, p. 319.

7. Criswell Freeman (ed.), *The Book of Southern Wisdom*. Nashville, Tenn.: Walnut Grove Press, 1994, p. 93.

8. Earl Black and Merle Black, *The Vital South*. Cambridge: Harvard University Press, 1987, pp. 85–86.

9. Aristotle, *The Politics*. New York: Vintage Press, 1969.

10. Machiavelli, *The Prince*. New York: Viking Press, 1978.

11. Gabriel A. Almond, "Comparative Political Systems," *Journal of Politics* 18 (1956): pp. 391–409.

12. Aristotle, *The Politics*, especially his critique of Plato in Book 2, and his establishment of the best regime by degrees, in Books 4 to 6.

13. V.O. Key, *Southern Politics in State and Nation*. 2d ed. Knoxville: University of Tennessee Press, 1977, p. 1.

14. Gabriel A. Almond and G. Bingham Powell, *Comparative Politics: A Developmental Approach*. Boston: Little, Brown, 1996, p. 23.

15. "Born Again Faith," *Time*, September 28, 1976.

16. Talcott Parsons, *The Social System*. New York: Free Press, 1951, p. 17.

17. Gabriel Almond and G. Bingham Powell, *Comparative Politics: A Developmental Approach*, p. 23.

18. V.O. Key, *Southern Politics in State and Nation*, p. 36.

19. Alfred A. Kroeber and Clyde Kluckohn, *Culture: A Critical Review of Concepts and Definitions*. New York: Vintage Books, 1963, p. 181.

20. The political science literature offers diverse approaches to the study of political culture. Representative discussions are in the following: Gabriel Almond and Sidney Verba, *The Civic Culture*. Princeton, N.J.: Princeton University Press, 1963. Donald J. Devine, *The Political Culture of the United States*. Boston: Little, Brown, 1972. John Kincaid (ed.), *Political Culture, Public Policy, and the American States*. Philadelphia: Institute for the Study of Human Issues, 1982.

21. Daniel J. Elazar, *American Federalism: A View from the States*, 3rd ed. New York: Harper, 1984.

22. In contrast to the self-interested politics of the individualistic culture, the moralistic one is dominated by the conception of a commonwealth with politics as an activity for the public interest. Ibid.

23. Christopher Cooper and H. Gibbs Knott, "Defining Dixie: Seeking a Better Measure of the Modern Political South." A paper presented at the biennial Citadel Symposium of Southern Politics, March 4–5, 2004, Charleston, S.C.

24. Shirley Ann Grau, "The Black Prince," in Young, Watkins, and Beatty (eds.), *The Literature of the South*, p. 13.

25. Thomas Jefferson, "Notes on Virginia," in Young, Watkins, and Beatty (eds.), *The Literature of the South*, p. 35.

26. Ben Robertson, *Red Hills and Cotton*. Columbia: University of South Carolina Press, 1942, p. 96.

27. Ralph David Abernathy, *And the Walls Came Tumbling Down*. New York: Harper & Row, 1989, p. 6.

28. Janice Holt Giles, *Forty Acres and No Mule*. New York: Houghton Mifflin, 1952.

29. Twelve Southerners, *I'll Take My Stand: The South and the Agrarian Tradition*. New York: Peter Smith, 1951.

30. C. Vann Woodward, *The Burden of Southern History*. Baton Rouge: Louisiana State University Press, 1960.

31. Southern Politics Collection, "Alabama," Vanderbilt University, Special Collections.

32. Rick Bragg, *All Over But the Southin'*. New York: Vintage Books, 1997, p. 58.

33. Gavin Wright, *Old South, New South: Revolutions in the Southern Economy Since the Civil War*. New York: Basic Books, 1986, p. 17.

34. Nashville *Tennessean*, February 9, 1969.

35. W.J. Cash, *The Mind of the South*. New York: Alfred A. Knopf, 1941, p. 89.

36. Brodus Mitchell, *The Rise of the Cotton Mills in the South*. Baltimore: Johns Hopkins University Press, 1921.

37. Southern Politics Collection, "Tennessee," Vanderbilt University, Special Collections.

38. C. Vann Woodward, *Tom Watson: Agrarian Rebel*. New York: Oxford University Press, 1938, p. 67.

39. *Sewanee Review,* Summer, 1948. Cited in: Young, Watkins, and Beatty, *The Literature of the South*, p. 602.

40. Quoted in Patrick Gerstner, "Religion and Mythology," in Charles Reagan Wilson, (ed.), *The Encyclopedia of Southern Culture*, p. 1722.

41. "Religious Regions," in Charles Reagan Wilson (ed.), *The Encyclopedia of Southern Culture*, p. 557. Martin B. Bradley, Norman M. Green Jr., Dale E. Jones, Mac Lynn, Lou McNeil, *Churches and Church Membership in the United States, 1990*. Glenmery Research Center, Atlanta, Ga., 1992.

42. Martin Luther King Sr. with Clayton Riley, *Daddy King*. New York: William Morrow, 1980, p. 195.

43. James Wooten, *Dasher: The Roots and Rising of Jimmy Carter*. New York: Warner Books, 1979, pp. 269–270.

44. Gabriel A. Almond and G. Bingham Powell, *Comparative Politics Today,* 6th ed. New York: Longman, 1996, pp. 47–50, 70–103.

45. Southern Politics Collection, "Tennessee."

46. Robert A. Caro, *The Years of Lyndon Johnson: Master of the Senate*. New York: Alfred A. Knopf, 2002, p. 218. The senator was Harry Byrd of Virginia.

47. Jay Tolson, *Pilgrim in the Ruins: A Life of Walker Percy*. Chapel Hill: University of North Carolina Press, 1994, p. 376.

48. Here quoted in Peter Applebome, *Dixie Rising*. New York: Random House, 1996, p. 14.

49. Compiled by the author from adding the GNP for each southern state. Also see: *The Economist*, May 16, 2002.

50. Daniel J. Elazar, *American Federalism: A View from the States*. 2d ed. New York: Thomas Y. Crowell, 1972, pp. 110–111.

51. Daniel J. Elazar, *The Metropolitan Frontier and American Politics*. New Brunswick: Transaction Publishers, 2003, p. ix.

52. See www.southnow.org. The program in Southern Politics, Media, and Public Life. School of Journalism and Mass Communications, The University of North Carolina at Chapel Hill.

53. Christopher Cooper and H. Gibbs Knott, "Defining Dixie."

54. Hubert Shuptrine and James Dickey, *Jericho: The South Beheld*. Birmingham, Ala.: Oxmoor House, 1974, p. 15.

2

History and Political Culture

"The South is a special case," wrote Pulitzer Prize–winning novelist and poet Robert Penn Warren, "it lost the war and suffered hardship . . . that kind of defeat gives the past great importance."[1] For many, the land south of the Potomac still exists mostly in the past, as much a state of mind as any geographical boundary. The memories, obligations, and hatreds from southern history formed a special culture, a unique expression of life unlike any other part of the American experience. "In a society bemused with innocence and optimism the South has lived with evils . . . and it does not believe that every evil has an easy cure."[2] Reminiscences of the past are shaped by the differing experiences of blacks and whites.

Historical circumstances left the South a minority culture within the larger nation. Its claim of regional uniqueness lay not in any success in making an impression on the rest of the nation, but in its ethical ideals and its battle for survival in opposition to the majority culture. History in the South is more than a chronicle of miseries and failures; it is also a kind of revelation, an unrolled scroll of prophecy about a land, a time, and a lost ideal. As Margaret Mitchell wrote in her 1936 novel, "Look for it only in books for it is no more than a dream remembered . . . a civilization gone with the wind."[3]

Black Southerners, and many white ones as well, would say, "good riddance" to the antebellum South, with its slavery, agricultural economy, and fierce devotion to lost causes. But even if the past is renounced, its memory remains like a shadow that guides present-day life and politics in a way unique in the whole country. "In that most optimistic of centuries in the most optimistic part of the world," wrote C. Vann Woodward about the twentieth century, "the South remained basically pessimistic in its social outlook and moral philosophy."[4]

The past becomes a part of culture, and anthropologist Clifford Geertz argues that, as a result, a way of life is "historically transmitted . . . either as shadows cast by the organization of society upon the hard surfaces of history, or as the soul of history."[5] Two points are central to exploring the relationship between southern his-

23

tory and the political culture. The first is that Southerners have had different attitudes and experiences from other Americans. The second is that, as a result of these experiences, they have different myths, rituals, and institutions in their political culture. In South Carolina, state employees can take a paid holiday in memory of the Confederate war dead; Sunday closing laws and limitations on liquor consumption are still the rule in many rural counties in the region. In black churches across the South a "Homecoming" celebration is an occasion when former members drive hundreds of miles to attend an extended Sunday worship service.

The region differs from the rest of the country in both behavior and attitude. The idea of southern exceptionalism has interested many from outside. One of the most important sources of writing about the South is the "foreign travel" literature of visitors passing through. From the time of the French aristocrat Alexis de Tocqueville, to contemporary journalists like Peter Applebome of the *New York Times*, those born outside the region find the South a fascinating study. "The American South," wrote de Tocqueville, "is more spontaneous, more spiritual, more open, more generous, more intellectual, and more brilliant."[6] Applebome is struck by southern distinctives when he writes about the 1995 Southern Baptist Convention in Atlanta, the conservative suburbs around the city, and the failure of the labor movement in South Carolina.[7] Tony Horowitz, another interloper born outside the region, is intrigued by southern Civil War reenactors who attend dozens of events in celebrations across the southern states.[8] All these writers find that the South persists as a distinct region in the face of cultural monotony and assimilation. The differences remain in the politics and social life of the region to this very day. To understand politics in the twenty-first century, it helps to have a reading on the past. The first premise of southern politics is a realization that the place remains a part of the country obsessed with looking back, and wondering why.

Memories of the Old South, with its feudal agricultural system, separate communities for blacks and whites, and despair over war, are mixed with more recent visions, of the New South of manufacturing dashed by Great Depression poverty, and the flush of postwar affluence. The twenty-first-century South has interstate highways, national television markets, and Internet connections to the rest of the world, making it as diverse economically, culturally, and racially as the rest of the country. But the rest of the country does not have a time when one group, to the total exclusion of half the native population, dominated the political and social order. The rest of the country did not spend a century at the window of economic prosperity watching as the nation fed at the table of industrial and economic expansion. And the rest of the country did not have to rationalize a system of social contradiction in a nation founded on the ideas of freedom and equality. The South is distinct in both its culture and its politics.

What history accounts for this southern uniqueness? During the period from 1629 to 1775 the United States was settled by at least four waves of English-speaking immigrants. While they had much in common, they differed from one another in many other ways, "in their religion, social ranks, historical generations, and also in the British regions from whence they came."⁹ The colonies of the South began with a distrust of central administration and a faith in smaller, more accessible local government. In time, the residents came to favor low taxes and individual initiative supported by the values of family and church. The agricultural economy supported a social structure of small towns with traditional family structures that emphasized conventional roles for women, that is, domestic homemaking, childrearing, and cooking. White supremacy was accepted, and then institutionalized, in defiance of democratic principles and ideals. The southern way of life was defended, first by the military, then by a one-party political system and legal institutions. The rural communities reinforced a reliance on moral and cultural values in defiance of modernity. As a result, the history of the South is a languid, unrelenting lament of virtuous exceptionalism in the midst of rampant poverty.

Southern politics at the dawn of the twenty-first century is the focus of this book, but the antecedent traits of that uniqueness are found in the historical epochs of the South. Political thought in other areas of the country was pragmatic and instructive; in the South it was romantic and inborn, derived from the living parts of the region. Other parts of the nation were in the mainstream of ideas and on the cutting edge of culture, but the South was backwater, hard scuffle, and poor. The North had virtuous theories of the wholesome inclinations of man, while the South had Calvinistic and Burkean doctrines of human depravity and the organic nature of society. The differences are examined in these historical divisions: the colonial era, the Civil War and Reconstruction times, the period of the New South and the Great Depression, and the more recent years of postwar development, economic growth, and social change.

"Southerners," wrote North Carolinian Jonathan Daniels, "are a mythological people, lost . . . in dreaming of days gone by."¹⁰ The "days gone by," remembered by Daniels and others, transmit the historical patterns of meanings, symbols, and the inherited conceptions about life that characterize the southern experience. Politics is a play on the stage of culture. Present behavior is guided by the familiar "way things are done," and politicians take their television cues today from what worked decades ago. The flatbed trailers of the past have been replaced by HDTV and the Internet, but the southern past echoes in heritage websites and the fiery, divisive rhetoric of talk radio. The South is changing; as a region it has changed more in the past half century than any other part of the country, but that change must be understood against the backdrop of what was acceptable behavior in the past. No political culture is static, and the theme of continuity amid change is one developed as these eras parade past.

The Colonial Era

From the beginning the South was different. The colonial origins of the region were the birthplace of its values, assumptions about life, and attitudes toward government, all of which contributed to its uniqueness. These differences were once less pronounced. The self-conscious South would become most evident in the antebellum Civil War and Reconstruction periods,. During the colonial era, four distinctions defined the culture and politics of the region, and from these sources sprang the legacy that became southern social and political uncommonness.

First, the early South differed from the northern colonies in the motivation for settlement. "If the Puritans established New England to be a City on a Hill, the early southerners portrayed their area as a new Garden of Eden."[11] The southern colonists came more for economic opportunity and social respect than utopian purity. John Rolfe and his Virginia settlers grew "brown gold," the tobacco that required constant attention and became the Jamestown colony's obsession. Georgia started as a philanthropic enterprise, the Carolinas were a string of plantation estates, and Virginia was a re-creation of rural England. The states of Alabama, Mississippi, and Louisiana began as commercial enterprises with extensive landholding and a slave labor force. No southern state began as a new "Christian Jerusalem."

Opportunities for improvement in the southern colonies lay in the availability of cheap, tillable land, a lush climate, and the long growing season. The South developed as an agricultural region in a feudal system, patterned more after the declining medieval lands of Europe, than any uniqueness of the American frontier experience. In Virginia settlers developed the land in a way to fulfill the English ideal of an aristocratic country estate, and that pattern was a model for the rest of the South. The arrangement of the plantation mirrored the structure of the entire southern social world. A small class of planters sat atop the class structure, and dominated society through control of soil, wealth, and political power.

The tradition of elite rule by a landed aristocracy saved commoners from the burden of political decisions by separating them from political power. Prominent families defined the style of the region, with their mansions and southern gentility. "The 'best' families [in Virginia] tended to intermarry and by mid-century [eighteenth] probably not more than a hundred families controlled the wealth and government of the colony."[12] Families along the James River were the social patricians of the state; their sense of "noblesse oblige" was a pattern that would carry America through its founding. Members of the middle class were sometimes related to the wealthiest planters. They established commercial and manufacturing interests and aspired to be gentry themselves, but landless men lacked dignity, and enterprise ranked below agriculture in social prestige. Deference to privilege characterized the well bred, who accepted the distinctions of class without question. At the time of the American Revolution, the Virginia House of Burgesses was an exclusive club where gentlemen discussed the affairs of state with sobriety and a supreme confidence.

Property tax requirements excluded white men at the bottom of the agrarian hierarchy from both social standing and political power. The class of poor agrarian whites, habitually landless, indentured, and unskilled, clung to the hope that one day they too would have land and position. Their livelihood depended on the economic fortunes of the elite, and, as tradesmen, they could expect little more than regular employment. In later times these landless whites would be disparaged as "rednecks," "crackers," and "hicks" who once existed to assist the landed elite. Later they would be an independent class in their own right.

African American slaves were at the bottom of this social structure, and their condition could only be described as desperate. The first slaves arrived in 1619 when a Dutch ship with twenty Africans docked in Jamestown, Virginia. Blacks were initially indentured servants, but later they were placed in perpetual servitude. As long as the institution of slavery existed, the southern planters could maintain high agricultural prices. Slave owners were not "bourgeois" in the sense that they resembled the landholding classes of Europe, but rather they were "laborlords" whose investment was in slaves.[13] The result was a doctrine of white supremacy, defined as a cultural belief that the excellence of southern society was dependent on the maintenance of Anglo-Saxon power and racial continuity. Slavery was officially recognized first in Virginia in the 1660s, and then elsewhere. One of the great agonies of slavery was that African men could not protect African women from European men, but European men brutally protected European women from African men. Life in the "peculiar institution" for slaves became a response to the alien environment around them through the creation of a separate culture with a unique language, religion, and community designed for survival.

The structure of Virginia social life was duplicated in other southern states, in Charleston and the low country of South Carolina, in plantation Georgia and North Carolina. These southern states mimicked the planter ideal of Virginia, whether it was the Creole planter in Louisiana, or the delta cotton farmer in Mississippi. The master of the plantation was neither the charming picture of romance and grace in books of reminiscences, nor the tyrant of abolitionist literature. Slavery was a brutal, but necessary, arrangement in the minds of most Southerners. The typical white landowner was a businessman who depended on slave labor, and was determined at all costs to protect his investment. Planters tended to move their capitalized labor often, taking little time to invest in the local infrastructure. "Gentlemen" were expected to offer themselves for public service. Each southern state had patrician families, established agrarian traditions, and a legacy of legislative dominance. The seriousness, wisdom, and rhetorical elegance of the period were reflected in the class-consciousness of southern life.

A second difference between the South and the North in the colonial period was the social role and daily practice of religion. Calvinistic New England reveled in its practical, common-law orthodoxy, heavy reliance on the Bible, and preoccupation with platforms, programs of action, and schemes of confederation. Residents of the Plymouth Bay Colony were single-minded men who risked everything to travel three thousand miles for an opportunity to build Zion in the new world. By contrast, the South practiced a relaxed and genteel refinement in matters of faith and community.

While the Puritans in Massachusetts wanted to "purify" the English church, the Anglicans of Virginia and the Carolinas were generally satisfied with the way things were in the mother country, and sought to duplicate that life in the new world. Virginia was divided into parishes, with English-trained clergy ministering to those who populated the estates. Religious freedom in the South was not utopian, or motivated by "purification," objection, or reform. Instead worship was a reflection of the home country, and drew on John Locke's philosophy of common sense.

The eighteenth-century gentlemen of Virginia, and the Carolinas, were persuaded that there should be no state censorship in matters of faith. A variety of non-Anglican faiths, such as Quakers, Presbyterians, Lutherans, German pietists, and Baptists, flourished in the South. "Gentlemen" were, of course, Anglican, but other traditions for those of a lower social class were tolerated. Collectively these practices laid the foundation for one of the region's most cherished heritages: "a strong faith in God without dictation by law of the form that faith should take."[14]

Beginning in 1800 itinerant evangelists carried the Christian faith from east coast wooden churches to "brush arbor" camp meetings and stump revivals across the South and into the wilderness west. They found a ready audience in the expanding homesteads and towns across Georgia, Tennessee, and Kentucky, and in the land to the Mississippi River. A regional spirit of plain preaching, unvarnished testimonials, and social acceptance came to characterize small town southern life. "Baptists almost came to own the Deep South except for tips of Florida, Louisiana, and Texas, where Catholics dominated."[15]

Christianity in the South faced a cultural paradox. The slaves, who heard the message of freedom in the Bible, found their masters turning the pages of the same book for a license to sanction human bondage. The frontier enthusiasm of revival appealed to the lower and more numerous segments of society, but no preacher dared condemn slavery. The culture of the South remained one where pious elites sanctioned racial domination and separation. In the course of time, slavery became so wedded to the economy and social structure that no minister dared to oppose it.

The frontier experience was a third factor crucial to the formation of the southern colonial character. Sectional conflicts developed within states as the frontier settlers moved from narrow strips of land strung out along the coast and inland communities, to the hinterland. Conflict was inevitable between the inland farmers and the tidewater aristocrats. The coastal economy of Virginia and North and South Carolina, for example, was marked by a high, white house overlooking acres of crops spread up and down a coastal plain. In the upstate interior, hard-working farmers scratched out a living by clearing acres of rocky, tree-infested land alongside hostile Indians. After the extinction of Indian claims in the area west of Georgia, the states of Mississippi (1817) and Alabama (1819) were added to the Union. Settlers occupied the vast region from Georgia to the Rio Grande during the years from the American Revolution (1776) to the annexation of Texas (1845).

Vignette 2.1   An Antebellum Justification for Slavery

Excerpts from: Josiah Priest, *Slavery, as It Relates to the Negro, or African Race: Examined in the Light of Circumstances, History and the Holy Scriptures.* Louisville, Ky.: W.S. Brown, 1849.

The words, *cursed Ham,* therefore, signify, in the Hebrew, that he had been *always* a bad person, even from childhood; for let it not be forgotten that Ham, at the very time he did that act, was more than a hundred years old (p. 93) . . . The appointment of this race of men to servitude and slavery was a *judicial* act of God, or, in other words, was a *divine* judgment (p. 98).

In this passage it is clear, that the law of Moses *peremptorily* directed, that *all* their perpetual slaves, or *bond* servants, should be procured from among the *heathen negro* race, the very people to whom the *curse* of Noah referred, and are *always* referred to as *heathens* (p. 112) . . . The term *heathen* therefore as used in the *law,* referred entirely to the race of Ham, who had been judicially condemned to a condition of servitude, more than eight hundred years before the giving of the law, by the mouth of Noah, the medium of the Holy Ghost (p. 113).

By this mode of phraseology what else can be understood than that while the Hebrews were forbidden to sell their own blood as *bondsmen* out of the country, they might, however, buy and sell *heathen* negro men for *bond* men, and thus traffic in them as an article of trade or commerce (p. 141) . . . But to make the fact still more clear, namely, that the Jews did actually deal in slaves of the negro race, see the book of Joel, third chapter . . . (p. 142). Here it is certainly stated that the Jews *might,* and actually *should,* sell the people of Palestine, who were of the race of Ham, the heathen negroes of old Canaan . . . (p. 143). Having, as proposed in the commencement of this section, shows that the law of Moses did *indorse* and *sanction* the enslaving of the race of Ham, as *denounced* by Noah, and that the Hebrews, through the whole Jewish history, acted toward them on *that* principle (p. 159).

If the passage is not thus understood, then it will follow that the Egyptian negroes, and consequently the whole negro race, are not human; for the prophet plainly says, that their flesh was as the flesh of asses; and asses are not human. To allow them, therefore, a place among the species called man, we are compelled to admit that interpretation (p. 181). JEZEBEL, the worst woman ever heard of in the annals of mankind, the wife of *Ahab,* one of the kings of *Israel,* not of *Judea,* was a negro woman, the daughter of ETHBALL, king of Zidonia (p. 187). If the Supreme Being has seen fit to endow this race with a less quantum of intellectual faculties, and with less attractive powers and persons, in all respects, than he has the white race—what then? Are we, therefore, to undervalue them on this account? We think not (p. 201).

The negroes of Africa, who are the descendents of the Egyptians, the Lybians, and the Ethiopians, all the same people, the race of Ham, the first negroes, for thousands of years, have made no advances in letters, or in any way approximating thereto; as in all Africa, among the negro tribes and kingdoms, not a *gleam* of the light of science, the precursor of which is the invention of *letters,* has appeared. Not a Hieroglyphic or symbol—no kind of painting . . . has appeared in all the vast regions of Southern Africa (p. 214).

In conclusion, therefore, from a view of the preceding facts, we are compelled to hold that it is absolutely certain, taking the whole history of both races, the whites and the blacks, into the account, that the *latter* are absolutely unequal and lower in mental abilities, and do not possess, *naturally,* the stamina of improvement as do the former; and that this difference is attributable alone to the wisdom of God, in the creation of the negro race, in the blood and being of Ham, their father; on which account it is as utterly impossible to elevate them to an equality with the whites; as it is to take away the blackness of their skins (p. 249).

"The magnet that drew men westward over the wilderness trails was cotton land."[16] The area below the Piedmont met the farmer's crop requirement of at least two hundred days between frosts.

The frontier promoted individualism, an impatience with formal institutions, and a distrust of government. The land required hard work and a respect for the Almighty who ultimately gave the increase. Many of the traits now called "southern," like an affinity for guns and violence, a fierce individualism, and a resistance to central political direction, were nurtured in isolated outposts away from the amenities and refinements of coastal life.

Black Southerners lived a different, and altogether separate, existence on the plantation and the frontier. Their cultural watersheds were the years from 1720 to 1780, when nearly two-thirds of the enslaved African population of the South were brought to the colonies. The staple crops of sugar, rice, indigo, and cotton required vast numbers of laborers, and this model of labor-intensive agriculture began early to differentiate the southern colonies from other English settlements. Notwithstanding evidence of kind masters, the bulk of evidence shows sunup to sundown work in situations of extreme cruelty. Slaves lived in poverty and despair, away from polite white society. Diaries of plantation owners are filled with accounts of slave resistance, work slowdowns, broken tools, pretended sicknesses, and resultant punishment. A climate of fear, coupled with the suspicion of an impending slave revolt, pervaded plantation life. The harshness of race was stamped on the region at birth.

African American culture grew into a caste system, with its own language, ideas about deity, social relations, and rituals of life. Slavery created a separate and isolated culture with unique music, dance, customs of childraising, crafts, and even language. In the first census of 1790, two million people lived above the Mason-Dixon line, and one million nine hundred thousand lived below it. One-third of the southern residents were black, and in some states—South Carolina for example—more than half the population was slave.[17]

The sectional conflict that led to the Civil War was basically economic. The agricultural southern economy was based on slave labor—without it businesses would collapse—and the seeds of that clash were sown in the colonial period. In the settlement of the frontier South, the models of plantation wealth in Virginia and the Carolinas were dominant. Small differences at the founding were magnified over time, and the accusing finger of history always returned to the slavery issue as the cause of the discord.

The fourth, and perhaps the most important, political difference between the South and the North in the colonial period was their separate views on the form the postrevolutionary government should take in America. The independence of the revolution resolved one set of critical questions about the relationship between the mother country and the colonies, only to raise new ones over how to divide power between the local and national governments. Those in favor of a stronger central government called themselves "Federalists," while their opponents were called "Antifederalists."

The split between the two groups matched divisions between the urban, market-oriented communities on the Atlantic coast who favored the new constitution and the backcountry rural inland areas that saw no reason for a strong, central government. The interior of North and South Carolina, and economically underdeveloped areas of southwestern Virginia and north Georgia, saw little benefit in a central government whose purpose was to tax them. The coastal cities, like Boston, New York, and Charleston, were eager to support the new government in an effective national policy to build public amenities and regulate foreign and interstate commerce.

Political differences between Federalists and Antifederalists were sharply defined in public debates. "A common Antifederalist argument during the ratification struggle of 1787–1788 was that they were the true federalists because they took their bearings from the principles of federalism laid down in the Articles . . . while the Federalists abandoned the principles of federalism and embraced a consolidated system."[18] Federalists portrayed the ratification as a critical turning point for the young republic that needed, in the words of John Jay, "safety of the people" best secured "by union against danger."[19] The Federalists won because they had a plan for recovery that was better than no plan at all.

The Antifederalists' most convincing argument was that the new Constitution lacked a basic bill of rights. They believed that the people were sovereign in the government, and the express reservation of power to them was the hallmark of good government. The people were the ones who set the rules, and selected a few to administer the power, which ultimately filtered back again to the people. The fact that the original document had no written guarantees of the people's right to assemble, worship, and have the right to trial by jury or to bear arms resonated with the southern population.

Over time the Antifederalist position would come to symbolize the southern position. The prevailing philosophy was that a culture rooted in an agricultural economy needed protection from a commanding central government intent on the expansion of power. Antifederalism emphasized individual sovereignty, limited government, and restrictions on taxes. The dawn of the American republic was a rare opportunity for the founders to grapple with fundamental ideas of government. The Tenth Amendment relieved Antifederalist fears about the provisions of centralization in the new Constitution. Southerners took a conservative, individualistic approach believing that government was at best a necessary evil.

Secession, the Civil War, and Reconstruction

The definition of the region south of the Mason-Dixon line as a unique cultural place was set in the colonial period, but over the next five decades the southern states became a distinct constituency. Never before, or since, has the South been more apart from the rest of the nation than in the antebellum years. Economic reliance on slavery was at the heart of this difference, ultimately dictating the particular virtues, interests, and ambitions of the area that would in the end require defense against northern interference.

The abolition of slavery in the North during the American Revolution created the opportunity for sectional conflict. Legislation was passed in Pennsylvania in 1780 to gradually abolish slavery. Court action in Massachusetts (1783) and unanimous acts in New York (1785) and New Jersey (1786) confirmed the legal sanctions that ensured the "peculiar institution" would wither away. Before the surrender at Yorktown the hope was that the values of US independence would serve as a basis to eradicate slavery, but southern states remained adamantly opposed to even the suggestion of such an idea.

The Northwest Ordinance of 1787 prohibited slavery and aristocratic inheritances in the new territory to guard against perpetual great estates. The Northwest Territory later became the states of Illinois, Indiana, Michigan, Ohio, and Wisconsin. Despite criticism at the time, "the Northwest Ordinance did more to perpetuate the Union than any document save the Constitution."[20] In this law the differences between West and South were spelled out in legislation and legal precedent. The provisions established equality as a guiding principle for settling the vast open spaces of the continent, and created an inevitable regional rivalry that pitted the South against the rest of the growing nation. This sectionalism was exaggerated by economic differences. Southerners resented the outflow of money from their pockets to the leaders of northern manufacturers who reaped the benefits of the tariff in the form of artificially elevated prices for their own goods.

The earliest expression of sectionalism in the new nation came not from the South, but from New Englanders opposed to the War of 1812. People in the northeast, living in the states of Massachusetts, Connecticut, and New York, depended the most on overseas trade. Representatives from these states all voted against the war. The western and southern areas of the country voted in a nationalistic fervor in favor of war. South Carolinian John C. Calhoun served as chairman of the House Foreign Relations Committee at the time, and reveled in the patriotic ardor of the moment: "The mad ambition, the lust of power, and the commercial avarice of Great Britain have left the neutral nations an alternative only between the base surrender of their rights, and the manly vindication of them."[21] Later this rhetorical venom about commercialism and a lust for power would be poured out on the supporters of the federal union. Calhoun, and Henry Clay of Kentucky, led a coalition of young congressmen from the frontier South and the newer states of the West in support of the war against ties to the European world.

After the war, Henry Clay emerged as the leader of negotiations to keep the Union together with the Missouri Compromise of 1820. This act established a balance between the admission of slave and free states. The country was beset with a

---

Vignette 2.2   John Caldwell Calhoun (1782–1850)

Born of Scotch-Irish ancestry in the upcountry of South Carolina, John C. Calhoun served in the federal government successively as congressman, secretary of war, vice president, senator, secretary of state, and again as senator. He entered Congress in 1811 as one of a handful of young nationalists urging war with England.

America experienced dramatic change from the close of the War of 1812 to the election of Andrew Jackson in 1828. The westward march of cotton contributed to overproduction and falling prices, a situation farmers in the South blamed on a tariff to protect manufacturers in the North. The issue of state versus national power was broached in a series of Supreme Court decisions, with the Missouri Compromise of 1820 revealing the depth of sectional cleavage over slavery.

Calhoun became the spokesman for the South when the very high tariff of 1828 drove the cotton states to the edge of rebellion. Convinced that his region suffered unduly from the tariff, Calhoun penned his "South Carolina Exposition" (1828), which was his first explicit statement of the doctrine of nullification.

What was nullification? Calhoun believed the Union was an agreement among states and powers were divided between the states and the national government. Supreme power, however, was not divided; since sovereignty must rest with either the states or the nation, Calhoun favored the former. He believed that since the states were sovereign before the Union was created, the Union was subordinate to the states. When a dispute arose between the two concerning the consti-

tutionality of an act of Congress, the Supreme Court could not sit in judgment; only the judgment of the original sovereign entity—the state—mattered in a dispute. "The great and leading principle is, that the General Government emanated from the people of the several states."

Calhoun believed a convention of the people should be called to vote on matters of constitutional dispute. If the convention declared an act of Congress null and void, operation of that act would be suspended in the boundaries of that state. The question of the relationship between the state and national government was resolved in favor of the states.

This was the doctrine of states' rights that guided the South in the years before the Civil War. Calhoun was a leading, if not *the* leading, defender of slavery and the agrarian economy. He also proposed the concurrent majority to protect southern interests in the legislature. When Congress again passed a tariff in 1832, Calhoun resigned the vice presidency to reenter the Senate and defend a decision by South Carolina to declare the tariff null and void within the state.

President Andrew Jackson and then Vice President Calhoun were sharply at odds over the extent of federal and state power. In 1830 at a dinner the president confronted Calhoun with a strong toast: "Our Union, It must be preserved." The startled Calhoun replied: "The Union, next to our liberty, most dear." For Calhoun, the states had originally been sovereign and were allowed to "interpose their sovereignty" to arrest the application of any law.

---

national paradox: slavery was crucial to the southern economy and, at the same time, a betrayal of national constitutional ideals. The agrarian values of the South clashed with the egalitarian settlement of the West and protectionist policies of the North. The expanding economy only showed this conflict in a larger public light.

Gradually the issue of national sectional separation became slavery, and it was Henry Clay and Stephen A. Douglas who forged the Great Compromise of 1850 to prevent national dissolution. By the terms of the law, California entered the Union as a free state, and a new boundary was drawn for Texas. Slavery was continued in the District of Columbia, but the slave trade was abolished there, and a more stringent fugitive slave law was enacted. A significant provision in the new law allowed the territories of Utah and New Mexico to vote as their constitutions directed, accommodating the nullification principle of John C. Calhoun.

Nullification was not a uniquely southern strategy; a number of northern states passed "personal freedom laws" in the 1850s seeking to invalidate the Fugitive Slave Act. Calhoun feared free states would outnumber slave states and eventually outlaw slavery. To protect the South he proposed the principle of "concurrent majority" whereby the minority could prevent domination with a veto of majority rule. "Calhoun recognized that any functionally negative power exercised by a section (the South) would contribute to a system whereby decisions were made jointly by the minority and the majority, and not by the majority alone."[22]

The southern economy continued to expand in the face of a national crisis. Baltimore, Washington, Richmond, Norfolk, and Charleston were the original slave trade centers. The rise of cotton production on what was once the frontier led to new slave trading centers in Montgomery, Memphis, and New Orleans. The planting, harvesting, and chopping of cotton became an exclusively southern passion that expanded with the economy. The greatest density of slaves was where cotton production was highest, and as cotton growing spread west, so did slavery. Eventually the forced servitude of black slaves was concentrated in a continuous "black belt," named more for the soil than the inhabitants, stretching from the tidewater of Virginia to the Carolinas through Georgia and Alabama to the Mississippi River and east Texas.

Slavery could not be separated from economics or from the social structure that came to support and defend it. Article One, Section Nine, of the Constitution forbade the importation of slaves after 1808, so the new slave centers were dependant on slave breeding in the upper South for agricultural expansion. Planters had little stake in community life since immovable land was a small part of their wealth, so they sold slave children and regularly moved to newer territory. When slavery was abolished, investment strategies changed and elites began to invest in their communities.

The most important institution for the separation of the races in the South was the Christian church. The Second Great Awakening (1820–1827) took place on the frontier where converts learned that their salvation was dependent more on them than on any divine plan by God. Seated on the "anxious bench" at a tent meeting, the changed souls were subject to dramatic, emotional, and heartfelt expressions of faith and conversion. Preachers like Lyman Beecher, Theodore Dwight Weld, and Charles Finney spread a gospel of individual responsibility and divine accountability.

**Vignette 2.3   The Grimke Sisters: Sarah Moore Grimke
(1792–1873) and Angelina Emily Grimke (1805–1879)**

These two daughters of a South Carolina planter were antislavery leaders and early agitators for women's rights. Sarah Grimke was born in 1792 and her younger sister arrived thirteen years later. Partly through the influence of an older brother, who was prominent in temperance and pacifist reforms, both women opposed slavery out of religious convictions.

On a trip to Philadelphia in 1819 Sarah was converted to Quakerism, and later so was her sister. Together they settled in Philadelphia where they became active in the abolition movement. They were the first salaried female spokeswomen in America, and the first to address men in public. Together they were the very picture of Quaker piety and purity, but they violated their southern honor as women and as antislavery crusaders.

The energetic Angelina published her "Appeal to the Christian Women of the South" in 1836, and South Carolina authorities threatened to arrest her if she returned to the state. Her older sister responded by writing "An Epistle to the Clergy of the Southern States" in the same year, urging churches to oppose slavery on Christian principle. These abolitionist writings were so contentious, that had the sisters returned to the South they might have been lynched.

The American Antislavery Society appointed them lecturers and sponsored them to speak in public. The prevailing attitude against such behavior led to their meetings being labeled "promiscuous assemblies." In the next year the sisters firmly linked the rights of slaves to those of women. They both attacked the "assumptions upon which southern society based its image of women."

Their feminist rhetoric created an uproar at the time, and none other than the leading abolitionist William Lloyd Garrison had to counsel them to emphasize the human rights of slaves before the political rights of women. Leading antislavery activist Theodore Weld married Angelina Grimke in 1838, and the sisters helped him with his abolitionist activities, including the operation of an interracial school in New Jersey, until their deaths.

The evangelists proclaimed that all men were brothers in the sight of God and deserved salvation. The moralistic sermons sometimes peaked with a question about how enslaved Africans in the United States would act if they were free. The tent meetings of the "awakening" crusades crossed state boundaries, traditional church denominations, and ethnic backgrounds. Over the course of time, antislavery was woven into the revival sermons, and the line between politics and religion evaporated. Church members spread the abolitionist movement from crusade to home gatherings, to neighboring meetings. Revivals in New York, Ohio, Pennsylvania, and Michigan led to a growth in antislavery sentiment.

The black church was born in these years of evangelism as freemen in the North joined together to write their own story of revival. The first Methodist General Conference for free blacks was formed in 1816 in Philadelphia.[23] Delegates from Baltimore and other cities agreed "that the people . . . should become one body, under the name of the African Methodist Episcopal Church."[24]

The call for emancipation began as a cry in these revivals and assemblies. The evangelical meetings had the collateral effect of imparting dignity to blacks in their daily struggles with white oppression. "In the deep South, Negroes and whites had, as in other places, worshipped together."[25] Later the slaves were granted separate services under strict white control. The rumor throughout the South was that black ministers would use preaching as a means to incite their race to insurrection. In spite of these warnings the African American church emerged as the one institution that could stand up to segregation and racial discrimination.

In a day when people accepted the Bible literally, white Southerners argued that the plight of black slaves was a heavenly affliction. Black skin color was a reminder of the sinful mark inflicted on Ham, the wicked son of Noah. Divine displeasure ordained slavery, which was defended as a positive good, assisting innately inferior beings in their struggle with nature. "Never before has the black race of Central Africa," wrote John C. Calhoun, "attained a condition so civilized and so improved, not only physically, but morally and intellectually."[26] Had not the Jews, God's chosen people, practiced slavery? Didn't the Ten Commandments mention "servants" three times? Didn't Paul urge the fugitive Onesimus to return to his master? "The proslavery churchmen of the South used the bondage of the soul to make more secure the bondage of the body."[27]

The religious debate anticipated political discord. The vacillations of pro-slavery churchmen led to denominational splits with the Methodists in 1844, the Baptists in 1845, and the Presbyterians in 1861. In the antebellum South, freedmen were expelled from many southern communities.[28] The slave insurrections led by blacks like Gabriel Prosser, Denmark Vesey, and Nat Turner were said to be a result of religious instruction, so the majority of white slave owners forbade both education and worship for their slaves. Revivals in northern churches led to cries for emancipation; in southern churches the same enthusiasm reinforced slavery.

The road to secession was paved with another distinction between North and South, that being social class. In 1831 Alexis de Tocqueville, the oft-quoted French visitor, observed that American democracy was characterized by something called "individualism." Unlike Europe, which had a structure of landed gentry whose responsibility it was to care for the lower classes, Americans emphasized self-reliance. "Individualism," according to de Tocqueville, "disposes each member of the community to sever himself from the mass of his fellows, and to draw apart with his family and friends; so that, after he has thus formed a little circle of his own, he willingly leaves society at large to itself."[29] He found this to be a distinctly US trait. Opposite this individualism was the political hierarchy of Europe, a structure that included de Tocqueville himself, and a tradition of other landed gentry who believed God intended them to rule.

De Tocqueville's visit in the 1830s coincided with a time when the colonial institutions of aristocracy, education, position, and wealth were being replaced by Jacksonian democracy, and rule by the "common man." In this transfer of power, the South stood as a US anomaly, a land ruled by an agrarian aristocracy with a sentiment for isolation and social exclusivism. Rule by the common man was not a familiar notion in the southern world. Jacksonian democracy was an irregular ideal in a place of landed gentry and elite rule. Money and class, more than common birthright, described society, and status, income, education, and lifestyle were associated with social rank in the South more than other places. Not surprisingly, de Tocqueville concluded his book with this insight: "Two branches may be distinguished in the great Anglo-American family, which have hitherto grown without entirely commingling; the one in the South, the other in the North."[30]

Southern racial distinctiveness was tied to another concern in community life, namely the special role of women in home life. Between 1830 and 1850 the cult of chivalry for white women became a major expression of southern romanticism. A white woman's role was restricted to "proper" conduct, with prescribed piety, purity, submissiveness, and domesticity the rule of the day. From the time of the revolutionary era, the South consistently lagged behind other regions of the country in implementing educational reform for its female population. The agricultural economy of the South kept women in traditional roles. "Whether her husband's farm was large or small, was planted by slaves, hired hands, or family, or was confined to one plantation or to several, the southern matron was a figure of formidable industry and talent."[31]

Black women were afforded no similar power on the plantation, and healthy family development was not a priority among slave owners. The abolitionist Frederick Douglass wrote that on the plantation where he was born, mothers were not allowed to take care of their children because their labor was needed elsewhere, so childrearing was "left to older women and grandmothers."[32] Race consciousness became definite in adulthood: black women did the cooking in the white home and the black children waited on the table. Slavery sealed the concubinage of slave women to white planters, their children, and overseers.

The economic, religious, and social differences between North and South were exacerbated by the unparalleled prosperity of the 1850s. Cotton was king, and southern planters capitalized on the overseas demand, but the North—it was alleged—held the cotton trade hostage with an unjust monopoly. In 1860 the Democratic Party made the ill-fated decision to hold its political convention in the city of Charleston. The hotels and boarding houses filled with "fire-eaters," men described by the press at the time as wanting to keep the cotton empire, protect the peculiar institution of slavery, and secede from the Union. On a cloudy Monday morning in April they got their way. The cotton-states delegates announced their withdrawal from the convention. Delegate Charles Russell of Virginia rose from the floor of the convention and called the crisis an "irrepressible conflict."[33]

From the perspective of history, the record shows the South deficient in every category necessary for military victory; in manufacturing and rail capacity, in population and reserves, they were far behind their northern opponents (Table 2.1).

Table 2.1   Union and Confederate Resources and Losses

Resources	Union	Confederate
Population	20,700,000	9,105,000 (total) 5,451,000 (white)
Manufacturing Entities	110,000	18,000
Manufacturing Numbers	1,300,000	110,000
Miles of Railroad	21,973	9,283
Estimated Troop Strength	2,100,000	850,000

Losses	Union	Confederate
Died in Battle	110,000	94,000
Died of Wounds	250,000	164,000

Sources: Berkin, et al., *Making America,* Boston: Houghton Mifflin, 1995, p. 410; Simkins and Roland, *A History of the South,* New York: Alfred P. Knopf, 1972, p. 237.

Enlistment volunteers came from a white population one-quarter the size of that in the North. Margaret Mitchell wrote after the Civil War that "Southerners can never resist a losing cause."[34]

In spite of these disparities, southern men entered the war with confidence and, to all but the most thoughtful, it seemed impossible that they could lose. Dr. J. H. Thornwell, a minister from South Carolina, proclaimed at the time that the "parties in this conflict are not merely abolitionists and slaveholders—they are atheists, socialists, communists, red republicans, Jacobins on the one side, and the friends of order and regulated freedom on the other."[35] The motto of the Confederacy was "Deo Vindice," for "God Vindicates," meaning that the Almighty would justify the southern cause on the field of battle. But in the end God did not vindicate, and after the war Southerners were left groping for an explanation of how the "infidels" could triumph on native soil once thought sacred. In battle after battle the Confederate army lost about the same number of killed and wounded as the Union army, but the population discrepancy meant reserves of material and men were exhausted far quicker in the South. The war touched every southern home: "To lose a war and then to have even the means of recuperation withheld is total defeat, and this is what the South experienced in the conflict."[36]

Each year of the war marked progress by the Union armies in their task to defeat the Confederacy. "While the Confederacy was bleeding internally because of blockade, inflation, desertion, disloyalty, and other ills, the armies of the United States were pressing forward determined to destroy the Confederate government and reincorporate its territories into the Union."[37] In 1861, the first year of fighting, the two sides were tentative in conflict. The Union forces suffered battlefield losses, but they effectively secured a blockade, occupied Northern Virginia, and took up positions in the west.

The full shock of the conflict became apparent in 1862, when the battle losses at Shiloh Church, in western Tennessee, exceeded 23,000 men. In that one afternoon both armies suffered five times the losses of Manassas. Americans had never known this type of horrific warfare, and the worst part was it was self-administered. In his novel about the battle of Gettysburg, Michael Shaara suggests a scene where a Union general surveys the battlefield as bodies were being laid out, "row after row, the feet all even and the toes pointing upward." The novel and character concluded that there was no divine spark in humans, they were all "animal meat: the Killer Angels."[38]

In the fall of 1862, the Army of the Potomac and the Army of Northern Virginia met at Sharpsburg, Maryland, along a creek named Antietam. At sunset on September 17, the day would become synonymous with the bloodiest single-day battle of the Civil War. "[Confederate General Robert E.] Lee had suffered only half as many casualties as he had inflicted in the course of the campaign . . . [but] the troops Lee lost were the best he had—the best he could ever hope to have in the long war that lay ahead, now that his try for an early ending by invasion had been turned back."[39]

The losses in Maryland anticipated the events unfolding in the penultimate year of 1863. Five days after the battle of Sharpsburg, President Lincoln issued his Emancipation Proclamation, set to go into effect on January 1 of the new year. Six months later, on June 30, 1863, a southern brigade searching for shoes encountered a Union cavalry unit near the town of Gettysburg, Pennsylvania. The subsequent battle proved to be the turning point of the war. In a desperate attempt to win in one move, General Lee sent eleven brigades in a mile-wide charge into the center of the federal lines on July 3, 1863. The gamble proved futile, and in those few minutes of Pickett's fateful charge the outcome for the South was sealed. "Just as the exhausted survivors of the final assault at Gettysburg were pulling themselves together, trying to find out who still lived, General Grant and General Pemberton were meeting under a flag of truce on a hill outside Vicksburg, Mississippi, agreeing to terms under which Pemberton and his army and the Vicksburg fortress and everything the Confederacy hoped for in the Mississippi Valley would the next day be surrendered."[40]

The defeat at Gettysburg and the surrender of Vicksburg devastated the Confederates, but the most lasting legacy of the war, and one that would influence politics in the South for decades, was yet to come. Union generals Ulysses S. Grant and William T. Sherman initiated a new type of warfare, "total war," waged not only against enemy troops but also against the civilian residents in order to destroy the morale and economic resources of the population. In his march Sherman cut a swath sixty miles wide that reeked of butchered animals and smoke from burned barns and abandoned farmhouses. After the war the Union general admitted that of the one hundred million dollars of destruction his armies wrought in Georgia, only twenty million were of military advantage.[41] Generations of Southerners persisted in making a distinction between Union generals who adhered to a code of conduct in battle, men like McClellan, Hancock, and even Grant; and the one who inaugurated a war of unlimited aggression—Sherman.

The defeat of the Civil War left the South poor, failed, and frustrated, emotions with which the rest of the country could hardly identify. A military defeat was followed by an economic collapse, social dismemberment, and political ostracism. The South went from a position of economic leadership to subsistence living, while the victorious North bounded into prosperity, optimism, and success. In the ashes of Shiloh, Antietam, and Gettysburg, the South discovered its cause "lost," and Charles Wilson Reagan aptly described the region as "baptized in blood."[42]

The legacy remained for generations. "Every third household in the South saw one of its members dead, a rate that was four times that of the North."[43] White Southerners identified the "Lost Cause" as a movement to enshrine the memory of the Civil War in every community. The mythology held that southern ideals were actually vindicated in defeat, and the bloodbath of war sanctified the values and beliefs of the region. A year after Appomattox, Confederate memorial associations were formed to care for the gravesites of the southern war dead and etch the memory of the Lost Cause into the regional psyche. "In the moment of death," wrote Robert Penn Warren, "the Confederacy entered upon its immortality."[44]

The legacy of soil and valor, a belief that while the chosen people lost a holy war, they emerged purified for a greater cause, came to dominate southern life and politics. White politicians regularly invoked a civil religion of sentimentality, conservatism, and southern identity to resist intellectual trends and social change. William Faulkner was part of this inheritance, and wrote about it nearly one hundred years later: "Who else could have declared a war against a power with ten times the area and a hundred times the men and a thousand times the resources, except men who could believe that all that was necessary to conduct a successful war was not acumen nor shrewdness nor politics nor diplomacy nor money nor even integrity and simple arithmetic, but just love of land and courage."[45] After the war, the population discovered that agrarian affection was not enough, and the South found itself an occupied country.

In the period of Reconstruction a new set of values came to the region. The period from 1865 to 1877 was a time when national efforts were made to incorporate the South back into the Union. Some Northerners approached this task in a spirit of revenge, others sought reconciliation, and idealistic reformers established schools and bureaus for reconciliation. A suddenly vibrant Republican Party, along with rapacious carpetbaggers, notorious native scalawags, and uninitiated freedmen all became active in the political process. Reconstruction abolished that most firmly rooted ideal of southern life—white supremacy. White Southerners determined in these years that no part of social or political relations could be changed to make blacks equal to whites.

The lasting legacy from the period was political. White Southerners came to hate consolidated political authority in a way no other part of the nation could fathom. The period was marked by rampant corruption in southern capitals, but the same could be said of the northern states. These were the years of the disgrace of the Grant administration in Washington, and the Tweed Ring in New York City. The public debt of southern state budgets soared, in Alabama from $7 million to $32 million, and in Louisiana from $14 million to $48 million; tax rates rose accordingly, 400 percent in Alabama and 800 percent in Louisiana.[46]

The most spectacular form of resistance was the midnight riding of the Ku Klux Klan and its kindred organizations. The small numbers of federal troops on hand for police duty were unable to protect blacks from physical attack. Insurrection took the form of the disruption of Republican meetings and intimidation of voters and candidates at election time. In the years of Reconstruction the southern economy was in ruins, the banks held only worthless Confederate money, acres of land stood idle, and white hearts brimmed with hatred for their former slaves who now dominated the political order.

At the same time, Reconstruction was a period of both success and frustration for black Southerners. Success came from voting participation. During Reconstruction and its aftermath, blacks were elected to local, state, and federal offices. For example, between 1869 and 1901 eight southern states elected a total of twenty black members of the US House of Representatives. Mississippi sent two blacks, though not simultaneously, to the US Senate. Significant numbers of blacks were elected to state government positions, but they were never in control to the point where they could neglect making alliances with peer white representatives. The number of black legislators was approximately 270 in 1868 and rose to almost 325 in 1872, but declined to barely 60 by the end of Reconstruction in 1877. During Reconstruction black legislators occupied 87 of 107 seats in the South Carolina House of Representatives and a black sat on the state Supreme Court. A black also occupied the position of secretary of state and treasurer in the Palmetto State. Mississippi, Louisiana, and South Carolina each elected black lieutenant governors, and a black in Mississippi served as speaker of the house.

African American success came in the form of political participation and improved economic opportunity, but frustration remained when at the end of the period they could point to only one tangible achievement: formal schooling. Occupational improvement reduced the illiteracy rate from 90 percent to 70 percent.[47] Former slaves migrated to towns and cities expecting jobs and homes; they found "carpetbaggers," a derisive term southern Democrats used to characterize northern opportunists who hoped to take advantage of the unstable politics of the time. New freedmen lived in overcrowded shanties with poor sanitation. In the face of opposition they established a system of public education, founded institutions for the mentally and physically disabled, and attempted to reform the prison system. The black leadership worked for civil and political rights, while their constituents wanted more tangible rewards, like ownership of land and educational opportunities. Outraged white leaders charged that corrupt officials led Reconstruction state governments. The new freedman voter was led by officials recruited for their allegiance, instead of business or professional men who had succeeded through accomplishment.

Extravagance, ignorance, and dishonesty marred Reconstruction rule, and while the crimes were not as bad as the legends they inspired, no amount of argument could convince anyone they were successful governments. White Southerners grudgingly accepted the abolition of slavery, but they could never agree to political rule by their former slaves or social rules that treated them as equals. White political opinion was split; some believed the invincibility of the Republican opposition could be divided by coalition, and others refused to abandon white supremacy. By 1869 some Democrats abandoned principle and accepted key Republican measures. Others refused. The "Myth of Reconstruction" was the belief among some whites that the old South, with its landed aristocracy, would one day be revived. A supine admiration for the past was increased if the injustices of Reconstruction were exaggerated. Margaret Mitchell's novel, *Gone With the Wind*, and D. W Griffith's movie, *The Birth of a Nation*, embodied this overstated nostalgia. The adherents longed for the past, and blamed the North and the black race for the disruption of social and political tranquility.

Rule by blacks and radical Republicans ended in a compromise that placed Rutherford B. Hayes in office after the presidential election of 1876 was thrown into the US House of Representatives. Hayes became president and the Republicans agreed to immediately withdraw federal troops and allow the southern states to govern themselves without northern or black interference.

> With troops out of the South and in a spirit of great conciliation, Congress removed other restrictions. In 1878 the use of armed forces in elections was forbidden. In 1894 appropriations for special federal marshals and supervisors of elections were cut off. In 1898 the last disabilities laid on disloyal and rebellious southerners were removed in a final amnesty.[48]

Why were Republican politicians and abolitionists willing to permit resegregation, a rebirth of racism, and the codification of Jim Crow within a generation of the Civil War? Historians have put forth a number of explanations, including latent northern racism, the rise of Social Darwinism with its survival of the fittest ethic, and the beckoning of westward expansion. C. Vann Woodward favors the latter explanation, "The reconstructed South came to be regarded in the eighties as a bulwark of, instead of a menace to, the new economic order."[49]

The Bourbon Era of southern history followed Reconstruction from the late 1870s until the turn of the century when the Democratic Party rose to govern the

South after the overthrow of Reconstruction. White supremacy meant more than a return to white dominance. It signified absolute elimination of blacks from every activity that involved any hint of equality with the white population. Typical of this attitude was "Pitchfork" Ben Tillman of South Carolina, who boasted that civilization was a product of white, Christian cultural evolution: "the superior race on the globe; the flower of humanity; the race responsible for the history of the world; and the achievements of the human family in a large degree."[50] Jim Crow laws, taken from a derisive name for a black minstrel, were enacted to separate whites and blacks in public and private facilities. The divided accommodations were codified in states across the South. In *Plessy v. Ferguson* (1896) the US Supreme Court upheld Jim Crow laws under the "separate but equal" doctrine providing for the segregation of blacks if they were provided "equal" public facilities.

The foremost change in southern agriculture after the Civil War was the rise of sharecropping, a market process that joined the freedman's desire for wages to the landowners need for labor. Whites reluctantly accepted the end of slavery and accommodated a new work routine of wages and credit. The effect of the new system was to keep black families in the local area and attach them to the land. In some cases blacks were able to make substantial economic progress in tenancy, but in most cases the landowner's lien destroyed individual initiative.[51] Another innovation in the postwar agrarian economy was the expansion of the vegetable and fruit industry. The development of rapid rail, and later truck farming, led to an expansion of peach farms in Georgia, and oranges, apples, and strawberries in South Carolina and Florida. The general expansion of perishable food to the markets of the North stimulated agriculture across the South. The longer growing season stretched from the eastern shore of Virginia to the lower Rio Grande Valley of Texas.

Gradually the southern farmer was caught in what amounted to an economic straightjacket: forced by credit to turn to cash crops and at the same time at the mercy of wholesalers, grain producers, and fertilizer distributors. Invariably, those farmers who were involved in production of the familiar crops of cotton and tobacco suffered the most. The crop-lien system forced both black and white farmers into economic dependency, and the system proved a disaster. The collapse of agriculture saddled the region with a legacy of poverty that would last until after World War II.

In the 1870s the bottom fell out of the cotton market and southern farmers revolted. The despair of farming across the South became a wail. The Grange, or Patrons of Husbandry, offered some hope with combined social activities, new methods of farming, and cooperative economic efforts. It answered the prayers of small farmers by declaring that federal legislation was needed to curb the profits of railroads and remedy the economic reversals. In the turmoil of the times white farmers in the region found common interests with the farmers of the West and Midwest. In the end the grandiose plans of buying and selling collapsed, and by 1878 the Grange was defunct across the South.

The discontent of the 1880s took the form of the Farmers Alliance. All across the South fiery political speeches decried the "money power" of Wall Street and the rising power of eastern urban commercial interests. The attitude grew that farmers were wealth producers, and other capitalists were parasites living off the sweat of the virtuous agrarians. The rhetoric of Ben Tillman (South Carolina) and Tom Watson (Georgia) was laced with the desirable qualities of the rural life and its impending destruction at the hands of evil outsiders.

The election of 1896 stands as one of the most important political contests in US history. The focus was on economic issues, with the debt-ridden farmers of the Midwest and South allied against "the idle holders of idle capital" of the northern cities. The defeat of William Jennings Bryan spelled the end of the Populist crusade, and made the rural South and the Democratic Party synonymous.

A New South and the Great Depression

The "New South" era inaugurated the twentieth century in the belief that the states of the Old South would shed their agrarian past, and embrace the promise of a shiny, new, urban and industrial future. Economic power shifted in the region from an agricultural aristocracy to men of industry and commerce. Ralph McGill hailed the "small town rich man" who owned the gin, cotton, or tobacco warehouse and controlled local credit as the new southern stereotype.[52] Tennessee Williams immortalized this life in his play, *Cat on a Hot Tin Roof*, and the movie *The Long Hot Summer* evoked this rural ideal.

Economic change happened in some communities, but the rural nature of the place resisted change. Economic development was synonymous with domination by northern capital, and reconciliation with former enemies. Reunification was unpopular in many quarters where residents remembered the northern invasion, especially Sherman's march. "New South" advocates of economic modernization, like Henry Grady of the Atlanta *Constitution* declared, "I see a South the home of fifty millions of people; her cities vast hives of industry; her country-sides the treasures from which their resources are drawn."[53] Tom Watson of Georgia, a red-headed populist with fire in his eyes, opposed the new industrial idealism of Grady. "If it means apology, abject submission—sycophancy to success—perish the thought . . . shame to Southern men who go to Northern banquets."[54] Watson was the first of a number of southern politicians who blamed the economic misery of the region on northern exploitation.

The spirit of regional antipathy against other parts of the country that characterized populism persisted into the new century. At root it was a movement to achieve economic reform for the agricultural classes in the Midwest and South. Southern leaders gained control of the Democratic Party and pursued change within its power structure. When Bourbon Era politicians abandoned them, they sought other allies, including black voters. The most radical of the populists declared that skin color bore no relation to political freedom and economic opportunity, and they asked for political equality. This brief alliance was shattered by the political defeat of populism in 1896, and destroyed by racism in the decades that followed. After this time "southern populism" was seen as a class movement directed against the economic elite who ostracized the poor.

White supremacy was maintained through control of the Democratic Party, whose primaries were tantamount to election. A southern commitment to low-wage labor and resource-exploitative industries, such as tenant farming and textiles, demanded a stable, conservative government not inclined to tax or regulate. Election victories were reserved for politicians who promised not to interfere. Tenant farming began as a way to get former slaves back to work, but by the beginning of the century, the system was the last refuge of poor blacks and whites with neither land nor equipment.

World War I proved to be a turbulent time in southern political and economic life. When faced with the sudden cutoff of European immigration, northern employers flooded the South with labor agents offering workers free transportation and an assurance of jobs at the end of the line. "Perhaps as many as a half million blacks went North between 1915 and 1920."[55] They were not alone; southern whites also left. Opportunity beckoned because wages were low in the South, and the industrial economy offered a chance for escape.

Back home, the New South supplemented a heritage of frustration with one of myth. A belief that economic regeneration was just around the corner only made the wishful thinking worse. With populism dying, the intellectual temper was set with a romantic optimism about the inevitability of progress. The South gradually regained the manufacturing capacity it lost in the depression years after the Civil War. Jeffersonian ideals of rural individualism lingered on in the twentieth century among the southern ruling classes, and they successfully halted the importation of northern capital for a time. Gradually business boosters touted the inevitability of southern industrialization. "Between 1909 and 1929 the South's share of the industrial output of the United States rose from 12 to 14 percent."[56] By 1929 business nationwide was showing weakness, and the agrarian economy in the South was slowing down. On October 24, 1929, the bottom fell out of the stock market, and, as prices continued to plummet, the agricultural economy "went South."

The clouds of the Great Depression eclipsed the myth of New South progress. By 1930, 79 percent of southern farmers owned no land; "once [they] had fallen into the trap of tenancy, they were kept there by ignorance, lack of opportunity, disease, social pressures, debt, and state and local laws."[57] Small towns and cities dominated the southern states, while railroads linked isolated farms to commercial cities, but the politics and social ideas remained the same rural and remote birthright unfamiliar to the rest of the nation. Because the economy was so dependent on agriculture, recession in the South featured poverty more severe than elsewhere, and worse than the border states.

Before the Great Depression, low-wage manufacturing jobs had begun to compete with farming as a source of livelihood in the twentieth-century South. Tomorrow came in the form of a more diverse economy. "Older industries, such as cotton textiles, tobacco, fertilizer, iron and lumber, expanded; among newer industries, petroleum, electric power, rayon, chemicals, and paper became important sources of wealth."[58] Leaders in the South described the place as rich in natural resources and now triumphant over its past. In truth, the little manufacturing that did come to the region failed to change the overall economic condition of the place as a whole. Incomes improved, but the social structure remained unchanged, with virtually all jobs in the new factories reserved for whites, while blacks were left with only janitorial or menial tasks.

The economy was rooted in family life that was similarly hierarchical in the 1920s. Most southern women were comfortable rooted in the familiar social roles associated with agrarian culture. Women of both races on tenant farms juggled and mastered a myriad of tasks that required physical endurance and skill. One author wrote of her grandmother in Georgia, where "the running of the household with its rituals and necessities, was a seven-day-a-week, fifty-two-week-a-year job that held Lee—and her black servants, who had to do the same jobs at home for their own families—captive."[59] Women in the South organized to influence public and social life through the church. Voluntary associations worked to support foreign missions, schools, and training seminars. The church was a haven for black women as well. They made their way to towns and cities, often taking domestic jobs. Once there they formed voluntary associations at their places of worship.

The political and social environment of the South dulled the appeal of the suffrage movement, which was gaining acceptance elsewhere. The states of Mississippi and Georgia refused to accept women's suffrage as the law of the land, claiming that the Nineteenth Amendment was passed too late to comply with state election law. The demand for the vote came at a time when political leaders were instituting poll taxes and literary tests to restrict participation by black Southerners, and women's suffrage was seen as yet another threat to the established order. The crusade against lynching was often women-led, so the demand for women's rights was seen as a radical cause.

The culture of the region created a "proper sphere" for white women that insulated them from the forces of modernity. Virtually every college sorority and fraternity had its beginnings on a southern campus. The myth arose of the southern belle who could sing your praises to the sky or slash you completely with the sweetest smile and the nicest words you did hear. Women were different in the South; the "Steel Magnolias" were feminine, strong, beautiful, and as elusive as a butterfly in spring, or such was the image.

The social system and the economic system both collapsed with the stock market in 1929. Agriculture, in decline after World War I and scarred by tenancy ever since, reached rock bottom and worse during the Great Depression. In 1933 average incomes in the South were 40 percent of what they were nationally, and many textile workers were on wage reductions, extended workweeks, and increased production schedules.[60] "I would see the cotton-mill people at the store," wrote Ben Robertson of his growing up years in upstate South Carolina, "their faces were pale . . . for they worked from before daylight until after dark, seventy hours a week."[61] The extent of this crisis is seen in Table 2.2, which shows the wholesale prices of key southern commodities during the Depression years.

The effects of the Depression were as much emotional as physical. The work weariness, coupled with a bleak future, sapped the populace of hope. The miseries were more than even the defeated South could remember. The fragile southern economy teetered on the brink of economic disaster. The average yearly per capita income went from $372 in 1929 to $203 in 1932.[62] Food prices dropped because of overproduction, which snowballed into farmers producing more to make up for the loss, resulting in a flooded market and still lower prices. In the region, despair became the acceptable social value exceeded only by fear. Hopelessness fueled radical politicians like Huey Long, who promised that in a vote for him "every man's a king, but no one wears a crown."[63] The Louisiana governor's proposal, adopted by Franklin D. Roosevelt (FDR) under the Agricultural Adjustment Act (AAA) of the New Deal, was that the federal government would pay farmers *not* to grow crops.

Tenant farmers suffered the most in these years. The system created a class of permanently poor agricultural workers without rights or guarantees. A picture of their life remains in the portrait by writer James Agee, and photographer Walker Evans, who were assigned by *Fortune* magazine in 1936 to collaborate on a series of articles with pictures about daily life in the Deep South. They lived in Alabama with three white families, sharing their food and sleeping in their cabins. Agee summarized their visit in prose written by candlelight on bare wooden floors as, "curious, obscene, terrifying, and unfathomably mysterious."[64] Black poverty was worse, summed up by bluesman Lonnie Johnson, "Hard times don't worry me, I was broke when it first started out."

Table 2.2 Wholesale Prices of Key Southern Commodities, 1925–1940

	1925	1928	1931	1934	1937	1940
Cotton[a]	$0.27	$0.19	$0.08	$0.12	$0.11	$0.10
Tobacco[b]	$24.79	$13.50	$12.20	$15.72	$24.19	$15.74
Textiles[c]	$0.36	$0.36	$0.35	$0.31	$0.20	$0.23

Source: Statistical Abstract of the United States, US Department of Commerce.
Notes: a. = per pound: b. = per 100 pounds; c. = per spool.

Vignette 2.4   Huey Pierce Long (1893–1935)

Huey Long emerged from the relatively poor hill country of northern Louisiana to transform forever the politics of his state and across the South. He was a great natural politician who looked, and often behaved, like a caricature of the redneck southern political stereotype of the region. At the time of his death in 1935, he was a serious rival to Franklin D. Roosevelt for the presidency.

Long began his political career as an advocate for poor people against the entrenched oil and planter interests of the state. Every southern state had a tradition of government by the elite, and Huey Long decided to take on the Old Regulars who lived in New Orleans and ran things statewide. He had a populist dislike for entrenched interests, and the oratorical powers to establish a mass following. Long lost the first time he ran, but won the governor's race in 1928 as an idealistic reformer who wanted to move the state forward. In the eight years he was a leader in Louisiana, four as governor and four as US senator, he created a political machine without precedent in US history. His wide popularity, use of official powers, and control of government through carefully chosen surrogates allowed him to concentrate virtually all power in his own hands. Long controlled the state as his personal fiefdom, silencing critics and intimidating opponents.

Throughout his political career Huey Long had a remarkable ability to tailor his presentation to win any audience. He could be brash, funny, iron-willed, brazen, folksy, or friendly; and his appearance alone was enough to excite a crowd. In 1932 he entered the US Senate where his rhetoric and disregard for tradition won him a national following. As the Depression widened and people looked for answers, Huey Long gave them in terms everyone could understand. Why was the country in such a condition? His answer was because wealth was concentrated in the hands of an economic elite, five hundred men on Wall Street made more money than all the farmers in the country combined.

First as a supporter of FDR, then as an opponent, Huey Long was always an advocate for redistribution of wealth. He believed the New Deal policies were inadequate for the problem at hand. Long began a national political organization entitled the Share Our Wealth Society, which had three million members at the end of just one year. The program promised each needy family an initial $5,000 and a guaranteed annual income of $2,500. The populist roots of Huey Long's appeal was in the black Share Our Wealth clubs, and with the former slaves who shared in the free school books, and improved state hospitals and public health services in the state. He once said, "I'm for the poor man. Black and white, they all gotta have a chance."

At the peak of his power, when he was positioning himself for a run at the presidency in 1936, Long was assassinated in September of 1935 by a Baton Rouge physician related to an anti-Long political appointee. No politician of his era, and few since, could match Long's popularity outside his region. Across the South he became a model for a popular leader who engendered blind loyalty from his followers.

The New Deal (1932–1940) of Franklin D. Roosevelt was a landmark effort to help the rural poor, identified in the South as the "Nation's Number One Economic Problem." Destitute farmers were the largest responsibility assigned to the Federal Emergency Relief Administration (FERA), especially southern tenants and sharecroppers. By the 1940s the farm programs were reaching more than 600,000 southern families, but this was far from a majority and it made little impact on agricultural tenancy.

Southerners were enthusiastic at first. Burnet R. Maybank, energetic mayor of Charleston, South Carolina, used emergency funds to spark the economy, expand water resources to bring in a paper mill, and build public housing projects.[65] The response by southern congressmen and senators in 1933 and 1934 was all that Roosevelt could have hoped for. "Like their Democratic colleagues from other regions, they gave the administration's proposals consistent and often enthusiastic support."[66]

Considering the widespread poverty and the "Solid South" political legacy of support for the national Democratic Party, enthusiasm for the New Deal should have remained uniformly high. It didn't. In Georgia, Governor Eugene Talmadge objected to the hourly wages paid on public works projects because he feared they would undermine the supply of farm laborers.[67] In Texas, Congressman Sam Rayburn initially supported the Emergency Relief Act of 1935, but later changed the entire program because people distrusted the planning and construction of rural electrification by government instead of local electric co-ops.[68] The national minimum wage was originally introduced to help the textile industry, but by 1939 the Works Projects Administration (WPA) minimums, while only 80 percent of those in the North, were still more than double the farm wage.[69] The deep-seated conservatism of the South made residents suspicious of federal programs, even in an hour of desperate need. New Deal "welfare giveaway" programs became a target for southern conservatives who maintained they encouraged laziness, government dependency, and cultivated a permanent underclass that was living on relief.

Residents of the South were used to hard times, but the 1930s were worse than anything before or since. The effects of Depression poverty are seen in Table 2.3, which shows the ranking of the southern region with the rest of the country, and among the southern states themselves, on a number of social and economic points. The measures are a rough indicator of the health of family life and domestic welfare in each state. Collectively they show that nine of the top ten states hardest hit by the Depression were in the South, and that all eleven of the southern states were among the thirteen most scarred by recession in the country. The rankings reveal that southern states were the poorest of the poor, and there were only limited effects of the federal and state programs designed to reverse the tide.

As Roosevelt assumed office the plight of southern farmers was desperate. The president believed that the family farm was an essential part of US life and needed to be saved. The Agricultural Adjustment Act encouraged farmers to reduce production by paying them not to plant. But the AAA and other "alphabet agencies" of the New Deal programs benefited large farmers, while small farmers, tenants, and sharecroppers continued to suffer in poverty. The AAA encouraged a "clearing of the land" of excess farm labor that contributed to the mass migration of Southerners northward in search of jobs. It also encouraged mechanization by consolidating ten-

Table 2.3   Rankings of Southern States for Selected Social Statistics in the Years of the Great Depression

	Infant Mortality Rate (1937)	Percentage of Illegitimate Births (1937)[a]	Poorest per Capita (1939)	Deaths Due to Influenza (1937)	Cumulative State Rank, South	Cumulative State Rank, National
Traditional States:						
Mississippi	18	4	1	2	3	3
Arkansas	23	12	2	3	6	6
South Carolina	3	1	4	12	1	1
Alabama	11	5	5	7	4	4
Louisiana	7	2	6	5	2	2
Emergent States:						
Tennessee	14	14	10	8	9	9
North Carolina	7	7	9	33	11	13
National States:						
Georgia	11	8	3	9	5	5
Virginia	6	9	14	14	8	8
Texas	4	21	11	6	7	7
Florida	17	11	7	16	10	11

Source: Statistical Abstract of the United States, 1942 and 1950
Note: a. Statistic not kept after 1950.

ant farm holdings into larger units. Roosevelt believed that the problem was the disproportion between agricultural and industrial prices, so the new programs imposed production quotas to raise prices. As a result, the Agriculture Adjustment Act unintentionally made the plight of small farmers worse.[70]

The appeal of the New Deal programs was feckless because all of the South's black population, and much of the white population as well, were unorganized and voteless. The Southern Democrats, who remained the most powerful members of Congress because of seniority, allied with the Republicans in an informal but effective anti–New Deal coalition. "With some 28 percent of the nation's population, the South received only 15.4 percent of the aid disbursed by the federal government in a typical Depression year such as 1937."[71] Nothing was easy in the South; and one reason the Depression hit so hard was that the economy was depressed well before 1929. Many plans ran into trouble from white administrators determined to maintain racial segregation. One New Deal administrator commented on a rural welfare program created to help both black and white tenant farmers: "White strikers were seldom molested as they marched, but whenever a predominantly Negro group attempted the tactic, its members ran great risks."[72] Programs aimed at the rural poor began to gradually cross racial lines, as the federal laws insisted on including the black poor as well as the white.

The most important industrial innovation in the years of the Great Depression was the development of hydroelectric power and its auxiliary steam-electric power. "The largest power developments of this section were the huge Murray Dam on the Saluda River in South Carolina, the six dams belonging to the Georgia Power Company, and the Catawba-Wateree River Developments in the Carolinas belonging to the Duke Power Company."[73] These developments were privately held and often resented by the customers.

The New Deal experiment that aroused the most public controversy was the Tennessee Valley Authority (TVA), created in 1933 as a form of welfare transfer payment for the unemployed. President Franklin Roosevelt suggested the construction of sixteen dams to speed economic development in seven southern states: Tennessee, Alabama, Georgia, Kentucky, Mississippi, North Carolina, and Virginia. The construction put thousands of people to work and gave opportunities for job training to an unskilled, rural work force accustomed to working on the farm. Above all, the TVA was a celebration of electric power in a part of the country without that modern amenity. With lights came hope. The agency provided power to eighty-three municipally owned power utility electric cooperatives over the next decade. Collectively it generated much of the power for the secret Oak Ridge nuclear plant and the production of aluminum for airplanes used during World War II.[74]

Republican presidential candidate Wendell Wilkie energetically attacked the TVA in the 1940 presidential election as an unjust expenditure of public funds, and an invasion by the government into the private sector. In 1938 the Supreme Court refused to invalidate the TVA, and the program was later seen as an aid to power production in the area. The purpose of the government programs was to help the rural poor, both black and white, but it didn't turn out that way. The Depression brought to a head the simmering racial animosity against blacks who were denied construction jobs and ousted as newsboys, barbers, waiters, janitors, and elevator operators. If a new plant opened or expanded, it was certain that only whites would be employed. The saying "Blood is thicker than water," meant blacks were dismissed if they stood in the way of white men deprived of employment.

Black residents decided to leave. Between 1860 and 1930 the black population continued to decline as more workers left for opportunities in cities in the North and Midwest. They left the ravages of the boll weevil, unemployment, and surging racism. The African American move from the South to the North, from country life to city ghetto, and from farm to factory is the story of one of the great social transformations of life in the United States. In the southern-based rural community, the masses of black tenants had a shared cultural matrix, but the urban experience was something new, and it discouraged any survival of southern culture.

What was it like to go from the rural South to the big city? Claude Brown described the arrival of African Americans in New York City this way: "The Georgians came as soon as they were able to pick train fare off the peach trees . . . from South Carolina where the cotton stalks were bare . . . the North Carolinians came with tobacco tar beneath their fingernails . . . descendents of Ham . . . twice as happy as the Pilgrims, because they had been catching twice the hell."[75] Between 1930 and 1950 the South lost 1.9 million black residents.[76] Poor white residents left too, fleeing to jobs outside the South and finding work anywhere they could. The cities of New York, Philadelphia, and Chicago became havens for Southerners earning wages with a hope of returning to a cheaper retirement. The expatriates left behind houses of peeling paint and missing boards, with wallpaper hanging like dead skin and worn wooden floors strewn with the relics of lost dreams.

World War II (1941–1945) accomplished what the New Deal could not. During the war US industrial output increased at an average rate of 15 percent per year. The government offered generous "cost plus" contracts, where Uncle Sam covered the complete cost of the project and simultaneously guaranteed a reasonable profit. Southerners found jobs in booming shipyards along the Atlantic and Gulf coasts in aircraft, machinery, and the petroleum industry. The intensification of southern industry was found in the example of Higgins Industries of New Orleans, Louisiana. Before the war the company produced shallow-draught boats for use in the bayous of the state, but after 1941 the designs for landing craft and patrol torpedo boats made Andrew Jackson Higgins a national hero.

The war effort had other effects not measured by an accountant's ledger. A substantial number of outsiders experienced the South for the first time. Half of all Americans who served in World War II spent some time at a southern military base. Southern white and black soldiers were exposed to new locales, ideas, and influence. The discrepancy between democratic values, for which the United States was fighting overseas, and the realities of racial practices back home were not lost on them. The war disturbed the economic and social isolation of the region.

The war economy reduced tenant farming in the South. Thousands of workers left for available jobs in war plants and industrial centers. The exodus lasted through the war years and for decades later. Work once done by tenants was taken over by heavy equipment. Beginning in the war years the size of the average farm doubled, and succumbed to a phenomenon beginning to characterize the rest of the economy—the corporate takeover.[77] Agribusiness became the norm in the South after the war, but family farms continued to struggle.

Textiles were another traditional industry changed by the war. Initially textile workers stayed on the farm and worked in the plants only when they were not needed for plowing, planting, or harvesting. The war demand gave year-round employment, as the industry produced uniforms, tents, and hundreds of other cloth items during those years. "Between 1939 and 1943 approximately 1.2 million new industrial jobs were created" in the South.[78] Many former sharecroppers left the farm for the demands of the military draft and the insatiable need for war industry workers.

Another contribution to the war effort was the redistribution of federal dollars in the form of military expenditures. "Tent cities" mushroomed across the South and basic training recruits often fell in love with the region, and many even married southern women and settled down to raise families in the postwar years. The military experience created a distinctive sense of community, one recaptured by active and retired personnel who moved to the South to spend their golden years.

Postwar Affluence

New industry came to the South in the postwar years to take advantage of a working population, cheap land, and available water and road transportation. The decades after the war offered the greatest economic surge in the region's entire history, and the first casualty of this growth was agriculture. Farmers acquired larger tracts of land, tractor power replaced animal muscle, livestock production increased, and new crops such as soybeans and peanuts became mainstream. For example, "in 1949 Georgia had 222,000 farm families; in 1969 it had 47,000."[79] The same was true in neighboring South Carolina, which had 137,558 farms in the state in 1940, and only 28,000 in 1982.[80] As trade factories, construction, and money concentrated in metropolitan areas, the long established pattern of rural southern agriculture began to disappear.

The Cold War moved Americans to the political right, and Southerners joined them in supporting collective security agreements, economic expansion, and increased military spending. Southern congressmen dominated defense committees in Congress and spent lavishly in their home districts in support of foreign commitments. Powerful congressional leaders like L. Mendel Rivers (South Carolina), John Stennis (Mississippi), Edward Herbert (Louisiana), and John Tower (Texas) protected the South. The Cold War was a boon to the southern economy. This was especially true for the US Army, which had twenty-four of forty-six major posts located in the South by 1980.[81] The South always had an affection for the military and, even during the contentious 1960s, the region proved a hospitable place to enlist, travel, serve, and retire.

The gradual expansion and improvement in the postwar southern economy left the legacy of incurable poverty in the past. Southern politicians were eager to expand military spending, but reluctant to appropriate money for human services and social programs. Governors, mayors, and chambers of commerce adopted a "go-go" growth ethic to attract outside capital and multinational corporations to the region. Inducements took the form of tax suspensions, special training programs, convenient plant sites, and transportation improvements. The ideals of limited government, unregulated growth, and states' rights endemic to the political culture were reaffirmed in this time. Southerners revisited the issue of unionization of manufacturing by 1947, and every state but Louisiana adopted right-to-work laws that prohibited making union membership a qualification for employment.[82] Challenges to the labor statutes in southern states were ineffective. The ethic of unbridled capitalism and a laissez-faire attitude to regulation came to characterize the region.

The South's climate and uncomplicated lifestyle proved an economic boom in the 1960s. Southern states learned how to scramble for nondefense dollars for infrastructure and development projects. Conservative southern politicians continually decried the expansion of the federal government in the postwar years, and at the same time held out their hands for ever-increasing amounts of federal aid and construction grants. Table 2.4 compares the average federal tax burden of each southern state with a select group of northern states. The comparison is of the per capita

Table 2.4 Average Per Capita Tax Burden and Per Capita Federal Aid, Defense Contracts, and Payroll in Southern and Selected States, 1965–1967

Southern States	Tax Burden	Federal Aid, Contracts, and Payroll
National		
Texas	291.42	444.79
Florida	268.95	285.58
Georgia	264.22	447.63
Virginia	257.68	426.52
Emergent		
North Carolina	228.20	239.71
Tennessee	224.92	240.90
Traditional		
South Carolina	175.11	264.06
Alabama	184.69	288.60
Arkansas	158.38	214.35
Louisiana	230.16	285.06
Mississippi	130.96	261.10
Selected Northern States		
Colorado	597.05	418.41
Illinois	580.72	418.41
Massachusetts	466.10	391.91
Minnesota	392.50	265.71
Nevada	408.07	345.58
New Jersey	410.97	258.53
New York	719.24	247.76
Ohio	492.94	239.71
Oregon	352.72	183.06
Wisconsin	352.55	150.98

Source: Statistical Abstract of the United States.

tax burden with the federal benefits returned—in this case to the benefit of every southern state—at the expense of other states.

The redistribution of federal dollars was the idea of President Lyndon Johnson, a native Southerner, whose Great Society programs (1964–1968) were designed to stimulate economic growth in depressed areas. The programs took money from the wealthy states and gave it to poorer states. Mississippi, for example, received twice the amount it paid in federal taxes. Large industrial states in the Midwest and Northeast, like Illinois and New York, subsidized southern growth through federal dollars. The paradox of this process was not lost on southern politicians who continued to support federal projects as long as they were spent in their home districts.

Each southern state received more from the federal government than it sent to Washington, and this federal transfer of funds reduced, but did not eradicate poverty. Southern congressmen insisted that states be allowed to administer the federal assistance programs without interference from Washington. Consequently, the system of eligibility and payment standards varied. Even though they received a disproportionate share of the federal funds, the southern states remained at the bottom of national per capita income rankings. The money from Washington helped, but did not dramatically alter the economy of southern states.

As the South experienced a long-awaited economic revitalization, the industrial North and Midwest began to slow down. The mounting labor and regulatory costs, along with higher taxes, led industrialists to move their plants to locations below the Mason-Dixon Line. Thanks to a host of factors, such as a hospitable climate, the development of air conditioning, water reclamation projects, the "right to work" status of southern states, available real estate, and new technologies of communication and transportation, individuals and new businesses from areas outside the South poured into the region.

While Detroit may have reigned as the "Motor City," at the rate automobile companies moved to the Southeast in the 1970s and 1980s, the region began to look like a new industrial center. In the 1980s, BMW, Mercedes, Nissan, Honda, General Motors, Ford, Toyota, and Hyundai all set up plants in the Southeast. "In South Carolina alone, the number of automobile workers jumped 225 percent since 1989, to 20,711 employees."[83] The automobile industry moved because of cheap labor and employees who were unlikely to unionize.

The new industrial centers obliterated a characteristic of regional life once thought permanent. For much of its history the South was a rural haven, the least urbanized area of the country. No city in the South had a population large enough to rank it as major, and only twelve cities in the region had enough population to rank them in the top fifty cities in the country. Small towns were common, but in the postwar years they were replaced by metroplexes like Dallas/Ft. Worth, Houston, Atlanta, and Charlotte, and sparkling new mid-sized cities like Jacksonville, Knoxville, and Austin.[84] Poor rural areas remained in the South, outside counties crisscrossed by interstate highways and exploding suburbs.

The great migration to urban areas in the postwar era led to an end of one of the most insightful of V. O. Key's observations about southern politics, "a powerful localism [that] provides an important ingredient of . . . factionalism."[85] Urbanization meant a disruption in the closely knit family ties and social connectedness that was such a part of the rural South. Harper Lee, for example, captured this togetherness well in her description of Maycomb County, the imaginary setting for her story, *To Kill a Mockingbird*: "New people so rarely settled there, the same families married the same families until the members of the community looked faintly alike . . . the present generation of people who had lived side by side for years and years, utterly predictable to one another."[86] Candidates for state office once pulled overwhelming majorities in their home counties and drew heavy support in adjacent counties. Rural politics was dominated by oligarchic county officials allied with local economic elites in a Byzantine patchwork of cliques and deals. Localism has not disappeared in the modern South, but now it is more centered in television media markets than hometown counties.

From 1970 to 1976 the region enjoyed a net population gain of nearly three million.[87] The new residents were younger and better educated. They seemed comfortable in the fast food restaurants, discount stores, and shopping centers that spread over the landscape. The influx of a new mass culture changed, but did not obliterate, the South's traditional value structure. Economic progress was embraced, but the region still favored small government and low taxes. Foreign investors were welcomed and their success often stemmed from an ability to accommodate southern values. For example, the Japanese management approach to automobile manufacturing was recognized by some as a throwback to the cotton mill communities of the late nineteenth- and early twentieth-century South. Rural crossroads and small towns accommodated urban commuters more than weekend farmers, but the preference for place and the pride of community lingered as important values.

Even in the new multicultural urban centers, family and religion continued as important distinctions of southern life. In many ways the region remained resistant to change. Of the ten states that failed to ratify the Nineteenth Amendment giving women the right to vote in 1920, only one was outside the South. Southern legislatures were crucial to the defeat of the proposed equal rights amendment (ERA) movement in the 1970s. Nine of the fifteen states that failed to ratify were southern, only Texas and Tennessee approved the amendment, and Tennessee later voted to rescind. Moral and cultural issues were as important as economic ones when it came to winning local and statewide elections.

With the election of Jimmy Carter in 1976 the rest of the country accepted the South as an equal. His nomination by the Democratic Party showed that the period of stepchild tolerance of the region was at an end. Moderate policies of business reform and growth, consumer protection, low taxes, and a care for the environment were what the country wanted in a leader, and the southern farmer embodied them in his life and political career. When Carter was inaugurated as governor of Georgia in 1971 he said in his address: "I say to you quite frankly that the time for racial discrimination is over."[88] The end of segregation, of racial separation and overt prejudice as an accepted social value, changed *the* basic premise of southern politics. "In its grand outline the politics of the South," wrote Key at midcentury, "revolves around the position of the Negro."[89] The civil rights movement altered the caste system of the South, and moved the region as whole into an era of mainstream politics. The change in race attitudes was the most important political realignment of southern politics since the firing on Ft. Sumter.

Jimmy Carter was not a successful president, but he was an authentic product of the region of his birth. His family had a sense of small-town noblesse oblige. He had deep religious convictions and social ethics that accepted African Americans as a central part of the Democratic Party, the South, and the nation. His election was a symbolic reunification of the South with the rest of the country, and recognition of southern values as emblematic of the country at large.

Summary

The political culture of the South grew from the colonial experience of an agrarian frontier to one of rule by an elite aristocracy infused with a paternalism of social dominance. An antifederalist sentiment viewed government as a means of maintaining traditional ways of life. In the antebellum years the culture flourished in a defense of slavery based on a biblical belief that whites were destined to rule the agrarian region. All these ideas were subject to the furnace of humiliation in the Civil War defeat.

In Reconstruction the ideal of white supremacy was reversed, until the reaction of Bourbon rule, when it returned with a vengeance. Economic discontent took the form of a populist revolt in the face of frustration. One-party politics led to rule by factions and personalities within a single political system. In the Great Depression the South suffered in incurable poverty. The postwar years brought economic recovery, population in-migration, and widespread urbanization. The changes altered, but did abolish, the historic suspicion of governmental authority. A feisty independence persists in the South and it is immune to changes in the culture.

A character in William Faulkner's novel, *Absalom, Absalom,* said of the South, "you can't understand it. You would have to be born there." Today about one-third of the nation partakes of that birthright. At the beginning of the twenty-first century, two patterns of politics are in evidence in the South. The first pattern is the persistence of a fragmented geographical allegiance in the face of urbanization. In Key's original study, many state political conflicts were explained as sectional disagreements between and among competing areas. For example, the political strife in Tennessee was explained as a compromise between Memphis Democrats and east state Republicans and Democrats. South Carolina was a competition between upstate residents of the Piedmont plateau and those who lived in the low country coastal plain. Key posited politics as a contest between geographical regions in the face of cultural change. These findings were consistent with those of Daniel Elazar, who found a combination of traditionalistic and moralistic political cultures joined together in the South.

Urbanization has dramatically altered, but not obliterated, these patterns. One effect of an urban South has been the homogenized nature of political campaigns for statewide elections. The US population that lives in the fifteen states known as the "sunbelt" encompasses the eleven southern states, and much of this population is absolutely urban. The Atlanta metropolitan area, for example, contains over half the population of the state of Georgia. Urbanization is closely tied to economic growth and it is championed by economic conservatives of the region. In most of the southern states that are examined here, half the population is in just a handful of counties. Three or four media markets, and sometimes as few as one or two, reach up to half the voting population in a southern state.

The second pattern emphasizes the social tensions that are prone to arise in this more concentrated setting. In the 1980s more and more US politics came to be explained in cultural rather than economic terms. The most visible component of the struggle is in divisive, highly emotional issues such as abortion, women's rights, homosexual rights, and the role of religion in public education and political life. The contemporary South is a deeply religious place, with churches in every neighborhood and at the intersection of major suburban crossroads. Moral issues such as whether or not to have a state-sponsored lottery, taking "God" out of the pledge of allegiance, and support for the Defense of Marriage Act defy geographic classification. Issues such as these form the agenda of the Religious Right, who have found a home in the GOP and the South.

Some political outcomes in the South are explained by the persistence of geographical divisions tied to religious and moral sentiment, but this conflict is now moderated by the dramatic economic and urban growth in each state and an influx of voters from other states. These two patterns of geographical competition tied to cultural conflict in urban areas are examined in Chapters 3, 7, and 8, but their significance should not be overlooked in the new politics of the South.

Southerners enjoyed a special "era of good feeling" after the bicentennial of 1976. The institutional pillars of the old order, Jim Crow segregation, rural and county domination of politics, one-party rule, disenfranchisement of voters, and legislative malapportionment were all relegated to the historical scrap pile. The new ethic supports uninterrupted economic growth, low taxes without unions, new industry, and suburban-grown privacy values. The new political campaigns employ television markets and direct mail campaigns in conjunction with last-minute phone calls to "push" suburban voters to the polls. The new politics of the new South is most apparent in the suburbs of emergent cities, the growth of which is explained in the next chapter.

Notes

1. Criswell Freeman, *The Book of Southern Wisdom*. Nashville, Tenn.: Walnut Grove Press, 1994, p. 131.

2. T. Harry William, *Romance and Realism in Southern Politics*. Athens: University of Georgia Press, 1961, p. 2.

3. Margaret Mitchell, *Gone With the Wind*. New York: Macmillan, 1936. This quote is from the familiar movie prologue.

4. C. Vann Woodward, *The Burden of Southern History*. Baton Rouge: University of Louisiana Press, 1960, p. 15.

5. Clifford Geertz, *The Interpretation of Culture*. New York: Basic Books, 1973, p. 1.

6. Alexis de Tocqueville, *Democracy in America*, trans. and ed. Harvey C. Mansfield and Delba Winthrop. Chicago: University of Chicago Press, 2000, p. 360.

7. Peter Applebome, *Dixie Rising: How the South Is Shaping American Values, Politics and Culture*. New York: Times Books, 1996.

8. Tony Horowitz, *Confederates in the Attic*. New York: Vintage Books, 1999.

9. David Hackett Fischer, *Albion's Seed: Four British Folkways in America*. New York: Oxford University Press, 1989, p. 6. Fischer shows that the great majority of Virginia's elite came from families in the upper ranks of English society, while the backcountry of the South was settled by North Britain immigrants.

10. Crisswell Freeman, *The Book of Southern Wisdom*, p. 130.

11. Charles Wilson Reagan, "History and Manners," in Charles W. Reagan and William Ferris (eds.), *The Encyclopedia of Southern Culture*. Chapel Hill: University of North Carolina Press, 1989, p. 583.

12. Daniel J. Boorstin, *The Americans: The Colonial Experience*. New York: Vintage Books, 1958, p. 103.

13. Gavin Wright, *Old South, New South: Revolutions in the Southern Economy Since the Civil War*. New York: Basic Books, 1986, p. 18.

14. Francis Butler Simkins and Charles Pierce Roland, *A History of the South*. New York: Alfred A. Knopf, 1947, p. 45.

15. Martin E. Marty, *Pilgirms in Their Own Land: 500 Years of Religion in America*. New York: Penguin Books, 1986, p. 175.

16. Ray Allen Billington, *Westward Expansion: A History of the American Frontier*, 3rd ed. New York: Macmillan, 1967, p. 319.

17. Charles Wilson Reagan, "History and Manners," p. 585.

18. W.B. Allen and Gordon Lloyd (eds.), *The Essential Antifederalist*. Washington, D.C.: University Press of America, 1985, p. vii.

19. John Jay, "No. 4," in Clinton Rossiter (ed.), Alexander Hamilton, James Madison, and John Jay, *The Federalist Papers*. New York: Penguin Books, 1961, p. 45.

20. Ray Allen Billington, *Westward Expansion*, p. 217.

21. Carol Berkin et al., *Making America: A History of the United States*. Boston: Houghton Mifflin, 1995, p. 238.

22. David M. Potter, *The South and the Concurrent Majority*. Baton Rouge: Louisiana State University Press, 1972, p. 6.

23. Martin E. Marty, *Pilgrims in Their Own Land*, p. 239.

24. Benjamin E. Mays and Joseph W. Nicholson, *The Negro's Church*. New York: Arno Press, 1933, p. 22.

25. Ibid., p. 26.

26. John C. Calhoun, "Speech on the Reception of Abolition Petitions" (February 6,

1837); in Michael B. Levy (ed.), *Political Thought in America: An Anthology,* 2d ed. Prospect Heights, Ill.: Waveland Press, 1992, p. 308.

27. Francis Butler Simkins and Charles Pierce Roland, *A History of the South*, p. 163.

28. C.G. Woodson, *The History of the Negro Church*. Washington, D.C.: The Associated Publishers, 1921, pp. 124–131.

29. Alexis de Tocqueville, *Democracy in America*. Edited and abridged by Richard D. Heffner. New York: Penguin, 1984, p. 193.

30. Alexis de Tocqueville, *Democracy in America*, trans. and ed. Harvey C. Mansfield and Delba Winthrop, p. 357.

31. Catherine Clinton, "Women on the Land," in Reagan and Farris, *The Encyclopedia of Southern Culture*, p. 1550.

32. Frederick Douglass, *Narrative of the Life of Frederick Douglass*. New York: Oxford University Press, 1963, p. 18.

33. Bruce Catton, *The Coming Fury*. New York: Doubleday, 1961, p. 35.

34. Criswell Freeman, *The Book of Southern Wisdom,* p. 131.

35. W.J. Cash, *The Mind of the South*. New York: Vintage, 1941, p. 83.

36. Richard Weaver, *The Southern Tradition at Bay*. Washington, D.C.: Regnery, 1989, p. 164.

37. Simkins and Roland, *A History of the South*, p. 237.

38. Michael Shaara, *The Killer Angels*. New York; Random House, 1974, p. 364.

39. Shelby Foote, *The Civil War: A Narrative*. New York: Random House, 1958, p. 702.

40. Bruce Catton, *Never Call Retreat*. New York, Doubleday & Co., 1965, p. 192.

41. Richard Weaver, *The Southern Tradition*, p. 52.

42. Charles Wilson Reagan, *Baptized in Blood: The Religion of the Lost Cause, 1865–1920.* Athens: University of Georgia Press, 1980, p. 4.

43. Charles Wilson Reagan, "History and Manners," in Reagan and Wilson, *The Encyclopedia of Southern Culture*, p. 588.

44. Robert Crisswell, *The Book of Southern Wisdom*, p. 94.

45. William Faulkner, "The Bear," *The Faulkner Reader*. New York: Random House, 1942.

46. Simkins and Roland, *A History of the South,* p. 274.

47. Ibid., p. 293.

48. John Hope Franklin and Alfred A. Moss Jr., *From Slavery to Freedom: A History of African-Americans*, 7th ed. New York: McGraw-Hill, 1994.

49. C. Vann Woodward, *Origins of the New South: 1877–1913*. Baton Rouge: Louisiana State University Press, 1951, p. 50.

50. Stephen Kantrowitz, *Ben Tillman: And the Reconstruction of White Supremacy*. Chapel Hill: University of North Carolina Press, 2000, p. 258.

51. Roger Ransom and Richard Sutch, *One Kind of Freedom*. New York: Cambridge University Press, 1977.

52. Ralph McGill, *The South and the Southerner*. Boston: Little, Brown, pp. 186–189.

53. C. Vann Woodward, *Tom Watson: Agrarian Rebel*. New York: Oxford University Press, 1938, p. 115.

54. Ibid., p. 126.

55. Gavin Wright, *Old South, New South*. New York: Basic Books, 1986, p. 198.

56. Francis Butler Simkins and Charles Pierce Roland, *A History of the South*. New York: Alfred A. Knopf, 1972, p. 460.

57. David Conrad, "Tenant Farmers," in Wilson and Ferris, *The Encyclopedia of Southern Culture*, p. 1412.

58. Simkins and Roland, *A History of the South*, p. 460.

59. Rosemary Daniell, *Fatal Flowers*. New York: Holt, Rinehart and Winston, 1980, p. 32.

60. Robert Hunt Lyman (ed.), *The World Almanac and Book of Facts for 1933*. New York: New York World Telegram, 1933, pp. 47 and 864.

61. Ben Robertson, *Red Hills and Cotton*. Columbia: University of South Carolina Press, 1942, p. 274.

62. John L. Robinson, "Great Depression," in Wilson and Ferris, *Encyclopedia of Southern Culture*, p. 623.

63. T. Harry William, *Huey Long*. New York: Alfred A. Knopf, 1969, p. 276.

64. James Agee and Walker Evans, *Let Us Now Praise Famous Men*. New York: Ballentine Books, 1939, p. 8.

65. George B. Tindall, *The Emergence of the New South: 1913–1945*. Baton Rouge: Louisiana University Press, 1967, p. 483.

66. Dewey W. Grantham, *The South and Modern America: A Region at Odds*. New York: Harper Collins, 1994, p. 921.

67. Kenneth Coleman (ed.), *A History of Georgia*. Athens: University of Georgia Press, 1991, p. 325.

68. D.B. Hartman and Donald C. Bacon, *Rayburn: A Biography*. Austin: Texas Monthly Press, 1987, pp. 295–296.

69. Donald S. Howard, *The WPA and Federal Relief Policy*. New York: Da Capo Press, 1973, p. 160.

70. David R. Contosta and Robert Muccigrosso, *America in the Twentieth Century: Coming of Age*. New York: Harper & Row, 1988, p. 167.

71. John L. Robinson, "The Great Depression," in *Encyclopedia of Southern Culture*, p. 623.

72. Donald H. Grubbs, *Cry from the Cotton*. Chapel Hill: University of North Carolina Press, 1971, p. 109.

73. Simkins and Roland, *A History of the South,* p. 468.

74. T.H. Watkins, *The Great Depression*. Boston: Little, Brown, 1993, p. 155.

75. Claude Brown, *Manchild in the Promised Land*. New York: Macmillan, 1965, p. vii.

76. Ronald Bailey, "Blacks in Northern Cities," in Wilson and Ferris, *Encyclopedia of Southern Culture*, p. 181.

77. Kirkpatrick Sale, *Power Shift: The Rise of the Southern Rim and Its Challenge to the Eastern Establishment*. New York: Random House, 1976, pp. 20–21.

78. Morton Sosna, "World War II," in Wilson and Ferris, *Encyclopedia of Southern Culture*, p. 674.

79. Kenneth Coleman (ed.), *A History of Georgia*, p. 351.

80. Ernest McPherson Lander Jr., *South Carolina*. Northridge, Calif.: Windsor Publications, 1988, p. 144.

81. Alvin R. Sunseri, "Military and Economy," in Wilson and Ferris, *Encyclopedia of Southern Culture*, p. 731.

82. F. Ray Marshall, "Organized Labor," in Reagan and Farris, *Encyclopedia of Southern Culture*, p. 1396.

83. *Greenville News*, October 26, 2002, p. 2E.

84. US Census Bureau, 2000.

85. V.O. Key, *Southern Politics in State and Nation,* 2d ed. Knoxville: University of Tennessee Press, 1977, p. 37.

86. Harper Lee, *To Kill a Mockingbird.* Warner Books, 1960, p. 131.

87. James C. Cobb, "Industry and Commerce," in Wilson and Ferris, *Encyclopedia of Southern Culture*, pp. 718–719.

88. Kenneth Coleman (ed.), *A History of Georgia,* p. 403.

89. V.O. Key, *Southern Politics,* p. 5.

3

The Demography and Geography of the South

History combined with the natural environment to make the culture of the South unique. Its history, geographic boundaries as marked by the Civil War, its conservative ideology, and its economic system based first on slavery and then on nonunion labor, stood in sharp contrast to the rest of the United States. The abiding image is of a place characterized by a rural way of life with a suffocating conventionality replaced by cities and technology that leapt old boundaries with the click of a mouse. Place is a part of the legacy, as Maya Angelou wrote in her autobiography, *I Know Why the Caged Bird Sings*: "What sets one southern town apart from another, or from a northern town or hamlet or city highrise . . . [is] the experience shared between the unknowing majority (it) and the knowing minority (you)."[1]

The region's habitats, whether coastal or interior, mountain, piedmont, or delta, established certain life patterns that tempered settlement, tradition, and politics. At first agriculture was dominant along the coast and interior waterways. The exploitation of forests expanded the agricultural system, which was later destroyed by the Civil War. In the first half of the twentieth century the region struggled to adapt to the industrial mandate so readily embraced by the rest of the country. By midcentury the dominance of geography was beginning to wane, but its effects would never disappear. After World War II, urbanization transformed a once unspoiled wilderness into a complex modern society connected by interstate highways.

While the physical geography of the South did not change, the population in each state migrated and shifted, and the use of natural resources adapted accordingly. Economic growth has historically been a function of size and population, natural resources, and the rate of social change in the region. Development in the South was uneven, but growth in the economy implied new resources that created new wealth. The social change that resulted in economic development slowly transformed the political process.

The figures in Table 3.1, comparing populations among the southern states for the years 1950 and 2000, show the growth and shifting patterns of population rank

Table 3.1   Area and Population of Southern States, 1950 and 2000

State	1950 Population[a]	National Rank	2000 Population[a]	National Rank	Area[b]	National Rank
Alabama	3,062	17	4,447	23	52,423	30
Arkansas	1,910	30	2,673	33	53,182	29
Florida	2,771	20	15,982	4	65,758	22
Georgia	3,445	13	8,186	10	59,441	24
Louisiana	2,684	21	4,468	22	51,843	31
Mississippi	2,179	26	2,844	31	48,434	32
North Carolina	4,062	10	8,049	11	53,821	28
South Carolina	2,117	27	4,012	26	32,007	40
Tennessee	3,292	16	5,689	16	42,146	36
Texas	7,711	6	20,851	2	268,601	2
Virginia	3,319	15	7,078	12	42,769	35
		% of National Population		% of National Population		% of National Area
Total Southern States	36,552	24	84,279	30	770,425	22

Source: Compiled by the author from the US Census (2000) and Nielsen Media research, www.neilsenmedia.com.
Notes: a. Population in thousands; b. Area in miles (including water).

and economic potential of the region. The South grew in relative population over this time, comprising 24 percent of the US population in 1950, and rising to 30 percent five decades later. The data show that Florida, which improved sixteen places from twentieth in population to fourth in fifty years, experienced the most dramatic growth.

In 1950 the southern states had surplus land to be developed. During the last three decades of the twentieth century they began filling with people, and population expansion was one reason for their economic development. Physical size and population, along with factors such as the availability of natural resources and the social makeup of a state, are important in explaining both economic growth and political potential.

The contrasts in evidence in Table 3.1 show that the southern states differ greatly in their range of population growth and national ranking. Texas, Florida, Georgia, and Virginia improved their population rank relative to other states in the same time period, while Alabama, Arkansas, and Mississippi dropped. While area and population do not determine economics or political development, they are important factors for understanding the subsequent political culture. The population changes in the years before and after 1950 were a result of several factors. First, the sharecropper tenant farmer system collapsed and five million blacks left the South for jobs elsewhere. They were replaced by in-migration of whites and a booming postwar defense economy. Second, the civil rights movement of the 1960s led to school integration and better education levels for black Southerners. Third, the federal government, as an enticement to desegregation, increased aid to public education and federal dollars flowed into the region to improve opportunity. Fourth, industries relocated to the region paying higher average wages than those found in agricultural jobs. Fifth, as natives left the South, better-educated workers moved in and they demanded better schools, substantially above the southern level.[2]

Geography cannot determine the political culture, but where people live within that geography, and what they do for a living, certainly influences social and political life. The history of the US South has been bound to the agricultural life of the region. From the beginning, the land and the farmer were among the most influential forces in shaping the southern economic, political, and cultural heritage. In the postwar years the South underwent a dramatic economic transformation. Improved household income levels in the years after the 1960s were hastened by public employment and training programs that enabled many poor individuals to begin the process of moving from farms to the emerging economy. Table 3.2 compares the percentage of the population employed in agriculture in 1950 with 2000. In 1950 a large agricultural sector meant a lower ranking on the state per capita income scale, but by 2000 farming had almost disappeared as a significant part of state employment.

By 2000 new techniques in agriculture changed southern rural life. Farmers acquired larger tracts of land, favored corporate techniques, and bought tractors. As

Table 3.2   Employment in the Agricultural Industry in the South, 1950 and 2000 (percentage of total employed)

State	1950	2000
Alabama	24.6	1.8
Arkansas	35.3	2.9
Florida	13.3	0.9
Georgia	22.1	0.8
Louisiana	18.3	1.7
Mississippi	42.2	2.6
North Carolina	24.9	1.8
South Carolina	26.2	0.7
Tennessee	21.9	1.1
Texas	16.2	1.2
Virginia	15.1	0.8
South Average	23.6	1.5
Nonsouthern States	9.3	0.8

Source: 1954 Statistical Abstract, US Census Bureau, Table 241; US Census 2000 Supplemental Survey, Table 3.

the size of the average farm and dependence on technology increased, the number of people employed in agriculture dramatically declined. Livestock production increased and new crops, such as soybeans and peanuts, grew where cotton was once planted as fewer and fewer farmers cut larger and larger slices of a bigger pie. Southern states at the millennium averaged less than 2 percent of their employment population in agriculture. This represents a dramatic departure from the past as diversification came with the slow, steady progress of adopting progressive, scientific means of farming.

The transformation of the region, and the narrowing of the income gap between the South and the rest of the nation, began at the turn of the twentieth century and accelerated after the Great Depression. Development in the region took off after the end of World War II. In 1980, for the first time, a majority of white Southerners—and a third of black Southerners—worked in middle-class positions, such as professional, technical, managerial, administrative, sales, and clerical jobs.[3] By the end of the century, the rural, small-town South was gone, replaced by neat suburbs along interstate highways outside of clean midsized cities.

The South developed thanks to a complexity of several factors—a hospitable climate made more appealing after the energy crisis of 1973, the convenience of air conditioning, cheap and available real estate, and new technologies of communication and transportation. New businesses and industries poured into the region. For most of its history the South was the least urbanized area of the nation. In 1950 only twelve cities in the region had enough population to rank them in the top fifty cities in the nation. By the 2000 census, seventeen southern cities were ranked in the top fifty cities, all of which had more than one million in their metropolitan area. Small towns, which were once common, now defined themselves as connected to the sparkling new cities.[4]

Table 3.3 shows the urbanization of the South in the years 1950, 1970, and 2000. "Urbanized" is defined as places with a population of 50,000 or more persons, including central cities and fringe areas, based on population density. The urbanized population figure is used because it best represents the movement of populace from rural to more densely inhabited urban areas between the points in time.

The rural character of the region is evident in the 1950 population figures in Table 3.3. South Carolina, Mississippi, North Carolina, and Arkansas averaged about one-tenth of their populations in urbanized areas in 1950, which was roughly one-fifth of the national (non-South) average. The southern urbanization figure was less that half the national average. The figures show that much of this population shift happened in the period 1950 to 1970. Virtually every southern state changed more in these two decades than in the two subsequent ones.

Table 3.3   Percentage of Population Living in Urbanized Areas

State	1950	1970	2000
Alabama	24.1	37.2	43.6
Arkansas	11.0	19.7	32.1
Florida	38.6	60.9	84.3
Georgia	27.2	41.0	61.2
Louisiana	35.4	46.8	56.7
Mississippi	4.6	14.5	23.9
North Carolina	12.7	23.9	46.7
South Carolina	11.4	25.1	46.7
Tennessee	29.8	37.9	52.1
Texas	36.5	61.8	71.0
Virginia	22.6	51.6	66.6
Non-South	52.5	62.7	70.9

Source: Compiled by author from US Census data.
Note: Urbanized is defined as places with a population of 50,000 or more persons.

Real estate development to accommodate in-migrants transformed bucolic farmland and crossroads into sprawling suburbs with gleaming office parks. In 1987 Earl and Merle Black summarized these economic gains by observing: "From the South's new middle class have emerged the society's most conspicuous models of success and achievement."[5] Members of the middle class living in new cities brought the southern states from the bottom of the economic ladder into the mainstream of US life.

Daniel Elazar's "civil communities" are an explanation of the mixture of local governments, interest groups, school districts, and chambers of commerce in counties and subcounties outside the boundaries of core cities. The delineation of a civil community is through its governmental jurisdictions, a municipal township, county, or special district. A resident of Plano, north of Dallas, lives in a civil community different from someone who resides in Arlington or Fort Worth. The people who live in Brentwood, or south Nashville, are different from those who own homes in Madison or Goodlettsville north of the city. In the postwar era, civil communities became "the effective government . . . and its progress in maintaining or improving [the] economic base and quality of life rest[ed] on the mobilizing ability of a key handful of civic leaders."[6] In dozens of civil communities that ring major cities, important decisions rest in the hands of experienced and invisible elite activists who influence the public agenda.

The civil community exists in a particular geography, with a cultural ambiance unique to the area. The universal fact of southern life is the climate. Once it favored a long growing season that served as the basis for the agrarian lifestyle, and distinguished the South from the rest of the country. "In that country," wrote Thomas Wolfe, "the very quality of the heavy air . . . is the soft thick gravy of time itself, sternly yet beautifully soaking down forever on you—and enriching everything it touches—grass, foliage, brick, ivy, the fresh moist color of people's faces and old gray stone with the incomprehensible weathering of time."[7] The region suffers from oppressive hot and humid summers, but has mild winters. The warm, humid climate, long growing season, and abundant moisture has had, and continues to have, a far-reaching effect on the region's lifestyle, economy, and culture. Today tourism is the new growth industry that flourishes in the climate. The mild temperatures along coastal areas and in mountain retirement communities are natural attractions. *Southern Living* magazine regularly features sections on gardens and outdoor amenities uniquely available in the region south of the Potomac River.

The original commitment to agriculture, especially to commercial crops such as cotton and tobacco, was made possible by a favorable climate and the rich soil. History in the South is indelibly linked to the fertile black soil that stretches from tidewater Virginia, through the Carolinas and across Georgia, central Alabama, the northwestern "Delta" region of Mississippi, and western Tennessee. The land is flat and fertile, lying below the uplands and hills that are in each state. The land of the

"Black Belt," was once famous for the rich, dark soil that produced crops in abundance.

Making up only a part of the total area of each southern state, the Black Belt counties—struggling with the problems of racial conflict and poverty—have also set the tone for politics statewide. In these places the political objective of whites was to maintain control by the minority in the midst of a black population majority. The toil of iniquity came in counties with names like Sunflower and Orangeburg, with populations that were 40, 50, 60, or even 80 percent black. A survey of Alabama's Black Belt in 2003 showed that "more than half the people are black; and almost everyone is poorer, unhealthier, less well-educated, and with worse jobs than those in the rest of the state."[8]

An emergent middle class is relatively new for the South. The traditional experience was one of lagging behind the rest of the country without much hope of catching up. Generations of Southerners after the Civil War clung to the myth of the rightness of their agrarian principles, which allowed them to resist the pull of Yankee industrialization and economic expansion. As a consequence of these beliefs, southern poverty became, in the words of historian C. Vann Woodward, "a long and quite un-American experience."[9]

At midcentury, the South trailed the rest of the nation in economic attainment. Table 3.4 shows the 1950 and 1987 per capita incomes for the United States and selected subregions. Per capita income is reported in 1987 dollars as a percentage of national income. In 1950, all major regions, except the South, were either above the national average or (in the case of the Plains states) within 3 percent of it. The South was 26 percent below the national average. The national average incorporates southern data, so a better standard of comparison is the combination of the three nonsouthern regions. The South's 1950 per capita was two-thirds (66 percent) of the nonsouthern per capita income average. In the Deep South, defined as the states of North Carolina, South Carolina, Georgia, Tennessee, Alabama, Mississippi, Arkansas, and Louisiana, per capita income was only 50 percent of the non-South figure.

In 1987 the southern figure increased 161 percent, far faster than the national average (119 percent) and the average for the nonsouthern states (109 percent). The South had the highest growth rate for the period 1950 to 1987. By 1987 the southern states were within 12 percent of the national average, and had narrowed the gap with all other areas of the country. What caused this increase? One economic study concluded that three factors proved exceptionally powerful in explaining the change: (1) gains in educational attainment, (2) rural to urban population shifts, and (3) increases in per capita employment.[10]

Table 3.5 examines the per capita income of individual states for 1950 and 2000. Their ranking in nominal dollars shows that in 1950 eight of the ten lowest ranking states in the United States were southern. The southern state with the highest per capita in 1950 was Texas, ranked thirty-first, in the bottom half of the

Table 3.4   Per Capita Income in the United States, 1950 and 1987

Region	1950 Per Capita Income[a]	1950 % of National Average	1987 Per Capita Income[a]	1987 % of National Average
United States	$7,059	100	$15,465	100
Nonsouthern States	$7,820	111	$16,375	109
Manufacturing Belt[b]	$7,937	112	$16,733	108
Southern States[c]	$5,197	74	$13,556	88
Plains States[d]	$6,848	97	$14,669	95
Western States[e]	$8,079	114	$16,269	101

Source: Leonard F Wheat and William H. Crown, *State Per-Capita Income Change Since 1950.* Westport, Conn.: Greenwood Press, 1995.

Notes: a. In 1987 dollars; b. The Manufacturing Belt includes New England (ME, NH, VT, MA, RI, CT), the Mideast (NY, NJ, PA, DE, MD, DC), and the Great Lakes (OH, IN, IL, MI, WI); c. The Southern States include the Peripheral South (VA, WV, KY, OK, TX, FL), and the Deep South (NC, SC, GA, TN, AL, MS, AR, LA); d. The Plains States include IA, KS, MN, MO, NB, ND, and SD; e. The Western States include the Rocky Mountain states (MT, WY, ID, CO, UT, NM, AZ) and the far West (WA, OR, NV, CA).

national rankings. The 1960s witnessed Lyndon Johnson's Great Society of "abundance and liberty for all," and programs such as food stamps, Medicaid, Medicare, aid to education, regional development, and housing programs flowed into the South. These governmental initiatives were visible and important, but they were less dramatic in explaining growth than the quiet, wholesale economic changes from the private sector, which mushroomed throughout the region. Restaurant and hotel chains, emerging computer technology, fast food franchises, and new manufacturing industry offered untold opportunity. After 1950 the South became part of the great US television culture, which buried the old life under expressways and suburban shopping malls.

Table 3.5 shows that by 2000 Virginia was a top twenty state in terms of per capita income, and much of the growth was due to the suburban ring of government workers and high-tech industries in the Washington, D.C., and Richmond areas, along with the military expansion in the Hampton Roads/Norfolk/Virginia Beach area. Other states experienced growth in the familiar sectors of real estate, business, and manufacturing. Florida, Georgia, and Texas were all ranked in the top half of the country in the 2000 listings of per capita income. At the turn of the twenty-first century, five of the bottom ten states in the rankings were still southern (Alabama, Louisiana, South Carolina, Arkansas, and Mississippi), but the prosperous states of Georgia, Florida, Virginia, and Texas established a path to national respectability. Every southern state improved its ranking from 1950 to 2000 except one, Mississippi, which remained last on both lists.

Table 3.5 States Ranked by Per Capita Income, 1950 and 2000[a]

	1950		2000
1.	District of Columbia	1.	Connecticut
2.	Delaware	2.	District of Columbia
3.	Nevada	3.	New Jersey
4.	New York	4.	Massachusetts
5.	Connecticut	5.	New York
6.	Illinois	6.	Maryland
7.	California	7.	Delaware
8.	New Jersey	8.	New Hampshire
9.	Washington	9.	Illinois
10.	Montana	10.	Colorado
11.	Massachusetts	11.	Washington
12.	Michigan	12.	Minnesota
13.	Ohio	13.	California
14.	Rhode Island	14.	**Virginia**
15.	Maryland	15.	Nevada
16.	Pennsylvania	16.	Rhode Island
17.	Oregon	17.	Pennsylvania
18.	Wyoming	18.	Hawaii
19.	Nebraska	19.	Michigan
20.	Indiana	20.	**Florida**
21.	Wisconsin	21.	Alaska
22.	Iowa	22.	Ohio
23.	Missouri	23.	Wisconsin
24.	Colorado	24.	**Georgia**
25.	Kansas	25.	Kansas
26	Minnesota	26.	**Texas**
27.	South Dakota	27.	Oregon
28.	North Dakota	28.	Nebraska
29.	Idaho	29.	Missouri
30.	New Hampshire	30.	Indiana
31.	**Texas**	31.	Vermont
32.	Utah	32.	**North Carolina**
33.	Arizona	33.	Iowa
34.	**Florida**	34.	**Tennessee**
35.	Vermont	35.	Wyoming
36.	Maine	36.	Arizona
37.	**Virginia**	37.	Maine
38.	New Mexico	38.	South Dakota
39.	Oklahoma	39.	North Dakota
40.	West Virginia	40.	Kentucky
41.	**Louisiana**	41.	**Alabama**
42.	**Georgia**	42.	**Louisiana**
43.	**Tennessee**	43.	**South Carolina**
44.	**North Carolina**	44.	Idaho
45.	Kentucky	45.	Oklahoma
46.	**Alabama**	46.	Utah
47.	**South Carolina**	47.	**Arkansas**
48.	**Arkansas**	48.	Montana
49.	**Mississippi**	49.	New Mexico
50.	*Alaska*	50.	West Virginia
51.	*Hawaii*	51.	**Mississippi**

Source: 1953 Statistical Abstract, US Census Bureau; US Census 2000 Supplemental Survey, Table 3.
Note: a. Alaska and Hawaii were not included in the 1950 rankings.

The economic ranking summarizes the evolution of southern states from a place at the bottom of the US economic pile in 1950, to one of mixed accomplishment at century's end. Much of the economic development and job creation in the South was fueled by international investments. Foreign automobile plants were located in the states of Tennessee, South Carolina, Alabama, and Mississippi in the last quarter of the twentieth century. Beginning in the 1980s, South Carolina's public and private sector leaders began a drive for more foreign investments and the state is now home to many international companies and has more jobs created by them than any state in the nation except Hawaii.[11]

This increase in income helped destroy the legacy of poverty and despair that haunted the South. The change was partly a result of the exposure the region received from the worldwide media coverage given the presidency of Jimmy Carter. The cultural and economic climate of the region received national attention because in the 1970s Plains, Georgia, was a favorite haunt of the press. One reporter described Carter's home with, "no plumbing in the house . . . an outdoor privy . . . the clapboard home was well shaded by a veritable forest of trees."[12] The news stories appealed to the national imagination of the South as a rural paradise, and even though the reality was far different from the stereotype, opportunity beckoned. Carter added to the image by working with the charity Habitat for Humanity after leaving office, showing the gracious side of southern hospitality.

Carter's life experience, moving from farmer to president, was a microcosm of what was happening all across the South. The economic base, labor market, and income levels in the region improved and closed the gap between it and the rest of the nation. The southern economy is now diversified with increasing numbers of investments by international firms offering wage levels above the national average. With negligible employment in agriculture, new industries mirror the country-at-large with service and high-tech jobs fueling the expanding economy. Some states (Virginia, Florida, Georgia, and Texas for example) have attracted more new economy industries and jobs than others (like Alabama, Louisiana, South Carolina, Arkansas, and Mississippi). These patterns, as will be demonstrated later, are important elements of the underlying conditions supporting subregional variations in shifts in political party allegiance.

The Urban Demography

The new unit of analysis for politics in the South is the metropolitan area with its accompanying media market. Since the 1980s a distinctive suburban politics has emerged in the United States. As suburbs became less dependent on the central cities, they developed their own way of thinking about national politics. An "ideology of localism," to quote Juliet Gainsborough in her book *Fenced Off*, developed around suburban life that fostered a decentralized and conservative ethic.[13] More and more, these characteristics apply to the new suburbs of southern cities.

The suburbs are a powerful voting bloc reached primarily by television. Originally, the cities of the nation had three television networks—CBS, NBC, and ABC—competing for audiences in a designated market. Cable television expanded the competition for viewers, but these markets have remained as units of analysis for decades. The commercial importance of a media market has grown as television stations reach across numerous counties and even state lines. Candidates for statewide office maximize their campaign expenditures to in-state media markets, trying to build from this base to communities and suburbs on the border of the state or in the rural areas.

In one sense a media market is a modern-day expression of Key's original "friends and neighbors" association that served as the basis for building winning coalitions in the rural statewide political races of yesteryear. In his midcentury work V. O. Key discussed the localism of southern rural politics, where candidates for office drew heavily from home and adjacent counties when they ran for office. Today candidates build their geographic campaign bases by expanding from one urban media market to another. It is not unusual to hear a candidate described as a "typical east Tennessee Republican," or a "south Georgia Democrat." In Mississippi "Delta politicians" evoke a stereotype and in South Carolina a "low country" politician is different than one from "upstate." Political campaigns build from one base to another, using targeted television commercials to introduce candidates and explain positions of importance to a particular audience.

The rise and reach of television markets in an urban area are the building blocks of the new southern politics. Poll results are often given to candidates showing their standing in important media markets, and candidates respond by pouring more money into various markets as a means of improving their prospects in various parts of the state. Candidates for office no longer work courthouse cliques or rely on the endorsements of local officials; instead, they use political consultants to craft appealing messages on television. Politics at the grassroots has given way to politics by direct mail, radio, and elaborate media campaigns using political commercials and "earned media" events for coverage by journalists. Campaigns today increasingly rely on expensive hired help: consultants, pollsters, and other campaign professionals to help turn out the vote.

Counties still serve as useful units to evaluate the political and social change in the South, but their usefulness must be placed in the new urbanized context. State statistics and election returns are county specific, and while there is a wide variation in the population and importance of each county, they collectively serve as the basis for the analysis of political and social change. The counties that make up a metropolitan statistical area—and its corresponding media market—are the basis of this analysis.[14]

In this chapter, I look at urban areas, with their associated media markets, as the building blocks to win political races statewide. The maps of each southern state show major cites that total to half the state's population. Why half the population? The barest majority of the state population is often compacted into just a few counties and cities. The bare majority criterion highlights the most crucial political regions of a state, and by examining partisanship in the largest media markets, and most important counties, a statewide pattern and consequent political strategy can be identified. Each map and accompanying table highlights the counties that contributed 50 percent, or as close to half as possible, of the state's population; there are more voters in the shaded counties (or parishes) than in the rest of the state combined.

Demography, not geography, is political destiny in a state. The two are related because urbanization tends to follow traditional geographic patterns. In this chapter the geography of each state is matched to the urban reality of politics in that state. The counties are ranked and classified as to their political importance, with the urban counties in metropolitan areas selected as most important. The size of each county is examined as the primary building block for urbanized political campaigns, and the significance of each county is explained in the context of its state politics. The analysis of each state follows the national, emergent, and traditional classifications identified in Chapter 1.

National States

Georgia

Georgia today, just like fifty years ago, can be divided into a semblance of a north-south sectionalism separated by a demarcation known as the fall line. The fall line between north and south Georgia is a geographical boundary marking the edge of the Piedmont Plateau leading to the coastal plains. About half the counties in Georgia are above the fall line, and about half are below it, but the population of the state is dramatically skewed toward the northern counties.

Georgia is a betrayal of its past and a promise of the southern future. Called the "Peach State," it produces less fruit than neighboring South Carolina. Immortalized as a plantation haven in *Gone With the Wind*, it is a state dominated by a single, great city. Its racial legacy was lost in a hail of preaching by a native, black son, Martin Luther King Jr., who became the youngest man to ever win a Nobel Prize. About the only thing that has remained constant in Georgia is the geography.

North Georgia is the Piedmont Plateau. Originally this upland region on the northern fringe of the cotton belt was a land of small farmers and isolated communities. Today it is synonymous with Atlanta, the convergence of three major interstate highways, the world's busiest airport, and over four million people. Map 3.1 shows this division. South Georgia is the nearly treeless Black Belt, which buckles the central part of the state to the coastal waterways. This area is as productive as any agricultural part of the country. The southern edge of the Black Belt is bounded by the Red Hills, a section of varying soil richness that attracted both plantations

Map 3.1   Georgia: Population Distribution

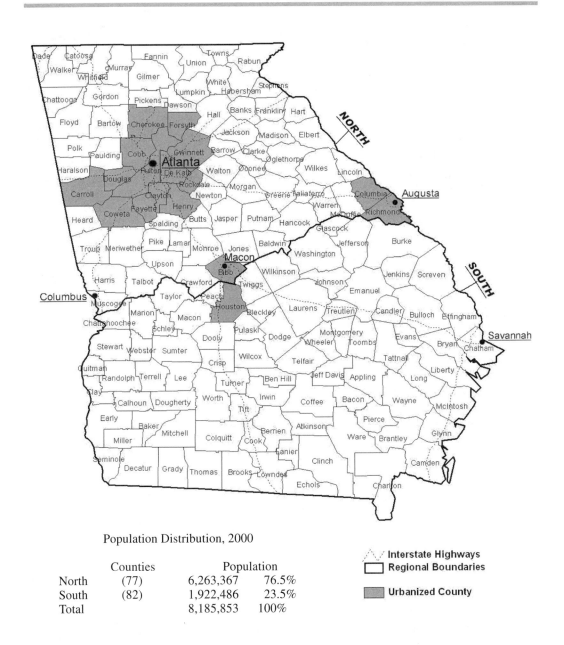

Population Distribution, 2000

	Counties	Population	
North	(77)	6,263,367	76.5%
South	(82)	1,922,486	23.5%
Total		8,185,853	100%

/\\/ **Interstate Highways**
☐ **Regional Boundaries**

▨ **Urbanized County**

and small farms. This is the part of the state with the legacy of coastal plantations, slavery, and cotton farming. It is to Tara in south Georgia that Scarlett O'Hara fled when federal armies invaded in the mythical story *Gone With the Wind,* and where Bethel Church served as a refuge for slaves in the stage play *Purlie.*

The northern counties were once piney woods, hills, and mountain streams. Today the city of Atlanta dominates not just the region, but remains the economic center of the state and the entire South. Atlanta is where William Tecumseh Sherman marched in 1864 to destroy the railhead hub of the southern rebellion, where Margaret Mitchell wrote her novel, and where Martin Luther King Jr. grew up. When the movie *Driving Miss Daisy*, about Miss Daisy Werthan and her black chauffer Hoke Coburn, won best picture in 1989, there was no more fitting setting than Atlanta in the years from 1948 to 1973. In the 1990s the city became what the Chamber of Commerce said it would be: "The World's Next Great City." The metropolitan area led Georgia into the ranks of a national state, with the 1996 Summer Olympics, and the CNN Broadcast Center next door to the World Trade Center.

The city of Atlanta has historically set the pace for the rest of the South. In 1947 one researcher wrote that he "has found it more difficult [to get an interview] in Atlanta than in New York, where frequently the prominence of the persons . . . was considerably greater than that of persons in Atlanta."[15] In the 1960s it was a "City Too Busy to Hate" in the civil rights struggle, and in the 1970s and 1980s it showed the benefits of economic development as its suburban counties swelled with new residents. But beneath the turbulent change associated with Atlanta's growth, and Georgia's prosperity, was a current of cultural continuity. For example, family and church still seem a part of the transition from the rural, racial politics of the past, to the new urban complexity with its multicultural lifestyles. Many of the state's most visible politicians, from Jimmy Carter to Andrew Young to Martin Luther King Jr., were identified by their religious faith as much as their party affiliation. Georgia has also accommodated cultural diversity in an exemplary way. Today the state has the third highest percentage of Hispanics of any state in the South, as well as a substantial black population. The variety of ethnicities is evident at the Metro stops in Atlanta, and is beginning to find its way into the suburbs that surround the city.

Originally the population of Georgia was sectional, with the populous rural south opposed to the small farmer and urban north. V. O. Key described this conflict as revolving around the personality of Eugene Talmadge and the antagonism between the Atlanta city center and the rural dominance of the county-unity system. One Georgian interviewed for the book *Southern Politics* patiently explained to Alexander Heard that "Georgia politics is divided into two factions: the Talmadge faction and the [anti-Talmadge] faction [and] . . . there are about 45 rural counties that can be bought outright."[16] The new politics of Georgia is a faint reflection of the past, with the reverse of the old and a new twist: Atlanta and everyone else. Half the population of the state is in the Atlanta metropolitan area.

They began calling it "Hot-lanta" in the 1970s, and the label is appropriate for a city that dominates nearly two dozen counties that circle it. Atlanta truly deserves the label "Capital of the South." No other state in the South is dominated by just one city the way Atlanta dominates Georgia. Amid the lush hills of north Georgia are gleaming office parks, industrial warehouses, and shopping centers connected by eight-lane interstate traffic arteries. The city is home to over four million people in the twenty-county Atlanta metropolitan area. It dominates transportation, recreation, and any other activity for one hundred miles from downtown. Atlanta was originally a rail center; today Hartsfield Airport and the interstate highway system make it a transportation crossroads for the entire region.

For more than fifty years the Atlanta Regional Commission (ARC) and its predecessor agencies have been the key source of information about the Atlanta area. The ARC oversees a ten-county area with a total population of 3.4 million.[17] The wealth of the city is at least as important as its size. Gwinnett County, a suburb with an affluent population, has a roadside advertisement that invites residents to the Mercedes-Benz dealership saying, "Stop by in your bathrobe." The Metro Atlanta area is defined as the ten counties of the Regional Commission, plus three others that are among the top twenty counties in the state in terms of population. The designation includes the areas north and west of Atlanta to the state line. Also included is Forsyth County east of the city, which was the fastest growing county in the nation from 1997 to 1998. The thirteen-county designation includes 46 percent of the state's population.

Georgia is a state with 159 counties. Twelve of the most populous are in the Atlanta area. Other areas of Georgia have important population centers in their own right and play a satellite, but still significant, role in state politics. The population distribution of Georgia is peculiar in that several important cities like Columbus, Savannah, and Augusta are located on the state border. Savannah is the second largest media market in the state, but it serves the residents of Hilton Head in next-door South Carolina as much as it does Georgia's residents. Similarly, Columbus straddles the Alabama border, and Augusta shares a media market with Aiken, South Carolina. The second largest market that encompasses Georgia residents alone is the Macon/Warner Robbins area in the central part of the state. Another area, about equal in population to the Macon/Warner Robbins city, is the Georgia share of the Augusta market on the eastern boundary of the state.

The population and media markets for these three areas are shown in Table 3.6. Together they contain over half the population of the state. A successful statewide political campaign is dominated by thoughts of Atlanta. Eight congressional districts touch on the Atlanta media market. The expense of advertising in the nation's ninth largest market drives up the cost of a statewide race, and diminishes the considerations of advertising in the markets of Savannah (79th), Augusta (114th), Macon (122nd), and Columbus (126th). Three metropolitan areas are selected to represent the most efficient use of resources in a statewide political race. Atlanta

Table 3.6   Georgia: Population Centers and Media Market Rank

Region/City	County	Population 2000	Media Market Rank
North Georgia			
Atlanta	1. Fulton County	816,006	9
Atlanta	2. Dekalb County	665,865	9
Atlanta	3. Cobb County	607,751	9
Atlanta	4. Gwinnett County	588,448	9
Atlanta	5. Clayton County	236,517	9
Atlanta	6. Cherokee County	141,903	9
Atlanta	7. Henry County	119,341	9
Atlanta	8. Forsyth County	98,407	9
Atlanta	9. Douglas County	92,174	9
Atlanta	10. Fayette County	91,263	9
Atlanta	11. Rockdale County	91,263	9
Atlanta	12. Cowetta County	89,215	9
Atlanta	13. Carroll County	87,268	9
	Subtotal	3,725,421	
North/South Georgia			
Macon/Warner Robbins	14. Bibb County	153,887	122
Macon/Warner Robbins	15. Houston County	110,765	122
	Subtotal	264,852	
North/South Georgia			
Augusta	16. Columbia County	199,775	114
Augusta	17. Richmond County	89,288	114
	Subtotal	289,063	
	Total	4,279,336	

Source: Compiled by the author from the US Census (2000) and Nielsen Media research, www.nielsenmedia.com.
Note: This total represents 52 percent of Georgia's population.

and Macon/Warner Robbins are the interior media markets; Augusta is a populous border city that offers a large population that is mostly Georgian. The Savannah media market is larger, but it offers a smaller domestic Georgia audience for television ads.

Statewide political campaigns are concerned with two geographical considerations. First, half the population of Georgia lives in one place. Second, much of a candidate's hard-earned money is being spent on people who live outside the state, in places like Auburn-Opelika, Alabama, and Aiken and Hilton Head, South Carolina, who cannot vote in Georgia. Such are the realities of present-day politics in what was once a state dominated by rural counties and a peculiar political arrangement, known as the "county-unit rule," designed to keep them in power. The Georgia legislature was once malapportioned to help rural counties stay in power; today it is dominated by one urban area, and the rural politics of yesteryear seem a quaint and distant memory.

Florida

For much of its history, Florida has been two states: one that extends over from the Georgia border and has identified with the racial and social traditions of the South, and the other whose tropical heritage is international and national in flavor. In the first part of the twentieth century most of Florida's population came from the states of Alabama, Georgia, and South Carolina. One of the oldest adages of Florida politics was, and remains: "the farther north you go, the farther south you are." Early in the twentieth century, migrants recreated the southern culture in the northern tier of counties, and the state had an economic and social culture like the rest of the region. The only exception was that Florida had a small black population compared to its neighboring Deep South states.

Now there is a new Florida. It is a region of rich Hispanic culture, tourism, and beach resorts along the Gulf of Mexico and the Atlantic seaboard to south Florida. Near Orlando, Mickey and Minnie Mouse have taken up residence and are at the center of a booming metropolitan area in the middle of the "Sunshine State." There are more hotel and motel rooms in Orlando than any other city in the United States. Families from the Midwest, East, and South now make plans to vacation in Florida at least once in their children's growing up years. As recently as 1940, Florida had more open acreage than any other state east of the Mississippi River. The state lacked the capital to spur development, so it exploited the one resource it had: land. The subsequent boom led to unprecedented development, from a forgotten swamp to a semitropical resort. Florida's population in the 1950s was less than its neighbor Alabama; in the 2000 census the state surpassed Alabama's population by 11.5 million. Florida has emerged as an empire, and it is one with a distinct culture and an international population.

Much of the state's uniqueness is attributable to its geography, which is a clue to its present political competitiveness. The rivers and wetlands in the central and southern part of the state isolate retirement communities from one another, and provide recreation for tourists. Enormous distances fragment Florida's population. For instance, from Key West in the south to Pensacola in the panhandle is approximately the same road distance as from Pensacola to Chicago. The state's southern region has historically been linked more to the Caribbean than the United States. Cubans settled in the Tampa Bay area, then later, in the 1960s, in Miami to escape Castro's domination of their homeland.

Despite all its diversity and dramatic population growth, the Florida electorate is amazingly compact. Map 3.2 shows that over half the population of Florida are in eight counties in the three largest media markets. The shaded metropolitan areas of

Map 3.2   Florida: Population Distribution

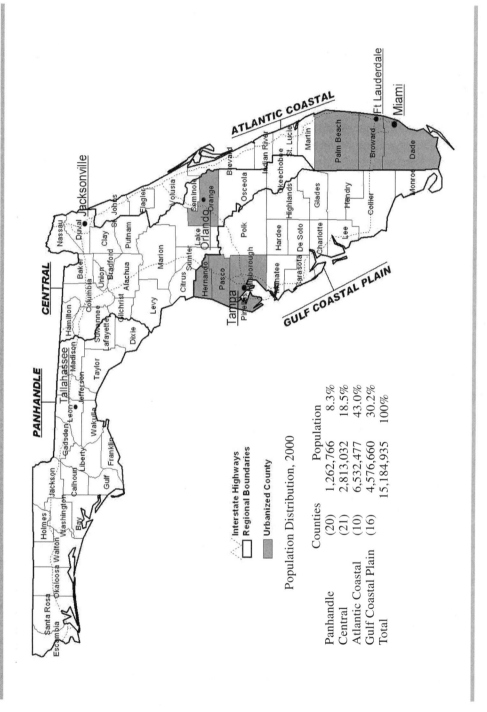

Population Distribution, 2000

	Counties	Population	
Panhandle	(20)	1,262,766	8.3%
Central	(21)	2,813,032	18.5%
Atlantic Coastal	(10)	6,532,477	43.0%
Gulf Coastal Plain	(16)	4,576,660	30.2%
Total		15,184,935	100%

Interstate Highways
Regional Boundaries
Urbanized County

Miami/Ft. Lauderdale, Tampa/St. Petersburg, and Orlando/Daytona Beach/ Melbourne have over eight million residents.

This population growth came in the second half of the twentieth century, when the international and multinational culture of Florida politics became dominant. The Florida economy went global and the political culture adapted accordingly. One-fifth of the economy of the state is based in tourism, and jobs are increasingly service oriented, especially to retired citizens. South Florida is a bridge to Latin America and the city of Miami is the gateway to the southern continent.

The culture of Florida is a dizzying set of migrations of individuals, families, and ethnic groups over time. In 1930 half of Florida's residents were born some- where else, and the in-migration of retirees has continued to the present day. This trend began in the 1940s when the New Deal policy of Social Security gave older Americans more money and a certain freedom to plan their retirement. In a telltale bit of social criticism, the state has been labeled as "God's Waiting Room" because of the number of elderly there. Florida is home to millions of older Americans familiar with the social, economic, and political aspects of retirement. The pattern first became apparent in the 1940s and 1950s as tens of thousands of Jews from the Northeast retired to the Miami area, while Midwesterners sold their homes to live in St. Petersburg. The graying of Florida had a dramatic effect on the culture of the state, but they were only part of the flood of new immigrants and citizens.

Most cities and communities in Florida came into existence since midcentury, so the whole state has a trendy feel of newness, experimentation, and freedom. The state has no income or inheritance taxes, and crime is a very important political issue for many older citizens. Florida was the first large state to allow a law for car- rying concealed weapons, and the National Rifle Association never fails to remind voters of this security at election time.

In Map 3.2 the state is divided into four regions. First, is the panhandle of the north, sometimes derisively called the "Redneck Riviera," because of its affiliation with the older southern culture. Politically this area is conservative with traditional churches and tourist venues to match the fine-grained sandy beaches. The second area is the fast-growing part of the state labeled as central Florida. It includes Daytona Beach, the city of Orlando, and development along the "I-4 Corridor" to Tampa Bay, making this region the largest media market in the state. Elsewhere, the grasslands and service-driven economy of central Florida is producing instant cities around manmade lakes, tourist traps, and golf courses. These areas are not urban, and they are not rural, rather they are a patchwork of affluent communities connect- ed by highways. Writer Pat Conroy described his Orlando years in a way that helps explain its attraction: "the happiest [days] of my childhood . . . a year spent fishing in a city dimpled with abundant lakes . . . smelling the spiced air . . . [and] climbing the trees to peel grapefruits, big as my head."[18]

The people who retired to the Gulf Coast, in the Tampa Bay/St. Petersburg area along Interstate 75, including many from the heartland of the Midwest, constitute the third area of the state. The Gulf coastal plain is a prominent population center in its own right, but it is dwarfed by south Florida. The fourth area in the state is the stereotype of luxury hotels, art deco, and affluent Jewish retirees living in the Miami-Dade, Broward, and Palm Beach counties along the eastern seaboard and Interstate 95. The Atlantic seaboard is the most populous of the four divisions shown on Map 3.2 and the ten counties on the Atlantic coast make up the most important political region, followed by that on the opposite Gulf Coast around Tampa Bay/St. Petersburg.

No fact is more apparent in Florida politics and culture than the recent explosion of population in the state. Florida's growth epitomizes strip development and means that political decisions based on one census can be obsolete by the next. The state is overspread with chaotic patterns of commercial development without a central business district. Endless walls of high-rise condominiums separate the beaches from the public transportation arteries along the Gold Coast of the Atlantic seaboard. The result of all this change means that zoning, environmental, and water issues tend to be fundamental to the political process. Despite general acceptance of the value of flood control, a complex of developments around Lake Okeechobee and the Kissamee River has awakened concerns about the future development of the state.

The greatest change in Florida's economic landscape in recent years has come from rapid industrialization in electronics, consumer goods, and apparel. Suburban shopping centers with reflective-window office parks house major electronic centers in cities like Melbourne and Orlando. The well-educated and ambitious entrepreneurs who work in these businesses are sensitive to global economic policies and the positions of politicians on world trade as they campaign for office. These newer business areas are not familiar with the rural-urban divisions that once dominated southern politics. In fact, in many Florida cities the incorporation boundaries extend far into the countryside, awaiting twenty-first-century growth.

Table 3.7 shows that in terms of demography, as well as geography, Florida has no real center. The state capital of Tallahassee is far from the rambunctious politics of Miami. The three counties of the Miami, Fort Lauderdale, and Palm Beach area have one-third of the state's population. The city of Miami recently changed its motto from the "Gateway" to Latin America, to the "Capital" of Latin America. Miami's patchwork, ethnic politics became famous after the 2000 election, when retirees on the Gold Coast who voted for Al Gore clashed with Latinos who supported George W. Bush. But it is important to remember that, despite televised "Miami Vice" images to the contrary, the City of Miami's politics and population are not Florida's.

The Tampa-St. Petersburg community on the west coast and the Orlando area in central Florida are growing more important in terms of politics, as the state population is shifting from the south to the developing counties along Interstate 4 in the middle of the state. This is the place George W. Bush exploited to win Florida in the 2004 presidential election. The counties in the Tampa/St. Petersburg metropoli-

---

Table 3.7 Florida: Population Centers and Media Market Rank

Region/City	County	Population 2000	Media Market Rank
Atlantic Coastal			
Miami/Ft. Lauderdale	Dade	2,253,362	15
Miami/Ft/ Lauderdale	Broward	1,623,018	15
Miami/Ft. Lauderdale	Palm Beach	1,131,184	15
	Subtotal	5,007,564	
Gulf Coastal Plain			
Tampa/St. Petersburg	Hillsborough	998,948	14
Tampa/St. Petersburg	Pinellas	992,482	14
Tampa/St. Petersburg	Pasco	344,765	14
Tampa/St. Petersburg	Hernando	130,802	14
	Subtotal	2,395,997	
Central Florida			
Orlando/Daytona Beach/Melbourne	Orange	896,344	20
	Total	8,299,905	

Source: Compiled by author from the US Census (2000) and Nielsen Media research, www.nielsen-media.com.
Note: This total represents 52 percent of Florida's population.

---

tan area are smaller than those in south Florida, but the media markets that encompass numerous contiguous counties with their associated communities are larger. The urban sprawl of central Florida extends from county to county with Orlando serving as the magnet for tourism and the epicenter of the new politics. In the next two decades this area is only going to grow in population and influence, and the state's power nationally will increase accordingly.

Virginia

Once called a "political museum piece," Virginia today is a model of economic growth and political change. The museum legacy remains though, in the tradition of conservative politics and patrician leaders. Virginians like George Washington, Patrick Henry, Thomas Jefferson, Richard Henry Lee, James Madison, and James Monroe created the republic and wrote the Constitution of the world's greatest democracy. The newer legacy of Virginia embraces leaders who understand developing sectors of the economy in service and technology industries that moved to the Commonwealth to make it competitive in global markets. Fairfax County, in the northern Washington, D.C., suburbs, has been dubbed the "Silicon Valley of the East."

A folk group from the "Old Dominion" describes its geographic shape as a "turkey on its belly," or "a chicken on its back." The political legacy is depicted with similar humor:

> She revels in the seasons,
> Shakes hands with the North,
> Hugs the Land of Dixie,
> While dancing on the Porch.[19]

The Virginia of today is rooted in the legacy of landed gentry from the past, while flirting with the affluence and diversity of the twenty-first century. The character of Virginia's migration differed dramatically from the Puritan character of Massachusetts. Virginia immigrants were "more highly stratified, more male-dominant, more rural, more agrarian, less highly skilled, and less literate."[20] At mid–twentieth century the ruling class was the courthouse machine of first governor, and then senator, Harry Byrd, who managed politics in the state for forty years after 1925. In the 1970s conservative Republicans won most statewide races, while Democrats held the legislature, but the main change was demographic long before it was political.

When V. O. Key wrote about politics in the Old Dominion, the state had four urban areas—today it has eight. The isolated cities of the 1950s have become a contiguous urban corridor that stretches from the northern boundary with West Virginia and Maryland to the southern border. The Virginia portion of the Washington, D.C., metropolitan area touches the Richmond area at the southern most tip of Spotsylvania County. Richmond, in turn, shares a boundary with the Norfolk/Virginia Beach/Hampton/Newport News metropolitan area. These three metropolitan areas (Washington, Richmond, and Virginia Beach) are the urban corridor of Virginia. The prominent growth pattern of the 1980s was along this Interstate 95 and Interstate 64 corridor.

The Tidewater area in the south, around the Navy bases in Norfolk, the shipbuilding yards in Newport News, and Army/Air Force bases in Hampton were at one end of this growth line. The other end includes the government employees and software entrepreneurs who live across the Potomac River from the nation's capital. Richmond, Chesterfield, and Henrico counties are a midway hub on this line. Virginia, like a number of southern states, grew more from in-migration than from a natural increase in its native population. The new residents were attracted to the economic opportunity and natural beauty of this urban corridor. The cities and counties along the interstates are the base of economic development in the state. Leave this urban and interstate axis, and the white-board fenced farms and stone houses of the state hearken back to a bucolic era long past.

Virginia keeps separate census statistics for incorporated cities and counties, but Map 3.3 shows that fifteen counties, along with their neighboring cities, contain

Map 3.3 Virginia: Population Distribution

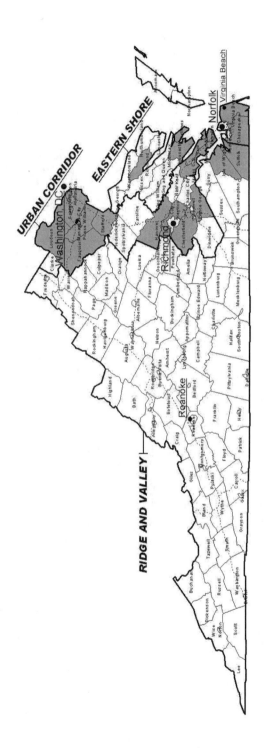

Population Distribution, 2000

	Counties	Population	
Eastern Shore	(13/0)	201,238	2.8%
Urban Corridor	(18/18)	4,529,097	63.7%
Ridge and Valley	(64/22)	2,383,118	33.5%
Total		8,049,313	100%

over 60 percent of the state's populace. This population is in three dominant media markets, with the Washington, D.C., and northern Virginia region being the largest. Although there are eleven Virginia counties in the Washington, D.C./Metropolitan MSA, only the six most populous are chosen for inclusion here.

David Brinkley wrote of a boom time in the District of Columbia and Virginia suburbs during World War II: "Government employment had more than doubled since the beginning of 1940, and more than five thousand new federal workers were pouring into Washington every month, often bringing their families with them."[21] In the decades of the 1990s the suburbs around Washington, D.C., grew at a less spectacular, but just as important pace. The new private entrepreneurs located in the suburbs where government employees once lived in quiet anonymity. Commuters in Fairfax County found the roadways jammed with yuppie venture capitalists as well as bureaucrats. High-tech office parks became home to affluent suburbanites whose interest was more in the economic, than the social, policies of the two political parties.

Government spending, especially defense, is important to the economy of Virginia. The military bases in Norfolk and Hampton, and a host of defense contractors around the beltway, testify to the role the military plays in state politics. Senator John Warner, chairman of the Armed Services Committee, is a native of the area having grown up in Washington, D.C. He shepherds money to state projects, and virtually all this economic activity is in the urban corridor.

The pattern of urbanization seen in the map is further explained in Table 3.8, which shows the separation of city and county statistics. This table shows the counties and cities in the metropolitan statistical areas of Norfolk/Newport News, Richmond, and the suburbs of Washington. Not surprisingly, the Washington suburbs are the largest in terms of population with nearly two million residents. Both Richmond and Norfolk have around one million residents each. These three areas, all connected by interstates and contiguous metropolitan designations, have nearly two-thirds of the state's population. Virginia may cultivate an image of white-fenced, genteel leisure with gentleman farmers and romantic cavaliers, but the reality is a modern corporate complex of interstate highways and research parks.

Texas

Texas won its independence in 1836. At the time, both the Spanish and Mexican governments did not allow slavery, but as southern immigrants came to the territory they brought their slaves with them. After the Civil War, African Americans were kept in submission by economic and political discrimination. Most of the black population was in east Texas, living in a social structure that was an extension of the Old South.

The southern values of separation and segregation were gradually abolished or absorbed into the vast landscape that is the rest of the state. Early settlers brought cotton farming to the "piney woods" of east Texas, but other types of farming and ranching became more significant further west. In the twentieth century the great

Table 3.8   Virginia, Urban Corridor: Population Centers and Media Market Rank

	Counties/Cities	Population 2000	Media Market Rank
Urban Corridor	Counties		
Washington/Northern Virginia	Fairfax	969,749	8
Washington/Northern Virginia	Prince William	280,813	8
Washington/Northern Virginia	Arlington	189,813	8
Washington/Northern Virginia	Loudon	169,599	8
Washington/Northern Virginia	Stafford	92,446	8
Washington/Northern Virginia	Fuquier	55,139	8
	Cities		
Washington/Northern Virginia	Alexandria City	128,283	8
Washington/Northern Virginia	Manassas	35,135	8
Washington/Northern Virginia	Fairfax City	21,498	8
Washington/Northern Virginia	Fredricksburg	19,279	8
Washington/Northern Virginia	Falls Church	10,377	8
Washington/Northern Virginia	Manassas Park	10,290	8
	Subtotal	1,982,061	
Urban Corridor	Counties		
Richmond/Petersburg	Chesterfield	276,800	58
Richmond/Petersburg	Henrico	262,300	58
Richmond/Petersburg	Hanover	86,320	58
Richmond/Petersburg	Prince George	33,047	58
	Cities		
Richmond/Petersburg	Richmond	197,790	58
Richmond/Petersburg	Petersburg	33,740	58
Richmond/Petersburg	Hopewell	22,354	58
Richmond/Petersburg	Colonial Heights	16,897	58
	Subtotal	929,248	
Urban Corridor	Counties		
Norfolk/Newport News	York	56,297	42
Norfolk/Newport News	James City	48,102	42
Norfolk/Newport News	Glouchester	34,780	42
Norfolk/Newport News	Isle of Wright	29,728	42
Norfolk/Newport News	Matthews	9,207	42
	Cities		
Norfolk/Newport News	Virginia Beach	425,257	42
Norfolk/Newport News	Chesapeake	199,184	42
Norfolk/Newport News	Newport News	180,150	42
Norfolk/Newport News	Hampton	146,437	42
Norfolk/Newport News	Portsmouth	100,565	42
Norfolk/Newport News	Suffolk	63,677	42
Norfolk/Newport News	Williamsburg	11,998	42
Norfolk/Newport News	Poquoson	11,566	42
	Subtotal	1,316,948	
	Total	4,228,257	

Source: Compiled by author from the US Census (2000) and Nielsen Media research, www.nielsen-media.com.

Note: This total represents 59 percent of Virginia's population.

mineral wealth of oil and natural gas reshaped the economy and stamped the culture of the state.

Honky-tonk songs and Hollywood legends describe Texas as silver-tipped boots, ten-gallon hats, and millionaires with shiny belt buckles. But the petroleum industry of yesterday has given way to a multinational population and a diverse economy today. German and Czech communities are in the central part of the state, the Mexican/Spanish influence of San Antonio and El Paso is now dominant, and today Houston has a vibrant black community. West Texas has rodeos and cowboys to match the plantations of east Texas, and interstates connect gleaming cities to some of the nation's most affluent and exclusive suburbs. The travel brochures today readily declare Texas as "It's Like a Whole Other Country."

The cumulative effect of migration and economic change resulted in the eight economic and geographic regions in evidence in Map 3.4. East Texas remains rural and biracial, but much of the population has migrated to the urban areas of Dallas and Houston, so it no longer plays a dominant role in politics or the economy. The Upper Gulf Coast has been an economic boom area for the state. Houston and Beaumont are oil and raw material centers for the entire country, and have added medicine, government, insurance, and banking businesses to their already flourishing economy. Houston is one of the largest metropolitan areas in the country, and as Larry McMurtry once wrote, "one sometimes wonders if Bowie and Travis and the rest would have fought so hard for this land if they had known how many ugly motels and shopping centers would eventually stand on it."[22] Extreme perhaps, but the rapid growth of Texas led to mushrooming cities consuming prairie land in huge gulps, and inviting the wrath of cowpokes weary with the change.

The area that benefited most from this economic expansion is north Texas. The region is a buffer between east and west, and the Dallas/Fort Worth area is the commercial and banking rival of Houston. Dallas was originally a rail center, and the "Metroplex" owes much of its growth in population to its geographic location. "Big D" stands as a prairie polyglot expression of J. R. Ewing, the Dallas Cowboys cheerleaders, and the First Baptist Church. It has a reputation as a wide-open town with unlimited opportunities for anyone willing to join the competition.

The "wildcatter," risk-taking culture nurtured in the oil patch of Texas abhorred government regulations and taxes. After John Kennedy was assassinated there in 1963, biographer Arthur Schlesinger described the mood of Dallas as, "longing for a dream world of no communism or overseas entanglements, no United Nations, no federal government, no labor unions, no Negroes, no foreigners—a world in which Chief Justice Warren would be impeached, Cuba invaded, the graduated income tax repealed, the fluoridation of drinking water stopped and the import of Polish hams forbidden."[23] This pejorative and disparaging description is more understandable given the resentment after the death of a president—but it also captures something of the spirit of north Texas.

West Texas, west central Texas, and the panhandle are the scarcely populated areas of Map 3.5, with ranching, irrigated farming, and petroleum exploration sup-plying most of the employment. Midland was the home of George H.W. Bush, whose son George W. Bush grew up playing little league baseball under cloudless skies. South Texas has a large population of Hispanics. Field laborers originally came north from Mexico for seasonal agricultural employment, then stayed as "ille-gals" because of the opportunity offered by an expanding economy. "By 1980 Texas ranked behind only California in its number of Spanish-speaking residents, second in its concentration of Vietnamese, third in African Americans, and ninth in American Indians."[24]

Texas is the second most populous state in the nation, and the heart of the new growth is around the three cities of Dallas/Fort Worth, San Antonio, and Houston. The eight regions of Texas contain over 20 million people in 254 counties, but half of the population is in just eight of them. The cities of Dallas/Fort Worth, San Antonio, and Houston comprise the "Texas Triangle," an accumulation of some forty-two counties that collectively contain 60 percent of the population of the state. The Texas Triangle follows Interstate 35 from Dallas/Fort Worth through Waco and Austin to San Antonio, then travels east on Interstate 10 to Houston, then returns up Interstate 45 to the Dallas/Fort Worth Metroplex. The north Texas, Dallas/Fort Worth area is the seventh largest media market in the United States. Along with Houston, which is the eleventh largest national market, Texas has two of the top three national media markets in the South.

In spite of its size and complexity, Texas is a simple state to analyze politically. Table 3.9 shows that, with over two hundred counties, half the population lives in just a handful of them, which are on the tips of the Texas Triangle. When Austin and Waco, two cities that lie along Interstate 35, are added to the Texas Triangle, the population totals to half that of the state. The statewide campaign strategy is to consolidate votes in the urban areas and then add support from sparsely populated counties. Cities like Lubbock or Corpus Christi, which would be major markets in other southern states, are incidental to the Texas political strategy dominated by the huge urban areas on the tips of the Triangle.

The new Lone Star swagger comes from the size and importance of the state in national politics. The Bush family has given the country two presidents from the same state within the same decade. In Washington, Senator Phil Gramm and Representatives Dick Armey and Tom DeLay led the GOP in its battles with the Clinton administration (1992–2000). Conservative candidates seeking political office in other states are often encouraged to hold fundraisers in Texas. The money and influence of Texas helps drive the national political agenda.

The ideal of the Texas cowboy, instant oilman fame, or the ranch spread of the "Dallas" television legend of the 1980s have gradually disappeared, and the new wildcatters are entrepreneurs in the personal computer, telecommunication, and real estate business who have risk taking in their blood. They collectively echo the same values as the petroleum mavericks, but they wear suits instead of Stetsons and

Map 3.4   Texas: Population Distribution

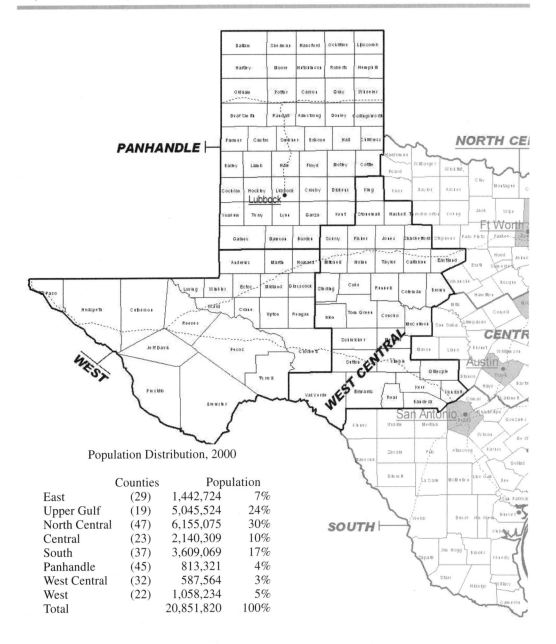

Population Distribution, 2000

	Counties	Population	
East	(29)	1,442,724	7%
Upper Gulf	(19)	5,045,524	24%
North Central	(47)	6,155,075	30%
Central	(23)	2,140,309	10%
South	(37)	3,609,069	17%
Panhandle	(45)	813,321	4%
West Central	(32)	587,564	3%
West	(22)	1,058,234	5%
Total		20,851,820	100%

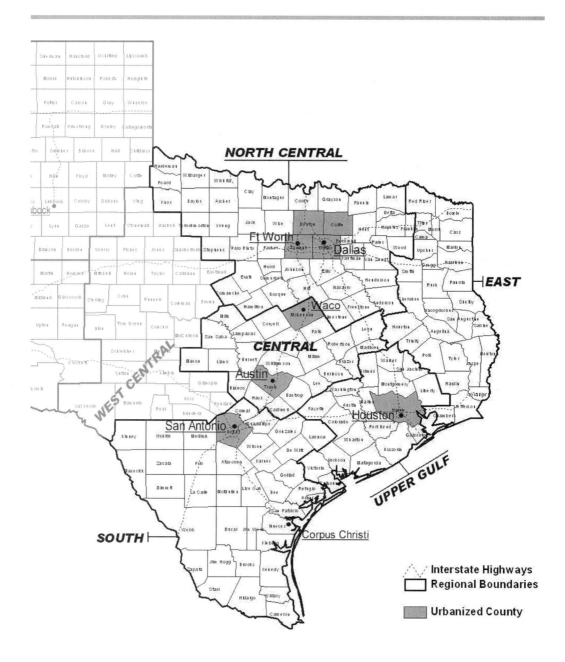

Map 3.5   Texas Triangle: Population Distribution

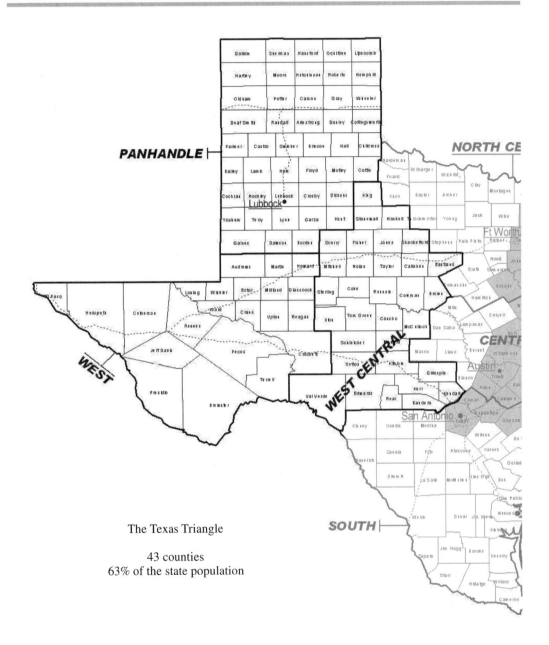

The Texas Triangle

43 counties
63% of the state population

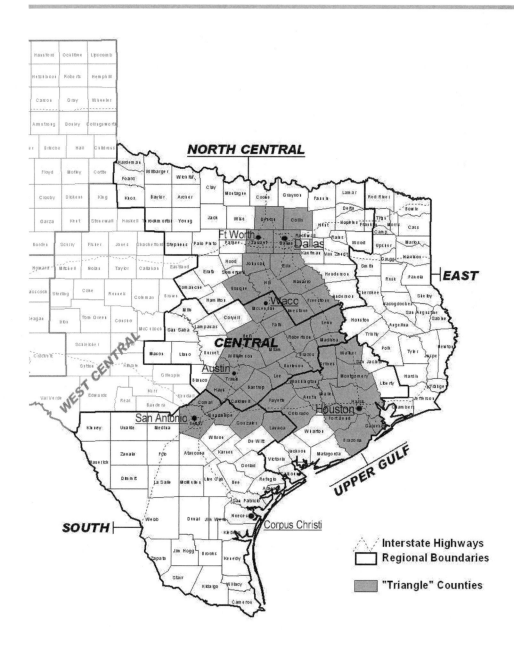

Table 3.9 Texas: Population Centers and Media Market Rank

Region/City	County	Population 2000	Media Market Rank
North Central Texas			
Dallas/Fort Worth	Dallas	2,218,899	7
Dallas/Fort Worth	Tarrant	1,446,219	7
Dallas/Fort Worth	Collin	491,675	7
Dallas/Fort Worth	Denton	432,976	7
	Subtotal	4,589,769	
Central Texas			
Austin	Travis	812,280	54
Waco	McLennan	213,517	95
	Subtotal	1,025,797	
South Texas			
San Antonio	Bexar	1,392,931	37
Upper Gulf			
Houston	Harris	3,400,578	11
	Total	10,409,075	

Source: Compiled by author from the US Census (2000) and Nielsen Media research, www.nielsen-media.com.
Note: This total represents 50 percent of Texas's population.

boots. The political culture is a product of the spirit of the oilfield, the ranch, and the Alamo. Texas politicians consistently emphasize a freedom from interference by government and self-reliant policies. The interstates connecting the cities of the Texas Triangle are modern-day pioneer routes of development for a state that treasures US individualism.

Emergent States

North Carolina

According to V. O. Key, North Carolina was a "closer approximation to national norms" than any other southern state.[25] In many ways the state has fulfilled that promise. It vies with Georgia for a population rank as the tenth largest state in the nation, and the Research Triangle Park between Raleigh, Durham, and Chapel Hill, is one of the nation's leading research centers. The nation's largest bank is headquartered in Charlotte, and the state has become a national financial center.

Yet, at century's end, North Carolina failed to make the conversion from a southern state of regional importance to one of national influence for several reasons. Unlike Georgia, the state has no population center; instead it has several metropolitan areas and thickly settled suburbs. The cutting-edge technology of the Research Triangle has not displaced the textile, furniture, and tobacco legacy in the rural regions of the state. Agriculture is still an important part of the economy here, and North Carolina effectively resists change with traditional Sunday blue laws, and a conservative social environment uneasy with rapid urbanization and the secular values that accompany it.

The state is justifiably proud of its tradition of racial moderation, with the first lunch counter sit-in movement being in Greensboro. But it is also a state where Ku Klux Klan radicals shot and killed black nationalists in 1979. North Carolina is a mixture of "Mayberry RFD" and some of the nation's best universities. Once home to one of the nation's most conservative US senators, it also has one of the most progressive research centers in the country and furnished the Democratic Party with a liberal running mate for vice president in 2004. North Carolina is not "behind" on any one indicator,; rather, compared to the national states, its rate of change has lagged. The persistent problem of widening income disparities keeps this state from matching the accomplishments of Florida, Virginia, Texas, and Georgia.

The paradox of North Carolina is that it is stocked with tradition-minded citizens who are interested in newer ideas. The state's rise from the bottom of the economic heap is founded on a belief that the funding of education and the development of an economic infrastructure would lead to income improvement. After upgrading its major universities and technical colleges in the 1950s and 1960s, North Carolina expanded its highway system and developed the "Research Triangle." Both the Research Triangle Park and the Research Triangle Institute came into existence in 1958, and have "become an international center for research, development and cutting edge technology."[26]

Map 3.6 shows that the three media markets of Charlotte, Raleigh-Durham, and Greensboro/High Point/Winston-Salem have 46 percent of the state population. When the coastal area of Wilmington is added, half the population is in just twenty-three counties. Since North Carolina has an even one hundred counties, half the population of the state is in less than a quarter of them.

Money magazine named the Raleigh-Durham area as the best place to live in the South for the year 2000. It is the second largest media market in the state with the attractions of low-cost housing, exceptional health care, cultural amenities, and a pleasing natural environment drawing residents nationwide. The Raleigh-Durham/Chapel Hill metro area has a population that ranks fifty-fourth of 318 metropolitan areas in the United States. In 1999, its per capita personal income was 12 percent above the national average, in an area of the nation with a below average cost of living. The Research Triangle brought national accreditation and a revived economy to the northern part of the state.[27]

The other booming metropolitan center of North Carolina is Charlotte, an area that includes Gastonia, North Carolina, and Rock Hill, South Carolina. In 2000 its

Map 3.6   North Carolina: Population Distribution

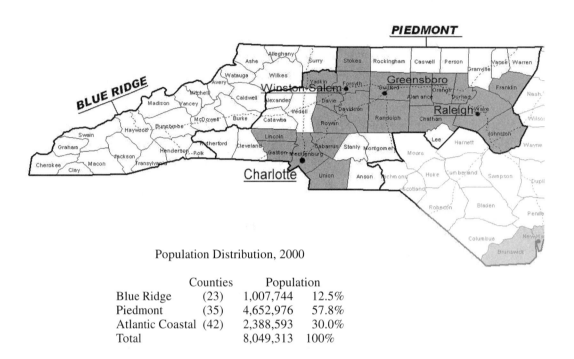

Population Distribution, 2000

	Counties	Population	
Blue Ridge	(23)	1,007,744	12.5%
Piedmont	(35)	4,652,976	57.8%
Atlantic Coastal	(42)	2,388,593	30.0%
Total		8,049,313	100%

MSA population ranked forty-second in the nation, while its per capita personal income ranked fifty-ninth. The fastest growing industries in the area were finance, insurance, and real estate. When North Carolina National Bank evolved into NationsBank, almost overnight Charlotte became a worldwide financial center, a leader in the new information technology, a global trade center, and home for international business. In 2000 the city had $774 billion worth of banking resources headquartered in its borders, an amount that ranked it second in the United States. Charlotte is home to both the Bank of America and First Union National Bank, and is also a branch of the Federal Reserve.

The third important media market in North Carolina, with a population over one million, is the Greensboro/Winston-Salem/High Point area. These cities have strong ties to the traditional industries of tobacco and textiles, but these industries are by no means the only economic enticements that the Winston-Salem MSA has to offer. It is home to the BB&T banking enterprises, making it yet another top financial center in the United States. Other corporations that have ties to the region

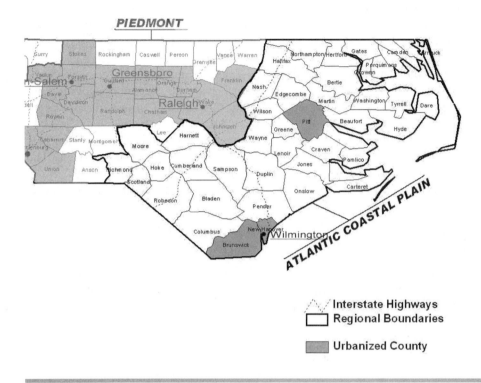

are Sara Lee, Tyco, Corning, and Krispy Kreme. *Entrepreneur* magazine has recognized Greensboro as a top five metropolitan area for small business.

Like other southern states, North Carolina has a seacoast boundary. Unlike its southern cousins it never had a major port like Charleston, South Carolina, or an inland waterway like the rivers from the Chesapeake Bay that reach into Virginia, to stimulate economic development. Instead the Outer Banks' island waterway attracts tourists, but its geography does not lend itself to extensive beachfront development. The exception to scarce coastal development is the military presence at Wilmington and up the coast to Jacksonville. Today the Wilmington-Jacksonville area is home to important military installations, most notably Fort Bragg Army Base, Pope Air Force Base, and the Camp Lejeune Marine Corps Base.

The population of North Carolina lies along an interstate highway arc of I-40, I-95, and I-85 from Charlotte to Greensboro to Raleigh-Durham and down to Wilmington. The state divides into three geographic regions: the Atlantic coast in the east, the middle Piedmont region, and the Blue Ridge Mountains in the west.

The Piedmont region has most of the population in the cities. The suburbs of Raleigh, Charlotte, and Greensboro are all connected by interstates and have experienced continuous development. The Piedmont area has over half the state's population, and the Piedmont interstate arc embraces the heart of North Carolina's population. The Blue Ridge Mountains in the west are home to a growing retirement population.

In 1950 the state had six metropolitan areas that held only 13 percent of the population. In 2000 North Carolina had eleven metropolitan areas, bulging with two-thirds of the state's population. Even with this accelerated growth and urbanized metropolitan areas, North Carolina failed to keep up with other states because its neighbors grew at an even faster rate. According to the Bureau of Economic Analysis, the state of North Carolina ranked thirteenth in 1980 and 1990, and twelfth in 1999 in Gross State Product. This ranking, while high, still placed North Carolina behind Texas, Florida, Virginia, and Georgia—all of whom ranked ahead of it on the national list.

Table 3.10 shows the urban connection of the population in the cities of Charlotte, Raleigh, and Greensboro. The infrastructure of North Carolina accommodates this growing economy. The rate of expansion is slightly above that of the United States as a whole, and proposed plans to improve the highway system, including those that encircle Raleigh, Winston-Salem, Greensboro, and Charlotte, will no doubt be enough to stimulate even more growth. The Piedmont plains are where the population has chosen to locate, with the Atlantic coastal areas of Greenville and Wilmington expanding rapidly since 1980. The mountains and coastline are borders to a booming economic triangle of the major cities. North Carolina has room and the opportunity to grow in the years ahead.

Tennessee

In the last three decades of the twentieth century, Tennessee became a part of the broad national culture, and—more importantly—the international economy. Multinational companies were attracted to the transportation infrastructure and readily available workforce in the state. Residents took pride in values of racial tolerance that were more than those of their rebel cousins and less than those of their Yankee neighbors. It proved attractive as a border state to immigrants drawn to the scenic beauty, cultural distinctiveness, and booming economy of the place.

Tennessee became predominantly urban, according to the census definition, in 1960. The ranking of its four largest cities—Memphis, Nashville, Knoxville, and Chattanooga—has not changed in forty years. The state has experienced economic and social stability in the face of a rising tourist trade, population expansion, and cultural change.

Among Tennessee's attractions are plentiful natural resources, a mild climate, a sophisticated infrastructure of highways and airports, and a trained labor force. A major draw for outside investors is the low cost of doing business in the state. It has no income tax, local taxes are low, and local governments frequently recruit busi-

Table 3.10   North Carolina: Population Centers and Media Market Rank

Region/City	County	Population 2000	Media Market Rank
Piedmont: Charlotte			
Charlotte	Mecklenburg	695,454	27
Charlotte	Gaston	190,365	27
Charlotte	Cabarras	131,063	27
Charlotte	Rowan	130,340	27
Charlotte	Union	123,677	27
Charlotte	Lincoln	63,780	27
	Subtotal	1,334,679	
Piedmont: Raleigh-Durham/Chapel Hill			
Raleigh	Wake	627,941	29
Raleigh	Durham	223,314	29
Raleigh	Johnston	121,965	29
Raleigh	Orange	118,227	29
Raleigh	Chatham	49,329	29
Raleigh	Franklin	47,260	29
	Subtotal	1,187,941	
Piedmont: Greensboro/High Point/Winston-Salem			
Greensboro	Guilford	421,048	44
Greensboro	Forsyth	306,067	44
Greensboro	Davidson	147,246	44
Greensboro	Almance	130,800	44
Greensboro	Randolph	130,454	44
Greensboro	Stokes	44,711	44
Greensboro	Yadkin	36,348	44
Greensboro	Davie	34,835	44
	Subtotal	1,251,509	
Atlantic Coastal: Greenville/New Bern/Washington			
Greenville	Pitt	133,798	106
Atlantic Coastal: Wilmington			
Wilmington	New Hanover	160,307	146
Brunswick	Brunswick	73,143	146
	Total	4,141,377	

Source: Compiled by author from the US Census (2000) and Nielsen Media research, www.nielsen-media.com.
Note: This total represents 51 percent of North Carolina's population.

ness by offering special tax breaks. These incentives led to budget shortfalls for state government after 2000, but the business culture remains strongly anti-union and pro-growth.

Tennessee has a history of influencing the nation at its grassroots. The music

Map 3.7   Tennessee: Population Distribution

Population Distribution, 2000

		Counties	Population	
East	(34)	2,119,505	37.2%	
Middle	(40)	2,069,976	36.2%	
West	(21)	1,499,802	30.0%	
Total		5,689,283	100%	

industry drew together the mountain bluegrass of east Tennessee, the country music tradition of the Grand Ole Opry in Nashville, and the Delta blues of Memphis to make Tennessee synonymous with instant celebrity and immediate wealth. Holiday Inns began as a chain of motels in the state, as did numerous fast food franchises and dozens of entertainment careers. Dreams are made and lost in Tennessee, especially in Nashville, where today's restaurant waitress might be tomorrow's country music legend.

Map 3.7 shows that of all the southern states, Tennessee retains the clearest geographical divisions identified by V. O. Key fifty years ago. The state is divided by the Cumberland Plateau in the east and the Tennessee River in the west, resulting in three grand divisions: east, middle, and west. The encircled stars of the Tennessee flag are emblematic of the state's three regions, but the geographical distance from west to east is enormous. It's as far from Memphis to Bristol, as from Memphis to the Canadian border. The cultural and political heritage of each region is unique and enduring. Size is the key to history. Memphis farms on the Mississippi Delta are very different from east Tennessee mountains and the politics are as vast as the geography.

East Tennessee had few slaves before the Civil War, and was unionist and Republican in its sentiments. Middle and west Tennessee held slaves and were Confederate in allegiance. The cities of Chattanooga, Knoxville, and the Tri-Cities

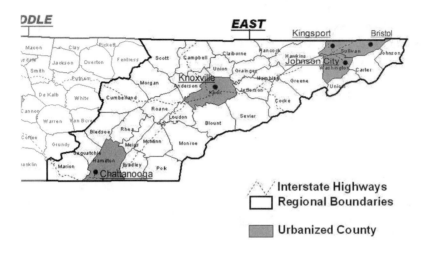

(Bristol, Kingsport, and Johnson City) are mountain metropolises in the same time zone that are geographically and culturally harmonious. Today east Tennessee has more than one-third of the population of the state, and the region stands as the Republican base for any statewide political campaigns.

Middle Tennessee, with the multicounty Nashville metropolitan area, is the largest media market in the state as well as the capital of government, business, entertainment, and manufacturing. In the 1980s Nissan built a plant in next-door Rutherford County and General Motors put a similar Saturn plant in Maury County, south of the city. Both of these automobile plants are less than an hour's drive from Nashville, and helped to energize the entrepreneurial spirit of the region.

The third area is Memphis, a place more like Mississippi than Tennessee, and called the "most rural-minded city in the South" by H. L. Mencken.[28] As a major city in the Delta area of the Mississippi River, it became a haven for black residents from the Mississippi backwaters trying to get away from their past on the farm. The city is home to blues music, agriculture, and black culture. It has a flavor of the Old South like no other city in the state.

Interstate 40 connects the east, middle, and west of the state. Tennessee's most populous area contains Knoxville in the east, with Nashville in the middle, and Memphis in the west. Memphis is the city with the largest one-county population in the state, the Nashville metropolitan area is the largest media market, and the populous cities of east Tennessee (Knoxville, Chattanooga, and the Tri-Cities) make it the largest of the three geographic regions.

Tennessee is an anomaly. It has no coastal lowland area; instead, it has an unusual mountain heritage wedded to a Mississippi slaveholding legacy. Despite its size, half the population is in four cities and nine counties. Table 3.11 shows the population of the three regions. In east Tennessee population is scattered among four media markets, while Nashville in middle Tennessee and Memphis in west Tennessee are each a single urban and media market.

Traditional States

Alabama

James Agee and Walker Evans penned the most impassioned and poetic lament of Alabama. "All over Alabama," Agee wrote in 1936, "the lamps are out . . . The roads lie there with nothing to use them [and] the fields lie there with nothing at work in them, neither man nor beast." This Depression image of agricultural poverty, evident in *Let Us Now Praise Famous Men,* haunts the state to this day.[29]

Table 3.11   Tennessee, Urban Counties: Population Centers and Media Market Rank

Region/City	County	Population 2000	Media Market Rank
East Tennessee			
Knoxville	Knoxville	382,032	62
Chattanooga	Hamilton	307,896	86
(Tri-Cities)/Bristol/Kingsport	Sullivan	153,048	93
(Tri-Cities)/Johnson City	Washington	107,198	93
	Subtotal	950,174	
Middle Tennessee			
Nashville	Davidson	569,891	30
Nashville	Rutherford	182,023	30
Nashville	Sumner	130,449	30
Nashville	Williamson	126,638	30
	Subtotal	1,009,001	
West Tennessee			
Memphis	Shelby	897,472	41
	Total	2,856,647	

Source: Compiled by author from the US Census (2000) and Nielsen Media research, www.nielsen-media.com.
Note: This total represents 50 percent of Tennessee's population.

Alabama had a raw frontier and backwoods quality with a history of racism, anger, and white trash in abundance. But it is also, as Rick Bragg writes, "the most beautiful place on earth . . . where gray mists hid the tops of low, deep-green mountains, where redbone and bluetick hounds flashed through the pines as they chased possums into the sacks of old men in frayed overalls, where old women in bonnets dipped Bruton snuff and hummed, 'Faded Love and Winter Roses.'"[30] The state is depicted in literature as uncivilized, unsanitary, and violent, for example, in Harper Lee's *To Kill a Mockingbird,* but it also is a place of undeserved scorn and untapped potential.

The legacy of backwardness was reinforced by television images in the 1960s, when the public protests of the civil rights movement showed a brutal, savage side of social relations in this Deep South state. Alabama was the location for most of the remembered pictures of the era, the snarling dogs of Birmingham, the assault by mounted police on the bridge at Selma, and the dramatic march from Selma to Montgomery along Highway 80 in 1965. National news reporters flocked to these cities during these years, and reported that Alabama remained benighted, cruel, and somehow out of touch with modern civilization.

Few states have a popular legacy of resistance to authority, an eagerness for improvement and rawness that can equal that of Alabama. The state history began when Jacksonian farmers sent Native Americans packing over the red clay hills to the reservation, and plantation farmers raised, and shipped, cotton from the dark Black Belt soil. Alabama was a state where the frontier was tamed with fierce determination. Birmingham became a symbol of the bare-knuckled life in the northern mountains with miners hacking away at the solid iron rock for the steel mills. Today the gouged out hillsides have given way to interstate highway exchanges, small factories, and Wal-Mart distribution centers. At the end of the twentieth century the raw and rural stereotype was tamed. Mercedes-Benz located a major automobile plant in the state, and Birmingham changed from a city of dogs attacking black demonstrators to one of genteel sophistication, with one of the nation's top medical centers.

Geographically, Map 3.8 shows that Alabama divides naturally into northern and southern regions, with the Black Belt, once cotton-growing south separated from the more mountainous north. In popular usage, the lower part of the state was the land of agriculture and slavery, while slaveless farmers and ambiguous political alliances dominated the upper part. South Alabama was once the heart of the "Old South" where dependence on one crop meant immediate profit and soil exhaustion. North Alabama was sparsely populated and resentful of downstate domination.

The population center of the state today is Birmingham, a four-county city that dominates finance, health care, and politics in the state. The city's economic potentates were once called "Big Mules," a term of derision invented by populist governors, like Jim Folsom, who opposed the limited vision the businessmen had for the state's future. The city has a distinct native feel, with Cherokee, Choctaw, and

Map 3.8   Alabama: Population Distribution

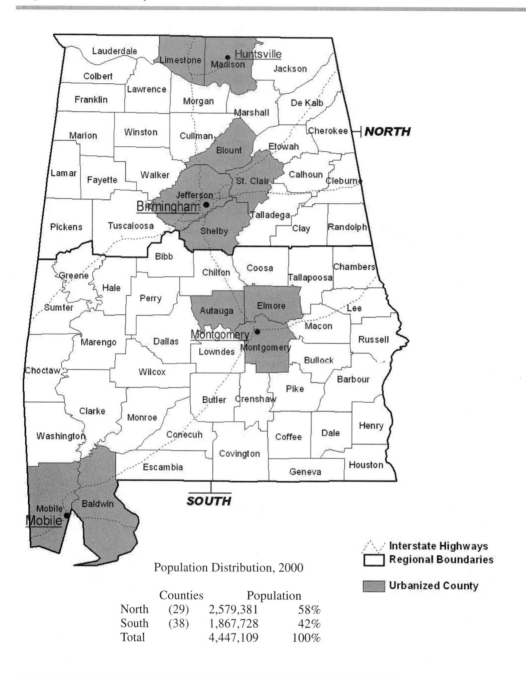

Population Distribution, 2000

	Counties	Population	
North	(29)	2,579,381	58%
South	(38)	1,867,728	42%
Total		4,447,109	100%

Chickasaw names for landmarks, creeks, and streets in the Jones Valley. At the beginning of the twentieth century Birmingham was the largest exporting venue for pig iron in the United States, and became known as the "Pittsburgh of the South." The heavy industrial economy gradually gave way to a more diverse one, including banking, computer services, and a medical complex for several states.

With Charlotte, Jacksonville, and Austin, Birmingham now has assumed regional importance. The city's influence is dominant in the state of Alabama, but the media market is not as large as Atlanta, Georgia, Charlotte or Raleigh-Durham in North Carolina, or Nashville in Tennessee. Table 3.12 shows that when the Birmingham numbers are added to nearby Huntsville, with its space and defense facilities, and the education complex in Tuscaloosa, the northern counties have approximately half the state's population.

Montgomery, in south Alabama, is a throwback to a different era. The city overlooks an oxbow bend in the Alabama River, and was once known as the

Table 3.12   Alabama: Population Centers and Media Market Rank

Region/City	County	Population 2000	Media Market Rank
North Alabama			
Birmingham	Jefferson	662,047	39
Birmingham	Shelby	143,293	39
Birmingham	St. Clair	64,742	39
Birmingham	Blount	51,024	39
	Subtotal	921,106	
North Alabama			
Huntsville	Madison	276,700	83
Huntsville	Limestone	65,676	83
	Subtotal	342,376	
South Alabama			
Montgomery	Montgomery	223,510	114
Montgomery	Elmore	65,874	114
Montgomery	Autauga	43,671	114
	Subtotal	333,055	
South Alabama			
Mobile	Mobile	399,843	63
Mobile	Baldwin	140,415	63
	Subtotal	540,258	
	Total	2,136,795	

Source: Compiled by author from the US Census (2000) and Nielsen Media research, www.nielsen-media.com.
Note: This total represents 48 percent of Alabama's population.

"Cradle of the Confederacy" in the decades after the Civil War. On the steps of the state capitol a bronze medallion marks the exact place where Jefferson Davis took the oath as president of the Confederacy. Today the area is home to a variety of military bases, state government buildings, and an ingrained legacy of political conservatism. South Alabama was the traditional agricultural area of the state. The cotton plantation culture is now replaced by manufacturing and service industries, but the social animosities and racial tensions remain. Farther south in Mobile is a city where the Tombigbee and Alabama rivers flow into the Gulf of Mexico. The city also serves as a population center for retirees and military personnel.

These four urban areas—Huntsville and Birmingham in the north, and Montgomery and Mobile in the south—have nearly half the population of the state in eleven counties. Alabama is not as urbanized as other southern states, but slightly less than half the state's population still reside in these four cities.

Arkansas

As part of the 1976 celebration of the American Bicentennial, the NBC television show "Today" produced a tribute to each state. The Arkansas segment featured the Ozarks, with the stereotype of a barefoot hillbilly bypassed by modernization. The two-term presidency of Bill Clinton, a backwoods success story who became a Rhodes Scholar and governor before winning the White House, changed the image of Arkansas. Like the state in which he was born, he appeared to be many things at the same time. No other modern politician seemed to so visibly win the public's support one moment, and lose its confidence the next. Arkansas had few natural resources or industrial advantages, but accomplished much in spite of these deficiencies. It is the smallest state in the South and the smallest between the Mississippi and the Pacific, yet it is one of the best known.

Poor farmers with little cash and fewer slaves originally settled Arkansas. The state never had a dominant planter class or economic elite; instead it was characterized by the hillbilly stereotype familiar to the "Today" viewers. The legacy of the "Arkansas Traveler," as an interloper with a humorous dialogue and a patchwork quilt, persists. Arkansas is part Mississippi and part Texas, part poverty and part opportunity. In the last quarter of the twentieth century the state became home to men like Sam Walton and Don Tyson, entrepreneurs who made huge fortunes through tough bargaining and breakthrough marketing ideas. But the stereotype of the state also exists, of agricultural stagnation, mobile homes, and lost dreams.

Arkansas never had a legacy of elite plantation owners or powerful businessmen to set the standards of proper political behavior in the state. Instead the state grew up with a populist flavor of individual initiative limited by agricultural poverty. The counties around Little Rock make the city the geographic and economic center of the state. As a media market, the middle-Arkansas area is far smaller than major cities in the national and emergent states of the South.

The state is divided into three regions, as shown in Map 3.9: the Mississippi

Map 3.9 · Arkansas: Population Distribution

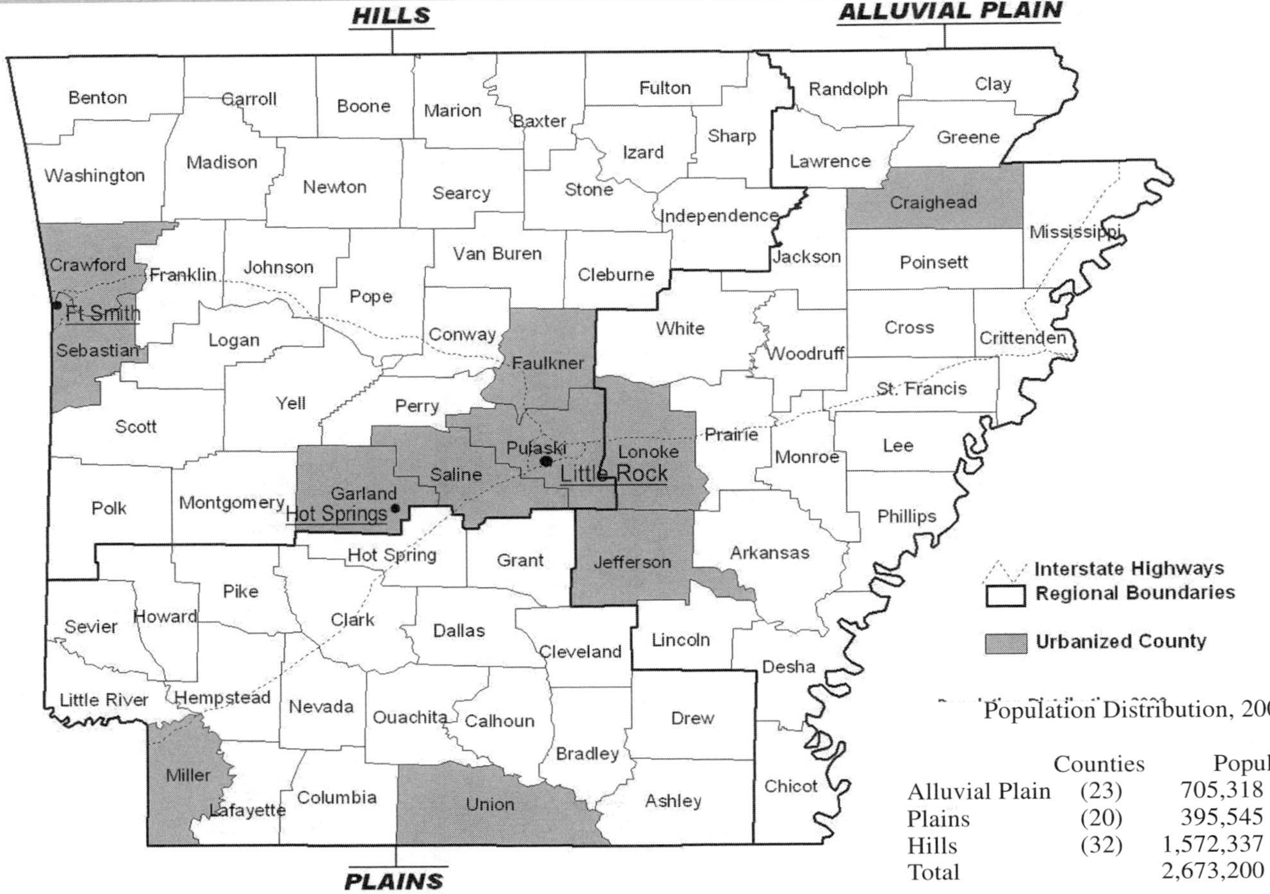

HILLS ALLUVIAL PLAIN PLAINS

Legend

Interstate Highways
Regional Boundaries
Urbanized County

Population Distribution, 2000

	Counties	Population	
Alluvial Plain	(23)	705,318	26%
Plains	(20)	395,545	15%
Hills	(32)	1,572,337	59%
Total		2,673,200	100%

County labels: Benton, Washington, Carroll, Madison, Boone, Newton, Marion, Searcy, Baxter, Stone, Van Buren, Izard, Fulton, Sharp, Randolph, Clay, Greene, Lawrence, Craighead, Poinsett, Cross, Crittenden, St. Francis, Lee, Phillips, Mississippi, Independence, Jackson, Woodruff, Monroe, Cleburne, White, Prairie, Arkansas, Lincoln, Desha, Chicot, Drew, Ashley, Bradley, Cleveland, Calhoun, Ouachita, Union, Columbia, Lafayette, Miller, Hempstead, Nevada, Clark, Dallas, Grant, Jefferson, Lonoke, Pulaski, Saline, Hot Spring, Garland, Perry, Faulkner, Conway, Pope, Johnson, Logan, Yell, Montgomery, Pike, Howard, Sevier, Little River, Polk, Scott, Sebastian, Crawford, Franklin

Cities: Fort Smith (Ft. Smith), Hot Springs, Little Rock

Delta counties along the alluvial plain, the flat plains to the border town of Texarkana, and the mountainous hills and wide valleys of the northwestern part of the state. The geography is uneven, with the alluvial plains being most distinct. This is the part of the state that looks to Memphis for its cultural connection, and bemoans the blues and despair that only natives along the Mississippi can know. The flat, marshy, lowlands along the Mississippi are the agricultural heartland with cotton, rice, and soybeans stored in huge warehouses.

The plains in the southern part of the state, along Interstate 30, are a throwback to other parts of the South. Rolling fields and leafy foothills characterize a part of the state more akin to east Texas and northern Louisiana. Texarkana sits on the border of Texas unable to decide whether to cast its cultural lot with the South or the West.

The Ozarks are the heart of the northwest region of the state. This corner of Arkansas has become a retirement and tourist area across the border from Branson, Missouri. The headquarters of Wal-Mart and Tyson's chicken empires are in the rounded green hills of the Ozarks. Interstate 40 bisects the state and all roads seem to converge in Little Rock. The city is the population and geographic center for the state, which has no other real metropolis. Little Rock is the state capital and focus of politics and economics.

Arkansas is still a rural state with four major media markets, the largest being Little Rock, which is fifty-sixth nationally, far below that of other major state centers in neighboring southern states. The cities in Table 3.13 contain 41 percent of the state's population, again, below that of sister states. Most southern states register half of their population in a few counties, but the rural nature of Arkansas means that most of the state is not metropolitan. Two major interstate highways connect the major population centers, with the growth sector being in the northwest corner along the Interstate 540 connector. In spite of its growth, and national visibility during the Clinton years, Arkansas remains largely undeveloped.

South Carolina

The state of South Carolina separates along a boundary that is political destiny at election time. The fall line divides the Piedmont Plateau and the northwestern third of the state, from the coastal plains in the south. Ten of South Carolina's forty-six counties lie in the upstate, thirteen in the midlands, and twenty-three are in what is known as the low country. These three divisions are shown on Map 3.10.

Charleston, and the coastal plains, retained strong ties to England, the Anglican Church, old world wealth, and the refinement of plantation life. The upstate was settled by Scotch-Irish and German farmers suspicious of the English, envious of plantation wealth, and dissenters from the Church of England. They were poor farmers, united in their abhorrence of low-country ways. "From the beginning the difference in our views was fundamental," wrote Ben Robertson in his upcountry memoir, *Red Hills and Cotton*, "one of us had to whip the other to a farewell and a

Table 3.13   Arkansas: Population Centers and Media Market Rank

Region/City	County	Population 2000	Media Market Rank
Mountain			
Little Rock/Pine Bluff	Pulaski	361,474	56
Little Rock/Pine Bluff	Faulkner	86,014	56
Little Rock/Pine Bluff	Saline	83,529	56
Little Rock/Pine Bluff	Lonoke	52,823	56
Ft. Smith/Fayetteville	Sebastian	115,071	107
Ft. Smith/Fayetteville	Crawford	53,071	107
Hot Springs	Garland	88,068	—
Subtotal		840,050	
Plains			
El Dorado	Union	45,629	134
Pine Bluff	Jefferson	84,278	—
Texarkana	Miller	40,443	—
Subtotal		170,350	
Mississippi Alluvial Plain			
Jonesboro	Craighead	82,148	180
Total		1,092,548	

Source: Compiled by the author from the US Census (2000) and Nielsen Media research, www.nielsenmedia.com.
Note: This total represents 41 percent of Arkansas's population.

frazzle . . . from 1750 to 1860 we lost to Charleston; since that time Charleston has lost to us."[31]

The state's political history reflected the economic, social, and cultural differences of regional distinctiveness. Two regions and two societies—low country and upcountry—defined the enduring political divisions. The wealthy planter and the slave economy of the low country had little in common with the small white farmers of the upstate.

> The just demands of the upcountry were neglected because of the low country's ignorance of conditions as well as because of the human propensity of those possessing power to retain it and the equally natural tendency of an old, wealthy, and cultured society to feel contempt for the new.[32]

The mingling of upstate and low country began in the twentieth century with textile manufacturing in the north and a more diverse tourist economy in the south. The upstate is home to a development corridor along Interstate 85. The midlands are dominated by the city of Columbia, in Lexington and Richland counties. The

Map 3.10   South Carolina: Population Distribution

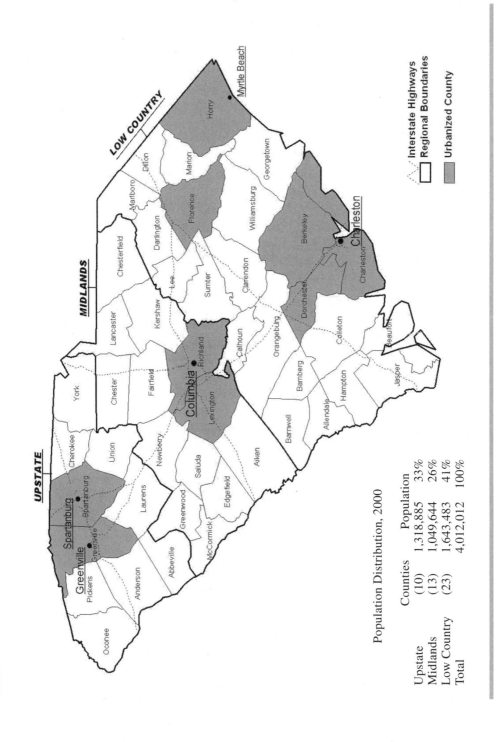

Population Distribution, 2000

	Counties	Population	
Upstate	(10)	1,318,885	33%
Midlands	(13)	1,049,644	26%
Low Country	(23)	1,643,483	41%
Total		4,012,012	100%

Vignette 3.1   Strom Thurmond (1902–2003)

Strom Thurmond became known as a South Carolina conservative fixture for nearly five decades in the US Senate, and in his political career earned a reputation for both steadfastness and political dexterity. When he retired at the turn of the twenty-first century he had defied the conventional rules of survival in US politics, and set records of longevity that are likely never to be surpassed.

Strom Thurmond's lifetime of public service brought notable accomplishments. He retired as US senator with the longest tenure, ran for president on a third-party ticket, won a statewide election on a write-in ballot, established the Senate filibuster record, changed his political party affiliation and won reelection to office, was a confidant or opponent of ten presidents, and married two beauty queens. He earned a reputation among some of being a right-wing naysayer, and among others of being an honest politician of down-home sincerity. Whatever else is said of him, Strom Thurmond was the supreme politician, changing with the times and outliving or neutralizing his opponents.

The Thurmond family roots lie deep in Edgefield County, an area of South Carolina that has produced ten governors, half as many senators, and a half-dozen lieutenant governors. Born the son of a politician, Thurmond spent his years after graduation from Clemson College as a school superintendent, state senator, and circuit judge. He served in World War II as a soldier who saw action in the D-Day invasion, eventually winning twelve military medals.

He returned home to run for governor. In 1947 Strom Thurmond moved into the state mansion as the first bachelor state executive since 1897. The next year he married Jean Crouch, a former Miss South Carolina Azalea Festival Queen who worked in his office. She was twenty-one and he was forty-six. Typical of the Thurmond work ethic is the legend that

he proposed by sending her a memo. To show that he was as fit and virile as any man twenty years his junior, the governor impressed a *Life* magazine photographer by doing a handstand for a picture. The image was destined to become famous in South Carolina political lore when an opponent sent it to every registered voter with the inscription: "We need a man who can stand on his feet and not his head."

Thurmond's staunch opposition to federally mandated integration thrust him into the national spotlight in 1948. Politically he was known as a fiery Southerner with the full panoply of racist and populist rhetoric. His contempt for the Truman civil rights platform inspired a run for the presidency, which garnered thirty-nine electoral votes. Buoyed by his new national reputation, he chose to challenge Olin D. Johnston in the Democratic primary for the US Senate in 1950. Johnston, who circulated the postcard of Thurmond standing on his head, defeated him by more than 24,000 votes.

In 1950 Thurmond left the governor's mansion to practice law in Aiken, South Carolina, but the unexpected death of US senator Burnett Rhett Maybank in 1954 created an opportunity to attain the seat that had eluded him earlier. In a surprise move, the Democratic Executive Committee picked a popular state senator to fill the remaining six-year term. An angry Strom Thurmond made that decision his main issue in a write-in campaign—and won by a large margin.

In Washington Thurmond's politics were described by one writer as "full of vinegar," but his career was a combination of firmness and flexibility. He filibustered for twenty-four hours and eighteen minutes against Lyndon Johnson's 1957 civil rights bill. His political gospel was a textbook of traditional conservatism: anticommunism, anti–gun control, in

(continues)

Vignette 3.1   Continued

favor of school prayer in public schools, and supportive of any initiative that reduced the size of the federal government. He changed political parties in 1964 and helped Richard Nixon win the presidency in 1968. In the Reagan administration he served as president pro tempore of the Senate, in theoretical line of succession to the presidency.

Most of Strom Thurmond's national reputation came from his life off the Senate floor. In January of 1960, Thurmond's wife, Jean, died from a brain tumor. After her death he cultivated the reputation as a Southern eccentric, attending receptions with five or six women on his arm. In the Nixon White House years, he announced that at age sixty-seven he was taking a new bride, this time to a twenty-two-year-old Miss South Carolina named

Nancy Moore. Though the two would separate in 1991, their union produced four children.

Strom Thurmond retired to Edgefield in 2002, at age one hundred. He is remembered by older voters as a feisty populist who fought against government intrusion, and by younger voters as a champion of Ronald Reagan's conservatism. He left his mark on southern politics as a survivor, a maverick, and a relic of Old South politics flourishing in the new era. He died on June 26, 2003, in Edgefield. After his death it was revealed that Thurmond had an out-of-wedlock child with a black woman. His daughter, Essie May Washington-Williams, had received support from Thurmond her whole life.

---

low country is spread out along a recreational and historic corridor from Hilton Head, through Charleston to Myrtle Beach.

The population breakdown for South Carolina is shown in Table 3.14. South Carolina is a small state with four million inhabitants in 2000, over half of whom live in four cities. Its major metropolitan areas are Greenville-Spartanburg, Columbia, Myrtle Beach, and Charleston. Collectively they are the four largest in-state media markets, and their total population is half that of the state. Interstate 26 connects three of these centers while the fourth, Myrtle Beach, lies off Interstate 95.

The cities of Greenville and Spartanburg, separated by a scant twenty miles, were once home to the state's bustling textile industry. Today many textile jobs are gone, but in their place hundreds of international companies have located in the region. The Interstate 85 development corridor from Charlotte, North Carolina, to Atlanta, Georgia, has attracted millions of dollars in development, and major companies like BMW and Michelin have chosen Greenville-Spartanburg as home.

In Columbia, the state has one of the more centrally located capitals in the country. Business, finance, and government prosper in Columbia, a city accessible within a two-hour drive from most areas of South Carolina. The midlands are connected to the historical tobacco-growing region of the state, and feature rolling plains and scattered lakes.

The city of Charleston, founded in 1670, is one of the oldest in the country.

Table 3.14 South Carolina: Population Centers and Media Market Rank

Region/City	County	Population 2000	Media Market Rank
Upstate			
Greenville/Spartanburg	Greenville	379,616	36
Greenville/Spartanburg	Spartanburg	253,791	36
	Subtotal	633,407	
Midlands			
Columbia	Richland	320,677	84
Columbia	Lexington	216,014	84
	Subtotal	536,691	
Low Country			
Charleston	Charleston	309,969	108
Charleston	Berkeley	142,651	108
Charleston	Dorchester	96,413	108
	Subtotal	549,033	
Low Country			
Myrtle Beach/Florence	Horry	196,629	109
Myrtle Beach/Florence	Florence	125,761	109
	Subtotal	322,390	
	Total	2,041,521	

Source: Compiled by the author from the US Census (2000) and Nielsen Media research, www.nielsenmedia.com.
Note: This total represents 51 percent of South Carolina's population.

Once the home of wealthy and prosperous planters, it has a reputation of clinging to its lost past. Pat Conroy's description in his book, *The Prince of Tides,* is typical: "The snobs of Charleston generally don't discriminate . . . they hate just about everybody."[33] The city has kept its older institutions and added new cultural centers, museums, and festivals. The attractions of low-country South Carolina include tourism, its medical and military centers, and the Charleston Port, one of the nation's busiest.

The Myrtle Beach area is the fourth population center of the state. The strip of restaurants, miniature golf courses, shopping centers, and entertainment venues make it a favorite playground for east coast vacationers. The fast-growing tourist industry of the state finds its home in Horry County, and its retirement communities are one of the growth industries in the state.

Other population centers are Aiken along the western boundary with Georgia, the Hilton Head development in Beaufort County (also near Georgia), and the Rock Hill area outside Charlotte, North Carolina. All are significant for state politics, but their border location makes them less interesting in statewide races. Each of these places is a satellite for an out-of-state population center. The state has emerged from an agricultural past into the bright light of a global economy. Any political candidate who seeks statewide office begins with a campaign plan that is centered around the three I-26 cities (Charleston, Columbia, and Greenville/Spartanburg) and the bustling tourist and retirement areas in Myrtle Beach.

Mississippi

Mississippi is named for the river that forms its western boundary and dominates the geography of the state. But historian David Cohn may have captured life in the state best when he wrote, "The Mississippi Delta begins in the lobby of the Peabody Hotel in Memphis and ends in Catfish Row in Vicksburg."[34] The place carries the weight of a tragic history, the beauty of an unspoiled river wonderland, and the dubious distinction of being last on virtually every important social and economic ranking in the nation. It has retained this ranking for some fifty years.

Mississippi gave the world writers like William Faulkner, Eudora Welty, Walker Percy, and Shelby Foote; at the same time it has the highest illiteracy rate of any state in the United States. It has a very traditional political structure, but this fact makes it oddly open to some innovations, such as riverboat gambling. It is the least urban of all the southern states examined, but metropolitan Jackson dominates its politics and cultural life, much like Atlanta does Georgia and Birmingham does Alabama. In one 1947 interview, Alexander Heard summarized politics in the state as he saw it. "I am mightily impressed by the seeming lack of any issues in Mississippi, the race issue is the only one that is talked about a lot [and] everybody is on the same side of it."[35] Indeed, race was the most important issue for both blacks and whites, but the differences between the two were vast.

Two historical tensions abide in Mississippi. The first is the conflict between blacks and whites, epitomized in Heard's observations and in the violence surrounding the integration of the University of Mississippi in 1962. The death of three civil rights workers in Neshoba County is further testimony to the heritage. The second legacy is the difference between the Delta planters and the poor farmers of the hills. Both legacies persist, and are interrelated, but it is the second that is most important when it comes to politics today.

Yoknapatawpha County was the mythical setting for the fiction of William Faulkner. The word comes from two Chickasaw words that mean "split land." That designation could apply to the state as a whole. Of all the southern states, only Mississippi retains the distinction given by V. O. Key: "the cleavage between the planters of the delta and the rednecks of the hills."[36] The division between east and west persists; Interstate 55, which stretches south from Mississippi to Louisiana, now institutionalizes what was once geographic.

Map 3.11 shows the two distinct, east-west, regions. The disenfranchisement of

Map 3.11   Mississippi: Population Distribution

Population Distribution, 2000

	Counties	Population	
Delta	(34)	1,401,818	46%
Hills	(48)	1,669,942	54%
Total		3,071,760	100%

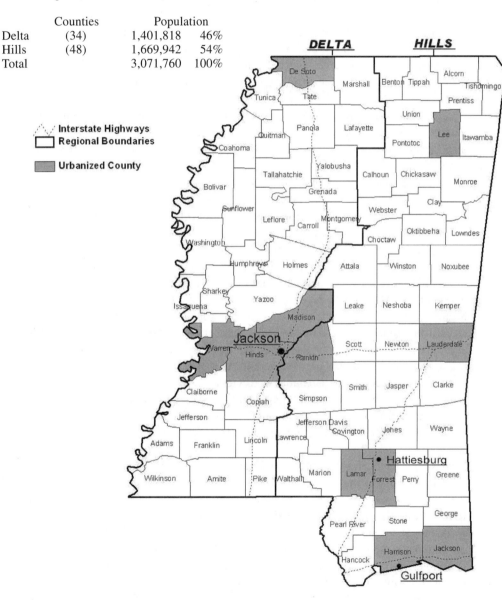

Interstate Highways
Regional Boundaries

Urbanized County

black voters led to white elite domination of the prosperous Mississippi Delta region, in contrast to the poor hills and piney woods counties of the east. The Delta was led by politicians opposed to the New Deal who supported segregation and the disenfranchisement of black voters, although they took a more paternalistic rather than hostile view, intending to improve health care and education for blacks. While Delta politicians howled about New Deal socialism, the region was a major beneficiary of government largesse. In 1934 some 44 percent of all AAA payments over $10,000 went to ten counties in the Delta. The aristocratic tendencies of Delta residents tempered graphic racist policies; instead they adopted a benign pastoralism in the midst of ironclad segregation.

The Hills were dominated by poor whites, receptive to the agrarian discontent themes the Greenback, Grange, Alliance, and neopopulist movements aimed at the dispossessed. Populist governors, like James K. Vardeman, who became known as the "Great White Chief," used graphic racial rhetoric to incite hill farmers. He once said of voting rights for blacks that there was "nothing in his [the black man's] individual character, nothing in his achievements of the past nor his promise of the future," that would entitle him "to stand side-by-side with the white man at the ballot box."[37]

The animosity between black and white, and the different expectations for the role of the blacks in society, divided the two regions. Racial tension moderated with new business gains and the rising tide of the Sunbelt economy. Rural counties relying on agriculture experienced population out-migrations as residents moved to the boom areas of Jackson, the Gulf Coast, the Tupelo-Columbus corridor, and the Memphis suburbs. The booming casino business in poor counties, like Tunica, transformed the landscape of the Delta. The Hills became home to small industry, and new companies met at the junctions and crossroads of small towns, escaping the agricultural legacy. The state's dominant metropolitan area, Jackson, has not been able to become what Atlanta is to Georgia, but it remains the population and political center of the state. At the same time Mississippi lacks a compelling economic center like the Research Triangle in North Carolina or a Texas Triangle population convergence to moderate and change the rural legacy.

Table 3.15 shows the continuing separations in Mississippi. Along the Mississippi River, from Memphis to Natchez, the fertile alluvial soil stretches two counties deep into the state. This was the area once home to huge plantations and the slaves who worked them. The black population later became sharecroppers, and finally full citizens. Rivers and some of the nation's poorest counties crisscross the Delta. Their vulnerability to natural disaster was exposed in 2005, when the costliest hurricane in US history slammed into Gulfport and drowned twelve coastal counties in a foot of water. Mississippi could scarcely afford any calamity, let alone one as devastating as Hurricane Katrina.

Once the city of Jackson was an isolated capital located in the lower part of the state and remote from the events of agricultural and plantation Mississippi. Today it is the central city in the state, and the focus of government and culture. As the largest city, it has the biggest in-state media market, but that ranking is still only the

Table 3.15   Mississippi: Population Centers and Media Market Rank

Region/City	County	Population 2000	Media Market Rank
Delta			
Memphis	Desoto	107,199	42
Delta			
Jackson	Hinds	250,800	88
Jackson	Rankin	115,327	88
Jackson	Madison	74,674	88
Delta			
Vicksburg	Warren	49,644	—
Hills			
Hattiesburg	Forrest	72,604	167
Hattiesburg	Lamar	39,070	167
	Subtotal	111,674	
Hills			
Biloxi/Gulfport	Harrison	189,601	157
Biloxi/Gulfport	Jackson	131,420	157
	Subtotal	321,021	
Hills			
Tupelo	Lee	75,755	131
Hills			
Meridian	Lauderdale	78,161	185
	Total	1,184,255	

Source: Compiled by the author from the US Census (2000) and Nielsen Media research, www.nielsenmedia.com.
Note: This total represents 42 percent of Mississippi's population.

eighty-eighth largest in the nation. Mississippi remains the least urban state in the South, and the combined population of its major cities amounts to only 42 percent of the state's population.

Louisiana

An impressed twentieth-century critic once said that Louisiana is not really an American state, but a "banana republic." It persists as a Latin enclave set in a country of Anglo-Saxon righteousness.[38] There is no denying that people in this state have a tolerance for political corruption unmatched in any other part of the country. The most natural divide, and the one most frequently used to partition the state, is by religion. V. O. Key commented on this separation: "Differences between the Protestant north and Catholic south furnished a convenient advantage to those who . . . would divide and rule."[39]

The northern part of the state is Protestant, and the southern part is Cajun Catholic. The traditional dividing line between the two areas varies; for purposes here Interstate 10 demarcates the two cultures. Map 3.12 shows the division between the two. The third source of votes, with a political culture unlike any other in the country, is the city of New Orleans, which is located in the southern parishes of the state. About New Orleans, John M. Barry says:

> No American city resembled it. The river gave it both wealth and a sinuous mystery. It was an interior city, an impenetrable city, a city of fronts. Outsiders lost themselves in its subtleties and intrigues. . . . Modern poker, the most secretive of games, was invented there. New Orleans had not only whites and blacks but French and Spanish and Cajuns and Americans (the white Protestants) and Creoles and Creoles of color (enough to organize their own symphony orchestra in 1838) and quadroons and octaroons.[40]

These three areas make Louisiana politics different from other places in the South, or the nation. The struggle is often between reform and conservative forces on the one side, and roguish populists who want to revamp the system and "throw the rascals out" on the other. There have been a lot of rascals through the years, and politicians like Huey P. Long and, later, Edwin Edwards, are creations unique to Louisiana. The political culture is related to geographical and natural disaster; the great Mississippi flood of 1927 changed the demographics and economy of the state for generations.[41] The future of Louisiana politics, and of the state itself, rests with how New Orleans recovers from Hurricane Katrina. Over a million persons were displaced by the storm, and many chose not to return. The actual cost of rebuilding New Orleans will be measured in human terms, not dollar amounts.

Progress has come to the state in the form of a more culturally diverse population and the mass culture that has equalized all of the South. In the spring of 1975 Vietnamese "Boat People" settled along the coast. The 1980 census registered a 178 percent increase in Asian population. Immediately after the fall of South Vietnam, two Louisiana Catholic dioceses resettled many Vietnamese refugees in the Orleans, Jefferson, Houma, St. Mary, Terrebonne, and Laforche parishes. The fishing and shrimp industries provided employment for many, as did the oil industry and offshore drilling. The 2000 census shows increasing numbers of Hispanics and Asians as well as the descendents of French Acadians who migrated to Louisiana from Nova Scotia. "Cajun Country" is a twenty-two-parish triangle in south Louisiana, outside the city of New Orleans, replete with a linguistic and foreign flavor unique in the South.

The history of the state bears the imprint of its main city. New Orleans was once the financial and international trading center of the South. It made some residents indescribably rich. Sugar, cotton, and indigo were the foundation of the agrarian economy, and later the discovery of sulphur in 1869, and oil in 1901, spurred

Map 3.12 Louisiana: Population Distribution

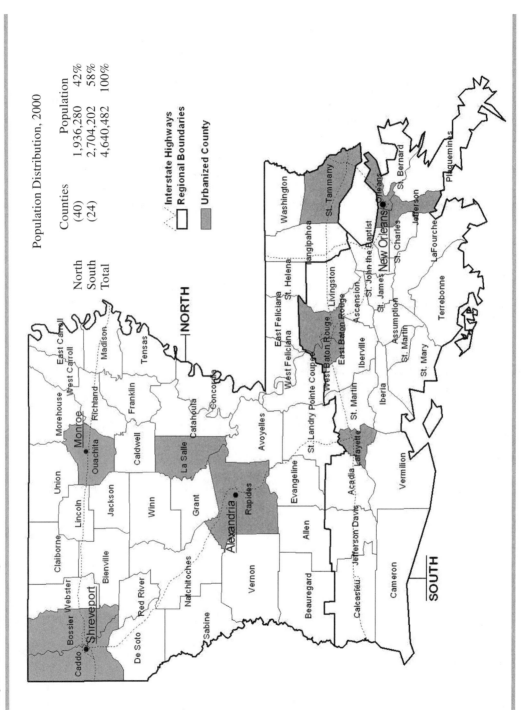

Population Distribution, 2000

	Counties	Population	
North	(40)	1,936,280	42%
South	(24)	2,704,202	58%
Total		4,640,482	100%

Interstate Highways
Regional Boundaries
Urbanized County

development. The great Mississippi flood of 1927 changed the city and seemed to hold back its future. New South cities like Charlotte and Miami, not to mention Atlanta, Dallas, and Houston, thrived and grew over the years. New Orleans fell far behind its old competitors, and the banks in Memphis now dwarf those in New Orleans. To this day Louisiana remains a major US domestic producer of oil and natural gas and the center of the southern, as opposed to the west Texas, petroleum refining and petrochemical manufacturing industry.

Louisiana became more urbanized in the last quarter of the twentieth century. Twenty of the sixty-four parishes reported a population of 50,000 inhabitants or more in the 2000 census. The largest are shown in Table 3.16. The metropolitan area of New Orleans is the media and population center for the state. The parishes around the city are home to over a million people. Together with Baton Rouge, New Orleans is the heart of Louisiana politics.

Summary

It seems almost quaint, in a time of sophisticated travel and Internet communications technology, to say that geography influences political and demographic des-

Table 3.16   Louisiana: Population Centers and Media Market Rank

Region/City	County	Population 2000	Media Market Rank
North Louisiana			
Shreveport	Caddo	252,161	79
Shreveport	Ouchita	147,250	—
Shreveport	Rapides	126,337	179
Shreveport	Bossier	98,310	79
Shreveport	La Salle	14,282	179
	Subtotal	638,340	
South Louisiana			
New Orleans	Orleans	484,674	43
New Orleans	Jefferson	455,466	43
New Orleans	East Baton Rouge	412,582	95
New Orleans	St. Tammy	191,268	43
New Orleans	Lafayette	190,503	125
New Orleans	West Baton Rouge	21,601	95
	Subtotal	1,756,094	
	Total	2,394,434	

Source: Compiled by the author from the US Census (2000) and Nielsen Media research, www.neilsenmedia.com.
Note: This total represents 52 percent of Louisiana's population.

tiny. The phenomenon of continuing large-scale migration to southern cities has changed the political culture in a way unimaginable decades ago. But environmental and geographic factors persist in explaining the patterns of southern politics. No image is more abiding about the South than the rural farmer laboring in the sun. But urbanization has changed this legacy, and dramatically modernized the South. Urban growth consolidated the population, facilitated economic growth, and altered the political map.

This change is summarized in Table 3.17, which shows the number of counties in each state needed to approach half of the state's population. Of the more than one thousand counties, parishes, and cities in the South, half of the population is in just 134 of them. This urbanization is especially apparent in the four national states (Georgia, Florida, Virginia, and Texas), where 8 percent of the total number of counties houses over half the population. The traditional states are less urbanized, especially Mississippi and Arkansas, but their population is nonetheless concentrated in several urban markets.

The urbanization of the South is probably the most dramatic aspect of the modernization and physical transformation of the region. Technological innovations, such as air conditioning, along with the interstate infrastructure, have encouraged

Table 3.17   Geographic Summary

State	Total Population[a]	Total Counties	MSA Counties	Number of MSA Destinations	50 Percent of Vote Counties	50 Percent of Vote Population[a]
National States						
Texas	20, 851	254	54	23	8	10,409
Florida	15,982	67	32	17	8	8,300
Georgia	8,168	159	44	8	17	4,279
Virginia	7,113	95/40	36/26	8	15/18	4,228
Emergent States						
North Carolina	8,048	100	35	12	23	4,141
Tennessee	5,689	95	27	7	9	2,857
Traditional States						
Louisiana	4,468	64	24	8	11	2,203
Alabama	4,447	67	21	12	12	2,225
South Carolina	4,012	46	19	7	9	2,042
Mississippi	2,844	82	9	4	11	1,184
Arkansas	2,673	75	10	5	11	1,092
Total	84,261	1,104	311	110	134	43,498

Source: Compiled by the author from the US Census (2000) and Nielsen Media research, www.neilsenmedia.com.
Note: a. Population figures are in thousands.

the development of large cities and industries in a part of the country known for its rural life in the midst of heat and humidity. Urban sprawl, suburbanization, congestion, and exploitation of available resources, such as water and forest, now characterize the South as well as the North. Competition for water reserves, an issue in western states, is now a part of southern politics. Air pollution is an issue along interstate highways in the urban cities that dot the landscape of the South. The southern states are becoming familiar with stream pollution, saltwater intrusion along the coast, and the lowering of water tables around cities.

Throughout history cities have played a prominent role in nurturing and transmitting culture, from high art to fads and fashions. Traditionally cities are sites of the great institutions of learning, where concentrations of population encourage innovation and challenges to traditional ways of doing things. For much of its history the South was rural and isolated from the mainstream of US life, but in the post–World War II years, the South joined the rest of the country in urbanization and suburbanization. The earliest southern cities, Charleston and Savannah for instance, were conduits of European culture connecting the new world with the old. Today, the cities of Atlanta, Charlotte, Dallas, and Houston are economic and culture-creating centers that influence the rest of the nation. The wellsprings of southern politics are in these urban areas.

Notes

1. Maya Angelou, *I Know Why the Caged Bird Sings*. New York: Random House, 1969.

2. Leonard F. Wheat and William H. Crown, *State Per-Capita Change Since 1950*. Westport, Conn.: Greenwood Press, 1995.

3. Ibid.

4. US Census Bureau, Table 18, "Population of the 100 Largest Urban Places: 1950," and Table 3, "Metropolitan Areas Ranked by Population, 2000."

5. Earl Black and Merle Black, *Politics and Society in the South*. Cambridge: Harvard University Press. 1987, p. 58.

6. Daniel Elazar, *The Metropolitan Frontier and American Politics*. New Brunswick, N.J.: Transaction Publishers, 2003, p. x.

7. Thomas Wolfe, "The House of the Far and Lost," from *Of Time and the River*. New York: Charles Scribner's Sons, 1934.

8. "Life After Cotton," *The Economist*, August 30, 2003, p. 21.

9. C. Vann Woodward, *The Burden of Southern History*. Baton Rouge: Louisiana State University Press, p. 26.

10. Wheat and Crown, Table 1.1, p. 3.

11. US Census Bureau, *Statistical Abstract of the United States: 2000*, 120th ed. Washington, D.C.: 2000, Table 134, p. 784.

12. Jane Wooten, *Dasher*. Nashville, Tenn.: Broaden Press, 1975, p. 87.

13. Juliet Gainsborough, *Fenced Off: The Suburbanization of American Politics*. Washington, D.C.: Georgetown University Press, 2001.

14. The general concept of a metropolitan area is one of a large population nucleus,

together with counties that have a high degree of economic and social integration with that nucleus. The Office of Management and Budget (OMB) defines metropolitan areas for purposes of collecting, tabulating, and publishing federal data. The metropolitan statistical areas used here are relatively freestanding places typically surrounded by nonmetropolitan counties. Unfortunately, there are two reasons why metropolitan statistical area (MSA) designations are not very useful when it comes to identifying the most important political areas in a state. First, the definition of an MSA often crosses state lines and blurs the political reality. In North Carolina and Georgia prominent population centers are on the border of the state. Second, the state can have so many metropolitan areas that it is impossible to rank them. For example, in Texas 85 percent of the population lives in twenty-three metropolitan areas, many of which are multicounty. The question remains: Which MSA's are most important?

15. Southern Politics Collection, "Georgia," Vanderbilt University, Special Collections.

16. Ibid.

17. The ten counties in the Atlanta Regional Commission are: Cherokee, Clayton, Cobb, DeKalb, Douglas, Fayette, Fulton, Gwinnett, Henry, and Rockdale. Source: www.atlreg.com.

18. Pat Conroy, *My Losing Season*. New York: Doubleday, 2002, p. 45.

19. The group is: EFO, Eddie from Ohio, and the song title is "Old Dominion."

20. David Hackett Fischer, *Albion's Seed: Four British Folkways in America*. New York: Oxford University Press, 1989, p. 231.

21. David Brinkley, *Washington Goes to War*. New York: Alfred A. Knopf, 1988, p. 107.

22. Larry McMurtry, *In a Narrow Grave: Essays on Texas*. New York: Simon and Shuster, 1968, p. 75.

23. Lawrence Wright, *In the New World: Growing Up With America, 1960–1984*. New York: Alfred A. Knopf, 1988, p. 15.

24. T.R. Fehrenback, *Lone Star: A History of Texas and Texans*. New York: Macmillan, 1995, p. 703.

25. V.O. Key, *Southern Politics in State and Nation*. Knoxville: University of Tennessee Press, 1970.

26. RTI International, "History," *Research Triangle Institute* (2001). http//www.rti.org/history.

27. *Money Magazine*. "Best Places 2000 Winners: Best in the South." October, 2001.

28. Gerald A. Capers, *The Biography of a River Town*. Memphis, Tenn.: Gerald Capers, 1966.

29. James Agee and Walker Evans, *Let Us Now Praise Famous Men*. New York: Houghton Mifflin, 1966, pp. 42–43.

30. Rick Bragg, *All Over But the Southin'*. New York: Vintage Press, 1997, p. 3.

31. Ben Robertson, *Red Hills and Cotton*. Columbia: University of South Carolina Press, 1942, p. 100.

32. Luther F. Carter and David S. Mann, *Government in the Palmetto State*. Columbia: University of South Carolina Press, 1983, p. 43.

33. Pat Conroy, *The Prince of Tides*. Boston: Houghlin Mifflin, 1986, p. 431.

34. Robert Crisswell, *The Book of Southern Wisdom*. Nashville, Tenn.: Walnut Grove Press, 1994, p. 134.

35. Southern Politics Collection, "Mississippi," Vanderbilt University, Special Collections.

36. V.O. Key, *Southern Politics in State and Nation*, p. 230.

37. Dale Krane and Stephen D. Shaffer, *Mississippi Government and Politics: Modernizers and Traditionalists*. Lincoln: University of Nebraska Press, 1992.

38. A.J. Liebling, "The Great State," in *The New Yorker*, May 28, 1960, and June 11, 1960, p. 100.

39. V.O. Key, *Southern Politics in State and Nation*, p. 160.

40. John M. Barry, *Rising Tide: The Great Mississippi Flood of 1927 and How It Changed America*. New York: Simon and Schuster, 1998, p. 213.

41. John M. Barry, *Rising Tide*.

4

The Racial Legacy

The secessionist firebrand William Lowndes Yancey proclaimed on the eve of the Civil War, "As for our history, we have made about all that has glorified the United States."[1] Whether Yancey was referring to the Declaration of Independence, the Bill of Rights, and judicial review, or the native traditions of agriculture, states' rights, and white supremacy is unclear. All these were southern legacies, but one came to characterize the region more than any other—white domination of the black race. Throughout its history, from the middle of the seventeenth century down to the dramatic changes of the 1960s, the region's ruling class dedicated itself to the domination of one race by another. Other areas of the country sympathized with white supremacy, and some even practiced it, but only the South embraced the ideal with the fervor that proudly wrote racial separation into laws and statutes, as well as the habits of everyday life.

Race is central to the definition of any political culture. In the United States the melting pot metaphor meant that various ethnic and socioreligious groups brought a variety of beliefs to be integrated into the new environment. Daniel Elazar begins his analysis of the American settlement by identifying "native" streams in the culture. These were the first settlers who founded colonies along the Atlantic seaboard from 1607 to the middle of the 1700s. In the South the settlements were based on slavery with an eye toward the social order of England. The plantation owner was a guardian and benefactor of his human property.

Slavery was once an integral assumption of life in the southern political system, protecting white, independent farmers from marketplace domination by northern capitalists. A central theme of southern politics was the political superiority of whites as an economic necessity for the preservation of the "Southern Way of Life." The system was vital for crop harvest and material survival. The social culture institutionalized separation of the races and the political system was designed to keep blacks in their proper place. Coretta Scott King wrote in her memoirs that in the segregated South, "Black children realize very early that there are places they cannot go."[2] Railroads, schools, theaters, hotels, restaurants, restrooms, water fountains, parks, public buildings, and even cemeteries were segregated in the South until the 1960s. In the 1950s and 1960s the virulent racism of the region steeled the resolve of civil rights demonstrators, even though they were armed only with their conscience, courage, and sense of justice.

White hegemony, and the importance of race-defining politics, was seen in V. O. Key's original work (1949), with his portrait of Mississippi and South Carolina as ruled by racial politics, and his explanation of the disenfranchising effects of the poll tax and literacy test in the South. Racial tensions were muted by the black exodus, with a first wave in the 1910–1930 period, and a subsequent exodus from 1940–1970. Simultaneously, the South experienced a growth in the population of non-Southerners moving in. In spite of these demographic changes, race remained a dominant force in politics.

A perpetual debate goes on about how much of the original racial legacy remains, and how different the South is from the rest of the country. Certainly in its literature, its national and local politics, its fierce insistence on a regional identification and chip-on-the-shoulder defensiveness, the South consistently defended first slavery, and then segregation. The culture of racism sanctioned discrimination in the workplace, in schools and churches, and in politics. Of all the southern political legacies, the racial one has figured most prominently in explaining the culture and politics of the region.

Under slavery the pattern of white domination rested on force and the accepted social and political norms of the culture. A political system founded on democratic ideals, yet embracing racism and discrimination, would hardly seem to be the stuff of Jefferson, Madison, and Washington, or the other Virginia giants who gave the nation, and the South, distinguished leadership before the Civil War. Yet the founders left intact a peculiar institution that contradicted the ideals they professed. When Confederate general Robert E. Lee surrendered to Union general Ulysses S. Grant at Appomattox courthouse on April 9, 1865, the two separate nations were supposed to become one. It never happened. Instead the South lapsed into a defense of honored and hallowed customs as justification to disenfranchise and economically exploit the black race.

The first significant postwar political change in racial laws was the ratification of the Thirteenth Amendment on December 6, 1865. It abolished chattel slavery and brought freedom to slaves in the Union border states (Maryland, Delaware, Missouri, and Kentucky) as well as those areas already under federal occupation (Tennessee, northern Virginia, and New Orleans). When the South was defeated on the battlefield, emancipation came to millions of enslaved Africans who were in bondage in the balance of the South. The newly freed slaves were a dominant presence in each southern state, and their status was an important political concern. As shown in Table 4.1, the 1860 census found that blacks were the majority in Mississippi (55.3%) and South Carolina (58.6%). They were less than half, but at least two-fifths, of the population in five other states—Alabama (45.4%), Florida

Table 4.1   Percentage Black Population in the Southern States, 1860–2000

State	1860	1870	1880	1890	1900	1910	1920	1930	1940	1950	1960	1970	1980	1990	2000
Alabama	45.4	47.7	47.5	44.8	45.4	42.8	38.4	35.7	34.7	32.0	30.0	26.2	25.6	25.0	26.0
Arkansas	25.6	25.2	26.3	27.4	28.0	28.1	26.9	25.8	24.8	22.4	21.8	18.3	16.3	15.9	15.7
Florida	44.6	48.8	47.0	42.5	43.7	41.0	34.0	29.4	27.1	21.8	17.8	15.4	13.8	13.5	14.6
Georgia	44.0	46.0	47.0	46.7	46.7	45.1	41.6	36.8	34.7	30.9	28.5	25.9	26.8	26.9	28.7
Louisiana	49.5	50.1	51.5	50.0	47.1	43.1	38.9	36.9	35.9	32.9	31.9	29.9	29.4	30.7	32.5
Mississippi	55.3	53.7	57.5	57.6	58.5	56.2	52.2	50.2	49.2	45.3	42.0	36.8	35.2	35.5	36.3
North Carolina	36.4	36.6	38.0	34.7	33.0	31.6	29.8	28.9	27.5	25.8	24.5	22.2	22.4	21.9	21.6
South Carolina	58.6	58.9	60.7	59.8	58.4	55.2	51.4	45.7	42.8	38.8	34.8	30.5	30.4	29.8	29.5
Tennessee	25.5	25.6	26.1	24.4	23.8	21.7	19.3	18.3	17.5	16.1	16.5	15.8	15.8	15.9	16.4
Texas	30.3	31.0	24.7	21.8	20.4	17.7	15.9	14.7	14.4	12.7	12.4	12.5	12.0	11.9	11.5
Virginia	43.3	41.9	41.8	38.4	35.6	32.6	29.9	26.8	24.7	22.1	20.6	18.5	18.9	18.7	19.6

Source: US Census Bureau.

(44.6%), Georgia (44%), Louisiana (49.5%), and Virginia (43.3%). The black portion of the population of the remaining southern states was less substantial, but still significant—North Carolina (36.4%), Texas (30.3%), Arkansas (25.6%), and Tennessee (25.5%).

The reform of black society lay at the heart of the Reconstruction effort. The original schemes were woefully inadequate to meet the economic and social requirements of so vast a population. Liberation from slavery did not result in the empowerment of former slaves. Marriage laws, rights to make contracts, acquire and hold property, sue and be sued, and other ordinary civil liberties were new to the black population. It is not surprising that fraud, abuse, and neglect characterized the period. The cast of characters included rapacious carpetbaggers, traitorous native scalawags, and numerous illiterate freedmen. The mere abolishment of slavery was but a first step for freedman citizenship.

The Fourteenth Amendment was ratified in 1868 to expand black rights. Its purpose was admittedly coercive, to force Reconstruction on the South, which had refused to even consider suggestions to bring the black man into the mainstream of social and political life. Likewise the Fifteenth Amendment was ratified two years later to prohibit states from using race as a basis to deny suffrage. The struggle of former slaves to become equal and independent citizens would continue for more than one hundred years. This chapter is divided into four epochs: the postbellum Reconstruction years, the period of New South enthusiasm at the turn of the century and beyond, the civil rights era, and the modern period.

Postbellum Reconstruction

Even though slavery was the issue that prompted the Civil War, black human rights and civil rights received little attention until after the congressional elections of 1866. Congressional or Radical Reconstruction for the next ten years (1867–1877) was a period when blacks enjoyed full civil and political rights for the first time. The emergence of Jim Crow laws was a throwback to segregation. The term was derived from a nineteenth-century minstrel character, and came to symbolize the southern system of legal segregation that emerged after the Civil War. This segregation meant that after 1877 black voters were subject to intimidation and systematic disenfranchisement. At the close of the nineteenth century blacks were again living as second-class citizens in a segregated society.

The foundation for the South's racial traditions rested with slavery codified by the US Supreme Court ruling in *Dred Scott v. Sandford* (1857). The ruling held that blacks (slave or free) were not citizens and did not have civil rights protected by the US Constitution. At the end of the Civil War freed slaves continued to occupy a subordinate position in a southern society still dominated by whites. Cruel injustices in the nineteenth century were the framework for the separate racial legacy so familiar to those knowledgeable about twentieth-century southern politics. The story of black and white became a Greek tragedy that never left the South's political stage.

The end of the Civil War marked the abolition of slavery, but it did nothing to remove the subordinate structure of inequality for blacks and the claims of white supremacy. When Abraham Lincoln was assassinated in April 1865, and Vice President Andrew Johnson, a Tennessee Democrat with states' rights sympathy, assumed the presidency, the abolitionists feared the worst. Johnson, as president, implemented Lincoln's reconstruction plan that included an offer of general amnesty (pardons) to all white Southerners, except for high Confederate civil and military officials and men of wealth, unless they obtained special presidential pardons. The repatriated Southerners had to take an oath of allegiance to the United States and accept the legislated measures abolishing slavery.[3]

The plan required the Confederate states to ratify the abolitionist provisions of the Thirteenth Amendment to the US Constitution. By the end of 1865 all southern states, except Texas, had complied with the provisions of the amendment, abolishing slavery, repealing their secession acts, and discharging their Confederate debt. President Johnson "appointed provisional governors in the Southern states, and legislatures based on white suffrage were called to modify their constitutions in harmony with that of the United States."[4] The requirement was that universal manhood suffrage, without reservations of race or color, be granted all inhabitants. This never happened. Johnson evaded the problem of black suffrage by leaving the solution of all race problems to ex-Confederates. Civil and voting rights for black males were not a requirement for the reentry of the seceded states under the Johnson plan, and the South moved quickly to enact "black codes" to limit the civil rights and liberties of former slaves.

The black codes were a legal response by southern governments that purported to bestow civil rights on newly freed slaves, both men and women. In actuality their purpose was the control of the black population. All across the South, new laws were passed that embodied the segregation in effect before the Civil War. For example, in Mississippi, blacks could acquire and dispose of personal property only in incorporated towns and cities. While innocuous on its face, the real intent of the statute was to keep the rural, agrarian African American population powerless. Black codes controlled former slaves with new vagrancy laws, prohibitions on the possession of firearms, curfews, and limitations on the ownership of property. Breaking these laws carried heavy fines. Convicted offenders who were unable to pay the fines had to work off their debts with white employers. The results were little different than the previous restrictions of slavery.

In sum, Reconstruction aggressiveness was matched by southern recalcitrance. The actions of South Carolina's constitutional convention of 1865 were typical of this resistance:

At a special session of the legislature in September, 1865, the so-called "black code" was passed . . . [their] nature . . . indicates that white South Carolinians could not conceive of Negroes as truly free agents in their relationship to the economy of the state.[5]

Actions by other southern leaders to force newly freed blacks into conditions like those resembling slavery opened the door for Congressional, or "Radical," Republican Reconstruction. Celebrations of southern history by whites greeted the congressional rulings. Whites set aside days to recall the heroism and nobility of the Confederate armies who sacrificed in the cause of states' rights, white supremacy, and the agrarian ideal. The celebration of southern valor helped unify the society in defeat, and gave a kind of civil religion to the racism of the region. The legacy of the "'Lost Cause'" also bestowed a cultural legitimacy on Confederate symbols, which would later be used to defend segregation.

In 1866 Republicans in Congress used their overwhelming majority to redefine Reconstruction for the southern states. The Congressional elections of 1866 were viewed as a national referendum on the proposed Fourteenth Amendment, granting citizenship to "all persons born or naturalized in the United States, and subject to the Jurisdiction thereof." This meant extending citizenship not just to former slaves in the South, but also to free blacks in the North who did not normally enjoy the full benefits of citizenship.

The election results, which handed Republicans a veto-proof majority, were taken as a mandate for reform. The Republican-dominated Congress acted quickly to challenge and repeal President Johnson's tepid plan for reconstruction. Congress, led by Northerners opposed to the empowerment of former Confederates as leaders in their native states, challenged Johnson and used their majority in Congress to impose a more radical form of reconstruction.

First, Congress refused to recognize the states readmitted to the Union under Johnson's plan. The Republicans wanted stronger standards before the subservient states were allowed back into the Union. Second, Congress passed legislation creating the Bureau of Refugees, Freedmen, and Abandoned Lands (i.e., the Freedmen's Bureau) in 1865 to provide aid and restoration services to the newly freed slaves. Legislation to extend the agency's life indefinitely was vetoed by President Johnson in February 1866. Congress quickly overrode Johnson's veto. A pattern of conflict was established when President Johnson twice vetoed other legislation between February and July 1866, and Congress overrode him again in July 1866. The Reconstruction acts were supplemented by legislation to prevent the president from frustrating the will of Congress. Finally, Congress passed the Civil Rights Act of 1866; subsequent Civil Rights Acts were enacted in 1870, 1871, and 1875, again over Johnson's veto. The Fourteenth Amendment passed in June 1866, and was sent to the states for ratification. It was intended to protect citizens (especially black citizens) from discriminatory actions by state governments. The next month

Tennessee became the first state readmitted to the Union after it ratified the amendment.

Congress remained in open conflict with President Johnson, and passed four other Reconstruction acts between March 1867 and March 1868. The measures were all designed to protect blacks and give them citizenship rights, but all stopped short of ensuring suffrage. The former Confederacy, excluding Tennessee, was partitioned into five military districts under the direction of military officers supported by federal troops, in a form of martial law. Each district was required to grant voting rights to all male citizens, excluding disqualified former Confederate rebels. The southern states were required to ratify the Fourteenth Amendment and rewrite their constitutions in accordance with its provisions before being readmitted to the Union. Readmission also extended the life of the Freedman's Bureau. Congressional Reconstruction disfranchised most southern voters and granted the vote to blacks, white Southerners loyal to the Union, and northern in-migrants.

All of the southern legislatures, except Tennessee, rejected the Fourteenth Amendment provision. Southern politicians took refuge behind racial barriers and solace in race-conscious rhetoric. Leaders like Generals Lee, Beauregard, and Longstreet advised cooperation to salvage a difficult situation. But others, like Ben Tillman in South Carolina, maintained that Reconstruction was breeding, "a conflict between the Caucasian and African races."[6] States' rights became a mantra to remain bitterly uncompromising in the face of inevitable change. The result was predictable.

In response to this insubordination, Congress enacted supplementary Reconstruction acts that faced the same Johnson veto. These Reconstruction acts authorized military commanders to supervise elections, and directed them to convene state constitutional conventions. Even though President Johnson narrowly interpreted the acts, and sought to slow down their implementation, more blacks than whites occupied voting lists in several states—Alabama, Florida, Louisiana, Mississippi, and South Carolina. Reconstruction had unintended benefits for Southerners who were opposed to the measures. Numerous non-property-owning whites became voters for the first time since the new state constitutions abolished the property qualification for voting. A few states permitted women to vote, and public education systems accepted both black and white students at separate schools in defiance of custom.

The Reconstruction acts were passed over the vetoes of the president and supplemented by legislation to prevent the executive from frustrating the will of Congress. In March of 1868 the fourth Reconstruction act allowed state constitutions in each state to be ratified by a simple majority vote. In the same month, the House of Representatives passed Articles of Impeachment against President Johnson for his obstructionism, but in May the Senate acquitted him by a single vote. In June of 1868 seven states—Alabama, Arkansas, Florida, Louisiana, North Carolina, and South Carolina—were readmitted to the Union and sent representatives to Congress. The Fourteenth Amendment was ratified in July, and the Freedman's Bureau ceased operation around the same time. In early 1870, the final three states—Mississippi, Texas, and Virginia—were readmitted to the Union.

Finally, in March 1870, the Fifteenth Amendment was ratified. It forbade abridgment of voting, "on account of race, color or previous condition of servitude." The amendment promised voting rights to southern freedmen as well as northern blacks, most of whom were prohibited from voting by state laws before its passage. Only a minority of nineteenth-century Northerners believed or practiced racial equality; for the most part they cared little about the plight of southern blacks except to fear that their relocation northward would undercut regional wages.

The period when outside influences dominated the South, and black participation played a dominant role in the government of the southern states, was known as Radical Reconstruction. It is usually dated from the summer of 1868 to the beginning of 1877. Thousands of Northerners settled in the South during Reconstruction. They represented a variety of hopes and purposes. Some were sincere missionaries of abolitionist ideas, who came to establish schools and churches. Others were fortune hunters and demagogues, who came south to capitalize on black misfortune. Some were Unionists looking for opportunity. The motives were as complex as human nature. The Reconstruction governments relied on the support of the newly enfranchised blacks, and the well-disciplined leadership of outsiders (known as scalawags and carpetbaggers by Southerners), to organize the electorate.

In the spring of 1870 black citizens began to exercise their newly granted rights to vote. Black candidates were elected to local offices, such as sheriff, or recorder of deeds, and state offices like superintendent of education, lieutenant governor, acting governor, secretary of state, state treasurer, and to both houses of state legislatures. In 1868 there were nearly 260 black southern legislators; the number peaked at around 325 in 1872 but declined to only 150 by 1876.[7] Black officials were influential in some states, but they were generally weaker than their white counterparts. Despite their population advantage, African Americans never controlled state government in any southern state. For a time, though, they did control the lower house of the state legislature in South Carolina. Blacks were elected to both houses of the US Congress, representing Alabama, Florida, Georgia, Louisiana, Mississippi, North Carolina, South Carolina, and Virginia. Public schooling, wages for black workers, and jury system reform were some of the issues that interested black elected officials.

Behind the façade of white acceptance of the new social order lurked a fierce determination by some to rid the states of black rule. Reaction to black voting and office holding was especially strong and violent. White resentment took the form of support for the most vengeful leaders, whose reaction was both shrewd and calculating. From 1867 to 1877 brutal acts of hostility against blacks were used to tighten the color line and create a more homogeneous society. Mob violence, especially lynching, ensured white supremacy by enforcing a kind of popular justice to regulate behavior in the region. This was particularly true for organized mob actions carried out by secret organizations, such as the powerful Ku Klux Klan (KKK) or the Knights of the White Camellia:

> Secret societies grew and spread when it became apparent to Southerners that their control was to be broken by Radical [Congressional] Reconstruction. For ten years after 1867 there flourished the Knights of the White Camellia, the Constitutional Union Guards, the Pale Faces, the White Brotherhood, the Council of Safety, the '76 Association, and the Knights of the Ku Klux Klan. Among the numerous local organizations were the White League of Louisiana, the White Line of Mississippi, and the Rifle Clubs of South Carolina.[8]

The secret societies were terrorist organizations. They used beatings, assassinations, and armed bands of horsemen at the polls to "redeem" the South from "Negro rule." Later, so-called Redeemer governments would be those led by these embittered white partisans who wanted to accomplish lasting reconstruction on their own terms, which were in opposition to those of the government in Washington. Whites sought to do by extralegal and illegal means what they could not do by law: exercise control over the black population and reestablish white supremacy. Through intimidation and violence, the objective of the secret societies was to prevent the implementation of the Fourteenth and Fifteenth Amendments.

Radical Reconstruction demands were again matched by Southern recalcitrance. The US Congress responded to this defiance by passing the Enforcement Act, or the so-called Ku Klux Klan acts in 1870 and 1871. The Enforcement Act sought to enforce the Fourteenth and Fifteenth Amendments and identified bribery, intimidation, and other actions to deny blacks their constitutional rights as federal crimes. The Ku Klux Klan acts strengthened federal authority to punish violent behavior against blacks by groups like the Klan. Shortly after the passage of the Ku Klux Klan acts, President Grant used their authority to impose martial law and suspend the writ of habeas corpus in South Carolina. In spite of this mandate, state and federal laws against the actions of antiblack organizations were generally ineffective.

Beginning in the 1870s white southern Democrats, or Redeemers, emerged to reclaim control of southern states from Republicans and blacks. These Democrats recouped management of state government and elections in Virginia and North Carolina in 1870, and in Georgia the following year. Laws that disfranchised former Confederates were repealed. Congress restored full citizenship to nearly all of the former Confederates. In 1874 Democrats gained controlled of both houses of Congress and by the end of 1875, Redeemer governments were in control in Arkansas, Alabama, Mississippi, and Texas. By 1876, Republicans controlled only Florida, Louisiana, and South Carolina.

The outcome of the 1876 presidential election ended Reconstruction. Samuel Tilden, the Democratic nominee, narrowly won the popular vote over Republican Rutherford B. Hayes. The electoral votes in three southern states—Florida, Louisiana, and South Carolina—were disputed, sending the election to Congress for resolution. In 1877, a bipartisan commission in Congress voted along party lines that Republican Hayes be awarded the disputed votes in what was termed the "Tilden-Hayes Compromise." To calm Democratic fears about the procedure, the Hayes supporters told influential white Southerners that railroads and public works would follow the Hayes election. But the main promise was that after the inauguration, the remaining federal troops in the South would be removed.

When native whites regained control of the South after 1877, their recollections of the period from Lee's surrender until the Tilden-Hayes compromise were bitter. White supremacy meant more than the resumption of political power; it signified absolute elimination of black rule from every social activity, and expungement of Reconstruction from the conscience of the South. Native white Redeemers gained control of the southern states and sought to return the South to a society that resembled pre–Civil War years.

Under Congressional Reconstruction, blacks voted and served in elected positions, and the federal government protected them against violent abridgements of their constitutional rights. Now all the security came to an end. White southern Redeemers rejected the changes forced on them by Republicans and the federal government. The bitter antigovernment rhetoric and fierce individualism that would characterize states' rights arguments for years to come had its genesis in these years. For white Southerners, the withdrawal of troops was tacit recognition of the legitimacy of states' rights, including the rights of state governments to regulate race relations in ways consistent with white supremacy.

Once free of federal intervention, the states resorted to a host of measures designed to maintain racial domination. They could now govern their internal affairs as they saw fit. For example, in 1882 South Carolina established the "Eight Box Law."

> The law of 1882 provided separate boxes for eight different classes of offices, national, state, and local. The intent of the "Eight Box Law" was ostensibly to provide an effective literacy test by requiring the voter to choose by the label the proper box for his ballot. In practice, however, it would be simple for elections managers to help those illiterates who would vote "right" and let others void their ballots through ignorance.[9]

The color line was tightly drawn in all similar political practices. The means of maintaining rule was to eliminate the opportunity for blacks to participate. Whites resorted to subterfuge and trickery to eliminate black participation, but intimidation was part of the culture as well. Reprisals were carried out against blacks who fought the new norms, and African Americans who even discussed politics were now advised to hold their tongue. Gradually the Republican vote began to disappear as a factor in southern politics. After 1885, southern representation in Congress became more Democratic and white. Florida's 1885 constitution repealed Reconstruction controls, and other southern states soon followed suit.[10]

Former Confederate political leaders worked tirelessly to assure Northerners that blacks were best served by white supremacy. Northerners listened because they were now tired of Reconstruction too, and no longer believed that national unity was possible. In northern minds the main hope for equality lay in economic ties between North and South. Private business interests and job growth, it was hoped, would eventually eclipse the legislative need for racial justice. The new attitude toward southern problems was embodied in the phrase the "New South." In Atlanta newspaperman Henry Grady's celebrated address before a sympathetic New York audience in 1886, he proclaimed that Southerners had been converted to the Yankee way; they were rejecting the idea of leisure, replacing politics with business, and sharing liberally with the black man in the region's mounting prosperity. The rhetoric said that the war was over, and economic success was just around the corner.

The economic and social ascendancy of the South was largely a myth. New South idealism was appealing because it offered Southerners a place at the economic table, but actual improvement was hard to find. Prosperity was promised, but remained an illusion. At the end of the century, economic circumstances were little better than after the Civil War, while the myth of the New South as a land rich, just, and triumphant remained. The profits from southern industry often wound up outside the region, and southern workers labored longer and earned less than their counterparts in the North. The Republican Party turned its attention away from the South to the huge business conglomerates driving economic expansion in the North and Midwest along with opportunities offered in westward expansion.

As the economic statistics told a morbid tale, attacks mounted from desperate populists tired of political promises. Many whites, especially small farmers and wage earners, were attracted to third parties, like the Greenbacks, Readjusters, and Independents. In the 1880s, the Greenbacks advocated readjusting the war debt with greenbacks ("poor man's money") rather than with gold or silver. To counter the appeal of third parties among small farmers and poor whites, some white Democratic leaders stooped to embrace black voters. In the 1890s the agrarian movement demanded that state and national governments use public authority to regulate banks and other businesses of commerce and industry to stop farm foreclosures, bankruptcies, and the rules of commerce and trade that favored big businesses and industry.[11] The economic panic was so severe in the South that white farmers formed alliances with blacks against the dominant business and industry conglomerates.

The agrarian movement, and the associated biracial People's Party, posed a direct threat to Democratic Party hegemony. The appeal was economic and not political, so—not surprisingly at election time—the old ways resurfaced, and the populist parties were crushed. With the aid of blacks and white Republicans, the

Vignette 4.1 "Pitchfork" Ben Tillman (1847–1918)

As an anti-Reconstructionist politician, Democratic activist, South Carolina governor, and US senator, Benjamin Ryan Tillman was the embodiment of white supremacy. He defined his world against the revolutions of black emancipation and Reconstruction. Tillman's rhetoric was legendary; he publicly boasted that "in 1876 we shot Negroes and stuffed ballot boxes." His vision and his voice helped to create the violent, repressive world of Jim Crow segregation in the South.

The roots of Tillman's racism lay in the white patriarchy typical of his birthplace in Edgefield County, South Carolina. He was only thirteen when the Civil War began, too young to join the more than three-fifths of the county's population who served in the Confederate army. On July 10, 1864, less than a week after the battle of Gettysburg, an army surgeon removed a cranial tumor that destroyed Tillman's left eye and gave him a fierce scowl. The young man may not have fought in the war, but he was imbued with the philosophy of white supremacy.

On July 8, 1876, Ben Tillman put his convictions to work in the Hamburg massacre. The town was a mostly black hamlet just across the river from Augusta, Georgia, and a few miles from Tillman's Edgefield County home. Tillman joined some seventy white men who besieged the town after a white man was killed. The Democratic guerillas selected several captives to be murdered in cold blood. Those executed included black militia members and a Republican town constable who had frequently fined or arrested white men. The men called their captives out one by one and executed them with a shot through the head, then on the way home stopped for a celebratory breakfast. Tillman said the incident was one of his proudest memories.

Throughout his public life Tillman struggled to mobilize farmers as a constituency for political power. He insisted that the coinage of silver would expand the circulating medium sufficiently to alleviate the credit crisis. Tillman wanted to transform his rural constituency with the slogan, "White Supremacy," and make his ideal into a description of a rural social reality. He understood, along with other southern politicians, that race was something more sub-jective than biological fact; it could determine partisan allegiance and behavior more than any other issue. In his mind, the term "racial equality" was an oxymoron; one race or the other would dominate, and if white men failed to rally together they would be conquered.

Tillman was an intense man, bitterly inhibited and spurred always by the belief that life and fate had treated him poorly. He was unattractive in appearance, quick-tempered, irascible, and mean. "White supremacy" was his social argument and political program all rolled into one. He hated the former African slaves, and blamed them for the economic plight of the region. It irritated him that the former slaves were free. In speeches he berated the black Africans as destructive forces of change: "the colored races [were] by common consent . . . articles of free trade among Caucasians everywhere."

As a politician Tillman wanted to mobilize not only the white man, but also ideas about white manhood. Education of the black race was a subject that excited him to near hysteria. The education of people not suited for it, he shouted to crowds of hot-eyed small farmers with mortgages and crop lines on their depressed acres, would bring a war between the races. His declarations incited violence and restrictions. The black race became the scapegoat of all the resentments small white farmers felt in their economic squeeze. By 1892 Tillman was the master of South Carolina politics.

The white race, in the senator's view, should preserve itself and dominate others. In his speeches he warned of a racial Armageddon where the "Southland will become a land of blood and desolation." The herds of "restless Negroes," Tillman warned, who roamed the southern roads from sawmill camp to labor gang were a threat to white women. "We must hunt these creatures down with the same terrified vigor and perseverance that we would look for tigers and bears."

When elected to the US Senate, he sought to arouse sentiment in the Congress to abolish the Fourteenth Amendment and nullify the Fifteenth. As a bitter foe of Grover Cleveland, he urged his followers in 1894 to "send me to Washington so I can stick my pitchfork in his [Cleveland's] ribs."

People's Party did score some isolated local victories across the South, and in 1894 they gained control of the North Carolina state legislature.[12] The Democrats responded with strident racial appeals, like those of "Pitchfork" Ben Tillman, playing the trump card of white supremacy. Politicians advocated agrarian reforms with provocative appeals of white supremacy. They sought political power for small white farmers while simultaneously disenfranchising African Americans and imposing segregation.

In the 1890s and early years of the twentieth century, blacks were stripped of their voting rights by the imposition of various requirements and conditions. Jim Crow laws were designed to restrict and segregate blacks. They became widespread in the 1880s. Property qualifications, residential requirements, poll taxes (a tax imposed on each voter before they exercised voting rights), educational qualifications, including understanding obscure legal and constitutional clauses, grandfather clauses (denying the right to vote to those whose grandfathers were slaves), and the white primary (established by the Democratic Party as a private organization to limit participation in primary voting) imposed drastic restrictions on voter registration among blacks and some poor whites.

Vigilante terrorism was a part of the intimidation as well. The bullying took many forms—among the most common were floggings, night visits to "regulate" enemies, tar-and-featherings, and lynchings. Violence was directed at blacks, to bring them into submission. As seen in Table 4.2, between 1882 and 1968, 3,029 blacks were lynched in the South.[13]

Table 4.2 Lynchings by State, 1882–1968

State	White	Black	Total
Alabama	48	299	347
Arkansas	58	226	284
Florida	25	257	282
Georgia	39	492	531
Louisiana	56	335	391
Mississippi	42	539	581
North Carolina	15	86	101
South Carolina	4	156	160
Tennessee	47	204	251
Texas	141	352	493
Virginia	17	83	100
Total: South	492	3,029	3,521
Total: Non-South	803	416	1,219

Source: Tuskegee Institute, "Persons Lynched Nationwide," Tuskegee, Alabama, 1969.

Before the Civil War, southern vigilantes inflicted death upon outlaws and individuals suspected of plotting slave insurrections. After the war, lynchings became more widespread and were usually directed at ex-slaves as a form of intimidation. Information on lynchings usually came from urban newspapers in each state. The figures in Table 4.2 show that 88 percent of black lynchings were in the South. "Among the states, Mississippi ranks first in lynchings from 1882 . . . Georgia is second . . . Texas third . . . and Louisiana fourth."[14]

Beginning in the 1890s, the various state laws, local ordinances, and customs that laid the ground rules for segregation and white supremacy were codified in state constitutions. Constitutional conventions to disenfranchise blacks from politics were approved in South Carolina (1895), Louisiana (1898), North Carolina (1910), Alabama (1901), Virginia (1902), and Georgia (1908). Virtually all African American voters were blocked from voting, but some whites were also disenfranchised resulting in a much smaller electorate. "In 1896 there were 130,344 blacks registered in Louisiana, constituting a majority in twenty-six parishes. In 1900, two years after the adoption of the new constitution, only 5,320 blacks were on the registration books, and in no parish did they make up a majority of voters."[15]

Before the institution of the "Australian ballot" in the 1890s, voter intimidation of blacks was widespread with the intent to keep them away from the polls. Later, the poll tax, and other forms of discrimination, reduced the size of the voting public all across the South. The imposition of a poll tax as a prerequisite for voting in Virginia's 1902 constitution had a devastating effect on the vote.

Whereas 264,240 Virginians had voted for the President of the United States in 1900, only 135,867 voted in the 1904 presidential election. Indeed, it was not until 1928 that the number of voters again reached the size of the 1900 turnout.[16]

Prerequisites for voting disenfranchised blacks and many poor whites, producing a small and durable electorate dominated by flamboyant politicians in primary elections. Voters were easily manipulated in the one-party South, and control required only a relatively few votes from "friends and neighbors" in surrounding counties, joining together to ensure Democratic victories.

Voting disenfranchisement was but one aspect in an effort to systematically relegate blacks to second-class citizenship. Mississippi led the way with legalized segregation, or Jim Crow laws, but in the 1880s and 1890s other southern states strengthened existing statutes and enacted new laws to separate the races and assign African Americans to subordinate positions in society. The black codes enacted in the mid-1860s to restrict the former slaves reappeared in a new guise.

The system of legalized segregation of blacks and whites in the public arena, in places like schools, hotels, restaurants, amusement parks, and recreational facilities, as well as buses and trains, became a fact of life during these years. School segregation laws were passed in nearly all southern states by 1890. Tennessee enacted laws requiring "separate but equal facilities" for transportation in the early

1880s; Florida, Mississippi, and Texas followed Tennessee's example, and most other southern states had similar laws on the books by 1894.

Between 1870 and 1884, the southern states passed laws banning miscegenation, or interracial marriages. The US Supreme Court sanctioned these actions. In 1883 the Court ruled the Civil Rights Act of 1875 unconstitutional, holding that the Fourteenth Amendment did not protect blacks from discrimination by private individuals and businesses. In a ruling on Louisiana's law establishing racial segregation of passengers on trains, the Court provided the justification for legalized segregation in *Plessy v. Ferguson* (1896). The Court ruled that the equal protection clause of the Fourteenth Amendment allowed states to provide "separate but equal facilities" for blacks, affirming the constitutionality of the doctrine.

At the close of the nineteenth century, blacks were free men and women, but they were denied full political and civil rights. White Democrats had returned to power in all of the southern states after 1877, and they were free to regulate internal affairs in their states, including race relations, without federal interference. With the disenfranchisement of black voters and the segregation of the races, the dark clouds of Jim Crow segregation overtook the sunshine of Reconstruction. "The *Plessy* decision, in effect, legitimated racial segregation, not only in transportation but in every aspect of life, including education, voting, public accommodations, employment, and so on."[17]

In 1895, Booker T. Washington, the most dominant and influential African American of his time, delivered his Atlanta Compromise Address before a predominantly white audience at the Cotton States and International Exposition in Atlanta. Washington did not challenge legal segregation and disenfranchisement; rather, he advocated accommodation:

> In all things that are purely social we can be as separate as the fingers, yet as the hand in all things essential to mutual progress. . . . The wisest among my race understand that the agitation of questions of social equality is the extremist folly . . . the opportunity to earn a dollar in a factory just now is worth infinitely more than the opportunity to spend a dollar in an opera-house.[18]

From 1895 until his death in 1915, Washington's accommodation of white control and black subordination in exchange for their acquisition of the skills to become productive members of the labor force was the law of the land. Washington's ideal demanded that social and political equality would have to be earned by blacks through participation and positive contributions in the southern economy.

The New South

The most important development in southern society at the time of the New South was the shift in economic control from an agricultural aristocracy to one of industry and commerce. The black population in the South took advantage of this change to leave the place of their birth and flee to the North and West. Those who stayed behind lived in a setting where white supremacy kept blacks in an inferior caste.

The aggrieved place of African Americans in the South did not provoke relentless opposition from outsiders, like the actions of the abolitionists before the Civil War. Instead, the nation ignored the problem because it was too busy growing and expanding, and the presumption among many of the common people in the rest of the country was that blacks probably deserved their inferior status. Segregation defenders argued that the system was "best" for both races, that blacks were "happier" with it, and that the old slave life "proved by experience" that separation of the races was best.

White supremacy went virtually unchallenged, and when opposition did arise, it was deflated using the constitutionality of states' rights as a fact of life. Whites took advantage of a truncated black vote, their economic destitution, and illiteracy, to employ physical intimidation and violence against the black population. The regnant power of racism was seen in the newfound respectability for the Ku Klux Klan. The grounds for KKK acceptance were sown with the popularity of D. W. Griffith's sympathetic and successful movie, *Birth of a Nation* (1915), based on Thomas Dixon Jr.'s novel, *The Clansman* (1905). In the movie the Klan saves the South from the anarchy of black rule by reuniting former wartime enemies in defense of white supremacy. The resurgent Klan was suddenly more visible, welcomed in social assemblies, and growing, with some two million members and numerous admirers outside the South.

Ralph McGill described the effect a Klan appearance had on an audience in Nashville, Tennessee, in the 1920s. "A small group of rabid Klansmen would appear on a Saturday night at a Salvation Army street meeting, drop a roll of bills, usually twenty-five or fifty dollars, on the drum, and silently walk away."[19] Parades, appearances in churches to make donations, and anonymous gifts to the needy combined to create a climate of respect and support among whites for a group whose real purpose was terror. The Klan practiced an effective mob psychology with the anonymity of hooded costumes, oaths of secrecy, and vigilante attacks on blacks. The revival of the Klan was one of the major news stories of the time, and its activities touched politics, crime stories, and the social calendar of southern cities. Social acceptance of Klan activities was captured in the movie, *O Brother Where Art Thou*, which replayed the stereotypes of racial separation and politics for a twenty-first-century audience. Popular respectability for the Klan kept blacks at bay.

Although the legal segregation of blacks continued, a movement for change gradually began to unfold. In response to the *Plessy* decision sanctioning segregation, some blacks responded with organized boycotts. In 1909 W.E.B. DuBois, a black opponent of Booker T. Washington's accommodation strategy, and a group of

Vignette 4.2   William Edward Burghardt DuBois (1868–1963)

As a historian, sociologist, editor, and social activist, W.E.B. DuBois did more to influence the strategy and tactics of the civil rights movement in the 1960s than any person of his era. He helped to organize the NAACP, gave it a newspaper voice, and provided blacks with a radical blueprint for social action.

DuBois was born in Great Barrington, Massachusetts, on February 23, 1868. He remained a New Englander in thought and action for the remainder of this life, and did not come to the South until 1885, when he enrolled at Fisk University in Nashville, Tennessee. Summer teaching in rural counties opened his eye to the plight of poor black Southerners in the Jim Crow South and galvanized his attachment to their plight. He determined to champion their cause. Upon graduation from Fisk he enrolled in Harvard University, where he earned a doctorate in 1888. His dissertation on the suppression of the slave trade was published in 1896, and after several teaching stops he returned to the South to teach sociology, economics, and history at Atlanta University.

When he returned to the South, W.E.B. DuBois fulfilled his lifelong ambition to assist the black race in its liberation. His third book, *The Souls of Black Folk* (1903), was a collection of essays on life in the South. His insight was that black Southerners had a "double-consciousness," meaning they were simultaneously American, aspiring to the ideals of equality and freedom, and black, trapped in a second-class system not of their making. With the publication of this book, DuBois became the leading intellectual spokesman in opposition to the "separate but equal" ideas of Booker T. Washington. He fought for social and political rights equal to those of whites: the rights of blacks to use public transportation, receive educational benefits, live anywhere they pleased, and vote freely. DuBois argued that African Americans should fight for these rights instead of following the economic rungs of self-improvement on the ladder of success outlined by Washington and his Tuskegee Institute.

DuBois was controversial in the South, so he moved to New York in 1910. There he founded and edited *The Crisis*, the monthly magazine of the fledging NAACP. For the next twenty-four years he used the publication as a vehicle to fight and record all forms of racial injustice. DuBois was influenced by socialist and Marxist ideas of liberation, and his ideas about racial change were controversial in the years of the Great Depression. He urged social revolution as an end in itself, and met each so-called advance for black American citizenship with criticism and skepticism. Finally, DuBois's ideas led to disagreements with the leadership of the NAACP, and he left the organization for good in 1948. Two years later he was arrested and tried as an unregistered agent for a foreign principal, but the judge acquitted him when the evidence was found to be insubstantial.

Unpopular and controversial even among his own followers, DuBois remained a radical voice for change. Late in his academic life he turned to fiction as an expression of the plight of black people living in the South and the nation. In 1961 DuBois was admitted to membership in the Communist Party of the United States, and shortly afterwards left to live in Ghana at the invitation of Kwame Nkrumah. In February of 1963, he renounced his US citizenship and became a citizen of Ghana. He died of natural causes on August 27, 1963, the day before the March on Washington to urge passage of civil rights legislation.

multiracial activists formed the National Association for the Advancement of Colored People (NAACP) to combat social injustice by fighting for black civil and political rights using litigation as a strategy.

Unlike the Klan, the NAACP dynamited no churches, burned no buses, and organized no mobs. What it did do was challenge white supremacy in the courts. Several early US Supreme Court rulings laid the foundation for the removal of restrictions on black voting, and the dismantling of Jim Crow laws. For example, in *Buchanan v. Warley* (1917), the Court outlawed a Louisville ordinance prohibiting integrated neighborhoods, signaling the Court's willingness to rule against some Jim Crow statutes. Two years earlier, in *Guinn v. United States* (1915), the Court declared the "'Grandfather Clause'" unconstitutional. The restriction stated that voters who had enjoyed the right to vote in 1867, and their lineal descendents, could be exempted from examinations like literacy tests. Since most blacks could not vote in 1867, these statutes effectively forced them to take the literacy tests and come under the thumb of the ruling white elites. Later in *Nixon v. Condon* (1932), the Court held that the Democratic Party in Texas performed a state function in holding a primary election and that its exclusion of blacks from primary elections was a violation of the Equal Protection Clause of the Fourteenth Amendment.[20] Although the Court reversed the *Nixon* ruling in *Grovey v. Townsend* (1935), in *Smith v. Allwright* (1944) the "white primary" was ultimately outlawed as a violation of the Fifteenth Amendment. In *Morgan v. Virginia* (1946), the Court struck down state laws advancing segregated facilities on interstate buses and trains. Racially restrictive covenants in housing contracts were prohibited in *Shelly v. Kraemer* (1948).

The litigation strategy employed by the NAACP enjoyed limited success, but southern political leaders continued to resist. Supreme Court rulings chipped away at Jim Crow laws, but the Court had no enforcement powers. Defiance meant that without a challenge to southern states' rights principles, judicial implementation would be compromised and white control and black subordination would continue. The Tilden-Hayes Compromise of 1877, and the states' rights principles upon which it was based, forbade federal intervention. The few African Americans able to vote in the South were unable to turn the tide, and black voters had little power to exert on state or national elected officials. In 1913, the NAACP staged a protest against President Woodrow Wilson's segregation of the federal government, but it resulted in no changes in hiring or firing. Blacks lacked the political power to get the president and Congress to pass legislation making something as outrageous as lynching a federal crime. The legal victories were important, but implementation or enforcement of them was absent. The intervention of the national government was a requirement before the southern system of white control and black subordination could be undercut.

Black Southerners, long denied the economic, social, and political rights so freely enjoyed by other Americans, endured even greater cruelty in the years of the

Great Depression. There was an unspoken, but almost universal, practice of employing blacks for menial work only at low wages. Their second-tier employment was justified because they were characterized as lazy, shiftless, and unreliable by dominant whites. The number of black female domestic workers increased in these years, while African American men found work in only select occupations. "[African Americans] enjoyed a virtual monopoly as Pullman porters and dining-car waiters . . . in the South's tobacco industry and around blast furnaces . . . [this] based on the assumption that the race possessed greater manual dexterity than the whites, and could endure heat better."[21] Black Americans received more equitable treatment nationally than they did in the South. In Chicago, Detroit, and Pittsburgh they joined labor unions, and received equal pay for equal work. The success of black relatives in other parts of the country was not lost on those trapped in the traditional caste system of the South.

The winds of change began to blow after World War II. The war was fought over racial issues, with the Aryan "superman" of Germany, and the "Divine Wind" of yellow-skinned Japanese militancy. Segregated black units, like the 99th Fighter Squadron and the Tuskegee Airmen "Red Tails," served in Europe with distinction on the front lines in contradiction of southern stereotypes. The egalitarian rhetoric of World War II produced a change in thought in the United States and helped to undermine the intellectual justification for racial segregation in the South. African American soldiers fought and died in both world wars, but black soldiers returning from the second conflict were more vocal about putting their lives on the line for freedom and democracy abroad, while being denied basic human and civil rights at home. When they were discharged, many black GI's left the South. Black migration to northern industrial centers allowed many natives to escape de jure segregation (separation by law) and a less racially structured society, but they found themselves in the midst of de facto separation (by the fact of housing and income) in their new neighborhoods.

Because of black out-migration, no southern state had an African American majority population in 1950. Mississippi had the highest black average at 45 percent, followed by South Carolina with 39 percent; then across the South the black population ranged from 13 percent to 33 percent in the remaining nine states (see Table 4.1 earlier). The moral paradox of the nation's professed belief in democratic creeds, and its continued regional racism brought global attention to the plight of the black South as the United States became the leader of the free world.[22] Communist critics in Eastern Europe and the Soviet Union delighted in the sanctimonious hypocrisy of US criticism of the "Iron Curtain" of Europe, while black Southerners lived restricted lives imprisoned in the segregated South. Eloquent expressions of US anticommunism rang hollow in the ears of African Americans facing discrimination every day.

The dignity and plight of black Americans was highlighted by two events in the postwar era. First, in 1946, Jackie Robinson became the first black baseball player to play in the major leagues. Born in Georgia and raised in California, Robinson responded to the challenge of integration by winning acclaim both on, and off, the field. Second, four years later, diplomat Ralph Bunche became the first black American to win the Nobel Peace Prize. Again, these accomplishments dispelled the stereotypes many in the United States had about the black race, and showed southern prejudice to be empty.

The confluence of several events made 1948 a watershed year in southern politics. First, the Democrats ended an interminable silence by both major parties on the issue of race relations when Harry S. Truman linked his campaign for the White House with the movement for equal rights. Second, the Deep South revolted against the Democratic Party in hopes that their abandonment would cause its defeat in the fall elections. The strategy failed when Truman still won the vote. "The Democratic party's new departure on civil rights policy was rooted in the growing importance of black voters in providing the margin of victory for Democratic candidates in key northern states."[23] The migration of black voters from the South had changed the electoral calculus in some large northern states making African Americans key to continued Democratic victories. In addition, the demise in the 1930s of the party's "two-thirds" rule for nominations stripped a united southern delegation of their ability to effectively veto a nominee.

Before 1948 major party nominees for Congress and the presidency embraced an understood principle of US federalism that said the central government should keep out of the internal affairs of states. The states' rights constitutionalism argument held that the states retained certain rights and powers that could not be taken from them. No national politician dared contradict such convictions, even though rulings by the Supreme Court allowed federal intervention. The regulation of race relations, including voting, was still left to the states. The results were devastating for black Southerners. In 1946 a faculty member at an African American college said that only one black person, a janitor at the college for women, was able to vote in Montevallo, Alabama.[24]

From the perspective of fifty-plus years it is hard to realize the difficulties facing a black person who wanted to vote in a southern state. The original interviews for Key's *Southern Politics* provide disturbing evidence of the widespread discrimination against blacks. In 1946 Peter Brown tried to pay his poll tax in Hale County, Alabama. A former extension agent who worked for the federal government in the early days of the New Deal, he seemed an ideal registrant. When he went to register, Brown was told the county had no record of him, and so the county could not accept his money for the poll tax that day. The next time Brown appeared, he found out the amount of his poll tax, but this time the county would not accept his check. He finally returned taking the exact change for his back poll taxes, which he laid on the counter of the tax assessor's office. The clerk had no choice but to mail Brown his receipt in accordance with the procedure for any other registrant.[25]

Paying the poll taxes was only the first step in a tedious and humiliating process. An interview with a black mail carrier active in the NAACP found that the Board of Registrars in Mobile, Alabama, would not always accept new voters. When black applicants arrived the white registrar would "take roughly fifteen minutes per applicant [and] indulge in 'slow down' tactics such as questioning the candidate in detail about the educational institution which he attended, questioning them in detail about where they lived . . . then [the registrar] would get up in the middle of the questioning and leave the room for maybe three or four minutes."[26] At the same time the board was registering white applicants at a much faster rate, while the black petitioners were forced to stand in line for several hours at a time on different days before being successfully enrolled.

Intimidation was a regular technique at the polling places on Election Day. In 1940 the Alabama Democratic Party declared that black voters would not be allowed to vote in any party primary. Even after the US Supreme Court handed down the *Allwright* decision on April 3, 1944, mandating black participation in Democratic Party primaries, state party officials refused to bend. The Alabama primary was on May 2, but black voters went away disappointed. Finally, a federal judge intervened, and black voters were allowed to vote, but not until 1946.

Control of the black vote was more conventional after they were registered. Vote buying was a frequent occurrence in both the black and white community of southern states. Black leaders would receive money from machine bosses and go into the community to purchase votes. The term "Boodlers" was used to refer to persons who sold their votes to the bosses. Before elections the NAACP regularly sent out postcards to qualified black voters, encouraging them to vote, and carrying a statement that it was unlawful to sell or buy votes in an election.

These cards were no help in Memphis, Tennessee, when V. O. Key interviewed locals about the Crump machine. The white power establishment used money, but also intimidation, to keep blacks in line. Preachers, businessmen, and community leaders gave black voters instructions on what was expected, and they dutifully followed suit. Anyone who strayed was reprimanded through hiring and firing practices, or verbal and political intimidation. When city contracts were revoked, relatives arrested, or persistent requests ignored, black community residents learned it did not pay to cross the Crump machine. "He [Crump] saw to it that the tax rate was low, that government was efficient, and that patronage went to the faithful . . . there [were] never any restrictions against Negroes voting so long as they voted right."[27]

All these practices were at issue in the presidential election of 1948 when President Harry Truman proposed a civil rights plank in the party platform that advocated an antilynching law, a permanent fair employment practices commission, desegregation of the armed forces, and elimination of the poll tax. At the Democratic Convention, Mayor Hubert Humphrey of Minneapolis convinced the delegates to approve the pro–civil rights plank. Two years earlier Truman had created a civil rights commission that issued a report calling for the federal government to pursue civil rights legislation. The combination of the recommendations in the commission report, *To Secure These Rights*, was a signal to white Southerners that the Democratic Party was prepared to leave them and seek federal civil rights legislation.[28]

Southern Democrats bolted from the presidential nominating convention. Six thousand delegates, mainly from Mississippi and Alabama, met in Birmingham to nominate Strom Thurmond, from South Carolina, and Fielding Wright, the former governor of Mississippi, for the States' Rights Independent (Dixiecrat) Party presidential ticket. Their hope was that the national Democratic ticket would fail without the electoral votes of the "Solid South." It didn't happen. Instead Truman narrowly won, and his loss of the southern states of Alabama, Mississippi, Louisiana, and South Carolina showed that the South was no longer crucial to a Democratic Party victory. The election of 1948 foreshadowed the future erosion of the Democratic Party's southern base.

The presidential election also showed that the national Democratic Party was prepared to take a stand on advancing civil rights for blacks through federal legislation, and to challenge the South's states' rights stance along with white supremacy. Thurmond's victories were in key states of the Democratic Party's coalition dating back to Roosevelt's first victory in 1933. The voting revealed that white Southerners would withdraw support from the Democratic Party nominee if the party's presidential nominee placed federal interference in state affairs and federal civil rights legislation on his legislative agenda. The southern position was reinforced by the leadership and committee positions held by southern Democrats in Congress. The southern resistance was poignant, but Southerners had not voted Republican to any significant degree since the Reconstruction years after the Civil War.

Black Southerners adopted a familiar strategy—they went to court. The NAACP Legal Defense Fund subsidized a coordinated assault on the barriers to education and voting rights for blacks. For attorney Thurgood Marshall, "the job was not so much winning his cases as getting a fair hearing on the record as the basis for subsequent appeal to higher, and, he hoped, friendlier courts."[29]

The realities of electoral politics and the proposed national civil rights legislation did not impede Supreme Court rulings. Two important decisions continued the trend of chipping away at *Plessy* and laying the foundation for a landmark ruling overturning it. In *Sweatt v. Painter* (1950), the Court ruled that denying black admission to the University of Texas Law School and the creation of a separate law school for blacks violated the Fourteenth Amendment because the separate law school for blacks was not equal to the older and prestigious University of Texas Law School. In the second case, *McLaurin v. Oklahoma State Regents for Higher Education* (1950), the Court struck down a policy of admitting blacks to a white university because the student's program of study was not available in the state's public college for blacks because they were isolated from their white counterparts in the classroom, library, and cafeteria. Both of these decisions were based on broad interpretations of the Equal Protection Clause of the Fourteenth Amendment and offered precedents for the eventual undermining of the "separate but equal" doctrine in *Plessy*.

Nearly sixty years after the *Plessy* ruling, the Supreme Court unanimously overturned the "separate but equal" doctrine of *Plessy* in *Brown v. Board of Education of Topeka* (1954). The Court consolidated cases challenging the constitutionality of school segregation in cases from Kansas, South Carolina, Virginia, and Delaware, and decided a companion case from the District of Columbia. In *Brown*, the Court issued an unqualified ruling declaring that separate educational facilities for whites and blacks were inherently unequal. "Chief Justice Earl Warren's remarkable opinion simply ignored the historical considerations and concentrated on the socio-psychological evidence that segregation imposed a 'feeling of inferiority' on Negro children."[30]

The Brown decision had broad cultural implications and ordered the dismantling of de jure segregation and the reign of white supremacy. The initial reaction to the Court's ruling was mixed. Although the Court's ruling was unequivocal, enforcement and implementation required political responses.

> There was the anticipated defiance in such states as South Carolina, Georgia, and Mississippi, whose governors had threatened to abolish public schools rather than permit white and black children to attend the same schools. Fiery crosses were burned in some Texas and Florida towns, and scattered groups of whites organized to resist the decision. If the *Knoxville Journal* surprised some, it spoke for many when it said, "No citizen, fitted by character and intelligence to sit as a justice of the Supreme Court, and sworn to uphold the Constitution of the United States, could have decided this question other than the way it was decided."[31]

The *Brown* decision, and the Supreme Court's demand for the dismantling of segregation, did not bring about immediate desegregation of the public schools. Reaction to the decision was mixed, largely because it dealt with the principle of de jure segregation and its constitutionality, not its enforcement.

> A year later, on May 31, 1955, in the second *Brown v. Board of Education* decision, [Chief Justice Earl] Warren ruled that the implementation of the desegregation decision should be handled gradually and, wherever possible, locally. The cases were remanded to the district courts with instructions to "take such proceedings and enter such orders and decrees consistent with this opinion as are necessary and proper to admit to public schools on a racially nondiscriminatory basis with all deliberate speed the parties to these cases."[32]

This was a victory for those who wanted to minimize the effects of the earlier decision and subsequent adjudication would be handled by federal district judges who owed their appointments to US senators opposed to the ruling. Together Brown I and II ordered the dismantling of dual public school systems and required that state and local officials proceed with "all deliberate speed." Clearly, the Court was mandating desegregation. The only question was how quickly desegregation would occur. Because public schools were the venue for desegregation, white parents responded to the decision by withdrawing their children from the public school system and enrolled them in private academies. The justification for the new schools went beyond race, but the number of private academies begun between 1954 and 1956 is too extraordinary to be mere coincidence.[33] The stage was set for the joining of political and judicial institutions with the battle moving to the political stage.

The Civil Rights Movement

A series of black protests that began with the Montgomery Bus Boycott of 1955–1956 became the most significant southern social movement of the twentieth century. With few exceptions, prior to 1955, African American challenges to white supremacy and black subordination were confined to litigation. The battles were spearheaded by lawyers in the courts with no participation by the population at large. All that changed after the *Brown* rulings.

The decision, "which represented an obvious threat to white supremacy, had ignited the sort of violent reaction always provided by challenges to the South's racial caste system."[34] Most of the population was inclined toward apathy and disgust, believing that after years of civil rights litigation nothing much had happened, and things would stay just about the same. White leaders were willing to excuse those who were violent against blacks because their actions contributed to the maintenance of white supremacy. This time it would be different. Numan V. Bartley wrote, "During the winter of 1958–59 massive resistance lost the initiative in southern politics."[35] First there was token integration, then the civil rights movement began a systematic dismantling of the region's most identifiable mannerism.

The protest movement was characterized by unconventional tactics, local protests, decentralized control, and a growing racial consciousness by the participants. Mass political movements by blacks, directed toward businesses and elected officials, were met with stiff resistance from white Southerners. The movement challenged the status quo by employing protest marches, boycotts, and the gradual but significant use of federal civil rights legislation, buttressed by Court rulings, to undermine Jim Crow laws.

The stage was set for a significant event, and it came with Rosa Parks's protest on December 1, 1955, in Montgomery, Alabama. Mrs. Parks's unplanned refusal to give up her bus seat to a white man was an outgrowth of gradually rising racial tension, and the event itself became a stimulus for mass protest through an organized boycott of the bus system. Rosa Parks had been secretary of the local branch of the NAACP, and her arrest mobilized the black community in support of the boycott. More support came on November 13, 1956, when the US Supreme Court upheld a

Vignette 4.3   E. D. Nixon (1899–1987) and Rosa Parks (1913–2005)

E. D. Nixon was a union organizer and friend of Rosa Parks who helped to recruit her to the Montgomery Improvement Association (MIA). The two of them were largely responsible for initiating the Montgomery Bus Boycott.

Nixon served as president of the Alabama branch of the Brotherhood of Sleeping Car Porters. He was known in the black community as a man who knew white policemen, judges, and clerks in town, and would go to see them about black grievances. Once he pushed his way into the governor's office and was the first black man since Reconstruction to put himself on the ballot for local office. He also served as president of the Montgomery chapter of the NAACP. In his capacity as a member of the Montgomery Improvement Association, Nixon met the new Baptist minister in town, Reverend Martin Luther King Jr., in 1955. He challenged the ministers to not let women take the lead in the protest. "We've worn aprons all our lives," he said, "It's time to take the aprons off."

Rosa Parks was born on February 14, 1913, in Tuskegee, Alabama, the daughter of a tenant farmer mother. She was raised in Montgomery where she attended Alabama State College and worked as a clerk and insurance saleswoman and, finally, as a tailor's assistant at the Montgomery Fair Department Store. As a former secretary of the NAACP, she also served as an assistant at communion services at the city's African Methodist Episcopal Church.

E. D. Nixon and Rosa Parks first met when he was president of Montgomery's struggling NAACP. Later she was hired by Nixon as secretary of the Montgomery chapter, and worked with him for several years. Despite her depiction as a waif, suddenly emboldened by a bus driver's abuse, Rosa Parks had a life history of standing up against racial mistreatment.

On December 1, 1955, she refused to give up her seat on a Montgomery bus to a white man and ignited the civil rights movement and the direct action strategy. For her act, Parks was arrested, which sparked a 381-day boycott of buses in Montgomery. The protest thrust Reverend Martin Luther King Jr., then an unknown twenty-six-year-old minister at the Dexter Avenue Baptist Church, into the national spotlight. "Rosa Parks was just the right person at the right time," E. D. Nixon later remarked. Nixon paid her bail and asked if she would be willing to serve as a test case to challenge the legality of Montgomery's segregation ordinances. After a discussion with her husband and mother, Rosa Parks agreed to become the "mother of the civil rights movement."

Two months after the boycott began, E. D. Nixon's house was bombed. Nixon was out of town at the time, but when he returned he joined King in leading the Montgomery Improvement Association boycott. Later Nixon and King were at loggerheads over the MIA's financial procedures, and the protests of Nixon and a number of other older activists led to their exclusion from protest plans.

Nixon is remembered as someone who connected the older civil rights movement, led by people like A. William Randolph and Eleanor Roosevelt, with the modern leadership of Martin Luther King Jr. In later years, Rosa Parks often expressed embarrassment at the adulation she received as a result of her notoriety. Rosa Parks passed away on October 24, 2005, at the age of 92, and was the first woman to lie in state in the US Capitol.

lower federal court's ruling, declaring that segregation of public transit was unconstitutional.[36] The civil rights movement had another legal victory and growing national visibility.

The *Brown* rulings were the linchpin for dismantling the system of white supremacy and black subordination. The tepid response to *Brown* by white Southerners soon turned hostile and defiant. Southern members in both houses of Congress in 1956 strongly denounced federal interference in state affairs and the usurpation of the authority of states in what they called the "Southern Manifesto." The document was little more than a condemnation of the *Brown* decision and a call for resistance using the states' rights argument for justification. The decisions of the Supreme Court in school cases were condemned as "a clear abuse of judicial power" and decried as "contrary to the established law, and to the Constitution." The eighty-two southern members of the US Senate and the House of Representatives pledged "to use all lawful means to bring about a reversal" of the *Brown* rulings, which they charged to be "contrary to the Constitution" and "to prevent the use of force in its implementation."[37]

The Southern Manifesto, originated by Senator Strom Thurmond of South Carolina and fueled by Senator Harry Byrd of Virginia, proclaimed the principles for "massive resistance" against race mixing and school integration. The public schools became the primary focus of civil rights activity as blacks and whites chose to work out the region's most serious problems in the laboratories of the schoolroom. Massive resistance "was an effort by [Virginia] to resist racial integration of its public schools even to the extent of closing down those schools under court order to desegregate."[38] State objections to federal interference were hallmarks of legal arguments against integration.

> "Massive resistance" became the battle cry in Virginia for those who wanted to fight even token compliance with the Supreme Court order. . . . Defiance was dressed in legalistic language and given a facade of respectability. . . . Other southern legislatures followed Virginia in adopting interposition resolutions "to resist this illegal encroachment upon our sovereign powers."[39]

James J. Kilpatrick, editor of the *Richmond News*, unearthed John C. Calhoun's "interposition" argument to justify southern resistance to integration. His wildly popular editorials were reprinted in newspapers across the South. Because respected white leaders supported continued segregation of the races, and said the Supreme Court decisions were illegal, the white populace saw nothing wrong with passive resistance or outright defiance of the Court rulings. State legislatures passed student assignment policies that dictated the closing of schools rather than sanctioning the admission of black students to all-white schools. For example, elected officials in Prince Edward County, Virginia, voted to close all county public schools rather than to admit black students to district schools. The Virginia General

Assembly created the State Pupil Placement Board to stall and prevent black student assignment to all-white schools by denying state school aid to those who allowed it.[40] Such were the common legal and political forms of "massive resistance."

The actions of black individuals and organizations seeking school desegregation in Virginia and Arkansas became the catalyst for the formation of the Citizens Council movement by whites across the South. "The Councils and allied groups provided the organization and inspiration for economic retaliation against Negro integrationists and any whites who dared to espouse their cause, but burgeoning segregationist organizations were more the result than the cause of the truculent southern mood."[41] The Citizens Councils were a white reaction to the organizational successes of the NAACP and perceived infiltration of communist-inspired groups advocating race mixing. They won the support of high elected officials, as well as business and professional groups, because they officially eschewed violence and cultivated civic respectability. There are no reliable membership figures on the number of whites who joined the councils, but "the South-wide figure probably never exceeded 250,000."[42] The Citizens Councils were organized across the South as a mechanism for ordinary white citizens to join forces in local communities with their state and federal elected officials to resist mandated racial integration.

In the end, the white supremacists and segregationists were unable to turn back the clock.

> Massive resistance failed to achieve the most cherished aims of its neo-bourbon proponents. The movement did not hold the South to an undeviating adherence to the caste system; it did not reestablish a pre–Civil War concept of states' rights; and it did not insulate the region from the intrusion of new ideas and social practices. Yet the real significance of massive resistance was not its failure, but the success it enjoyed in stabilizing political patterns.[43]

Proof of federal power and national resolve came when President Dwight D. Eisenhower sent federal troops and the National Guard to Little Rock, Arkansas, in the fall of 1957 to guarantee school desegregation. The action prevented Governor Orval Faubus, and mobs of sympathetic whites, from stopping nine black students from attending classes at all-white Central High School. The incident received national publicity and proved to be an unexpected boon to the forces of desegregation because it caused a widespread reassessment of racial attitudes and social values across the South, and the nation at large.

Further federal intervention also came with the passage of federal civil rights legislation. The Civil Rights Act of 1957 was the first post-Reconstruction civil rights law to be enacted. Over the objections of southern US senators and representatives, and a record-breaking filibuster (24 hours and 18 minutes) by Senator Strom Thurmond, the federal law sought to secure black voting rights and established a bipartisan US Civil Right Commission. The Civil Rights Act of 1957, though lacking real strength, advanced the theory that the protection of black voting rights would equip them for warding off discrimination in other areas. "Pass one civil rights bill, no matter how weak, and others would follow."[44] Once passed, a bill could be amended or altered and the symbolic effect of "starting something," for sixteen million blacks who had watched every other bill die, could not be measured.

The Civil Rights Act of 1960 strengthened the 1957 Civil Rights Act and opened the door for sending federal registrars into southern states to assist in black registration. The incremental steps represented by the passage of the civil rights legislation was significant because "the conservative Republican–Southern Democratic coalition, which had been invincible on civil rights issues (particularly procedural ones), was splintered and defeated by a cooperative effort between northern Democrats and liberal Republicans."[45]

The currents of change, though incremental, were ushering in a new era. The success of the Montgomery Bus Boycott catapulted Reverend Martin Luther King Jr. into the leadership of the Southern Christian Leadership Conference (SCLC) and the voice of nonviolent protest to racial segregation. Reverend King became the leader of the civil rights movement, especially in the South. His nonviolent strategy was designed to protest the oppression of blacks and the denial of their basic human rights in a country whose actions contradicted the Declaration of Independence, the US Constitution, and the principles of democratic self-government. Mass black protests and demonstrations against racial injustices confronted the white power establishment with its hypocrisy, and elicited from the world sympathy for the black crusade. The litigation strategy of the NAACP was now supplemented by protest as a means of social change. Black mobilization for political activism became the dominant strategy for confronting white supremacy and marshaling the power of the national government in support of racial equality in the face of white southern recalcitrance.

The second major phase of the civil rights movement began on February 1, 1960, when four black college students in Greensboro, North Carolina, sat at a lunch counter reserved for whites. The sit-in movement, and the accompanying freedom riders of the early 1960s, were visible aspects of the direct action social protest strategy.[46] Students in the sit-in movement were affiliated with NAACP youth chapters, but they initiated the protest on their own. Service was denied the students, but no arrests were made. Over the next several days hundreds of black students descended on Woolworth's. The students were cursed and jeered by whites, but the sit-ins spread to other cities. They went first to black colleges: North Carolina cities such as Winston-Salem (Winston-Salem State College), Durham (North Carolina College), Raleigh (Shaw University and Saint Augustine's College), Charlotte (Johnson C. Smith University), and Fayetteville (Fayetteville State College), Elizabeth City (Elizabeth City State College), and Concord (Barber-

Scotia College). Later in the spring semester, sit-ins sprang up in cities with black colleges and elsewhere in Virginia (Richmond, Hampton, Norfolk, Portsmouth) and Tennessee (Nashville and Chattanooga), and Montgomery, Alabama. The initial sit-in protests were peaceful, but when they spread to other cities, the students became more assertive. The first violence between black and white youths happened in Portsmouth, Virginia.

> The sit-ins brought to the surface interracial tensions that had long been suppressed in the South, and they stimulated a process of self-realization among blacks that would continue through the decade . . . nonviolent direct action was a starting point for the emergence of a new political consciousness among oppressed people.[47]

The third phase of the civil rights struggle began with the "Freedom Riders" of 1961. Blacks and sympathetic whites organized the Congress of Racial Equality (CORE) that year, and began to test the implementation of the Interstate Commerce Commission's 1955 racial discrimination policy on interstate bus facilities in waiting rooms at Trailways and Greyhound bus stations from Virginia to Mississippi. Between Virginia and Georgia the Freedom Riders were greeted with integrated restaurant service in some locations and closed waiting rooms in others. Violence awaited them when they crossed the Alabama state line. White mobs viciously attacked the riders near Anniston and at the Birmingham bus station. CORE activists decided to discontinue their efforts, but student activists vowed to persist.

A central aspect of the CORE strategy was to bring white kids from the North directly into the civil rights struggle in hopes that the media attention would put pressure on the Kennedy administration. When parents of college students began to call Washington and demand protection for their children, federal bureaucrats paid closer attention to the enforcement of civil rights rulings. Other organizations, like the Southern Christian Leadership Conference, Nashville Student Movement, Student Nonviolent Coordinating Committee, plus nonaffiliated individuals, joined the original Freedom Riders in the Deep South. They were all examples of grassroots direct action that forced blacks and whites, including white public officials, to confront the politics that evoked white supremacy.

Protest politics was an outgrowth of the Montgomery Bus Boycott model established by Reverend Martin Luther King Jr. The strategy enabled powerless blacks to use protest as a political resource.[48] Powerless groups, lacking sufficient resources to secure desired outcomes from white political leaders, engaged in protest to gain national attention and elicit a response from belligerent Southerner mobs and public officials. Their visible activities motivated third parties, such as federal officials, non-Southerners, and sympathetic white Southerners to press for corrective actions.

This pattern of confrontation reached its zenith in Birmingham, Alabama, in 1963, which was the culmination of the fourth phase of the civil rights effort. The events in Birmingham came after challenges in Mississippi and Alabama were met with violent resistance. In the previous fall, whites rioted and two people died in reaction to the enrollment of James Meredith, the first black student at the University of Mississippi. In June 1963, in Jackson, Mississippi, Medgar Evers, the field secretary of the NAACP for the state, was gunned down as he walked from his car in his driveway to his home.[49]

The Birmingham protest was orchestrated by civil rights leaders to expose segregation to the glare of nationwide media attention. The planners sought to mobilize poor and working-class blacks, who were sympathetic with the movement but not active, to become foot soldiers in the protests. Reverend Martin Luther King Jr., and thousands of demonstrators, were arrested. In one of the marches schoolchildren kneeled before firemen and police; in another the police turned German shepherd dogs loose on the demonstrators, sprayed them with high-powered water hoses, and then arrested them. The media images singed the conscience of Americans watching from coast to coast, and one hundred years of southern life was condensed to a few minutes of television tape.

The most violent incident associated with the Birmingham protests took place on a placid Sunday morning in September 1963. Four young black girls attending Sunday school were killed when a bomb exploded at the Sixteenth Street Baptist Church, a meeting place for the demonstrators in Birmingham. Years later, three members of the Ku Klux Klan—Robert E. Chambliss, Thomas E. Blanton, Bobby Frank Cherry—were convicted of murdering the four girls. At the time, violence and murderous acts by white supremacists were expected, yet their actions galvanized the resolve of many non-Southerners to pass stiff federal civil rights laws to protect black voting rights.

The passage of this federal legislation was the fifth, and final, phase of the civil rights movement in the United States. In the 1960 presidential election, John Kennedy campaigned for a comprehensive civil rights act with enforcement mechanisms, and signaled his support for Reverend Martin Luther King Jr.'s civil rights leadership, endearing himself to over two-thirds of the blacks eligible to vote. Kennedy's civil rights bill was stalled in debate at the time he was assassinated in November 1963. When Lyndon Johnson ascended to the presidency, he promised to continue Kennedy's legislative program, including a new civil rights law.

Lyndon Johnson was an odd champion for civil rights. He was a Southerner, "and Texas was part of the South . . . southern heritage [means] a great deal to me."[50] Yet Lyndon Johnson would become the greatest champion of black Americans, and of all Americans of color, because of his identification with their downtrodden status. As shocked and dismayed citizens across the country attempted to make sense of the Kennedy assassination, President Johnson seized the moment and used his considerable power of persuasion to move bottled-up bills to enactment as a way to honor President Kennedy.[51]

His campaign for legislation was helped by tragic events. In June of 1964, three civil rights workers, living in Mississippi to help register black voters, disappeared. Two months later President Johnson sent military personnel to Mississippi to help search for the killers. The bodies were discovered in Philadelphia, Mississippi. The investigation found that the three civil rights workers—a black, a white, and a Jewish male—had been arrested for speeding and then released by the local sheriff to members of the Ku Klux Klan. The death of these three students made passage of new civil rights laws practically inevitable.

Public opinion, guided by the determined leadership of Johnson, used the success of the civil rights movement as a backdrop to break up the conservative coalition in Congress.[52] Conservative midwestern Republican senators, led by Everett Dirksen, voted to pass the bill. The 1964 Civil Rights Act restored citizenship and political rights black Americans lost in the nineteenth century. The key provisions:

- barred discrimination in public accommodations that involved interstate commerce, such as theaters, hotels, and restaurants;[53]
- forbade employers from discrimination in employment on the basis of race, color, religion, national origin, and gender;
- granted the federal government authority to file lawsuits to desegregate public facilities and schools;
- permitted the federal government to withhold federal funds from programs, such as education programs, which were administered in discriminatory ways;[54]
- extended and enhanced the power of the Civil Rights Commission, created in the 1957 act, to investigate civil rights violations and make recommendations to Congress; and
- attempted to deal with the denial of the right to register to vote for most southern blacks through uniform standards, such as the completion of the sixth grade as proof of literacy.

The 1964 act was the most far-reaching civil rights legislation since Reconstruction, legally moving blacks from a position of second-class citizenship and subordination to full citizens before the law. For the first time since Reconstruction, white supremacy was dealt a fatal blow.

The voting rights provision in the 1964 Civil Rights Act represented progress over previous acts, but its enforcement depended on the US attorney general to investigate patterns of discrimination and then take legal action. The process was tedious and fraught with opportunities for delay. The murder of the three civil rights workers engaged in voter education in Philadelphia, Mississippi, along with other acts of violence and terrorism against civil rights activists, created an environment for stronger voting rights protections.

In the first months of 1965, Martin Luther King Jr. organized demonstrations to protest discriminatory voter registration practices in counties around Selma,

Alabama. Some of the counties in south Alabama were majority black in population, but had less than one hundred registered African American voters. Following the death of Jimmie Lee Jackson, and an attack on civil rights marchers as they crossed the Edmund Pettus Bridge in Selma, Alabama, Reverend King led demonstrators on a highly publicized march from Selma to Montgomery. The subsequent protest on the grounds of the state capitol called for stronger voting rights legislation. President Johnson persuaded Congress to once again break the resistance to effective voting rights legislation from southern members and enact the legislation.

Nicholas Katzenbach, attorney general during the Selma crisis, recalled Johnson's instructions: "he said, 'I want you to write the toughest voting rights act that you can devise.'"[55] Congressional hearings documented that federal antidiscrimination statutes were insufficient for overcoming the resistance to enforcement of the Fifteenth Amendment by southern local voter registrars and state officials.

President Johnson signed the Voting Rights Act into law in August of 1965. The act secured the right to vote for blacks and other minorities by eliminating preconditions to voting and abolishing the reasons southern officials gave for limiting black participation. Key provisions of the act included:

- suspension of literacy tests, and other tests, used to discriminate;
- authorization of the appointment of federal registrars in any state or county where fewer than 50 percent of the eligible voters were registered (seven southern states initially comprised these "covered jurisdictions");
- requirement of covered jurisdictions, under Section 5 of the act, to obtain "preclearance" for all new voting practices and procedures from either the US attorney general or the Federal District Court for the District of Columbia; and
- application, under Section 2 of the act, of a nationwide prohibition of the denial or abridgement of the right to vote based on race or color.

The act did not prohibit the use of poll taxes as a precondition to voting, but directed the attorney general to challenge their use.

At the time of its enactment the most imposing barrier to the black franchise was the literacy test in seven southern states. In contrast to the Civil Rights Act of 1964, which was opposed by overwhelming numbers of Southerners, the Voting Rights Act was supported by almost one-third of the populace. Passage of the 1965 act resulted in federal registrars traveling to areas of the South with under 50 percent black registration where literacy or character tests were used. Even when fairly employed, which was rare, the exams had the effect of keeping a disproportionate number of blacks from registering.[56]

The next year Attorney General Katzenbach challenged the obstructions, and in *Harper v. Virginia State Board of Elections* (1966), the United States Supreme Court struck down Virginia's poll tax as unconstitutional under the Fourteenth

Amendment. The Voting Rights Act was renewed and extended by Congress in 1970, 1975, and 1982 (for twenty-five years) to include Hispanics, Alaskan natives, American Indians, and Asian Americans. In 1975, the act was extended to all or parts of ten states beyond the original seven. The constitutionality of the Voting Rights Act was upheld by the US Supreme Court in *South Carolina v. Katzenbach* (1966).

The 1964 Civil Rights Act, along with the 1965 Voting Rights Act, was the culmination of a struggle for African Americans that began following the Tilden-Hayes Compromise to gain enforcement of the Fourteenth and Fifteenth Amendments. For black Southerners the denial of full citizenship and political rights, except for the few Reconstruction years, was overcome once again through the efforts of the federal government in the face of resistance by most southern leaders and officials. Atlanta Mayor Ivan Allen's testimony before the US Senate Committee on Commerce on July 26, 1963, in favor of the passage of the 1964 Civil Right Act captured the significance of both pieces of federal legislation and the primacy of federal action.

> I want to emphasize again . . . that now is the time for legislative action. We cannot dodge the issue. We cannot look back over our shoulders or turn the clock back to the 1860's. A hundred years ago the abolishment of slavery won the United States the acclaim of the whole world when it made every American free in theory. Now the elimination of segregation, which is slavery's stepchild, is a challenge to all of us to make every American free in fact as well as in theory—and again to establish our Nation as the true champion of the free world.[57]

The moral imperative in the conflict between the ideals of a democratic state and the provisions of the US Constitution were reconciled in the mid-1960s, resulting in equality for blacks before the law regardless of state, county, or town of residence.

By the mid-1960s almost half of all African Americans lived outside the South. Once the civil rights movement abolished official discrimination in the South, it was broadened to include the eradication of de facto segregation and discrimination elsewhere. Blacks were confined to teeming urban ghettos and subject to discrimination in employment and promotion in major cities across the country. In 1966 Dr. Martin Luther King Jr. took the campaign for racial dignity north, to the residential segregation of Chicago. Gradually it became clear that the civil rights movement was becoming the first casualty of the Vietnam War, and Dr. King's criticism of US foreign policy took the spotlight off the plight of black Americans. As the protests spread, the mood of the movement for black rights became fiercer, and the outbreaks of racial violence that occurred in northern and western cities were different from the controlled protests in the South. The violence in northern cities flared spontaneously and engulfed the whole country in a media riot. At the height of these demonstrations, thousands of blacks roamed the streets, burning and looting.

The militant wing of the protest embraced violence, and took suggestive names like the Black Panthers and "Black Power." Dr. Martin Luther King Jr. refused to join forces with the militants, and was criticized by them for his passive measures. Rioting continued in the ghettos across the nation during the summer of 1966, and through the "long hot summer"[58] of 1967. In that year, outbreaks occurred in seventy-five communities with 130 deaths. As the leading figure in the movement for black civil rights, Martin Luther King Jr. was blamed for the outbreaks and discouraged by the militancy of the movement. "The Dr. King of August [1967] was far more militant, more pessimistic and more dispirited."[59] Undeterred, King planned a "poor people's" march on Washington in the spring of 1968 to dramatize the need for government programs to eradicate poverty. In early April of 1968, he led a demonstration in Memphis in support of the city's garbage workers, who were mostly black. On the night of April 3, Dr. King addressed a mostly black audience saying:

> I just want to do God's will. And He's allowed me to go up to the mountain. And I've looked over. And I've seen the promised land. I may not get there with you. But I want you to know tonight that we as a people will get to the promised land.[60]

The next day his veiled prophecy was tragically fulfilled when an assassin's bullet struck him down. His death brought to an end the national racial crisis that had gripped the nation for over a decade. The nation watched the funeral on television, and Congress passed the Civil Rights Acts of 1968 as a memorial to Dr. King. The act forbade discrimination in the sale or rental of property; "open housing" was a last legacy of the civil rights crusade. The most public expressions of rage, grief, and hope for the black movement died with the funeral for Dr. King, as his dream became reality in the causes he pursued.

The Modern Period

The end of legal racial separation provided blacks with valid protection against white supremacy, altering the legacy of white domination and black subordination before the law. The civil rights movement bridged the racial divide that had separated the races in the South. Blacks became political actors, and began to win rewards from the political system. In 1964, 73 percent of white Southerners were registered voters, but the portion for blacks was only 36 percent. By 1969, the portion of white registrants was 84 percent and the black portion stood at 65 percent.[61] In memory of the civil rights movement, black voters supported Democratic Party candidates in overwhelming numbers.

After a time, blacks became candidates for elected offices themselves and enjoyed success in local elections and in races for seats in state legislatures and the US House of Representatives. Doug Wilder, a Democrat elected in 1986, became the first African American to win a statewide office (lieutenant governor), and it was in Virginia no less. Though blacks were now political actors, racial block voting meant they were largely elected to office from predominantly black constituencies. Wilder's triumph was a glaring exception to this rule. African Americans in the post-1965 era became consistent and reliable voters for black and white Democratic candidates. Racial polarization and block voting have been tempered by black support for white Democrats.

By promoting legal remedies for discrimination, and winning elections, blacks were able to build a national consensus for their cause. In the 1970s the busing of pupils from one neighborhood to another for reasons of racial balance was an integration method endorsed by the Supreme Court. The policy threatened neighborhood school solidarity and was opposed by a majority of whites.[62] The size and social proximity of the black population in southern cities and towns meant that schools in the region were the most integrated in the country by the middle of the decade of the 1970s. The legacy of white supremacy had melted in the face of continued integration.

In 1974 the Supreme Court ruled against busing across school district lines to achieve integration between suburban areas and the inner city. Major cities in the South began to resegregate along class, instead of racial, lines. Affluent suburbs, largely inhabited by Anglo middle-class families, ringed downtown multicultural areas. Affirmative action programs, originally instituted to assist blacks in employment, gradually came in for legal challenges. Across the South, the policy of affirmative action was widely perceived as favoritism to members of minority groups. In 1978 the Supreme Court outlawed the use of quotas to aid racial minorities in university admission policies, but permitted the use of race to achieve diversity in schools, workplaces, and in public employment.[63]

These trends in the 1970s had the effect of fragmenting the civil rights movement and alienating the ideals of equality that were once widely popular in the white community. The legacy of racial polarization continued in voting patterns. The Republican Party became ascendant as more and more whites abandoned the Democratic Party. The end of legal segregation and the exercise of the vote by blacks largely removed race baiting and overt appeals to white supremacy from southern campaigns and elections. Low taxes, small government, resistance to federal government intervention and mandates, and conservative positions on social issues galvanized white Southerners into the Republican Party. Blacks, by contrast, joined a minority of white Southerners still loyal to the Democratic Party and became the most reliable base for the party that today is in the minority across the southern region.

In the 1990s black Southerners received a windfall in representation with the creation of majority/minority congressional districts. This was a direct result of amendments to the Voting Rights Act, especially the 1982 extension that passed both houses of Congress by veto-proof majorities. These provisions were subsequently widened by the *Thornberg v. Gingles* (1986) decision that adopted criteria for testing claims of vote dilution of minorities. After the decennial census, state legislatures redrew congressional districts to accommodate black representation. This was done at the insistence of federal courts, and sometimes by federal courts themselves, and resulted in increased minority representation in state legislatures as well as the US Congress.

The irony of creating majority black congressional and legislative districts is that Republicans struck an immediate alliance with black Democrats to draw districts mandated by the Voting Rights Act. Republicans found themselves the beneficiaries of legislation they opposed. "When heavily black areas were cut from several districts, many white Democrats lost their strategic advantage."[64] The consolidation of black voters had the collateral effect of allowing Republicans to contest white Democrats in districts where the latter had lost a considerable amount of their base support. Black representation in Congress increased dramatically from two in 1949, to thirty-eight in 2000.

The effects of racial redistricting were fairly obvious. Southern congressional districts once represented by white centrist Democrats gave way to conservative Republicans and liberal black Democrats. The policy effects are less apparent, but after 1994 it is clear that conservative Republicans gained at the expense of moderate Democrats.[65]

The Future Prospects

Since 1950 decisive political developments modified everyday racial life in the South. Social changes, such as those emanating from the Supreme Court's school desegregation rulings in *Brown v. Board of Education* in 1954 and the massive resistance of many white Southerners to that decision, spread across the South. The expansion and success of the civil rights movement in the 1960s undermined the superordinate/subordinate pattern of race relations in the region. The subsequent participation by black voters in Democratic politics, and the recent growth in the Republican Party of white conservatives, dramatically altered the tenor of southern elections. This effect had national implications. The establishment of southern political power began with the election of Jimmy Carter as president in 1976, followed by Ronald Reagan's dependence on the South for votes in 1980, followed by George Bush's victory in 1988, then Bill Clinton's dual successes in 1992 and 1996, and finally George W. Bush's victories in 2000 and 2004.

The participation by African Americans in the political system permanently changed politics in the South. The decisive event that enshrined black enfranchisement and participation in the region was passage of the Voting Rights Act in 1965. This law suspended preconditions to voter registration such as the literacy tests that had been used by white local registrars to bar blacks from the polls, banned the poll tax (the Twenty-Fourth Amendment to the US Constitution, adopted in 1964, outlawed the poll tax in federal elections) as a state suffrage requirement, and gave the president the authority to send federal examiners into the South to register African Americans. The Voting Rights Act transformed the virtually all-white southern electorate to a mixture of blacks and whites generally, with black voting majorities in many towns, cities, and counties. The immediate effects of the act are seen in Table 4.3, which shows black voting participation approaching levels characteristic of whites.

Two factors have historically determined voter turnout levels in the South. The first, and most important, was legal restrictions on suffrage. These limitations were designed to disenfranchise large portions of blacks and poor whites. The second factor limiting participation was the degree of party competition. The Democratic primary once existed to disproportionately disenfranchise the Republican Party, favored by blacks. Any populist parties that challenged the established order were overwhelmed by Democratic dominance. "The result was a period of Democratic allegiance and domination that extended into the middle of the twentieth century."[66]

The increase in black voter registration and the subsequent appearance of black elected officials in the late 1960s altered the South's political landscape. At the beginning of the decade, 28 percent of eligible black adults were registered; by 1971, 58.6 percent were registered voters.[67] The Voting Rights Act did not immedi-

---

Table 4.3   The Voting Rights Effect: Registered Black Voters, 1965–1971

	1965		1971	
State	Percent of White VAP[a]	Percent of Black VAP[a]	Percent of White VAP[a]	Percent of Black VAP[a]
Alabama	69.2	19.3	78.5	54.7
Arkansas	65.5	40.4	61.4	80.9
Florida	74.8	51.2	64.7	52.9
Georgia	62.6	27.4	68.8	64.2
Louisiana	80.5	31.6	77.7	56.6
Mississippi	69.9	6.7	69.7	59.4
North Carolina	96.8	46.8	60.6	44.4
South Carolina	75.7	37.3	49.7	45.8
Tennessee	72.9	69.5	67.3	65.6
Texas	N/A	N/A	56.8	68.2
Virginia	61.1	38.3	59.6	52.0
Regional Average	72.9	36.8	65.0	58.6

Source: Charles V. Hamilton, *The Bench and the Ballot.* New York: Oxford University Press, 1973.
Note: a. VAP = Voting Age Population, which was 21 years and over in 1965 (except in Georgia) and 18 years and over in 1971.

ately translate into black political power. In 1970, the number of black officials nationwide stood at 1,469, by 1980 the number had grown to 4,850, in 1990 it stood at 7,335, and at the end of the twentieth century the total was 8,936.[68] African Americans were registering to vote and assuming places of leadership in both state and federal offices. Significantly, black voters and officeholders have been extremely loyal supporters of the Democratic Party, but they have suffered as one-party rule was replaced by two-party competition.

Unimagined possibilities for African Americans became reality at the end of the twentieth century. For example, Table 4.4 shows that in several southern states representation is beginning to approach the minority population of the state. Alabama, for example, has a black population that totals 26 percent, and minority representation in the state senate of 23 percent and in the state House of Representatives of 26 percent. Black participation is not limited to state offices. The sixteen representatives in Congress from the region have changed the texture of politics in every southern state. The populism of black voters, and their tendency to vote together in the Democratic Party, makes them a crucial part of state political governance.

A key concept in Daniel Elazar's development of a theory of political culture was the migratory streams and historical experiences that various immigrant groups brought to their new locations. Newer ethnic and socioreligious groups have their own patterns of culture to integrate into the southern environment. In the last quarter of the twentieth century southern states, and southern cities, filled with immigrants from Central and South America. Growing ethnic issues involving Spanish-speaking citizens are now part of the political fabric of every southern state, especially Florida and Texas. Some cities, like Miami and San Antonio, have Hispanics as the largest population constituency. Table 4.5 shows the Hispanic minority in every southern state, which increased dramatically in the decade of the 1990s. In the states of Texas and Florida the minorities of black and Hispanic together are closer to being majorities.

Latinos are poised to officially overtake blacks as the largest minority in the country in the next census, and are a growing presence in every southern state. They now have reached 37 million nationally according to the US Census Bureau, and there are an estimated 10 to 12 million illegal Mexican immigrants in the United States. In the Dallas–Fort Worth area alone, one-third of the population was identified as of Hispanic descent in the 2000 census. Much of the new urban population in the South is Latin American, not just Mexican.[69] Some southern cities like Miami and San Antonio have a historic Latino history and culture.

The Hispanic population in Florida is especially important to the politics of that state. Cubans in south Florida, and Latinos elsewhere, are crucial blocs for both parties at election time. In 2004 Mel Martinez used his name and ethnicity to win a seat in the US Senate, and became the first Hispanic-surnamed senator from the South. The Latino population is not only the largest minority, it is also growing by

Table 4.4   Black State Legislators in the South, 2001

	State Senate			State House			Total State Legislature		
State	Number of Black Legislators	Total Seats in Chamber	Percent Held by Black Legislators	Number of Black Legislators	Total Seats in Chamber	Percent Held by Black Legislators	Number of Black Legislators	Total Seats in Chamber	Percent Held by Black Legislators
Alabama	8	35	23	27	105	26	35	140	25
Arkansas	3	35	9	13	100	13	16	135	12
Florida	6	40	15	16	120	13	22	160	14
Georgia	11	56	20	36	180	20	47	236	20
Louisiana	9	39	23	22	105	21	31	144	22
Mississippi	11	52	21	35	122	29	46	174	26
North Carolina	7	50	14	18	120	15	25	170	15
South Carolina	7	46	15	24	124	19	31	170	18
Tennessee	3	33	9	14	99	14	17	132	13
Texas	2	31	6	14	150	9	16	181	9
Virginia	8	40	13	10	100	10	15	140	11
Total	72	457	16	229	1,325	17	301	1,782	17

Source: Hastings Wyman's *Southern Political Report* 556, May 21, 2001.

Table 4.5   Hispanic Population of the Southern States, 1990–2000

State	1990 Population	1990 Percentage	2000 Population	2000 Percentage	% Growth
Alabama	24,629	0.6	63,142	1.5	156.4
Arkansas	19,876	0.8	58,322	2.2	193.4
Florida	1,574,143	12.2	2,587,957	16.6	64.4
Georgia	108,922	1.7	367,592	4.6	237.5
Louisiana	93,044	2.2	122,682	2.8	31.9
Mississippi	15,931	0.6	32,972	1.2	107.0
North Carolina	76,726	1.2	392,599	5.0	411.7
South Carolina	32,741	0.9	98,777	2.5	201.7
Tennessee	30,551	0.7	159,244	2.9	421.2
Texas	4,339,905	25.5	6,642,697	32.7	53.1
Virginia	160,288	2.6	295,048	4.3	84.1

Source: 1990 data from US Statistical Abstract, 2000 data from US Census 2000, Supplemental Survey, "State Rankings—Statistical Abstract of the United States," Table 21, available at www.census.gov/statab/ranks.

over 3 percent a year, compared with 0.6 percent in the rest of the population. They arc also getting richer; Hispanic income now accounts for about 8 percent of US GDP, and is expected to reach 10 percent by the next census in 2010. Latinos are highly concentrated, with 75 percent in just seven states, two of which—Texas and Florida–are in the South. They are the youngest population group in the country, and the target of DVD and CD market advertising.[70]

Aside from Texas and Florida, Hispanics are new to the Southeast. In 1980 Georgia had barely 100,000 Hispanic residents, ten years later the census takers found nearly 400,000 living there, and by 2002 the estimate was a half million. Table 4.5 shows a similar pattern across other southeastern states. Research has found that Hispanics participate in politics at lower rates than whites or blacks, and they are much less likely to register to vote.[71]

Urban growth is pulling the South into a new regional alignment, more Sunbelt than southern, and more contemporary than traditional. The Old South of black and white distinctives is being washed away by urban and multicultural similarities. Recent research on southern Jews showed that they held political opinions similar to those outside the region. Southern birth and residence do not moderate southern Jewry, "they tend to hold different views than their non-Jewish neighbors."[72] Middle-class minorities now live in suburbs beside white neighbors. Today the cities of Orlando, Dallas, Houston, Atlanta, and Charlotte have more in common with other cities of similar size in the rest of the nation than with the rural South forty miles outside their city limits.

Historically the South has been called the most "native" region of the country. Short story writer Elizabeth Spencer captured the southern view of the world outside the South as one not to be trusted. "There were Yankees 'up there' we said to ourselves, looking north; the other southern states, like neighboring counties, offered names that could be traced in and out among one's connection and might prove acceptable."[73] Many white Southerners could trace their ancestry back to settlers who arrived before 1850, and sometimes before 1800. Black families were similarly anchored in the South, since virtually all African Americans were once cogs in the agricultural machines of the plantations. The region could not attract foreign immigrants because of limited economic opportunities and social xenophobia. The lack of diversity raised the tension between black and white and kept outside immigration at bay. However, concomitant with the extension of full citizenship and political rights to southern blacks was a growing in-migration of non-Southerners.

Table 4.6 shows native-born population of southern states in 1950 and 2000. In 1950 over nine-tenths (90.6 percent) of the population in the South was native born and bred; by 2000 only about three-quarters (77.7 percent) of the population hailed from Dixie. The in-migration of non-Southerners brought differences to a region not known for its social diversity. Even after this influx, the South had a higher native-born population than the rest of the nation. These newcomers, many from northeastern and midwestern states, brought their own values with them from another political culture. Sometimes their values have been absorbed by the traditional southern political culture; at other times they have been a change agent in their new communities. John Shelton Reed mentions how southern opposition to handgun regulation eventually became the national position, and how attitude "convergence brought about by the 'Southern' pattern [is] spreading."[74]

The South looks and feels different today than it did a half century ago. The population growth rates of most southern states have exceeded the national average for several decades.[75] Many of the newcomers are members of minority groups. In the 1970s, the flood of Asian and Latin American immigrants gave a new texture to southern culture and politics. Hispanics came to the region as migrant workers or laborers in low-wage jobs. They first appeared in Texas and Florida; later their numbers swelled to those seen in the earlier tables. They competed with blacks and low-income whites for wages and social services. Hostility to new immigrants took the form of opposition to federal government programs for bilingual education and affirmative action programs.

Asian refugees came at the end of the Vietnam War and settled in odd places. "Indochinese Hmong tribesmen came to Selma, Alabama, and Memphis, Tennessee. Vietnamese peasants settled along the Gulf Coast where they fell into competition with struggling shrimpers and fishermen."[76] Children of immigrants

Table 4.6 Percentage Native-Born Population in the Southern States, 1950 and 2000

State	1950				2000			
	Native to State	Native to Other Southern State	Total Southern Nativity	Non-Southern Nativity	Native to State	Native to Other Southern State	Total Southern Nativity	Non-Southern Nativity
Alabama	80.08	8.71	88.79	2.62	73.40	15.07	88.47	11.53
Arkansas	77.17	12.31	89.48	9.92	63.90	15.29	78.71	21.46
Florida	45.68	28.85	74.53	26.27	32.70	12.97	42.43	56.64
Georgia	85.43	9.30	94.73	3.54	57.80	18.27	81.00	19.20
Louisiana	84.71	9.15	93.86	4.06	79.40	11.14	89.78	10.22
Mississippi	88.89	7.99	96.88	2.47	74.30	16.87	91.09	8.91
North Carolina	87.43	8.40	95.83	3.43	63.00	14.97	81.80	19.00
South Carolina	87.90	8.67	96.57	2.58	64.00	17.52	82.29	16.94
Tennessee	80.04	13.25	93.29	6.27	64.70	17.41	82.72	17.41
Texas	78.42	8.94	87.36	11.75	62.20	8.90	81.33	28.08
Virginia	74.36	10.43	84.79	14.45	51.90	17.68	64.72	35.29
South Average	79.09	11.45	90.54	7.94	62.48	15.10	78.59	22.24

Source: US Census Bureau.

excelled in public school classrooms, entered the military, and won admission to prestigious national universities. Table 4.7 compares the ethnic composition of the present-day South with 1950 and 1980 figures, the latter year being one when comparative data are available from the census. Beginning in the 1980s, African Americans who earlier left the region began to return as retirees, and many young blacks were attracted by the region's new economy, now divorced from the legacy of legal segregation.

Today the South is less homogenized than the myth of white men in overalls sitting on country store porches drinking R.C. Colas and eating Moon Pies. But the southern landscape has not been altered uniformly. Change has been most rapid in cities, least rapid in rural areas, with the Hispanics gathered in pockets of south Texas, the tip of Florida, and in urban areas throughout the South. The influx of nonwhite newcomers has already transformed politics in south Florida and its impact is being felt in Texas, Virginia, and Georgia. In the twenty-first century, Hispanics and Asians will become prominent political actors in southern communities and states. In the states of Texas and Florida, minorities are approaching the majority of the population.

No aspect of southern politics is more distinct than that of race. Once, the politics of white supremacy and the Democratic Party were synonymous. No more. The reasons for the Democratic Party demise vary, but a sophisticated analysis of racial attitudes in the 1972 presidential election contends that race played the major role in the realignment of US politics in the 1980s. Edward C. Carmines and James A. Stimson conclude their book, *Issue Evolution: Race and the Transformation of American Politics,* by saying that "racial issues had become a permanent feature of partisan divisions and ideological cleavages, they were embedded in the very fabric of US politics."[77] The authors argue that racial issues moved from the halls of Congress, to the activists of both parties, to a position where they are aligned as an integral part of the normal struggle for political power.

Critics of this explanation argue that it is class, not race, that caused the racial polarization.[78] For whatever reason, black Southerners, because of their experience with civil rights, view government as a positive force in addressing social and economic ills, and look to the federal government for leadership and financial resources. The Republican Party consistently believes that less government is better government. The black vote is the major base of support for the Democratic Party throughout the South; black support in the Republican Party is infinitesimal.

The racial divide in the South is evident in the social bases of the Republican and Democratic parties as well. The affluent middle class of whatever race tends to favor the Republican Party, but few blacks are in evidence here. Instead, examples of black and white racial politics are seen almost exclusively in the Democratic Party. The future of racial politics is not in the historic dispute of black and white relations. The growing Hispanic, non-native-born, and Asian populations make the older biracial politics obsolete. The future of racial politics is not in the past, but in

Table 4.7 Ethnic Diversity in Southern States as a Percentage of Total Population, 1950, 1980, and 2000

State	1950			1980						2000					
	White	Black	Other	White	Black	Hispanic[a]	Asian	Native American	Other	White	Black	Hispanic[b]	Asian	Native American	Other
Alabama	67.9	32.0	0.01	73.8	25.6	0.8	0.2	0.20	0.2	70.9	25.1	1.5	0.7	0.44	0.7
Arkansas	77.6	22.3	0.07	82.7	16.4	0.8	0.3	0.41	0.3	79.4	15.3	2.2	0.8	0.45	0.1
Florida	78.2	21.8	0.08	84.0	13.8	8.8	0.6	0.20	1.5	65.8	14.5	16.6	1.5	0.19	0.3
Georgia	69.1	30.9	0.04	72.2	26.8	0.4	0.4	0.14	0.4	63.7	28.0	4.6	2.0	0.24	0.2
Louisiana	67.0	32.9	0.16	69.2	29.4	2.4	5.4	0.29	0.5	63.1	31.3	2.8	1.0	0.58	0.2
Mississippi	54.6	45.3	0.17	64.1	35.2	1.0	4.3	0.25	0.2	60.9	36.2	1.2	0.6	0.25	0.1
North Carolina	73.4	25.8	0.77	75.8	22.4	1.0	0.3	1.10	0.4	70.5	20.3	5.0	1.6	1.11	0.2
South Carolina	61.1	38.8	0.07	68.8	30.4	1.1	0.4	0.19	0.3	67.1	28.2	2.5	0.9	0.33	0.1
Tennessee	83.9	16.1	0.03	83.5	15.8	0.7	0.3	0.11	0.2	79.7	15.0	2.9	1.3	0.16	0.2
Texas	87.2	12.7	0.09	78.7	12.0	21.0	0.8	0.28	8.2	52.2	10.4	32.7	3.0	0.41	0.2
Virginia	77.8	22.1	0.09	79.1	18.9	1.5	1.2	0.18	0.6	70.7	18.6	4.3	4.3	0.19	0.3
Non-South	93.7	5.2	0.57	85.4	8.8	6.3	1.6	0.75	3.4	71.8	8.5	12.3	4.5	0.79	0.4

Source: 1953 Statistical Abstract, US Census Bureau, Table 25; 1982–1983 Statistical Abstract, US Census Bureau, Table 36; US Census 2000 Supplemental Survey, Table 1.

Notes: a. Includes people of Hispanic origin of any race—not excluded from 1980 White, Black, Asian, Native American, and Other numbers.
b. Hispanic origin of any race—excluded from 2000 White, Black, Asian, Native American, and Other numbers.

the multicultural politics that confront all of US society, not just residents of its South.

Racial conflict between black and white has always been the most visible negation of whatever was commendable about the South. No matter how much one admired southern virtues, be they the genteel manners, bravery in battle, or courage in defeat—there was always the memory of slavery, sharecropper tenancy, and white supremacy. For every word of forgiveness by a leader like Martin Luther King Jr. there was a southern politician like Ben Tillman or Lester Maddox who needed exoneration. The debate as to how much of southern politics is governed by class divisions, as opposed to racial ones, continues. One thing is clear, the legacy of white supremacy was the abiding memory of life in the region, and its presence was all the more paradoxical given the deep Christian religious practices in evidence in southern communities.

Notes

1. Peter Applebome, *Dixie Rising*. New York: Random House, 1996, p. 13.
2. Coretta Scott King, *My Life with Martin Luther King, Jr.* New York: Holt, Rinehart & Winston, 1972, p. 47.
3. John Hope Franklin and Alfred A. Moss Jr., *From Slavery to Freedom*. 7th ed. New York: McGraw-Hill, 1994, pp. 223–224.
4. Ibid., p. 225.
5. George Brown Tindall. *South Carolina Negroes: 1877–1900*. Columbia: University of South Carolina Press, 1952, p. 7.
6. Stephen Kantrowitz, *Ben Tillman: And the Reconstruction of White Supremacy*. Chapel Hill: University of North Carolina Press, 2000, p. 53.
7. J. Morgan Kousser, *Colorblind Injustice: Minority Voting Rights and the Undoing of the Second Reconstruction*. Chapel Hill: University of North Carolina Press, 1999, p. 19.
8. Franklin and Moss, *From Slavery to Freedom*, p. 249.
9. Tindall, *South Carolina Negroes*, p. 69.
10. Mary L. Frech and William F. Swindler (eds.), *Chronology and Documentary Handbook of the State of Florida*. Dobbs Ferry, N.Y.: Oceana Publications, 1973.
11. Norman Pollack (ed.), *The Populist Mind*. New York: Bobbs-Merrill Company, 1967.
12. Hugh Talmage Lefler and Albert Ray Newsome, *North Carolina: The History of a Southern State*. Chapel Hill: University of North Carolina Press, 1963.
13. National Association for the Advancement of Colored People, "Thirty Years of Lynching in the United States," April 1919.
14. Charles Regan Wilson and William Ferris, *Encyclopedia of Southern Culture*. Chapel Hill: University of North Carolina Press, 1989, p. 175.
15. Franklin and Moss, *From Slavery to Freedom*, p. 261.
16. Ralph Eisenberg, "Virginia: The Emergence of Two-Party Politics," in William C. Harvard, (ed.), *The Changing Politics of the South*. Baton Rouge: Louisiana University Press, 1972, pp. 40–41.
17. Lucius J. Barker, Mack H. Jones, and Katherine Tate, *African Americans and the American Political System*. Upper Saddle River, N.J.: Prentice Hall, 1999, p. 123.

18. Louis R. Harlan (ed.), *The Booker T. Washington Papers,* Vol. 3. Urbana: University of Illinois Press, 1974, pp. 583–587.

19. Ralph McGill, *The South and the Southerner.* Boston: Little, Brown & Co., 1959, p. 129.

20. Barker, Jones, and Tate, *African Americans and the American Political System,* p. 221.

21. Francis B. Simkins and Charles P. Roland, *A History of the South.* New York: Alfred A. Knopf, 1972, p. 509.

22. Franklin and Moss, *From Slavery to Freedom,* p. 413.

23. Earl Black and Merle Black, *The Vital South.* Cambridge, Mass.: Harvard University Press, 1992, p. 95.

24. Southern Politics Collection, "Alabama," Vanderbilt University, Special Collections.

25. Ibid.

26. Ibid.

27. Ralph McGill, *The South and the Southerner,* p. 99.

28. Barker, Jones, and Tate, *African Americans and the American Political System,* p. 221.

29. Richard Kluger, *Simple Justice: The History of Brown v. Board of Education and Black America's Struggle for Equality.* New York: Alfred A. Knopf, 1976, p. 223.

30. Donald O. Dewey, *Union and Liberty: A Documentary History of American Constitutionalism.* New York: McGraw-Hill, 1969, p. 297.

31. Franklin and Moss, *From Slavery to Freedom,* p. 413.

32. Dewey, *Union and Liberty,* p. 298.

33. Richard A. Pride and J. David Woodard, *The Burden of Busing.* Knoxville: University of Tennessee Press, 1985.

34. Michael Belknap, *Federal Law and Southern Order.* Athens: University of Georgia Press, 1987, pp. 51–52.

35. Numan V. Bartley, *The Rise of Massive Resistance.* Baton Rouge: Louisiana State University Press, 1969, p. 341.

36. *Gayle v. Browder,* 352, US 903 (1956).

37. *Congressional Record,* 84th Congress Second Session, Vol. 102, part 4 (March 12, 1956). Washington, D.C.: Government Printing Office, 1956, pp. 4459–4460.

38. Eisenberg, "Virginia: The Emergence of Two-Party Politics," p. 51.

39. Jack Bass and Walter DeVries, *The Transformation of Southern Politics.* New York: New American Library, p. 346.

40. Virginius Dabney, *Virginia: The New Dominion.* Garden City, N.Y.: Doubleday & Company, pp. 535–544.

41. Bartley, *The Rise of Massive Resistance,* p. 83.

42. Neil R. McMillan, "Citizen's Councils," in Charles Wilson Reagan and William Ferris (eds.), *Encyclopedia of Southern Culture,* p. 203.

43. Bartley, *The Rise of Massive Resistance,* p. 340.

44. Robert A. Caro, *The Years of Lyndon Johnson: Master of the Senate.* New York: Alfred A. Knopf, 2002, p. 893.

45. Stephen K. Bailey, *Congress in the Seventies.* 2d ed. New York: St. Martin's Press, 1970, p. 67.

46. Clayborne Carson, *In Struggle: SNCC and the Black Awakening of the 1960s.* Cambridge, Mass.: Harvard University Press, 1969, pp. 9–18; Bryan Fulks, *Black Struggle.* New York: Laurel-Leaf Library, 1969, pp. 270–272.

47. Carson, *In Struggle,* p. 12.

48. Michael Lipsky, "Protest as a Political Resource," *American Political Science Review* 62 (December 1968): pp. 1144–1158.

49. In 1994 Byron De La Beckwith, a white supremacist, was convicted for the murder of Evers following two failed previous attempts.

50. Robert A. Caro, *The Years of Lyndon Johnson: Master of the Senate*, p. 716.

51. Richard E. Neustadt, *Presidential Power*. New York: John Wiley & Sons, 1960.

52. Bailey, *Congress in the Seventies*, pp. 63–82.

53. The US Supreme Court upheld the constitutionality of Congress using the interstate commerce clause to forbid discrimination in public accommodations in *Heart of Atlanta Motel v. United States* (1964). The regulation of interstate commerce was a right explicitly given Congress in Article I, Section 8 of the Constitution. Beginning with John Marshall's decision in the case of *Gibbons v. Ogden* (1824) the federal courts established the precedent of interpreting interstate commerce broadly, which provided the background for sections of the Civil Rights Act of 1964.

54. This tactic had been advocated for many years by Adam Clayton Powell, the black congressman from Harlem, New York.

55. Howell Raines, *My Soul Is Rested*. New York: Putnam, 1977, p. 371.

56. Chandler Davidson and Bernard Grofman (eds.), *Quiet Revolution in the South*. Princeton, N.J.: Princeton University Press, 1994, p. 31.

57. Ivan Allen Jr., Mayor of Atlanta, Hearings Before the US Senate, Committee on Commerce. *A Bill to Eliminate Discrimination in Public Accommodations Affecting Interstate Commerce*. Eighty-Eighth Congress, First Session, July 26, 1963, p. 867.

58. William Manchester, *The Glory and the Dream*. New York: Little, Brown, 1973, pp. 1079–1081.

59. David J. Garrow, *Bearing the Cross*. New York: Vintage Books, 1988, p. 572.

60. Ibid., p. 621.

61. Steven F. Lawson, *Black Ballots*. New York: Columbia University Press, 1976, p. 331.

62. Pride and Woodard, *The Burden of Busing*.

63. *University of California Regents v. Bakke*, 438, US 265 (1978).

64. James M. Glaser, *Race, Campaign Politics, and Realignment in the South*. New Haven: Yale University Press, 1996, p. 183.

65. David Lubin and Stephen Voss, "The Missing Middle: Why Media-Voter Theory Can't Save Democrats," *Journal of Politics* 65 (2003): pp. 227–237; Kenneth Shotts, "Does Racial Redistricting Cause Conservative Policy Outcomes? Policy Preferences of Southern Representatives in the 1980s and 1990s," *Journal of Politics* 65 (2003): pp. 216–226; Dewey Clayton, *Journal of Black Studies* 33 (2003): pp. 354–388.

66. Terrel Rhodes, *Republicans in the South: Voting for the State House, Voting for the White House*. Wesport, Conn.: Praeger, 2000, p. 2.

67. Steven F. Lawson, *Black Ballots*.

68. Joint Center for Political and Economic Studies, *National Roster of Black Elected Officials, 1970, 1980, 1990*. Washington, D.C.: Joint Center for Political and Economic Studies. David A. Bositis, *Black Elected Officials: A Statistical Summary, 1999*. Washington, D.C.: Joint Center for Political and Economic Studies, 2000.

69. *The Economist*, January 25, 2003, p. 37.

70. *The Economist*, August 14, 2004.

71. Charles S. Bullock III and M.V. Hood III, "Tracing the Evolution of Hispanic Political Emergence in the Deep South." Paper presented at the biennial Citadel Symposium on Southern Politics, March 4–5, 2004, Charleston, South Carolina.

72. Kenneth D. Wald and Ted G. Jelen, "Religion and Political Socialization in

Context: A Regional Comparison of the Political Attitudes of American Jews." Paper presented at the biennial Citadel Symposium on Southern Politics, March 4–5, 2004, Charleston, South Carolina.

73. Elizabeth Spencer, "The Gulf Coast," in Suzanne W. Jones (ed.), *Growing Up in the South: An Anthology of Modern Southern Literature*. New York: Signet Classics of Penguin Books, p. 9.

74. John Shelton Reed, *The Enduring South: Subcultural Persistence in Mass Society*. Chapel Hill: University of North Carolina Press, 1986, p. 92.

75. Susan A. MacManus, "Demographic Shifts: The Old South Morphs Into the New." Paper presented at the biennial Citadel Symposium on Southern Politics, March 4–5, 2004, Charleston, South Carolina.

76. "Nativism," in Charles W. Reagan (ed.), *The Encyclopedia of Southern Culture*, p. 417.

77. Edward G. Carmines and James A. Stimson, *Issue Evolution: Race and the Transformation of American Politics*. Princeton, N.J.: Princeton University Press, 1989, p. 137.

78. This is the argument of Jeffrey M. Stonecash, *Class and Party in American Politics*. Boulder, Colo.: Westview Press, 2000.

5

Religion and Southern Politics

On Friday, July 10, 1925 an accepted assumption of small town southern life came under national scrutiny. John Scopes, a young biology teacher at a public high school, was brought to trial to test the legitimacy of Tennessee's newly passed anti-evolution law. Scopes was accused of violating the statute by teaching evolution in his classroom. The case ballooned into one of the great media events of the twentieth century, with the South under as much scrutiny as any legal statute.

Dayton, Tennessee, was a small community of some 2,000 people in the eastern part of the state. Days there were typical of places all across the South. The social interaction in such communities revolved around churches, where religious life was synonymous with family life. James Agee wrote of living in these times in his masterpiece, *A Death in the Family*, set in nearby Knoxville, ten years earlier. In one scene a female character relates that, "God showed her only what she knew already: that come what might she must . . . trust in God . . . put my trust in Him."[1]

The faith exemplified in Agee's character saturated virtually every southern town, and the Scopes trial exposed it to national inspection. The theme of the coverage at the time was a clash between two worlds: that of the rural South, opposite the emerging secular and sophisticated, urbane and humanistic nation. The southern agrarian and religious ideal was personified by William Jennings Bryan, the "Great Commoner" from Nebraska, who was a defeated presidential candidate and Christian believer. Opposite him were Clarence Darrow and a host of New York and Chicago intellectuals and secular sophisticates.

The legal question at issue in the trial was the state legislature's right to establish a school curriculum, a point lost in the press coverage. Scopes admitted after the trial that he probably missed teaching the chapter on evolution anyway. It didn't matter. "Darrow's aim at Dayton was to discredit fundamentalists, and, with the help of his friend, H. L. Mencken, he did that in a famous bit of testimony that was never heard by the jury or entered into the trial record."[2] Darrow asked Bryan, "Did you ever discover where Cain got his wife?" and the Great Commoner replied, "I never tried to find out." Under Darrow's sharp questioning it became clear that Bryan had not thought carefully about many of his views of biblical literalism.

The most widely publicized misdemeanor case in US history ended with neither side claiming victory. As a result of the Scopes trial, the anti-evolutionary law "became a symbol of pride and regional identity."[3] By popular referendum the people of Arkansas enacted the region's third anti-evolution statute in 1928; Louisiana followed soon after, and Texas barred the mention of it in state-approved textbooks. School boards throughout the South imposed limits on teaching evolution, and such restrictions enjoyed widespread support in local communities.

The Scopes trial showed that few things are more critical to the life of a culture than its definition of the sacred. Yet, as Rodney Stark has written, "it is [hard] to understand why Gods were long ago banished from the social-scientific study of religion."[4] Textbooks on US politics regularly conclude that religion is not, and never has been, a significant factor in the development of US political institutions. Secular scholarship ruled religion in decline in advanced industrial societies, and ignored its influence in the political realm.

Yet religion has emerged as an important political factor in US politics, and especially in the study of southern politics. "Religious groups may take the initiative in political action, but they may also react to the decisions of government and other political actors."[5] Since government now has more regulatory power to establish policies that affect the major functions of religious groups, the faithful have responded when they felt threatened. This is especially true in the South, which has a feisty independence wedded to a fierce piety. That streak was readily apparent in the Scopes trial.

The image of the South suffered when the trial ended, and the comparison was stark: backwoods, half-educated yokels and crackpot preachers versus cultured urban modernists, skeptical of revealed religion. The conservative, Protestant Christian religion was an understood cultural norm in every southern community, and church life sustained countless social customs. Local politics, community benevolence, and the standards of courtship and marriage all involved some aspect of church affiliation. Eudora Welty spoke for generations of writers when she said, "[we] were blessed in one way or another; if not blessed alike . . . by the King James version of the Bible. . . . Its cadence entered into our ears and memories for good . . . the evidence, or the ghost of it, lingers in all our books."[6] The "Bible Belt" lifestyle was unquestioned as a way of right living, and accepted by both black and white Southerners. But in 1925 H. L. Mencken denounced Christianity as a "childish theology founded upon hate," and its fundamentalist adherents as "rustic ignoramuses" who knew nothing "that was not in Genesis."[7]

Mencken's dispatches from Dayton were syndicated across the country, and depicted Southerners in a way that affects generations to this very day. "In the trial by public opinion and the press, it was clear that the twentieth century, the cities, and the universities had won a resounding victory, and that the country, the South, and the fundamentalists were guilty as charged."[8] Within five years, despite strong feelings by many Americans that evolutionary teaching was wrong, all legislation forbidding its being taught in the public schools was repealed.

The trial highlighted one of the most important aspects of southern life, and one intimately connected to politics and elections in the region. The affinity for Protestant fundamentalism was, and remains, an abiding trait of life in the South. The term "fundamentalism" comes from a series of pamphlets published from 1910 onwards entitled, "The Fundamentals: A Testimony of Truth." They represented a reaction to two tendencies in Protestant denominations: (1) a rationalizing of the faith with "higher criticism" to play down the supernatural aspects of Christianity and appeal to the modern scientific mind, and (2) a replacement of concern with personal righteousness by a desire to improve life in the social and political world.

Both black and white evangelicals in the South believed that social improvement came from individual conversion and regeneration. In the black community religion fostered a civic culture of protection that supported civic activism like voter drives and campaign activism, as well as protest and criticism of existing institutions. A study of black activism during the civil rights protests of the 1960s found that mainstream protest was supported from the pulpit. A survey in 1984, the same year that Jesse Jackson campaigned for the presidency, found that 60 percent of African Americans reported that they were encouraged to vote at their place of worship, and 10 percent reportedly worked for a political candidate through religious institutions. In the contours of Afro-Christianity, "life is a struggle, but we have something within us that tells us we are more than what is seen on the outside."[9]

Both black and white churchgoers believed religion was always "better felt than telt," to quote the Scottish proverb. Their acceptance of the Bible, and its application to everyday living, was—and remains—the single best explanation for the predominantly conservative, traditional heritage of southern beliefs and values. Fundamentalist Southerners insist that the Bible is the word of God, that miracles really did happen, and that a convert must be "born again." A key to understanding southern politics is to grasp this fact of life about the region south of the Potomac River.

In 1947 a party official in Florida was asked why counties in the state, usually reliably Democratic, suddenly reversed themselves and went 75 percent for Republican Herbert Hoover in 1928. He had a one-word reply: Catholicism.[10] The religious affiliation of the Democratic nominee, Alfred E. Smith, was enough to send most of the party's loyalists scurrying to the other side. In the words of Michael Barone about the southeastern states, "[they are] one of the most religious places on the planet."[11] Churches in the South were so much a part of the community as to be indistinguishable from it. In mocking God and revealed religion, Clarence Darrow—and the rest of the nation—was holding the South up for ridicule.

Southerners were historic Newtonians; they believed in absolute, unchanging laws of science—physical as well as moral laws. When Jefferson spoke of the "laws of nature and nature's God" in the Declaration of Independence he asserted an absolute truth on which Christians and Deists could agree. One hundred eighty years later, when Martin Luther King Jr. preached from the prophet Amos and declared, "let justice roll down like a river, righteousness like a never-failing stream," he appealed to an audience that believed the same thing. Finally, in 1973 when North Carolina senator Sam Ervin spoke as chair of the Senate Select Committee on Presidential Campaign Activities investigating the Watergate scandal, he said the laws of God in the seventh verse of the sixth chapter of Galatians declared: "Be not deceived. God is not mocked; for whatsoever a man soweth, that shall he also reap."[12] Such was Sam Ervin's, and the South's, verdict on the misdeeds of Richard Nixon even though many had voted for him. God-given, absolute, unchanging laws revealed through scripture characterized life in *both* the white and black culture of the South.

Across the rest of the country absolute laws of social and ethical morality were coming in for criticism and abuse. In the 1870s and 1880s it became clear to many religious leaders that the Enlightenment's trust in human reason and science was a better guide to cultural enrichment and religious affection than the literal dictates of scripture. The modernism of the time resonated with the biology of Charles Darwin, the philosophy of William James and John Dewey, the "new" history of James Harvey Robinson and Charles Beard, and the physics of Albert Einstein.[13] The secular view argued that the present humanistic world was infinitely wiser than the biblical one of prophets, burning bushes, and missionary journeys. The rest of the country longed for the South to join them in the twentieth century. But many Southerners would not leave their traditional ways; instead they sought a separate identity in what they saw as the apostate nation.

Southern White Evangelicals

Conservative Protestant Christianity, and its followers in the South, did pass through a wilderness after the Scopes trial, but they did not enter the grave.[14] The major Protestant denominations split into mainstream and fundamentalist camps. In the South the latter outnumbered the former. Even though Christian arguments for reality and morality were rejected by many leading minds in the universities of the country, such notions remained a vital part of southern life. After losing a number of public battles, including the rejection of biblical inerrancy by the Presbyterian Church, the religious conservatives regrouped.[15] They formed independent denominations, Bible churches, parachurch and revivalist organizations. They did not stop at church formation, but built their own schools, Bible colleges, and hospitals, and launched a myriad of newspaper and religious publications.

Much of the rest of the country wrote off biblical literalism as incompatible with modernity. Mainstream culture saw the South as an anomaly, and believed that secularism would eventually spread with educational opportunity and economic improvement. In spite of these forecasts, the South stubbornly refused to change. Evangelical ministers kept their congregations together and launched a critique of modernity using the most modern form of communication: radio.

Charles Fuller, and his *Old Fashioned Revival Hour*, was the model of this response. In 1939, his program was heard over 152 stations on the Mutual Broadcasting System, reaching an audience of some ten million listeners. Four years later Fuller's broadcast was heard on over 1,000 stations, and his gospel association was buying 50 percent more radio time than the secular client in second place. Radio evangelists reached a large and sympathetic audience in the small communities and farms of the South. Radio was the most popular form of communication and family entertainment on the farm, connecting rural homes and communities together in a seamless web of worship.

The religious programs were a comfort in a part of the country mired in the Depression and away from the tides of change that were sweeping urban areas. The denunciation of secularism, and its resistance by the faithful, became a hallmark of conservative Protestant sermons heard on the radio and preached in southern pulpits. For many in the region the crusade against modernity was a central element of their faith. "Modernism and the theory of evolution, they were convinced, had caused the catastrophe [of World War I] by undermining the Biblical foundations of American civilization."[16]

In the South, modernity was labeled as a movement to abandon religious ideas for the acceptance of the secular culture. They believed that liberal reformers in the North saw God's hand in cultural improvement, not in individual salvation. Conservative preachers, on the other hand, responded that the survival of civilization was their principal concern, and there was no hope for cultural renewal except in a return to the Christian faith and its collateral principles. For Bible-believing evangelicals, the Nietzsche-inspired Third Reich in Germany, and the emperor worship of Japan, were prime examples of non-Christian belief. In the case of Europe, modernity was seen as a prelude to outright apostasy. The world crisis caused people to return to organized religion as a source of comfort and faith, and the southern fundamental churches grew in influence and power as a result.

The conservative churches were concerned about the modern world, but they were also concerned with the modern state. In the dictatorships of World War II they saw increasing centralization of political institutions and state domination of public life. They feared government encroachment at home, and the growth of the state made it increasingly difficult for them to worship without simultaneously addressing the evils of the political control of modernity.

In 1941 a number of conservative churches, alarmed at the continuing advance of perceived state-sponsored secularism, joined to form the American Council of Christian Churches (ACCC). The next year, a larger body of evangelicals, also disturbed over mainstream church infidelity and growing secularism, formed the National Association of Evangelicals (NAE). At first these organizations avoided taking political stands, but they gradually shifted from an emphasis on individual spiritual experience to an indictment of secular culture, communism, and the diminished regard for the Bible in the values of general culture.[17]

After World War II, the conservative evangelical Christian groups organized to broadcast the gospel and confront the culture. On Memorial Day in 1945, as the first troops made their way home from Europe after the German surrender, a Youth for Christ (YFC) rally was held in Chicago where seventy thousand young people gathered on Soldier Field. Their preacher was Billy Graham, a man with southern roots, who rose in prominence at YFC rallies and soon became the featured evangelist. During the 1950s the Billy Graham Evangelistic Association held crusades throughout the country, and later in locations all around the world. The collective result of this effort was to move southern evangelicalism from the backwaters of neglect into the mainstream of culture. Religious conservatism was a respectable belief on the postwar national stage basking in the glow of US military virtue, victory, and exceptionalism.

Insofar as YFC had a political orientation, it was largely conservative, and gradually elements of anticommunism, mixed with the impending arrival of a righteous millennium judgment, crept into the preaching. The revivalists regarded communism as an unvarnished evil, "anti-God, anti-Christ, and anti-American." From the 1960s forward, numerous conservative politicians sought to align themselves with the fundamentalist Christian crusades. "Primarily because he was a Southerner, he registered to vote as a Democrat," but Billy Graham's most lasting effects were with Republicans: Eisenhower, Nixon, and later, Reagan.[18] His association with conservatives in the GOP was a major influence on the decision of many white middle-class southern churchgoers to abandon their decades-old allegiance to the Democratic Party, and vote Republican, at least at the presidential level. Graham shot to the top of the "Most Admired Americans" list and his advice mattered in the 1960s, which was a time of sit-ins, pray-ins, boycotts, pickets, and rioting on a scale not seen before in US history.

In the 1960 presidential election, evangelical preachers warned their congregations not to vote for John Kennedy's Catholic theology or his liberal politics. Even after his important talk in Houston, Texas, where Kennedy directly addressed the issue of his religion, opposition "was more open in the South, [and] it was felt in all sections."[19] Lyndon Johnson helped carry many southern states for the Democrats in 1960, but conservatives in the party soon objected more to Kennedy's New Frontier policies than his religion.

After the JFK victory, the evangelical response was not to mix religion with politics, but the decade didn't cooperate with that separation for long. The Food and Drug Administration (FDA) soon approved "the Pill," a female oral contracep-

Vignette 5.1   Reverend Billy Graham (1918–)

Reverend Billy Graham is the best-known Protestant preacher in the United States. He has spoken to more than 200 million people worldwide in his many crusades. Graham was a confidant of ten US presidents, and former president George H. W. Bush called him "America's pastor."

William Franklin "Billy" Graham was born on November 7, 1918, in Charlotte, North Carolina. When Graham was fifteen years old he fell under the influence of a spellbinding evangelist named Mordecai Ham, and later was deeply influenced by another evangelist from Alabama, named Jimmie Johnson. He was converted in 1936 at Bob Jones College, and subsequently enrolled at Wheaton College outside Chicago for further training. There he met and married Ruth Bell, the daughter of China medical missionaries. They were married in 1943 a few months after graduation, and Graham became pastor of a small church in Chicago.

In Chicago Graham was introduced to broadcast evangelism and, in 1947, issued his first book, *Calling Youth to Christ.* In the summer of 1949 he became nationally famous after an evangelistic campaign in Los Angeles. As his evangelistic career blossomed, Graham instituted practices to give his efforts a high degree of integrity and financial accountability. In 1950 he began a half-hour radio program, and two years later began a newspaper column, "My Answer," which was syndicated in newspapers nationally.

Throughout the 1950s Graham conducted numerous crusades around the world, and helped fund a leading evangelical magazine, *Christianity Today,* in 1955. As television became more widespread, he adopted the new medium into his crusades. The visual broadcasts opened doors for Graham to meet powerful US political figures, and he met privately with many world and national leaders.

By the 1960s Graham was such a public figure that his actions took on a political cast. He was criticized during these years for failing to use his status more aggressively for social causes. Graham met privately with Dr. Martin Luther King Jr. and together the men shared their optimism about the potential for a series of crusades that would convert racially mixed audiences. Billy Graham insisted that his evangelical meetings be open to all people as a symbol of the importance of racial equality. The evangelist worked behind the scenes to lower racial tension in cities across the South. A few months after the bombing of the Sixteenth Street Baptist Church in Birmingham, he held a nonsegregated crusade in the city. These efforts were not enough to quiet his foes, who criticized him for accommodating nonbelievers and for not doing enough for civil rights.

Throughout his career Graham tried to avoid political issues, such as race and war, but sometimes his involvement with political leaders has been costly. In 1960 he supported Richard Nixon for the presidency, and endorsed him again in 1968 and 1972. Graham was often a guest at Nixon White House gatherings, and considered himself something of a confidant of the president. After the Watergate scandal, however, Graham realized that Nixon had used him as a pious screen to hide the administration's wrongdoings. Embarrassed, Graham withdrew from the political arena.

Billy Graham's influence might be worldwide, but he remains a peculiar American, and a distinctly southern figure. His rise from a North Carolina farm boy to become a companion of presidents, his simple faith and unvarnished record are a model of southern values endemic to the region. In the 1990s the aging Graham gradually reduced his schedule and placed his son, Franklin, in a position to succeed him following his death.

tive that reduced a significant barrier to nonmarital sex. In 1962 the Supreme Court banned state-sponsored prayer and Bible reading in public schools and for the first time religious conservatives sensed that power was being redistributed to the opponents of traditional Christian values. In their eyes the liberal welfare state itself became the single most important advocate of secularism in the society.

The 1960s brought a new set of challenges to southern churchgoers. They were confronted with the hypocrisy of racial separation, the unquestioned support of US foreign policy in places like Vietnam, and the sex education curriculum—with banned public prayer—in local schools. The issue of greatest moral consequence, and the one that sparked the most dramatic political confrontations of the decade, was racial.

Prior to 1963 Birmingham, Alabama, was a city with a split personality. On the one hand was the sobriquet designated by the city chamber of commerce as the "City of Churches," and on the other was the "Bombingham" designation for the number of racial incidents in the city since the end of World War II. In the spring of 1963 it became a battleground of the conscience. The rhetoric on both sides was laced with Christian symbols. Black protesters were "tearing down the walls of a racial Jericho," led by a modern-day prophet, Reverend Martin Luther King Jr. White resistance was justified as a biblically mandated injunction against race mixing, communism, and the Eastern religion of Ghandi. Protest leaders were accused of being communist infiltrators, and the nonviolence that guided their precepts was described as the first rumblings of a Soviet takeover. The mixture of religion and politics was complete when black believers showed up in white churches on Sunday morning to partake of communion. The ritual of Sunday morning church attendance, taken for granted by residents as a part of everyday life in the region, now became political theater.

Southern religious habits came in for national scrutiny in the televised civil rights demonstrations; once again the comparisons were not favorable. Private schools across the South were classified as "resegregation academies." Even when parents and administrators said they enrolled their children in private schools for religious reasons, the suspicion was that their explanations masked a deeper racial animus. The private school movement in the South was not seen as a reaction to cultural change, but as a subterfuge for racial exclusion.

The decade of the 1960s (and the early 1970s) was a time of increasing controversy and acrimony with religious language used to both integrate the schools and oppose integration; support the war in Vietnam, and protest it; and to advocate equality for women, yet say that their God-given place was in the home. In the last years of the decade the concern among conservative Christian churchgoers was more with the drift of US culture than any racial animosity. The Warren Court gradually lifted prohibitions against books, movies, and other materials previously banned or restricted as obscene. The Supreme Court's decision prohibiting organized prayer in schools set in motion a reaction to the values of the public schools.

Moral clarity, and the stimulus for involvement by religious conservatives in politics, came in a Supreme Court decision the next decade. In 1973 the Court ruled in *Roe v. Wade* that state abortion statutes were illegal. Most European countries provided abortion free and justified it when undertaken for reasons of health. The United States went down a different path, declaring abortion a constitutional right. It would be hard to design a way of legalizing abortion that could stir up more controversy. *Roe v. Wade* did as much as anything else to make US politics what it is today. Until the 1960s, politics was defined by a combination of economic issues and the legacy of government involvement beginning with the New Deal. Republicans were rooted in the business and professional elites; the Democrats were rooted in the trade unions, the urban political machines, and the ethnic minorities. White Southerners of all classes voted Democratic. The Republican Party was headquartered in the Yankee northeast and the agricultural Midwest.

But after 1973, social values started to trump economic issues. Abortion, like civil rights, began to redefine politics. The *Roe* decision legalized abortion on demand and excluded the unborn from the definition of "persons" protected by the Fourteenth Amendment. Shocked out of their sleep by the *Roe* decision, countless religious conservatives attacked what they saw as the moral and social crisis of their time. When roused, they were ready to join other conservatives who had been active ever since the failed Goldwater campaign of 1964, and together they would become the "New Religious Right."

"Of all the shifts and surprises in contemporary political life, perhaps none was so wholly unexpected as the political resurgence of evangelical Protestantism in the 1970s."[20] The abortion issue helped drive millions of northern Catholics and southern evangelicals into the Republican Party. A Gallup poll taken in the spring of the year after the *Roe* decision found that the South was leading the country in opposition to abortion.

Gallup Poll
March 8–11, 1974

Question: Do you favor or oppose the Supreme Court ruling on abortion?

	Favor	Oppose
East	52%	40%
Midwest	41%	49%
West	59%	29%
South	29%	52%

After the initial decision, abortion gradually became a more accepted part of the US social culture. Yet support for it always lagged in the South. The *Roe* decision cited an implicit constitutional right to privacy, and lit a smoldering fire of resentment that ignited the southern evangelical community to oppose state expansion of any implied constitutional rights. The Court set loose a string of subsequent rulings such as: whether constitutional provisions should be extended to protect homosexuals, the permissive distribution and protection of pornography, and the constitutional debate that galvanized southern voters in a way no individual ever could—the equality of women.[21]

The South regularly showed the least amount of enthusiasm for these new cultural initiatives. As the decade of the 1970s drew to a close, the statistics told a tale of cultural change unlike any imagined by a southern preacher. During the decade, divorce increased 67 percent, families headed by unwed mothers rose 356 percent, and 17 percent of all children were born out of wedlock.[22] For Southerners the numbers were proof positive of governmental apostasy. For them the solution to all these problems was a restoration of traditional morality, and the bedrock location of that ethic was in southern churches.

The shift in politics from classic issues of economics and foreign policy, to deep-seated moral and religious values was diagnosed by a sociologist in 1991 who traced the roots of the discord back to the disruption of the 1970s. James Davidson Hunter, in his book *Culture Wars*, defined the new conflict as one between *orthodox* notions of traditional family and community based on a transcendent authoritative truth, and *progressive* notions that adopt changing patterns in culture as a way of adapting modernity to a new form.[23] The crisis of cultural authority in the United States was a collision between the two worldviews.

Confessing evangelical Christians in the South saw themselves as members of the *orthodox* camp. They rushed into the public square to restructure US civic values, politics, and the culture at large. Preachers in the South came to the forefront of the emerging conservative religious crusade to defend traditional values. Among the newly prominent spokesmen of the emerging movement were: Jerry Falwell, Charles Stanley, James Robison, Pat Robertson, D. James Kennedy, and Jim Bakker. Reverend Billy Graham was a silent partner in the coalition. What they all had in common, aside from offering political commentary on social issues with their preaching, was that they were each based in a southern state. Falwell was a lifelong resident of Lynchburg, Virginia; Charles Stanley was in Atlanta; James Robison's church was in the Dallas–Fort Worth area; Pat Robertson was in Virginia Beach; D. James Kennedy was in Florida; Jim Bakker was in Charlotte; and Billy Graham was from North Carolina.

The new "televangelists," as they were called, might differ on issues of religious doctrine, but they agreed that the source of moral decline was "secular humanism," defined as the imposition of secular views on the private enclaves of the faithful. The term had an amorphous meaning, but its focus became the government-sponsored programs that denied transcendent moral principles and substituted conventional values in their place. Since much of this imposition came with the imprint of government, in schools, regulatory rulings, and judicial mandates, the new conservative religious advocates thought the best solution was to get government into the hands of believers who supported traditional moral values. For this to happen, evangelical Christians in the South—the proponents of the orthodox vision—had to set aside their inhibitions against involvement in politics and seek out candidates for support.

The Carter Presidency

The presidential election of 1976, celebrating the US bicentennial, was an ideal opportunity for southern "born-again" Christians to influence US politics in a dramatic way. For the first time in a long time, they could elect one of their own to office. Jimmy Carter seemed to be just the right man at the right time. He was as southern as sunshine on peaches, and his life experiences resonated with millions of native voters. On the back of his campaign biography, *Why Not the Best?,* he described himself as a former governor of Georgia, farmer, engineer, naval officer, nuclear physicist, Christian, and American. Early in the book Carter recalled his growing-up years in Plains, Georgia, "and each Sunday we attended Plains Baptist Church, where my father was a Sunday school teacher."[24]

Carter was not retiring about his religious beliefs, but he did not wear them on his sleeve either. When reporters asked him about his religion, he patiently explained his conversion, the "born-again" Christianity of which he was an advocate, and why he believed religious faith was a valuable asset in politics. Jimmy Carter seemed to be the answer conservative evangelical voters needed to restore the country to its roots, and halt the slide of secular culture. Numerous southern religious leaders, from Martin Luther King Sr. to Pat Robertson, endorsed Carter for president.

Carter won the election of 1976 because he accidentally touched two strands of future conservative power: the Sunbelt economic base and Protestant evangelicals. The Democratic Party was not comfortable with either cord, and after a while, neither was Carter. Religious conservatives were roundly attacked by the administration for brazenly entering the political arena, and then expecting rewards. One member of the White House staff at the time quipped that applications for jobs in the administration had to be reprinted with two questions: "What year were you born?" and "What year were you born again?" Evangelicals responded with a defense that their activities should follow the pattern of grassroots political activism established in the 1960s.

Soon, there were indications that southern support for Jimmy Carter might be premature, and he might not be the great hope white evangelicals envisioned. In October of 1976 candidate Carter gave a long interview to *Playboy* magazine that received national media attention. Reverend Jerry Falwell heard of the interview and criticized Carter for granting the favor of an exclusive to such a magazine as *Playboy.* Much to his surprise, Falwell received a phone call from Jody Powell, Carter's special assistant, demanding that the minister refrain from such public criticism of the candidate. Falwell was surprised, and a little pleased, that what he had said caused such a stir with a presidential contender. Michael Cromartie suggests "that the revival of conservative Protestant political involvement, at least for its fundamentalist wing, began with a single phone call."[25]

Once in office Jimmy Carter was a disappointment to those who thought he would promote conservative Christians to visible offices. The southern evangelicals who supported him found that he did not press for action on social issues like school prayer and abortion. No sooner had he won the nomination than the insurgent feminist wing of the party demanded a change in his personal abortion position and demanded support for the Equal Rights Amendment. The 1976 Democratic Party platform, the first written since the controversial *Roe* decision, was vague and recognized the legitimacy of both pro-life and pro-choice views.

To conservatives Carter seemed powerless to stop the groups who disagreed with his southern constituency. The president advocated passage of the Equal Rights Amendment, did not condemn homosexual unions as valid expressions of family life, and kept up federal funding of abortion. The White House Conference on Families ended with spokesman Jody Powell giving an expansive definition of a family and concluding, "when Jimmy Carter spoke of family and healing wounds and divisions and so forth, he was thinking of family in that broad sense."[26]

Evangelicals in the South did not share the sentiment. They believed the definition of family was clear in scripture, and they did not think any US president could change it. The failure of Jimmy Carter, one of their own, to substantiate the meaning of the word "family" proved that the evangelical trust in him was unwarranted. When the time came for re-election, the Bible-quoting Baptist president lost the support of the Bible-believing voters in the South.

The final break came in 1978 when the Carter administration tightened standards for the tax-exempt status of church-operated schools, requiring that the percentage of a school's student body drawn from racial minorities be increased. Many private schools were in the South, and, while most of them were integrated twenty years after the *Brown* decision, they resented federal intrusion into the makeup of their student body and advice on the character of their curriculum. The disillusionment with Carter was a perfect opportunity for the conservative religious right strategists to bring together an alliance of Protestant fundamentalists, Catholic right-to-lifers, and independent Christians with opposition to abortion as the litmus issue.

Ralph Reed, who would become a Christian activist in the succeeding decade, recalls a visit Jimmy and Rosalynn Carter made to Atlanta to campaign for the Equal Rights Amendment in 1980. To pacify feminists in the Democratic Party, Carter called members of the state Senate off the floor so he could lobby them personally, or have them call him on the telephone. Georgia insiders knew that the amendment was destined for defeat in Georgia. The outcome was a foregone conclusion, but Carter faced a tough primary battle with Ted Kennedy, and he needed to show the activist feminists in the Democratic Party that he was committed to their agenda.[27]

Ronald Reagan, George H. W. Bush, and the New Religious Right

The organized Religious Right that burst into public consciousness before the 1980 election had been developing for a very long time. The movement was originally a loose and poorly articulated collection of TV evangelists, renegade mainline clergymen, coordinating committees, and conservative political activists. A clear organizational structure emerged from three organizations: Christian Voice, a coalition of several pro-family groups on the West Coast led by author-lecturer Hal Lindsey and actor Pat Boone; Religious Roundtable, a group of prominent Southern Baptist pastors and related evangelicals, who sponsored a number of workshops for pastors; and Moral Majority, founded by Jerry Falwell, which was a collection of independent, fundamentalist and mainline ministers concerned about the drift of the country. All three groups were active in fundraising, campaign mailings, and the establishment of opposition research and position papers in 1979.

One writer recalls that the Christian Right was originally begun by Richard Viguerie, Paul Weyrich, and Howard Phillips, two Catholics and a Jew, who were politically active before the 1980 election. "They saw the possibility of a conservative movement based on social and moral issues."[28] Together they persuaded Jerry Falwell, a popular fundamentalist Baptist minister in Lynchburg, Virginia, to lead an organization they named the Moral Majority.

The groups of the Religious Right worked on a number of related fronts, but they had one geographic base: the South was home for them all. Virginia was the base for Falwell's Moral Majority, and Pat Robertson's massive Christian Broadcasting Network, affiliated with Christian Voice, was a neighbor in Virginia Beach. Falwell and Robertson had doctrinal and theological differences with one another, but they were in agreement that the cultural crisis had reached the boiling point.

The Religious Roundtable began as a meeting in a hotel near the Dallas–Fort Worth airport where leaders like Billy Graham, Charles Stanley, Adrian Rogers, Pat Robertson, and Rex Humbard met to discuss the need for a united response to address the crisis in government and its marginalization of evangelicalism. The decision to hold training sessions for pastors, who attended the meeting at D-FW airport, foreshadowed a visible presence in the upcoming presidential election. One minister after another took a microphone during the meeting to complain about the Carter presidency and its effect on life in their community. Newspaper columnist Bob Novak attended a "Campaign Training Conference" for ministers in Georgia and concluded that "Jimmy Carter's goose was cooked because I saw the intensity of these people."[29] As late as 1965 Jerry Falwell had castigated his fellow clergy for taking part in the march at Selma, Alabama. Now ministers who had earlier disdained politics took the lead in educating their congregations about the evils of "secular humanism," and the responsibility Christians had to be active in the public arena.

Francis Schaeffer, a pastor who wrote extensively during this period, authored a best-selling book entitled *A Christian Manifesto* that argued, "the State must be made to feel the presence of the Christian community."[30] In the 1970s it did. Members of the Christian Right believed their moral attitudes were closer to the preferences of the majority of Americans, and more mainstream than those in evidence on movie screens, television sets, and in classrooms of state universities. They believed that a liberal elite controlled the federal government, the national media, and the great research universities. This combination of secular humanist values and concentrated power was thwarting their conservative agenda.[31]

Jerry Falwell, for one, thought the first responsibility of the newly organized Christians was to get their name and agenda recognized by voters before the 1980 election. Falwell's public campaign made him the subject of countless television interviews and shifted the spotlight of media attention to the cultural agenda. His visibility reduced the newsworthiness of related efforts like those of the Religious Roundtable. A Gallup poll in December of 1980 found that "40 percent of a national sample had heard of the Moral Majority . . . the surveys taken in the South and southwest found levels of recognition almost twice the national figure."[32] Congregations and pastors associated with the Religious Right preached on the subject of cultural decay, they registered voters in the narthex of their churches, and assisted in the distribution of literature to church members in the weeks before the election. Objective estimates were that the Religious Right registered about two million voters, many of them for the first time, prior to the 1980 election.

As the November deadline approached, Ronald Reagan seemed an unlikely hero for the New Christian Right. He was divorced and remarried, his performance as a parent was suspect, and he won fame and fortune in the movie and television industries, regularly vilified for their contribution to moral decay. As governor of California he signed into law a liberal abortion statute, he was not a regular churchgoer, and his tax return showed that he contributed less than 1 percent of his income to charitable and religious causes. Reagan connected with the southern constituency even though he was taciturn about his Christian beliefs. When asked if he was "born-again" the former California governor responded by giving his church affiliation and asking the questioner to pray for him.

What Reagan did have was a feel for evangelical believers that Carter lacked. Maybe it was his Disciples of Christ churchgoing background, or his mother's legacy of regular instruction from the Bible. Whatever it was, Reagan was the one candidate who seemed able to speak directly and effectively to the newly empowered born-again constituency. A Gallup poll in September of 1980 found that "more than half of the evangelicals said they were more likely to vote for a candidate who shared their religious convictions."[33] While all three men in the presidential race—

John Anderson, Ronald Reagan, and Jimmy Carter—claimed to be Christians, only Reagan could offer a conservative economic agenda, a "standing tall" foreign policy, and convictions similar to the evangelicals on the crucial social issues. To conservatives in the South, Ronald Reagan had policies to go along with his public witness.[34]

The Republican platform that year reflected the conservative ideologues in public display and the influence of the New Religious Right. Gone was the earlier support for the Equal Rights Amendment, and in its place was a plank supporting a constitutional amendment to outlaw abortion and a recommendation that opposition to abortion be a prerequisite for any federal judgeship. In contrast to earlier GOP conventions, this one had few ideological victims bleeding in the aisles after votes on the new platform. The Reagan campaign team constantly played the role of healer and party unifier among diverse groups, and while many thought the final platform too conservative, the party as a whole was able to unite behind the nominee. The new tenor of presidential politics was set at the end of Reagan's acceptance speech, when the standard bearer asked for a moment of silent prayer, and then closed with a benediction, "God Bless America."

Any lingering doubts about Ronald Reagan's support from the Religious Right vanished when he came to Dallas's Reunion Arena on August 21, 1980, to address the Religious Roundtable. Seventeen thousand people filled the seats, along with fifty to sixty million television viewers gathered to hear the speech by the then nominee destined to be called the "Great Communicator." Reagan opened by stating the obvious: "I know this event is nonpartisan, so you can't endorse me, but I want you to know that I endorse you." To an audience used to hearing fiery evangelists, Reagan warmed their hearts with an endorsement of tuition tax credits, his complaint that the Supreme Court had expelled "God from the classroom," and his observation that everybody in favor of abortion had already been born. At the end of the speech Reagan invoked his legendary storytelling ability to say that if shipwrecked on an island and able to choose but one book to read for the rest of his life, he would choose the Bible. The speech brought thunderous applause in Dallas and established the GOP nominee as the candidate with values like those of conservative white Christian voters.[35]

Before the election, major media pundits and election forecasters predicted a contest too close to call. The experts assumed the undecided voters would split down the middle. They didn't. Democratic voters defected to Reagan in unprecedented numbers. Every southern state but Jimmy Carter's beloved Georgia went for Ronald Reagan in 1980. The effects of this election on subsequent presidential races are seen in Table 5.1, which shows US presidential electoral vote by party from 1952 until 2004. Before 1980 the South was almost perfectly competitive, with the Republicans holding a very slight 51 percent to 49 percent advantage when electoral votes were at stake for president. Since 1980 the region has given 88 percent of its electoral vote to the GOP, including total loyalty in 1984, 1988, 2000,

Table 5.1 US Presidential Vote by Party Affiliation

	1952	1956	1960	1964	1968[a]	1972	1976	1980	1984	1988	1992	1996	2000	2004
National States														
Georgia	D	D	D	R	AI	R	D	D	R	R	D	R	R	R
Florida	R	R	R	D	R	R	D	R	R	R	R	D	R	R
Virginia	R	R	R	D	R	R	R	R	R	R	R	R	R	R
Texas	R	R	D	D	D	R	D	R	R	R	R	R	R	R
Emergent States														
North Carolina	D	D	D	D	R	R	D	R	R	R	R	R	R	R
Tennessee	R	R	R	D	R	R	D	R	R	R	D	D	R	R
Traditional States														
Alabama	D	D	D	R	AI	R	D	R	R	R	R	R	R	R
Arkansas	D	D	D	D	AI	R	D	R	R	R	D	D	R	R
South Carolina	D	D	D	R	R	R	D	R	R	R	R	R	R	R
Mississippi	D	D	b	R	AI	R	D	R	R	R	R	R	R	R
Louisisana	D	R	D	R	AI	R	D	R	R	R	D	D	R	R
Republican Total	4	5	3	5	5	11	1	10	11	11	7	7	11	11
Percent Republican	36%	45%	27%	45%	45%	100%	9%	91%	100%	100%	63%	63%	100%	100%

Source: Statistical Abstract of the United States.
Notes: a. In 1968 George Wallace ran as a third-party candidate on the American Independent (AI) ticket; b. In 1960 Mississippi cast its electoral votes for Harry Byrd.

and 2004. One of the major reasons for this allegiance was the conservative social agenda advocated by Republican candidates, which remains very popular with white southern evangelical voters. The 1980 presidential election was a watershed in patriotism, piety, and politics and it changed the tenor of southern politics.

Words and symbolic reassurances—more than deeds—characterized the Reagan administration once it was in office. After the election, Senate Majority Leader Howard Baker and president-elect Reagan jointly announced that the "social agenda" would have to wait for at least a year to allow the new administration to focus on the economic recovery. Later evangelical supporters were crushed to hear that Sandra Day O'Connor, an upper-class activist who favored the Equal Rights Amendment, and legalized abortion, was to fill the first vacancy on the Supreme Court.

The administration was able to immediately cut taxes, but seemed reluctant to assist in the passage of controversial legislation like a bill to limit abortions. Surgeon General C. Everett Koop, probably the most visible evangelical conservative in the administration, pledged in his confirmation hearings not to use his post as a platform to campaign against abortion. Once confirmed, Koop found himself dealing with the new plague of AIDS, and his proffered solutions of increased sex education and condoms only served to alienate the evangelical voters who once championed him.

In spite of these disappointments, evangelical Christians in the South remained strong supporters of Ronald Reagan. As the 1984 campaign season rolled around, Jerry Falwell declared at a press conference that "Ronald Reagan is the finest president in my lifetime . . . if we were to give grades to a president, I would give him nothing less than an 'A.'"[36] Others were less enthusiastic, but Christian conservatives remained hopeful that in the second term the Reagan administration would finally address the social issues that were the base reason for their interest in politics. There was some concern that the agenda was not being pushed, and at the same time some satisfaction that the administration was at least sympathetic with the cause. The main advantage evangelicals had in the 1980s was that the White House door was open, something not characteristic of the Carter years.

Access to the White House meant implicit support for other policies of the administration, not only initiatives on moral and social issues, but also Reagan's stated positions on economic and foreign policy. The conservative argument that government should be smaller and less intrusive found a home in the hearts of religious conservatives worried about the tax-exempt status of their schools and churches. As the second Reagan term expired, amid an AIDS crisis at home and the Iran-Contra scandal abroad, Religious Right leaders began to wonder who would be the champion of their cause in 1988.

Pat Robertson, son of a US congressman, Phi Beta Kappa graduate of Washington & Lee University, Yale Law School, and New York Theological Seminary, offered himself. Though he had never been elected to any political

Vignette 5.2   Pat Robertson (1930–)

Born the son of a Democratic US senator from Virginia, Marion Gordon "Pat" Robertson turned from a career of law to one of televised religion and made himself one of the most influential leaders of the Christian Right political movement in the Reagan era of the 1980s.

Robertson's early education was in the public schools of Lexington, Virginia, but he finished high school at the elite McCallie School in Chattanooga. He returned to his hometown to graduate from Washington & Lee University in 1950. After serving as a Marine Corps officer during the Korean conflict, he completed a law degree at Yale Law School in 1955.

Despite a promising education, Robertson never practiced law; instead he went to work as a corporate executive. Shortly afterward he had a profound conversion experience and dedicated himself to Christian ministry. He went to seminary and became an ordained Baptist minister in 1961.

Robertson embarked on an enterprise that would become his signature—the Christian Broadcasting Network. The ministry was begun in a small television station near Virginia Beach, Virginia, supported by pledges from seven hundred faithful supporters. The "700 Club" quickly became popular with Christians for its mix of news and commentary, interviews with prominent believers and newsmakers, and biblical homilies. Ultimately the program would appear on 275 television stations and was translated into the languages of sixty countries.

As the Christian Broadcasting Network grew, CBN University (later Regent University) followed in its wake in 1978, and was followed in the 1980s by other Christian organizations. Two political interest groups, the Freedom Council and a legal-assistance project to help Christian causes known as the National Legal Foundation, soon appeared in the public eye. In the late 1980s Robertson's programs were raising some $240 million per year.

In 1987 Robertson was presented with a petition of some 3.3 million names urging him to run for political office; he subsequently resigned his church offices and launched a campaign for the 1988 Republican presidential nomination. His campaign embraced themes of conservative America, fiscal conservatism, opposition to homosexuality and abortion, moral conservatism on issues of sexual conduct and pornography, and a return to prayer in the public schools. Early in the campaign, aspects of his personal background and relatively unorthodox sides of his personal theology came to light. Robertson's war record was questioned, his personal sexual ethics examined, and his charismatic theology subjected to public scrutiny. As a candidate, Robertson had surprisingly early success in the Iowa and Minnesota caucuses as well as the South Dakota primary, but he was decisively rejected by southern voters—many of whom were members of conservative churches—in the decisive "Super Tuesday" primaries that year.

After his unsuccessful presidential bid, Robertson returned to his cable television empire and helped found the Christian Coalition as a grassroots, issue-oriented army of faithful voters. The Coalition proved very successful in articulating the social agenda of the Religious Right of the United States, and monitoring the positions of various candidates for office with their "voter guides," which were distributed in churches prior to elections. Many subsequently attributed the GOP triumph in the 1994 midterm congressional elections to the efforts of Robertson and his organization.

In 1997 Robertson astonished the media world when he resigned the presidency of the Christian Coalition and sold his International Family Entertainment corporation to Rupert Murdoch, a media mogul known for taking the low moral road. The profits from the sale were used to endow Regent University and promote worldwide evangelism.

At the turn of the century, Robertson remained a powerful force in Republican and conservative politics. By criticizing secularism and deep-seated popular discontent with select cultural values, he won for himself and his organization a considerable following, amid much controversy.

office, Robertson had advantages other candidates could only dream about. He had a proven television presence, a fundraising operation in place from his *700 Club* network show, and he had one more advantage that gave him an edge in the primaries that year—he was a Southerner. In the election year of 1988 the southern states banded together to hold their primaries in early March to give a conservative flavor to the tickets of both parties early in the election cycle. A win on Super Tuesday could propel any candidate to the nomination, and Robertson appeared to have an early edge.

Unfortunately for Pat Robertson, and the Religious Right as a whole, it was a bad time to be a religious broadcaster. In the spring of 1987, Jim and Tammy Faye Bakker's PTL (Praise the Lord) Network and Heritage USA theme park near Charlotte, North Carolina, collapsed in an embarrassing series of stories of gross exploitation, misuse of funds, mismanagement, and sexual misbehavior. The press began an intense investigation of all television ministries, including a background check of Pat Robertson and found that his oldest son had been conceived well before he and his wife were married. These early setbacks were overcome in February of 1988 when the televangelist presidential candidate, carried by his grassroots organization, finished a surprising second place behind Bob Dole, but ahead of George Bush in the Iowa caucuses.[37]

Just before the Super Tuesday vote in the South, another television preacher scandal broke when Jimmy Swaggart made headlines with a prostitute in a motel room on the outskirts of New Orleans. A survey at the time found that nearly two-thirds of Americans had an unfavorable opinion of television evangelists.[38] Pat Robertson found himself answering questions about his views on the separation of church and state. When George Herbert Walker Bush took a resounding victory in the South Carolina primary, then followed up with a series of wins in other southern states, the Robertson campaign folded its tent in early March and left the field to the vice president from Texas, who won every primary on Super Tuesday and every electoral vote in the South the following fall.

The election of George H. W. Bush in 1988 was really an endorsement of a third term for Ronald Reagan. George Bush was a man who brought dignity to the Oval Office, but his administration was plagued by divided government and an unpredictable economic cycle that abruptly ended his term. Bush adopted Texas as his home after World War II, but his roots were in New England, Yale, and Wall Street. Republican losses in Congress reduced the party margin in Congress, and Bush's power as president to sustain his vetoes. The conservative social agenda was largely ignored as Bush devoted most of his term to the ill-fated budget deal of 1990 and the Gulf War.

George Bush may not have been a native Southerner, but he was very popular in the region. In 1988 he carried every southern state, and the depth of his appeal is shown in a state like Florida, where he received over 60 percent of the vote and won every county but one. Once in office Bush ordered the bureaucracy to interpret laws in ways that pleased Christian Right activists and provided many symbolic benefits to conservatives in the way of support for pro-life positions and by mentioning their issues in his speeches. Still, many conservative evangelicals became disenchanted with his administration when he broke his "no new taxes" pledge in office.

Two issues occupied the attention of southern evangelical voters in the 1980s and early 1990s. The first was the emergence of the new Christian Right organization to replace the Moral Majority in US politics. The second was the struggle for control of the Southern Baptist Convention, the largest and most important Protestant denomination in the South, and the nation. Together, these two movements, and the political events they helped inspire, led the South into the arms of the Republican Party.

The Christian Coalition

In June of 1989 Reverend Jerry Falwell announced that he was folding the Moral Majority to return to his duties at Thomas Road Baptist Church and Liberty University. Liberal pundits greeted the announcement with glee, proclaiming that the preacher's retirement signaled the collapse of the New Christian Right in US politics. The *New Republic* concluded that the religious movement had "self-destructed."[39] What the critics didn't realize was that a new pro-family movement was rising, phoenix-like, from the ashes of the first.

Pat Robertson's 1988 presidential campaign was the political crucible for energizing thousands of conservative political activists, many for the first time. The volunteer lists were consolidated to form a new grassroots organization. At first the Christian Coalition was a low-budget, no-frills, volunteer-driven, fundraising behemoth that projected training up to fifty thousand volunteers in the field and starting chapters in each of the three thousand US counties. Its new director, Ralph Reed, targeted his legions for the heartland of the country. "Our values were popular, particularly in the South and Midwest, but also in unlikely regions of the country, and we enjoyed a strong demographic base of support from evangelicals and Roman Catholics."[40] The Christian Coalition used personal computers, faxes, the Internet, home school networks, and a savvy direct mail operation to mobilize thousands of households. The grassroots political methodology was taken from person-to-person evangelism techniques used by Robertson to build membership in his church, and later his television ministry.

The Christian Coalition was one of a handful of organizations to pick up the mantle of leadership in the conservative Christian community, and its techniques were typical of others in the movement. "The Christian Coalition, Concerned Women for America, and Focus on the Family and its political arm, The Family Research Council [had] active state and local affiliates in most areas and . . . built a sophisticated infrastructure to mobilize and inform their members."[41] The combined total of the individuals mobilized by the Christian Right is impossible to

---

Vignette 5.3   Ralph Reed Jr. (1961–)

Ralph Reed gained national recognition as the executive director of the Christian Coalition during the term of Bill Clinton's presidency (1993–2000). Under his leadership the Christian Coalition became a potent grassroots organization facilitating followers and believers. Reed became a prominent national spokesman for conservative Christians, many of whom resided in the South, and subsequently applied his skills as fundraiser and strategist to the Georgia Republican Party.

Ralph Eugene Reed Jr. was born in 1961 and grew up in Miami, Florida, and Toccoa, Georgia. His introduction to politics came in 1976 when he helped a family friend run for Congress. In the early 1980s he worked on the campaign of Georgia congressman Mack Mattingly, who invited him to intern in his office after the election. Reed stayed in Washington to work for the Republican National Committee in Ronald Reagan's 1984 reelection bid.

After the presidential election, Reed entered graduate school to pursue a PhD in history at Emory University. His dissertation, entitled "Fortress of Faith: Design and Experience at Southern Evangelical Colleges, 1830–1900," forecast an interest in the role of faith and politics. Reed's academic career was sidetracked in 1989, when unsuccessful presidential candidate Pat Robertson asked him to help form a new organization to mobilize Christians into politics.

Reed's memorandum suggested a grassroots organization to teach Christians about politics and hold elected officials accountable for their votes on crucial matters of policy. Robertson promised to back the initiative by raising funds, and Dr. Reed and his wife, Jo Anne, moved to Virginia Beach, Virginia. From this modest beginning, the Christian Coalition grew into a formidable group that claimed to have 1.7 million members with over 1,700 chapters in all fifty states by 1996.

The high point of Christian Coalition influence came in the 1994 midterm elections, when members helped the Republican Party capture the US House of Representatives. In that election Reed claimed to have distributed over 60 million voter guides evaluating candidates for office. In the years after that electoral victory, Ralph Reed regularly appeared on television talk shows to rebut Clinton administration spokespersons, defending his policies and justifying his personal behavior.

After Clinton's aborted impeachment, Reed stepped down as the executive director of the Christian Coalition and started a political consulting firm in Atlanta, Georgia. He was subsequently elected chair of the Georgia Republican Party, where he helped engineer the election of Republicans in the 2002 midterm elections.

---

measure because of duplicate membership lists and the secondary effect of political activism. The organizations communicated to their members with newsletters complete with action alert bulletins and explicit instructions about which officials to contact, and what arguments to make, when lobbying.

When the Supreme Court ruled in the *Webster v. Reproductive Health Services* decision in July of 1989 that states could pass some restrictions on abortion, the new organizations set out on a massive lobbying campaign. The first Christian Coalition guides were distributed in 1990 in seven states, and in June of that year the conservative organizations took out full-page ads in the *Washington Post* and *USA Today* decrying taxpayer-funded support for the National Endowment for the Arts (NEA). The NEA sparked a furor by funding controversial artists like Andres Serrano who portrayed a crucifix in a jar of urine, and Robert Mapplethorpe whose exhibits featured homoerotic photographs. The Christian Coalition, in concert with other groups, worked in 1991 to help Clarence Thomas, an African American, win confirmation to the US Supreme Court.

Support from these organizations, labeled as the "New Religious Right" by the media, helped some moral conservatives win office under the Republican Party banner. But there were also some high-profile losses, and these grabbed national attention as well. In 1994 the state of Virginia witnessed a battle between the Christian Coalition–backed candidate Oliver North, and incumbent Democrat Charles Robb. Dissident Republicans ran an independent candidate in the general election to assure North's defeat. In the presidential elections of 1992 and 1996, the Coalition supported Pat Buchanan, who was defeated first by George Bush and then by Bob Dole.

Christian Right involvement was more successful at the state and local level. Grassroots activity began with select candidate recruitment, when challengers were offered an array of services to help with their campaigns. Christian Right candidates often entered Republican primaries. In 1994 the influential magazine *Campaigns and Elections* reported that the Christian Right was the dominant faction in eighteen states, including eight of eleven in the South. The Coalition had substantial influence in thirteen others, including two in the South.[42] Altogether ten of eleven southern states were under the influence of the Christian organizations. Only Tennessee was exempt from its dominant influence.

In the 1990s the Christian Right made an effort to increase its representation on elected school boards. Such local-member elections were usually low-information contests where few citizens bothered to vote, and those who did could usually recognize only a few names on the ballot. The outcome of such elections was important to the curriculums and activities of students in local communities. The Coalition candidates in these early campaigns faced well-organized and well-funded opponents with National Education Association (NEA) backing. Even when not successful, Christian conservative campaigns were helpful in defining the local political agenda and shaping policy outcomes.

The Southern Baptist Controversy

In the 1980s and 1990s the Southern Baptist Protestant denomination was embroiled in a controversy that had a direct influence on politics and elections in the South. The controversy raged over ten years, until the victorious conservatives finally purged their foes from the Southern Baptist agencies and seminaries. The Baptist controversy was more than a theological dispute; it was part of a larger cultural crisis in the South and the nation.

No other major religious denomination has shaped white southern culture more than the Southern Baptist Convention (SBC). Organized in 1845, after a disagreement with northern members over slavery and sectionalism, the SBC is the second largest religious body in the United States, and the largest in the South. Over half of all Southern Baptists are in five southern states: Texas, Georgia, North Carolina, Tennessee, and Alabama. The states with the highest population of Southern Baptists are: Mississippi, Alabama, Oklahoma, Tennessee, and Kentucky.[43] The Southern Baptist Convention has more churches than any other religious body in the nation, and the prominent corners of most southern cities are home to their buildings.

One growing-up-southern memoir recalled a childhood where the church was central to every activity, and the guardian of every thought. "The child who had been Raised Right was not only Saved, but had spent a large part of his formative years in the House of the Lord . . . from Sunbeams through BYPU, from Sunday school to prayer meeting, from Those Attending Preaching to Those With Prepared Lessons, everything was counted . . . [and] so was everybody."[44] Such was the pattern all over the South.

The denomination retains a traditional emphasis on local church autonomy, but a general theological consensus prevails with coordinated activities and a yearly "Convention" system of church government. Southern Baptists are biblically conservative, and their theology has influenced politics and culture in the South. One Southerner recalls that, "revival in the church occurred during laying-by time for the dirt farmers . . . it involved a march down the aisle to shake the preacher's hand, a vote of admission by the church membership, and a Sunday afternoon immersion . . . while the congregation lined the bank and sang, 'Shall We Gather at the River?'" This "Old Time Religion" image of the white South began to change in the 1960s and 1970s.

With the end of segregation and Jim Crow, the South became part of the Sun Belt, and its theology came in for criticism from moderate elements within the church that were uncomfortable with the historic conservatism of biblical literalism. In 1968 the convention approved a resolution that asked for social action in race relations and antipoverty efforts, and confessed complicity in the injustice done to blacks. This bold stance moved the SBC into the nexus of politics, and resulted in two militant, ideological factions struggling for control of the largest US Protestant denomination. This battle raged from 1979 to 1991.

Conservative critics at the time contended that the leadership of the SBC had opened the doors of the denomination's agencies and entities to blatant theological liberalism, especially at the SBC's six seminaries.[45] The relationship between theology and politics is oblique, but readily apparent on Election Day. Political science research confirms that religious traditions and coalitions now structure party politics, and are potent predictors of behavior even when economic factors come into play. In times of peace and prosperity the importance of church attendance and conservative values are quite strong.[46] A study of Baptist ministers found that most were open to the appeal for political activism because they saw the cultural effects in their churches each week. The organizational influence of the Christian Coalition was quite strong.[47]

The controversy over these issues divided the SBC beginning in 1979 when a conservative group, the Baptist Faith and Message Fellowship, aimed at affecting the selection of the next president of the Southern Baptist Convention. The reasons given for the split were theological: whether the Bible was, or was not, the infallible Word of God. Also at issue was whether or not the nation's largest Protestant denomination would be more vocal on issues like opposition to abortion, homosexuality, and support for school vouchers and prayer.[48] The conservative wing of the SBC supported Adrian Rogers, pastor of the 10,500-member Bellevue Baptist Church in Memphis, Tennessee. Rogers won on the first ballot and conservatives assumed most of the control of the denomination. Control of the presidency was crucial in Southern Baptist affairs since the president appointed members of the convention committees that, in turn, controlled the nominations of trustees and denomination agencies and seminaries.

The plan for the conservative takeover was to win the presidency for a hand-picked candidate, then use the appointment power aggressively to expand their influence. The task had to be repeated time and again. The number of appointments, and terms of office, were such that it would take consecutive years to fully impanel agency boards with conservative members. Conservatives won every election for president of the SBC for the next decade after Rogers's initial victory. Gradually, professors and seminary administrators who did not hold to a literal interpretation of the Bible were replaced. Moderates responded that the tactics of the new majority were a violation of Christian doctrine, the Baptist stance on separation of church and state, and little more than an overt attempt to join the denomination to the Moral Majority. The majority didn't care. The convention elected men like Charles Stanley, a popular television evangelist and president of the convention in the mid-1980s. Stanley was also a founding member of the Moral Majority.[49]

The power struggle within the Southern Baptist Convention gave key figures in the new Christian Right control over the nation's largest Protestant denomination, and resulted in stronger ties between that religious body and the Republican Party. By 1986 the transformation was complete for the GOP and its candidates. Republican presidential hopefuls George Bush, Jack Kemp, and Pat Robertson all showed up at the SBC Convention that year. Prominent Baptists served on the board of the American Coalition for Traditional Values (ACTV), an organization that coordinated the registration of an estimated 1.5 to 2 million evangelical voters in 1984. The vast majority of these registrants voted Republican.

The convention repeatedly affirmed its opposition to abortion, homosexuality, and the ordination of women to the pastoral office. The affirmation of these positions by the Southern Baptists was part of the steady movement to the right among regular churchgoers, and a key element in Republican elective gains in the South. In the words of a study on the relationship between the SBC and the GOP, "there are a number of religious forces at work in *Southern* politics that have national ramifications."[50] The link between Baptist belief and Republicanism was forged in the 1980s.

The majority white denomination provided large numbers of voters to the Republican Party, and played a critical role in the long-range rise of the GOP to a majority status in the South. The convention regularly adopted conservative positions on issues and the effect of the conservative Baptist theology saturated the South in an unquestioned political orthodoxy that shaped cultural vales and influenced the local political agenda. County school curricula, books in the public library, and displays in newly built art museums all indirectly felt the effects of the SBC.

Some individual Baptists felt the call to political office as strongly as their preachers did to the pulpit. In one instance the calls were synonymous. Reverend Mike Huckabee served as president of the Arkansas Baptist State Convention from 1989–1991 as an ordained minister. The convention had over 1,200 churches in Arkansas with nearly 500,000 members across the state. At the end of his tenure as state Baptist president, Huckabee ran for governor in 1998 and won with 60 percent of the vote.[51]

The election of successive conservatives to the presidential office of the SBC gradually moved the denomination back to its conservative theological roots. In June of 1991 a normally reserved President George Bush emotionally praised the convention for its "rock-solid" values. The president was greeted by raucous applause, and promised to work for voluntary prayer in schools and restated his opposition to federally funded abortions.[52] That same year, the SBC welcomed retired Marine Lt. Colonel Oliver L. North, Prison Fellowship director Charles W. Colson, and former Moral Majority leader Jerry Falwell. In the wake of the first Iraq war, the delegates to the convention waved US flags and sang patriotic hymns.

Yet in the ensuing presidential election, many in the denomination gave their allegiance to an all–Southern Baptist Democratic ticket, headlined by Arkansas governor Bill Clinton (Immanuel Baptist Church) and Senator Al Gore (Mt. Vernon Baptist Church).[53] Clinton quoted from the Bible in his inaugural address and, for a time, his appeal in the South was quite strong. But the affection many Baptists, and Southerners in general, had for the ticket disappeared when the new administration supported gays in the military. In the 1990s the SBC reaffirmed a "submissive" role for women in marriage, and opposition to homosexuality as normal sexuality— including gays in the military. The support for tuition vouchers for private schools clashed with the Clinton administration support for public schools. Church members who disagreed with the SBC positions were not obligated to leave, but many chose to do so. Jimmy Carter announced that he was leaving the SBC in 2000, the same year that Bill Clinton decided he would do the same. At century's end there were numerous southern denominations that ordained women, embraced homosexual rights, and took a less than literal view of the Bible. But none of them could match the size, power, and influence of the Southern Baptist Convention when it came to cultural hegemony.

"Baptist Republicanism has developed through a complicated history," but all along it was rooted in the culture of the Old South.[54] In rural and suburban communities the Southern Baptist Church was, and remains, the guardian of religious orthodoxy and political permissibility among the white population. A study in 2004 concluded that social conservatives exercised either a "strong" or "moderate" influence in forty-four Republican state committees, and the Baptist churches in each state were home to many of the political activists.[55]

Compassionate Conservatism

The conservative texture of southern politics frequently found expression in the election of like-minded candidates, but regional sentiments seldom appeared as doctrines of public policy. The South was defined by what it was *against*: higher taxes, federally sponsored health care, and welfare. The rest of the nation had no idea what it was *for*. That changed in the 1990s when the term "faith based" became synonymous with a newer approach to social policy.

In 1992 a little-known journalism professor named Marvin Olasky, at the University of Texas in Austin, published a book entitled *The Tragedy of American Compassion*.[56] The book presented a history of the nation's welfare system. It showed how, a century before the federal government became involved in the provision of social services, thousands of local, faith-based charitable agencies and churches waged a war on poverty much more successfully than that of the national government. In articles and speeches, Olasky argued that local organizations were better suited to deliver social programs because they had the knowledge and flexibility necessary to cope with local needs.

When George W. Bush was preparing to run for governor of Texas in 1994, he, and his key adviser Karl Rove, met with Olasky. The ideas of a host of social thinkers were combined into a series of programs collectively entitled "compassionate conservatism." The ideas were rooted in political conservatism, arguing that government should have a limited role in the lives of citizens, and allow individuals to express themselves in volunteer associations. Compassionate conservatism rejected the conventional wisdom, that government programs were enough to solve social problems. The federal agencies, according to Olasky and other critics, had actually made the situation worse. They sought to move the GOP social programs away from welfare spending, to a positive program of local opportunity.

Olasky's book disappeared when it was published in 1992, but two years later, then incoming Speaker of the House Newt Gingrich mentioned it repeatedly as a plan for reforming welfare. In the Washington welfare debates of 1995 and 1996 conservatives argued that the poor were not passive, and would be amenable to overtures that emphasized personal responsibility and self-reliance. Workfare, an alternative to the older government system, was a success in Governor Tommy Thompson's Wisconsin, Governor John Engler's Michigan, and Mayor Rudolph Guiliani's New York City. In Texas, the prescriptions of compassionate conservatism were in place from El Paso to Texarkana, and had resulted in a shrinking welfare budget. The collective philosophy and prescriptions were embodied in the 1996 Welfare Reform Act, but even then some conservatives argued that the act sacrificed sacred compassionate conservatism principles for expediency.

Marvin Olasky, and other reformers, envisioned successful government welfare programs as being those transferred from government bureaucracies to private institutions where they would be administered on faith-based diversity. In Texas, Governor George W. Bush adopted the phrase, "compassionate conservatism," and proposed a substantial change in the way government officials dealt with charities. For example, in Houston the Texas prison system turned a facility over to the Christian Ministry, Prison Fellowship. The "Innerchange" program was based on an eighteen-month prerelease program that emphasized Bible-based studies as an alternative to traditional incarceration plans.

As he prepared to run for the presidency, Bush proposed an expansion in federal charitable deductions to support private and religious programs.[57] In his campaign, Bush argued that faith-based groups would succeed where secular organizations failed because they helped change a person's heart before behavior. The faith-based aspect of the programs had a special appeal in the South, where thousands of churches engaged in extensive "mercy-ministry" programs.

The appeal of compassionate conservatism to churchgoing Southerners was immediate and dramatic. The proposed programs were based on the biblical conviction that treatment of social ills must have a moral purpose. The drug, youth, and prison programs in the compassionate conservative policy notebook emphasized allowing people the opportunity to maximize their own capabilities. The premises were optimistic about the ability of individuals to do a better job of helping themselves, and favored the marketplace as the vehicle for self-improvement. More importantly for Christians in the South, the programs fit with their deeply rooted preconceptions of how faith should be expressed in their neighborhoods and communities.

For years volunteers in Christian organizations argued that a heart-change, spiritual correction was necessary before a drug addict, pregnant teen, or prison offender could change his or her life. Government programs forbade evangelism, so thousands of Christian volunteers avoided government service and began privately funded, or church-sponsored programs instead. Compassionate conservatism allowed these Christians to join with the federal government without sacrificing the integrity of their beliefs. The compassionate conservative social agenda languished in congressional committee in the first term of the George W. Bush administration, but the promise of its enactment was enough to keep conservative Christians loyal to the Republican Party.

In 2003 Alabama provided a test for compassionate conservatism. That year Governor Bob Riley, who was elected by a 3,120 vote margin, launched a campaign to persuade the state's voters to endorse a $1.2 billion tax increase—the largest in its history. Riley's reasons were a restatement of the liberal Social Gospel with a conservative twist. He told the *Birmingham News* that the biblical mandate to "take care of the least among us" required a restructured tax system. "It is immoral," he said in a newspaper interview, "to charge somebody making $5,000 an income tax."[58]

As a member of the US House of Representatives, Bob Riley voted like a traditional conservative Republican with the personal ethics of a devout Southern Baptist. In the governor's mansion he faced a colossal $675 million budget deficit, and sought to synthesize compassionate conservatism and the Social Gospel of government concern into a campaign for larger government. Voters in Alabama saw a contradiction in the rhetoric, and Riley's actions split his political base. The Christian Coalition of Alabama declared its opposition to the tax package, while the national Christian Coalition called the plan "visionary and courageous." Liberal mainline Protestant organizations supported the governor's plan, while the more numerous evangelical Protestant churches said the governor was perverting Judeo-Christian principles in his campaign.

In the end, Riley's crusade to persuade voters to go into the booth and sanction a tax increase for religious reasons proved futile. On September 9, 2003, the electorate rejected the proposal by a two to one margin. Only in the South could such a crusade for economic justice be waged with biblical quotes. The tenets of compassionate conservatism won out in the end. The argument that the poor should be directed to churches and faith-based charities, instead of government offices, trumped the campaign for more taxes.

Polls taken before the vote showed that 69 percent of prospective voters favored the referendum, but on the day of the election more than two out of three Alabama voters rejected the plan. Respondents favored some parts of the program, but voted down the entire package.[59]

The 2004 Presidential Election

The 2004 presidential election highlighted the importance of religious and moral issues in politics.[60] Religious attitudes and conservative values topped security issues and the war in Iraq as major problems on Election Day. Faith issues, like gay marriage, stem cell research, and abortion were key flashpoints in those who went to the polls in November. Five months earlier the Supreme Court of Massachusetts said that the state could no longer forbid homosexuals to marry. After the ruling same-sex couples in various towns in New Mexico and New York obtained licenses to marry for a short period of time. Although none were able to register their marriages, the controversy helped explain the unanimous support George W. Bush received on Election Day.

In a survey of southern voters taken well before the election, in February of 2004, over three-quarters of those surveyed believed that religious values were important in determining political beliefs. When asked which political party had more leaders with strong moral character, Republicans were chosen more frequently, but the differences were quite dissimilar between the races. African Americans believed Democrats had more leaders with strong moral character, while whites gave this distinction to Republicans.

To evaluate the effects of religion and its salience with voters, partisans were asked if they thought the opposing party was "sinful." "Approximately 25 percent of identifiers in both parties believe the other party was 'sinful.'"[61] The level of concern for moral and religious issues was such that a quarter of the party activists believed the opposing party was not just philosophically wrong, but in rebellion against the Almighty.

The 2004 presidential election was saturated with spiritual overtones. The magnitude of George W. Bush's reelection, and the overwhelming triumph of amendments banning gay marriage in eleven states, combined to make moral values the top issue at the ballot box. Pundits swiftly labeled the 2004 election as the fruit of the "Bible Ballot," and the activities of the "values voters" as decisive. The growing importance of "God and Country" became an issue of large political significance.

Catholic bishops around the country exhorted their flocks from the pulpit not to vote for politicians who flouted church teaching on homosexuality and abortion. John Kerry, a Roman Catholic with a New Englander's reticence about discussing his personal beliefs, found himself in the eye of the storm. By contrast George W. Bush's Methodist and born-again Christian faith, which he discussed with ease, gave him a clear advantage with the values constituency.

According to a poll by the Pew Forum on Religion and Public Life, about 85 percent of Americans said religion was important in their lives and 72 percent said it was important that the president have strong moral beliefs. A Pew survey of voters in the 2004 presidential election found that 63 percent of voters who attended religious services more than once a week said they would vote Republican, while 62 percent of voters who rarely attended services said they would vote Democrat.

The southern states united behind the GOP platform with its clear positions against abortion rights, stem cell research, and support for a constitutional amendment banning gay marriage. John Kerry's suggestion that a president didn't need the South to win the nation's highest office was proven false. If nothing else, the election results confirm the importance of religion as a fundamental base in the politics of the South. In many ways, the religious South precedes the emergence of the political South. The high-commitment communities of evangelical white

Protestants, black Protestants, and controversy in the mainline denominations over issues like the ordination of gay clergy added fiery conflict to the generally halcyon nature of southern religious life. "At the millennium, the soul of the South is being reincorporated into the politics of the nation with religious groups peculiar to the southern experience anchoring both major party coalitions."[62]

The African American Church

The irony of religious devotion and churchgoing by black and white Southerners was not lost on those who sought to reform race relations in the era of the 1960s. Martin Luther King declared that "eleven o'clock on Sunday morning is the most segregated hour in America." But King's irritation with the established church extended to the black community as well as the white. "I'm sick and tired of seeing Negro preachers riding around in big cars and living in big houses and not being concerned about the problems of the people who made it possible for them to get these things."[63]

Race was the most important factor by which religious membership was determined in the South. From the beginning, African American participation was severely limited by law, by tradition, and by the whims of white society. Religious institutions were racially segregated, yet black and white members shared a similar theology: conservative Protestant, Baptist, or Methodist. Nearly all of what has been said about "southern religion," its emotional content, fundamentalist basis, and community spirit, applies to both racial groups. Black religion has its roots in white religion, but more precisely in obedience to white domination.

The earliest effort to bring Christianity to slaves in America was the Anglican Society for the Propagation of the Gospel in Foreign Parts, established in the early eighteenth century.[64] Except for a few slaves baptized into white churches, no blacks were Christians. Although slaves were finally "in church," it was not "their church," and the incongruities of the southern white church's faith and practice were everywhere apparent. Slaves who yearned for spiritual nourishment had to steal away to swamps, "hush harbors," or their own quarters where they consoled one another, prayed, and sang. These escapes were infrequent and African Americans saw their salvation as a subset of that of their master.

The black church came into existence fully committed to the private religious conversion, what one member called the "God struck me dead" experience, but also with the concern to destroy the evil slave system that existed in defiance of Christian teaching.[65] The emphasis in black churches was reeducation against the idea that black people were cursed by God, or that they were destined to forever be "hewers of wood and drawers of water." The comfort and security of God's love was offered as an antidote to the harsh reality of daily life. The black church was the primary resource for information about, and safety on, the Underground Railroad.

Vignette 5.4   Martin Luther King Sr. (1897–1984) and Martin Luther King Jr. (1929–1968)

Martin Luther King Day commemorates Martin Luther King Jr. and his accomplishments, but his legacy of leadership in the black community stretches back two generations to his maternal grandfather.

The Reverend A. D. Williams was a leading minister in Atlanta in the early years of the century, and was also the senior pastor at Ebenezer Baptist Church on Auburn Avenue. He insisted that any suitor for his daughter, Alberta, be well educated. So it was that, at the age of twenty-one, Martin Luther "Daddy" King enrolled in the fifth grade at the Bryant School and worked his way through seminary at Morehouse College.

In 1926 Reverend King married Alberta Williams, and five years later succeeded his father-in-law as pastor of Ebenezer Baptist Church. "Daddy" King led voter registration drives in the 1930s, and won national acclaim championing the efforts of Atlanta's black teachers to win pay equal to that of white teachers. In the 1950s, his son's ministry eclipsed his.

Martin Luther King Jr. grew up on Auburn Avenue and attended Morehouse College like his father. He wasn't planning to enter the ministry, but fell under the influence of Dr. Benjamin Mays, who convinced him that the pulpit could be both personally fulfilling and socially productive. After graduating from Morehouse in 1948, King attended Crozer Theological Seminary, where he finished a doctorate in 1955.

By this time Martin Luther King Jr. was married and pastor of the Dexter Avenue Baptist Church in Montgomery, Alabama. He made his first mark on the civil rights movement by mobilizing the black community of Montgomery to join a 382-day boycott of the city's bus lines. As leader of the Montgomery Improvement Association he experienced arrest and the bombing of his

home, until finally in 1956 the US Supreme Court declared bus segregation unconstitutional.

After the Montgomery Bus Boycott, Martin Luther King Jr. returned to Atlanta to become co-pastor of Ebenezer Baptist Church and lead the Southern Christian Leadership Conference in a campaign for civil justice. As leader of the SCLC he developed a philosophy of nonviolence that he shared with other communities around the country.

In 1963 his nonviolent tactics were put to their most severe test in Birmingham, Alabama. The mass protest for fair hiring practices and desegregation of department store facilities precipitated police brutality toward marchers before a national television audience. King was arrested, but his voice was not silenced as he wrote "Letter from a Birmingham Jail" to refute his critics. The letter was addressed to white clergy in Birmingham who found the SCLC campaign there "unwise and untimely."

In the summer of 1963 King was the principal speaker at the historic March on Washington where he delivered his famous "I Have a Dream Speech." *Time* magazine named him "Person of the Year" in 1963, and a few months later he received the 1964 Nobel Peace Prize. The next year King took on the challenge of voter registration in Selma, Alabama, which resulted in passage of the 1965 Voting Rights Act.

When he adopted opposition to the war in Vietnam as a part of his civil rights crusade, King came in for criticism by the NAACP and the Urban League. He turned his attention from the issue of civil rights to what he thought was directly related to the Vietnam struggle: poverty. With this goal in mind, King began to plan another massive march in Washington, D.C., but interrupted his plans to

(continues)

Vignette 5.4 Continued

support the Memphis sanitation men's strike. There he was killed on the balcony of the Lorraine Motel, just off Beale Street, on April 4, 1968.

The father lived to bury his son, and the next year he buried his second son, A. D., who drowned in a swimming pool. In spite of these tragedies, "Daddy" King carried on as a respected and influential leader of the civil rights movement. Then, on the last Sunday in June of 1974, an assassin murdered his wife,

Mrs. Bunch King, in a pew at Ebenezer Baptist Church.

Reverend Martin Luther "Daddy" King Sr. supported Jimmy Carter in 1976 and 1980. He died in 1984. "There were students in northern colleges," he wrote before his death, "who expected me to harbor a lot of anger and a lot of hatred for white people. And I said to them, as quietly as I could, that this wasn't true and never would be."

In one sense, slaves lived in a world closer to the supernatural than their masters. Whites, despite all their talk about the nearness of God, were property owners and master users of technology that took most of the mystery out of life. They were part of the established order that manipulated the physical and social environment by mechanical means. They had less need for God. In black homes, by contrast, religion was in the realm of the spirit, because the realities of life—death, heartbreak, desertion, and defeat—were much closer at hand. In the black community, God's acts in history were there to bring "liberty to the captives," mirroring "the crucified Christ and the Lord of the Apocalypse, Daniel and Joshua, Moses and Jesus, present experience and hope."[66]

When the slave era ended with the northern victory of the Civil War, the black church became independent and sponsored schools, savings societies, insurance companies, banks, and a variety of social services to assist the former slaves. Black churches were the one community institution that could effectively resist white domination. Communal values were reinforced through weddings, funerals, church "homecomings," and family reunions—all of which were rooted in the black church. These occasions provided venues for self-expression, affirmation, and leadership in the community. By default, black preachers became political advocates and community spokesmen. Spiritual nurture and social reform were twin responsibilities in the black pulpit.

Christian denominations, like the African Methodist Episcopal Church (AME), various Pentecostal churches, and the largest black association, the National Baptist Convention, flourished in the black neighborhoods and rural bypasses of the South. In the part of the country notorious for poor education, the black church provided trained men—and later women—for the pulpit. The publishing houses of the black denominations circulated information and provided resources immune to white censorship.

The religious exercises of the black church created a world away from white society. The pulpit message of forgiveness and forbearance helped the weak and powerless make the oppressor irrelevant. Christianity kept the black population from being destroyed by their social and economic circumstances. Consistent with their commitment to equality, blacks regularly expressed Christian love for all people, including their white oppressors.

In the years after World War I hundreds of thousands of African Americans left the South, placing churches in the region at risk. At the turn of the century 90 percent of the US black population lived in the South; sixty years later only about half lived there.[67] The church had traditionally provided a kind of social safety net in the rural southern community, but this collapsed in the years of the Great Depression. A pioneering study of the African American churches in the summer of 1930 found uneducated ministers tending churches in debt with less than half the membership giving regularly and consistently to the work.[68] Even in crisis, the black church survived as the one place southern African Americans could go for social acceptance and reassurance.

The two historic values of the black church, individual spiritual nurture and social reform, were joined in the civil rights movement of the 1960s. The moral dimensions of the conflict afforded black activists an opportunity to recruit white Christian allies in an effort to express their faith through action. Private convictions became public morality on television screens and in newspapers around the country.

Black Theology and the Civil Rights Movement

The difference between black and white Christianity in the South is that the former was born in slavery, and the latter flourished in freedom. One black writer described the contrast in the two traditions: "the message of the Bible did not come to us in monasteries, in theological libraries or in debates with philosophers and kings, but in hidden meetings out of earshot of the patrollers, under the lash of plantation overseers, and in the dilapidated, impoverished ghettos of a hundred cities."[69] Black theology may have begun in secret, but the civil rights movement gave it public testimony.

The social side of the faith was carried by powerful preachers with a gift for oratory. Martin Luther King Jr. was himself the son of a preacher, and in his education and philosophy of ministry are clues about the public relevance of black theology. In racially mixed classes at Crozer Seminary in Chester, Pennsylvania, King encountered higher biblical criticism and the liberal social gospel of Walter Rauschenbusch.[70] The Social Gospel followed philosophical pragmatism and held that the only test of truth was action. The clearest expression of faith was its ability to inspire the moral conscience, specifically social action. In his last year of seminary King read Reinhold Niebuhr's *Moral Man and Immoral Society,* which attacked the Social Gospel's premise that a steady advance of reason and good will would follow enlightened education on social injustice. "The white race in America," warned Niebuhr, "will not admit the Negro to equal rights if it is not forced to do so."[71] These theories of social action affirmed the public and political aspects of the Christian faith.

Black history and black theology joined in the civil rights movement at the same time. The behavior and rhetoric of black demonstrators became a part of US "civil religion": defined as a set of religious sentiments honoring tolerance, equality, freedom, patriotism, duty, and cooperation in society. On these values Protestant, Catholic and Jew, black and white, North and South, rich and poor could all agree. "The American civil religion, as expressed in our national rites and symbols, is in fact a central source of coherence in American public culture, holding together various and even contradictory elements of its tradition."[72]

The civil rights demonstrations began as a religious awakening, predicated on faith. Martin Luther King Jr. liked to tell the story of a prayer he uttered at midnight on January 27, 1955, in the darkest hour of the Montgomery Bus Boycott. "I could hear an inner voice saying to me: 'Martin Luther, stand up for righteousness. Stand up for justice. Stand up for truth. And lo I will be with you.'"[73] The prayers, piety, and biblical language of nonviolence brought the theology of the black church into the mainstream of US life.

Two competing perspectives are in evidence for the role that religion plays in black political activism. The first is the "opiate" argument, which insists that Afro-Christianity promotes otherworldliness. The second perspective is the inspiration theory, which argues that religion plays a central role in black politics catalyzing the collective involvement of members to action. Frederick C. Harris concludes his study of black political activism by saying that it is "multifaceted and, in some instances, ambiguous," but the bulk of evidence contradicts critics who argue that religion fosters passivity.[74]

The appeal of religious nonviolence was especially strong in the South, where black and white audiences were accustomed to being upbraided by ministers. Martin Luther King Jr. regularly spoke before audiences to invoke the image of America as it *could* be, as well as what it *should* be. This message was not as well received in urban neighborhoods of the North, far removed from the premises of revealed religion. Less than a week after the Voting Rights Act was passed in 1965, rioting broke out in the black ghetto of Watts, in Los Angeles. As he walked through the litter of Watts, Martin Luther King Jr. was greeted with hostility and verbal abuse.[75]

Urban racial conflict in the North and West was different from southern racial conflict. One of the ironies of the civil rights movement was that its nonviolent success in the South inspired rioting and violence in the North. Watts stirred copycat violence in cities like Chicago, Hartford, San Diego, Philadelphia, and Springfield, Massachusetts. The path of urban rioting would continue in over one hundred cities between 1965 and 1968. The work of removing legal barriers and attacking state-sponsored segregation in the South was more peaceful than the despair and cynicism of northern ghettos. One explanation for the difference, perhaps *the* major explanation, was that the religious culture of the South created receptivity to nonviolent change, not apparent in northern neighborhoods.

The controversy of the political movement was cloaked in theological language. The most eloquent statement of the nonviolent philosophy was Martin Luther King's "Letter from a Birmingham Jail," addressed to white Christian and Jewish sympathizers critical of the movement. The civil rights demonstrations in the South gave common ground for all in the United States to unite behind the movement. In the ringing climax of his "I Have a Dream" speech, King included everyone: "we will be able to speed up that day when all God's children, black men and white men, Jews and Gentiles, Protestants and Catholics, will be able to join hands and sing in the words of the old Negro spiritual, 'Free at last, Thank God Almighty, we are free at last.'"[76]

The civil rights movement established black churches as the venue for politics in the African American community. Subsequent political campaigns involved mandatory appearances in the pulpit for aspiring candidates. The Association of Black Pastors in each southern state became one of the most powerful groups in politics, and their position on issues like a lottery referendum, or a gay rights amendment, or their endorsement of a primary candidate could be decisive in an election. Black pastors, like Jesse Jackson and Al Sharpton, sought the Democratic presidential nomination.

Summary

The apocryphal story is told of a regular churchgoer who retired from business and decided to spend his golden years writing a book about church architecture. The man traveled the nation visiting churches, and, in his first stop in California, he found a room off the sanctuary that had a golden telephone on a small table with a sign reading: "Call Heaven for $10,000." The writer asked the pastor about the room and the minister said, "You can call God on that phone, but it is going to cost you to talk to him." Everywhere the man went, from Colorado to Illinois to New York, he found the same golden phone with the same sign. Finally, the man crossed into Mississippi and entered a small Baptist church. Again he found the golden telephone, but this time the sign read: "Call Heaven for $.25." The man found the pastor of the church and told him of all his travels and then asked why the call was so cheap. The pastor shrugged his shoulders and said, "Son, you're in the South now, it's a local call."

An understanding of religion and politics is essential to interpreting political behavior in the US South. Religious views have infused politics in the region from colonial times to the present day. Movements to end slavery, prohibit the sale of alcoholic beverages, and grant citizenship to African Americans in the 1960s all had their impulse in religious convictions. No single attribute or collection of conditions can satisfactorily explain the continuing awareness of a separate South, but religion would have to be included on the list.

Viewed against the backdrop of this history, any definition of political culture must include the sacred values, institutions, and social groups that operate in the public arena. Perhaps the only regional attitude as distinctive as race in the South is religion. "Religion has been a primary force in conserving regional identity to the present day."[77] Known colloquially as the "Bible Belt," the Southeast is distinguished by a conservative, fundamentalist orientation to the Christian faith that has avoided the secularizing influence of science and the accompanying control over nature that shaped the rest of US culture.

The theological orthodoxy that permeates white southern Protestantism is a mixture of biblical literalism, Scottish "common sense" rationalism, and English apologetics. A strong belief in the rights of the individual stems from the belief that God has a special concern for his chosen people. This view is anchored in the biblical doctrine of "original sin," meaning the idea that man is morally flawed and lacks perfection. Religion remains the most important and effective public institution in local community life. Allegiance to faith has fueled a popular stereotype of religious extremism and inflexibility among those who attend church services in the region.

Church attendance is related to the innate conservatism of the South. With 30 percent of the population, the eleven southern states contain 41.6 percent of the communicant, confirmed full members of churches in the United States. South Carolina has about the same population as Connecticut, but it has nearly two and one-half times as many churches.[78] Church attendance and activities play a prominent role in family and community life, and since the 1970s religion has begun to influence politics as well.

With its diversity of Bible-believing denominations, Christianity unites an otherwise fiercely independent constituency around unspoken, but widely accepted, values. As Flannery O'Connor said, "I think it is safe to say that while the South is hardly Christ-centered, it is most certainly Christ-haunted."[79] Churches reinforce southern culture and ideals of economics, politics, morality, and race. Although religion and the church are as important in the lives and politics of southern blacks as they are for southern whites, the New Christian Right is largely a movement of white Southerners.[80] Table 5.2 compares the religious affiliation of residents of the United States and each southern state. The Baptist population is about three times the national average in the southern states of Georgia, Tennessee, Mississippi, South Carolina, Arkansas, and Alabama. Presbyterians and Episcopalians are over the national average in the states of Virginia and South Carolina. The southern states are heavily Protestant and Orthodox denominations, Jews, Mormons, and Catholics are underrepresented.

Table 5.2 Religious Affiliation by State, 2000 (percentage of population)

	USA	South	Georgia	Florida	Virginia	Texas	N. Carolina	Tennessee	Alabama	S. Carolina	Mississippi	Arkansas	Louisiana
Roman Catholic	43.9	24.5	10.2	39.5	20.5	37.8	8.6	6.3	6.2	7.2	7.4	7.6	52.6
Protestant													
Baptist	16.9	39.1	48.3	20.6	28.8	32.1	46.1	51.0	59.4	49.2	62.5	58.6	30.2
Methodist	7.3	11.9	15.6	7.1	16.6	8.9	18.4	13.6	13.6	16.3	15.5	11.8	6.1
Lutheran	5.4	2.0	0.3	2.5	2.9	2.6	3.0	1.0	0.5	3.4	0.4	2.0	0.8
Pentacostal	3.8	4.8	6.8	5.4	5.1	4.0	4.4	4.7	3.1	6.9	3.4	5.4	3.5
Christian/Disciple	2.9	3.9	1.8	2.3	3.6	5.0	2.5	9.8	5.4	1.3	3.4	7.0	1.3
Presbyterian	2.8	3.4	3.6	3.2	5.4	1.8	6.4	5.1	2.7	6.7	2.5	1.8	0.9
Episcopalian	1.6	2.0	2.0	2.3	4.3	1.5	2.2	1.2	1.9	2.8	1.4	0.9	1.3
United Church of Christ	1.2	0.4	0.1	0.7	0.8	0.1	1.4	0.0	0.1	0.0	0.0	0.0	0.1
Eastern Orthodox	0.3	0.2	0.1	0.4	0.3	0.0	0.2	0.0	0.0	0.2	0.3	0.0	0.0
Mormons	3.0	1.2	1.2	1.5	1.8	1.3	1.1	0.8	0.8	1.1	0.8	0.9	0.6
Jews	4.3	2.5	2.6	9.6	2.6	1.1	0.7	0.6	0.4	0.6	0.0	0.1	0.6
All Others	7.2	4.1	7.2	7.2	7.3	3.8	5.0	12.2	5.9	4.3	2.4	3.9	2.0
Total	100.0	100.0	100.0	100.0	100.0	100.0	100.0	100.0	100.0	100.0	100.0	100.0	100.0
Total Adherents as percent of population	50.2	50.2	44.8	44.1	41.6	55.5	45.4	51.1	54.8	47.6	54.6	57.1	58.8

Source: Edwin S. Gaustad and Philip L. Barlow, *New Historical Atlas of Religion in America.* New York: Oxford University Press, 2001.

The impact of this distinctiveness is a culture characterized as having an unabashed and forthright dependence on God in the middle of a gleaming secular culture. The Christian story relates a theme of human destiny born to Edenic perfection, lost in a fall, and capable of being revived into a "born again" state. "It's a very Southern story, one of redemption through faith, in a region where there was a solid religious South before there was a solid political one."[81] When relating to its historical experiences, especially slavery and the Civil War defeat, the white South sees itself as a faithful Judah to an apostate Israel, and the black South as the children delivered from slavery. The Bible, with its tales of paradise and human destiny, is the South's ultimate text.

The changing demographics of the South, especially the growing Hispanic population, serve to highlight a role the Roman Catholic Church plays in politics in the region. In Florida, Louisiana, and Texas, Catholics are the largest affiliation in the state. Nationally, Catholics are the largest denomination of Americans, and on social issues like gay marriage and abortion their voice is compelling among the faithful.

In the late 1950s and 1960s the civil rights movement drew heavily on the institutional and ethical resources of the black church to appeal to the conscience of the white Christian establishment. The movement, squarely planted in the black church, confronted and challenged the contradictions in white Christian morality and white supremacy for its maintenance of segregation and black inferiority.

The legacy of Christian activism continued in 1995, when Alabama circuit judge Roy S. Moore posted the Ten Commandments in his courtroom, and into 2003 when Moore had the same tablets placed in the foyer of the Supreme Court building of the state. In a society that prizes tradition, nothing is more sacred than religion with its attendant moral uprightness. James Dickey wrote of this vision when he described the mood in a southern church as, "an intensity of gentleness beyond any description and in silence a sense of congregation like layers of souls, close to each other, caring."[82]

The religious affection of white Southerners is the most tangible component in the cultural struggle over the emotional issues of abortion, legalized gambling, women's rights, homosexual rights, and the role of prayer in public schools. These conflicts are symptomatic of larger cultural struggles to shape and define the fundamental assumptions of US public and private life. The South is a partisan participant in the contemporary battle between orthodox and progressive religious life.[83] Though not completely transformed, the social landscape in the South is a growing mixture of traditional conservative values with more moderate and progressive ones mixed in the context of race and a more diversified social base for politics. The configuration of partisan allegiances in the South has led to a rebirth in the conservative view of the role of government, and the qualifications of individuals who should occupy positions of political leadership.

In the postwar era, prominent religious movements arose in the region to maintain an association between explicit faith commitments and government. For example, Christian organizations have advanced proposals for government to return prayer to the public schools, and offer vouchers to families who want their children to attend private religious schools. The impulse to return Christianity to the "Naked Public Square" is strongest in the US South, and the connection between religion and politics is most obvious there. In the South, candidates for public office usually make their faith commitments explicit in campaign commercials and brochures. The stand they have on issues like abortion rights, homosexual rights, school vouchers, and public prayer can determine election success or defeat. These issues arise in the new patterns of political partisanship emerging in the eleven southern states.

Notes

1. James Agee, *A Death in the Family*. New York: Grosset and Dunlap, 1957, pp. 57–58.
2. Garry Wills, *Under God: Religion and American Politics*. New York: Simon and Schuster, 1990, p. 98.
3. Edward J. Larson, *Summer for the Gods*. New York: Basic Books, 1997, p. 221.
4. Rodney Stark, "Why Gods Should Matter in Social Science," in *The Chronicle of Higher Education*, June 6, 2003.
5. Kenneth D. Wald, *Religion and Politics in the United States*. 2d ed. Washington, D.C.: Congressional Quarterly, 1992, p. 38.
6. Eudora Welty, "One Writer's Beginnings," in Suzanne W. Jones (ed.), *Growing Up in the South: An Anthology of Modern Southern Literature*. New York: Signet Classics of Penguin Books, 2003, p. 39.
7. Marion Elizabeth Rodgers (ed.), *Mencken and Sara: A Life in Letters*. New York: McGraw-Hill, 1987.
8. George M. Marsden, *Fundamentalism and American Culture*. New York: Oxford University Press, 1980, p. 186.
9. Frederick C. Harris, *Something Within: Religion in African-American Political Activism*. New York: Oxford University Press, 1999, p. 61.
10. Southern Politics Collection, "Florida," Vanderbilt University, Special Collections.
11. Michael Barone, *The Almanac of American Politics*. Washington, D.C.: National Journal, 1972–2004.
12. Irwin Glusker (ed.), *A Southern Album: Recollections of Some People and Places and Times Gone By*. New York: A&W Visual Library, 1975.
13. D.G. Hart, *Defending the Faith: J. Gresham Machen and the Crisis of Conservative Protestantism in Modern America*. Philipsburg, N.J.: P & R Publishing, 1994, p. 6.
14. The term "religious conservative" is used to include evangelical, fundamentalist, and charismatic Christians who identify themselves as theologically conservative Protestants. There are differences in style, but almost all of them hold to two convictions: (1) a literal interpretation of the Bible, and (2) a belief that one must have a "born again" experience of conversion. Virtually all of them are politically conservative.
15. Bradley J. Longfield, *The Presbyterian Controversy*. New York: Oxford University Press, 1991.

16. George M. Marsden, *Fundamentalism and American Culture*, p. 3.

17. Richard John Neuhaus and Michael Cromartie (eds.), *Piety and Politics: Evangelicals and Fundamentalists Confront the World*. Washington, D.C.: Ehtics and Public Policy Center, 1987, p. 72.

18. William Martin, *With God on Our Side: The Rise of the Religious Right in America*. New York: Broadway Books, 1996, p. 41.

19. Theodore C. Sorensen, *Kennedy*. New York: Harper & Row, 1995, p. 219.

20. Kenneth D. Wald, *Religion and Politics in the United States*, p. 223.

21. *New York Times Co. v. Sullivan*, 376, US 254 (1964); *Miller v. California*, 413, US 15 (1973); *Lemon v. Kurtzman*, 403, US 602 (1971); *Wisconsin v. Yoder*, 406, US 295 (1972); *Griswold v. Connecticut*, 381, US, 479 (1965); *Roe v. Wade*, 401, US 113 (1973).

22. Neuhaus and Cromartie, *Piety and Politics*, p. 77.

23. James D. Hunter, *Culture Wars*. New York: HarperCollins, 1991, pp. 107–132.

24. Jimmy Carter, *Why Not the Best?* Nashville, Tenn.: Broadman Press, 1975, p. 19.

25. Michael Cromartie, "Religious Conservatives in American Politics: 1980–2000." The Witherspoon Fellowship Lectures, Family Research Council, March 16, 2001.

26. William Martin, *With God on Our Side*, p. 178.

27. Ralph Reed, *Active Faith: How Christians Are Changing the Soul of American Politics*. New York: Free Press, 1996, p. 93.

28. Steve Bruce, *Conservative Protestant Politics*. New York: Oxford University Press, 1998, p. 149.

29. William Martin, *With God on Our Side*, p. 207.

30. Francis A. Schaeffer, *A Christian Manifesto*. Westchester, Ill.: Crossway Books, 1981.

31. *Wall Street Journal*, October 13, 1980, p. 18.

32. Neuhaus and Cromartie, *Piety and Politics*, p. 81.

33. *New York Times*, September 7, 1980.

34. *Wall Street Journal*, September 11, 1980.

35. William Martin, *With God on Our Side*, pp. 214–215.

36 . Ibid., p. 239.

37. *New York Times*, February 12, 1988.

38. *New York Times*, March 6, 1988.

39. Sean Wilentz, "Strength for the Journey," *New Republic*, April 25, 1988, and reported in the *Washington Post*, June 12, 1989.

40. Ralph Reed, *Active Faith*, p. 132.

41. Clyde Wilsox, *Onward Christian Soldiers: The Religious Right in American Politics*. Boulder, Colo.: Westview Press, 1996, p. 61.

42. John F. Persinos, "Has the Christian Right Taken Over the Republican Party?" *Campaigns and Elections*, September 21–24, 1994.

43. www.sbc.net.

44. Ferroll Sams, *The Whisper of the River*. New York: Viking Penguin, 1984, p. 3.

45. *Washington Post*, June 8, 1979.

46. Kenneth W. Wald, Dennis E. Owen, and Samuel S. Hill Jr., "Churches as Political Communities," *American Political Science Review* 82 (1988): pp. 531–548; Charles W. Dunn (ed.), *Religion and American Politics*. Washington, D.C.: CQ Press, 1989; David Legge and Lyman A. Kellstedt, *Rediscovering the Religious Factor in American Politics*. Amonk, N.Y.: M. E. Sharpe, 1993.

47. Jim Guth, "The Mobilization of a Religious Ethic: Political Activism Among Southern Baptist Clergy," in *Christian Clergy in American Politics*, Sue Crawford and Laura Olson (eds.). Baltimore: Johns Hopkins Press, 2001, pp. 139–156.

48. *Washington Post*, May 16, 1980.

49. Ibid., June 10, 1986, June 14, 1986.

50. Oran Smith, *The Rise of Baptist Republicanism*. New York: New York University Press, 1997, p. 191.

51. *Little Rock Democrat-Gazette*, June 2, 1991.

52. *Atlanta Journal and Constitution*, July 10, 1992.

53. Ibid.

54. Oran Smith, *The Rise of Baptist Republicanism*, p. 205.

55. *The Economist*, May 17, 2003, p. 28.

56. Marvin Olasky, *The Tragedy of American Compassion*. Washington, D.C.: Regnery Gateway, 1992.

57. Marvin Olasky, *Compassionate Conservatism*. New York: Free Press, 2000.

58. *Birmingham News*, May 19, 2003; *Talon News*, August 22, 2003. Also see: Lisa San Pascual, "The Social Gospel Lays an Egg in Alabama," *Religion in the News* 6, no. 5 (Fall 2003), pp. 11 and 25.

59. Robert A. Bernstein and Jim Seroka, "Alabama's Tax Reform: What Went Wrong and Why?" Paper presented at the biennial Citadel Symposium on Southern Politics, March 4–5, 2004, Charleston, South Carolina.

60. Lyman Kellstedt, John Green, Corwin Smidt, and James Guth, "The Soul of the South: Religion and the New Electoral Order," in Charles S. Bullock III and Mark J. Rozell (eds.), *The New Politics of the Old South: An Introduction to Southern Politics*. 2d ed. Lanham, Md.: Rowman & Littlefield, 2003, pp. 283–299.

61. Matthew Corrigan, "Consequences of Partisan Realignment in the South." Paper presented at the biennial Citadel Symposium on Southern Politics, March 4–5, 2004, Charleston, South Carolina.

62. Kellstedt et al., "The Soul of the South," p. 295.

63. Taylor Branch, *Parting the Waters: America in the King Years*. New York: Simon and Schuster, 1988, p. 695.

64. Andrew Billingsley, *Mighty Like a River*. New York: Oxford University Press, 1999, p. xx.

65. Milton C. Sernett (ed.), *African American Religious History*. Durham, N.C.: Duke University Press, 1999, p. 69.

66. Donald C. Mathews, *Religion in the Old South*. Chicago: University of Chicago Press, 1977, p. 214.

67. Thomas C. Holt, "Black Life," in *Encyclopedia of Southern Culture*, p. 136.

68. Benjamin E. Mays and Joseph W. Nicholson, *The Negroes Church*. New York: Institute of Social and Religious Research, 1933.

69. Gayraud S. Wilmore and James H. Cone, *Black Theology: A Documentary History, 1966–1979*. New York: Orbis Books, 1979, p. 3.

70. Taylor Branch, *Parting the Waters: America in the King Years, 1954–1963*. New York: Simon and Schuster, 1988, pp. 74–75.

71. Ibid., pp. 82–83. The quote is from Reinhold Niebuhr, *Moral Man and Immoral Society*. New York: Westminster John Knox Press, 2002, p. 253.

72. E.D. Hirsch Jr., *Cultural Literacy*. Boston: Houghton Mifflin, 1987, p. 99.

73. David Garrow, *Bearing the Cross: Martin Luther King, Jr. and the Southern Christian Leadership Conference*. New York: Vintage Books, 1988, p. 58.

74. Frederick C. Harris, *Something Within*, p. 65.

75. William Manchester, *The Glory and the Dream*. New York: Bantam Books, 1974.

76. Stephen B. Oates, *Let the Trumpet Sound: The Life of Martin Luther King, Jr.* New York: Harper & Row, 1982, p. 262.

77. Francis Butler Simkins and Charles Pierce Roland, *A History of the South*, New York: Alfred A. Knopf, 1952, p. 299.

78. Martin B. Bradley, Norman M. Green Jr., Dale E. Jones, et al., *Churches and Church Membership in the United States, 1990*. Atlanta: Glenmary Research Center, 1991.

79. Flannery O'Connor, *Mystery and Manners*. New York: Farrar, Straus and Giroux, 1961, p. 44.

80. Steve Bruce, *The Rise and Fall of the New Christian Right*. New York: Clarendon Press, Oxford, 1988, p.181.

81. Peter Applebone, *Dixie Rising*. New York; Random House, 1996, p. 28.

82. James Dickey, *Jericho: The South Beheld*. Birmingham, Ala.: Oxmoor Press, 1989.

83. James Hunter, *Culture Wars*.

6
Political Partisanship

The dominance of a one-party political system in the South after the Civil War into the mid–twentieth century belies the existence of partisanship and conflict in elections. The competition between and among rival Democratic factions could be just as vicious as any battle between Democrats and Republicans, and was likely to be more personal. Huey Long called a baldheaded opponent, "Turkey Head," and Lyndon Johnson once said an antagonist was so stupid he "couldn't pour piss out of a boot with the instructions written on the heel." The rural character of the South produced no-nonsense politicians who communicated on a base level with their constituents. The rhetoric was homespun and connected with common values of simple people. Sam Rayburn, the acerbic Texas congressman once said, "There are no degrees of honesty. A man is either honest, or he isn't."[1]

In the South ambitious politicians to represent these constituents were plentiful, but because of the one-party system, opportunities to win important offices were rare. Politics was dominated by small-town rich men who knew US senators and congressmen as "friends," and could write to Washington about a job for someone in the community. Local elites "knew people" in the governor's office and made contributions during campaigns to the right man at the right time. This led to intraparty competition and fierce contests for relatively unimportant offices. Sometimes the factions were based on geography, sometimes on powerful personalities, and sometimes on long-standing animosities, but always they led to colorful and contentious contests.

Following Reconstruction, the disenfranchisement from political participation of practically all blacks, and many white have-nots, decimated the Republican and Populist parties in the South. Between 1910 and 1950 the Democrats monopolized state offices and deterred serious opposition in general elections. November elections were empty rituals with the outcome known before the voting booths ever opened. On average less than one-fifth of eligible voters showed up to vote in these

215

years. The economic, social, and political institutions were so enmeshed with each other that this lack of participation was a source of regional pride, and any criticism of elections being determined by anything other than primaries was seen as disloyal.

The skill of southern Democrats was most apparent in the way they used the "Solid South" base at election times. One person interviewed for V. O. Key's book shared the experience of a visit from a Washington insider trying to raise money for Franklin Roosevelt's reelection campaign bid in 1944. The man addressed a group of mill workers in South Carolina urging them to contribute $1.00 each for FDR. The crowd was respectful, but silent and unenthusiastic. When the talk was over a member of the audience came up and said they certainly appreciated the campaign worker coming over and talking to them, and they were interested in what he said. But the speaker should realize that he was asking the mill workers to vote for Roosevelt and also contribute a dollar, when the workers usually got *two* dollars for voting. In other words, the visitor needed to pay the audience three dollars to get his contribution.[2]

White elites effectively limited voter access to resources for competition in elections. Old-style southern politicians controlled elections by co-opting opponents, or resorting to intimidation and election fraud. Democratic one-party rule had another, more nefarious, origin. Party leaders historically came from Black Belt counties, and knew that single-party rule controlled participation by blacks. The most virulent racism was born in the rural rhetoric of backwoods campaigns. White domination was guaranteed as long as there was one political party. Rural poverty and control by county governments perpetuated this system through limited voting and elite rule.

One-party rule was really no-party rule, with the only competition being factions within the Democratic Party itself. The rural agrarian economy provided no opportunity or channel for significant political protest activity. The political culture of the South accepted only modest levels of government activity as legitimate. Southerners were suspicious of collective action by government, no matter how appealing the promises. Of course not all spurned the idea of public works. WPA projects dotted the landscape of southern communities and after World War II the region would rally to secure federal grants and military installations. Others rejected the New Deal, and then the Great Society, and looked unfavorably on any government activity as an intrusion into their individual lives.

The tables in this chapter capture in a summary measure the change from a one-party factional political party system, to one with two parties. At first the year-by-year percent Republican measure condenses the change in representation for federal and state offices. These changes are summarized in turn by a measure that captures the change in a single number for both the federal- and state-level offices.

Political Culture and Political Realignment

The political culture is the framework of values that places limits on individuals and group activity. Political parties shape the overall tone and style of political activity in a state or region. According to Daniel Elazar, some political cultures emphasize participation more than others, and one of the characteristics of the "traditionalistic" and "individualistic" political culture is that it looked unfavorably on energetic governmental activity.[3] Research has confirmed that moralistic cultures have higher turnout rates than the individual and traditional cultures characteristic of the South.[4] Political culture can help explain one of the abiding features of southern politics, that of nonparticipation by voters in the region.

Political parties are key to the political culture because they "orient people toward the basic elements in the political system."[5] Political parties function as organizations that run candidates for public office and have the allegiance of part of the electorate. In democracies two or more political parties compete for public office and provide stability for the system as a whole. One-party domination and a lack of participation by the populace means that elected officials can govern without accountability. That was the legacy in the political culture of the South where factions within a loose one-party system contended for dominance at election time.

A comparison of voter participation in presidential elections is shown in Table 6.1. The table shows registration and voter turnout in 1952 and 2000 for each southern state, and these states are compared to the nation as a whole. A comparison of the votes cast, and the voting-age population in 1952 shows an abysmal rate of participation by citizens in these states. The differences, while enormous at midcentury, had moderated by the year 2000.

Since the appearance of Elazar's theory, several scholars have explained the nonparticipation in evidence in Table 6.1. Ira Sharkansky found that among the forty-eight continental states, high scores on traditionalism were related to less developed governmental bureaucracies, lower governmental expenditures, lower tax efforts, fewer public services, lower public employee salaries, and lower voter participation.[6] As urbanization forced government to expand services, voters began to register and participate.

One-party domination by the Democratic Party was the rule at midcentury, with the first major defections occurring in 1952 when Dwight Eisenhower ran for president. In that election Tennessee, Texas, and Virginia voted Republican. Two Democratic US senators represented each of the eleven southern states. Every member of the US House of Representatives from the region, except three from east Tennessee, belonged to the Democratic Party.

The party composition of state elected officials confirmed one-party rule. Democratic Party allegiance was total at the state level. Every one of the eleven states had a Democratic governor. The state senates were 100 percent Democratic, except for Georgia, North Carolina, and Virginia—they were 90 percent. Tennessee

Table 6.1   Political Participation and Voting, 1952 and 2000 Presidential Elections

State	1952		2000	
	Percent of Voting-Age Population Voting[a]	Percent of Registered Voters Voting[b]	Percent of Voting-Age Population Voting[a]	Percent of Registered Voters Voting[b]
Alabama	24.8	N/A	50.0	65.9
Arkansas	38.3	73.0	47.8	59.2
Florida	50.4	73.8	50.6	68.1
Georgia	30.5	50.7	43.8	66.9
Louisiana	40.3	61.7	54.2	64.7
Mississippi	24.3	N/A	48.6	57.1
North Carolina	52.6	N/A	50.3	56.9
South Carolina	29.4	60.1	46.6	64.3
Tennessee	45.2	N/A	49.2	65.3
Texas	42.3	N/A	43.1	62.4
Virginia	31.4	92.3	53.0	74.0
South	37.2	N/A	48.8	64.0
Non-South	69.6	N/A[c]	52.7	68.7

Sources: 2000 data available at www.fec.gov/pages/2000turnout/reg&to00.htm. 1952 data: Population, US Census Bureau, 1958 Statistical Abstract, Table 446; Registered Voters, US Census Bureau, 1955 Statistical Abstract, Table 398; Votes Cast, US Census Bureau, 1953 Statistical Abstract, Table 356.

Notes: a. Voting age includes citizens 21 years old and over prior to 1971 (except for Georgia) and 18 thereafter; b. Registration not reported in some states and marked N/A for lack of either records or requirement for voter registration. Numbers reported for Arkansas, Florida, Georgia, and Louisiana are from 1952; for South Carolina, 1950; and for Virginia, 1949; c. Not relevant due to large number of states either not requiring or not reporting voter registration.

was the most competitive two-party state, and it was still 85 percent Democratic. The Democrats dominated state lower houses: Florida, Mississippi, Louisiana, South Carolina, and Texas were exclusively one-party Democratic in their lower legislative chambers. The partisan make-up of the remaining lower house legislatures in the South were at least 90 percent Democratic, with the single exception to the monolith again being Tennessee, and it was 77 percent.

Fifty years after Key's seminal study, the partisan allegiance in the South, with a more urbanized, affluent, and diverse electoral base, is completely transformed. In the 2000 presidential election, every one of the eleven southern states (although Florida's vote was disputed for a time) voted in the majority for Republican George W. Bush. Their loyalty was repeated four years later. After 2004, only four of the twenty-two US senators were Democrats, a drop from unanimity fifty years ago to a ratio of less than one-quarter. The only states with at least half Democratic representation in their US House of Representatives delegations were: Arkansas (50 percent) and Mississippi (50 percent). The redistricting in Texas led to GOP domination in 2004, with Republicans controlling two-thirds of the delegation. The other southern states were majority Republican in representation in the US House, and GOP prospects were bright given the redistricting after the 2000 census.

The partisan transformation at the federal level was trickling down to the state level where Democratic domination lingered. Democratic governors were found only in four states in 2004: Tennessee, Virginia, Louisiana, and North Carolina, with the latter winning reelection that year. Six states—South Carolina, Virginia, Georgia, Tennessee, Florida, and Texas—had Republican majorities in their state senates in 2004. Most state senates were competitive between typically white suburban Republicans and minority urban or rural Democrats. The only exception to this pattern is Arkansas, which continued to be three-quarters Democratic. The lower houses of the state legislatures have changed dramatically as well—those in Florida, Virginia, Georgia, Texas, and South Carolina are run by the Republicans. The other southern states are two-party competitive at this level, with only Louisiana and Arkansas being dominated by the Democrats. After the 2004 election each party controlled half of the houses of the southern legislatures, the first time in modern history that Democrats did not control a majority of the southern legislative chambers.

The changes since 1950, from a region dominated by one-party Democratic allegiance with a diminished electoral base, to one that has two competitive parties, including a strong Republican presence, with all citizens eligible to vote and influential in national politics—is the focus of this chapter. V. O. Key crystallized the theory of electoral realignment when he wrote "A Theory of Critical Elections" in 1955, a few years after completing his book on southern politics. Three major political scientists contributed important work after Key: E. E. Schattschneider, James L. Sundquist, and Walter Dean Burnham.[7] Innovative additions were made to the realignment interpretation in the 1970s and 1980s.[8] In 2002 David Mayhew reviewed the realignment discussion by proposing fifteen claims in four broad categories that summarized the findings on political realignment and critical elections.[9]

The political history of the South is synonymous with its legacy of one-party politics. Given the changes in the region, it is proper to explain how and when this subculture underwent a party realignment. That means a set of elections in which the electorate responds to a powerful issue that changes the political order. Mayhew argues that the claims of realignment can be grouped into four categories: (1) a dynamic of periodicity, much like a business cycle, (2) a group of necessary preconditions, causes, or properties that come before the realignment, (3) a cluster of issues that can be related to ideology, and (4) an associated change in government policy. These four claims of realignment were met in the southern subculture by the presidency of Ronald Reagan.

The Republican Party constituted a historical minority in US politics in 1980, and was only a faint memory in the South. In this critical election, Ronald Reagan made himself and the party he led into a majority force for change. Like the South, Reagan was a throwback to a different era, and comfortable with that fact. The GOP nominee frontally attacked Jimmy Carter's record and made himself the heir to southern values. The first requirement of realignment is periodicity. The realignment cycle emerges approximately every thirty years or so, and is fueled by the tension between inertia and concentrated bursts of change. The last clear national realignment was 1932, but a significant election in the South was in 1948. The Dixiecrat revolt meant the cycle of realignment would occur in the Carter presidency, and had the Georgian been able to mold the South back into the national Democratic Party, the realignment timing would have been met. Carter failed, but Ronald Reagan did lead the South into a national party, albeit one that was familiar to few in the region. The Carter disappointment, and Reagan's landslide victory, allowed the South to disengage from the Democrats and embrace the GOP. If the delayed independence of Southerners in 1948 is taken as a benchmark, then the 1980 realignment is right on schedule.

The second realignment requirement is that its preconditions are met when new cleavages appear, often in ideological polarization. "For one reason or another . . . good showings by third parties tend to stimulate, or at least take place shortly before, realignments."[10] In 1980 John Anderson ran as a moderate independent with Republican roots, hoping to force Reagan off to the right, and Carter, if not to the left, at least into obscurity because of his failed presidency. Anderson lost. The country, and the South in particular, wanted more ideological leadership. As a reporter at the time put it, Reagan "played the chords: moderation, resentment of government, unhappiness at the economic situation, disappointment at Carter, [and his] experience in California."[11] The Reagan rhetoric echoed that of George Wallace about government intrusion and failure, the difference was that the California governor had a smiling, sunny, optimistic manner of articulating antigovernment conservatism to southern audiences.

The third element of realignment is concerned with issues. For James Sundquist a cluster of related issues, like slavery in the 1850s or the role of government in the Great Depression of the 1930s, forced a new dominant voter cleavage. No similar calamity presented itself in the 1980 election, but it did not have to. Walter Dean Burnham contends that an increase in ideological polarization can force realignment just like a crisis.[12] Ronald Reagan capitalized on the failed presidency of a native southern son to discredit him and embrace the conservative values endemic to the region. Reagan wanted a constitutional amendment to limit abortions, he had a plan to revive the economy without raising taxes, and he wanted government's role trimmed and adjusted, but not abandoned. Ronald and Nancy

Reagan led the crowd in the singing of "God Bless America," and ended his rallies with a prayer. Jimmy Carter did none of these things, and as a result the former Georgia governor lost his geographical base in 1980.

The realignment discussed here is not national in focus, but regional; it is not the US culture that is at issue, but the subculture of the South. The final requirement for realignment is a change in government policy, "a turning point in the mainstream of national policy formation."[13] In sum, the public expresses its will on crucial issues that determine subsequent elections. The Reagan election was watershed in determining the size and role of government. Even Bill Clinton, the first two-term Democrat since FDR, would begin his State of the Union address with the words, "the era of big government is over." It was Ronald Reagan who ended the era of the New Deal and the Great Society.

The change in social and economic patterns in the South helped precipitate this realignment. In this chapter the changes in partisanship are summarized in tables documenting the change—but the analysis is not limited to summary tables. The explanation for partisan transformation involves more than numbers. The political culture of the South is the context for shifts in economic and social conditions, but it is also the source for the continuity between the past and the present. In many respects it is the underlying stimulus for changes in political party fortunes.

V. O. Key's classic state-by-state analysis of southern politics confirmed one-party rule founded on three distinct southern institutions: the near total dominance of the Democratic Party, disenfranchisement of black voters, and the pervasive ethos of Jim Crow rule. In a chapter entitled "Is There a Way Out?" Key indicated future two-party competition might be rooted in the factions within the Democratic Party.

> A single party . . . dominates the South, but in reality the South has been Democratic only for external purposes, that is, presidential and congressional elections. The one-party is purely an arrangement for national affairs. . . . The Democratic Party in most states of the South is merely a holding company for congeries of transient squabbling factions, most of which fail by far to meet the standards of permanence, cohesiveness, and responsibility that characterize the political party.[14]

The rudimentary elements of party competition, which would subsequently become the Republican Party, existed within the factions of the Democratic Party. Key argued "the extent to which the Democratic Party divides into two party-like factions or veers toward a splintered factional system in the various states" was discerned by examining the percentage of the total vote polled by the two leading candidates for governor in the first Democratic primary.[15] Key found that Tennessee, Virginia, and Georgia were bifurcated, while Florida had a multiplicity of factions. Arkansas, South Carolina, Texas, and Mississippi had multiple Democratic factions too, which he characterized as "friends and neighbors" associations within one party. North Carolina, Alabama, and Louisiana occupied a middle ground between the bifurcated state Democratic parties and the states of multiple factions.

Key's analysis at mid–twentieth century showed in the single-party South—where victory in the Democratic primary was tantamount to election—a latent factionalism was more the rule than genuine party competition. The splintering of the Democratic primary vote was used as an indicator of party division. Fifty years ago Key declared that Virginia stood alone as a state where one faction, the "Byrd Machine," dominated. Arkansas, South Carolina, Texas, Mississippi, and Florida were wide-open systems where the strongest factional candidate could not expect much more than a third of the primary vote.[16]

In the 1970s the institutional forces Key identified as maintaining Democratic Party dominance in the South began to crumble.[17] The civil rights movement and the Voting Rights Act of 1965 granted full citizenship and political rights to previously disenfranchised blacks, and removed the restrictions to voter registration that excluded most of them from political office. The involvement of the Supreme Court in the question of vote dilution was established in the case of *Baker v. Carr* (1962) that held legislative apportionment subject to court jurisdiction. In *Reynolds v. Sims* (1964) the Court decided that because Alabama's legislative districts contained unequal numbers of voters, the state's apportionment diluted the votes of inhabitants in heavily populated districts and violated the equal protection clause of the Fourteenth Amendment. The resulting reapportionment revolution required the legislatures to draw new districts on the basis of population equality. Economic, social, and demographic changes began to sweep the South, challenging its distinctive regional qualities and Key's three distinct institutions (the Democratic Party, black disenfranchisement, and Jim Crow rule). These changes ended one-party domination.

The level of Republican identification in the South changed at the national level with the election of Eisenhower in 1952, and by 1980 the trickle had become a flood. Republican growth came from newcomers, conservative rural Democrats, and suburban middle- and upper-class voters who changed their political allegiance. Bass and DeVries commented in 1977, "The forces of social and economic change that have stirred political trends in the South will continue to exert pressure toward two-party political competition."[18]

The close connection between the federal government and the Democratic Party transformed the southern social base of state politics. The change in the status of blacks from political objects to political participants, especially in Democratic Party politics, drove a wedge into the party. The Republican Party pursued a "southern strategy," with a subtle—and not so subtle—rhetoric fashioned to lure southern white voters from their traditional Democratic allegiance.

William Havard argued in 1972 that for the first time since 1948, regional antipathy toward the national Democratic Party by southern white voters coalesced around the 1968 presidential candidacy of George Wallace and began a shift in

Democratic Party loyalty in the decade of the 1970s. Alabama governor Wallace originally captured the national spotlight in fiery opposition to civil rights. That image, however, overshadowed his more lasting legacy as a spokesman for white working-class resentment and general opposition to big, intrusive government.

Republicans built on these antifederal sentiments in their "southern strategy," devised by Lee Atwater and Kevin Phillips. The plan was to capitalize on southern resentment of big government, and Ronald Reagan exploited these anxieties fully in 1980. Democrats continued to flourish at the state and county level, but southern states turned Republican at the federal level. Havard wrote in 1972 that, "with the Republican Party increasingly competitive in the evolving and wavering South, with the defection from the Democratic Party fluctuating wildly in the Deep South, and with the general decimation of state Democratic organizations throughout much of the region, it would be hard to categorize the politics of the South as anything but a 'no-party' system."[19]

The polarizing element in southern politics was the sledgehammer effect of the newly enfranchised black voters. As more and more blacks became loyal supporters of the national Democratic Party, white Southerners broke their traditional Democratic allegiance. The wedge between blacks and whites not only transformed the social base of the Democratic Party, but also contributed to subregional variations in emergent Republicanism. Tennessee and North Carolina had part of their history in the Republican Party. South Carolina immediately had a viable Republican Party when Strom Thurmond switched parties in 1964, while GOP growth in Georgia and Arkansas was much slower. Havard concluded that the South might ultimately divide into two groups: a majority white Republican Party opposed by a black minority party.[20]

Earl and Merle Black announced in the 1980s that "Democratic monopolization of southern politics has ended, and Republicans now vigorously contest most major elections." A caveat followed, as the authors noted that Republicans were not yet competitive for all types of offices, or in all parts of the South.[21] Since the Great Society of the 1960s, Republican presidential candidates have fared well among white Southerners, especially those of the middle- and upper-class ranks. It took longer for southern Republicanism to "trickle-down" to nonpresidential statewide elections, but Black and Black confirmed in 1987 "the traditional Democratic domination of statewide elections in the South has vanished."[22]

Twenty-five years ago Republican strength was more advanced in the peripheral South (Virginia, North Carolina, Tennessee, and Texas) than in the Deep South (South Carolina, Georgia, Alabama, Mississippi, and Louisiana). Since Ronald Reagan's presidential victory in 1980, Republicans are competing better across the entire South for a wider range of offices than ever before. "Approximately two-thirds of the white vote went to Republican nominees for president, US senator and US representative in 1996."[23] Gains among traditional white voters are offset by African American losses; in presidential elections Republicans seldom attract more than 10 percent of the black vote. At the end of the twentieth century the partisan transformation was complete. "Reagan's presidency was the turning point in the South."[24] The combination of shifting economic, cultural, and religious loyalties made the South competitive and changed the texture of politics nationally.

Levels of Political Change

Modernizing forces ultimately altered the social order and the "Solid South" loyalty to the Democratic Party began to unravel. The last time all eleven former Confederate states voted Democratic in a national presidential election was in 1944. Since the 1940s the social, economic, and racial landscape of the South has been transformed by the emergence of a two-party system, economic growth with multinational corporations, and the presence of an expanding middle class. The splintering of the Democratic monolith was begun by inroads by the Republican Party at the presidential level, then statewide offices, with more modest Republican gains in sub-statewide positions.

Central to any explanation of partisan change is the notion of political "dealignment," meaning the "decline in the centrality of parties to citizen political orientations and behavior."[25] The dealignment perspective in US politics means that voters' partisan loyalties are substantially and permanently weakened. This perspective has had appeal in the South because for years the Republicans held an edge at the presidential level, while Democrats were dominant in offices down the ticket.[26] Scholars have argued that dealignment has run its course because Republicans continued to win offices at all levels and the rise of independent identifiers—arguably the most important indicator of dealignment—is really nullified when people are asked how they are "leaning" in an election.[27] When independent leaners are added to partisans, the South comes close to the realignment ideal.

In sum, the evidence suggests that dealignment may have been overstated and, especially in the South, partisan development and electoral competition have led to a restructuring. The tables in this chapter will show that politics in the South is rather stable, with predictability tied to residence in urban and suburban areas.

Change trickled-down from presidential races to lower ones. Southern sentiment for the candidacy of Dwight Eisenhower or Richard Nixon was transferred to an occasional GOP candidate for the US Senate or governor. Once a Republican won a statewide race, it was easier for a US House candidate to win an open seat when a Democrat retired. Ultimately Republicans began to capture statewide seats. Landslide electoral victories by the GOP, like those in 1972 and 1980, were very influential in spreading partisan change.

The development of southern Republican strength has been from the top down: meaning the earliest change was at the presidential level, then filtered down to the statewide offices, congressional seats, and then into the state legislature. Initially the percent Republican electoral figure was quite high in both terms for Dwight D. Eisenhower. The states of Texas, Florida, Virginia, and Tennessee voted for Ike twice. The Kennedy/Johnson, or Boston/Austin, ticket was helpful in reclaiming the Solid South legacy for the Democratic Party in 1960.

The rise of racial politics in reaction to the civil rights movement, government expansion with the Great Society programs, and the war in Vietnam came to dominate politics in the 1960s. In 1964 the South stayed loyal to the Democrats, but even in the landslide years the Republicans made significant inroads in the traditional southern states. George Wallace was identified as an antiblack candidate in that election, and the term "backlash" was introduced into the political lexicon to describe him. Later the ideas of Wallace would be used by Reagan to entice southern voters into the GOP. In 1968 Wallace helped erode the lock Democrats had on the South. The Wallace campaign spoke forcefully about what Richard Scammon and Ben Wattenberg called the "Social Issue."[28]

Political discourse that election year was a complex of concerns over "law and order," racial tensions and rioting, family values at home and the Vietnam War abroad. In 1968 George Wallace carried five southern states (Georgia, Alabama, Arkansas, Louisiana, and Mississippi) and received forty-six electoral votes. His campaign against government waste and intrusion helped deliver the presidency to Richard Nixon in 1968, and foreshadowed the rise of the Reagan domestic agenda in the 1980s.

Political realignment in the South received a dramatic boost when the southern states were rocks in the Nixon landslide victory of 1972. Every southern state voted Republican that year, and every electoral vote—save one in Virginia awarded to an independent candidate—was in the GOP column as well. A complete reversal took place four years later when native son Jimmy Carter took the White House and carried every southern state but Virginia.

For a brief shining moment after the Carter victory, the Democratic Party stood at the apex of political power in the United States. In the words of Michael Barone, Jimmy Carter's inauguration after the Watergate scandal was "Democratic government as far as the eye could see."[29] Inside the beltway it was thought that the Democrats would hold onto the executive branch for eight years, and it was impossible to envision how they could lose either house of Congress. After all, Democratic domination of Congress had been virtually unchallenged since 1932. Staffers on the Hill basked in unbroken tenure as leaders on important committees. Democrats expected to nominate a solid majority on the Supreme Court, and fill vacant judicial appointments with loyalists. The state governments were as heavily and solidly controlled by Democrats as any time in history.

For a time, Carter became a cultural icon, and made Southerners, and their way of life, fashionable in Washington and across the country. Prior to his election southern politicians only merited the presidential office as vice presidential nominees (Andrew Johnson and Lyndon B. Johnson) who subsequently succeeded to the presidency. After 1976, southern senators and governors could legitimately harbor aspirations for the nation's highest office without explanation or apology.

Jimmy Carter envisioned presiding over a sweeping national reformation of sorts, a reorganization of all things federal, a reshaping of the tax system, and a reinfusion of human rights into foreign policy. He produced instead a presidency of good intentions and diligent work habits, but failed leadership and lost opportunities. Most importantly for Southerners, "the tragedy of the Carter presidency is that he . . . foolishly squandered those good wishes [of his constituency]."[30] In the 1980 presidential election Carter lost every southern state except his native Georgia.

The election of Ronald Wilson Reagan in 1980 was the most significant event for the country, and for the South, in forty years. Some said Reagan was catapulted into the nation's highest office by anger over Carter-era interest rates and the humiliation of the Iranian hostage crisis and that he was untried as a leader. Some feared the conservatism of the Reagan presidency would be moderated by the realities of governing. In the end all the guesswork about the fortieth president was wrong; Reagan presided over a dramatic transformation of US life. "Reagan's presidency was the turning point in the evolution of a competitive, two-party electorate in the South."[31]

From the perspective of twenty-five years it is clear that the dramatic election of 1980 foreshadowed the collapse of the Democratic Party at the presidential level. Since that year the southern electorate has embraced the GOP with the fervor Scarlett O'Hara had for Ashley Wilkes. Only in 1996, when Florida slipped away from the Republican fold, has the South fallen below the three-quarters electoral support it achieved in 1980 for the Republican nominee. In most elections, 1984, 1988, 2000, and 2004, the electoral support has been unanimous. In sum, since 1980 the South has given the Republicans roughly half the electoral votes needed to win the presidency.

Support for the Republicans in Congress was not as dramatic as that for president, but the southern trend was a growing obedience in the same direction. Table 6.2 shows US Senate representation for every presidential year from 1952 to 2004. Southern states had no senators from the GOP until 1961, when John Tower won a special election after Lyndon Johnson was vice president. In 1964 Strom Thurmond switched parties, and two years later, Thurmond, Tower, and Howard H. Baker Jr. from Tennessee all won as Republicans.

In 1972 when Richard Nixon won the presidency with a "southern strategy" in place, the trickle-down of two-party politics was everywhere apparent. Former Nixon aide William Safire invented the term "southern strategy," which became an attack phrase by liberal journalists to attribute racial animus to any opposition to desegregation or busing that might be well received by southern whites. Later the term became synonymous with any Republican policy designed to pry conservative whites from their allegiance to the Democratic Party.

Table 6.2   US Senate Seats by Party Affiliation, 1952–2004

	1952		1956		1960		1964		1968		1972		1976		1980		1984		1988		1992		1996		2000		2004	
	D	R	D	R	D	R	D	R	D	R	D	R	D	R	D	R	D	R	D	R	D	R	D	R	D	R	D	R
National States																												
Georgia	2	0	2	0	2	0	2	0	2	0	2	0	2	0	1	1	1	1	2	0	1	1	1	1	2	0	0	2
Florida	2	0	2	0	2	0	2	0	1	1	1	1	2	0	1	1	1	1	1	1	1	1	1	1	2	0	1	1
Virginia	2	0	2	0	2	0	2	0	2	0	1a	1	1a	1	1a	1	0	2	1	1	1	1	1	1	0	2	0	2
Texas	2	0	2	0	2	0	1	1	1	1	1	1	1	1	1	1	1	1	1	1	1	1	0	2	0	2	0	2
Emergent States																												
North Carolina	2	0	2	0	2	0	2	0	2	0	1	1	1	1	0	2	0	2	1	1	0	2	0	2	1	1	0	2
Tennessee	2	0	2	0	2	0	2	0	1	1	0	2	1	1	1	1	2	0	2	0	2	0	0	2	0	2	0	2
Traditional States																												
Alabama	2	0	2	0	2	0	2	0	2	0	2	0	2	0	1	1	1	1	2	0	2	0	0	2	0	2	0	2
Arkansas	2	0	2	0	2	0	2	0	2	0	2	0	2	0	2	0	2	0	2	0	2	0	1	1	1	1	2	0
South Carolina	2	0	2	0	2	0	1	1b	1	1	1	1	1	1	1	1	1	1	1	1	1	1	1	1	1	1	0	2
Mississippi	2	0	2	0	2	0	2	0	2	0	2	0	2	0	1	1	1	1	0	2	0	2	0	2	0	2	0	2
Louisiana	2	0	2	0	2	0	2	0	2	0	2	0	2	0	2	0	2	0	2	0	2	0	2	0	2	0	1	1
Total	22	0	22	0	22	0	20	2	18	4	15	7	17	5	12	10	12	10	15	7	13	9	7	15	9	13	4	18
Republicans	0%		0%		0%		9%		18%		32%		23%		45%		45%		32%		41%		68%		59%		82%	

Source: Statistical Abstract of the United States.
Notes: a. Virginia senator Harry Byrd was an independent who was a member of the Democratic Caucus; b. Strom Thurmond switched to the Republican Party in 1964, and was reelected in 1966.

The marshaling of southern voters worked. Every southern state voted for Nixon for president, and every national southern state but one (Georgia) had a Republican senator by that time. After Reagan's election in 1980, Republican southern representation in the US Senate approached half of all senators, a number exceeded in the last years of the Clinton administration. Resistance to Republican incursions in the Senate remained most obdurate in the traditional southern states that only began to weaken by electing candidates when Democratic incumbents retired after Reagan's victory in 1980. The national and emergent states had split representation during the 1980s.

Democrats slowed the erosion when Bill Clinton was elected president in 1992, but after the GOP retook the Senate in the 1994 midterm election, the rout was on. George W. Bush's vigorous campaigning for US House and Senate candidates in 2002 and 2004 led to Republican domination by his second term. The GOP swept every southern Senate seat in 2004.

Bipartisan southern representation in the US Senate changed US politics. For decades the filibuster was as sacred as Excalibur in the hands of southern senators to guard their home states against the passage of civil rights laws. Because of their seniority, southern senators exercised a pervasive and persuasive influence on the decorum, oratory, and pace of work in the most venerated of US institutions. The original architects of the US Constitution, men like James Madison and Charles Pinckney, were themselves Southerners whose ideas about political procedure framed the founding of the institution.

For much of the twentieth century the enormous power held by southern committee chairmen was unlike anything known in US politics. The legendary "Southern Caucus," twenty-two senators who met in the offices of Richard B. Russell of Georgia, was sufficient to stop any threatened legislation in the prewar and postwar years. For example, in January and February of 1938, an outbreak of lynching in the South prompted antilynching bills to be introduced by nonsouthern senators. When the time came to vote, the sponsors could not muster even a simple majority, let alone the needed two-thirds to stop the filibuster.

At midcentury the Southern Caucus met, agreed upon tactics, and left meetings in a solid front. The Southerners entered together in an unspoken, but very clear, show of unity to Congress. Robert Caro quotes an unnamed reporter in the Press Gallery of the Senate at the time who whispered to a colleague, "The South has arrived."[32] Collectively, the southern coalition decided what issues made the legislative calendar and when they were considered. The committee chairs could expedite or halt favored legislation.

This bloc of parliamentary power disappeared when southern states began to send Republicans to the US Senate, but it reemerged in the guise of the GOP in the twenty-first century. Bill Frist of Tennessee became majority leader and guided a fragile coalition of Republicans in the Senate from 2000 onward. Senators like George Allen of Virginia and Richard Shelby of Alabama shepherded the president's programs through committee and were spokesmen for Bush administration

---

Vignette 6.1   Richard B. Russell (1897–1971)

Richard Brevard Russell was a legislative force so dominant in the US Senate that he was called the South's greatest general since Robert E. Lee. He was a masterful legislative strategist who fought against federal civil rights legislation and increased agricultural subsidies for farmers while expanding government spending for national defense. He was a principled partisan, whose leadership set the agenda for postwar politics in the United States.

Russell was born in Winder, Georgia, on November 2, 1897. His father was a state legislator who became chief justice of Georgia's Supreme Court, and the son followed in his father's footsteps by earning a law degree at the University of Georgia in 1918 and practicing law in his hometown. A political career was born in 1921, when Russell won election to the Georgia House of Representatives where he became speaker at age thirty, and the state's youngest chief executive in 1931.

When the incumbent US Senator died in 1932, Russell won the special election for the seat. From 1933 until his death in 1971 he was the unofficial dean of the US Senate. He made himself a master of Senate rules and procedure, and combined his knowledge with an impressive ability with people. His gentle, warm, and friendly manner delivered in a musical southern drawl had an effect on his colleagues who deferred to him on legislative matters.

This respect came from Russell's knowledge and expertise, but also from his tendency to avoid publicity. The senator from Georgia devised compromises and allowed others to take the credit. He was so successful at keeping his name out of the papers that he was frequently not even mentioned when the bills

passed even though he was largely responsible for the result. Russell preferred the anonymity because he had what was more important to him—respect and power without equal in the premier US political institution.

For twenty-six years Richard Russell was either chairman or dominant member of the Senate Armed Services Committee. From this base he became the leading Senate expert on national defense. In the rubble of World War II, he became convinced that in any future war the enemies of the United States should be made to feel the full vengeance of military dominance. In the decades of the Cold War there was no more militant defender of US military superiority than Dick Russell. Although an advocate of a strong military, Russell opposed the commitment of US troops in Southeast Asia. However, once the president made the decision to commit troops to the conflict, and the senator's advice was overruled, he supported the military action.

For thirty-eight years Richard Russell tried to bring the resources of the federal government to help US farmers. He played a major role in providing funds for rural electrification, soil conservation, and government-insured mortgages. He was proudest of his fight for the national school lunch program.

The cause for which he is most remembered was his leadership of the southern wing of the Democratic Party. He was the chief strategist in southern efforts to defeat or weaken civil rights bills. His name was placed in nomination for the presidency at the Democratic Party conventions of 1948 and 1952, but his southern roots and opposition to civil rights kept him from the nomination.

Richard Russell died in Washington on January 21, 1971.

---

policies. The widened majorities after 2004 led to administrative reform and judicial appointments.

A pattern similar to that in the Senate is seen in House elections, although the influence was less pronounced in the latter because of its size and complexity.

Table 6.3 shows that House member results lagged behind the allegiance southern states gave Eisenhower and Nixon in the 1950s. The New Deal witnessed the emergence of a coalition of conservative Republicans and Democrats that dominated wartime and postwar politics. The Republican–Southern Democratic coalition was united in opposition to the unpopular wartime agency and expanding federal government. "In the 78th Congress, the Republicans won more roll-call victories than did the Democrats and were able to amend noncontroversial legislation almost at will."[33] The conservative coalition controlled the Committee on Rules, where two southern Democrats consistently voted with four Republican members to keep Roosevelt administration bills from reaching the House floor.

In the postwar years the patterns of partisan growth were similar—but slower—than the Republican percentages for the US Senate. The suburbanization, and urbanization, of the South in the decades of the 1960s and 1970s slowly changed congressional representation. The patterns of urban dominance, so apparent in the maps and tables of Chapter 3, began during this time period. GOP congressmen usually won their first seats in reapportioned suburban districts. After the 1970 census, southern Republicans emphasized political realignment and spent time trying to convert southern Democratic officeholders to their cause.

The Reagan presidency offered the opportunity for conservative Democrats to switch and ally themselves with the popular conservative Republican president. In late 1985 three dozen southern Democrats arrived at the White House for a meeting with President Reagan. They came to renounce their party and pledge themselves in allegiance to the Republican legislative agenda. They became known as the "Blue Dogs," and one senior presidential aide subsequently described their session with the president as a "naturalization ceremony," but it was also the end of the Democratic Solid South in the House of Representatives.

Typical of the congressmen who embraced Reagan was Phil Gramm of Texas, a conservative economist who benefited from the Reagan opportunity. Elected as a Democrat, he converted to become a Blue Dog conservative who helped enact Reagan's tax rebate measure in 1981. When threatened with retaliation by the Democratic Party in Texas, Gramm switched parties, and won his House seat as a Republican. The Gramm model was a prototype of what was happening to the entire region, but his allegiance was not yet in evidence in congressional elections. Only about one-third of the congressmen were in the GOP at decade's end.

Gradually, the political conservatism in the South became a spawning ground for the Republican Party. In the decade of the 1980s the population in the South's suburban counties grew at twice the national average. Cobb County, outside the city of Atlanta, grew by over 50 percent in this period and its experience was typical of many southern cities. The congressman for much of Cobb County in the 1970s and early 1980s was Dr. Larry McDonald, a Democrat and former head of the John Birch Society, a conservative anticommunism group popular in the Cold War era. McDonald's rabid conservatism fit the area he represented until his death

Table 6.3 US House Seats by Party Affiliation, 1952–2004

	1952		1956		1960		1964		1968		1972		1976		1980		1984		1988		1992		1996		2000		2004	
	D	R	D	R	D	R	D	R	D	R	D	R	D	R	D	R	D	R	D	R	D	R	D	R	D	R	D	R
National States																												
Georgia	10	0	10	0	10	0	9	1	8	2	9	1	10	0	9	1	8	2	9	1	7	4	3	8	3	8	6	7
Florida	8	0	7	1	7	1	10	2	9	3	11	4	10	5	11	4	12	7	10	9	10	13	8	15	3	8	8	17
Virginia	7	3	8	2	8	2	8	2	5	5	3	7	6	4	1	9	4	6	4	6	7	4	6	5	3	7[a]	3	8
Texas	22	0	21	1	21	1	23	0	20	3	20	4	22	2	19	5	17	10	8	19	9	21	17	13	13	17	11	21
Emergent States																												
North Carolina	11	1	11	1	11	1	9	2	7	4	4	7	9	2	7	4	6	5	8	3	8	4	6	6	5	7	6	7
Tennessee	7	2	7	2	7	2	6	3	5	4	5	3	5	5	6	3	6	3	6	3	4	5	4	5	4	5	5	4
Traditional States																												
Alabama	9	0	9	0	9	0	3	5	3	5	4	3	3	4	4	3	5	2	5	2	4	3	2	5	2	5	2	5
Arkansas	6	0	6	0	6	0	4	0	3	1	3	1	3	1	2	2	3	1	3	1	2	2	2	2	3	1	3	1
South Carolina	6	0	6	0	6	0	6	0	5	1	4	2	2	5	2	4	3	4	4	1	3	3	2	4	2	4	2	4
Mississippi	6	0	6	0	6	0	4	1	5	0	3	2	3	2	3	2	4	1	4	1	5	0	3	2	3	2	2	2
Louisiana	8	0	8	0	8	0	8	0	8	0	7	1	6	2	6	2	4	4	4	4	4	3	2	5	2	5	2	5
Total	100	6	99	7	99	7	90	16	80	26	74	34	81	27	69	39	73	43	77	39	77	48	54	71	52	72	50	81
Republicans	6%		7%		7%		15%		25%		31%		25%		36%		37%		34%		38%		57%		58%		62%	

Source: Statistical Abstract of the United States.
Note: a. Virginia had one independent in 2000.

Vignette 6.2   Sam Rayburn (1882–1961) and Lyndon B. Johnson (1908–1973)

Two Texas legislators, Sam Rayburn and Lyndon Johnson, one a Speaker of the US House and the other a US Senate majority leader and later president, dominated US politics in the 1950s and 1960s. The older man was a substitute father for the younger, and together they set the agenda for politics in the postwar era.

Samuel Taliaferro Rayburn served as Speaker of the US House of Representatives longer than any man in the nation's history. Born in Roane County, Tennessee, to the son of a Confederate soldier, the family moved to Texas when the boy was five. At the age of sixteen he entered Mayo Normal School, now East Texas State University. Three years after graduation Rayburn won election to the Texas House of Representatives. While in Austin he attended law school and won admission to the bar. In 1912 he led a field of eight candidates for the US House of Representatives seat in the Democratic Party primary, assuring his election in the overwhelmingly one-party state of Texas.

Rayburn was renominated and reelected from the district twenty-three times. Known as a devoutly loyal party man, he became a lieutenant of the influential Texas congressman, John Nance "Texas Jack" Garner. In 1932 he directed Garner's unsuccessful campaign for the presidency. Rayburn was heavily involved in the negotiations that put Garner on the national ticket. When Roosevelt won the presidency, Rayburn became a workhorse legislator for the New Deal programs. In 1937 he became Democratic majority leader, and three years later, Speaker. From this position he assisted Lyndon Baines Johnson's rise to power.

Johnson was born near Johnson City, Texas, the small community founded by his forebearers. He graduated from Southwest State Teachers College in San Marcos and, after teaching school, became the Texas director of the National Youth Administration. NYA was a New Deal program to help employ youth during the Depression. In the same year that Rayburn became Democratic majority leader, Johnson won an eight-way race for congressman from the Tenth District of Texas.

In Washington, Johnson became the adopted son that bachelor Sam Rayburn never had. Lyndon would invite "Mr. Sam," as he called him, over for dinner. In turn Rayburn invited the junior congressman and prodigy to the hideaway, "Board of Education" meetings in the Capitol where a select group would "strike a blow for liberty" with a late afternoon drink. The room was furnished with leather easy chairs and a sofa, a desk at which Rayburn presided, and a picture of Robert E. Lee on the wall. With the exception of Johnson, the attendees were powerful committee chairs and senior leaders in Congress.

Together Rayburn and Johnson protected oil and gas interests and played a major role in national politics. Rayburn would rule the House with an iron hand, and, after a loss in 1941, Johnson would win a savagely fought campaign for the US Senate in 1948. In 1954, with the Democrats in command of both houses, Johnson became the youngest man ever to be Senate majority leader. Johnson's legendary leadership in the Senate came under the tutelage of Sam Rayburn.

In 1960 Johnson briefly opposed John F. Kennedy for the Democratic presidential nomination, then—in a move that shocked the country—went on the ticket as vice president. Rayburn opposed the move, but after a face-to-face meeting with Kennedy he agreed that the move would unite the Democratic Party and lead to victory in the fall. But Rayburn would not live to see his protégé serve as president; the Speaker died of cancer on November 16, 1961, in his beloved Bonham, Texas.

Lyndon Johnson assumed the presidency after the tragic assassination of Kennedy on November 22, 1963. After winning a landslide election in 1964, he embarked on an ambitious reform program to combat poverty, provide health insurance for the elderly, and enforce civil rights statutes. The "Great Society" was destined to be the first casualty of the Vietnam War.

Johnson's quest for reelection in 1968 was halted by antiwar activism and he stayed in Washington only long enough to witness the inauguration of longtime political foe, Richard M. Nixon. He returned to his beloved LBJ ranch where he died of a massive heart attack on January 22, 1973.

in 1983, which occurred when a Soviet fighter jet shot down Korean Airlines flight 007 with McDonald and 268 other passengers aboard. After McDonald's death, Cobb County was represented by Newt Gingrich, architect of the Republican takeover of Congress in 1994, and later Speaker of the US House of Representatives.

The Bill Clinton presidency became the political graveyard for the Democratic Party in the South. In 1992 the South gained nine congressional seats as a result of the census redistricting. All went Republican in the election that year, one that saw a Democratic governor from the region win the presidency. In the 1994 midterm elections, Republicans went from a 48 to 77 deficit in the House in the eleven Deep South states, to a 64 to 61 advantage. In the 1994 midterm election that advantage expanded to a 71 Republicans to 54 Democrats spread. The Senate results mirrored those in the House, and went from 9 Republicans and 13 Democrats, to a 13 Republicans and 9 Democrats reversal in 1994. In the annals of Republican lore, few elections could match the midterm accomplishment of 1994. "The election saw the Republicans gain fifty-two seats in the House of Representatives and regain control for the first time in forty years."[34] The GOP won back the Senate and key governor's races in New York and Texas, where George W. Bush began his march to the presidency.

The Clinton legislative agenda of gays in the military, a tax increase, and a new government health program did not sit well with white voters in the South. After the 1994 debacle the South had more Republican congressmen than Democratic, and for the first time it was fashionable to run at any level as a Republican. Typical of the new insurgent change was Lindsey Graham, a feisty one-term South Carolina state legislator who won an open-seat election in 1994 and became the first Republican to represent his district in Congress since the 1870s. In 2002 Graham succeeded the legendary Strom Thurmond in the US Senate.

The trickle-down of Republican victories was slower in the state houses and state senates as shown in Table 6.4 and Table 6.5 respectively. The figures for GOP growth are almost the same for both legislative bodies, single digits until the 1968 election, teen numbers until Reagan's second term, then a gradual upswing in Republican representation reaching the low forties by century's end.

For decades the office of state legislator embodied the stereotype of a white male lawyer, evolving country bumpkin, who railed against Yankee capitalism while sporting racial slurs. Most southern legislators only met in biennial sessions, and when they gathered they passed a flurry of bills at the behest of a governor.

Whatever the validity of the stereotype, it began to change in the 1960s and 1970s. The pattern of GOP representation tracked the growth of urban living in the South. The first representatives to claim Republican seats in the state legislatures were usually from suburban districts drawn after a decennial census. The Democratic Party outside the South permitted conservative members to exert considerable influence within their respective states, and maintain their near monopoly on power in state legislative bodies.

Table 6.4   State Senate Seats by Party Affiliation, 1952–2004

	1952		1956		1960		1964		1968		1972		1976		1980		1984		1988		1992		1996		2000		2004	
	D	R	D	R	D	R	D	R	D	R	D	R	D	R	D	R	D	R	D	R	D	R	D	R	D	R	D	R
National States																												
Georgia	53	1	53	1	53	1	44	9[a]	48	7[a]	48	8	52	4	51	5	47	9	45	11	41	15	34	22	32	24	22	34
Florida	37	1	37	1	37	1	42	2	32	16	25	14[a]	29	10[a]	27	13	32	8	23	17	20	20	17	23	15	25	14	26
Virginia	38	2	37	3	38	2	37	3	34	6	33	7	35	5	31	9	31	9	30	10	22	18	20	20	18	22	16	24
Texas	31	0	31	0	31	0	31	0	29	2	28	3	28	3	23	7[b]	25	6	23	8	18	13	14	17	15	16	12	19
Emergent States																												
North Carolina	48	2	47	3	48	2	49	1	38	12	35	15	46	4	40	10	38	12	37	13	39	11	30	20	35	15	29	21
Tennessee	29	4	27	6	27	6	25	8	20	13	19	13[a]	23	9[a]	20	12[a]	23	10	22	11	19	14	18	15	18	15	16	17
Traditional States																												
Alabama	35	0	35	0	35	0	35	0	34	1	35	0	35	0	35	0	28	4[c]	28	6[b]	28	7	22	13	23	12	25	10
Arkansas	35	0	35	0	35	0	35	0	34	1	34	1	34	1	34	1	31	4	31	4	30	5	28	7	27	8	27	8
South Carolina	46	0	46	0	46	0	46	0	47	3	43	3	43	3	41	5	36	10	35	11	30	16	26	20	22	24	20	26
Mississippi	49	0	49	0	49	0	52	0	52	0	50	2	50	2	48	4	49	3	44	8	39	13	34	18	34	18	29	23
Louisiana	39	0	39	0	39	0	39	0	39	0	38	1	38	1	39	0	38	1	34	5	34	5	25	14	26	13	24	15
Total	440	10	436	14	438	12	435	23	407	61	388	67	413	42	389	66	378	75	352	104	320	137	268	189	265	192	277	245
Republicans	2%		3%		3%		5%		13%		15%		9%		14%		16%		23%		30%		41%		42%		47%	

Source: Statistical Abstract of the United States; The Council of State Governments.

Notes: a. one independent; b. one vacancy; c. three independents.

Table 6.5 State House Seats by Party Affiliation, 1952–2004

	1952		1956		1960		1964		1968		1972		1976		1980		1984		1988		1992		1996		2000		2004	
	D	R	D	R	D	R	D	R	D	R	D	R	D	R	D	R	D	R	D	R	D	R	D	R	D	R	D	R
National States																												
Georgia	202	3	202	3	203	2	198	7	169	26	151	29	157	23	156	23[d]	154	26	144	26	128	52	106	74	104	74[e]	81	99
Florida	90	5	89	6	88	7	102	10	77	42	78	42	92	28	81	39	77	43	73	47	71	49	59	61	43	77	36	84
Virginia	91	7	94	6	96	4	89	11	85	15	65	20[b]	78	17[c]	74	25[a]	65	33[e]	59	39[e]	58	41[a]	51	48[a]	47	52[a]	37	61
Texas	150	0	150	0	150	0	149	1	142	8	133	17	132	18	114	35[d]	98	52	93	57	92	58	82	68	78	72	62	88
Emergent States																												
North Carolina	106	14	107	13	105	15	106	14	91	29	85	35	114	6	95	24[d]	82	38	74	46	78	42	59	61	62	58	63	57
Tennessee	80	19	78	21	80	19	75	24	49	49[a]	21	48	66	32[a]	57	39[de]	62	37	59	40	63	36	61	38	61	38	53	46
Traditional States																												
Alabama	105	1	106	0	106	0	104	2	106	0	104	2	106	2	100	4[d]	87	12[cd]	58	17[f]	82	23	72	33	67	38	63	40[i]
Arkansas	97	3	97	2[a]	99	1	99	1	96	4	99	1	96	4	93	7	91	9	88	11[a]	89	10[a]	86	14	70	30	72	28
South Carolina	124	0	124	0	124	0	124	0	119	5	103	21	111	12	107	17	96	27[d]	87	37	73	50	52	71[a]	53	71	50	74
Mississippi	140	0	140	0	140	0	122	0	122	0	119	2[a]	118	3[a]	115	4[de]	116	6	112	9[a]	93	27[e]	84	36[e]	86	33[h]	75	47
Louisiana	100	0	101	0	101	0	103	2	105	0	101	4	101	4	95	10	91	14	86	17[g]	88	16[a]	78	27	71	34	67	37[j]
Total	1,285	52	1,288	51	1,292	48	1,271	72	1,161	178	1,089	221	1,168	149	1,087	227	1,019	297	960	356	915	404	790	531	742	577	659	661
Republicans	4%		4%		4%		5%		13%		17%		11%		17%		22%		27%		30%		40%		44%		50%	

Source: Statistical Abstract of the United States.

Notes: a. one independent; b. fifteen independents; c. five independents; d. one vacancy; e. two independents; f. three vacancies; g. two vacancies; h. three independents; i. two independents; j. one independent.

In some state legislatures a mini-coalition emerged of conservative Democrats and newly elected Republican legislators from the suburbs. Southern legislatures considered fewer bills per session and enacted a higher proportion of all bills introduced in session. An urban-rural tension arose in the governing coalition with suburban Republicans favoring home rule for their municipalities, while rural Democrats clung to their historic legislative dominant position. Gradually in the 1960s and 1970s the continued leftward drift of the national party drove white voters into the waiting arms of the GOP. Throughout the 1990s white voters complained about the Clinton excesses and unwillingness to address the underlying problems of US society. The cities in southern states continued to provide more representation to the various state legislatures until, at century's end, Florida, Virginia, and South Carolina were controlled by the Republicans, and other states, like Tennessee, were trending that way.

Inasmuch as there is a pattern in evidence in these two tables it is that national and emergent states became more two-party competitive, while the traditional states—with the exception of South Carolina—remained Democratic. The tables show that conservative white Democrats can still survive in the South, but their future is in jeopardy. Following the 1990 census, the Republican Party formed an alliance with the NAACP to create more black majority districts—resulting in more black candidates for Congress and the diminished number of white southern Democrats.

The Ranney Index of Party Competition

Political parties transact the important business of transferring power in the body politic. Of all the aspects of political power, the most important has been interparty competition. While the previous tables show unmistakable growth in Republican allegiance, there is no summary measure to register how this partisan change is collectively influencing politics in the South.

The most widely used, and effective, measure of party competition is the Ranney Index of Party Competition. The Ranney Index first appeared in 1965 and has been updated six times since. The index, based entirely on state offices (governor, state senator, state representative), is a good indicator of any change in two-party politics in any state over time.

The Ranney Index appeared in each of the seven editions of a text on state government written by Herbert Jacob and Kenneth Vines entitled *Politics in the American States* (1965). Ranney authored the original chapter on political parties that contained his index for the first three editions of the book. All subsequent editions of the classic text contained party competition analyses derived from the original Ranney Index measure, but updated by other scholars. In the 1965 edition of the Jacob and Vines text, the Ranney Index of Party Competition covered state offices (governors, state representatives, and state senators) during the 1946–1963 period.[35] Ranney found that eight southern states (South Carolina, Georgia, Louisiana, Mississippi, Texas, Alabama, Arkansas, and Florida) were Democratic-dominant states. The three other states (Virginia, North Carolina, and Tennessee) were modified Democratic-dominant.

In subsequent editions of the text the Ranney Index revealed a sustained drift into the Republican Party. In the sixth edition (1996) the Ranney Index covered the 1989–1994 period. By this time the transformation from one-party dominance was nearly complete.[36] Not one southern state was found to be one-party Democratic. Five states (Arkansas, Louisiana, Georgia, Mississippi, and Alabama) were the only remaining modified one-party Democratic states. Six states (Tennessee, North Carolina, Texas, Virginia, Florida, and South Carolina) were two-party competitive. For the first time in over one hundred years the majority of the states in the South were out of the Democratic fold. In the seventh edition (1999), which covered the 1995–1998 period, only Arkansas, Georgia, and Louisiana were found by the Ranney Index to be modified one-party Democratic. No southern state was one-party Democratic. The remaining eight states were two-party competitive.

While there is some overlap in the periods covered, the trend is unmistakable. In some seven editions of *Politics in the American States* the Ranney Index has chronicled deterioration in Democratic allegiance at the state level. The shortcoming of the original Ranney measure is that it was appropriate only for state offices like governor, state representative, and state senator. Even at this level, with few exceptions, politics became two-party competitive.

Measures of Party Competition in 2004

The measure of party competition developed by Austin Ranney (1965) is adapted for use in this book. The original measure required an examination of two different aspects of competition: interparty competition for control of government (the governor and state legislature) and electoral competition (the percentage of votes won in state elections). The widely used and longstanding Ranney measure is a composite of competition for control of government and uses Democratic and Republican allegiance as a base measure. The actual measure has several components:

1. Proportion of Success: the percentage of votes won by the parties in gubernatorial elections and the percentage of seats won by the parties in each house of the legislature.
2. Duration of Success: the length of time the parties controlled the legislature.
3. Frequency of Divided Control: the proportion of time the governorship and the legislature were divided between the two parties.

Ranney used these three dimensions to calculate his index of interparty competition, which was done for various time periods between 1946 and 1998. The major drawback of the Ranney Index is that it has only been used for state offices; here it is adapted for federal elections.[37] The same dimensions Ranney defined for state competition are applied to federal offices using the president as a substitute unit for the governor, and the US Senate and congressional delegations as replacements for chambers in the state legislature.

The assumption here is that party competition at the federal level (US Senate races, the presidency, and congressional seats) influences competitiveness for gubernatorial, state senate, and state house levels. In addition, the measures assume that the growth of party competition in a state cannot be divorced from national trends.

The presence of television imports national issues to the state level, and forces local politicians to take positions on issues of national importance even though they have no influence on the outcome. A large part of the growth of the Republican Party in the South is due to the aversion white voters have to the "liberal trends" of the national Democratic Party. The assumption here is that voters do not clearly distinguish between national and state issues, and that votes for a party at the national level are a prelude to votes at the local level. The Ranney Index is adapted to national politics with the following measures.

1. Proportion of Success: the percentage of votes won by the parties in presidential elections and the percentage of seats won by the parties in the US Senate and House of Representatives.
2. Duration of Success: the length of time the parties controlled the national legislative delegation.
3. Frequency of Divided Government: the proportion of time the presidency, House, and Senate were divided between the two parties.

Like the measure for state party competition, the federal measure calculates the dimensions of interparty competition for select years between 1948 and 2004. The index is a measure of the control of government, with a score of 0 indicating complete Republican control and a score of 1.0 indicating absolute Democratic control. At its midpoint (.500), control of government is evenly split between the two parties, indicating a highly competitive environment.

Ranney used his index to classify states by party control, but his measure is only for competition at the state level. Here we use the Ranney measure for federal competition (Table 6.6), then compare with the traditional measures for state elections (Table 6.7). The final composite measure is used to classify states as to party control for both federal and state elections (Table 6.8). The following classifications and categories were originally used by Ranney and are appropriate for this study.

.8500 or higher: one-party Democratic
.6500 to .8499: modified one-party Democratic
.3500 to .6499: two-party competition
.1500 to .3499: modified one-party Republican
.0000 to .1499: one-party Republican

The values of the Ranney Party Control Index are initially calculated for federal offices from the years 1948 to 2004 in six-year increments to accommodate the four-year presidential elections. The six-year time period accommodates the full cycle of political change at both the state and federal level. Given the off-year election dates for some state offices, and the need to see what effect upset victories might have on subsequent races, the six-year period allows trends to emerge. The figures for 2004 are at the beginning of a new cycle and are for just one election, but they are very revealing. Before calculating these values for the southern states it is necessary to explain how their importance has changed for national politics since V. O. Key wrote his book in 1948. The Ranney measure of state party competition is applied to federal elections from 1948 to 2004, with complete measures through the midterm elections of 2002. These races for US Senate, House of Representatives, and president are shown in Table 6.6.

The numbers in the table show that two-party competitions arrived for federal offices in the 1964–1970 period with Tennessee, Texas, Florida, Virginia, and South Carolina slipping below .6500 into the two-party columns and North Carolina nearly there with a score of .6579. The range of figures for two-party competition is .3500 to .6499, and by the Reagan election of 1980 every southern state was two-party competitive at the federal level, except Virginia and North Carolina, which were now modified one-party Republican (.3499 or lower). This means that southern states were shifting their allegiance to the Republican Party during the decade of the 1970s, when native son Jimmy Carter was in the White House.

Beginning with the second Clinton administration in 1996, three of the four southern states in the national category (Texas, Georgia, and Florida) were recording scores below the .3500 range, meaning they were becoming modified Republican in allegiance. Virginia was a curious case, shifting from modified Republican during the 1980s to two-party competitive in the 1990s. Both emergent states of Tennessee and North Carolina were modified Republican, meaning their index scores are below .3500, at the federal level by the second Clinton administration. Two of the traditional southern states, Mississippi and South Carolina, were the only states in that category that changed in their political allegiance to modified Republican by the year 2000 (below .3500). Louisiana, Arkansas, and Alabama retained enough Democratic allegiance to be classified as two-party competitive at the federal level.

The figures in Table 6.6 show a complete transformation at the federal level of the South from modified one-party Democratic allegiance in the 1950s to modified

Table 6.6 Federal Measures of Southern Party Competition, 1948–2004

	1948–1954[a]	1956–1962	1964–1970[a]	1972–1978	1980–1986	1988–1994[a]	1996–2002	2004–
National States								
Georgia	0.7881	0.7861	0.6720	0.4883	0.4883	0.4975	0.3841	0.2189
Florida	0.7344	0.7852	0.6077	0.6533	0.4153	0.3958	0.4031	0.3109
Virginia	0.7078	0.6818	0.5950	0.1976	0.1843	0.4299	0.3264	0.1817
Texas	0.7629	0.7288	0.6088	0.5920	0.4010	0.3968	0.2834	0.1778
Emergent States								
North Carolina	0.7545	0.7265	0.6579	0.5171	0.3031	0.3157	0.3567	0.2129
Tennessee	0.6975	0.6805	0.4691	0.3726	0.4621	0.5135	0.2788	0.2445
Traditional States								
Alabama	0.7058	0.7666	0.8659	0.6194	0.4330	0.6367	0.2190	0.1642
Arkansas	0.7720	0.7534	0.6863	0.6353	0.6385	0.5888	0.4474	0.5488
South Carolina	0.6873	0.6833	0.5571	0.4339	0.3546	0.3573	0.3560	0.1855
Mississippi	0.7371	0.7431	0.6574	0.5490	0.3944	0.3249	0.2931	0.1706
Louisiana	0.7320	0.7374	0.7143	0.6626	0.5346	0.6211	0.4931	0.2304

Source: Compiled by author.

Note: a. Figures do not reflect votes for independent candidates (Strom Thurmond in 1948, George Wallace in 1968, and Ross Perot in 1992).

Key:

.8500 to 1.000: one-party Democratic

.6500 to .8499: modified one-party Democratic

.3500 to .6499: two-party competition

.1500 to .3499: modified one-party Republican

.0000 to .1499: one-party Republican

one-party Republican rule by 2004. If the figure after the 2004 presidential election persists, then every southern state—with the exception of Arkansas—will be listed in the GOP column for president, US Senate, and US House of Representatives. According to the Ranney measure two national states, Virginia and Texas, along with Alabama, South Carolina, and Mississippi, are on the edge of becoming one-party Republican. Any doubt that the South has switched allegiance firmly from the Democrats to the GOP was erased on November 2, 2004. Not only did George W. Bush defeat John Kerry in every southern state, but Republicans won all contested Senate seats and gained in the US House of Representatives.

These results confirm that the dramatic transformation in partisan allegiance seen in Table 6.6 is reflected in present-day elections. On an intuitive level it is clear that Texas is a more Republican state than, say, Arkansas. The predictive ability of the Ranney Index is shown in Table 6.7. The first column of the table shows the ranking of the eleven southern states on the Ranney Index in the 1996–2002 period. Alabama, with a score of .2190, is the state with the lowest index score making it a moderate one-party state, while Louisiana (.4931) is a two-party competitive state. The second column ranks the states as to their margin of allegiance in the 2004 presidential victory by George W. Bush. For example, in 2004 Bush won Alabama by a 63 percent to 37 percent margin, while the president carried Florida by only a 52 percent to 47 percent spread. The Spearman's rho correlation coefficient of .5637 shows a moderately strong relationship between the Ranney Index and GOP allegiance at the presidential level in the subsequent election.

Table 6.7 Ranney Index Comparison for the 2004 Presidential Election

Ranney Index Rank on Federal Measure 1996–2002	Rank Order of Bush Victory Margin 2004
1. Alabama	1. Alabama
2. Tennessee	2. Texas
3. Texas	3. Mississippi
4. Mississippi	4. South Carolina
5. Virginia	5. Georgia
6. South Carolina	6. Louisiana
7. North Carolina	7. Tennessee
8. Georgia	8. North Carolina
9. Florida	9. Arkansas
10. Arkansas	10. Virginia
11. Louisiana	11. Florida

Spearman's Rho = +0.5637

The transformation from Democratic to Republican Party allegiance was much slower, but still pronounced, at the state level. Table 6.8 records the transformation of party allegiance at the grassroots by using the same unit of analysis developed by Ranney and other scholars in *Politics in the American States*. These states were originally solidly Democratic; some were monoliths—meaning that *every* state office was in the hands of one party—in the years when V. O. Key wrote *Southern Politics*. The findings at the end of the six-year period, 1996–2002, is that every state but Mississippi, Arkansas, and Alabama have scores of between .3320 and .6499, making them two-party competitive throughout the state. If the 2004 scores are indicative of the future for local offices, then Arkansas and Louisiana are returning to the Democratic fold. Overall, the scores in Table 6.8 show deterioration in Democratic dominance over time, with the figures decreasing from left to right in the table.

The idea that party politics trickles down from the national races to state elections is apparent when the figures in Table 6.6 and Table 6.8 are compared. The transition of party allegiance at the national level began in the 1964–1970 period, but it was not until after the 1996–2002 period that state governments felt the full effects of the GOP surge. The 2004 figures for state offices reflect the trend seen at the national level, but at a less dramatic rate. North Carolina, Arkansas, and Louisiana are resurgently Democratic, while Florida, South Carolina, Virginia, and Texas are modified one-party Republican. The most dramatic change was in Georgia, where Sonny Perdue's election in 2002 coupled with redistricting flipped the state into the GOP column by 2004. The emergent states of Tennessee and North Carolina have divergent stories. Tennessee Democrats lost the state senate in 2004, and while it remained two-party competitive the prospects for the GOP are bright. North Carolina has halted the Democratic erosion and remains within the shadow of one-party allegiance. The same can be said of the traditional states of Alabama, Arkansas, and Mississippi.

The twin Bush victories in 2000 and 2004, along with redistricting, portend GOP success as the new century wears on. Several states showed a consistent Republican emergence *after* Ronald Reagan's election in 1980. By the time George Bush took office in 1988, Texas, Virginia, and Florida were all two-party competitive in statewide offices in the national state category classification. The effects of two-party competition were apparent in the emergent states as well. North Carolina and Tennessee share a border and a mountainous Republican Party heritage. Both these states were two-party competitive at the state level at the end of the Reagan-Bush years.

South Carolina, Mississippi, and Alabama, in the traditional southern states classification, were voting competitive at the state level by 1988. Most southern states were competitive by the 1988–1994 period. In this period only Louisiana, Arkansas, and Georgia resisted the Republican trend to remain modified one-party Democratic.

Table 6.8 State Measures of Southern Party Competition, 1948–2004

	1948–1954[a]	1956–1962	1964–1970[a]	1972–1978	1980–1986	1988–1994[a]	1996–2002	2004–
National States								
Georgia	0.9907	0.9920	0.7407	0.8668	0.8673	0.7913	0.6182	0.2809
Florida	0.9440	0.8960	0.6493	0.7370	0.6855	0.5766	0.3320	0.2167
Virginia	0.8846	0.8716	0.7641	0.4692	0.6920	0.6391	0.4292	0.3677
Texas	0.9772	0.9296	0.8956	0.7704	0.6452	0.5760	0.4366	0.2668
Emergent States								
North Carolina	0.7889	0.6719	0.8117	0.7704	0.6684	0.6009	0.6204	0.6653
Tennessee	0.8579	0.8228	0.6819	0.5467	0.4887	0.6313	0.5778	0.5620
Traditional States								
Alabama	0.9587	0.9651	0.9393	0.9325	0.7942	0.5227	0.6667	0.6474
Arkansas	0.9461	0.9362	0.7518	0.8539	0.7984	0.8413	0.6715	0.7191
South Carolina	1.0000	0.9995	0.9024	0.7178	0.7647	0.4523	0.4216	0.2793
Mississippi	0.9956	1.0000	0.9108	0.9047	0.8677	0.6156	0.6616	0.5748
Louisiana	0.9950	0.9756	0.9421	0.9390	0.7355	0.8228	0.5970	0.6870

Source: Compiled by the author.

Note: a. Figures do not reflect votes for independent candidates (Strom Thurmond in 1948, George Wallace in 1968, and Ross Perot in 1992).

Key:

.8500 to 1.000: one-party Demoncratic
.6500 to .8499: modified one-party Democratic
.3500 to .6499: two-party competition
.1500 to .3499: modified one-party Republican
.0000 to .1499: one-party Republican

Summary

Table 6.9 shows the combined measures of state party competition by averaging the figures in the previous two tables together. This summary measure encapsulates all the trends discussed in this chapter. Collectively they show a dramatic realignment from the Democrats at midcentury to two-party competition and largely Republican allegiance at the federal level in the next century. The combined figure shows a consistent migration to the GOP. More than fifty years ago V. O. Key described the Republican Party this way: "it scarcely deserves the name of party. It wavers somewhat between an esoteric cult on the order of a lodge and a conspiracy."[38] How different things are today in terms of party competition from what they were at midcentury.

The Ranney Index measure in Table 6.9 is a single-digit summary of state and federal races from 1948 to 2004. In the 1950s five of eleven states were one-party Democratic, and the rest were modified one-party Democratic. By the 1980s all but two were two-party competitive, and in the 1990s all were. By 2002 four states (Texas, Florida, Virginia, and South Carolina) were on the verge of becoming modified Republican states, meaning that the GOP is the presumed favorite in races from state legislature to president of the United States.

Today the South has become a home not only for two-party competition, but also as a breeding ground of viable national presidential candidates. The last four presidential elections have featured candidates who came from states that are the subject of analysis in this book. One of the oldest shibboleths in politics is, "no Democrat has ever won the White House without the South," and that proverb was sustained once again in 2004.

Disentangling the change and continuity in the region's traditional political culture, social and economic development, government reforms, and a new breed of political leaders is the key to understanding the transformation in party politics that is sweeping the South. Equally important is the struggle between traditional conservative southern political values and more moderate political forces. In the new southern political landscape, the Democratic Party has been largely displaced as the holder of the allegiance of traditional southern conservatives.

The presence of Republican voters is now a fact in the South. The next chapters will outline the patterns of voting in each state and the importance of urban areas in the new political competition.

Notes

1. D.B. Hardeman and Donald C. Bacon, *Rayburn*. Austin: Texas Monthly Press, 1987, p. 428.
2. Southern Politics Collection, "Georgia," Vanderbilt University, Special Collections.
3. Daniel Elazar, *American Federalism: A View from the States*. 3rd ed. New York, Harper & Row, 1984, p. 130.

Table 6.9 Combined Measures of Southern Party Competition, 1948–2004

	1948–1954[a]	1956–1962	1964–1970[a]	1972–1978	1980–1986	1988–1994[a]	1996–2002	2004–
National States								
Georgia	0.8894	0.8891	0.7062	0.7967	0.6778	0.6444	0.5012	0.2499
Florida	0.8392	0.8406	0.6285	0.6954	0.5504	0.4862	0.3675	0.2638
Virginia	0.7962	0.7767	0.6796	0.3242	0.4382	0.5345	0.3778	0.2748
Texas	0.8699	0.8292	0.7522	0.6398	0.5231	0.4864	0.3600	0.2223
Emergent States								
North Carolina	0.7717	0.6992	0.7348	0.6380	0.4883	0.4583	0.4886	0.4391
Tennessee	0.7770	0.7547	0.5755	0.4597	0.4764	0.5724	0.7283	0.3478
Traditional States								
Alabama	0.8323	0.8614	0.9026	0.7760	0.6135	0.5797	0.4429	0.4058
Arkansas	0.8591	0.8448	0.7191	0.7446	0.7185	0.7147	0.5595	0.6339
South Carolina	0.8437	0.8414	0.7298	0.5989	0.5597	0.4048	0.3732	0.2324
Mississippi	0.8664	0.8716	0.7841	0.7267	0.6311	0.1703	0.4774	0.3727
Louisiana	0.8635	0.8565	0.8282	0.8008	0.6350	0.7219	0.5450	0.4587

Source: Compiled by the author.

Note: a. Figures do not reflect votes for independent candidates (Strom Thurmond in 1948, George Wallace in 1968, and Ross Perot in 1992).

Key:
.8500 to 1.000: one-party Democratic
.6500 to .8499: modified one-party Democratic
.3500 to .6499: two-party competition
.1500 to .3499: modified one-party Republican
.0000 to .1499: one-party Republican

4. Norman Luttberg, "Classifying the American States," *Midwest Journal of Political Science* 15 (November 1971); Charles Johnson, "Political Culture in American States," *American Journal of Political Science* 20 (August 1976), pp. 491–509; Ira Sharkansky, "The Utility of Elazar's Political Culture: A Research Note," *Polity* 2, no. 1 (Fall 1969), pp. 68–83. Robert Blank, "Socio-Economic Determinism of Voting Turnout: A Challenge," *Journal of Politics* 36, no. 3 (August 1974).

5. Walter A. Rosenbaum, *Political Culture*. New York: Praeger, 1975, p. 4.

6. Ira Sharkansky, "The Utility of Elazar's Political Culture, A Research Note," *Polity* 2 (Fall 1969), pp. 65–83.

7. V.O. Key Jr., "A Theory of Critical Elections," *Journal of Politics* 17 (1955), pp. 3–18; E.E. Schattschneider, "United States: The Functional Approach to Party Government," in Sigmund Neumann (ed.), *Modern Political Parties: Approaches to Comparative Politics*. Chicago: University of Chicago Press, 1956; E.E. Schattschneider, *The Semisovereign People: A Realist's View of Democracy*. New York: Holt, Rinehart and Winston, 1960; James L. Sundquist, *Dynamics of the Party System: Alignment and Realignment of Political Parties in the United States*. Washington, D.C.: Brookings Institution, 1973, rev. ed. 1983; Walter Dean Burnham, *Critical Election and the Mainsprings of American Politics*. New York: Norton, 1970.

8. Paul Allen Beck, "A Socialization Theory of Partisan Realignment," in Richard G. Niemi (ed.), *The Politics of Future Citizens*. San Francisco: Jossey-Bass, 1974; Jerome M. Chubb, William H. Flanigan, and Nancy H. Zingale, *Partisan Realignment: Voters, Parties and Government in American History*. Beverly Hills, Calif.: Sage, 1980.

9. David R. Mayhew, *Electoral Realignments: A Critique of an American Genre*. New Haven: Yale University Press, 2002.

10. Ibid., p. 21.

11. John F. Stacks, *Watershed: The Campaign for the Presidency, 1980*. New York: New York Times Books, 1981, p. 238.

12. Walter Dean Burnham, *Critical Elections and the Mainsprings*, p. 7.

13. Walter Dean Burnham, "Party System and the Political Process," in William Cameron and Walter Dean Burnham (eds.), *The American Party Systems: Stages of Political Development*. New York: Oxford University Press, 1967.

14. V.O. Key, *Southern Politics in State and Nation*. 2d ed. Knoxville: University of Tennessee Press, 1977, p. 16.

15. Ibid., pp. 16–17.

16. Ibid., pp. 277–316.

17. Jack Bass and Walter DeVries, *The Transformation of Southern Politics*. New York: New American Library, 1976, p. 4.

18. Ibid., p. 405.

19. William Havard, *The Changing Politics of the South*. Baton Rouge: Louisiana State University Press, 1972, pp. 690–691.

20. Ibid., p. 729.

21. Earl Black and Merle Black, *Politics and Society in the South*. Cambridge, Mass.: Harvard University Press, 1987, p. 259.

22. Ibid., p. 291.

23. Charles S. Bullock and Mark J. Rozell (eds.), *The New Politics of the Old South*. Lanham, Md.: Rowman & Littlefield, 1988.

24. Earl Black and Merle Black, *The Rise of Southern Republicans*. Cambridge, Mass.: Belknap Press of Harvard University Press, 2002, p. 25.

25. Harold Stanley, "Southern Partisan Changes: Dealignment, Realignment or Both?" *Journal of Politics* 50 (1988), pp. 65–88.

26. Earl Black and Merle Black, *The Vital South*. Cambridge, Mass.: Harvard University Press, 1992; Nicol Rae, *Southern Democrats*. Oxford: Oxford University Press, 1989.

27. Bruce E. Keith, David B. Magleby, Candice J. Nelson, Elizabeth Orr, Mark C. Westyle, and Raymond Wolfinger, *The Myth of the Independent Voter*. Berkeley: University of California Press, 1992.

28. Richard M. Scammon and Ben J. Wattenberg, *The Real Majority*. New York: Coward, McGann and Geoghpean, Inc., 1971, p. 40.

29. Michael Barone, *Our Country*. New York: Free Press, 1990, p. 559.

30. Clark Mollenhoff, *The President Who Failed*. New York: Macmillan, 1980.

31. Earl Black and Merle Black, *The Rise of Southern Republicans*, p. 25.

32. Robert Caro, *The Years of Lyndon Johnson: Master of the Senate*. New York: Alfred A. Knopf, 2002, p. 96.

33. D.B. Hardeman and Donald C. Bacon, *Rayburn*, p. 287.

34. Lewis L. Gould, *Grand Old Party: A History of the Republicans*. New York: Random House, 2003, p. 465.

35. Austin Ranney, "Parties and State Politics," in Herbert Jacobs and Kenneth N. Vines (eds.), *Politics in the American States*. Boston: Little, Brown, 1965, pp. 63–70.

36. John F. Bibby, Cornelius P. Cotter, James L. Gibson, and Robert J. Huckshorn, "Parties and State Politics," in Virginia Gray, Herbert Jacob, and Robert B. Albritton (eds.), *Politics in the American States*. Glenview, Ill.: Scott Foresman/Little, Brown, 1990, pp. 90–93.

37. Ranney used three dimensions to calculate his index of interparty competition, which are updated here. Specifically, the figures are the average percentage of the popular vote won by Democratic gubernatorial candidates; the average percentage of seats held by Democrats in the state senate, in all legislative sessions; the average percentage of seats held by Democrats in the state house of representatives in all sessions; and the percentage of all gubernatorial, senate, and house terms that were controlled by the Democrats. The federal measure substituted presidential outcomes for gubernatorial, US Senate for state senate, and the US House delegation for the state legislative make-up. Washington domination was replaced for that at the state capital. Austin Ranney and Willmoore Kendall, "The American Party System," *American Political Science Review* (1954), pp. 477–485; Austin Ranney, "Parties and State Politics," pp. 63–70.

38. V.O. Key, *Southern Politics in State and Nation,* p. 277.

7
The Republican Electoral Surge

In the 1970s southern political practices came to resemble more closely those of the rest of the nation. The election of Jimmy Carter in 1976 conferred a newfound respectability on the region. Ronald Reagan's victory four years later was due in no small part to the enthusiasm of southern voters who abandoned Carter and embraced the Republican Party. The support for Reagan, and the conservative agenda of the Republican Party, was rooted in the white middle-class voters filling up the suburbs around major metropolitan areas across the region.

Chapter 3 presented a profile of the urban southern population in each state. The maps in that chapter showed the dramatic transformation of the South from a region of rural havens and farms to modern cities with homogenized shopping malls and eight-lane interstate highways for commuters. In each southern state a handful of counties held between 40 percent and over one-half the state's population. Demography, not geography, is now political destiny in the South. The media markets in three or four urban areas often touch a majority of the state's population, enough to win a statewide election. The new politics of the South revolves around this urban reality, and the ability of the GOP to exploit the suburban advantage explains their rise to dominance in presidential elections.

This refitted electorate has laid to rest some of the oldest southern political aphorisms. For example, the traditional leanings of east Tennessee meant "the Republicans had to come over the mountains with a 100,000 vote margin" to win. But our earlier analysis of urbanization in the "Volunteer State" shows that there are plenty of communities full of Republicans outside Chattanooga, Nashville, and even Memphis. In the state of Alabama, the "Big Mules" in Birmingham are in the suburbs, not the downtown businesses anymore. Texas is dominated by population centers on the points of a triangle, not the rural communities that required Lyndon Johnson to campaign for office in a helicopter. In short, the new urban politics has changed the way candidates seek statewide office.

Another change came with the concentration of minorities in cities. The push

249

for civil liberties and civil rights for blacks began in the urban community with allies among affluent, well-educated whites in the late 1960s and early 1970s.[1] Their support for an egalitarian culture for civil rights, free speech, and a permissive social culture alienated middle-class whites and drove them away from the Democratic Party. As the Democrats mobilized black votes, they became more dependent upon black support, especially in urban areas. The size and cohesion of the black vote is central to any understanding of urbanization effects on southern voting patterns. "For Democrats the essential task is to combine virtually all the black vote with enough white votes to produce a majority. . . . Republican candidates . . . typically require landslide white majorities since they cannot depend on any sizeable contribution from blacks."[2] There is a generally accepted 60 percent target of the white vote that Republican statewide candidates need to win in most states of the South.

The legislative term-limits movement, which blossomed nationally in the 1990s, also had an effect on southern politics. The campaign to impose limitations on the number of years that elected officials can remain in office had its base in the public's dissatisfaction with government. It began in the 1990 election when voters in California, Colorado, and Oklahoma approved initiatives that imposed term limits. Twenty-one states adopted these measures, although some subsequently voted to repeal term limits, or had existing laws overturned by state courts.[3]

To examine the effect of black resettlement, term limits, and urbanization upon political partisanship and the metropolitan population, so evident in Chapter 3, the counties of each state are placed in a partisan context by evaluating their allegiance in the voting patterns of presidential elections. The last five presidential elections are used to evaluate county-by-county allegiance to the Democratic and Republican parties in each state. The presidential elections of 1988, 1992, 1996, 2000, and 2004 are compared because the post-Reagan realignment, as measured by the Ranney Index in the previous chapter, was evident in this time period. Several of the nominees were southern, or unabashedly claimed southern roots: George Bush, Bill Clinton, George W. Bush, Al Gore, and John Edwards. The allegiance they inspired, or failed to inspire, is a rough indicator of the deeper party loyalty voters have at the grassroots.

The Ranney Index figures in the previous chapter confirm that two-party competition began at the presidential level, then trickled down to statewide offices, like congressional races, and finally into the state legislatures. For example, Texas became two-party competitive for federal races in the 1964–1970 period, and became competitive at the state level in the 1980–1986 period. In the 2002 midterm elections, for the first time in history, Texas Republicans won every statewide office while also controlling both houses of the state legislature. In the same way, Georgia became two-party competitive at the federal level in the same 1964–1970 period. It was less two-party competitive at the state level in the decade of the 1990s until election night 2002, when a Republican won the governorship for the first time since Reconstruction. In sum, the presidential races are the wellsprings from which party realignment flowed.

This conviction about party politics, and the realignment of southern voters, is based on the book V. O. Key wrote about political participation, and nonparticipation, after he published his work on politics in the South. His last book, *The Responsible Electorate*, argued that voters respond to the past when they enter the voting booth, not the future.[4] Key drew an explicit distinction between *prospective*, or future, voting; and, *retrospective*, or past, voting. Recently scholars have expanded on Key's concepts of retrospective voting, using the economic assumptions of Anthony Downs.[5]

The perspective of rational choice retrospective voting, developed by Morris Fiorina, maintains that voters are more oriented toward outcomes than policy means to achieve them, and that voters evaluate incumbents based mainly on what has been done in the past.[6] The implication is that voters pay little attention to promises about what will be done. Retrospective evaluations are used in making comparisons among the alternatives available on Election Day. Fiorina finds citizens monitoring party promises and performance over time based on party identification, which they use to assign responsibility for current societal conditions and evaluate ambiguous platforms. Retrospective voting maintains that human beings simply find it easier to get information about what has gone on in the past, than to try and guess what might happen in the future. When they enter the voting booth they are conscious of their past voting decisions in similar circumstances.

The effect of Fiorina's retrospective model is useful for explaining voting behavior in the South, and is seen in two dramatic elections in 1948 and 1968. Earl Black and Merle Black argue that the adoption of the civil rights plank by the Democratic Party in 1948 stimulated the exodus of white Southerners from the party. Later, George Wallace's American Independent Party attacked the racial and social liberalism of President Lyndon Johnson's Great Society. Together, these two elections "symbolize the decline and fall of presidential Democracy."[7]

Partisan realignment in the South for Republicans was halted by Jimmy Carter's victory in 1976. For a time it appeared that the historic affinity Southerners had for the Democratic Party would be revived. But it was not to be. "Reagan's presidency was the turning point in the evolution of the competitive, two-party electorate in the South."[8] The conservative policies and rhetoric of the Reagan presidency made Republican partisanship respectable. All across the South, "Good Ole Boys" started putting Reagan/Bush stickers on their pickup truck bumpers.

These ideas are helpful in emphasizing partisan realignment in the South. Some southern voters cast a ballot for Eisenhower in 1952, or for Nixon in 1968, or for Reagan in 1980. The results of those elections encouraged them to consider supporting other Republicans in subsequent races. In the five elections selected here, at the end of the twentieth century and into the next, voters could choose between

Southerners running for president in both political parties. The issue for southern voters was no longer region; it was now ideology.

The maps in this chapter show Republican or Democratic allegiance through these five (1988–2004) presidential contests. Counties were designated as urban by their geographic descriptions in Chapter 3; here a partisan tint is added to the analysis. A Republican or Democratic allegiance in every election from 1988 to 2004 is a good indicator of bedrock sentiment and realignment in that county. The allegiance of neighbors influences other neighbors in suburban subdivisions, and is evident in bumper stickers and yard signs that announce allegiance and go a long way in helping others to make up their mind about a candidate. Television commercials in an urban market can influence thousands of voters prior to Election Day. In this chapter this presidential allegiance is examined for every county in each of the eleven southern states. Questions include: Which counties are the Republican Party base, and which are the Democratic Party base, or are they divided in their allegiance and up for grabs on Election Day? Except for the black voters in urban areas, the suburbs are fertile grounds for Republican candidates. Special attention is devoted to the partisan allegiance of the urban counties identified in Chapter 3, because they contain around half the state's population.

The assumption here is that these maps indicate how party politics trickles down from the presidential level, and the examination of national elections sets the pattern for subsequent statewide and substate races. The Ranney Index calculations in Chapter 6 show that every state, with the exception of Florida, had a figure showing greater allegiance to the Democratic Party at the state level than the federal one. GOP wins in Washington are gradually translated to victories in state politics. The goal in every presidential election is for a candidate to "win" a state by getting 50 percent, plus one, of the vote in that state. Since Republicans have had so much success in the South at the presidential level, subsequent candidates for statewide office use the voting results evident in presidential elections as a pattern for them to follow. Campaigns spend money in media markets that maximize exposure to their base vote. As in earlier chapters, the states will be examined in order from national, through emergent, to traditional states.

National States

Georgia

Politics in Georgia has historically been split between metropolitan Atlanta and the rural areas of the state. V. O. Key called Georgia "Rule of the Rustics," and the antagonism between urban and rural areas was exploited for political purposes. Today Atlanta dominates Georgia's politics. The city was home to both Martin Luther King Jr.'s tolerant racial attitudes and a booming economy. The rural counties led the state in voting for segregationist Lester Maddox in 1966, and George Wallace in 1968. But the politics of race changed with the explosive urbanization of

Atlanta, and the election of Jimmy Carter as governor in 1970. Carter placed a portrait of Martin Luther King Jr. in the state capitol and honored the legacy of the civil rights movement in his speeches. With Carter's election, the politics of Georgia ceased being mostly about race, and became more and more about urban growth and economics.

The animosity between urban and rural areas is deep seated. "The deadliness of the county unit system," said a county judge in 1947, "is that it is obviously undemocratic . . . violates the principle of representative government . . . [and] gives petty [bosses] in 50 or more counties absolute rule."[9] The Georgia county-unit system allocated at least one house seat to each of the state's 159 counties, and then apportioned an additional forty-six seats based on a complicated population formula. The result was, as Charles S. Bullock has noted, that "three tiny counties with a few hundred voters each could easily offset the Atlanta vote, and in the days of boss-controlled counties, manipulating the rural vote was far easier than campaigning successfully in large urban counties."[10] The county-unit rural system was abolished in 1962, but the tension between Atlanta's large, downtown black population and the fast-growing suburbs remains.

The politics of urban and suburban growth, tax policy, transportation, and land use are issues that favor Republicans in the new demographic context. The 1980 election was a benchmark for the GOP in Georgia. That was the year Jimmy Carter was beaten for the White House, and Democrat Herman Talmadge lost his Senate seat to Republican Mack Mattingly. Carter carried his home state in his final presidential campaign, but population trends were growing for the Republicans in future races. Lower taxes and support for the military, along with a tradition of a conspicuous expression of public religious faith, escorted Republican Paul Coverdell into the US Senate in 1992, and tightened all statewide races in the 1990s. "During the 1990s, Georgia grew faster than any other state east of the Mississippi and gained two seats in Congress."[11] The culmination of this GOP trend was in 2002, when Republican Saxby Chambliss defeated incumbent Democrat Max Cleland in the midterm US Senate election.

Prior to this midterm victory, the trend of Republican electoral victories provided evidence for split-level realignment, with successes at the presidential level gradually filtering down to lower-level offices. "The growth of the Republican Party—and the corresponding decline in Democratic dominance—has been gradual and marked by frequent reversals of fortune."[12] The Republican tide began in the ring of counties around Atlanta, and flowed into the rural areas alienated from the agenda of the national Democratic Party. Georgia elected Democratic senators, first Sam Nunn and then Zell Miller in this period. Both were conservative on issues of gun control, defense, and the social agenda, and neither embraced the controversial policies of the national party. One of Sam Nunn's last acts before retiring as US senator in 1994 was to lead the legislative opposition against gays in the military, this despite the fact that Georgia voted for Bill Clinton in 1992.

Vignette 7.1   The Talmadge Legacy:
Eugene Talmadge (1884–1946) and Herman Talmadge (1913–2002)

Eugene Talmadge and his son Herman epitomized a style of politics that evoked a fanatical loyalty from rural Georgia supporters who were drawn to their defense of agrarian values in the face of social change. Gene Talmadge was renowned for his pugnacity, which pleased the small farmers of the state who elected him governor in 1932.

Born the second of six children, and the oldest son, of a Forsyth County farming family, Eugene Talmadge finished law school and purchased farm property along Sugar Creek in Telfair County. He began his statewide political career in 1926 when he defeated the establishment candidate for the office of commissioner of agriculture. From this platform he was elected governor.

Talmadge was a natural campaigner. Slight of build, with horn-rimmed glasses and dark hair across his forehead, he would "shuck off" his coat at a political rally, exposing a pair of red suspenders, and launch into a fiery tirade against his opponents. His style evolved from populist agrarian to virulent racism. He gained notoriety as a stereotypical southern demagogue, the "Wild Man from Sugar Creek."

"Ole Gene," as he was called, drew crowds of 20,000 to 30,000 for rallies in small towns throughout Georgia. His rhetoric conjured up vivid images of a righteous rural life embodied in biblical Israel, surrounded by a materialistic, philistine culture hostile to southern values. In many ways, Gene Talmadge represented the agrarian response to the vast changes associated with the emergence of modern America. An older time of autonomous rural communities was collapsing in the face of an urban juggernaut of industrial life.

By 1936 Talmadge was solidly in the antilabor, anti-Negro, intrusive government, "stop-Roosevelt" camp of the Democratic Party. He backed Huey Long for the presidency and, after the Louisiana governor was assassinated, helped form the "Constitutional Jeffersonian Democratic" party that nominated the Georgia governor for president. After a time out of politics, Talmadge again returned to the governor's chair in 1940. This time he became embroiled in a feud with the University of Georgia, resulting in a fired dean and the university's temporary loss of accreditation.

Herman Talmadge, who would attain the office of US senator, followed in the footsteps of his father. After finishing a law degree from the University of Georgia, he practiced in Atlanta until his father died in 1946. In a quirk of fate he was elected to the governorship by the state legislature in 1947, where he served for sixty-seven days then vacated the office after a decision by the Georgia Supreme Court went against him.

One of V. O. Key's *Southern Politics* interviewers was in the lobby of the Henry Grady Hotel less than two hours after the Georgia Supreme Court ruled against Talmadge. "Whee-ee! Hooray for Appling County," shouted a legislator as he left the elevator, "we showed 'em now." "Whee-ee! The rootin'-tootin' representative from Applin', the first county on the list." It seems that "Uncle" Alec Tuten joined a host of other anti-Talmadge legislators drinking bourbon on the fourteenth floor of the hotel in celebration of the ruling. The merriment and back-slapping continued with "Uncle Alec" declaring, "I'll kick ole Tom [Mitchell, the acting governor's] hat off." Such was the elation surrounding the most notable defeat of the Talmadge machine in Georgia history.

The son kept the agrarian rhetoric, but abandoned the antics that were not appropriate before a television audience. Herman Talmadge's zenith as a politician came when he was a member of the Senate Watergate

(continues)

Vignette 7.1   Continued

Committee. John Ehrlichman, domestic policy adviser to President Nixon, was before the committee to defend the idea that the president had the inherent power, in the name of national security, to commit acts otherwise illegal.

In front of a national television audience, Talmadge asked Ehrlichman if he was familiar with the English common law premise that held no matter how humble a man's cottage, even the King of England could not enter it without this consent. Ehrlichman replied that the principle had been eroded by practice over the years. To which Talmadge responded:

"Down in my country we still think it is a pretty legitimate principle of law."

In that response, Herman Talmadge appeared to the nation at large to symbolize the values of the southern country lawyer with simple agrarian values, who understood right or wrong better than his more powerful neighbors. Talmadge was elected as a Democrat to the Senate in 1956, 1962, 1968, and again in 1974. After his moment in the media sun, he was denounced by the Senate in 1979 for financial mismanagement, and lost his bid for reelection in 1980.

The Atlanta suburbs are home to largely affluent white voters who repeatedly elected Newt Gingrich to Congress in the 1980s and 1990s. The "smaller government and less taxes" Republican theme, which came from talk radio hosts, resonated well in suburbs and exurbs for commuters stuck in traffic along interstate highways around the city. The trend was echoed in the state's congressional delegation that rose from 39 percent Republican in 1990, to 73 percent in 2002. Continued Democratic control of both houses of the general assembly and the governor's office in the 1990s enabled the party to gerrymander legislative and congressional districts in their favor. But this advantage was offset by Republicans joining forces with African Americans to draw majority black districts. In spite of their majority, Democrats found it hard to hold their advantage in the state house chambers.

Georgia has an unusual history when it comes to presidential politics. It was the second most Democratic state in John Kennedy's 1960 victory, went for Goldwater in 1964 and George Wallace in 1968, and then voted heavily Republican in 1972 in a protest against George McGovern. When native son Jimmy Carter ran in 1976 and 1980, the state proved a powerful base. In the 1980s and 1990s a strong in-migration around Atlanta and shifting allegiance in the urban centers made for close races. Bill Clinton won the state by 13,000 votes in 1992, and Bob Dole took it by a margin of only 27,000 votes in 1996. The George W. Bush victory in 2000 was more convincing, 56 percent, and improved to 58 percent in 2004.

The patterns of voting for presidential elections are seen in Map 7.1, which shows an inner-core of Democratic black allegiance in the downtown Atlanta metro counties of Fulton and DeKalb. These urban counties, which are about half black

Map 7.1   Georgia: Political Partisanship in Presidential Elections, 1992–2004

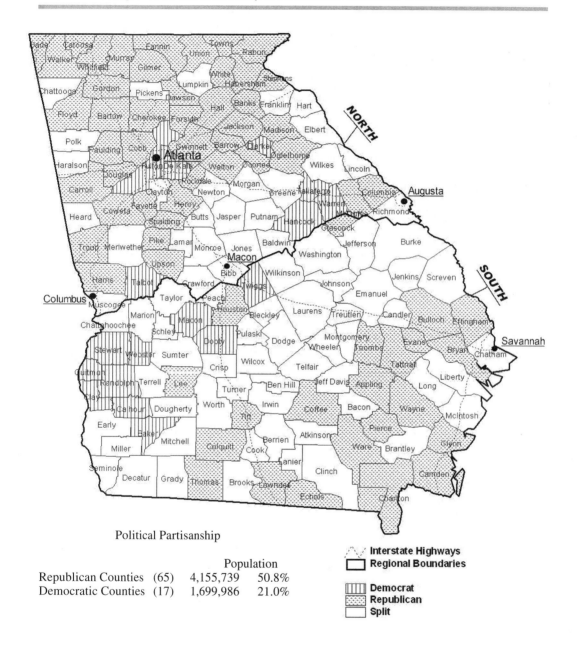

Political Partisanship

		Population	
Republican Counties	(65)	4,155,739	50.8%
Democratic Counties	(17)	1,699,986	21.0%

Interstate Highways
Regional Boundaries

Democrat
Republican
Split

and stocked with urban professionals distrustful of the Republican social agenda, cast about 22 percent of the statewide vote in the Democratic column.

The suburbs, with a strong GOP allegiance, cast about one-third of the state vote in the presidential race. These neighborhoods are home to middle-class white conservative voters who supported Newt Gingrich in the 1990s, and translated that allegiance to the GOP thereafter. Their values are, as Peter Applebome wrote in 1996, "low tax[es], low union, strong work ethic, strong commitment to family and community."[13] The rest of the state has slightly less than half the statewide vote. The map shows that Republicans also do well in the state's Atlantic coast retirement regions.

A Democratic victory in Georgia requires overwhelming support of African Americans and about 40 percent of the white vote. Presidential candidates under the Democratic mantle have the hardest time attracting traditional white support, and "in the last four elections the Democrat has failed to exceed a third of the white vote."[14] Most of the counties in north Georgia are Republican, while Democrats do well in the swath of Black Belt counties in the middle of the state. The fast-growing south Georgia counties are increasingly Republican, while Democrats are mired in the stagnant rural counties.

The shaded counties in Map 7.1 voted Republican in every presidential election from 1988 to 2004. Since over three-quarters of Georgia's population are in the northern part of the state, the donut counties around Atlanta are the bedrock base of the GOP statewide. For example, Forsyth County voted 84 percent for George W. Bush in 2004. In the 2000 presidential election, the ten counties around the city of Atlanta supplied nearly one-third (32 percent) of the total vote George W. Bush received in Georgia. Thirty-two counties outside Atlanta in north Georgia added another 20 percent of the GOP vote.

Earlier, in Chapter 3, seventeen counties were identified in Georgia that collectively held over half the state's population in three media markets. They are shown again in Table 7.1 with their presidential partisanship percentages for the elections from 1988–2004. The table shows that thirteen of these identified counties voted Republican in every one of the past five presidential elections. Two counties, DeKalb and Fulton, with 1.4 million residents, voted Democratic each time and were the anchor of the Democratic Party in Georgia. They delivered nearly two-thirds of their vote to Clinton and Gore in these elections. Other Democratic counties are along the fall line in central Georgia.

The map and table show that the Democratic base is small and shrinking, while the Republican counties are expanding in major population areas. The ring of suburban counties around Atlanta averaged over 60 percent loyalty to the GOP in the four presidential races. The margins in these counties are so overwhelming that losses in dozens of smaller downstate counties are inconsequential by comparison. In the 2000 presidential race Republicans captured the rural, nonmetro vote as well as the suburban vote. Map 7.1 confirms that essentially half the population of the

Table 7.1   Georgia: Presidential Election Partisanship, 1988–2004

Region/City	County	Republican Average 1988–2004	Democrat and Third-Party Average 1988–2004
North Georgia			
Atlanta	Fulton	39%	61%
Atlanta	Dekalb	33%	67%
Atlanta	Cobb	61%	39%
Atlanta	Gwinnett	64%	36%
Atlanta	Clayton	41%	59%
Atlanta	Cherokee	69%	31%
Atlanta	Henry	63%	37%
Atlanta	Forsyth	71%	29%
Atlanta	Douglas	60%	40%
Atlanta	Fayette	67%	33%
Atlanta	Coweta	63%	37%
Atlanta	Carroll	60%	40%
Atlanta	Rockdale	61%	39%
North/South Georgia			
Macon/Warner Robbins	Bibb	45%	55%
Macon/Warner Robbins	Houston	58%	42%
North/South Georgia			
Augusta	Columbia	71%	29%
Augusta	Richmond	45%	55%

Note: The total population of these counties represents 52 percent of the state population.

state (51 percent) lived in counties that voted Republican five straight times in the presidential races, while only 21 percent resided in counties that voted Democratic that often. Most noticeable in Table 7.1 is the margin by which the Republican counties in the Atlanta area supported the GOP presidential candidates. Many suburban counties voted 60 percent and more, for the Republicans.

The key to any GOP victory in Georgia is to rally the white suburban voters around Atlanta, then add the isolated communities on the borders to the north Georgia base. The Democratic strategy requires that a national candidate dilute the Republican suburban vote to the point where the rural and urban (both black and white) vote can capture the state. This has not happened in Georgia since the Carter races of 1976 and 1980, and the Clinton victories in 1992 and 1996, when the Republicans won these counties with barely 50 percent of the vote.

In terms of electoral success, the decade of the 1990s saw Republicans gain in statewide races, but their success stalled out at offices for governor, US senator, and other statewide offices. In a survey of county party chairs, Republicans were optimistic, believing their party organizations were gaining strength; while Democrats perceived more mixed trends.[15] Some of this Democratic pessimism surfaced in 2002 when incumbent senatorial candidate Max Cleland failed to win the necessary votes in the Atlanta suburbs that he had won six years earlier, and Saxby Chambliss squeaked out a narrow victory. It received a double emphasis in 2004 when native son Zell Miller gave a fiery speech at the GOP convention. Georgia voted in another GOP senator that year, and went for George W. Bush by a 48 percent to 41 percent margin.

Florida

Florida is different from any other state in the South. It was historically underpopulated, and then experienced an eruption of in-migration that made it one of the nation's most populous and important states. It has huge Hispanic (including Cuban) populations, a smaller black population, and an enormous elderly segment sixty-five years old or older. When joined together, the various populations of Latin Americans, retirees, and out-of-state immigrants collectively make Florida the fourth most populous state in the 2000 census, and the most changed southern state in the past fifty years. Approximately 16 percent of Florida's population speaks a language other than English at home. The state has one of the nation's most buoyant economies, from tourism and retirees, but also in services and trade.

V. O. Key described politics in Florida after World War II as, "every man for himself," meaning that the geography and diversity of the state discouraged political cohesions and any idea of consistent party or "machine" politics. A key to Florida's uniqueness was its small black population, which historically limited the ability of politicians to play the race card in political elections. What Key could not foresee was the massive population growth that would ultimately determine contemporary politics in the state. Elderly arrivals partake of no single political tradition, and there is no common frame of reference to explain state politics. Elderly voters in the 1960s were mostly Republican with affluent backgrounds. The retirees of the 1980s were more diverse, and many were blue collar Democrats moving south to capitalize on an inflated housing market.

The transition to a competitive political environment was fueled by three forces: (1) in-migration of large numbers of conservative, middle-class people from the North and Midwest, (2) in-migration of elderly persons, and (3) traditional Democrats deciding to change parties. "In 1980 nearly two-thirds of registered voters were identified as Democrats . . . by 2000 less than one-half were registered Democrats."[16]

Florida is a state without one dominant metropolitan area. Miami's Dade County casts 14 percent of the state's vote, and the three counties on the Gold Coast—Dade, Broward, and Palm Beach—have one-third of the electorate. Yet the

Miami media market is smaller than that of Tampa and St. Petersburg. While half the population of the state is in a handful of counties, Florida still has ten major television markets. Over 90 percent of the state population lives in incorporated metropolitan areas, making it the South's most urban state. This means that any politician who wants to be known statewide must fly around constantly to get on local newscasts. Orlando and Daytona Beach are home to the tourist and citrus industry, but there are literally dozens of smaller communities, from Naples to Pensacola, that house a diverse population needed for any party victory.

The collision of the older Florida, located in the northern part of the state with a population of blacks and whites, and the retirees from New York Jews to Catholics and Protestants from the Midwest, along with the Cubans and other Hispanics from Latin America, produced a unique political culture. All these factors make Florida elections unpredictable and subject to startling fluctuations at the presidential level and related statewide races. In presidential races the state trended Republican after 1945, then went for Jimmy Carter in 1976. Voters turned against Carter in 1980 as the state began electing Republicans to newly created congressional seats. In 1988 virtually every county voted for George H.W. Bush. "The trend toward an increasing number of Republican and Independent voters means that Democratic candidates are no longer assured of victory."[17] The GOP won control of the Florida state senate in 1994, and the state house in 1996, while voting for Bill Clinton in his second term.

The 2000 presidential election revealed the razor-thin partisan balance of Florida before the whole nation, but Jeb Bush won a convincing reelection in 2002, and his brother followed suit two years later. The Atlantic Gold Coast in south Florida, with about one-third of the statewide population, is heavily Democratic with Jewish voters and retirees. The Tampa/St. Petersburg area is competitive, while the northern panhandle, from Jacksonville to Pensacola, is Republican. In 2004 none of the nail-biting drama of four years earlier was in evidence since the state went to George W. Bush by a 52 percent to 47 percent margin.

This pattern is shown in Map 7.2. The map shows that the Republican base vote in Florida is largely in nonmetro counties, and totals to less than one-third of the electorate. The major urban cities of Miami and its adjacent counties are Democratic; they total more than one-third of the population. A final third of the counties change their allegiance.

No image of the 2000 election is more abiding that that of election officials counting various contested ballots in counties around the state. The statistical tie showed that George W. Bush received 537 more votes than Al Gore, and this margin was decided by the 739 vote difference Bush gained from federal absentee ballots. The competitiveness of the Florida electorate is seen in the map with over 30 percent of the population living in counties that voted Republican for presidential candidates in the 1990s and early twenty-first century, and 44 percent of the electorate living in counties that voted Democratic every time during the same time

Map 7.2   Florida: Political Partisanship in Presidential Elections, 1992–2004

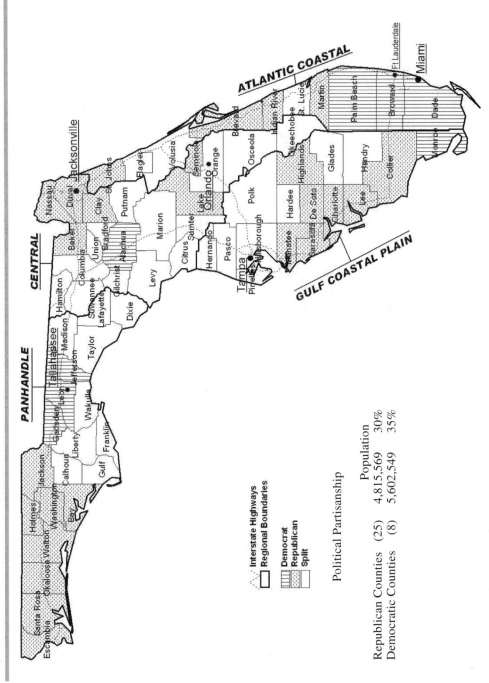

Political Partisanship

		Population	
Republican Counties	(25)	4,815,569	30%
Democratic Counties	(8)	5,602,549	35%

Interstate Highways
Regional Boundaries

Democrat
Republican
Split

ATLANTIC COASTAL

CENTRAL

PANHANDLE

GULF COASTAL PLAIN

period. Most of the electorate resides in competitive counties for presidential races.

The state was not always as competitive as it was in 2000. In 1988 every county but one voted Republican, but in the 1990s it became a fierce battleground.[18] In 1992 and 1996 Florida was the only one of the four largest states in the country to be seriously contested, with Bush winning it in 1992, and Clinton taking it in 1996. The 2000 election has become part of US political history, and the Florida legacy of "hanging chads" and delayed reporting of results is likely to keep historians busy for decades to come as they try to see who really won. Ultimately Bush was awarded Florida and the presidency, and the legacy of the "Sunshine State" as the scene of the closest US presidential election was indelibly stamped on a generation of voters.

Table 7.2 shows the partisanship of the urban counties in the presidential elections. Together with Map 7.2, the table shows the highly competitive nature of presidential and statewide contests in Florida. Democrats have a near majority in the urban counties of Miami and Tampa/St. Petersburg. Democratic strength is also in black precincts that voted 90 percent for Gore in 2000 and turned out in unprecedented numbers. The Republicans are dominant in the less populated areas, especially in the panhandle from Pensacola to Jacksonville. From looking at the map and table it is hard to see how the state voted for the GOP in four of the last five presidential elections.

Table 7.2   Florida: Presidential Election Partisanship, 1988–2004

Region/City	County	Republican Average 1988–2004	Democrat and Third-Party Average 1988–2004
Atlantic Coastal			
Miami/Ft. Lauderdale	Palm Beach	38%	62%
Miami/Ft. Lauderdale	Broward	38%	62%
Miami/Ft. Lauderdale	Dade	44%	56%
Gulf Coastal Plain			
Tampa/St. Petersburg	Hernando	44%	56%
Tampa/St. Petersburg	Hillsborough	47%	53%
Tampa/St. Petersburg	Pasco	44%	56%
Tampa/St. Petersburg	Pinellas	44%	56%
Central Florida			
Orlando/Daytona Beach/Melbourne	Orange	49%	51%

Note: The total population of these counties represents 52 percent of the state population.

Republicans win the state by attenuating the Democratic vote in the eight metropolitan counties that have over 52 percent of Florida's vote, and outpolling Democrats in the nonmetro counties. In the 2000 election, Gore bested Bush in the metropolitan counties that had over half the state's population, but Bush was dominant in the nonmetro counties. The same pattern was repeated in 2004, with one notable exception. Republicans carried virtually every county in the Tampa/St. Petersburg area, upping their margin by some three to five percentage points. The GOP push along the Interstate 4 corridor, from Orlando to Tampa Bay, made the margin for the Republicans in 2004.

The cliffhanger election of 2000 belies an underlying partisan stability in Florida politics. There is evidence of a "top-down" realignment from the presidential races to lesser offices. This Republican advance "penetrated elections for US Senate and governor from 1986 onwards, but came to structure cabinet office elections more gradually with a culmination of this realignment in the 1990s."[19]

A geographic north-south divide exists in the Florida electorate. For much of the state's history elections were decided in north Florida and the panhandle, but now the majority of the state's population lives south of Interstate 4, a major transportation artery that divides Florida from Daytona Beach to Tampa Bay. With the exception of heavily populated Jacksonville north of this line, the geopolitical center of gravity is in the center and southern counties. In 2000 the GOP won every county in the panhandle, and thirteen of fourteen in central Florida, a pattern that was repeated four years later. The competitive counties on the Atlantic coast along Interstate 95 went Democratic, while the Gulf coastal plain counties shifted into the GOP column. These small changes in partisanship were enough to swing the state into George W. Bush's column. This strategy was duplicated in 2002 with Jeb Bush's gubernatorial victory, which served as a model for the 2004 presidential race.

Virginia

In 1952 Senator Harry S. Byrd maintained what was called a "golden silence" about the presidential election. As a Democrat he could not endorse a Republican candidate, but he would not comment on the prospects of Adlai Stevenson and the Democrats statewide either. It was no surprise, then, when Virginia voted for Eisenhower in 1952 and 1956, and for Nixon in 1960. Lyndon Johnson used his charm to court Senator Byrd in 1964, and the state joined the rest of the country in the landslide Democratic win that year, but in 1976 and 1980 Virginia was the most Republican of the southern states. When Jimmy Carter won the White House, the Commonwealth was the *only* southern state to back GOP nominee Gerald Ford.

As the national Democratic Party moved to the political left, the conservative members of the Byrd machine gave their support to the Republican Party. In the 1970s the small-town lawyers and bankers, who were the heart and soul of the organization, were swamped by an in-migration population flood. The Washington suburbs were 5 percent of the statewide vote in the postwar years; by 1970 they were 21 percent. The Tidewater area around Norfolk was 13 percent of the vote in 1940; by 1970 it was 22 percent. Today these suburbs are the heart of politics in the "Old Dominion." The new residents of the urban corridor, the area from Washington, D.C., to Richmond and Norfolk, were progressive on race issues, and helped elect Linwood Holton as governor in 1969. Holton was a Republican who made a point of enrolling his daughter in the predominantly black Richmond public school system, and calming the rhetoric about racial division.

In the late 1970s conservatives held both US Senate seats and nine of the ten Virginia seats in the US House. Harry Byrd Jr. ran as an independent, and after he retired in 1982 the machine once dominated by his father existed only as a memory. Between 1951 and 1980 Virginia elected more Republican governors than any southern state.[20] But their domination ended in 1981 when Charles W. "Chuck" Robb, the son-in-law of Lyndon Johnson, won the governorship. "Robb's victory and gubernatorial leadership had a profound impact on state politics," and inaugurated a decade of Democratic dominance in the 1980s.[21] While the rest of the South swooned for Reagan's GOP appeals for the first time, Virginia abandoned the Republicans and flirted with moderate Democrats. Robb ran as a fiscal conservative, and presided over a booming economy that enabled him to pump money into education. As a fiscal conservative, with conventional views on race, he fit the pattern of attitudes in the urban corridor of the state.

The conservative mold cast by Holton, and copied by Robb, emphasized economic growth and a polite social agenda. Such a pattern well accommodated the national GOP, and Virginia remained a safe Republican state for presidential elections and many statewide ones as well. Chuck Robb's strategy of courting Republicans with conservative economic policies, while keeping a more liberal social agenda, energized the Democratic Party in the state. In the 1980s Democrats won statewide offices with this formula, the capstone being Doug Wilder's victory for governor in 1989. Wilder's accomplishment as the first elected black governor, in a venerable southern state no less, attracted national and international press attention. His margin of victory was less than 7,000 votes out of 1.8 million cast, and showed that the sentiment of Virginia was still conservative and rooted in the GOP ideology.

The seeds of GOP dominance were sown by Republican victories and intraparty squabbles during Wilder's governorship. His public feud with Senator Charles Robb split the Democratic Party, and his arguments with the legislature over black-majority districts caused more hard feelings. In the 1980s Virginia was solidly Republican for Ronald Reagan and for George Bush. The state's proximity to Washington kept the GOP agenda in the minds of state residents. The northern suburbs were increasingly caught up in the economic boom, the Tidewater area was pro-military, and conservative suburbs dominated the Richmond area.

Vignette 7.2   Doug Wilder (1931–)

The most important symbol of the changing politics in the South was the election of L. Douglas Wilder as governor of Virginia in 1989. Wilder himself commented on the significance of his victory when he said his office would be "just blocks from the White House of the Confederacy and just miles from the segregated neighborhood where I grew up." The aspirations of US blacks to assume an equal place in southern political life were personified in Wilder's victory.

Lawrence Douglas Wilder was born in the segregated Richmond neighborhood of Church Hill. His father's parents had been slaves in nearby Goochland County, and were sold to separate owners after their wedding. Grandfather Wilder needed a pass to visit his wife on Sundays. Douglas Wilder was the seventh of eight children born to Robert Wilder, a salesman who supervised agents for a black-owned insurance company. As a youth he shined shoes, delivered papers, and waited tables at clubs and hotels while attending segregated Armstrong High School.

Wilder graduated from all-black Virginia Union University in 1952, and served in the Korean War. It was in the integrated military that Wilder showed his gift for leadership. He was promoted to sergeant and won the Bronze Star for heroism at Pork Chop Hill in 1953. After the *Brown v. Board* decision in 1954 showed the power of judicial review, Wilder entered law school at Howard University. He returned to Church Hill in 1959 and opened a thriving law practice.

In 1969 Wilder won a three-way contest and became the only black in the forty-member state senate. He was typecast as a liberal and was the only member to vote against capital punishment and for Martin Luther King Jr.'s birthday as a state holiday. Over the years, Wilder earned a reputation as a shrewd, pragmatic politician who often allied himself with the centrist establishment.

In time he became one of the most influential politicians in Richmond, and in 1985 determined to run for lieutenant governor. He immediately encountered opposition from Democratic Party regulars who feared his presence on the ticket might spell defeat for others down the ticket. But Wilder refused to accept the conventional wisdom about black politicians, and went on to a 52 percent to 48 percent victory, becoming the first black candidate ever elected to statewide office in the South since Reconstruction.

By 1989 Wilder was in a strong position to repeat his statewide triumph, this time for the governor's office. He was the unanimous choice of the Democratic Party, but in the general election he faced a Republican who attacked him on his liberal voting record and his pro-choice stand on abortion. Polls had Wilder comfortably ahead, but on election night he won by a razor-thin margin of only 6,741 votes.

As governor, Wilder fell into a feud with Senator Charles Robb that culminated in allegations by the governor of phone tapping and a criminal investigation. The Wilder-Robb break damaged the state Democratic Party for a decade. When Wilder announced on September 13, 1991, after only two years in the governor's mansion, that he was forming an exploratory committee to seek the Democratic presidential nomination, his support statewide began to drop noticeably. Wilder subsequently dropped his presidential campaign bid, and returned to his duties as governor.

Since Virginia does not allow governors to hold consecutive terms, Wilder stepped down in 1994. He subsequently taught political science at Virginia Commonwealth University in Richmond and continued to practice law.

The Republican strength in Virginia is in the rural areas as well. Map 7.3 shows GOP domination along the urban corridor and in the nonmetro areas. Nearly half of the Virginia population lives in counties and cities that voted Republican five straight times, while only 16 percent of the population lives in counties and cities with a similar Democratic allegiance. The map confirms Republican dominance in presidential politics is practically complete, with a huge geographical base that is loyal to the GOP. The hidebound conservatism of the place keeps Democrats at bay.

In 1993 former congressman George Allen capitalized on this mood to win a convincing victory for governor. Allen campaigned on a platform of lower taxes, longer prison sentences, and no parole. Once in office he worked to build the Republican Party by recruiting candidates and adopting issues popular at the national level. In 1995 he gathered state GOP candidates on the steps of the capitol to reveal a ten-point "Pledge for Honest Change," modeled after the success of the "Contract with America" sponsored by the GOP in nearby Washington.

The tenor of politics in the state is evident in the career of Senator John Warner, who has been regularly elected since 1978. Warner is from the D.C. area and considers himself a guardian of national defense issues, a position that helps his standing in the Tidewater area of the state. The antiterror efforts of the 1990s, and the initial decade of the twenty-first century, rely on the training of elite units in places like Newport News, Virginia.

The Warner-Allen strategy of conservative social policies and defense-oriented politics, so popular at the national level, are just as successful in Virginia. The conservative ideological orientation of the electorate provided the foundation for subsequent victories by former attorney general James Gilmore, and state legislators down the ticket. Gilmore's pledge to cut car taxes was popular, and ran on the tracks laid by Allen. As a result, "the Virginia political landscape has undergone profound changes in the modern era."[22]

Virginia remains one of the most Republican states at the presidential level, but beneath that allegiance lurks a Democratic rebirth. In 1996 Bill Clinton lost the state by a mere two percentage points. Four years later George W. Bush won by a more convincing eight percentage points. Despite its proximity to the White House and national affairs, the state has not figured prominently in presidential politics.

Although many Virginians prefer to think of the Commonwealth as rural and its citizens as tied to the land, the population of the state is centered along the interstates from northern Virginia to Richmond, and to Hampton Roads and Newport News. The vast majority of the growth in the urban corridor has occurred in the outer suburbs, and as Table 7.3 shows, these counties (Fauquier, Loudoun, Hanover, Chesterfield, Glouchester, and York) are zealously Republican. They have experienced astonishing growth. For example, in the decade of the 1990s, Loudoun County outside Washington, D.C., grew by 55 percent, Stafford County by 44 percent, and Spotsylvania County by 35 percent.

By contrast, the central cities have smaller populations and their devotions to

Map 7.3 Virginia: Political Partisanship in Presidential Elections, 1992–2004

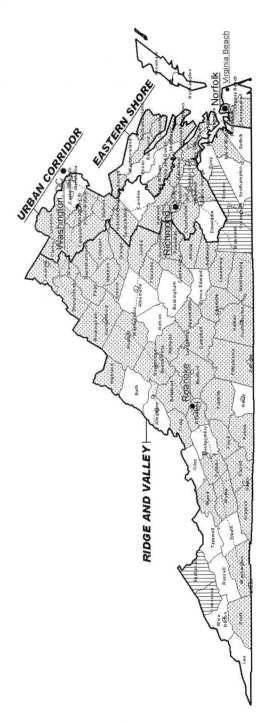

Political Partisanship

		Population	
Republican Counties	(64/16)	3,327,637	47%
Democratic Counties	(7/13)	1,157,062	16%

Legend:

Interstate Highways
Regional Boundaries

Democrat
Republican
Split

Table 7.3 Virginia: Presidential Election Partisanship, 1988–2004

	County/City	Republican Average 1988–2004	Democrat and Third-Party Average 1988–2004
Urban Corridor	Counties		
Washington/Northern Virginia	Arlington	36%	64%
Washington/Northern Virginia	Fairfax	50%	50%
Washington/Northern Virginia	Fauquier	61%	39%
Washington/Northern Virginia	Loudoun	55%	45%
Washington/Northern Virginia	Prince William	54%	46%
Washington/Northern Virginia	Stafford	59%	41%
	Cities		
Washington/Northern Virginia	Alexandria	36%	64%
Washington/Northern Virginia	Fairfax	50%	50%
Washington/Northern Virginia	Falls Church	39%	61%
Washington/Northern Virginia	Fredricksburg	45%	55%
Washington/Northern Virginia	Manassas	56%	44%
Washington/Northern Virginia	Manassas Park	55%	45%
Urban Corridor	Counties		
Richmond/Petersburg	Chesterfield	63%	37%
Richmond/Petersburg	Hanover	68%	32%
Richmond/Petersburg	Henrico	57%	43%
Richmond/Petersburg	Prince George	59%	41%
	Cities		
Richmond/Petersburg	Colonial Heights	71%	29%
Richmond/Petersburg	Hopewell	54%	46%
Richmond/Petersburg	Petersburg	23%	77%
Richmond/Petersburg	Richmond	33%	67%
Urban Corridor	Counties		
Norfolk/Newport News	Glouchester	60%	40%
Norfolk/Newport News	Isle of Wright	55%	45%
Norfolk/Newport News	James City	58%	42%
Norfolk/Newport News	Mathews	60%	40%
Norfolk/Newport News	York	61%	39%
	Cities		
Norfolk/Newport News	Chesapeake	53%	47%
Norfolk/Newport News	Hampton	46%	54%
Norfolk/Newport News	Newport News	49%	51%
Norfolk/Newport News	Poquoson	72%	28%
Norfolk/Newport News	Portsmouth	41%	59%
Norfolk/Newport News	Suffolk	48%	53%
Norfolk/Newport News	Virginia Beach	57%	43%
Norfolk/Newport News	Williamsburg	45%	55%

Note: The total population of these areas represents 59 percent of the state population.

the Democratic Party provide a smaller statewide base. The city of Arlington in the D.C. area, Petersburg, and inner-city Portsmouth are Democratic strongholds. As the suburbs exploded, the central cities shrank in comparison, and the result was a strengthening of the grip the GOP held on the state.

Texas

The Alamo, Texas Rangers, and the myth of instant wealth have given politics in Texas a special independent flair. Author John Steinbeck once wrote, "Texas is more than a state in the union. It is a state of mind."[23] The quote, along with its vast landscape, invited the belief that the state is a nation unto itself. Today the rural Texas of oil wells, cattle, and tumbleweeds has given way to an economy of trade, manufacturing, and finance. Texas is now one of the most urbanized and industrialized states in the country. The silicon chip, invented by an engineer who worked for Texas Instruments, has revolutionized the economy of the state—and the nation. The pattern of rapid suburban growth changed the culture and politics of the place.

Like the rest of the states in the former Confederacy, Texas had a solid one-party Democratic allegiance through most of the twentieth century. At the turn of the nineteenth century when the writer O. Henry (William Sidney Porter) was a Texas newspaperman, he said: "We have only two or three laws, such as against murdering witnesses and being caught stealing horses, and voting the Republican ticket."[24]

Eisenhower carried the state in 1952 and 1956. Elections were once intramural battles between local conservative and national liberal Democrats, with the former dominating politics in the state and the latter dominating politics in Washington. Texas divided itself into two groups, the conservative Democrats and the liberal Democrats. Businesses in the state sided with the former to advance their interests. Railroad, cattle, then oil, energy, and construction allied themselves to the conservative Democrats in positions of power. As Robert Caro wrote of Lyndon Johnson, whose rise to power was underwritten by archconservatives, "He was helping New Dealers with the money of men who hated the New Deal."[25]

Democrats fought bitter primaries but coalesced on Election Day. It was the differences between the two factions that led to Jack Kennedy's fateful decision to come to Dallas in 1963 to unite the party before the 1964 presidential election. Reconciliation proved impossible. In time the conservative interests who supported John B. Connally went into the GOP, and the liberal faction who backed Ralph Yarborough stayed with the Democrats.

The word "Republican" was anathema until the election of native son Lyndon Johnson in 1964. When LBJ won the presidency Democrats held all thirty-one seats in the Texas senate, and 149 of 150 in the state legislature. The congressional delegation was an army that followed the national party dictates when it came to spending programs, and the allegiance of representatives to Sam Rayburn or LBJ was legendary. But the enchantment began to wear thin when the liberalism of the national Democratic Party clashed with the homespun values of the Lone Star State; politicians liked to say they were a "Texas Democrat," or a "conservative Democrat."

In the 1950s and 1960s, Texas values became America's values. Sam Rayburn stood before the graduating class of Syracuse University in June of 1956 and said, "Men are not angels [and] it is not, therefore, criminal that inequalities should exist among us. But it would be criminal if we should ignore them."[26] This frontier ethic of Texas equality became the Great Society of the 1960s. On Wednesday, November 27, 1963, Johnson was introduced to a joint session of Congress as "our former colleague." In the aftermath of John Kennedy's assassination a Southerner speaking in the unmistakable accent of his own region said, "We have talked long enough about equal rights. . . . It is time to write the next chapter—and write it in the books of law."[27] In a sense, Texas ethics helped to write the civil rights legislation of the 1960s.

Finally, the liberal domination of the national Democratic Party led to realignment at the grassroots. When President Johnson signed federal civil rights legislation in the mid-1960s he remarked that he was, "signing away the South for the next fifty years."[28] Maybe it is the "independent" spirit of the oil and natural gas industry, or the deep moralistic political culture of the West, or the legacy of the Alamo—for whatever reason, Texas retains a deep-seated conservative strain. Every high school student in the state takes Texas history, and they remember the independence of the Texas Republic, the Confederate veterans who returned to an agricultural depression, and the ruggedness of a trail drive as depicted in the book, *Lonesome Dove*. With the emergence of the Republican Party, these interests began to gravitate to the GOP.

George Herbert Walker Bush, the scion of a rich, eastern Republican family, who made millions as an independent oilman in Texas, led the realignment. After two terms in Congress he lost a statewide race to Lloyd Bentsen, but recovered to become director of the Central Intelligence Agency, ambassador to the UN, special envoy to China, vice president, and then president. He claimed native status; and his son, George W. Bush, cited his Texas record in the 2000 presidential campaign. Texas, and the frontier ethos, became synonymous with power in Washington. One of the applause lines in George W. Bush's acceptance speech at the 2004 Republican convention came when he rebutted critics who said he had a swagger by saying he came from a state where that was called "walking."

Map 7.4 shows the domination of Republicans in the state. Texas has arguably been one-party GOP for a generation and Republicans have won five of the last seven gubernatorial elections, although they didn't win the first one until 1978. The statewide Republican trend began with the election of John Tower to the US Senate in 1961. Allegiance was sparse for a time. In 1968 Republicans elected two state senators and eight legislators. The legacy of the Vietnam War, and Lyndon

Johnson's sudden decision to not seek the presidency in a second term, opened voters to a new way of doing politics. In the 1972 Democratic governor's race, Dolph Briscoe won by three points over Republican Hank Grover. Texas's growing number of conservative Republicans began winning elections, first in Dallas, then in the western suburbs of Houston, and then in other cities across the state. The fast-growing areas of Harris County were the political base for congressman, then senatorial candidate, and finally vice president and president, George Bush. "Hence, a remarkable transformation had taken place. . . . Texas was now a powerhouse on the national stage."[29] The map shows that two-thirds of the Texas population lives in counties that have voted Republican in every presidential election since 1988. In the same time period the Democratic base was in counties that held only 10 percent of the state's population.

It was conservative Republican president Ronald Reagan's landslide election in his second term of 1984 that broke the Democrats' hold on Texas. That was the same year that a former Texas A&M economics professor, named Phil Gramm, ran for the US Senate and attained a 59 percent to 41 percent victory over Democrat Lloyd Doggett. It may have been in Texas during these years when George Bush was vice president that the term "liberal" came to be associated with anyone linked with the Texas Democratic Party. From Texarkana to El Paso, whites changed their allegiance to that of Reagan, and then to adopted son George Bush.

In 1988 the national tickets with Texans in each party resulted in a Bush-Quayle win over Dukakis-Bentsen by 56 percent to 43 percent. The last statewide office winner in the Democratic Party who won a contested race in the national spotlight was Ann Richards, for governor in 1990. The Democratic Party strength in the countryside collapsed in 1994 when George W. Bush carried 189 of 254 counties.

The suburban strength of the Republican Party is seen in Table 7.4 where Republicans carried the areas around Dallas, Waco, and Harris County. The reach and strength of the GOP is most evident in Map 7.4, which shows the counties at the tips of the Texas Triangle that voted for the GOP in presidential elections. The map shows the counties of west Texas, the panhandle, and upper Gulf being solidly Republican and that twenty-four of the forty-two counties of the Triangle voted GOP in every election. Texas was very good to George W. Bush in 2000 and 2004. He won Dallas, Houston, and even San Antonio on the tips of the Triangle. In the remaining counties he outpolled Gore and Kerry by a ratio of two to one. The same pattern was evident in the Rick Perry victory over Tony Sanchez in the 2002 gubernatorial race. Given the allegiance to Republicans in the hinterland, all any GOP candidate need do is split the urban areas, and Table 7.4 shows that they are doing just that, and the statewide political outcome is a foregone conclusion.

The Democratic base is in the Latino vote in south Texas and far west Texas, the black vote in central cities, and isolated rural counties in other areas. The increasing influence of the minority population in the state, particularly Mexican

Map 7.4   Texas: Political Partisanship in Presidential Elections, 1992–2004

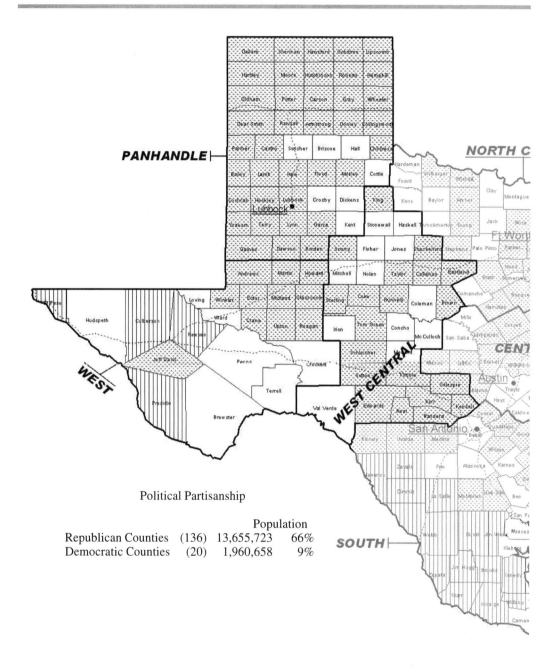

Political Partisanship

		Population	
Republican Counties	(136)	13,655,723	66%
Democratic Counties	(20)	1,960,658	9%

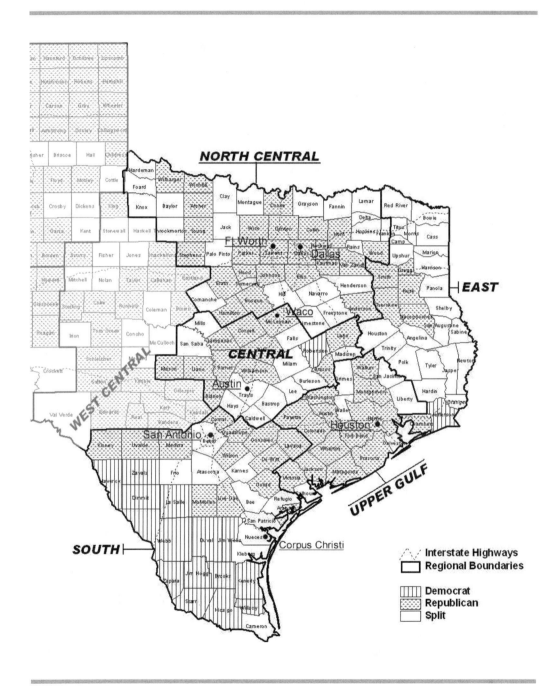

Table 7.4   Texas: Presidential Election Partisanship, 1988–2004

Region/City	County	Republican Average 1988–2004	Democrat and Third-Party Average 1988–2004
North Texas			
Dallas/Ft. Worth	Dallas	49%	51%
Dallas/Ft/ Worth	Tarrant	55%	45%
Dallas/Ft. Worth	Denton	62%	38%
Dallas/Ft. Worth	Collin	66%	34%
Central Texas			
Waco	McLennan	55%	45%
Austin	Travis	41%	59%
South Texas			
San Antonio	Bexar	49%	51%
Upper Gulf			
Houston	Harris	52%	48%

Note: The total population of these areas represents 50 percent of the state population.

Americans, should bring smiles to the faces of Democrats. These counties are reliably Democratic, but in 2002 Republican gubernatorial nominee Rick Perry took 35 percent of this Hispanic vote. Texas is reliably Republican and has generated national politicians like George Bush, Phil Gramm, and George W. Bush for the nation's highest office. It remains a country-sized state, and it is very difficult and expensive to run a statewide campaign here. All in all, the state with the Lone Star seems tailor-made for the Republicans to continue a string of victories.

Emergent States

North Carolina

North Carolina is one of America's growth states, but at the same time it retains a sentiment of rural melancholy. The culture is a mixture of progressive and tradition-minded citizens, a place with one of the nation's leading research centers complete with the latest computer technology, and a governor who declared in 1999 that the elimination of outhouses was one of the priorities of his administration. A former senator, Jesse Helms, was synonymous with conservative Republican causes; another senator, John Edwards, sought the Democratic presidential nomination in 2004 with one of the most liberal voting records in the US Senate. The state is a paradox of new and old values.

For most of its history, the differences between east and west explained the politics of North Carolina. The Tidewater area of the east was pro-British, while the Piedmont and mountains were anti-British. The coast was involved in commerce and trade, while the interior had smaller farms and a more independent spirit. North Carolina was one of the last of the thirteen original colonies to ratify the Constitution because the document did not contain a section guaranteeing fundamental civil liberties. Their delay was largely responsible for the first ten amendments to the Constitution, known today as the Bill of Rights.

In the Civil War most of the slaves were in the east, while the western part of the state retained considerable Union sentiment. In the prohibition vote of 1908 the east voted wet, while the west voted dry. The historic dividing line between the two areas was the fall line, which divides the Piedmont hills from the rest of the state. In Chapter 3, North Carolina was divided into three major topographical regions, each with a historically distinctive economic and cultural base. The Atlantic coastal plain, or the historical Tidewater area, has a large black population and its white residents retain Democratic, and isolationist, voting habits. The cities of the Piedmont, the second area, are populous with downtown Democrats and Republican-leaning suburbs. The history here is of a vivid independence and unpredictability. This is the area of the state with textile, tobacco, and furniture making, alongside banking and information technology. The mountains in the western part of the state, the Blue Ridge area, are sparsely populated and fiercely Republican in political allegiance.

Map 7.5 shows that North Carolina has a presidential GOP base that is equally at home in the metropolitan and rural areas. The state voted Republican in Ronald Reagan's 1980 triumph and every election since. In 2000 George W. Bush captured 56 percent of the metropolitan vote and 56 percent of the nonmetro vote. The map shows that about half the population of the state resides in counties that have voted Republican five straight times. The Democratic base is much smaller, with only 10 percent of the population living in counties that were similarly loyal.

In the 2000 Census, North Carolina competed with Georgia as the nation's tenth largest state. The population lies along an interstate arc of highways I-40 and I-85, from Charlotte in the south, to Greensboro and Raleigh-Durham, down to Wilmington on the coast. Despite its dramatic growth, the state has no dominant urban area. The Piedmont counties contain most of the population in the cities of Charlotte, Raleigh, and Greensboro.

These regional distinctives of North Carolina have made it politically competitive in statewide contests, but the Tarheel State leans Republican at the presidential level. In the early years of the twentieth century the relatively small black population left the state free of the racist demagoguery practiced in neighboring states of the Deep South. A calm attitude on race and established urban areas led to predictions of a GOP takeover in the last third of the century. In 1968 Richard Nixon carried the state, and four years later conservative senator, and soon to be state personality, Jesse Helms won a US Senate seat. Helms used his position as a Raleigh news broadcaster

Map 7.5   North Carolina: Political Partisanship in Presidential Elections, 1992–2004

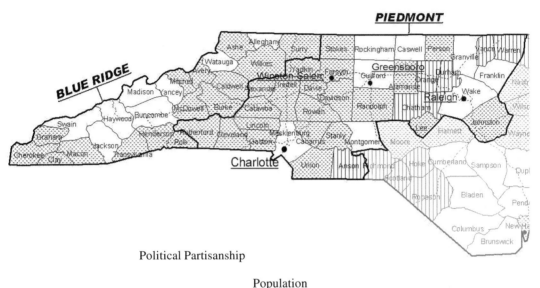

Political Partisanship

		Population	
Republican Counties	(49)	3,856,660	48%
Democratic Counties	(17)	920,293	11%

to dilute the Democratic vote in the Tidewater area, and score well in the smaller towns and suburbs of the Piedmont. His five victories in US Senate races led to the identification of a new voting bloc in North Carolina politics: "Jessecrats." By appealing to rural white conservative Democrats, Helms gained the needed margins of victory in closely fought elections. His campaigns were over his staunch conservative stances, yet he centered the battle not on his ideas, but on his opponents' ideas.

Once elected, Jesse Helms staked out positions on the conservative right opposing abortion and state-funded sex education programs, putting curbs on the federal judiciary, increasing defense spending, and favoring prayer in the public schools. His sympathy for conservative causes attracted national attention and his Congressional Club, organized initially to retire his 1972 campaign debt, became an extremely successful political action committee. The PAC provided funds and technical assistance for conservative causes and candidates, inside and outside of North Carolina.

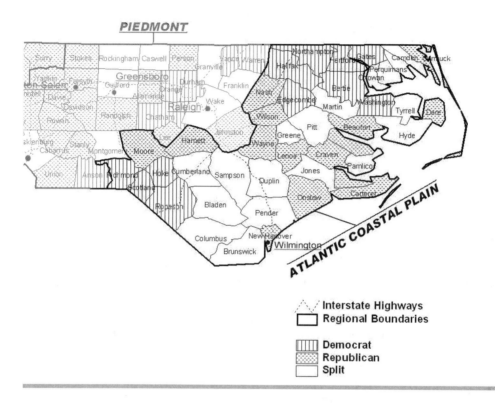

The conservatism of the state changed national politics in 1976 when, after five straight losses, Ronald Reagan started denouncing the Panama Canal Treaty and won his first primary victory over Gerald Ford in the Tarheel State. That victory, earned with the blessings of Senator Jesse Helms, kept Reagan's presidential hopes alive until 1980. Despite North Carolina's Republican and conservative bent, there are those who think such a trend is bound to change.

In their book, *The Emerging Democratic Majority*, authors John Judis and Ruy Teixeira use the state as an example of the moderate future available for southern Democrats. The minority vote, along with "professional women and other relatively liberal whites in the state's growing postindustrial areas are the base of the Democratic vote."[30] According to the authors, these high-tech regions are composed of postindustrial workers who tend to be ethnically diverse and more complex in their political orientation. These "ideopolises," as the authors call them, want to work and live in communities that reflect an openness and tolerance of ideas. The Research Triangle in the northern part of the state, and the city of Charlotte are identified as such areas in North Carolina.

Patterns of presidential partisanship are shown in Table 7.5. The Greensboro and Charlotte areas are Republican, while the Raleigh area, and especially the Research Triangle Park in Durham, are staunchly Democratic. Statewide, forty-nine counties were Republican in allegiance, and seventeen were base Democratic counties. The partisanship of counties is important because during the 1990s race and politics came together in a redistricting controversy that stretched until the next

Table 7.5   North Carolina: Presidential Election Partisanship, 1988–2004

Region/City	County	Republican Average 1988–2004	Democrat and Third-Party Average 1988–2004
Piedmont			
Charlotte	Cabarras	62%	38%
Charlotte	Gaston	64%	36%
Charlotte	Lincoln	60%	40%
Charlotte	Mecklenburg	50%	50%
Charlotte	Rowan	61%	39%
Charlotte	Union	62%	38%
Piedmont			
Raleigh	Chatham	45%	55%
Raleigh	Durham	36%	64%
Raleigh	Franklin	47%	53%
Raleigh	Johnston	61%	39%
Raleigh	Orange	35%	65%
Raleigh	Wake	50%	50%
Piedmont			
Greensboro	Almance	58%	42%
Greensboro	Davidson	63%	37%
Greensboro	Davie	68%	32%
Greensboro	Forsyth	53%	47%
Greensboro	Guilford	49%	51%
Greensboro	Randolph	67%	33%
Greensboro	Stokes	62%	38%
Greensboro	Yadkin	70%	30%
Atlantic Coastal			
Greenville	Pitt	50%	50%
Atlantic Coastal			
Wilmington	Brunswick	51%	49%
Wilmington	New Hanover	53%	47%

Note: The total population of these areas represents 51 percent of the state population.

census. The litigation meant that different plans were used for three successive elections—1996, 1998, and 2000.[31] Republicans aspired to extend their support for presidential candidates further down the ballot, and Democrats hoped to capitalize on their moderate legacy and retain control of the state legislature. Both achieved partial victories, with Republicans winning both US Senate seats by 2004, and Democrats tightening their hold on the governor's office and both houses of the state legislature.

The Democratic vote remains in the eastern part of the state, and the urban ideopolises around Raleigh. In the 2000 presidential election the twenty nonmetropolitan counties carried by Gore all had African American populations of 25 percent or higher. The Republicans remain strong in the Blue Ridge Mountains and the suburban Piedmont. The patterns in the table and the map are not reassuring for Democrats despite predictions of an emerging majority. Nearly half the state's population lives in counties that voted Republican in every presidential election from 1988 to 2004. Five of the eight ideopolises, identified by Judis and Teixeira as trending Democratic, voted for Elizabeth Dole, the victorious Republican candidate for US Senator in 2002. Three of them voted for George W. Bush two years later.

The state retains a dual political character. The largest segment of the population is the tradition-minded, white, suburban voter who is strengthened by the religious revivals of Reverend Billy Graham, and later his son, Franklin. They vote Republican and support rock-ribbed conservative candidates like Jesse Helms, John East, and Lauch Faircloth. The other element in North Carolina is the progressive impulse that builds good schools and universities, develops the infrastructure for business relocations, and encourages change. The liberal progressives support candidates like Jim Hunt and John Edwards. No doubt much of the state's population gravitates back and forth between these two poles, and for that reason the state is competitive in each election.

Tennessee

Tennessee has been defined geographically because of its size. The political divisions match the landscape, and have their roots in the Civil War. The state took two votes on secession, and the Union sympathizers were mainly farmers in the eastern mountains whose posterity voted solidly Republican in presidential races. The Confederate counties in middle and west Tennessee have long been Democratic, and their allegiance set the tone for politics statewide. In the original 1946 interviews for Key's book, the defeated Republican candidate for governor opined that "not being a damn fool he knew he did not have much chance of being elected . . . [but] the Republican Party had 40 percent of the voters . . . [and] men came to him with tears in their eyes when he had finished speaking expressing gratitude that somebody is carrying the banner and expressing the fervent hope that somehow, some day a real two-party contest can be developed."[32]

Key's work discussed the rivalry among the three regions, and to some extent the tearful wish of those listeners was realized in the party competition of today. The enduring nature of the political divisions is one of the uncanny features of politics in the state, where rural-urban differences are not as important here as the traditional geography. The state produced presidential candidates in the 1990s from the traditional state subdivisions: Vice President Al Gore hailed from middle Tennessee, and former governor, presidential candidate, and later US senator Lamar Alexander came from east Tennessee. The allegiance to geography and party has moderated with the dizzying pace of urbanization and economic transformation that swept over the state, but the geographic divisions still have relevance.

The resurgence of the Republicans had its origins in the economy of World War II. The cheap electric power of the TVA enabled Democratic politicians like Estes Kefauver and Albert Gore Sr. to win US Senate seats and adopt a moderate agenda on issues like civil rights and labor legislation. Both had national political profiles with Kefauver running as the Democratic nominee for vice president in both 1952 and 1956. When the Democratic Party embraced civil rights in the 1960s, disaffected conservatives shifted to the Republican Party. The turning points were 1966, when Howard Baker won a US Senate seat as a Republican, and 1970 when Winfield Dunn was elected governor. The growing affluence of many Tennesseans, including a number of new residents who had relocated to the state, caused natives and newcomers to take another look at the Republican Party, whose fiscal conservatism appealed to their upwardly mobile ambitions.

Tennessee has never had a large black population, 16 percent in 2000, half of whom lived in, or around, the city of Memphis in the western part of the state. Much like North Carolina, the state has little history of the racial politics that characterizes so much of the Deep South. Tennessee is the ultimate border state. Nashville is a city with a tolerant racial history, recognized as one of the first cities to desegregate after the *Brown v. Board* decision of 1954. This moderate history has changed politics, and leaves issues of economic growth and taxation as the centerpiece of most political campaigns.

This state, like a number of others in the South, has a strong history of military service. That legacy proved important in 1970, when Republican upstart Bill Brock beat venerable Democrat Al Gore Sr. who had become a critic of the Vietnam War. As the Democratic Party came under the control of the political left, the Republican positions seemed more in tune with the conservative populist voters in the state.

Richard Nixon nosed out George Wallace by four percentage points to win the state in the presidential election of 1968, and repeated the trick again in 1972. The president's subsequent disgrace in the Watergate scandal, and the neighborliness of Georgia-born Jimmy Carter, resulted in a Tennessee return to the Democratic fold in 1976. The presidential races of the 1980s gave the Republicans encouragement, as Tennesseans contributed to the defeat of Jimmy Carter in 1980 after going heavily for him in 1976. The state remained Republican in 1984 and again in 1988.

In 1992 Democrats returned to power when native senator Al Gore Jr. was put on the national ticket with Bill Clinton. That year the Democrats won the state in the presidential sweepstakes, took the post of governor, both US Senate seats, and a majority of the state legislature seats as well. But Democratic government, "as far as the eye could see," was short-lived. Republican Fred Thompson, and later Senate Majority Leader Bill Frist, defeated Democrats in 1994 and again in 1996. The state remained presidentially Democratic in 1996, but in a surprising display of independence, voted against native son Al Gore Jr. in the razor-thin 2000 election. Had Al Gore received his home state's eleven electoral votes, he would have been president. In the statewide presidential vote Bush won by a margin of 79,421 votes out of over two million cast.

Map 7.6 shows the allegiance Tennessee developed for the GOP in the decade of the 1990s to the 2004 presidential election. The analysis includes elections when Gore was on the national Democratic ticket. Despite his presence, over one-third of the state population lived in counties that voted Republican every time.[33] The GOP bastion remained east Tennessee, which was as dependably Republican in 2000 as it was during Reconstruction, and virtually every period since. The Republican base is in the Chattanooga, Knoxville, and Tri-Cities area, the state's most populous division. Memphis anchors traditionally Democratic west Tennessee, and the Nashville area is competitive. In 2000 Bush and Gore tied in the eight county totals for Memphis, Nashville, Chattanooga, Knoxville, and the Tri-Cities, but Bush carried the nonmetro counties, and this vote ensured his victory in the state. The margin in 2004 was substantial for George W. Bush who carried the east Tennessee base, suburban middle Tennessee, and the west Tennessee city of Jackson along with the Memphis suburbs.

A survey of party chairs and activists in 2001 concluded that "party activists in [both political parties] of Tennessee have reasonably vital local party organizations in many counties."[34] This seesaw political allegiance is apparent when the US Senate races are examined. East Tennessee was the base for Howard Baker, and later governor and senator, Lamar Alexander. Jim Sasser was from middle Tennessee, as were Al Gore Sr. and Jr. West Tennessee, home of the once powerful Crump machine, has become a hotly contested area when the Republican suburbs are compared to the Democratic downtown of Memphis.

Tennessee's swing to the Republican Party began in the 1970s, when the suburbs around Nashville filled up with ambitious couples capitalizing on the booming economy. In the decade of the 1980s, "both political parties in Tennessee continued to enjoy some success at the polls, but . . . neither party became the dominant one."[35] Table 7.6 shows the bedroom communities in Rutherford, Sumner, and Williamson counties supplied the GOP with substantial margins in each presidential race. The east Tennessee Republican base remained solid in the Tri-Cities, Knoxville, and Chattanooga areas. The political behavior of these cities is virtually indistinguishable from the rural counties around them, and together they provide Republicans with a cohesive geographical base.

Map 7.6   Tennessee: Political Partisanship in Presidential Elections, 1992–2004

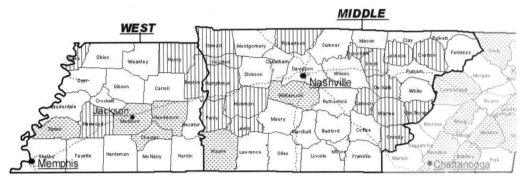

Political Partisanship

		Population	
Republican Counties	(29)	2,137,985	38%
Democratic Counties	(20)	353,954	6%

Table 7.6   Tennessee: Presidential Election Partisanship, 1988–2004

Region/City	County	Republican Average 1988–2004	Democrat and Third-Party Average 1988–2004
East Tennessee			
Knoxville	Knoxville	56%	44%
Chattanooga	Hamilton	54%	46%
Tri-Cities	(Bristol-Kingsport) Sullivan	60%	40%
Tri-Cities	(Johnson City) Washington	59%	41%
Middle Tennessee			
Nashville	Davidson	43%	57%
Nashville	Rutherford	53%	47%
Nashville	Sumner	54%	46%
Nashville	Williamson	65%	35%
West Tennessee			
Memphis	Shelby	44%	56%

Note: The total population of these areas represents 50 percent of the state population.

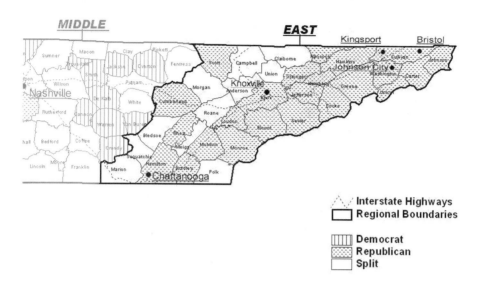

The shift in allegiance around Nashville meant the Republicans had expanded their statewide base westward, and were able to win races by taking two of the three geographical regions. When the votes of a city like Jackson in west Tennessee are added to the eastern Republican base, then the GOP can legitimately lay claim to majority party status. The results of recent elections confirm this suspicion. The Republican revolution in the state is all the more striking given that the political loyalties are quite deep. The legacy of father Al Gore to his son was not enough to overcome the newer inheritance of economic growth and feisty conservatism.

Traditional States

Alabama

"Moons, red with the dust of barren hills," says a stanza of the 1930s anthem *Stars Fell on Alabama*, "an emancipation of malevolence that threatens to destroy men through dark ways of its own." The texture of Alabama politics is captured in these lyrics celebrating the raw emotions of human conflict that have been such a part of life and culture in the state.

When Alabama is mentioned, the racial history is the most dominant memory in the minds of most Americans. This was the birthright that haunted Hugo Black, the US senator who became a Supreme Court justice in 1937 and joined the majority in the famous *Brown v. Board* decision after having once been a member of the Ku Klux Klan. The capital city of Montgomery was witness to the bus boycott in 1955 that launched the civil rights movement. In the 1960s, the state became synonymous with the crusade for racial equality. Later, Selma would be remembered as the symbol for voting rights for African Americans.

The populist side of Alabama politics was seen in the antics of James Elisha "Big Jim" Folsom, who won the governorship in 1946 and 1954. Alexander Heard was conducting interviews shortly after Folsom won his first term. Several people interviewed were impressed with Big Jim's style, especially his impatience with traditional political organizations in rural areas. One explained that the future governor became very angry at his campaign manager and insisted that "he didn't want to sit in a hotel room talking to two-bit politicians and lose the election."[36] Folsom's personality carried him to victory and one of his opponents conceded that "if the people think you are just home folks you have a certain victory." A campaign with the slogan, "The Little Man's Big Friend," was destined to succeed, especially when Folsom's speeches emphasized better roads and schools, opposition to racial discrimination, and support for women's rights. On the stump, Folsom's overpowering personality and oratory were compelling, but his drunkenness ruined him after a 1962 television appearance, and he was finished in statewide politics.

In the 1960s the racial tenor was set by George Wallace, a political protégé of Big Jim Folsom, who began his political career as a racial moderate, but decided to play the "race card" after his gubernatorial defeat in 1958. Wallace was known as Alabama's "Fighting Judge," whose legacy of state political domination was set in 1962 when he was first elected governor on a segregation pledge. For the next twenty-four years, until he retired from political office in 1986, Wallace was the spokesman for the side of politics that was against change in the racial order and social structure, and the expansion of the federal government.

From the symbolic "stand in the schoolhouse door" to his presidential campaigns, George Wallace positioned himself in the 1960s as the prototype segregationist–states' rights spokesman for the South. The Alabama governor became one of the nation's most vocal critics of federal power. He dominated the national political agenda with a message directed at the blue collar and working-class people who suffered economic reversals in any recession, and hated the anti-Vietnam movement, school busing, and the intrusion of the federal government into their everyday lives. The political dominance and longevity of Wallace retarded the development of the Republican Party in the state, but the governor's appeal would ultimately become Ronald Reagan's appeal, and the latter's message of alienation was central to the conservative resurgence nationally in the 1980s.

The most lasting effect of Wallaceism was the drawing of Alabama Democrats, and others across the South, away from the national party to a third party led by the Alabama governor, then into the arms of the Republican Party. Forty years of populist and racial politics marked the change in Alabama as whites long ago accepted integration with a corresponding commitment to a reduced role for the federal government. Typical of this changing allegiance was businessman Forrest "Fob" James, who first won election to governor as a Democrat (1978–1983), then served a second term as a Republican (1994–1999). Current US senator Richard Shelby switched parties the day after the 1994 election, and has prospered as a conservative Republican in this once solid Democratic state.

Map 7.7 shows that three-quarters of Alabama's population live in counties that voted Republican five straight times, while only 5 percent reside in counties that were similarly loyal to the Democrats. The Republican counties are the most populous, while the Democrats are in the traditional Black Belt that spans the state. In the 2004 presidential election Alabama voted for George W. Bush by a greater percentage than his native Texas.

Alabama's flirtation with Republicans at the presidential level began in 1948 with Strom Thurmond's third-party candidacy, and culminated with Goldwater's successful 1964 presidential candidacy. Edward Carmines and James Stimson argue that this Alabama exodus of white voters from the Democratic to the Republican Party is a textbook example of partisan realignment based on race. They contend that race, and issues associated with it, is a polarizing concern strong enough to drive the white population away from the Democratic Party.[37] "By carrying the state, Goldwater showed that white Alabamians would vote Republican and Democratic loyalties could not be taken for granted at the presidential level."[38]

Politics statewide is a contest between Democratic forces aligned with the Alabama Educational Association, monolithic black voters, and trial lawyers on one side, and Republican business interests and white suburbanites sympathetic to the lower taxes and less government theme of the GOP on the other. Map 7.7 shows the geographical cleavage in the state. Every metropolitan area voted Republican, while the south Alabama Black Belt served as the base for the Democrats. Nearly three-quarters of the state's population lives in counties that voted Republican in every presidential election in the 1990s to 2004.

In the 2000 presidential election George W. Bush received a higher share of the state's metropolitan than nonmetropolitan vote. The north Alabama vote is decidedly Republican, while the Black Belt is the Democratic base in the central part of the state. The Alabama coast is replete with luxury vacation homes and retirees, and is a growing base of GOP support. The urban areas proved especially loyal in 2004 with George W. Bush winning Mobile by 65 percent to 35 percent, and Birmingham by 63 percent to 37 percent.

In spite of urbanization, politics in Alabama still has a north-south flavor. The federal government transformed northern Alabama counties along the Tennessee River with a TVA project, and then expanded its influence with the Tennessee-Tombigbee waterway project. People in these areas appreciate federal largesse, and "cutting pork" is not a winning theme here for Republicans, hence the counties'

Map 7.7   Alabama: Political Partisanship in Presidential Elections, 1992–2004

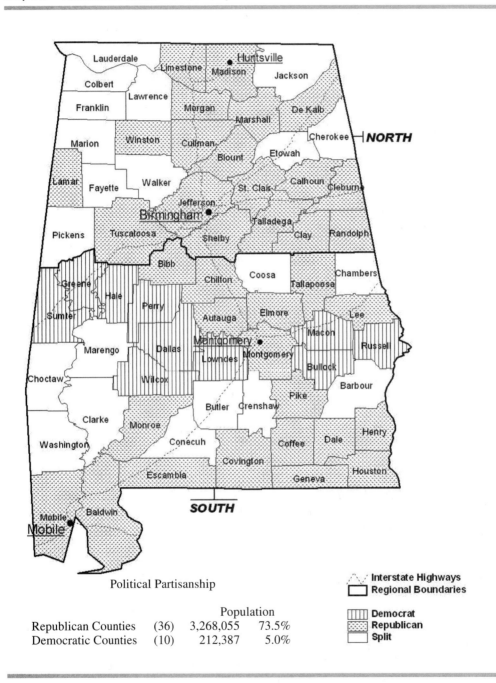

Political Partisanship

		Population	
Republican Counties	(36)	3,268,055	73.5%
Democratic Counties	(10)	212,387	5.0%

Interstate Highways
Regional Boundaries
Democrat
Republican
Split

Democratic loyalty. The federal government funds medical research in Birmingham, the NASA facilities in Huntsville, and various other projects in the state. The better-educated professional and technical residents in the lush, green hills of cities like Huntsville and Birmingham combine high-tech expertise with traditional values.

Politics in south Alabama is still racially polarized, with African Americans voting Democratic and most whites aligned with the Republican Party. "Blacks make up 25 percent of the voters at the polls in 2000 and went 11 to 1 for Gore over Bush . . . whites who considered themselves members of the religious right constituted 23 percent of the voters and broke 4 to 1 for Bush."[39]

Table 7.7 shows that the city of Birmingham is the effective center of the state and the major metropolitan area. It has shed its legacy of violence from the civil rights era, and now stands as one of the newest southern cities. Racial polarization reminiscent of barking dogs and water hoses remains in the housing patterns, as most blacks live in the city itself or in factory towns north of Red Mountain, while whites populate leafy suburban housing developments. A new city has grown up along the freeways leading to and from the downtown area in surrounding counties. The suburban city is strongly Republican and overwhelms black allegiance at the presidential level. The same can be said of the environs around Mobile,

Table 7.7   Alabama: Presidential Election Partisanship, 1988–2004

Region/City	County	Republican Average 1988–2004	Democrat and Third-Party Average 1988–2004
North Alabama			
Birmingham	Jefferson	53%	47%
Birmingham	Shelby	76%	24%
Birmingham	St. Clair	69%	31%
Birmingham	Blount	66%	34%
North Alabama			
Huntsville	Madison	56%	44%
Huntsville	Limestone	58%	42%
South Alabama			
Montgomery	Montgomery	50%	50%
Montgomery	Elmore	67%	33%
Montgomery	Autauga	66%	34%
South Alabama			
Mobile	Mobile	56%	44%
Mobile	Baldwin	68%	32%

Note: The total population of these areas represents 48 percent of the state population.

Montgomery, and suburban Huntsville. Collectively, they make Alabama one of the most Republican states in the country when it comes to presidential elections.

Arkansas

One image from Arkansas scarred a generation and changed US history at the same time. In 1957 six-term governor Orval Faubus defied the federal government by preventing the integration of Little Rock Central High School. Television, still in its infancy, beamed images of green-clad national guardsmen with their weapons shouldered to protect a handful of black students going to school with whites for the first time. This was the national image of Arkansas until 1992, when Governor Bill Clinton celebrated his presidential victory in Little Rock.

With Bill Clinton's inauguration in January of 1993, many residents hoped their native son would wipe away the legacy left by Faubus, but when the former governor left office at century's end, Arkansas residents were as ambivalent as ever about their reputation in the national eye. Clinton's upset victory for the presidency was historic in terms of national politics, but it was also Arkansas's bid for national respectability. Later, the president's mistakes became theirs. When independent counsel Kenneth Starr closed down his office in 1996 he had achieved fourteen convictions, including Governor Jim Guy Tucker who was forced to resign that same year. The idea that something is awry in the political fabric of the state persisted into the next century.

Despite its traditional and rural conservatism, which would suggest an affinity for the Republican Party, Arkansas has a history of one-party Democratic domination. Politicians like John McClellan and William Fulbright achieved seniority in Washington and represented Arkansas with a gravity that captured the national spotlight in the 1960s. In the House of Representatives, Wilbur Mills ruled the Ways and Means Committee like a personal fiefdom for sixteen years. The antics of Arkansas politicians in Washington, like Wilbur Mills's affair with stripper Fannie Fox, served to enrich the Li'l Abner/Ozark stereotype of barefoot hicks chasing loose women in the rural Arkansas hills. The events of the 1960s and 1970s did little to change this image, and Bill Clinton in the White House only institutionalized it. In retirement the former president has chosen to spend little time in his home state.

The truth about Arkansas is different from the stereotype, but the popular conception of it as backwoods, primitive, and poor remains. Part of this reputation is by design. The state extols its characteristic features as a means of attracting tourist dollars. Travel and tourism in Arkansas, "The Natural State," ranks as the third largest industry behind food and health services.[40]

The rural and small-town culture of the state makes for conservative bedrock politics, and Democratic allegiance continues in the face of liberal policies in the national platform and growing GOP clout elsewhere in Dixie. Arkansas reacted negatively to the cultural changes of the 1960s and 1970s. Residents supported the

Vietnam War and the police, while they opposed gun control and the US Supreme Court's expansion of civil liberties. One-party politics and the lack of an opposition party in the state prevented any partisan realignment.

In presidential elections Arkansas was a "Solid South" Democratic state from 1953 to 1972. The Nixon landslide estranged voters from the national party in 1972, but that alienation was restored in Carter's election of 1976. Reagan's election in 1980 popularized the Republican appeal here, as elsewhere in the South, and the drift into the GOP camp began at that time. It was arrested by the Clinton triumph in 1992.

Arkansas voted 53 percent for Bill Clinton in 1992, and 54 percent four years later. Both these margins by a native son candidate were less than the 56 percent statewide figure achieved by George H. W. Bush in 1988. In 2000 Arkansas voted only 46 percent for Al Gore, while George W. Bush won the state with 51 percent of the vote. Four years later Bush's margin expanded to 54 percent. The abiding conservatism of Arkansas fits well with the GOP philosophy, and the one-party label may be fading in the state. The allegiance of voters to the Democratic Party began to change and surfaced in the election of Mike Huckabee (1998) and Tim Hutchinson (1996). Still, today this state is one of only two in the South with the reliably Democratic stamp still in place when it comes to statewide races.

Map 7.8 shows the allegiance of Arkansas voters in the years 1988 to 2000. The results show that Arkansas is more conservative, even if it is not as Republican, as its neighbors. Adjustments in the partisan calculations for native son candidate Bill Clinton were made here, but unlike Tennessee where Al Gore was left in the analysis, here other statewide races are used to show partisanship statewide. The results of the victorious Dale Bumpers victory over Mike Huckabee in 1992, and the Republican victory of Tim Hutchinson over Winston Bryant for the US Senate in 1996 are substituted instead of the Clinton landslides. The map does *not* include results from the 2004 presidential election because George W. Bush carried many counties that had previously voted Democratic in every election from 1988 to 2000.

These races give an accurate picture of grassroots partisanship, and they show shifting allegiance in most counties. The map reveals that Arkansas is more competitive in presidential politics than its historic one-party label would indicate. Republican allegiance is in the northwest corner, offset by Democratic loyalty along the Mississippi alluvial plain. In the 2000 presidential election virtually every county north and west of Little Rock voted Republican, and those counties south and east went mostly Democratic. The same pattern was evident in 2004. Early in the election cycle Arkansas was listed as a "battleground state," but in the last month polls showed a decisive shift to George W. Bush, who carried it by nine percentage points. Most of the cities are competitive in statewide races, and neither party has a strong urban geographical base in a close race.

Map 7.8 shows partisanship evenly split between the two parties. In presiden-

Map 7.8   Arkansas: Political Partisanship in Presidential Elections, 1992–2004

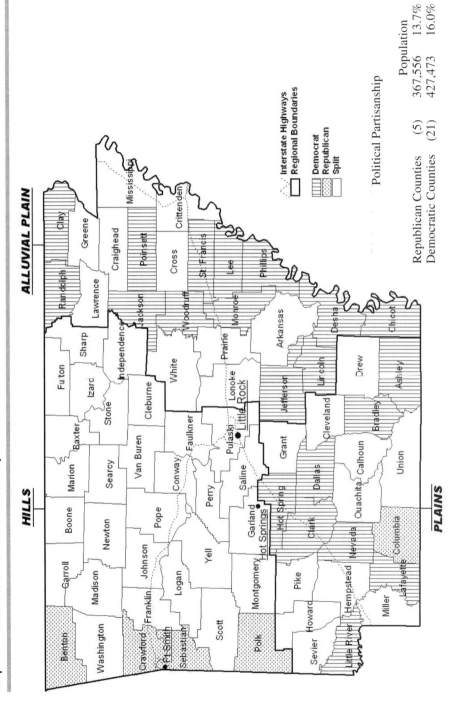

Interstate Highways
Regional Boundaries

Political Partisanship

- Democrat
- Republican
- Split

		Population	
Republican Counties	(5)	367,556	13.7%
Democratic Counties	(21)	427,473	16.0%

tial races, Arkansas voted for former governor Bill Clinton, but flirted with Republicans in races down the ticket. After the 2000 election residents had a Republican governor, US senator, and one congressman representing the northwest corner of the state. In the 2002 midterm elections Republicans lost the Senate seat Tim Hutchinson held, as voters switched back to the Democratic Party.

The competitiveness of Arkansas politics is apparent when the urban areas are examined in Table 7.8. Arkansas is less urban than other southern states, so the eleven counties in the table only contain slightly more than 40 percent of the statewide population. The embryonic emergence of Republican allegiance is seen in the suburbs of the city of Little Rock, in Ft. Smith, and in Rogers and Bentonville in northwest Arkansas, but most cities in the state are within a few percentage points of being evenly divided between the two parties when Republicans win the state.

South Carolina

Ever since former senator Strom Thurmond provided critical votes to nominate Richard Nixon at the 1968 Republican National Convention, South Carolina has been one of the GOP's strongest southern states. It was not always this way. In the

Table 7.8 Arkansas: Presidential Election Partisanship, 1988–2004

Region/City	County	Republican Average 1988–2004	Democrat and Third-Party Average 1988–2004
Mountain			
Little Rock/Pine Bluff	Pulaski	55%	45%
Little Rock/Pine Bluff	Faulkner	59%	41%
Little Rock/Pine Bluff	Saline	63%	37%
Little Rock/Pine Bluff	Lonoke	65%	35%
Mountain			
Ft. Smith/Fayetteville	Sebastian	62%	38%
Ft. Smith/Fayetteville	Crawford	66%	34%
Hot Springs	Garland	54%	46%
Plains			
El Dorado	Union	59%	41%
Pine Bluff	Jefferson	34%	66%
Texarkana	Miller	58%	42%
Mississippi Alluvial Plain			
Jonesboro	Craighead	53%	47%

Note: The total population in these areas represents 41 percent of the state population.

1944 presidential election, South Carolina was the nation's most Democratic state, but the tradition began to slip after that peak. James F. Byrnes, who was the state's most significant political figure having served in FDR's cabinet, the US Senate, and on the US Supreme Court, shocked Democratic leaders when he supported Dwight D. Eisenhower in 1952. Byrnes was considered the leading candidate for the Democratic vice presidential nomination in 1944, but was vetoed by northern urban constituencies. His defection was an early sign that power was shifting in the Democratic national party. Later Byrnes backed Richard Nixon and Barry Goldwater. The betrayal of the Democratic Party by the state's most visible politician showed that the "Solid South" legacy in the state was at an end.

Democratic presidential candidates still carried South Carolina in 1952, 1956, and 1960, but the margins of victory were never comfortable. John Kennedy squeaked by with a majority of just 10,000 votes in 1960, thanks largely to the support of then Democratic governor, and later US senator, Ernest "Fritz" Hollings.

The commitment of the national Democratic Party to civil rights ruptured the traditional allegiance South Carolinians had to the party in the decade of the 1960s. South Carolina has a large black population, and the state regularly voted Democratic, but allegiance deteriorated during the Johnson presidency. Although loyal to Democrats at the grassroots level, white voters in the state found the Republican Party more comfortable in presidential voting as they increasingly turned aside from the national Democratic Party platform.

The 1964 election happened during the middle of the civil rights movement and before the enactment of the Voting Rights Act. The election was memorable in statewide political lore because white voters crossed over to pull the lever for Republican Barry Goldwater and voted with the GOP in large numbers for the first time. Millionaire textile magnate Roger Milliken, a conservative activist with a strong anti-union premise, bankrolled an energetic recruitment and organization effort for the Republican Party. He was helped by Strom Thurmond's defection from the Democratic Party with the attendant respectability it brought to those active in state politics. In ten presidential elections since 1964, the Republican presidential candidate has failed to carry the state only once—in 1976 when its next-door neighbor, Governor Jimmy Carter, led southern voters back into the Democratic fold.

Desegregation and school busing played a major role in redefining political allegiance in the 1972 race. Senior US senator Strom Thurmond pointedly criticized the Nixon administration for some of its stands on achieving racial integration goals, and much of the state seemed sympathetic to the candidacy of George Wallace, until his shooting in 1972. Four years later South Carolina began a flirtation with Jimmy Carter, whose background in Plains, Georgia, mirrored that of many white residents in the state. When Carter appeared at the Firecracker 400 stock car race in Darlington in 1976, he seemed to be speaking the language white voters in the Palmetto State wanted to hear, but the association proved short-lived.

Carter's endorsement of liberal social programs, coupled with the "malaise" that accompanied his leadership, proved uninspiring to state voters. Four years later the Republicans presented Ronald Reagan as a presidential candidate who would stir the hearts of South Carolina conservatives in a way no national Democrat ever could. Reagan drew his support from the white, urban middle class, the business community, old segregationists opposed to federal intrusion, and recently arrived Northerners. The number of issues where voters in South Carolina supported the president began to expand during the Reagan years: states' rights and civil rights were joined by concerns like prayer in the public schools, welfare reform, crime, and abortion. Reagan set a tone for rolling back the federal government and the Great Society programs of the 1960s and 1970s, enabling him to capitalize on the antigovernment fervor in the state. Many white state natives took a paternal pride in the guitar-picking antics of native son Lee Atwater as he made headlines in Washington and engineered George Bush's win to succeed Reagan as president in 1988.

Map 7.9 shows that more than twenty of the state's forty-six counties voted Republican in every presidential election from 1988–2004. James Edwards won only fourteen counties in his 1974 victory as the first Republican governor since Reconstruction. In 1986 Republican Carroll Campbell won seventeen counties in his 51 percent to 49 percent triumph. The presidential victories of the late 1980s, 1990s, and in 2000 and 2004 were in twenty counties with 70 percent of the state's population.

The urban counties, with nearly three-quarters of the state population and straight-ticket Republican allegiance, contrast sharply with the twelve counties that were straight Democratic in their vote but have only 9 percent of the state's population. The Republican advantage is in the upstate and the midlands, while the Democratic loyalty is in rural Black Belt counties in the low country.

The order of Republican presidential primaries thrust the state into national politics beginning in 1988. That year political consultant Lee Atwater flew into the state to confer with GOP leaders and shift the GOP primary to the Saturday before Super Tuesday primaries across the Southeast. The early March date helped George Bush win a smashing victory over Bob Dole and Pat Robertson. The state again proved decisive in national Republican primaries four years later, when George Bush won with two-thirds of the vote, discrediting Pat Buchanan's claims to represent southern state values and social conservatism. Republican presidential nominees carried South Carolina in 1992 and 1996, but they were not successful nationally.

The role South Carolina played in national politics changed in the millennium election of 2000. George W. Bush limped into the state after losing badly to John McCain in New Hampshire. Before a national television audience the Texas governor declared that South Carolina was "Bush Country," and his subsequent ten-point victory forecast his eventual nomination and general election victory. On stage at

Map 7.9   South Carolina: Political Partisanship in Presidential Elections, 1992–2004

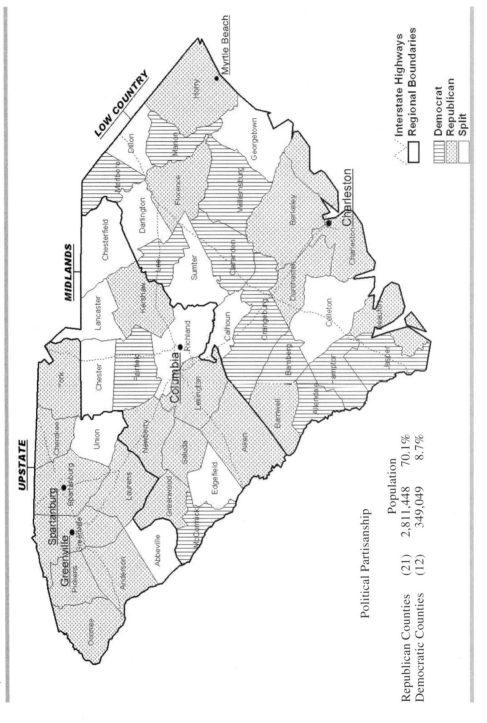

Political Partisanship

		Population	
Republican Counties	(21)	2,811,448	70.1%
Democratic Counties	(12)	349,049	8.7%

Legend:
- Interstate Highways
- Regional Boundaries
- Democrat
- Republican
- Split

the GOP national convention that year, with the nomination firmly in hand and confetti and balloons in the air, George W. Bush walked to the edge of the platform to mouth a silent "thank you" to the South Carolina delegation.

The pattern most in evidence in South Carolina since midcentury is the urban nature of the state as shown in Table 7.9. The nine urban counties, with over half the state population, are dramatically Republican. "The rules are slightly different in South Carolina," writes one observer. "Republicans on the far right wing have a generally easier time gaining acceptance within the party's primaries and organizational hierarchy, owning to the influence of religious and racial white conservatives."[41] Every urban county, except Richland in the Columbia area, voted overwhelmingly for the GOP in the last five presidential elections. It is this base vote that has allowed Republicans to win statewide by carrying fewer than half the counties; the margin of victory in urban areas offsets the traditional rural allegiance to the Democratic Party.

Mississippi

"You don't love because," wrote William Faulkner of this deepest of southern states, "you love despite." The theme of tragedy, often elegiac, is in Mississippi as a celebration of the human spirit, human fortitude, courage, and endurance without an ultimate triumph. Regardless of its past, there is much to celebrate in the state.

Table 7.9   South Carolina: Presidential Election Partisanship, 1988–2004

Region/City	County	Republican Average 1988–2004	Democrat and Third-Party Average 1988–2004
Upstate			
Greenville-Spartanburg	Greenville	63%	37%
Greenville-Spartanburg	Spartanburg	59%	41%
Midlands			
Columbia	Richland	42%	58%
Columbia	Spartanburg	69%	31%
Low Country			
Charleston	Charleston	52%	48%
Charleston	Berkeley	57%	43%
Charleston	Dorchester	61%	39%
Low Country			
Myrtle Beach	Florence	55%	45%
Myrtle Beach	Horry	56%	44%

Note: The total population of these areas represents 51 percent of the state population.

In the recent three decades Mississippi has emerged, but it still ranks last on most national scales of economic welfare and social progress. Education reforms have narrowed the gap between the state and the rest of the nation, but the difference between Mississippi and everyone else remains the most salient fact of life for anyone who lives there.

In spite of improvement, Mississippi is the quintessential southern state. All the things associated with trite southern clichés: magnolia-scented evenings, antebellum mansions, and tarpaper shacks can be found beside double-lane roads in the state. The stereotypes of literary genius, like William Faulkner and Eudora Welty, were born out of the adversity that is Mississippi's history. Welty wrote of the state in 1941, that natives "endure something inwardly—for a time secretly; they establish a past, a memory; thus they store up life."[42]

The state's culture is a traditional one, characterized by a long-standing planter class and a social system of established families dedicated to the preservation of the status quo. The state never adopted progressive ideas or embraced social change with any enthusiasm. History made Mississippi a very conservative place. At the presidential level it has voted Republican in each of the last seven presidential elections.

Democrats survive by pledging allegiance to a conservative social agenda and supporting education as a way for state improvement. Funding for better schools has become a mantra of political campaigns in both parties, and the money for change has come from riverboat gambling revenues. Mississippi has thirty-one casinos, and is number three nationally in gambling revenues behind Nevada and New Jersey.[43]

The place of African Americans has always been a central issue in Mississippi's political culture, and for generations that niche was defined by white landowners. "Historically, there has been no questioning the racial imperative of Mississippi's traditional elite."[44] Delta planters used black laborers on their farms and poor whites indulged in race-baiting demagoguery to secure their position. But the civil rights movement, especially the Voting Rights Act of 1965, changed all that. Because of black out-migration, African American voters cannot win statewide elections at will. They must work with white voters, and the party that has benefited the most from the bargain is the GOP.

Mississippi's march into the Republican Party began in the civil rights struggle of the 1960s. The Democratic national party estranged white voters at the same time it galvanized black allegiance. The state voted for the Dixiecrat ticket in 1948 and for Goldwater in 1964, went over 60 percent for Wallace in 1968, and 87 percent for Nixon four years later. Mississippi came within a breath of voting for Ford in 1976 and has remained Republican in every presidential election since. It was George Bush's number one state in his defeat of 1992, and Ross Perot's worst state nationally. Despite its proximity to Bill Clinton's Arkansas, Mississippi remained devoted to the GOP in the decade of the 1990s.

Republican allegiance is rooted in issues like defense, crime, taxes, and cultural values.

The state's landslide support for Richard Nixon in 1972 led to a statewide exodus of white voters from the Democratic Party. This allegiance is seen in Map 7.10 where the more populous hill country and the counties contiguous to Interstate 55 are either competitive or loyal to the GOP. The Delta counties, with their high black population, have a checkered loyalty to the Democratic Party. Over 60 percent of the state's population lives in counties that voted Republican in the recent presidential elections, while the Democratic base has only 16 percent of the state's population. Clearly the piney wood hills of east Mississippi are the Republican base counties.

The Hills have a disturbing racial history. Early neopopulists, such as James Vardeman, employed blatant and graphic racist rhetoric to attract the Hill farmers. In the 1903 gubernatorial race Vardeman said the Declaration of Independence did not apply to African Americans. This rhetoric was toned down among Delta planters who saw such demagoguery as impolite. Counties today still divide along racial lines, but a host of social and economic issues remain as the best explanation for realignment to the GOP.

Modern differences go deeper than race. "No matter how it is described, at the root of the struggle were real economic and social cleavages which gave the conflict its defining characteristics."[45] The "planters" of the Delta, and the "rednecks" of the Hills, were a division that went beyond geography. For example, the Hills supported prohibition, while the Delta opposed it. These distinctions were mentioned by V. O. Key in 1949, and institutionalized with the construction of Interstate 55 in the 1960s. Map 7.10 confirms the partisanship of Mississippi voters in the presidential elections of the 1990s and the new century.

In 2000 Mississippi voted for George W. Bush 58 percent to 41 percent; in 2004 the margin was 60 percent to 40 percent. Mississippi's rural nature and sizable African American population, make it one of the few states in 2000 where George W. Bush did better in metropolitan areas than rural ones. The electorate remains polarized by race, with 82 percent of whites voting Republican and 96 percent of blacks voting Democratic. The difference now is that the black vote is small because of out-migration in the counties that border the Mississippi River.

"While much has changed in the landscape of electoral politics . . . one thing has remained constant. . . . Mississippi has always been a bulwark of southern conservative ideas and values, regardless of which political party appears to have the upper hand."[46] The remarkable thing about Mississippi politics is the unusually large margins voters give the GOP in statewide races. Ten of eleven counties in Table 7.10 voted Republican, and two—Rankin in Jackson and Lamar in Hattiesburg—were over 70 percent in GOP allegiance. The suburbs around Jackson, Hattiesburg, and Biloxi average nearly 60 percent loyalty to Republican candidates.

Map 7.10   Mississippi: Political Partisanship in Presidential Elections, 1992–2004

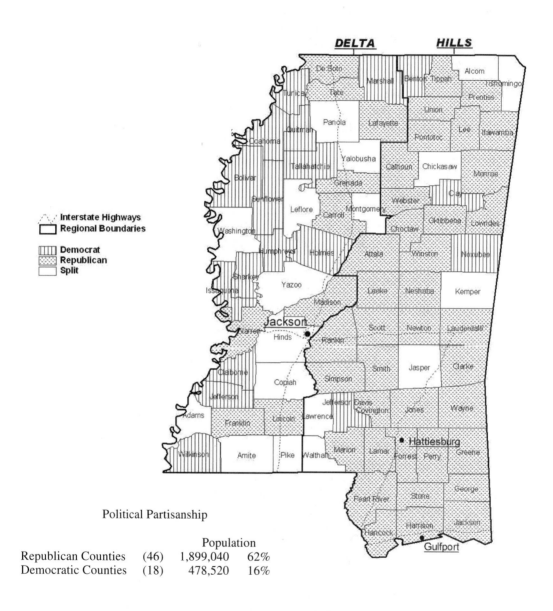

Interstate Highways
Regional Boundaries

Democrat
Republican
Split

Political Partisanship

		Population	
Republican Counties	(46)	1,899,040	62%
Democratic Counties	(18)	478,520	16%

Table 7.10   Mississippi: Presidential Election Partisanship, 1988–2004

Region/City	County	Republican Average 1988–2004	Democrat and Third-Party Average 1988–2004
Delta			
Memphis	Desoto	66%	34%
Jackson	Hinds	46%	54%
Jackson	Rankin	75%	25%
Jackson	Madison	60%	40%
Vicksburg	Warren	55%	45%
Hills			
Hattiesburg	Forrest	60%	40%
Hattiesburg	Lamar	73%	27%
Biloxi/Gulfport	Harrison	60%	40%
Biloxi/Gulfport	Jackson	65%	35%
Tupelo	Lee	61%	39%
Meridian	Lauderdale	65%	35%

Note: The total population of these areas represents 42 percent of the state population.

Mississippi defies urbanization, with only a little more than one-third of the vote in metro areas, and the state continues to have many rural counties that rely on agriculture. The boom areas of the economy are Jackson, the Gulf Coast, and the Memphis suburbs. These areas collectively have over 40 percent of the state population.

Louisiana

In the spring of 1959 *Time* magazine solemnly declared that then governor Earl K. Long of Louisiana had gone, "just plain crazy," and that the people of Louisiana were finally getting the government they elected, and deserved. The legacy of eccentricity became a badge of honor. Politics here has always had the flavor of a third world tribal battle, with colorful personalities, an accepted degree of corruption, and a legacy of no-holds-barred conflict and demaguery.

In the state of Louisiana the rules are always changing, and constantly open for interpretation. For example, in 1975 Louisiana adopted an open primary with all parties running on the same ballot. The state's second primary, held in December, is a result of a 1997 Supreme Court ruling that the state had to hold its first primary on national Election Day. If in the primary a candidate receives a majority vote (50 percent or higher), then he/she is automatically elected and there is no runoff election. However, if no candidate receives the majority, then a runoff election between the top two candidates (regardless of party) from the primary determines the winner. Candidates from the same party can end up in the runoff, as well as candidates from opposite parties. It is not unusual to find Louisiana having runoff elections in December, long after the rest of the country has finished up a month earlier.

At first Louisiana looks like its sister southern states, with a high black population and a history of Democratic allegiance. But appearances can be deceiving. The political culture is a mix of France, America, Africa, and the Caribbean. In 2003 GOP voters nominated a thirty-two-year-old unknown son of Indian immigrants, who was Catholic and conservative. He lost in the general election, but somehow it seemed appropriate for the state to break the stereotype of what a Republican candidate should be. Louisiana has produced a colorful parade of candidates, from Huey Long and Edwin Edwards to David Duke and "Buddy" Roemer.

The politics in Louisiana continues to be a split between the French Catholic population in southern Louisiana, the white Anglo-Saxon Protestant populace in the north, with New Orleans as a diverse French and Creole ambience. In the bayous of southern Louisiana outside the city of New Orleans the population is of French descent and devoutly Roman Catholic. The black population is significant and active in opposition to the GOP social agenda. Yet an alliance of north and south is possible on the social issues like abortion and homosexual rights. Not surprisingly, Louisiana has one of the most restrictive abortion statutes in the nation, and became the first state to offer covenant marriages in which couples could agree not to be covered by no-fault divorce laws.

Northern Louisiana has a larger black population and more traditional southern allegiance to issues of race and the role of government. With few exceptions, the north has dominated the state's politics since 1960, leading voters into Goldwater's column in 1964 and George Wallace's in 1968. In 1972 Louisiana went for Nixon, returned to the Democratic fold for Carter in 1976, and then stayed Republican until 1992, when the state went for Clinton and the Democrats twice. In 2000 Louisiana supported Bush, and again proved loyal to the president in 2004.

Al Gore's base was the New Orleans MSA, but Bush carried the nonmetro parishes and the areas north of Interstate 10. While Louisiana has never played a prominent role in national politics, it remains one of the most competitive southern states when it comes to presidential elections. It came closer than any other southern state to voting for Michael Dukakis in 1988. In 1992 the state cast the highest vote for Bill Clinton and Al Gore of any southern state except their native Arkansas and Tennessee. Economics is a driving issue in each statewide election because of the collapsing domestic oil industry and the shaky infrastructure. The state closed highway rest stops in the 1980s, and laid off state workers in times of recession.

Map 7.11 omits the results of the 2004 presidential election because George W. Bush snatched several traditionally Democratic counties. The map shows the Democratic strength to be in the south, with scattered Republican strength in the New Orleans suburbs and pockets in north Louisiana and cities like Shreveport.

Map 7.11   Louisiana: Political Partisanship in Presidential Elections, 1992–2004

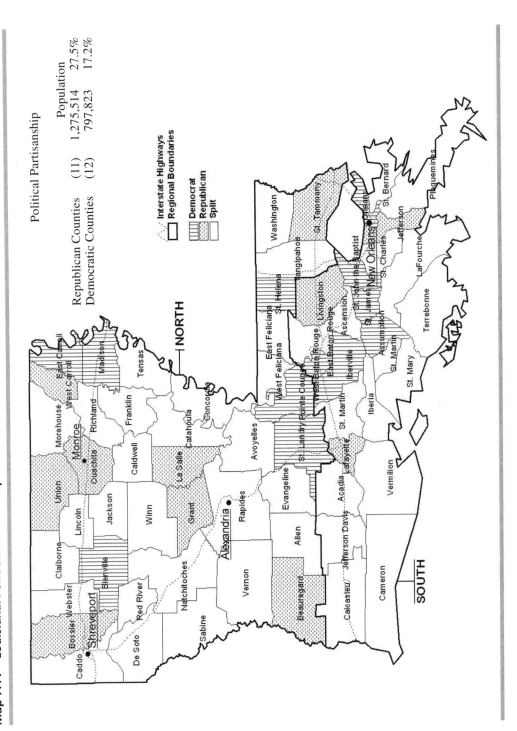

Political Partisanship

		Population	
Republican Counties	(11)	1,275,514	27.5%
Democratic Counties	(12)	797,823	17.2%

Interstate Highways
Regional Boundaries

Democrat
Republican
Split

The 2000 census showed a dramatic growth in the black population of the state. "The state's white population increased 1 percent in the 1990s and its black population increased 12 percent in the same time period."[47] The Democratic showing in 2000 rested heavily on the loyalty of African Americans in the New Orleans parish. Gore carried neighboring St. John the Baptist and St. James parishes as well, but the margins were narrow. Bush did well in the nonmetro parishes. The allegiance of black and white to the Democratic and Republican parties respectively, is one of the major reasons why the state is so competitive.

Politics in Louisiana is remarkable for the persistence of Old South racial divides in the face of urbanization, and the changes of a new century. "Politics has been revolutionized in two ways . . . the Republican Party, which was virtually non-competitive in Louisiana elections, has emerged to almost parity with the once-dominant Democratic Party . . . [and] African Americans, who compose almost one-third of the population, have risen from formal suppression to positions of power."[48] The Old South roots are seen in the 1991 election, where onetime Ku Klux Klan legislator David Duke finished two percentage points behind in the governor's race. The new politics is seen in the gleaming development along the interstate highways and the advance in offshore oil production. The state is beset with tensions of corruption, race, and reform, which are beneath the surface of each election.

The competitiveness of Louisiana politics is evident in Table 7.11, which

Table 7.11   Louisiana: Presidential Election Partisanship, 1988–2004

Region/City	County	Republican Average 1988–2004	Democrat and Third-Party Average 1988–2004
North Louisiana			
Shreveport	Caddo	48%	52%
Shreveport	Ouchita	58%	42%
Shreveport	Rapides	54%	46%
Shreveport	Bossier	60%	40%
Shreveport	La Salle	63%	37%
South Louisiana			
New Orleans	Orleans	25%	75%
New Orleans	Jefferson	58%	42%
New Orleans	East Baton Rouge	52%	48%
New Orleans	St. Tammy	66%	34%
New Orleans	Lafayette	56%	44%
New Orleans	West Baton Rouge	43%	57%

Note: The total population in these areas represents 52 percent of the state population.

shows most of the counties in the state up for grabs in any election. The suburban base, which usually serves as a platform for Republican expansion, is smaller and less potent than in other states. The downtown counties in Shreveport and New Orleans are solidly Democratic and few of the suburbs have the allegiance of the GOP in numbers sufficient to offset rural voter sentiments. Unlike other southern states, Louisiana remains competitive in each election cycle.

Summary

The partisan patterns for each state are summarized in Table 7.12. One conclusion stands out, the decade of the 1990s was a time of dramatic partisan change: Virtually half (48 percent) of the population of the South lives in counties that voted Republican in five straight presidential elections. By contrast only 15 percent of the population lives in counties with a similar Democratic allegiance for the same time period.

The implications of this may not be self-evident. Elections are not county winner-take-all contests, and just because a majority of voters vote the same way does not mean that the minority could not triumph in the next election. But the size, consistency, and margin of allegiance in the maps and tables show that the large urban

Table 7.12   National Presidential Elections, 1988–2004

State	Total Population[a]	Total Counties	GOP Counties	State Population	Democratic Counties	State Population
National States						
Georgia	8,168	159	65	4,155,739	17	1,699,986
Florida	15,982	67	25	4,815,569	8	5.602,549
Virginia	7,078	95/40	64/16	3,327,637	7/13	1,157,062
Texas	20,851	254	136	13,655,723	20	1,960,658
Emergent States						
North Carolina	8,048	100	49	3,856,660	17	920,293
Tennessee	5,689	95	29	2,137,985	20	353,954
Traditional States						
Alabama	4,447	67	35	3,268,055	10	212,387
Arkansas	2,673	75	5	367,556	22	427,473
South Carolina	4,012	46	21	2,811,448	12	349,049
Mississippi	2,844	82	46	1,899,040	18	478,520
Louisiana	4,468	64	11	1,275,514	12	797,823
Total	84,261	1,049	486	40,570,926	163	13,959,754

Note: a. Population in thousands.

centers in the southern states now dominate politics there. The partisan allegiance in the major media markets is a reliable guide to future voting behavior. Past voting patterns are as reliable a predictor as can be found to suggest what might happen in future elections.

Demographic and economic improvement has produced a change in voting. More blacks have registered in the South, and created a more liberal base for the Democratic Party. New minorities have come in through immigration, and they have created an additional base for both Democrats and Republicans. In the South, the party of FDR can still do well among the less affluent, both white and non-white. Still, it is the Republicans who have benefited most from economic growth and electoral change, and it is the middle class that has flocked to the GOP banner.

In his book, *Class and Party in American Politics*, Jeffery Stonecash argues that this growth is because "class has displaced other sources of political division."[49] Both parties have a political base, but in the South the GOP is better able to motivate the turnout of its constituency through campaign appeals. The GOP appeal is the middle-class appeal. In suburbs from Fairfax County to Plano, Texas, millions of voters live in similar civil communities. The Home Depot stores, six-lane interstate commuter arteries, churches, schools, parks, and recreational areas combine to produce a homogeneous political culture. The Republicans have benefited most from the class allegiance in these suburban communities.

The importance of this county-by-county allegiance is especially significant if one accepts the premises of retrospective voting. That model holds that voters are unclear on the specifics of economic and foreign policy of candidates, but they are very clear on their feelings about the *results* of those policies. Ronald Reagan broke the presidential hold Democrats had on the South in 1980 and 1984. The verdict on his presidency was good; Reagan ended his term of office very near his high points.

An examination of poll results of both Reagan terms shows that he never fell below 50 percent approval ratings in the South.[50] If citizens vote in the future on the basis of past judgments, then the southern verdict was that a Republican change in the 1980s was worth the risk. If, as Fiorina's retrospective model declares, elections are less about where society should move and more about where it has been, then the prospects of Republican domination of at least presidential races, and other statewide contests as well, are good.[51]

Chapter 3 showed that half the population of the South lives in just 134 counties, and this compacting of the southern electorate has a critical influence over politics and governance. This chapter reveals that 106 of these counties voted Republican in the elections from 1988 to 2004. The pattern in Table 7.12 shows that contiguous suburbs that ring major southern cities are an engine of votes for the Republican Party in statewide elections. To reach the urbanized mass of voters in metropolitan areas candidates put more emphasis on television advertising, media markets, radio ads, and direct mail, along with personal visits to shopping malls.

Political campaigns today are waged with print advertising, direct mail, and elaborate media campaigns in compact media markets. Television commercials are the laser-guided bombs of a political campaign, able to target the discrete opinions of voters and appeal to sentiments captured in surveys. At one time, the Democratic Party in each southern state was responsible for rallying the faithful on Election Day. No more. Today the parties are basically relegated to the role of raising money to buy more television ads.

The television campaign ads are bought in the largest media markets, and touch a large middle-class audience that is increasingly inclined to vote Republican at the presidential level. The success of GOP candidates down the ticket shows that this allegiance is gradually trickling down. Republican statewide victories reinforce the loyalty suburban residents already have to the GOP.

Most of all, television ads provide information about candidates and campaigns to the majority of voters who read and research very little on those running for political office. In short, politics is television, and television is politics—second only to the candidate in importance to a campaign. Increasingly across the South, Republicans have a distinct advantage in statewide campaigns because all their allegiance is in tightly compacted suburbs. In the next chapter we will show how Democrats are able to overcome this advantage.

Notes

1. Everett Carl Ladd Jr. and Charles Hadley, *Transformations of the American Party System*. New York: W.W. Norton, 1975, pp. 195–200.

2. Earl Black and Merle Black, *Politics and Society in the South*. Cambridge, Mass.: Harvard University Press, 1987, p. 143.

3. Idaho voted to repeal term limits; state courts in Massachusetts, Nebraska, and Washington declared them in violation of their state constitutions. Sarah McCally Morehouse and Malcolm E. Jewell, *State Politics, Parties and Policy*. Lanham, Md.: Rowman & Littlefield, 2003, pp. 231–232.

4. V.O. Key, *The Responsible Electorate*. Cambridge: Harvard University Press, 1966.

5. Anthony Down, *An Economic Model of Democracy*. New York: Harper & Row, 1957.

6. Morris Fiorina, *Retrospective Voting in American National Elections*. New Haven: Yale University Press, 1981.

7. Earl Black and Merle Black, *Politics and Society in the South*, pp. 261–262.

8. Earl Black and Merle Black, *The Rise of Southern Republicans*. Cambridge, Mass.: Belknap Press, 2002, p. 25.

9. Southern Politics Collection, "Georgia," Vanderbilt University, Special Collections.

10. Charles S. Bullock III, "Georgia: Still the Most Democratic State in the South?" in Charles S. Bullock III and Mark J. Rozell (eds.), *The New Politics of the Old South*. 2d ed. Lanham, Md.: Rowman & Littlefield, 2003, p. 54.

11. Ibid., p. 53.

12. John A. Clark, Audrey A. Haynes, Brad Lockerbie, and Jason Seitz, "Georgia: Partisan Parity in the Peach State," *American Review of Politics* 24 (Spring 2003), p. 35.

13. Peter Applebome, *Dixie Rising*. New York: Times Random House, 1996, p. 45.

14. Charles S. Bullock III, "Georgia," p. 65.

15. John Clark et al., "Georgia," p. 50.

16. Michael J. Scicchitano and Richard K. Scher, "Florida: Political Change: 1950–2000," in Charles S. Bullock III and Mark J. Rozell (eds.), *The New Politics*, p. 250.

17. Ibid., p. 264.

18. The Bush presidential landslide in 1988 so distorted the picture of state partisanship that another race was substituted for the calculation of state partisanship in this chapter. The 1988 Senate race between Connie Mack and Buddy MacKay gave a better picture of statewide allegiance, and is used here to compare with subsequent presidential races.

19. Jonathan Knuckey, "The Structure of Party Competitiveness in the South: The Case of Florida." Paper presented at the biennial Citadel Symposium on Southern Politics, March 4–5, 2004, Charleston, South Carolina.

20. Larry Sabato, *Goodbye to Goodtime Charlie*. Washington, D.C.: Congressional Quarterly Press, 1983.

21. Mark J. Rozell, "Virginia: The New Politics of the Old Dominion," in Bullock and Rozell, *The New Politics,* p. 139.

22. Ibid., p. 149.

23. John Steinbeck, quoted in Peter Applebome, *Dixie Rising*, p. 14.

24. "Laws and Order," by O'Henry in *Everybody's Magazine*, New York (September 1910).

25. Robert A. Caro, *The Years of Lyndon Johnson: The Path to Power*. New York: Alfred A. Knopf, 1982, p. 663.

26. D.B. Hardeman and Donald C. Brown, *Rayburn*. Austin: Texas Monthly Press, 1987, p. 421.

27. Tom Wicker, *JFK and LBJ*. Baltimore: Penguin Books, 1968, p. 169.

28. T.R. Fehrenbach, *Lone Star*. New York: Macmillan, 1968, p. 705.

29. Frank B. Feigert, Dawn Miller, Kenda Cunningham, and Rachel Burlage, "Texas: Incipient Polarization," *American Review of Politics* 24 (2003), p. 185.

30. John B. Judis and Ruy Teixeira, *The Emerging Democratic Majority*. New York: Scribner, 2002, pp. 72–78.

31. Charles Prysby, "North Carolina: The Development of Two-Party Competition," in Bullock and Rozell, *The New Politics*, pp. 167–172. The North Carolina chapter has an extended discussion of the redistricting controversy.

32. Southern Politics Collection, "Tennessee," Vanderbilt University, Special Collections.

33. I considered replacing the 1992, 1996, and 2000 election results with other statewide races because the presence of Al Gore Jr. on the national ticket would distort voting patterns. The results of Table 7.6 include the Gore candidacy because the presidential patterns were clearer in showing allegiance other than the substituted races, which were overwhelmingly Republican. The counties displayed in Table 7.6 show loyalty to Democratic and Republican candidates in all four presidential elections despite the presence of Al Gore on the national Democratic ticket.

34. John M. Bruce, John A. Clark, Michael M. Gant, and Linda M. Daugherty, "Tennessee: A Maturing Two-Party System," *American Review of Politics* 24 (2003), p. 180.

35. John Lyman Mason, "Tennessee: Politics and Politicians that Matter Beyond State Borders," in Bullock and Rozell, *The New Politics*, p. 180.

36. Southern Politics Collection, "Alabama," Vanderbilt University, Special Collections.

37. Edward G. Carmines and James A. Stimson, *Issue Evolution*. Princeton, N.J.: Princeton University Press, 1989.

38. Harold W. Stanley, "Alabama: Republicans Winning the Heart of Dixie," in Bullock and Rozell, *The New Politics*, p. 82.

39. Ibid., p. 92.

40. Michael B. Dougar, *Arkansas Odyssey*. Little Rock: Rose Publishing, 1994, p. 599.

41. John C. Kuzienski, "South Carolina: The Heart of GOP Realignment in the South," in Bullock and Rozell, *The New Politics*, p. 40.

42. Eudora Welty, "Old Mr. Marblehall," in Thomas Daniel Young, Floyd Watkins, and Richmond Croom Beatty (eds.), *The Literature of the South*. Rev. ed. Glenview, Ill.: Scott, Foresman & Co., 1968, p. 889.

43. Michael Barone and Richard Cohen (eds.), *The Almanac of American Politics*. Washington, D.C.: National Journal, 2001, p. 855.

44. Joseph B. Parker (ed.), *Politics in Mississippi*. Salem, Wis.: Sheffield Publishing Co., 1993, p. 4.

45. James F. Lea, "The Political Culture of Mississippi," in Joseph B. Parker (ed.), *Politics in Mississippi*, p. 6.

46. David A. Breaux and Charles E. Menifield, "Mississippi: A Study in Change and Continuity," in Bullock and Rozell, *The New Politics*, p. 110.

47. Michael Barone and Richard E. Cohen, *The Almanac of American Politics*, p. 667.

48. Wayne Parent and Huey Perry, "Louisiana: African Americans, Republicans and Party Competition," in Bullock and Rozell, *The New Politics*, p. 130.

49. Jeffrey M. Stonecash, *Class and Party in American Politics*. Boulder, Colo.: Westview Press, 2000, p. 129. Stonecash concludes that "race issues matter, but they do not appear to matter more for lower income groups than others."

50. George C. Edwards III, *Presidential Approval*. Baltimore: Johns Hopkins University Press, 1990, pp. 91–113.

51. Morris P. Fiorina, *Retrospective Voting in American National Elections*. New Haven: Yale University Press, 1981, p. 6.

8

The Democratic Response in Statewide Races

In 1942 Ben Robertson captured his childhood understanding of life on a South Carolina farm this way: "We own more land than Democrats and Baptists ought to."[1] For decades white Southerners believed in those three things: the land, the Democratic Party, and the Baptist Church. During the Great Depression the order of allegiance might have been different. Millions in the region survived on the governmental subsidies of FDR's New Deal, and Democrat and southern became synonymous.

Yet in politics, as in life, things are not static for long. The political loyalty of the southern past gradually deteriorated and became a fertile field for the cultivation of new allegiances. A movement away from single-party devotion began in the postwar years, and ended in the 1980s, when two-party competition came to virtually every statewide race in the South. The Republican message of lower taxes and less government forged Ronald Reagan's electoral majority. His landslide included the entire West, the South except for Jimmy Carter's Georgia, and the Midwest except for Vice President Mondale's Minnesota. The base of the GOP majorities, built in the 1980s, was a wide swath of states called "The Republican L." It took in the Rocky Mountain region, with Alaska thrown in, the Plains states, and the entire South. In 2000 these states had a total of 233 electoral votes, with 270 needed to win. Bill Clinton cracked the "L" in his two-term presidency, but it reemerged in 2000 for George W. Bush, and again in 2004.

Republican domination, so evident in the South in the years from 1988–2004, and shown in a county-by-county analysis in the previous chapters, trickled-down to statewide races like governor, US senator, and US congressman. Democratic control disappeared, but it was not replaced by Republican rule. Ninety-three statewide, nonpresidential elections were contested in the South between 1990 and 2000: Republicans won 61 percent of these, and Democrats won 39 percent. The rough 60/40 split shows Republican strength, but not command like the "Solid South" Democratic majorities of old.

How have the Democrats withstood the Republican onslaught, and the emergence of two-party competition, after the Reagan victories of the 1980s? How have they been able to win in their new minority status? An initial explanation is that the historic allegiance white Southerners had for the Democratic Party remained, but it suffered a steep decline since its heyday at midcentury. A GOP consultant tells the story of a man who came to see him in 1994, when a Democratic congressman retired to open a seat to fierce competition in the fall election. The visitor sat in the office with his hands on his knees and declared that he was going to vote Republican in the upcoming election. He explained that his vote was the first ever in his family for a Republican, and that none of his relatives knew of his decision. The visitor went on to recount a tearful memory of going with his grandfather to stand beside the railroad tracks in a silent salute as the train bearing FDR's body passed from Warm Springs, Georgia, back to Washington, D.C.

"Now," the man said in a whisper, "I'm going to break a deathbed promise I made to my grandfather and vote for your candidate." The consultant was moved, and to break the uncomfortable silence he offered the man a brochure on the GOP candidate and a bumper sticker for his pickup. But the visitor refused, and said with a sigh, "I said I'd vote for him, but I'm not ready to tell anyone else about it just yet."[2]

That's the way it was all across the South: millions of white Southerners were willing to vote Republican in the silence of the voting booth, but in public they still considered themselves Democrats. Converts to the GOP preferred to vote in primaries by mail, with an absentee ballot, rather than risk showing up on Election Day to publicly declare their allegiance by walking to the Republican side of the precinct room. The obligation to Democrats was especially pronounced in state legislatures. Table 6.8, presented in Chapter 6, shows that in the 1970s only two southern states (Tennessee and Virginia) were two-party competitive at the state level. In 1976, 91 percent of the state senators in the South, and 89 percent of the state legislators, were Democratic in party allegiance.

Earl Black and Merle Black discuss how Democratic state legislatures and governors reapportioned state legislative seats and congressional districts to favor themselves in the face of increasing urbanization. Democrats could survive in Republican suburbs by being conservative, and then moderate, on issues of national importance like defense, gun control, and abortion. With racial integration a new political calculus arose. The biracial arithmetic worked best in the Deep South, where a mixture of race and urbanization meant that "extraordinary white majorities were required for Republican victories."[3]

The grassroots Democratic memory kept Republican hegemony at bay, but this all changed in the 1980s. The annals of US partisan change have seldom, if ever, witnessed a more dramatic transformation than that which occurred in the South from the 1980s through the 1990s. The Republican surge gathered momentum with victories in the 1994 midterm election, and for a while it seemed unstoppable in the

South. At the national level, leadership of the GOP shifted to men like Newt Gingrich from Georgia, Phil Gramm from Texas, and Trent Lott from Mississippi. Many southern voters who had always voted Democratic changed their affiliation virtually overnight. "While the South has continued to be the most Republican region in the 1990s, Democrats made a comeback when their [national] ticket boasted not one, but two Southerners."[4] Southern Democrats came to believe that their only hope of winning the White House rested on finding a candidate, like Bill Clinton, who could break the Republican monopoly on the South's electoral votes.

In the early 1990s Democrats found an issue that allowed them to stop the Republican realignment, and recover their balance and competitiveness. The issue was education, and the policy was to fund schools from lottery revenues. No issue was closer to the hearts of Southerners than the schooling of their children. For generations its pursuit was characterized by a quest for quality outside the region because the native schools at all levels were so bad. When Jack Burden, the protagonist in Robert Penn Warren's novel *All the King's Men*, tells his mother that he is going to the state university she responds, "Oh, Son . . . why don't you go to Harvard or Princeton . . . or even Williams. . . . They say it's a nice refined place."[5] Discontent came because school terms were shorter in the South, per pupil expenditures were lower, and teachers were poorly trained and pitifully paid.

The lackluster performance of southern schools was rooted in three unique aspects of the history and culture of the region. First, the rural nature of the South emphasized family, religion, and personal relationships more than the instruction from government-funded schools. Church Sunday School programs, finishing schools for women, and military colleges for men all stressed character over the cultivation of the intellect; the pursuit of books was secondary to the social graces. Second, the South suffered under the double curse of a huge school-age population and a low level of taxable wealth. In the antebellum South, slavery led to a "use-it-up-and-move-along" attitude toward the land since slave owners were mobile and had little incentive to invest in infrastructure like schools. Later, "the belief that the South as a region would not capture the return on investments in education, especially for blacks, was one reason why industrial employers so often joined planters in opposing increases in spending on schools."[6]

Ferroll Sams recalls his elementary school years in rural Georgia as eleven grades were housed in a two-story building for a student body of two hundred fifty. "In those Depression days before a distant entity called government had concerned itself with providing basic necessities and with preventing the psychological effects of cultural deprivations, it was interesting to observe how" difficult it was for parents to provide their children with something as luxurious as art supplies.[7]

Third, state political leaders were unwilling to support schools because they feared increased education dollars would be spent on blacks. Black education was in "separate but equal" facilities that were poor cousins to the white schools, and no self-respecting white man wanted to spend money on schools with the prospect of having to upgrade the black programs at the same time. In the postwar period the historic educational differences between the South and rest of the nation moderated, but schools in the region still lagged behind the rest of the country in achievement and prestige.

These are some of the reasons why the Democratic message of educational reform had a siren song effect on southern voters. In the 1990s Democrats promised to reverse the legacy of second-class schools with dedicated lottery money for public education. Gambling had been celebrated in southern culture from Mark Twain's portrayal of the riverboat gambler on the Mississippi to country music singer Kenny Rogers's 1970s hit song, "The Gambler." The other side of gambling was opposition in the pulpits of Christian churches, where it was condemned as an expensive vice that exploited the poor across the various states. In the educational lottery the southern aversion to games of chance was overcome by the proffered benefits to education. The Midas appeal of a "clean," statewide lottery was seen as a way to painlessly close the gap between schools in the South and the rest of the nation.

After 1994 every Democratic governor in the South, along with a host of like-minded legislators, made education the centerpiece of their agenda. Proposals ran the gamut, from promoting preschool programs to college scholarships for high school graduates who wanted higher education. These programs were approved in referendums with the promised proceeds earmarked for K–12, remedial, or trade school programs, or college scholarships. Some Republicans took notice of these political winds, and followed the lead of Governor George W. Bush whose educational agenda was central to his victories in Texas. Yet, all across the South, it was Democrats who benefited politically from the issue of educational reform. The Republican mantra of less government, lower taxes, and opposition to gambling seemed stingy by comparison. Democratic governor Zell Miller of Georgia began a trend of spending that others soon followed.

The Democratic political strategy was designed to carve the middle-class white voters away from the Republican Party, insisting that support for free-market economics and the values of the Religious Right were unhelpful to them. Middle-class white women voters, the so-called Soccer Moms who were concerned about the education of their children, were open to the plea of better neighborhood schools and scholarships for their college students. These suburban women were often college-educated and worked to supplement the family income for public school kids who wanted to attend college upon graduation.

A second factor aiding the Democratic rebirth was the grassroots allegiance voters in many rural areas still had for the party. The term "Yellow Dog Democrat" was a label given voters who wouldn't vote Republican if the Democratic nominee were a yellow dog. The Great Depression left many Southerners faithful to the New Deal Democratic Party of Franklin D. Roosevelt. Families in some areas of the South had only known representation by Democrats at the state and county levels.

For them there was but one political party. Their allegiance, much like that of the visitor to the Republican consultant, was understood in statewide races.

The third source of Democratic and twenty-first-century strength in the South remains the African American vote on any Election Day. The loyalty of black America is the foundation for Democratic strategy when it comes to statewide elections. In downtown areas of major cities, and on rural farms, the support for the Democratic Party is absolute in black neighborhoods. The vote in the black community often tops 90 percent for a Democratic candidate in a statewide race. Postelection analysis focuses not on the loyalty of African Americans, but on the size of their turnout. Democrats often lose when black turnout is low and African American enthusiasm can be the difference between winning and losing. Even though some black leaders complain that their support is taken for granted, almost no African Americans are outspoken Republicans. A substantial and united black vote is the necessary component for Democrats to win on Election Day.

A fourth, growing, source of Democratic support in elections is the increase in outside-of-the-South migration to the region. For two decades one of the forces feeding the expansion of the Republican Party was the in-migration of tax-averse retirees. But this same population appreciated Social Security and resented threatened Republican cuts in social programs that benefited the elderly. The retirees were wary of the GOP agenda on issues like abortion, homosexual rights, and prayer in public schools. When it came time for the newly arrived Southerners to choose between a public lottery for education, and a tax increase on their newly purchased homes, they favored the former.

Surveys of party activists in 1991 and 2001 consistently found that many of them are relatively new to activism, with Republicans showing a strong tendency toward the conservative side of the ideological spectrum, and Democrats spread more evenly from left to right. Republicans tend to be more loyal to their national party platform than Democrats. The newness of the GOP at the local level means that they were generally more optimistic about their party's chances in future elections, while Democrats were less sanguine. Two surveys in Alabama, for example, found that "in both 1991 and 2001 Republicans [were] more likely to say that their party [had] gotten stronger, rather than weaker, with regard to both 'overall' organization and more specific activities such as campaign effectiveness, fund raising and candidate recruitment."[8]

Democrats can divide the states in the South into three categories based on their measures of state competition as presented in Chapter 6, and the county-by-county allegiance in Chapter 7. The eleven southern states are grouped into these categories: (1) reliably Republican, (2) two-party competitive, and (3) traditionally Democratic. The type of state dictates the tactics and strategy for Democratic candidates.

The first category is for states that are reliably Republican in any statewide election, be it presidential, gubernatorial, or US Senate. These states have a Ranney party competition figure that shows the state as strongly Republican in national races, and trending the same way in state races. Each state has a substantial urban/suburban geographic base vote, and an allegiance to the Republican Party on Election Day. The five states that are "Reliably Republican" are Texas, South Carolina, Alabama, Tennessee, and Mississippi. The best way for Democrats to win in these states, be it at the presidential or the statewide level, is for the Republicans to make a mistake on a policy issue or be touched by scandal. In 1998 South Carolina governor David Beasley angered conservatives by advocating removal of the Confederate flag from the state capitol and opposing the introduction of video poker gambling. Beasley's popularity plummeted, and an unknown legislator named Jim Hodges won the governor's race. In 2000, Republican governor Don Sundquist in Tennessee proposed a state income tax to balance the state budget. The Republicans lost the state's executive seat two years later. Absent Republican controversy, or the personal unpopularity of a politician, a Democratic victory is unlikely in these states.

The second group of states is two-party competitive. These are states where the combined Ranney Index hovers around .500, meaning the population is evenly divided in political allegiance for all races from the top to the bottom of the ticket such that no party has an advantage. Victory on Election Day in these states depends on uniting the base Democratic vote with dissident Republicans and new-comers to forge a minimal winning coalition. Two states—Florida and Georgia—are graded as competitive states where two-party competition is the norm, and two others—North Carolina and Virginia—are similarly up for grabs, especially along the latter's urban corridor. North Carolina and Virginia were once more Republican than they are in 2006; the attrition of the GOP is credited to the issues and candidates seized upon by Democrats to market their programs. Most of this success is at the county and state legislative level.

Finally, the third group in our classification is of states that remain traditionally Democratic in the face of cultural, urban, and political change. Two states—Louisiana and Arkansas—are in this category. At midcentury V. O. Key described Arkansas as being one-party Democratic. Fifty years later change has come, but Arkansas's allegiance to Bill Clinton and a host of other Democrats remains strong. Louisiana is trending Democratic as well.

In any southern election, a Democratic strategy for statewide success requires a candidate able to rekindle the enthusiastic, historic allegiance white voters once felt to the party, joined to a solid black vote. The so-called wedge issue for this trans-formation was education in the 1990s. Black support was enhanced by registration and get-out-the-vote campaigns to improve turnout on Election Day. While Republicans relied on television in media markets to stimulate voters, Democrats adopted a grassroots strategy of: (1) collecting rural counties, (2) attaching them to downtown black voters, and (3) attenuating the suburban vote.

Democratically controlled legislatures worked to keep GOP presidential victories from filtering down by moving important elections to off years. Among the southern states only North Carolina holds its gubernatorial contest in presidential election years. Virginia, Louisiana, and Mississippi elect governors in odd-numbered years, in large measure to limit the electoral opportunities for Republicans. Between 1965 and 1985, nine southern states amended their constitutions to allow governors to succeed themselves in office. Prior to this time many southern governors were limited to one four-year (or two-year) term, with no consecutive reelection permitted. When amended to allow two-term reelection, the possibilities of Republicans building a statewide party through control of the governor's office were increased.

Another element in any political campaign, of whatever partisan stripe, is often overlooked: enough money to be competitive in a statewide race. While Republicans campaign in suburban malls and broadcast television commercials in select markets, Democrats rely on cheaper grassroots techniques like backyard barbecues, door-to-door organization, and buses for transportation to the polls. But no amount of local Democratic support can overcome a huge discrepancy in fundraising. To remain competitive, Democrats must have about the same amount of money as their GOP opponents.

The proverb, "Money is the mother's milk of politics," remains as one of the more enduring political sayings. Candidates may win statewide elections for a host of reasons besides money, but none can win without it. In the original 1947 interviews for V. O. Key's book *Southern Politics*, the ready availability and corrupting influence of money was a frequent topic of conversation. The $15,000 limit on campaign costs in Florida was routinely ignored. Instead, candidates regularly spent between $40,000 and $50,000 without fear of penalty. When the runoff was added in, the total cost of winning the Democratic primary could be $100,000 to even $200,000.[9] Today a statewide race in Florida costs at least $8 million, all regulated by state laws. An insider close to Huey Long in Louisiana declared the "Kingfish" spent between $500,000 and $600,000 on his statewide campaigns, almost all of it in cash and none of it traceable. Elections today in Louisiana cost $5 million, and a 2003 study of campaign finance laws gave the state a grade of C-minus on this legislation, which was significantly better than most southern states, who failed miserably.[10]

When it comes to running a political campaign, incumbency, name recognition, and issues all matter—but they are meaningless if the candidate does not have enough money to be competitive. Media-driven campaigns dictate that candidates have resources sufficient to buy television time and improve their prospects of winning. Anyone associated with a political campaign knows that for a candidate to win there must be enough money to compete with an opponent on television. A competitive budget and media campaign by a Democrat doesn't guarantee victory, but without such resources a candidate can be guaranteed defeat.

Financial disclosure laws for gubernatorial races vary from state to state, so comparable data is difficult to find. In federal races, however, candidates are required to file uniform disclosure forms. Table 8.1 compares the amount of money spent by Democratic and Republican candidates in recent senatorial races. The table shows that only once, in 1996 in Georgia, was a Democrat able to defeat a better-funded Republican opponent. In that race Max Cleland was a well-known Georgia public figure who served in the Carter administration and had substantial name recognition statewide. Bob Graham in Florida and Fritz Hollings in South Carolina outspent their Republican rivals so the financial noncompetition label was in their favor rather than their Republican rivals. Democrats lost most races where

Table 8.1   Financial Expenditures in Selected Senate Races

State	Year	Democratic Candidate	Republican Candidate	Outcome/Democratic Candidate
Financially Competitive				
South Carolina	2004	$5,273,942	$8,990,448	Lost/Tenenbaum
Georgia	2000	$2,533,746	$1,093,408	Won/Miller
Florida	2000	$6,535,832	$8,664,112	Won/Nelson
Virginia	2000	$6,610,252	$9,995,980	Lost/Robb
North Carolina	1998	$8,331,382	$9,375,771	Won/Edwards
Tennessee	1994	$5,020,515	$7,017,424	Lost/Sasser
Alabama	1990	$3,437,073	$1,853,869	Won/Heflin
Alabama	1996	$2,284,801	$3,862,359	Lost/Bedford
Arkansas	1996	$1,577,838	$1,604,014	Lost/Bryant
Arkansas	1998	$3,122,776	$1,093,007	Won/Lincoln
South Carolina	1996	$1,913,574	$2,632,682	Lost/Close
Louisiana	1996	$2,504,815	$1,878,242	Won/Landrieu
Financially Noncompetitive				
Arkansas	2004	$6,423,226	$106,741	Won/Lincoln
Georgia	1996	$2,926,391	$9,858,955	Won/Cleland
Florida	1998	$5,094,581	$1,487,498	Won/Graham
Virginia	1996	$5,819,157	$11,600,424	Lost/Warner
Texas	1996	$978,862	$14,078,131	Lost/Morales
Texas	2000	$4,602	$3,518,862	Lost/Kelly
North Carolina	1996	$7,992,980	$14,589,266	Lost/Gantt
Tennessee	1996	$792,969	$3,469,369	Lost/Gordon
Tennessee	2000	$173,406	$4,664,737	Lost/Clark
Alabama	1992	$2,807,764	$149,578	Won/Shelby
South Carolina	1998	$4,968,456	$2,143,278	Won/Hollings
Mississippi	2000	$40,349	$3,663,052	Lost/Brown
Louisiana	1998	$3,858,472	$364,073	Won/Breaux

Source: Compiled from Federal Election Commission reports available at www.fec.gov.

they were not competitive financially. The fundraising discrepancies, and the political defeats, were most noticeable in Texas, Tennessee, and Mississippi.

Democrats won about half the contests when they were financial equals, and did best in states that were two-party competitive. Bill Nelson used his experience to win a US Senate seat in Florida in 2000, and John Edwards vaulted to victory in 1998. The 2000 election cycle was the year Arkansas was one of the most Democratic states in the region but voted for George W. Bush for president. In each case, Democrats were financially resourceful in states that were potentially winnable. The secret to victory was timing, the right race in the right state with enough money, in a year when the outcome was not contingent on factors like a presidential election or a scandal.

The analysis in this chapter examines the pattern of Democratic victories in states across the South. In some states the record of two-party competition in statewide races is so spotty that the state is effectively in the hands of the GOP when it comes to handicapping votes for president, governor, or senator. A Democrat can still win in these states when they are a minority, but only if the Republicans divide their allegiance on Election Day by scandal or a particularly divisive policy. Tennessee and Virginia are two states where Democrats won the governor's race in 2002 and 2001 respectively after Republicans alienated voters with their policies. In other states, the competition between the two parties is even, and maps are used to show the county-by-county competition as well as the results in the identified urban counties.

National States

Georgia

A message on twin water towers beside Interstate 85 in Gwinnett County outside Atlanta proclaims: "Success Lives Here." The sign summarizes life in communities and commuter suburbs amid strip malls with Home Depot and Chick-fil-A stores in abundance. But the water towers could also be the motto of the Georgia Republican Party, since it flourishes along with the azaleas and the highways. The previous chapter showed that the donut counties around Atlanta are the wellsprings of political realignment statewide.

In spite of this urbanization and steady Republican growth, Georgia remains a competitive state, one that has remained tenaciously Democratic at the grassroots. All the elements necessary for a Democratic victory are in place in the Peach State: a legacy of devoted Democratic Party loyalty, a large and loyal black population, and an agrarian culture. The state was the last one in the former Confederacy to elect a Republican to the governor's office, and that not until 2002. Two-party competition, a substantial in-migration of non-Southerners, a well-funded slate of candidates, and a population accustomed to loyalty to the Democrats sustained the party in races from president to state legislator. The true strength of the party was—and remains—the loyalty of black voters in downtown Atlanta and in rural areas throughout the state.

The combination of these elements is embodied in the career of a politician like Zell Miller, who won the governor's office in 1990, and served as US senator at the turn of the millennium. Miller is a product of the state political culture that produced Richard Russell, Sam Nunn, and a host of lesser Democratic officeholders in Georgia. All these successful candidates were experienced politicians, conservative on issues like national defense and gun control, faithful to the Democratic Party legacy of support for the little guy, and a belief that successful candidates should spend time in rank before seeking higher office. The loyalty of Georgia voters to these types of candidates stretches back decades.

Zell Miller's career is typical of that for a southern Democrat. He hails from north Georgia with a folksy manner and a keen sense of public opinion. Miller worked for Lester Maddox in the last two years of that controversial governorship, ran the state Democratic Party when Jimmy Carter was governor, and was elected lieutenant governor in 1974 where he held office for sixteen years. He was elected governor in 1990 and 1994 with a policy proposal—the HOPE scholarship program of state lottery funds for scholarships—that proved astonishingly popular.

Once in the governor's office, Miller appointed the first black woman to the state Supreme Court, strengthened drunk driving laws, and started boot camps for first-time offenders to the criminal justice system. He tried, and failed, to get the legislature to remove the Confederate stars and bars from the Georgia flag. He called for getting guns out of schools and an income tax cut for retirees. In short, he kept the conservative social agenda, much like Sam Nunn did in the US Senate in Washington, and at the same time moved for social change on select issues.

In July 2000 Miller was appointed to the Senate to complete the term of Republican Paul Coverdale who died in office, and won reelection in his own right in a special election that fall. In Washington, Zell Miller carried out a promise he made to be bipartisan, supporting John Ashcroft for attorney general in the George W. Bush cabinet, and co-sponsoring Bush's tax program. He was rumored to be considering a change of party in May of 2001, but denied any such intention in a public press conference. Miller's conservative sentiments were embodied in his book about the Democrats entitled, *A National Party No More*.[11]

Miller addressed the Republican National Convention in September of 2004 as a Democrat concerned about the ideals and drift of his party. As a Southerner he recalled the years of bipartisanship that once characterized lawmaking and discussion in the country. "Time after time in our history, in the face of great danger, Democrats and Republicans worked together to ensure that freedom would not falter. . . . But not today." After reciting a legacy of accomplishment Miller concluded, "But don't waste your breath telling that to the leaders of my party today [who think] America is the problem, not the solution."

The career of Zell Miller, and his concluding address to the Republican Party, is a metaphor for millions of former southern Democrats who have changed parties in the past decades. His career is an example of a successful southern Democratic politician surviving in a competitive, two-party state. His lottery scholarship program was so popular it helped elect Democratic governors in the two neighboring states of South Carolina and Alabama in 1998. He was familiar and trusted, so that when he pushed a moderate social agenda on the crucial race issue, appointed visible African Americans to prominent office, and advocated a new state flag, voters were not alarmed. On issues of crime, defense, gun control, and taxes, Zell Miller took positions that the press described as moderate, but really they were more Republican than Democratic.

Miller's senatorial race, which is one of the three races examined here, is shown in Map 8.1. The map shows the county-by-county pattern of Democratic successes in the late 1990s and 2000. In 1996 Max Cleland was elected to the US Senate as a capstone to a political career. Two years later, Roy Barnes won a close gubernatorial race against Guy Milner, the man who started the Norrell temporary agency and spent lavishly from his personal fortune. Finally, in 2000 Zell Miller defeated Mack Mattingly in a race for the US Senate. The counties in Map 8.1 are shaded by their loyalty to either the Democrats or the Republicans in *all three* of these races.

The patterns in Map 8.1 show how Democrats were able to win, sometime against better-funded opponents. First, the Democrats were able to reclaim the rural, agrarian south Georgia base, which was once the lifeblood of the party. These counties are sparsely populated, but they add up. Democrats carried 102 of 159 counties in all three elections they won statewide. Seventy of the more than one hundred counties that voted Democratic were in the loyal, but lightly settled south Georgia region. This part of the state has a longstanding history of populist loyalty to the Democratic Party, and these candidates were able to reawaken that memory.

Second, Democrats were able to make significant inroads in the north Georgia base of the GOP. The counties south and southwest of Atlanta joined their downstate cousins just over the line in south Georgia. These counties formed a solid, and necessary, base. The popularity of Democratic candidates was enough to split the Republican loyalty in northeast and southwest Georgia. The candidate with the most appeal to these normally loyal Republicans was Zell Miller.

Finally, and most importantly, Democrats broke the lock Republicans had in the Atlanta suburbs. The counties that make up metropolitan Atlanta have over half the population of the state and are the focus of any political campaign. In most cases, the difference between a Democratic victory and defeat is the double-digit percentage swing in the vote of the Atlanta suburbs.

The importance of the suburban swing vote in Georgia's largest city is seen in Table 8.2. The table contrasts the margins of victory for Republicans in presidential

Map 8.1   Georgia: Political Partisanship in Statewide Elections

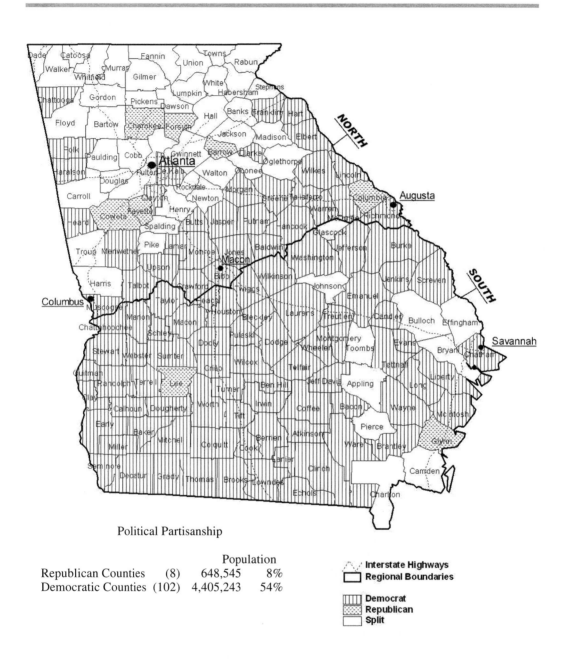

Political Partisanship

		Population	
Republican Counties	(8)	648,545	8%
Democratic Counties	(102)	4,405,243	54%

Interstate Highways
Regional Boundaries

Democrat
Republican
Split

Table 8.2 Georgia: Electoral Margins of Victory, by Party

Region/City	County	Republican Average in Victory	Democrat and Third-Party Average in Defeat	Republican Average in Defeat	Democratic Average in Victory	Difference
North Georgia						
Atlanta	Fulton	39%	61%	37%	63%	−2%
Atlanta	Dekalb	33%	67%	28%	72%	−5%
Atlanta	Cobb	61%	39%	53%	47%	−8%
Atlanta	Gwinnett	64%	36%	58%	42%	−6%
Atlanta	Clayton	41%	59%	34%	66%	−7%
Atlanta	Cherokee	69%	31%	62%	38%	−7%
Atlanta	Henry	63%	37%	57%	43%	−6%
Atlanta	Forsyth	71%	29%	66%	34%	−5%
Atlanta	Douglas	60%	40%	51%	49%	−9%
Atlanta	Fayette	67%	33%	60%	40%	−7%
Atlanta	Coweta	63%	37%	58%	42%	−5%
Atlanta	Carroll	60%	40%	48%	52%	−12%
Atlanta	Rockdale	61%	39%	55%	45%	−6%
North/South Georgia						
Macon/Warner Robbins	Bibb	45%	55%	38%	62%	−7%
Macon/Warner Robbins	Houston	58%	42%	47%	53%	−11%
North/South Georgia						
Augusta	Columbia	71%	29%	61%	39%	−10%
Augusta	Richmond	45%	55%	39%	61%	−6%

Note: The total population of these areas represents 52 percent of the state population.

elections (shown in the previous chapter) with the margins won by Democrats in statewide victories. The column labeled "Difference" in the table is the percentage contrast in the Republican vote in a winning and losing effort. The differences between a winning and losing campaign are in evidence in this chapter. The figures show how much fall-off there must be for the Democrats to win. These are Georgia's most populous counties, and the percentages can be deceiving. A vote swing by the margins in the five most mercurial counties (Clayton, Douglas, Carroll, Rockdale, and Cobb) as indicated by the percentages in the last column of Table 8.2, would move more than 33,000 votes from the Republicans to the Democrats, or vice versa, in an election year. Recall that Bill Clinton won Georgia in 1992 by a mere 13,000 votes, and that Bob Dole carried it four years later by a similarly small 27,000-vote margin, and the importance of the swing vote in just five Georgia suburban counties becomes apparent.

The swing votes in the Atlanta suburbs are the difference between victory and defeat for any Democrat in any statewide race in Georgia. But victory on Election Day is not just a matter of percentage wins in crucial counties; it is also dependent on turnout. In 2002 Georgia shocked the nation by electing a GOP governor for the first time in one hundred years, and at the same time turned out an incumbent Democratic senator. The vote percentages of the Atlanta suburbs in the 2002 election were such that the Democrats could have won, but *turnout,* and an alienated rural constituency unhappy with the state flag decision, allowed the Republicans to take a narrow victory.

Florida

The 2000 presidential election was a snapshot of the division of political loyalty in this state. Stamped on the minds of television viewers are contentious press conferences, made-for-television demonstrations, and convoluted legal explanations of a recount. The entire controversy took place in a part of the country with palm trees and well-tended lawns basking in sunshine as the rest of the country shivered through a December winter. The political separations in Florida are deeply etched, and are also unique to the diversity of the political culture of one of the nation's most populous states.

Florida has a smaller black population than other southern states, a huge Latino base, and a disproportionately large elderly constituency. The diverse population, and widespread economic success of the state, means that a religious controversy over a statewide lottery or the Confederate battle symbol on the state flag, are *not* issues here like they are elsewhere in the South. The base to which Democrats appeal begins with the elderly, many of whom revere the legacy of FDR. They remember the Democratic Party of the New Deal and postwar prosperity. The message of supposed Republican cuts in Social Security and veterans' benefits, along with tax cuts for the wealthy, helped Democrats here. The traumatic events of the 1960s—Vietnam and civil disorders—shook the allegiance of many retirees to the

Democratic Party, and opened their ears to Republican appeals of less intrusive government, but they mostly remember the past. As a result the competition for older voters is keen.

The size and population of the state, along with its mixture of ethnic groups, make statewide elections much like presidential contests—where the personality of the candidates overshadows the issues and party affiliation. A statewide election in Florida has a flush of television commercials, and requires extensive travel with endless personal appearances. Democrats dominate the Atlantic Gold Coast along Interstate 95, and win statewide races by attracting votes in nonaligned counties in central and Gulf Coast Florida. Democrats dominate the urban areas, but Republicans counter this advantage by winning the panhandle and the Gulf Coast plain along with the Cuban vote in south Florida.

The state is very competitive, and political elections are the exact opposite of the "let go and relax" attitude cultivated by travel and tourist advertisements. Name recognition matters here; in 2002 Jeb Bush followed his brother's razor-thin victory for president with a shining triumph (56 percent to 43 percent). Democrats have their own popular candidates and the one with the most "Zell Miller–like" appeal is former governor, senator, and, for a time, 2004 presidential candidate, Bob Graham. Like Miller, Graham has been in politics most of his adult life and has earned the trust of voters.

Bob Graham was first elected to the state House of Representatives in 1966, when he was thirty. He was elected governor in 1978, and won the office a second time in 1982. In 1986 Graham won the US Senate seat against an incumbent Republican. Once in office he was labeled a moderate because of his hard line on crime and opposition to Fidel Castro. Graham broke with the Clinton White House decision to return Elian Gonzalez to Cuba, and he supported the Gulf War resolutions and campaign finance reform.

In a state with a huge elderly population, Graham made medical and healthcare funding major issues in his political career. He was an early advocate of prescription drug coverage for this constituency. Such positions made him very popular throughout the state, and no Republican could effectively challenge him in an election. Graham's career is a model of success for Democrats in a competitive state with a diverse political geography.

The county-by-county analysis of voter allegiance is shown in Map 8.2 for three statewide races in which Democratic candidates won. The first race is the gubernatorial election that Jeb Bush lost to Lawton Chiles in 1994. In spite of a national tide for Republicans, Chiles beat the younger Bush brother that year in a squeaker election. In 1998 popular senator Bob Graham won by a near two to one majority. While Florida voters narrowly voted for George Bush in 2000, they voted for Democrat Bill Nelson by a more comfortable 52 percent to 48 percent margin.

The previous analysis of presidential voting in Florida showed the near majority domination by Democrats in urban areas, at the same time that Republicans were

Map 8.2   Florida: Political Partisanship in Statewide Elections

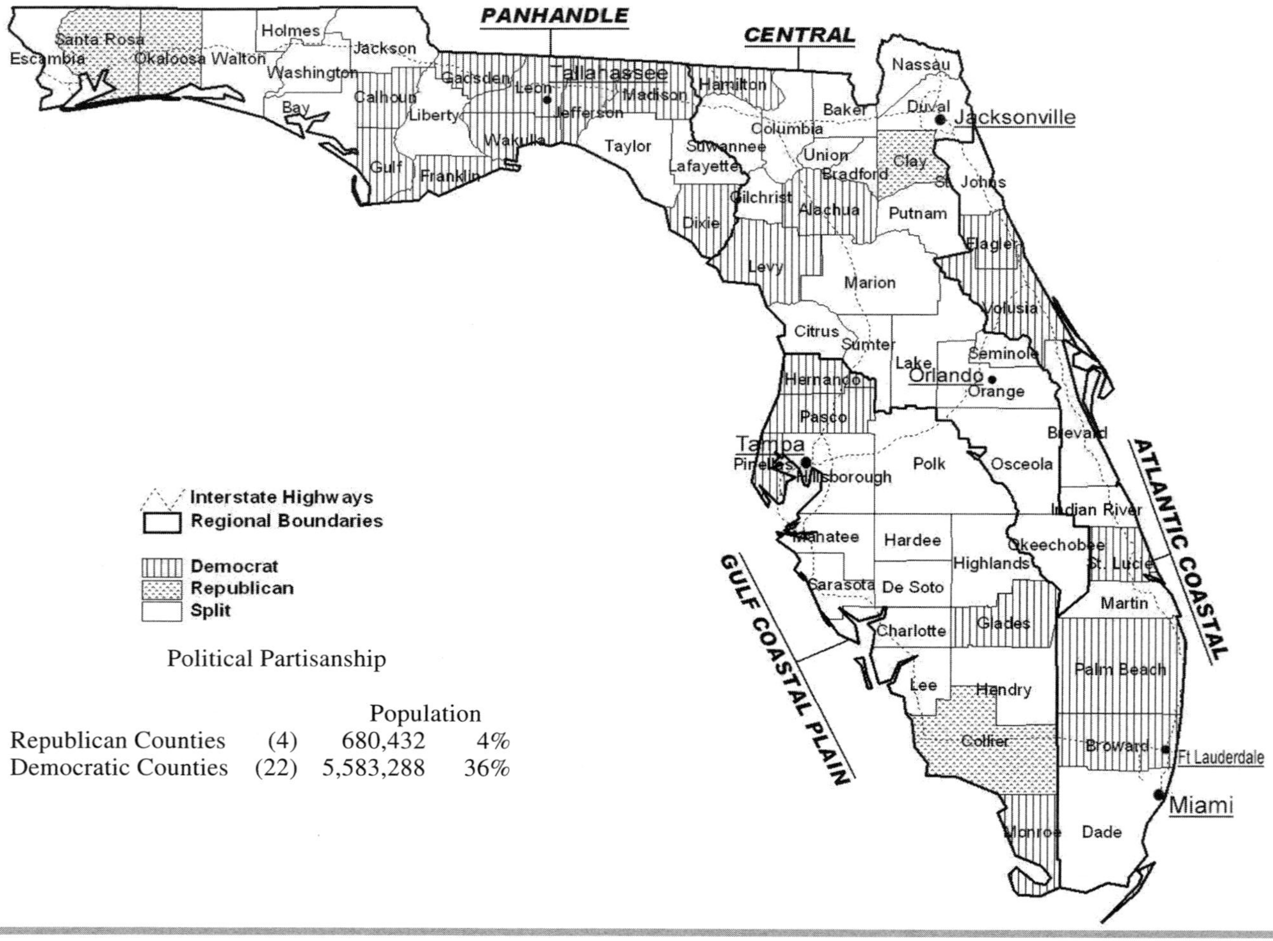

Interstate Highways
Regional Boundaries

Political Partisanship

- Democrat
- Republican
- Split

		Population	
Republican Counties	(4)	680,432	4%
Democratic Counties	(22)	5,583,288	36%

Table 8.3   Florida: Electoral Margins of Victory, by Party

Region/City	County	Republican Average in Victory	Democrat and Third-Party Average in Defeat	Republican Average in Defeat	Democratic Average in Victory	Difference
Atlantic Coastal						
Miami/Ft. Lauderdale	Palm Beach	38%	67%	34%	66%	–4%
Miami/Ft. Lauderdale	Broward	38%	62%	30%	70%	–8%
Miami/Ft. Lauderdale	Dade	44%	56%	39%	61%	–5%
Gulf Coastal Plain						
Tampa/St. Petersburg	Hernando	44%	56%	44%	56%	—
Tampa/St. Petersburg	Hillsborough	47%	53%	47%	53%	—
Tampa/St. Petersburg	Pasco	44%	56%	43%	57%	–1%
Tampa/St. Petersburg	Pinellas	44%	56%	55%	56%	–11%
Central Florida						
Orlando/Daytona Beach/Melbourne	Orange	49%	51%	46%	54%	–3%

Note: The total population of these areas represents 52 percent of the state population.

strong in the panhandle and northern counties. In these statewide races the independence of the electorate is shown when *neither party has a near majority advantage in the state*. In Map 8.2 forty counties are unshaded, meaning they divided their allegiance in at least one of the three Democratic victories. Most of Florida is not aligned with either party in these statewide races. Seven counties have never voted with one party for more than two elections in a row; they switch back and forth depending on the candidates and the contest. The deciding majority in any race in Florida is not aligned with either party at the beginning of the campaign. The strategy of a statewide campaign is to appeal to these independent voters who make up the deciding margin in any race.

V. O. Key proclaimed at midcentury that "Florida is different," and "in its politics it is almost literally every candidate for himself."[12] We see the same trait fifty years later as the independent streak of the Florida electorate remains. The populous counties in south Florida (Broward and Palm Beach) remain Democratic, but their neighbors (Dade and Martin) are competitive. Similarly, those on the Gulf coastal plain (Pasco, Pinellas, and Hernando) are Democratic, with Hillsboro being up for grabs in any election.

Table 8.3 shows that more than half the population of the state is in just eight counties, all of them dominated by Democrats. When successful statewide, the Democratic candidates must drive up their base votes in these urban counties. The percentage difference for Democrats in the last column of the table appears small, but the actual number of votes in question is enough to determine the outcome of an election; for these eight counties we are talking about more than 215,000 votes. In 1994 Lawton Chiles defeated Jeb Bush by 63,940 votes in the governor's race. Victories by Bill Clinton in 1996 and Bill Nelson's Senate race in 2002 were by a mere 300,000 votes out of more than five million cast. A swing of some 200,000 votes in these counties is enough to determine the outcome.

The three counties of the Miami/Ft. Lauderdale area (Palm Beach, Broward, and Dade) constitute the most important area for Democrats. The percentage difference here in victory and defeat translates into some 184,000 votes. Notice that the four counties in the Gulf Coast cities of Tampa and St. Petersburg are only marginally Democratic and three of the counties are trending Republican.

The irony of Florida politics is that Democrats dominate the urban areas of this most urban of southern states, while Republicans win elections. The state voted four out of five times for the GOP presidential nominee, the Republicans control Florida's governorship, both statehouse chambers, and eighteen of twenty-five congressional seats. Nonmetropolitan areas determine election outcomes in this state, and Democrats must do well outside the major cities if they expect to win.

Virginia

It was the most improbable victory in the most unlikely of states. In 2001 a decade of unbroken losses for Democrats was ended when Mark R. Warner won a special election for governor. He managed to overcome the Old Dominion's reliably Republican classification and his victory stands as a shining example of how a candidate's centrist politics can capture victory in a conservative southern state.

Warner was a former liberal Democrat who campaigned against a lackluster opponent by declaring himself outside of politics. "I'm running as a Democrat and I'm proud to be Democrat, but quite frankly, I don't believe the politics of the twenty-first century are going to be decided by the R's or the D's."[13] Warner ran as an anti-politician, who held the tired old ways of the past in contempt. It was a strategy that allowed Independents and Republicans to vote for a man who described himself as a businessman conservative. Warner also had personal wealth, some $200 million in a technology fortune, and he spent freely from his personal resources.

As a candidate Warner put together a message that acknowledged his Democratic Party affiliation, but declared that he was at root a "Virginia conservative." "I support the death penalty. I'm against gay marriage [and] I support the Second Amendment."[14] He spent a substantial amount of money on early television ads, introducing himself and delivering a reassuring message to Virginians that he was a safe alternative to the Republican candidate. He was also able to capitalize on a Republican feud that divided the GOP leaders and frustrated voters. Previous governor James S. Gilmore alienated some Republican leaders over how to shape and finance the state's annual budget in the midst of an economic downturn. Disaffected Republicans joined with independent voters to form a group called "Virginians for Warner."

Warner's victory, along with that of Chuck Robb against Oliver North in another strife-torn campaign in 1994, shows the Democratic strategy in bold detail. Map 8.3 is a county-by-county analysis of these two races. Democratic success was especially striking in south and southwest Virginia. The rural allegiance is reminiscent of the Byrd machine that dominated the politics of the Commonwealth in past decades. But the secret to Warner's victory lay in the way he broke GOP domination of the urban corridor.

Warner's victory capitalized on voter discontent because of layoffs and a weak economy. The mostly mountainous communities of rural Virginia treasured both gun rights and union membership. The Democrats supported both in Warner's race. Warner focused on economic growth, public education, and the need for fiscal caution in budget matters. He avoided divisive social issues such as gun control, abortion, the death penalty, and gay rights to give voters a reason to return to the party many had abandoned, but held in sentimental fondness.

A voter, interviewed by the *Washington Post* two months before the election, summed up the strategy: "There'd be a lot more Democrats if it weren't for abortion and gun control."[15] After the election, leading Republicans complained that the only reason the Democratic Party won was because its nominee effectively ran as a Republican. "The election also was characterized by huge ticket-splitting, as the

Map 8.3 Virginia: Political Partisanship in Statewide Elections

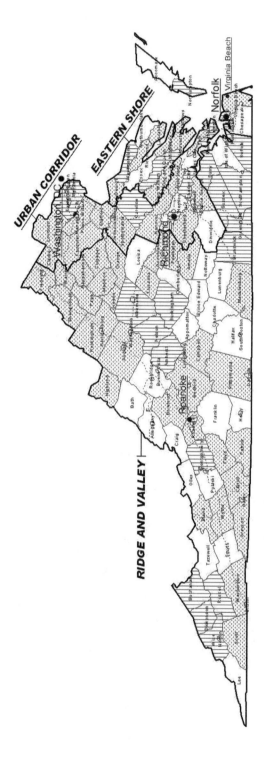

Political Partisanship

		Population	
Republican Counties	(48/9)	2,799,701	39%
Democratic Counties	(21/25)	3,062,838	43%

Table 8.4 Virginia: Electoral Margins of Victory, by Party

Region/City	County/City	Republican Average in Victory	Democrat and Third-Party Average in Defeat	Republican Average in Defeat	Democratic Average in Victory	Difference
Urban Corridor	Counties					
Washington/Northern Virginia	Arlington	36%	64%	28%	72%	-8%
Washington/Northern Virginia	Fairfax	50%	50%	43%	57%	-7%
Washington/Northern Virginia	Fauquier	61%	39%	58%	42%	-3%
Washington/Northern Virginia	Loudon	55%	45%	53%	47%	-2%
Washington/Northern Virginia	Prince William	54%	46%	53%	47%	-1%
Washington/Northern Virginia	Stafford	59%	41%	58%	42%	-1%
	Cities					
Washington/Northern Virginia	Alexandria	36%	64%	29%	71%	-7%
Washington/Northern Virginia	Fairfax	50%	50%	46%	54%	-4%
Washington/Northern Virginia	Falls Church	39%	61%	31%	69%	-8%
Washington/Northern Virginia	Fredricksburg	45%	55%	40%	60%	-5%
Washington/Northern Virginia	Manassas	56%	44%	55%	45%	-1%
Washington/Northern Virginia	Manassas Park	55%	45%	58%	42%	+3%
Urban Corridor	Counties					
Richmond/Petersburg	Chesterfield	63%	37%	62%	38%	-1%
Richmond/Petersburg	Hanover	68%	32%	66%	34%	-2%
Richmond/Petersburg	Henrico	57%	43%	52%	48%	-5%
Richmond/Petersburg	Prince George	59%	41%	59%	41%	—
	Cities					
Richmond/Petersburg	Colonial Heights	71%	29%	71%	29%	—
Richmond/Petersburg	Hopewell	54%	46%	54%	46%	—
Richmond/Petersburg	Petersburg	23%	77%	21%	79%	-2%
Richmond/Petersburg	Richmond	33%	67%	28%	72%	-5%

(continues)

Table 8.4 Continued

Region/City	County/City	Republican Average in Victory	Democrat and Third-Party Average in Defeat	Republican Average in Defeat	Democratic Average in Victory	Difference
Urban Corridor	Counties					
Norfolk/Newport News	Glouchester	60%	40%	56%	44%	-4%
Norfolk/Newport News	Isle of Wright	55%	45%	50%	50%	-5%
Norfolk/Newport News	James City	58%	42%	48%	52%	-10%
Norfolk/Newport News	Mathews	60%	40%	54%	46%	-6%
Norfolk/Newport News	York	61%	39%	53%	47%	-8%
	Cities					
Norfolk/Newport News	Chesapeake	53%	47%	52%	48%	-1%
Norfolk/Newport News	Hampton	45%	54%	36%	63%	-8%
Norfolk/Newport News	Newport News	49%	51%	42%	58%	-7%
Norfolk/Newport News	Poquoson	72%	28%	64%	36%	-8%
Norfolk/Newport News	Portsmouth	41%	59%	33%	67%	-8%
Norfolk/Newport News	Suffolk	48%	52%	45%	55%	-3%
Norfolk/Newport News	Virginia Beach	57%	43%	52%	48%	-5%
Norfolk/Newport News	Williamsburg	45%	55%	38%	62%	-7%

Note: The total population of these areas represents 59 percent of the state population.

GOP handily won the race for attorney general and picked up a remarkable twelve seats in the House of Delegates races."[16] The first key to victory for Warner, and other Democrats, is that a successful challenger must have financial competitiveness and issue definition along with candidate appeal.

Table 8.4 shows that the second key to success for Democrats in this reliably Republican state was the attrition of GOP margins in the Norfolk/Newport News metropolitan area at the southern end of the urban corridor. Successful Democratic candidates in the victories analyzed have increased their margins in both cities and counties. The average difference between winning and losing for Democrats in the urban corridor is small—around four percentage points in an average election. Since the corridor has 59 percent of the state's population, a percentage change of four points can translate into some 70,000 to 100,000 votes out of more than 2 million cast.

A third reason for the allegiance of voters to the Democratic Party is the enthusiasm black voters have for the nominee. In Warner's victory, former governor Douglas Wilder gave an endorsement and stumped the state on his behalf. The support of Wilder was critical in the mercurial Norfolk/Newport News and Hampton Roads communities. Richmond is unflinchingly Republican, but Norfolk varies in its GOP allegiance. Virginia benefited more than many states from the Voting Rights Act of 1965 because the state had historic low participation rates tied to the Byrd Machine. When black voters registered in historic numbers, the prospects of the Democratic Party improved. Expanded participation had a downside in that Democratic candidates could be victimized by low participation and turnout on Election Day.

Texas

Michael Barone has written that "Texas is the counterweight to New York in presidential politics."[17] In 2004 the state cast thirty-four electoral votes for George W. Bush, and New York cast thirty-one votes for the Democratic nominee. A Democrat has not won a significant statewide race in Texas since Ann Richards defeated Clayton Williams in 1990 and that victory, in a campaign of notorious negative slurs, was by a mere two percentage points.

The bellwether race in the state was in 1988, when native senator Lloyd Bentsen joined Michael Dukakis to square off against favorite son George Bush who ran with Dan Quayle. The Democrats garnered only 43 percent of the vote that election, and Republicans have dominated every meaningful contest since. For these reasons Texas is classified as reliable Republican and a desert for Democratic candidates.

The growing Hispanic population in Texas makes ethnic politics crucial here, but Democrats have not been able to capitalize on this advantage. In 2002 Laredo banker Tony Sanchez spent freely from his own fortune and lost. The candidacy of a native Hispanic who was well financed did not stimulate turnout for Democrats.

Map 8.4   North Carolina: Political Partisanship in Statewide Elections

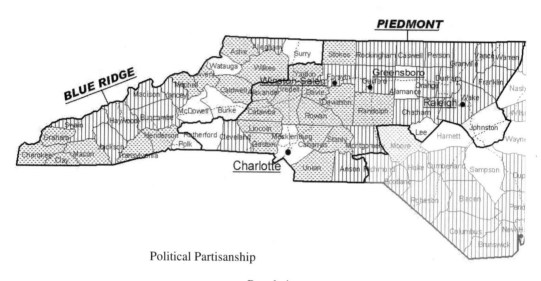

Political Partisanship

		Population	
Republican Counties	(26)	1,853,305	23%
Democratic Counties	(57)	4,292,450	53%

Republicans often garner at least a quarter, and often a third, of the Latino vote, making it difficult to capitalize on the black-Hispanic alliance necessary to defeat the largely white Republican Anglo vote. Another problem Democrats have in this state is the absence of an avuncular Democrat, with a Zell Miller or a Bob Graham appeal, who could reassure voters in a statewide race. John Sharp, a "New" Democrat who was state comptroller, came close, but lost in two statewide races. Lloyd Bentsen and Lieutenant Governor Bob Bullock are gone from the public stage in Texas, and no successor has been found to approach their popularity. Democrats have tried to win elections with a minority appeal to Hispanic voters, and with African Americans and proffered social programs. The demographics are promising, but so far no unified and coherent campaign strategy—with enough money—has emerged to attract white crossover voters to achieve victory. For these reasons there are no maps or tables for Democrats in Texas.

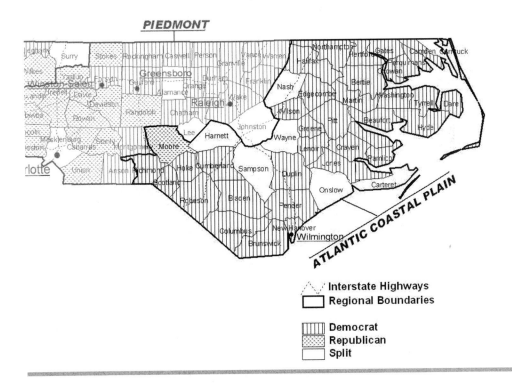

Interstate Highways
Regional Boundaries

Democrat
Republican
Split

Emergent States

North Carolina

In the spring of 1972 Jesse Helms walked into a small hardware store in the Piedmont Village of Rockwell to campaign. There he bumped into his opponent, incumbent senator Everett Jordan. Both men broke into laughter, and joked with each other about the outcome of the race before they departed.

The incident reveals something about state campaigns here. A polite formality prevails: "Within the confines of one-party government, it [North Carolina] never tolerated outright bigots of the stripe found in other [southern] states."[18] Something in the culture of the state led to a decent and responsible respect for political opponents in political contests. Maybe it is the "Mayberry" image of small town neighborliness, or the deeply ingrained religious culture that causes opponents to curb their rhetoric. Some commentators believe the influence of world-class universities

Vignette 8.1 Hunt vs. Helms, 1984

At the time it was the most highly publicized and expensive race for a southern US Senate seat in modern political history. The race pitted a rock-ribbed conservative, incumbent Republican against a moderate Democrat and southern governor. Some said it was a showdown between the Old South and the New South, antigovernment and progovernment, Republican and Democrat—but in the end it was an old-fashioned, mud-slinging contest that cost an estimated $25 million.

Jesse Helms grew up in the southern Piedmont village of Monroe, once the center of a cotton-growing economy. While working his way through Wake Forest College, he dropped out to work for the *Raleigh News and Observer* newspaper. He enjoyed the job so much that he made journalism his career, and in 1948 went to work for a small radio station, WRAL, as news director. There he fell under the influence of the station owner, A. J. Fletcher, who used the station as a platform to campaign for conservative US senator Willis Smith.

When Smith won, Helms went with him to Washington, then returned to North Carolina as executive director of the state banking association and editor of its trade magazine. In 1960 Helms returned to WRAL as a television commentator, with his broadcasts heard on seventy rural radio stations and reprinted in some two hundred newspapers. This exposure made Jesse Helms a household name across eastern North Carolina, and in 1972 he capitalized on his popularity to successfully run for the US Senate.

Jim Hunt's family was from the small community of Rock Ridge in the eastern Carolina coastal plain. The family was committed to the land and as a high school student Hunt was involved in the state Junior Grange, replete with the political ethic of FDR's New Deal. Hunt attended North Carolina State University where he served as vice president of the North Carolina Young Democrats. In 1960 he worked on the successful gubernatorial campaign of Terry Sanford and subsequently entered law school. In his second year of law school Hunt became national college director for the Democratic National Committee and moved to Washington, delaying his graduation.

Young Jim Hunt identified with the blossoming liberalism of the early 1960s and the Kennedy years, but he also realized that such convictions had to be moderated in a state like North Carolina. Both Jesse Helms and Jim Hunt won elections in 1972, the former to the US Senate and the latter to lieutenant governor. Four years later Hunt won an astonishing 65 percent of the vote against his Republican adversary in the race for governor. His personal popularity outweighed questions of liberalism or conservatism, and he awoke to the label of a rising star in the New South politics.

As the 1984 election year dawned the two men squared off in a battle to decide not only the office, but the future of North Carolina politics. The election was a referendum on southern partisanship, and the future of the GOP in the South. Richard Whittle, a former North Carolina reporter who wrote for the *Los Angeles Times–Washington Post* Service, predicted in 1983 that, "Barring an act of God, Helms can't win." Hunt led by six percentage points in most polls, and in a state where Democrats outnumbered Republicans three to one, his prospects looked bright.

But the senior senator from the state had help from on high. In Dallas's First Baptist Church on the Sunday after the Republicans nominated Ronald Reagan for a second term, Reverend Jerry Falwell declared from the pulpit: "Senator, you are a national treasure. . . . We can't do without you." That same week thirty-second commercials began airing all

(continues)

Vignette 8.1   Continued

across North Carolina with the president proclaiming, "I cherish my friendship with Jesse Helms, and I need his honesty and his patriotism in the United States Senate."

Both candidates canvassed the country raising money, and in September the race turned negative. Helms followed a disappointing performance in the first public debate with a television campaign that repeatedly asked: "Where do you stand, Jim?" The incumbent senator's campaign strategy was to align Hunt with the floundering Mondale campaign, while Helms embraced the popular programs of Ronald Reagan. The Helms campaign ran a hard ad against racial quotas that led to charges of bigotry from the Democrats. Jim Hunt ran on his record, and the popularity he had acquired after twelve years in office. The Democrat was a better debater, and held his own in the October televised contests.

In the end the long campaign, lavish

expenditures on television, and vitriolic exchanges resulted in political overexposure and a near dead-heat in votes. What began as an ideological referendum on the future of the state ended as a personal mission of search and destroy. One estimate said the Tarheel electorate was subjected to some twenty thousand television commercials. After nearly eighteen months of television ads, and approximately $25 million, the two candidates split the state.

Jesse Helms prevailed by 86,000 votes out of more that 2.2 million cast. The vote margin was a tangible 52 percent to 48 percent victory that belied the closeness of the race. Both men continued their careers in public service. Senator Helms reigned as chair of the Foreign Relations Committee during the Bush and Clinton administrations, and Jim Hunt served two more terms as governor.

---

at Chapel Hill and Durham, along with an attentive press, have fostered a climate of respect and tolerance in political campaigns. For whatever reason, the competitive politics of the Tarheel State are more genteel.

This legacy was sorely tested in 1984 when incumbent senator Jesse Helms faced former governor Jim Hunt. In that election fifty-two of the state's 100 counties voted Republican and forty-eight voted Democratic. The contest was fierce and the results historic; in the end the divisions of that race portended subsequent patterns within the state. The Republican strength was, and remains, in the small towns and villages of the central and western Piedmont, as well as the western mountains. The Democrats dominate the northeastern rural areas and the dominant urban centers around Raleigh-Durham. The state is very competitive, but the patterns of allegiance are stable.

Map 8.4 shows the county-by-county allegiance for four Democratic victories. In 2000 Mike Easley won the governor's office succeeding Jim Hunt who won it twice before. This was the first time the Democrats held the governorship three consecutive times since the 1960s. Easley repeated his triumph in 2004. The 1996 Hunt gubernatorial victory, and the 2000 and 2004 Easley victories, are three of the four races. The last one is the important victory of John Edwards against Lauch

Table 8.5 North Carolina: Electoral Margins of Victory, by Party

Region/City	County	Republican Average in Victory	Democrat and Third-Party Average in Defeat	Republican Average in Defeat	Democratic Average in Victory	Difference
Piedmont						
Charlotte	Cabarras	62%	38%	55%	45%	−7%
Charlotte	Gaston	64%	36%	55%	45%	−9%
Charlotte	Lincoln	60%	40%	54%	46%	−6%
Charlotte	Mecklenburg	50%	50%	48%	52%	−2%
Charlotte	Rowan	61%	39%	54%	46%	−7%
Charlotte	Union	62%	38%	58%	42%	−4%
Piedmont						
Raleigh	Chatham	45%	55%	40%	60%	−6%
Raleigh	Durham	36%	64%	29%	71%	−7%
Raleigh	Franklin	47%	53%	41%	59%	−6%
Raleigh	Johnston	61%	39%	53%	47%	−8%
Raleigh	Orange	35%	65%	29%	71%	−6%
Raleigh	Wake	50%	50%	42%	58%	−8%
Piedmont						
Greensboro	Almance	58%	42%	51%	49%	−7%
Greensboro	Davidson	63%	37%	55%	45%	−8%
Greensboro	Davie	68%	32%	61%	39%	−7%
Greensboro	Forsyth	53%	47%	46%	54%	−6%
Greensboro	Guilford	49%	51%	43%	57%	−6%
Greensboro	Randolph	67%	33%	61%	39%	−6%
Greensboro	Stokes	62%	38%	55%	45%	−7%
Greensboro	Yadkin	70%	30%	62%	38%	−8%
Atlantic Coastal						
Greenville	Pitt	50%	50%	41%	59%	−9%
Atlantic Coastal						
Wilmington	Brunswick	51%	49%	42%	58%	−9%
Wilmington	New Hanover	53%	47%	45%	55%	−8%

Note: The total population of these areas represents 51 percent of the state population.

Faircloth in 1998. Edwards's accomplishment propelled him onto the national stage, and was the foundation of his 2004 presidential bid. The map shows that Democrats carried fifty-seven counties each time they won.

The Democratic Party base electorate is in the Atlantic coastal plains in the eastern part of the state. The affinity between the coastal areas of North Carolina and the Democratic Party, in this state as well as the entire South, is historic. The low-lying regions of each state were once home to large plantations and to a substantial black population. Today the plantations are gone, but the black population, and a corresponding allegiance to Democrats, remains. In North Carolina, the coastal plain is the geographic base for any statewide Democratic victory, but to seal that win in this competitive state, the urban centers along the interstate highways from Charlotte, Raleigh, Greensboro, and Wilmington must be added to the vote in the coastal plain.

Each political party in North Carolina has a geographic base, and the key to electoral victory is to consolidate that allegiance before the election. The magic number in statewide races appears to be fifty, half the number of counties in the state. Successful Republican presidential campaigns, identified in the previous chapter, averaged forty-nine counties in winning four straight times. For Democrats the spread of the electorate in urbanized areas dictates that they win over half the total number of counties.

The figures in Table 8.5 compare the two-party percentages of urban areas in victory and defeat. Every county in the Charlotte area voted Republican, but by different margins. The largest county, Mecklenburg, is evenly divided in both Democratic victory and defeat. The Raleigh/Durham area is the mirror opposite of Charlotte, with every county but one voting Democratic. Greensboro, and the urban counties along the interstate highways to the coast are mixed in their political allegiance. Elections are won or lost along this corridor.

The three metropolitan areas of Charlotte, Raleigh/Durham, and Greensboro are roughly comparable in population, and as Table 8.5 shows, elements in each of them change their loyalty at the margins for any race. It is important for any Democrat to drive up the percentages in the Raleigh area, and reduce the corresponding margins in the Greensboro suburbs. This appears to be what Mike Easley did in his successful 2000 gubernatorial victory.

Tennessee

It was the celebration that never was. In downtown Nashville the War Memorial Auditorium stage was dressed for rejoicing in the election of home state senator, and vice president, Al Gore as president. The legacy of Andrew Jackson, Estes Kefauver, and Al Gore Sr. was to be reborn as the prodigy of a moderate southern state entered the Oval Office. But the red, white, and blue bunting had to be put back in storage because Gore lost his home state by 80,000 votes in 2000.

One commentator wrote after the controversial election of 2000 that, "The fact

Map 8.5   Tennessee: Political Partisanship in Statewide Elections

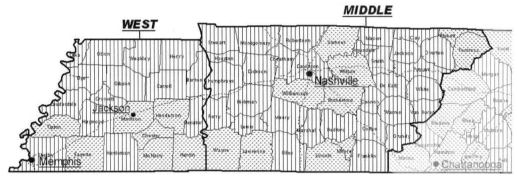

Political Partisanship

		Population	
Republican Counties	(41)	2,340,680	41%
Democratic Counties	(54)	3,349,203	59%

that native son Al Gore was unable to win here as the representative of the incumbent party in a time of peace and prosperity suggests that Tennessee is likely to be out of reach for presidential Democrats in the near future." That same commentator called the governor's race in the Volunteer State "highly competitive" and concluded: "Regardless of the nominees, expect a close race."[19]

Some revenge was extracted by the Democrats who maintained control of both statehouse chambers, and five of the nine congressional seats, as well as the governorship in 2004. Republicans take some consolation from the victories in both US Senate seats, but Tennessee is more competitive than the "Reliably Republican" presidential tag would indicate. The grassroots allegiance to conservative values keeps it in the GOP column.

Party rivalry in Tennessee can be deceiving. Gore's presence on the national ticket gave the state a two-party competitiveness that was disingenuous. On the night Tennessee voted for George W. Bush, it had two Republican US senators, a Republican governor, and a congressional delegation that was majority GOP. In short, the east Tennessee Republican allegiance, mentioned by V. O. Key, had gradually spread to envelop the suburbs and then the state.

Republican hegemony was derailed in 2002 when the second-term leadership of Governor Don Sundquist came under fire for proposing a state income tax. Tennessee is one of seven states in the country that has no income tax, and when the sitting governor proposed one in conjunction with a reduced sales tax, he was

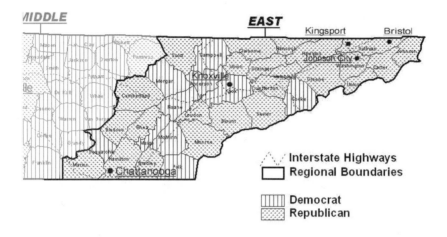

booed at Republican meetings. Sundquist became the object of radio talk show chatter, and found his vetoes being overridden with bipartisan majorities in the legislature. Motorists descended on Legislative Plaza in downtown Nashville to honk their horns outside the chambers and intimidate the governmental process into rejecting higher taxes.

In 2002 Nashville Democratic mayor, Phil Bredesen, won the gubernatorial race because of widespread discontent with Republican policies. His victory stopped a string of GOP statewide triumphs that stretched from 1994. The Bredesen-Hilleary race of 2002 is the *only one* analyzed as an example of a Democratic triumph in this state. Bredesen won by promising to oppose an income tax and using his experience in the healthcare industry to fix TennCare, the bankrupt Medicaid system in Tennessee. He also opposed gun control and supported educational improvements. Even so, the race was the closest one for governor since 1896, with Bredesen winning 51 percent to 48 percent.

Because Map 8.5 totals population figures in each county, the Republican and Democratic figures are larger than the actual vote a candidate received in the election. The patterns in the map, however, are familiar. They show the east Tennessee Republican base opposite west Tennessee loyalty to the Democratic Party, a division first identified by V. O. Key in his discussion of the Crump Machine in Memphis. In the 2002 election there is one anomaly; the Knoxville media market was flooded with Bredesen commercials and voted narrowly Democratic. The pains

Table 8.6   Tennessee: Electoral Margins of Victory, by Party

Region/City	County	Republican Average in Victory	Democrat and Third-Party Average in Defeat	Republican Average in Defeat	Democratic Average in Victory	Difference
East Tennessee						
Knoxville	Knoxville	56%	44%	50%	50%	−6%
Chattanooga	Hamilton	54%	46%	53%	47%	−1%
Tri-Cities	(Bristol-Kingsport) Sullivan	60%	40%	58%	42%	−2%
Tri-Cities	(Johnson City) Washington	59%	41%	59%	41%	—
Middle Tennessee						
Nashville	Davidson	43%	57%	39%	61%	−4%
Nashville	Rutherford	53%	47%	51%	49%	−2%
Nashville	Sumner	54%	46%	50%	50%	−4%
Nashville	Williamson	65%	35%	58%	42%	−6%
West Tennessee						
Memphis	Shelby	44%	56%	42%	58%	−2%

Note: The total population of these areas represents 50 percent of the state population.

of the state spending crisis were especially sharp at the University of Tennessee, and related state agencies in metropolitan centers across the state. The result was the mayor of Nashville did well in Knoxville, and when Nashville and Knoxville were joined to the Democratic stronghold of west Tennessee and Memphis, the Democrats held a statewide majority.

The revival of substantial Democratic strength in Tennessee coincided with partisan deadlock. In a sense it could be said that the Bredesen victory reflected a national trend. In Tennessee the Democrats went from a position of the comfortable majority to a competitive minority. The Bredesen victory broke a string of Republican successes, and served as a pattern for southern success.

This urban partisanship is shown in Table 8.6. The swing vote is especially sharp in Knoxville, and in Williamson County south of Nashville/Davidson County. Knoxville is the anchor of the east Tennessee Republican bastion, and Williamson County is a bedroom community of Nashville communities. When these two Republican bastions gravitated to the Democratic Party the fate of the GOP was assured.

Traditional States

Alabama

Few states are more conservative than Alabama, and in most elections that means the state votes Republican. But as the *Economist* magazine noted in 2002, "politics in Alabama can be peculiar."[20] Peculiar is a good word to describe a governor who declared himself "the little man's big friend," and one who installed his wife in office when he could no longer serve. It is peculiar when a judge gets elected as Chief Justice of the Supreme Court after defending a public display of the Ten Commandments, and taking his appeal to the state Supreme Court. The same word applies to a host of politicians who won office in the 1980s as Democrats, and were reelected as Republicans in the 1990s.

The irony of this change is that Democrats have a long and rich history of leadership in Alabama. In every family are members who remember the antics of "Big Jim" Folsom or George Wallace, and the populist politics that are special in the culture of the state. It was once the country's most Democratic state in partisan allegiance, but has now become one of the nation's most Republican.

Almost alone, Bill Clinton changed the politics of Alabama.

In 1993 Senator Richard Shelby said the Clinton program was "high on taxes and low on spending cuts," and switched parties. Former governor Fob James soon followed suit, and won the gubernatorial contest in 1994. At the grassroots, Democrats still run the state, they control the legislature and supervise redistricting, but their strength wanes in statewide races. Each year the declared allegiance of everyday voters becomes more inclined to support Republicans instead of Democrats for state office.

Map 8.6   Alabama: Political Partisanship in Statewide Elections

Political Partisanship

		Population	
Republican Counties	(11)	725,637	16%
Democratic Counties	(34)	2,135,762	48%

Table 8.7   Alabama: Electoral Margins of Victory, by Party

Region/City	County	Republican Average in Victory	Democrat and Third-Party Average in Defeat	Republican Average in Defeat	Democratic Average in Victory	Difference
North Alabama						
Birmingham	Jefferson	53%	47%	42%	58%	–11%
Birmingham	Shelby	76%	24%	65%	35%	–11%
Birmingham	St. Clair	69%	31%	56%	44%	–13%
Birmingham	Blount	66%	34%	56%	44%	–10%
North Alabama						
Huntsville	Madison	56%	44%	44%	56%	–12%
Huntsville	Limestone	58%	42%	49%	51%	–9%
South Alabama						
Montgomery	Montgomery	50%	50%	43%	57%	–7%
Montgomery	Elmore	67%	33%	62%	38%	–5%
Montgomery	Autauga	66%	34%	60%	40%	+4%
South Alabama						
Mobile	Mobile	56%	44%	46%	54%	–10%
Mobile	Baldwin	68%	32%	63%	37%	–5%

Note: The total population in this area represents 48 percent of the state population.

The drift of Alabama Democrats away from the national party is epitomized in the political career of Richard Shelby, who grew up in Birmingham the son of a steelworker. Shelby went to Tuscaloosa where he finished an undergraduate degree at the University of Alabama in 1957, and a law degree in 1963. In 1978 Shelby ran for the US House as a Democrat, and in 1986 he upset incumbent Republican Jeremiah Denton, a former Vietnam prisoner of war, in the race for the US Senate. One week after the Republicans seized control of the US Senate in 1994, he changed parties. "You don't know how I feel," Shelby declared, "as a conservative Democrat in the Democratic Party, you're in the minority."[21] The Republicans opened their arms to receive him and he was allowed to keep his committee seniority.

In time, Alabama's politics followed those of Richard Shelby. The historic allegiance of agrarian voters in overalls who were Democratic changed to suburbanites in minivans who voted Republican. The surprise win of Democrat Don Siegelman for governor in 1998, then, is a pattern worth studying for what happens when the Republican majority divides. Republicans split between Fob James and Winston Blount, and Siegelman was able to conclude, "Fob has done for me what I could never do for myself: Divide the Republican Party and at the same time unite the Democratic Party."[22]

Siegelman followed the 1990s formula for electoral success: a united black vote, isolated rural support, and an appeal to suburban voters with his advocacy for a statewide lottery. He promised $150 million for merit-based college scholarships and prekindergarten programs, and won by a 58 percent to 42 percent margin. The new governor had scarcely finished taking the oath of office before pulpits across the state erupted in attacks on the statewide lottery. Siegelman's forces outspent the lottery opponents three to one, but the Bible Belt opposition was fierce and determined in churches and shopping malls. In October of 1999 Alabamians rejected the lottery by a 54 percent to 46 percent margin.

The Democratic governor was left without his key issue, not to mention the money, to build a consensus with Republican values in a conservative state. His experience was an embodiment of the puzzles described by James Glaser in *Race, Campaign Politics, and the Realignment in the South*: "the Democratic Party has become more closely identified with blacks, which has led to even further white defections," and yet "even as a majority of whites turned Republican, southern Democrats have continued to win."[23] Siegelman's agenda embraced higher teacher salaries, strict penalties for drunk driving, and restrictions on abortion. All in all, his programs were well received, but his improved standing suffered in the recession of 2001. When expected revenues fell short of projections, Siegelman got the blame. He lost a bid for reelection by 3,120 votes after a controversial recount. Republican Bob Riley won by opposing tax increases and with calls to limit spending to the previous year's revenues.

Map 8.6 shows the two Siegelman races, a victory in 1998 and an extremely narrow defeat in 2002. Usually only Democratic victories are used in these maps to

show patterns of partisan strength, but Alabama had a victorious Democratic senator who won in 1992, then changed parties and the state has no recent statewide
examples of a Democratic triumph. The map shows that the Democratic vote is in
the Black Belt region that buckles the state from border to border, and in the western counties that abut the state of Mississippi. In presidential elections the northern
counties are historically Republican in allegiance, but in Siegelman's races they
aligned with the Democrats.

To see how Democrats can win a statewide race in Alabama, the votes are examined in the major cities of Birmingham, Huntsville, Montgomery, and Mobile. These
results are shown in Table 8.7. Siegelman scored significant victories in the populous
urban counties that carry the bulk of the population in each city. The contrast between
Democratic victory and defeat is especially sharp in the counties of Jefferson
(Birmingham), Madison (Huntsville), Montgomery (Montgomery), and Mobile
(Mobile). Collectively these four counties have over one-third of the population of
the state, and there was a 10 percent variation in Republican victory and defeat.

In 2002 the Alabama governor's race was the closest contest in the nation.
Siegelman won the black vote and carried largely white counties in northwestern
Alabama, but his margins in Birmingham were narrower than 1998, and the differences were enough to prove his undoing. The race showed that Alabama could be
competitive, but it is trending Republican. The roadblock to complete realignment
to the GOP lies in the significant black population that is enthusiastically
Democratic.

Arkansas

Today Arkansas stands as a reliably Democratic island in a sea of Republican
southern neighbors. The small town grassroots loyalty voters have to the party of
FDR, JFK, and LBJ remains. The patterns of one-party allegiance V. O. Key wrote
about fifty years ago persist, although they are attenuated by urban diversity and
growth. Today, Democrats in the state are in the familiar position of trying to balance the leftist interests of their party's national supporters with a state that is turning more conservative and uncomfortable with the national party.

The Clinton era stamped the politics of this state with a legacy few governors
in the South have been able to match. His victory in 1978, defeat in 1980, then
reelection in 1982 for a decade-long rule, established Democratic hegemony in
Arkansas when sister southern states were flirting with Ronald Reagan's brand of
GOP conservatism. While politicians in neighboring states changed their party
affiliation, those in Arkansas remained proud Democrats.

Part of the legacy is rooted in the agrarian history of the state. Between 1940 and
1960 Arkansas lost population as displaced farm workers moved to other states in
search of better jobs. The Democratic Party became the refuge for those who stayed
behind, and litters of "Yellow Dog" Democrats were born in those years. Bill
Clinton's boyhood experience was typical. In the summer of 1966 he showed up at

Map 8.7   Arkansas: Political Partisanship in Statewide Elections

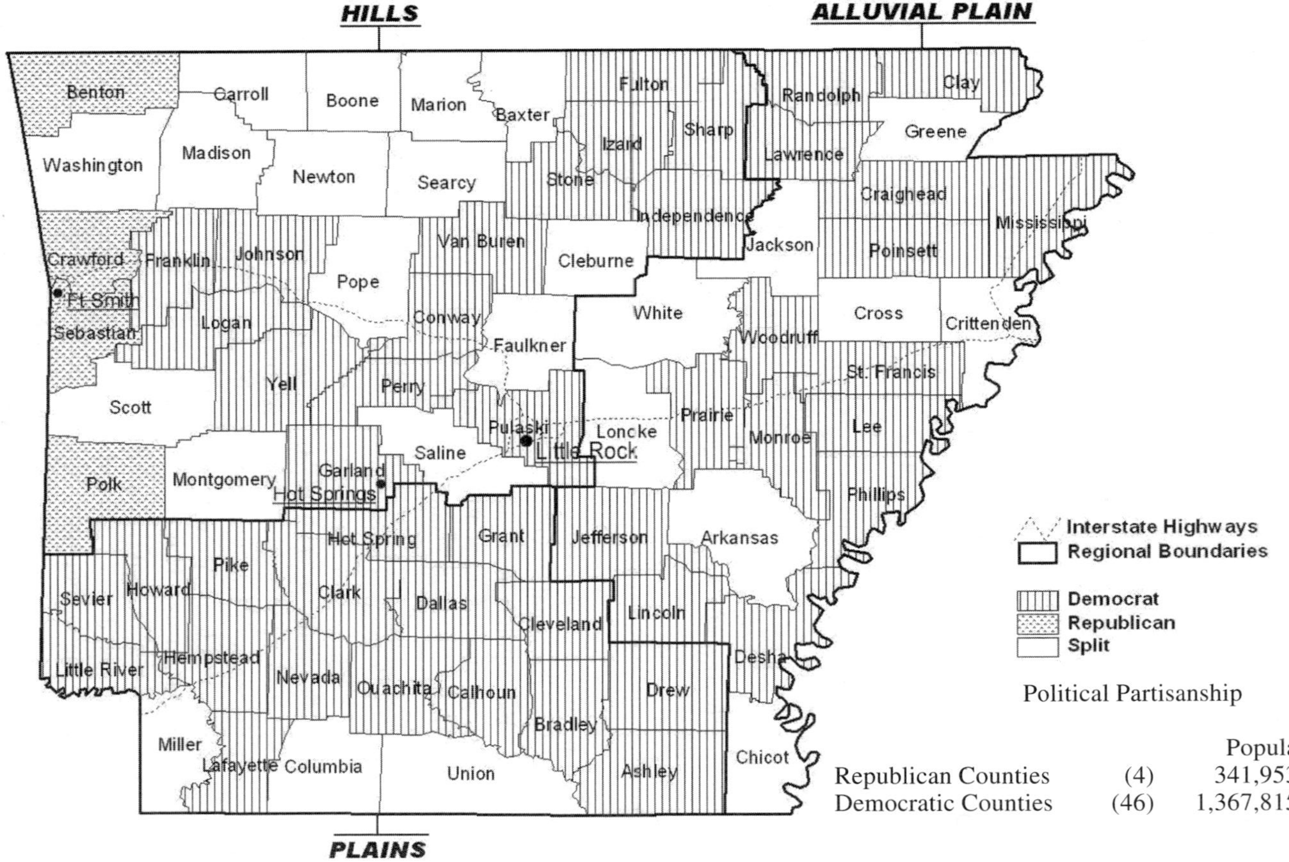

ALLUVIAL PLAIN

HILLS

PLAINS

Clay
Greene
Mississippi
Randolph
Lawrence
Craighead
Poinsett
Crittenden
Fulton
Sharp
Independence
Jackson
Cross
St. Francis
Lee
Phillips
Izard
Stone
Cleburne
White
Woodruff
Monroe
Baxter
Van Buren
Faulkner
Prairie
Arkansas
Desha
Chicot
Marion
Searcy
Conway
Pulaski
Lonoke
Lincoln
Drew
Ashley
Boone
Newton
Pope
Perry
Saline
Little Rock
Jefferson
Cleveland
Bradley
Union
Carroll
Madison
Johnson
Yell
Garland
Hot Spring
Grant
Dallas
Ouachita
Calhoun
Benton
Washington
Franklin
Logan
Montgomery
Hot Springs
Clark
Nevada
Columbia
Scott
Pike
Howard
Hempstead
Lafayette
Crawford
Ft. Smith
Sebastian
Polk
Sevier
Little River
Miller

Interstate Highways
Regional Boundaries

Democrat
Republican
Split

Political Partisanship

		Population	
Republican Counties	(4)	341,953	12.8%
Democratic Counties	(46)	1,367,815	51.2%

Table 8.8 Arkansas: Electoral Margins of Victory, by Party

Region/City	County	Republican Average in Victory	Democrat and Third-Party Average in Defeat	Republican Average in Defeat	Democratic Average in Victory	Difference
Mountain						
Little Rock/Pine Bluff	Pulaski	55%	45%	37%	63%	−18%
Little Rock/Pine Bluff	Faulkner	59%	41%	47%	53%	−12%
Little Rock/Pine Bluff	Saline	63%	37%	48%	52%	−15%
Little Rock/Pine Bluff	Lonoke	65%	35%	47%	53%	−18%
Mountain						
Ft. Smith/Fayetteville	Sebastian	62%	38%	55%	45%	−7%
Ft. Smith/Fayetteville	Crawford	66%	34%	56%	44%	−10%
Hot Springs	Garland	54%	46%	47%	53%	−7%
Plains						
El Dorado	Union	59%	41%	48%	52%	−11%
Pine Bluff	Jefferson	34%	66%	30%	70%	−4%
Texarkana	Miller	58%	42%	47%	53%	−11%
Mississippi Alluvial Plain						
Jonesboro	Craighead	53%	47%	41%	59%	−12%

Note: The total population of these areas represents 41 percent of the state population.

the Marion Hotel to work on the campaign of Judge Frank Holt. "In signing up with the Frank Holt campaign . . . Young Bill was introduced as . . . a bright boy who goes to school up east . . . [and] was a favorite of the Democratic Party establishment."[24]

Party factions in Arkansas might differ over personality, say over Orville Faubus or J. William Fulbright, but when it came to elections they were all Democrats. In the 1970s Senators Dale Bumpers and David Pryor began their terms as ideological moderates, then drifted into a more liberal stance over time. It was a pattern that Bill Clinton would emulate.

The geographical base of Democratic strength is shown in Map 8.7 for four statewide races, all for the US Senate. In 1992 Dale Bumpers defeated a GOP newcomer, Mike Huckabee, for the right to represent Arkansas in the US Senate. Four years later Tim Hutchinson became the first Republican senator from Arkansas since 1879. His base was the counties west and north of Little Rock. In 1998 Blanche Lincoln defeated another newcomer, Fay Boozman, in the race between two women in this notoriously conservative state. Mark Pryor, son of former governor David Pryor, kept the Democratic presence in Washington when he defeated incumbent senator Tim Hutchinson in 2002. The final race was Blanche Lincoln's reelection in 2004.

The map shows a stark geographical pattern of partisanship. The plains of south Arkansas, along with like geography on the eastern boundary of the Mississippi River, are fertile Democratic counties. The alluvial plains are home to a substantial black population, and when their allegiance is joined to middle-class white voters in central and southern Arkansas, Democratic domination tops 50 percent.

The overlapping allegiance of voters in the four Senate races belies the closeness of partisanship across Arkansas. Table 8.8 shows that Republicans run up large margins in the Little Rock, Ft. Smith, and Fayetteville suburbs; while Democratic strength is in the sparsely populated counties in the hinterland. When Democrats win the GOP attrition in the suburbs is severe, as much as 18 percent in some counties, and into the double-digits in many others. Arkansas is the least urban of all the southern states, so Republican suburban strengths are easily offset by rural allegiance. The newspaper with the largest in-state circulation is the *Arkansas Democrat-Gazette*, so the arrival of a daily paper is yet another reminder of the historical partisan pattern.

Arkansas is classified as a traditionally Democratic state, but that label distracts from the occasional Republican allegiance in the state. The presidential vote shows that the Arkansas electorate is moving away from one-party partisanship and toward two-party competition. But in 2004 Democrats still had three of four congressional seats, both US Senate seats, and the state house and senate.

South Carolina

The depth of Democratic dominance at the state level in South Carolina was evident in 1924, when then US senator Cole Blease heard that the GOP presidential

Map 8.8 South Carolina: Political Partisanship in Statewide Elections

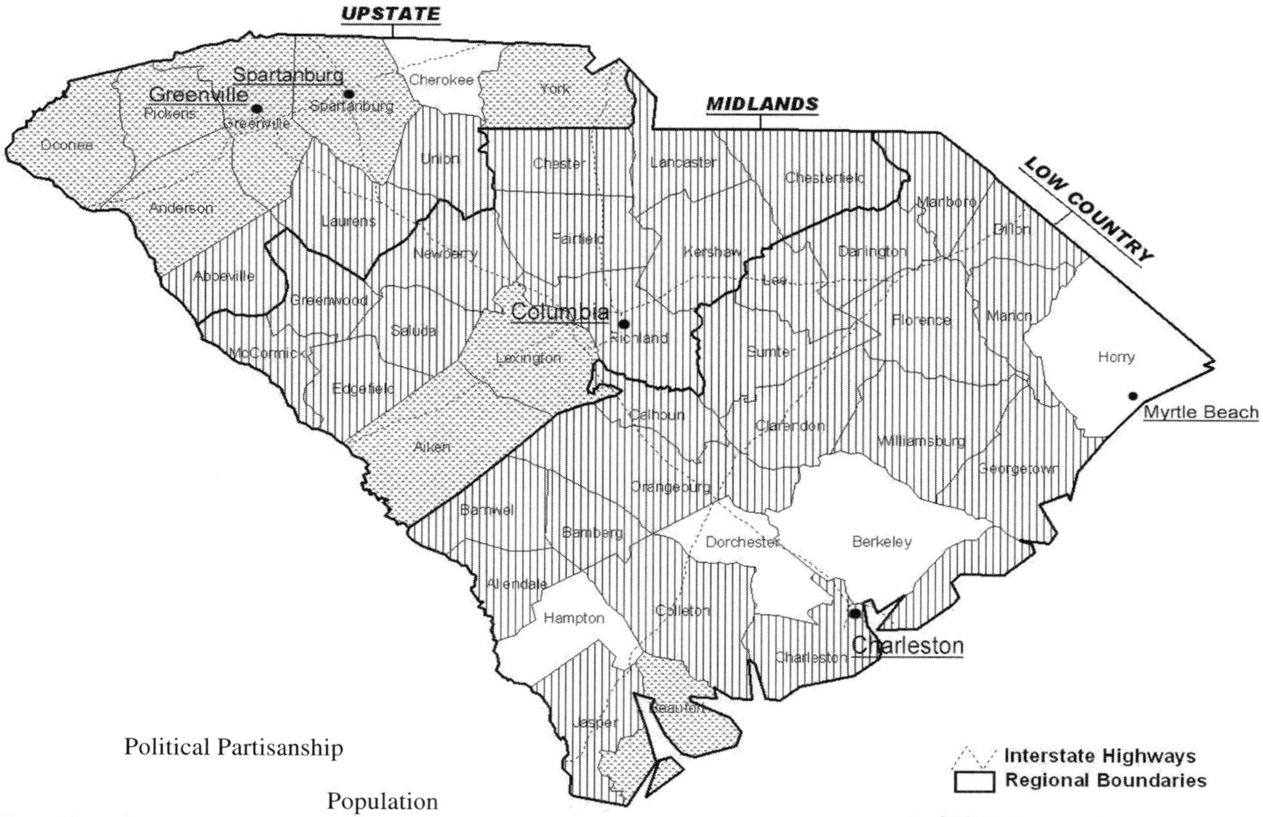
UPSTATE
MIDLANDS
LOW COUNTRY
Spartanburg
Greenville
Columbia
Myrtle Beach
Charleston
Oconee
Pickens
Greenville
Spartanburg
Cherokee
York
Anderson
Union
Chester
Lancaster
Chesterfield
Marlboro
Dillon
Laurens
Fairfield
Kershaw
Darlington
Abbeville
Newberry
Lee
Greenwood
Saluda
Richland
Florence
Marion
Horry
McCormick
Lexington
Sumter
Edgefield
Calhoun
Clarendon
Williamsburg
Aiken
Georgetown
Orangeburg
Barnwell
Bamberg
Dorchester
Berkeley
Allendale
Hampton
Colleton
Charleston
Beaufort
Jasper
Interstate Highways
Regional Boundaries
Democrat
Republican
Split

Political Partisanship

		Population	
Republican Counties	(9)	1,620,236	40.3%
Democratic Counties	(32)	1,882,160	46.9%

Table 8.9   South Carolina: Electoral Margins of Victory, by Party

| County | Presidential | | Statewide | | |
	Republican Average in Victory	Democratic Average in Defeaat	Republican Average in Defeat	Democratic Average in Victory	Difference
Upstate					
GSP: Greenville	63%	37%	59%	41%	–4%
GSP: Spartanburg	59%	41%	53%	47%	–6%
Midlands					
Columbia: Lexington	69%	31%	58%	42%	–11%
Columbia: Richland	42%	58%	37%	63%	–5%
Low Country					
Charleston: Charleston	52%	48%	41%	59%	–11%
Charleston: Berkeley	57%	43%	45%	55%	–12%
Charleston: Dorchester	61%	39%	48%	52%	–13%
Low Country					
Myrtle Beach: Florence	55%	45%	47%	53%	–8%
Myrtle Beach: Horry	56%	44%	50%	50%	–6%

Note: The total population in these areas represents 51 percent of the state population.

candidate received 1,123 voters out of 50,131 ballots cast in South Carolina. "I'm not surprised he got 'em," muttered Blease, "but I can't believe the Department of Elections had the nerve to count 'em."[25] Such was the reality of Democratic allegiance at the state level in South Carolina.

All this began to change with the civil rights movement, which put Democrats in the state at odds with their national party. The first crack in the traditional monolith appeared in 1948 and expanded in 1964, when Strom Thurmond changed parties, and the result trickled-down ten years later when the Republican nominee for governor, James B. Edwards, won office after the Democratic nominee was disqualified. Edwards was an oral surgeon from Charleston who had earlier won a primary election over retired Army general William Westmoreland. He capitalized on the "fresh face" image Republicans were able to generate with their conservative rhetoric, and hopes ran high in GOP circles that the trend would continue.

In the next election, the expected GOP realignment did not materialize. Control of the governor's mansion again returned to the Democratic Party in 1978 when Dick Riley carried every county in the state but one. Riley set a standard of leadership and popularity that few in either party have been able to match. His administration gained the confidence of the Democratic-led legislature and instituted a number of educational reforms. Riley's popularity led to a then unprecedented second four-year term. His success, and integrity, subsequently landed him the job as secretary of education for eight years in the Clinton administration. Within the state, Riley established a reputation that rose above politics.

The US Senate delegation from South Carolina was split in 1966, with Democrat Fritz Hollings opposite Republican Strom Thurmond on most issues. That partisan division would last thirty-six years. In 2002, at age 100, Thurmond stepped down to be succeeded by Republican Lindsey Graham. Stability at the national level left competition only at the state level. Republicans won the governorship in 1986, 1990, and 1994, but in 1998 their string of victories was broken by Jim Hodges, a little-known Democratic legislator from Lancaster County. Hodges identified the wedge issue to divide Republican voters enough to win office. The concern was South Carolina's notoriously poor schools, and the challenger promised to rescue education through a statewide lottery. The Democrats used the promised lottery issue, and the incumbent's personal unpopularity, to skin suburban voters away from the GOP. The success of a lottery in nearby Georgia, where revenues were used to finance scholarships at state universities and increase funding in the public schools, was enough to entice suburban voters to reject the status quo and give Hodges a victory.

Exit polls showed that almost a third of the voters calling themselves conservative voted for Hodges. A strong African American vote helped as well, with 40 percent of the Democratic vote coming from blacks. Those who were concerned about education, the economy, and taxes voted for Hodges, while voters distressed about gambling and ethics stayed Republican.[26]

Even though South Carolina has a conservative Republican image nationally, in 1998 Democrats were able to reelect Fritz Hollings to the US Senate and win the governor's office after a twelve-year hiatus.

Map 8.8 shows county partisanship for these three races. Democrats won three times in the 1990s, two in 1998, and the Hollings victory in 1992. The map shows that the upstate remained Republican, as did the Columbia suburb of Lexington and the Hilton Head community in Beaufort County. Democrats swept the midlands and the low county. Senator Hollings was from Charleston, and he always had a base of political support in the lower part of the state.

The strategy of the two parties is apparent from the information in the map. Democrats begin with a solid black voter base that is usually around 25 percent or more of the turnout in general elections, and very cohesive. On any Election Day at least 90 percent, and sometimes much more, of the African Americans go out to pull the Democrat lever. "For Democrats the essential task is to combine virtually all the black vote with enough of the white vote to produce a majority in the total electorate."[27] Democrats are at a disadvantage in urban areas, but the rural allegiance to the party remains strong.

Republicans, on the other hand, enjoy a huge numerical and popular advantage among whites, but the vote is not unified. Table 8.9 shows that the contest is over the suburban independent voter, who is nominally conservative but suspicious of political parties and open to occasional self-interested appeals. This is especially true of low-country voters who can be persuaded to abandon the GOP on occasion. If these voters are content with the Republican platform and candidate, then they win; but if an issue divides the conservative suburbanites, then the Democrats win. Democrat Jim Hodges used this tactic successfully in 1998 when he used the lottery issue to defeat incumbent Republican governor David Beasley in a rough-and-tumble gubernatorial election.

Table 8.9 shows that most of the attrition in the Republican vote was in the midlands and the low country. An unspoken, but very real, political legacy in the state holds that one of the two US Senate seats will belong to the city of Charleston, the home of former Senator Fritz Hollings. In 2002 and 2004 the adage was erased when voters sent two upstate congressmen, Lindsey Graham and Jim DeMint, to the US Senate. The low country has become home to thousands of retirees, who are normally sympathetic to the GOP, but they also have a frisky independence that causes them to flirt with new candidates and ideas.

Mississippi

Someone once asked Mississippi writer Eudora Welty why a state with such a high illiteracy rate has produced so many writers. Her reply bespoke the sentiment of generations of Mississippians. "Because," she said, "we have a lot of explaining to do." Justification of the past, with all its hidden foibles and secrets, is a lifelong occupation in this state.

No state in the South has a more militant history of opposition to racial change than this one. The name is synonymous with violence, hate, and the old ways. That obstinacy may be rooted in the statistic V. O. Key identified at midcentury: the state has a higher proportion of black population than any other in the South. In the 2000 census Mississippi still had the highest black population of any southern state.

For decades the Democratic Party was the guardian of the status quo in Mississippi. Politicians like James Eastland and John Stennis ran for office by explaining what they could do for the state as members of the majority party. Voters listened, and sent incumbents to Washington time and again. Even so, "Mississippi politics in the end reduces itself to a politics of frustration."[28]

The frustration came from all the promises unfulfilled, and all the hopes dashed on the rocks of a rude social reality. In the 1960s the federal antipoverty programs were going to remake the state, and in the 1990s it was gambling revenues that would change education levels. Each time the result was the same: Mississippi was last.

Political change came in 1978, when the retirement of James O. Eastland precipitated a split in the Democratic Party and Republican Thad Cochran won with a 45 percent plurality. In office, Cochran voted to extend the Voting Rights Act and to establish the federal Martin Luther King Jr. holiday. He developed a reputation of

Map 8.9   Mississippi: Political Partisanship in Statewide Elections

DELTA   **HILLS**

Interstate Highways
Regional Boundaries

Democrat
Republican

Political Partisanship

		Population	
Republican Counties	(37)	1,532,060	54%
Democratic Counties	(45)	1,312,598	46%

Table 8.10 Mississippi: Electoral Margins of Victory, by Party

Region/City	County	Republican Average in Victory	Democrat and Third-Party Average in Defeat	Republican Average in Defeat	Democratic Average in Victory	Difference
Delta						
Memphis	Desoto	66%	34%	50%	50%	–16%
Jackson	Hinds	46%	54%	44%	56%	–2%
Jackson	Rankin	75%	25%	71%	29%	–4%
Jackson	Madison	60%	40%	60%	40%	—
Vicksburg	Warren	55%	45%	56%	44%	+1%
Hills						
Hattiesburg	Forrest	60%	40%	51%	49%	–9%
Hattiesburg	Lamer	73%	27%	61%	39%	–12%
Biloxi/Gulfport	Harrison	60%	40%	54%	46%	–6%
Biloxi/Gulfport	Jackson	65%	35%	58%	42%	–7%
Tupelo	Lee	61%	39%	50%	50%	–11%
Meridian	Lauderdale	65%	35%	60%	40%	–5%

Note: The total population of these areas represents 42 percent of the state population.

effective constituency service, and support for programs like low-income school lunch programs, grants for black colleges, and loans for farmers. His pleasant personal demeanor and avoidance of racial invective helped spread Republican popularity.

When the Republicans became the majority party in the US Senate during the Reagan administration, Cochran ran as an incumbent who could get things done. He has used his position on the Appropriations Committee to fund defense programs that help employ people back home. In the process he has helped make voting Republican respectable in a state where it was once unthinkable. Trent Lott, first elected to the US Senate in 1988, was the beneficiary of this new allegiance. From 1996 until 2001 he was the GOP majority leader in the Senate. Unfortunately, the position carried little institutional power and Lott survived as an orderly and well-organized leader. His dismantling came in 2002 when he mentioned that in 1948 Mississippi voted for retiring South Carolina senator Strom Thurmond. The storm of press criticism and the tepid support of his fellow Republican senators led to Lott's resignation as majority leader. Once again, the racial legacy of Mississippi rose to cost a Washington politician his reputation.

"Mississippi's Senate politics, therefore, has basically involved a straightforward shift from conservative Democrats elected by whites to conservative Republicans still elected by whites."[29] The pattern of voting in the state remains overtly racial, and divides along the line separating the Delta flatlands from the wooded Hills.

Map 8.9 shows the county partisanship for a lone Democratic victory in a sea of Republican triumphs. In November of 1999 Democrat Ronnie Musgrove won the governor's office by a 49.6 percent to 48.5 percent margin. Musgrove is from Tocowa and was elected lieutenant governor in 1995. The governor's campaign was a contest between Musgrove and former congressman Mike Parker. The election was the closest in Mississippi history, and Map 8.9, when compared to the one showing Republican victories in the previous chapter, shows that Musgrove ran ahead of national Democrats in northeast Mississippi. The Delta counties remained the base of the Democratic vote, and the two candidates split Jackson, with Musgrove taking Hinds County, and Parker winning next-door Rankin County. In politics, Mississippi embodies the deepest elements of a southern state, and the Delta counties have the richest farmland, and some of the poorest people, in the region.

Mississippi law states that pluralities are unacceptable for winning statewide office, so the gubernatorial election was decided by the state house of representatives. After a tedious tabulation, reminiscent of the Florida recount, the candidates were tied with sixty-one legislative districts apiece. In the state house, Democrats held a big majority, and Musgrove was finally elected by a margin of 86 to 36.

Table 8.10 compares the Musgrove victory with the presidential margins in the previous chapter. The table shows that when Democrats win, the margins are reduced for Republicans in the populous counties of Desoto (Memphis area), Forrest and Lamar (Hattiesburg), Lee (Tupelo), and Lauderdale (Meridian). The losses for Republicans in these counties, along with the Musgrove victories in the northeast part of the state, sealed Parker's loss. This analysis, like that in Tennessee, shows how closely divided the electorate is in the reliably Republican state. But it also shows how a Democrat can emerge from the conservative political culture and win statewide office.

Democratic momentum was stymied in 2003, when Haley Barbour won the governor's mansion after the largest turnout in Mississippi state history. Barbour began his career in politics as director of political affairs in the Reagan White House, then served two terms as chairman of the Republican National Committee, including the 1994 elections when the GOP won control of both houses of Congress. His standing in the majority party proved an asset in 2005 when Hurricane Katrina devastated the state, and the close relationship between the governor and President Bush smoothed the way for aid to reach the Magnolia State. Barbour surprised skeptics, and alienated part of his constituency, when he signed a bill in October to allow the state's gambling casinos to move inland. In light of this success, it seems unlikely that Democrats can make much headway with voters over the way the governor handled hurricane relief.

Today Mississippi still ranks fiftieth on many scales. Yet for many natives of the state the sentiment is the same it was for writer Willie Morris, who wrote in 1954, "I know Mississippi and I loved what I saw."[30]

Louisiana

A twentieth-century observer once wrote: "Louisiana politics is of an intensity and complexity that are matched, in my experience, only in the Republic of Lebanon."[31] The southern part of the state is a Mediterranean maze and the northern part is Dixie conservative. New Orleans is a third part, different from the rest of the state, and the nation as well.

The free spirit of indulgence in New Orleans and south Louisiana permeates the politics of the state. Louisiana grants a level of political license to its politicians that is unknown to the rest of the country. As Willie Stark, the Huey Long–like character in Robert Penn Warren's masterful book, *All the King's Men*, says, "Do you think half the things I've done were clear, distinct, and simple in the constitution of this state?"[32] The politics of Louisiana are not clear, nor are they distinct or simple, but they have been Democratic and populist for most of recent history.

From 1928 to 1986, a Long—or Long relative—held elective office in Louisiana. "The Long experience has strengthened Louisiana's already strong predispositions—tolerance for corruption, disinterest in abstract reform, and taste for colorful extremists regardless of their short-term means or long-term ends—in a way that helps explain the rise and fall of such unlikely politicians as the four-term

Map 8.10   Louisiana: Political Partisanship in Statewide Elections

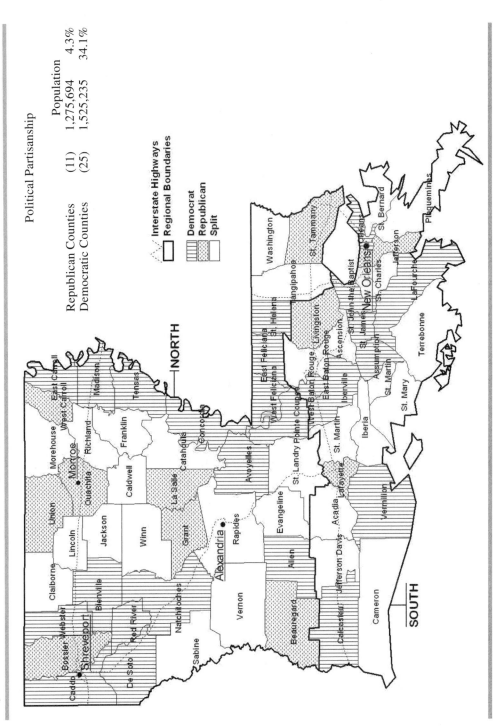

Political Partisanship

		Population	
Republican Counties	(11)	1,275,694	4.3%
Democratic Counties	(25)	1,525,235	34.1%

Interstate Highways
Regional Boundaries

Democrat
Republican
Split

Table 8.11   Louisiana: Electoral Margins of Victory, by Party

Region/City	County	Republican Average in Victory	Democrat and Third-Party Average in Defeat	Republican Average in Defeat	Democratic Average in Victory	Difference
North Louisiana						
Shreveport	Caddo	48%	52%	47%	53%	–1%
Shreveport	Ouchita	58%	42%	54%	46%	–4%
Shreveport	Rapides	54%	46%	50%	50%	–4%
Shreveport	Bossier	60%	40%	54%	46%	–6%
Shreveport	La Salle	63%	37%	60%	40%	–3%
South Louisiana						
New Orleans	Orleans	25%	75%	21%	79%	–4%
New Orleans	Jefferson	58%	42%	54%	46%	–4%
New Orleans	East Baton Rouge	52%	48%	49%	51%	–3%
New Orleans	St. Tammy	66%	34%	65%	35%	–1%
New Orleans	Lafayette	56%	44%	55%	45%	–1%
New Orleans	West Baton Rouge	44%	57%	41%	59%	–2%

Note: The total population of these areas represents 52 percent of the state population.

Governor Edwin Edwards and the onetime Ku Klux Klan leader and state legislator, David Duke."[33] Louisiana politicians have a knack of speaking to common people in everyday situations.

Map 8.10 shows the parish allegiance of Louisiana voters in three elections in the late 1990s. In 1996 Mary Landrieu, the oldest child of nine of the former mayor of New Orleans, Moon Landrieu, won election to the US Senate. In the same election, Bill Clinton won a convincing thirteen percentage point decision over Bob Dole. The third race was Mary Landrieu's narrow win in 2002, when she was the target of the National Republican Committee's effort to unseat her after her narrow victory six years earlier and George Bush's presidential win in 2000. In 2002 both parties made Louisiana a priority, and Landrieu's 52 percent to 48 percent win defied pundit predictions.

The map shows that the parishes with Democratic allegiance border the Mississippi River. The first Democratic axis is from East Carroll through Baton Rouge to the parishes around New Orleans ending in LaFourche Parish. A second pocket of Democratic allegiance is in the parishes outside and around Shreveport, and off Interstate 10 in the southwestern part of the state. Collectively, the parishes that voted Democratic in all three elections have a little more than one-third the state's population. The map confirms that Louisiana is a two-party competitive state.

When Democrats win statewide races they add parishes contiguous to the base parishes. In Mary Landrieu's 2002 victory, eight of nine parishes that joined the majority were next to base parishes that were three times loyal to the Democratic Party. Unlike the other southern states in our analysis, the secret of a Democratic victory is not seen in the urban areas of the state. Table 8.11 compares the Republican and Democratic percentages in victory and defeat. With the exception of heavily Democratic Orleans parish, home to the city of New Orleans, the difference between a Democrat win and loss is quite small. Democratic victories do not come from suburban areas deserting the Republican Party; instead the secret to winning lies elsewhere.

In keeping with the history of the state, the pattern for success in Louisiana is unique. Democrats win by consolidating the rural, not the urban areas. The parishes in the northwest corner and along the Mississippi River are crucial to any statewide victory. Gambling and urbanization are less important factors here, and the media markets do not dominate elections the way they do in other states. Instead, the crucial vote for a statewide victory is in the parishes that switch loyalty from election to election.

The future of Louisiana politics rests on the survival, or revival, of the city of New Orleans after the Hurricane Katrina disaster. The city is wedged between the Mississippi River on the south and Lake Pontchartrain on the north, and is below sea level, a saucer waiting to be filled. The hurricane flooded the city, killing hundreds of people and stranding thousands. In the weeks afterward, residents fled to shelters nationwide. Months after the waters receded, the population was less than one-quarter what it was before the August storm. Ray Nagin, the Democratic mayor of New Orleans, blasted the federal government for its slow response. For generations the Democratic vote in Louisiana was dependent on the turnout of voters in the largely black precincts of New Orleans. Now the streets and neighborhoods where those voters lived are vacant, and the future of two-party politics in the state depends on where—and how—the city returns to life.

Summary

V. O. Key stated in the 1946 original memo justifying the writing of *Southern Politics* that the region was a distinct political entity for two reasons. The first was the high black population in states in the South, and the second was the predominance of strength held by the Democratic Party, "so consistently that we have what is called a 'one-party' system."[34]

Today, one-party politics is dead in the South, but two-party competition has not replaced it. Instead the states vary as to their competitiveness and allegiance to either party. In the same election southern voters have voted Republican at the presidential level, and changed their loyalty to Democrats for governor or US senator. Over time Texas became a reliably Republican state, while Arkansas retained its one-party Democratic moniker V. O. Key gave it fifty years ago.

What all the southern states have in common is the burgeoning of the modern metropolitan South, and it is difficult to see how this growth helps Democrats. As the population increasingly chose to live in and around cities, the electorate became more concentrated and the politics changed accordingly. Two-party politics accompanied the increase in urban living, but the metropolitan vote is not unified, instead it is divided by partisans and ideological differences. As Juliet Gainsborough describes in her book, *Fenced Off*, state conflicts can involve differences between suburbs and central cities.[35] When threatened with urban problems, suburbs can mobilize along ethnic and racial lines.

For Democrats to overcome Republican advantages in the suburbs they must unite the African American vote, both urban and rural, around a popular and moderate white candidate. The ensuing campaign must entice independent-minded mall shoppers into their camp. This was the strategy followed by Jim Hodges in South Carolina (1998) and Mark Warner in Virginia (2002), and by a host of candidates for decades in Georgia. The Texas delegation of 2002, which unsuccessfully offered minority candidates for the offices of governor and US senator, shows the relevance of this strategy.

Rural areas have not lost their clout in the face of this metropolitan consolidation. Central downtown areas, heavily populated with African Americans who vote Democratic, are ringed by white suburbs that are Republican in allegiance. It is not unusual for the two to cancel each other out, leaving the rural areas to decide the outcome. In the 2000 presidential election Bush and Gore ran fairly even in important metropolitan areas, but Bush ran stronger in the nonmetro areas. The pattern was repeated in the presidential election of 2004.

Notes

1. Ben Robertson, *Red Hills and Cotton*. Columbia: University of South Carolina Press, 1942, p. 8.
2. Personal interview with David Woodard, in the fall of 1994.
3. Earl Black and Merle Black, *The Rise of Southern Republicans*. Cambridge, Mass.: Belknap Press of Harvard University, 2002, p. 148.
4. Charles S. Bullock III and Mark J. Rozell (eds.), *The New Politics of the Old South*. Lanham, Md.: Rowman & Littlefield, 2003, p. 3.
5. Robert Penn Warren, *All the King's Men*. New York: Harcourt, Brace and Jovanovich, 1946, p. 119.
6. Gavin Wright, *Old South, New South: Revolutions in the Southern Economy Since the Civil War*. New York: Basic Books, 1986, p. 176.
7. Ferroll Sams, *Run with the Horsemen*. New York: Viking Penguin, 1982, p. 55.
8. The surveys of party activists are in Charles D. Hadley and Lewis Bowman (eds.), *Southern State Party Organizations and Activists*. Westport, Conn.: Praeger, 1995; John A. Clark and Charles Prysby (eds.), *American Review of Politics* 24 (Spring, 2003).
9. Southern Politics Collection, "Florida," Vanderbilt University, Special Collections.
10. www.pewtrusts.com/campaigndisclosure (2003).
11. Zell Miller, *A National Party No More: The Conscience of a Conservative Democrat*. Macon, Ga.: Stroud & Hall, 2003.
12. V.O. Key, *Southern Politics in State and Nation*. 2d ed. Knoxville: University of Tennessee Press, 1977, p. 83.
13. *Washington Post*, October 28, 2001.
14. Ibid., September 4, 2001.
15. Ibid.
16. Mark J. Rozell, "Virginia," in Charles S. Bullock III and Mark J. Rozell (eds), *The New Politics of the Old South*. 2d ed. Lanham, Md.: Rowman & Littlefield, 2003, p. 149.
17. Michael Barone, *The Almanac of American Politics: 2002*. Washington, D.C.: National Journal, 2001, p. 1447.
18. William D. Snider, *Helms and Hunt: The North Carolina Senate Race, 1984*. Chapel Hill: University of North Carolina Press, 1985, pp. 7–8.
19. Michael Barone, *The Almanac of American Politics*, pp. 1413, 1409.
20. Quoted in *Mobile Register*, April 28, 2002.
21. Earl Black and Merle Black, *The Rise of Southern Republicans*, p. 304.
22. Michael Barone, *The Almanac of American Politics*, p. 58.
23. James Glaser, *Race, Campaign Politics, and the Realignment in the South*. New Haven: Yale University Press, 1996, pp. 23, 196.
24. David Maraniss, *First in His Class: A Biography of Bill Clinton*. New York: Simon & Schuster, 1995, p. 75.
25. Harry S. Dent, *The Prodigal South Returns to Power*. New York: John Wiley and Sons, 1978, p. 3.
26. www.lexisnexis.com. Associated Press, "Key Findings from South Carolina Exit Poll," November 4, 1998.

27. Earl Black and Merle Black, *Politics and Society in the South*. Cambridge, Mass.: Harvard University Press, 1987, p. 143.

28. V.O. Key, *Southern Politics in State and Nation*, p. 230.

29. Earl Black and Merle Black, *The Rise of Southern Republicans*, p. 119.

30. Willie Morris, *North Toward Home*. New York: Dell Publishing, 1967, p. 141.

31. T. Harry Williams, *Huey Long*. New York: Alfred A. Knopf, 1969, p. 194.

32. Robert Penn Warren, *All the King's Men*, p. 136.

33. Michael Barone, *The Almanac of American Politics*, p. 661.

34. Southern Politics Collection, Vanderbilt University, Special Collections.

35. Juliet F. Gainsborough, *Fenced Off: The Suburbanization of American Politics*. Washington, D.C.: Georgetown University Press, 2001.

9
Leaders and Legislators

The journalists liked to call them "colorful." It was a word that masked the oftentimes outlandish behavior and rhetoric of southern politicians. In June of 1946, *Life* subscribers opened their magazines to read about the gubernatorial campaign of Jim Folsom, shown visiting Cullman, Alabama. Most of the pictures were standard campaign fare, with the candidate shaking hands and speaking on the stump, but one showed how "Big Jim" ended each working day. Folsom's naked six-foot-eight-inch frame was lathered up as he "sat in a bathtub so small he had to raise his bent knees as high as his shoulders."[1] He was a "colorful" campaigner.

Once in office the publicity was just as vivid. Expenses at Folsom's governor's mansion often ran to four hundred dollars a day, mostly for food and liquor. The rumor was that the booze was purchased from a tiny crossroads general store owned by Folsom's cousin in Cullman, Alabama. He was accused of siring children outside his marriage and in partial reprisal bought a state yacht and named it after his striking young wife, Jamelle. Whenever he was accused of something he responded with a plea of guilty. "Always enlarge on it, especially if it ain't so . . . you go on denying something, they'll say, hell, he's guilty."[2]

Exaggeration was at the heart of the "colorful" politicians of the South. In his first campaign for governor of Louisiana, Huey Long paced up and down with what one New Orleans reporter called a "panther tread." As he talked on he would gesticulate, rumple his hair, take off his coat and tie, then loosen his collar and shirt. One female voter said his appearance made her nervous. "I didn't know what he was going to take off next."[3]

On June 12, 1935, Huey Long engaged in a filibuster that gripped the attention of the whole nation. He talked continuously for fifteen and a half hours, lecturing on the Constitution, Judah P. Benjamin (the Confederate secretary of state from Louisiana), and a detailed description of how to fry oysters and prepare potlikker. Huey Long was the "colorful" senator from Louisiana.

The vividness of southern politics lived on in 1966, when George Wallace held his wife's hand as she ran for governor of Alabama. She stood aside and listened when he said, "I'm fighting this outlaw, beatnik crowd in Washington that has just about destroyed the federal government—and I'm trying to save it."⁴ Wallace's wife won, and he moved in down the hall from the governor's office to act as her adviser. The former governor, as well as his wife, was "colorful." Taken as a group, southern governors and legislators are a diverse lot, but they have one thing in common: a history of extravagant showmanship, violent expression, and memorable rhetoric in promoting the politics of the sectional faith.

How is it that a part of the country oriented to conservative values, fundamental Christianity, and sobriety produced so many legislators and governors who stood in stark contrast to those values? Part of the answer lies in the rural localism that once was a feature of southern politics. Historically, most natives of the South were comfortable and secure in their small communities. The state capital was a place of unfamiliar power, and what was known was suspect, given the amount of money involved and the way it was spent, so the rural population was willing to vote for most any candidate who promised to represent them against hostile values. The localism of the South left it vulnerable to the appeal of charismatic leaders, promising reform, who were at the same time bent on self-promotion. Imagine the campaign scene in east Texas, to workers in a cotton field, when a helicopter appeared overhead and these words came from on high like thunder: "Hello, down there! This is your friend, Lyndon Johnson, your candidate for the United States Senate. I hope you'll vote for me on Primary Day. And bring along your relatives to vote, too."⁵ The novelty of the visit alone was enough to swing an election.

The twentieth century trampled the seclusion of the South into oblivion, and its politicians gradually changed their ways to adapt to the new television motif. But the Mayberry-like historical isolation of the place left its citizens victims of promises made by candidates on courthouse lawns to men dressed in coveralls and women in gingham dresses. The original mismanagement of government in the South was made worse because the voters adored those who made their lives more difficult. The loyalty of an uneducated populace to a charismatic leader persisted in the face of a mountain of evidence confirming corruption of the public purse. It didn't matter what the facts were; if the people believed something was real it was real in its consequences. When Huey P. Long died in 1935, one hundred thousand people turned out for the funeral. Almost all were poor whites, who remembered Long's "Every Man a King" economic appeal. In Georgia, Governor Gene Talmadge defended himself to his constituents by saying, "Sure I stole, but I stole for you," and all was forgiven.⁶

All this was part of the "colorful" tradition of southern political leadership. It was part of a political culture that indulged the leaders because someone else had always made the important decisions for the voters. Behavior in public office, which was scandalous elsewhere, was commonplace in the South. It was not *that* unusual for house Democrats in the 2003 session of the Texas legislature to leave the state to avoid a quorum because a redistricting bill threatened the party's state senators and congressional incumbents. After all, in 1979 twelve liberal Texas state senators "broke quorum" and went into hiding from the Texas Rangers so they wouldn't have to vote on a presidential primary bill they opposed. The "Killer Bees," as they were called at the time, prevailed on the floor of the house by attracting national publicity for unconventional behavior. The Ardmore (Oklahoma) Democrats and the Albuquerque (New Mexico) Democrats of 2003 fame were only keeping alive a Texas tradition that stretched back decades. In fact, eccentric behavior, both personal and professional, was synonymous with politics in the South.

Overlooked in the press coverage of the colorful antics and verbal hyperbole of southern politicians is the fact that they presided over some of the largest, and most important states in the country. Honest people were left speechless in the face of their elected leaders' notorious antics and publicity stunts. No matter how significant a record an elected politician compiled for integrity and trustworthiness, it could be wiped out in an instant by a governor's or legislator's outrageous behavior. The reputation of a state and its leaders was affected nationwide.

Robert Penn Warren, author of the 1946 Pulitzer Prize–winning book *All the King's Men*, once shared the story of a trip he made from the West Coast back to the South shortly after Huey Long was assassinated. At gas stations and motels on the trip, perfect strangers walked up to engage him in conversation about life and politics in Louisiana when they noticed his license plate from the state. That trip was one reason why Warren decided to write his novel, which was a thinly veiled chronology of the rise to power of a demagogue in a poor southern state. The antics of southern politicians were an obsession with national journalists, especially in the Depression and postwar years.

Present-day governors and state legislators in the South wrestle with the legacy of eccentric personalities and "country bumpkin" politicians from the past who spouted racial slurs and were careless about the details of government. Virtually every southern state has some tale to tell. The political machines of Byrd and Crump in Virginia and Tennessee, respectively, impressed V. O. Key. The conservative antics of Jesse Helms and Strom Thurmond became legend in North and South Carolina. The racial invectives of a Ben Tillman, James K. Vardeman, or George Wallace were imputed to the whole region.

The roots of the stereotypes are historical, in that political power in the South was originally reserved for the few, the elite, who spoke for dominant economic interests in the state. The traditional culture dictated a passive electorate. Populist appeals produced eccentric candidates who could capture the agrarian population isolated from one another and vulnerable to verbal manipulation. V. O. Key classified the southern states as "loose factional systems" that discouraged political opposition and conflict. Southern governmental efficiency came in the "Bourbon" era after Civil War Reconstruction, when carpetbagger extravagances were corrected by lower budgets, reduced credit, and minimal taxation. Salaries for public officials were fixed at absurdly low levels and political power was vested in state legislatures instead of state executives.

Elected officials were put in office to protect the status quo, and not to initiate reforms. A leader's rhetoric and antics were little more than flag-waving patriotism coupled with racial appeals about a mythical past suddenly threatened by outside ideas. Almost no changes ever took place. Some politicians were colorful because they were willing to play the "race card." Take, for example, the political career of Ellison D. "Cotton Ed" Smith, a US senator from South Carolina, who earned his nickname organizing farmers across the southeast into the Southern Cotton Association. Smith attracted national recognition when he twice walked out of the 1936 Democratic National Convention in Philadelphia—once when a black minister gave the invocation and again when a black congressman was presented as a speaker. The "Phillidefy Story" was Cotton Ed's contribution to political rhetoric in his home state. On the stump, Smith's audience requested a version of the "Phillidefy Story," which grew larger in each retelling. A description of city life, freethinking Yankee ideas, and the threat they posed to regional values became his signature in his native state. Smith proclaimed, "White supremacy . . . can no more be blotted out in the hearts of South Carolinians than can the scars which Sherman's artillery left on the State House in Columbia."[7]

The state of South Carolina, and the voters across the entire region who shared Smith's racial views, paid a price for these antics. In the 1930s New Deal insiders ignored Smith, despite his chairmanship of the Senate Agriculture and Forestry Committee. He remained popular in his home state, with a secure political future but without influence in Washington and largely ineffective.

No Roosevelt initiative was more suspect among southern leaders than the president's efforts on behalf of blacks. President Roosevelt appointed African Americans to federal offices in the North, and granted federal relief on the basis of need instead of race. Cotton Ed labeled the New Deal, "the most tragic era of American life." Roosevelt retaliated by trying to unseat the crusty old spellbinder in the 1938 US Senate race. This campaign was part of FDR's broader effort following the failure of his "court-packing" plan. Smith was reelected, but his victory proved pyrrhic. When he returned to Washington he was a marked man. All federal patronage in the state was taken from Smith's hands and he was unwelcome at the White House. In short, his antics cost him any opportunity to help the people he represented. A gesture by a constituent summed up the changing reality for Smith when the senator received a miniature celluloid doghouse with a picture of himself inside. "I've spent thirty-one years in the Senate," groaned Cotton Ed with a nod toward Roosevelt's office up Pennsylvania Avenue, "and now I'm in the doghouse."[8]

Smith was not alone. The more attention southern leaders attracted nationally, the stronger their reputations were at home, but the greater damage they did to their constituents in the eyes of the nation. The problems of underdevelopment were ignored by leaders caught up in the histrionics of their own populist political campaigns and press attention. The ideal of southern leadership centered on the ability to get elected, and that often involved flamboyant antics delivered to win party primaries that catered to the "bumpkin" stereotype. Governing was secondary to getting elected, and some of the administrations of southern politicians were as inept as any in the nation's history.

The persistence of southern "color" in the governor's office, and the effects leadership has on life in an entire state, make a discussion of state executives necessary. This chapter first examines the governor's office in southern states, and then the legacy of regional leadership in the state legislature. In time these offices escaped, along with the rest of the region, the stereotypes and constraints of the past. In the South, the institutions were slow to change because of statutory and constitutional restrictions, but eventually the native suspicion of state politicians was overcome by the needs of an urban electorate bathed in the problems of modernity.

Southern Governors

In the minds of voters, the governor sits at the apex of power and influence in a state, but that image can be misleading. The powers of the gubernatorial office were severely circumscribed at the nation's founding because of reaction to the strength of most colonial governors. The English government exercised authority through the royal governor as an agent of the crown, and officials had broad discretionary power. "He arrived in his domain," records a history of the time, "with elaborate instructions to implement his prerogatives."[9]

Colonial governors had the power to summon and dissolve the legislature and appoint officials, they served as commander-in-chief of the military and could issue royal proclamations. Some governors were weak and others unpopular. The most famous was Sir William Berkeley who came to Virginia in 1642 and held office until 1677. But the success and length of his tenure was the exception; few governors stayed long term and most tired of contending with the colonial demand for self-government.

After the American Revolution the new state constitutions drew upon the foundations of English law to empower legislatures over executives. Despite what was said in preambles about the sovereignty of the people, the southern states were run by landed aristocrats with the education and breeding to exercise control over the populace. Legislative power meant greater freedom for oligarchies to regulate who participated in elections and ran for office. In South Carolina, for example, an individual voter was required to have twenty-five acres or more of land; a state senator had to be worth 2,000 pounds and a governor must show a net worth of 10,000 pounds.[10]

The general populace of the southern states accepted the leadership of their economic and social superiors, and the governor was not expected to advocate the cause of the common people. Instead, he was expected to provide institutional care of the state's businesses in agreement with the ruling elites. The major power of the office was military, with state constitutions designating him as commander-in-chief. Executive terms were short, and while some states allowed succession, the governor's power was subservient to that of the legislature.

Gradually the governor's office benefited from the popularity of the presidential example. After Andrew Jackson's robust presidency, suffrage was expanded and the job shifted to one of administration. The major executive task was filling vacant appointments and coordinating departments created by the legislature. An effective governor had to deal with the politics of personalities and issues. Governors had neither the constitutional authority nor the personal power to control their own branch of government. A so-called long ballot meant voters elected a number of constitutional officers, and governor had to share power with other politicians who won statewide races just like he did. Executives were not expected to be problem solvers; instead they had more ceremonial and ambassadorial duties.

In the early decades of the twentieth century the Progressive movement influenced the conduct of the office. "In general they sought to impose a greater measure of social order, to foster economic opportunity and development, and to protect the weak and unfortunate in deserving cases."[11] Reforms required government empowerment and regulation, so states adopted new statutes to facilitate these developments.

The statewide Democratic primary, implemented in all southern states by 1915, meant that voters could elect reformers to railroad and public utility commissions. Huey Long used his election to the Louisiana Railroad Commission in 1912 at the age of twenty-five as a platform for publicity to later run for governor.[12] Reform governors, like Hoke Smith of Georgia and Napoleon Broward of Florida, strengthened the authority of boards and commissions that regulated the railroads. The agrarian population responded by reelecting southern populist reformers.

In some cases the governor was able to control the state through his management of the Democratic Party. Originally the candidate had to pull together a coalition large enough to ensure his nomination, and once in office he had to manage his party's legislators and policy agenda. Ambition for reelection or advancement was the major informal requirement for office. In times of recession the state was able to offer jobs to people for political loyalty. Again, Huey Long used the power of state contracts to rise to power, "because he could offer jobs to people who would go with him."[13] The power of appointments, and patronage at their disposal, increased the influence of state executives.

The Great Depression of the 1930s pointed out just how paltry state power was when faced with the massive social problem of unemployment and population displacement. The states were unable to dispense even piecemeal remedies and the main job of the state executive consisted of begging for help. Southern governors were depicted as "Good-time Charlies," meaning that they raged against the conditions and their fear of federal power, while at the same time asking Washington to help address their most pressing problems. In the South, the behavior of governors attracted national attention, and collectively they gave the impression that the governors' mansions were inhabited by eccentric clowns.[14]

The most notorious antics were by Huey P. Long, who conducted the affairs of state from his bedroom and once received the commander of a German warship in green pajamas. These were the years when Germany was rearming, and the snub of a military captain had international diplomatic repercussions. Long devised a scheme for federal spending far more lavish than anything Franklin Roosevelt proposed, and was the greatest threat to FDR's presidency before his assassination in 1935. Millions outside the South admired Huey Long's daredevilry, irreverent bad manners, and outspoken audacity. But Louisiana was not alone in having flamboyant personalities in the gubernatorial office.

W. Lee "Pass the Biscuits Pappy" O'Daniel entered Texas politics in 1938 after 54,446 radio listeners urged him to run for office. At campaign rallies his son and daughter would pass through the crowd holding little flour bags labeled "Flour: not Pork" for donations. The campaign played on the popularity of country music with a band, "The Light-Crust Doughboys," useful in drawing a crowd. He had absolutely no previous political experience, in fact he had never even cast a vote, but he toured the state in a red circus wagon with his daughter, Molly, and fiddler son Patty Boy. He drew the largest crowds in the history of Texas politics.

In the election "Pappy" O'Daniel won without a runoff with 30,000 more votes than the next eleven candidates combined. In office he vetoed legislation, passed off the most serious political questions with a quip, and appointed inexperienced men to run the most important departments of state government. When asked what taxes he would propose for the debt-ridden Lone Star State, he said "no power on earth" could make him say. The voters loved him, and reelected him governor in 1940 by an even larger margin than two years earlier. In the 1941 US Senate primary O'Daniel beat Lyndon Johnson by 1,311 votes, most collected in questionable voting practices in rural south Texas counties.[15]

Another 1947 *Life* magazine article featured the antics of Alabama governor "Kissin'" Jim Folsom, this time at an "Air Day in Texas" event near Harlingen, Texas. Photographers caught Folsom kissing seven different Texas beauties, and these were the closed-eyes, on-the-lips variety of passion not usually seen in magazines, let alone featuring a sitting governor. The next morning Folsom ordered beer with his breakfast, then smacked his lips and loudly proclaimed to all within earshot, "Only thing better than beer, is whiskey."[16] Pictures of the governor in his undershirt, unbuttoned trousers, and socks without shoes made respectable Southerners cringe with embarrassment.

The South was full of these images. Louisiana governor James Houston

Vignette 9.1 Edwin Edwards (1927–)

In a state known for flamboyant politicians, Edwin Edwards emerged in the 1970s and 1980s as the most controversial, powerful, and quotable governor since Huey Long. "People say I've had brushes with the law," said Edwards. "That's not true. I've had brushes with overzealous prosecutors." In the end the zealots won. Edwards was convicted in federal court in 2000 on seventeen counts of fraud and racketeering, and sentenced in 2001 to ten years in federal prison and fined $250,000.

A Cajun from Markville, where his parents were sharecroppers, Edwards graduated from LSU law school at age twenty-one. He settled in Crowley, where he practiced law as one of two local attorneys who conducted business in both English and French. Edwards often used French in dealing with older clients, and translated their statements into English for court proceedings.

Edwards drew on his Cajun constituency for support in his political career, first for the Crowley City Council in 1954, then the Louisiana state senate and the US Congress from 1965–1972. In the 1972 Democratic primary Edwards won by only 5,400 votes out of over a million cast and cruised to a comfortable victory over the Republican candidate in the general election.

Edwards was the first governor elected from Cajun Louisiana, and he remained in the public limelight throughout his years as governor. He would win office four times, and could be described as the best kind of politician in the worst possible kind of way. Glib and colorful, Edwards was a powerful stump speaker, and yet at ease with television. Once when asked who was the greatest politician he'd seen in Louisiana in his lifetime, he responded: "My lifetime? It would have to be every time I shave and look at him in the mirror."

Edwards's rise from poverty contained the seeds of his eventual destruction. He was an inveterate womanizer and dealmaker who was particularly fond of gambling. In 1983, while campaigning for his third term as governor, Edwards adopted the slogan, "Laissez les Bon Temps Rouler" (Let the Good Times Roll). They did, and the governor was indicted, but not convicted, for mail fraud, obstruction of justice, and public bribery regarding the sale of hospital certificates. The collapse of the petroleum market in the mid-1980s left the state in a deep financial crisis and eroded Edwards's popularity.

In typical Louisiana fashion, Edwards saved the best for last. In 1991 he entered a runoff election for governor that drew national attention when he faced former Klansman David Duke. Virtually every political leader in the state, Republican and Democrat alike, and even the Republican president of the United States George Bush, endorsed Edwards. The popular campaign slogan advised: "in a choice between a racist and a crook, vote for the crook." Edwards won, and immediately established the Louisiana Lottery.

Legalized gambling expanded in the state to include riverboat casinos, land-based casinos, and video poker. In 1995 the US Attorney's Office in Baton Rouge released transcripts of wiretaps and tape recordings between a video-poker operator and prominent Louisiana politicians. Gradually the evidence began to point to Edwards who was eventually convicted of fraud and racketeering over a scheme to extort money from applicants for casino licenses. The man who once described an opponent as "taking an hour and a half to watch *60 Minutes*" was sentenced to prison at age seventy-five.

"Jimmy" Davis balanced a country music career with the duties of office for two terms, 1944–1948 and 1960–1964. His hit, "You Are My Sunshine," remains the Louisiana state song to this very day. "Ole" Gene Talmadge liked to campaign in red galluses as he traveled to rural county seats in Georgia to rail against outsiders, and South Carolina governor-elect Strom Thurmond stood on his head before cameras to impress his wife-to-be. He garnered nationwide notoriety in *Life* magazine for the feat (November 4, 1954).

No other part of the country could rival the South when it came to flamboyant politicians, be it the tricks of the legislature or the behavior of ruling governors. Somehow it is not surprising to hear that Louisiana governor Earl K. Long considered himself: "40 percent Catholic and 60 percent Baptist . . . [and was] in favor of *every* religion, with the possible exception of snake-chucking [because] anyone who presumes to know how he stands with Providence [so much] that he will let a snake bite him . . . deserves what he's got coming to him."[17] Nor was it unusual to learn that Governor Earl Long was subsequently committed to the state mental institution by his wife after he ran off with New Orleans stripper Blaze Starr. To the chants of "Yea, Uncle Earl; Yea, Uncle Earl," the judge rapped his gavel and declared "case dismissed" on the charge of insanity.

Racism was part of the color. In January of 1967, when the South was in the midst of the most dramatic change in its history, the civil rights movement sparked a white backlash in one of the region's most progressive states. Lester Garfield Maddox was elected governor of Georgia, and celebrated by peddling a bicycle backwards down Peachtree Street in Atlanta. For a decade prior to his election, Maddox made himself a symbol of white resistance to integration. In a city that prided itself on racial toleration, he advertised that his fried chicken restaurant, the Pickwick, was a place where the management had the right to refuse service to anyone.

In 1964 he attracted national attention when he refused to obey the recently passed Civil Rights Act by denying service to blacks and distributing axe handles to his supporters in a show of defiance to the new law. He won the gubernatorial election of 1966 with little financial support and no assistance from established political leaders. Aside from the antics of the chief executive in the national press and on television, the Maddox administration was uneventful. In fact, it may have been the foundation for Jimmy Carter's legislative progressivism four years later. The two men remained personal and political rivals for years to come, Maddox clinging to the past while Carter embraced the future.

The antics of southern politicians were not unique to the Depression or the racial acceptance of the civil rights movement. In 1979, when state legislatures in the South were passing constitutional reforms to strengthen the hand of the governor as a chief executive, one elected official was abusing the privilege. Tennessee governor Ray Blanton ordered the commutations of twenty-four convicted murders and twenty-eight other prisoners before his signing frenzy ended with the early swearing-in of his successor.[18] One of the prisoners allegedly involved in the pardon-selling scheme was James Earl Ray, the convicted assassin of Martin Luther King Jr. Blanton was elected with the slogan, "We Need that Ray of Blanton Sunshine," but his administration collapsed in disgrace three days before the inauguration of Lamar Alexander—appropriately enough, at night. Tennessee has a history of political moderation, two-party competition, and respectable representation, but the Blanton fiasco made the state a national spectacle.

There are other tales of outlandish activity by southern politicians, be they mayors, legislators, or governors. Local officials were known to alter election returns upon request, and county judges were political operators as much as judicial ministers. A mayor in Nashville was said to "work better drunk than any other one did sober." Suffice it to say in summary that the poverty, despair, and one-party political tradition were a cultural stage on which the elected actors strutted in comedic form. However, this is not to deny that many governors had notable accomplishments. Huey Long developed the infrastructure of Louisiana, Jimmy Davis left office with a budget surplus, and Jim Folsom improved Alabama's schools. Yet what makes them memorable is not their policy accomplishments, but their public behavior in office. Most of these antics began in the years of the Great Depression, when governors had neither the money nor the power to change the conditions of their state, but the reasons were deeper than the historical times. The office of governor was weak; the job paid next to nothing and attracted a certain type of personality. The occupants were figureheads, and they behaved accordingly.

The Modern Era

The low expectations for southern governors began to change after World War II, along with the economic fortunes of the region. The absence of a well-defined, competitive two-party election system still meant that they could compensate for a lack of official power with histrionics, but most were accountable to fierce intraparty competition as a substitute. The coming of two-party politics increased the responsibilities of office and attracted more appealing candidates. The Democratic primary victory was no longer tantamount to winning the election, and the electorate gradually became more independent. When states had to provide better highways, infrastructure, and regulation of development, accountability came with campaign promises. The civil rights movement muted the overt racism of political campaigns, and party competition led to more intense electoral combat.

Another change in southern politics, as well as national politics, was the emergence of television as a medium for candidates and officials to communicate with the electorate. Television focused more attention on the informal aspects of the office than print journalism. Each day politicians had to offer on-camera comments about legislation and appear at media events, to give short talks for local news station coverage. The emergence of the new medium ruined the career of someone like "Big Jim" Folsom of Alabama. In 1946 Folsom crisscrossed the rural areas of the state with his "Strawberry Pickers" band and a corn-shuck mop with wooden bucket and the words "Suds for Scrubbing" to symbolize his determination to "scrub out the capitol from basement to flag pole." An Alabama farmer interviewed in 1947 summed up Folsom's appeal: "Us poor farmers have been left out in the past, and we think that Big Jim is interested in us and will do something for us for a change."[19] He won two terms. But when he entered the 1962 primary, Folsom had to make a final campaign talk on television. He appeared drunk on camera, could not remember the names of his sons when he introduced them, and broke into a spontaneous singsong chant of "Me too!" to describe the programs of his opponent.[20] In the primary he finished third, as people went to the polls to ask: "Did you see Jim Folsom drunk on TV last night?" Folsom's alcoholism was a political liability anywhere, but what was disguised, and even funny, before a rural audience was tragic in the sterile television studio.

Gradually governors learned how to cope with the new media environment. A group of political scientists has written, "Probably the most significant source of informal power available to governors is their relationship with the public through the media and through other modes of contact."[21] Governors now planned news conferences and issued press releases to control evening news coverage in local media markets instead of mounting stages to speak spontaneously. In the modern era most southern governors limited their access to the media for fear that a misstatement could disrupt their planned political agenda. Television election campaigns created blow-dried politicians instead of trailer-bed orators. Chief executives now stood before joint sessions of the legislature with polished, compact addresses watched by statewide constituents who expected a political delivery appropriate for a professional image. It didn't take long for the natural aptitude of southern politicians to blossom before television audiences just like they once did for crowds on the county square. First, Jimmy Carter, then Bill Clinton and George W. Bush rose from southern governorships to the US presidency. Their accomplishments in office were a negation of past memories, of colorful governors who were unable to help their constituents.

The southern culture traditionally dictated that the office of the governor be structurally very weak. In the southern states budget development was often a shared responsibility with the legislature. The concept of plural state executives remains in the number of separately elected executive branch officials, like lieutenant governor and attorney general. For the chief executive this means working with other officials who have a claim to statewide political success. The appointment powers of southern governors were less than other states, and often required legislative approval. Until recently, many chief executives in the South could not succeed themselves, and two-year terms were used for those that could.

A state's constitution is the basic framework for operating government, constraining political power and limiting the scope of government. The typical southern state constitution has several revisions, numerous amendments, and is often quite lengthy. Alabama, for example, has the longest state constitution in the country, 5,204 provisions compared to only 240 in the federal Constitution. Southern states have had more constitutions than other states because their history of rebellion required at least one and sometimes numerous reconstitutions of state government. They were among the earliest colonies, and their Civil War recalcitrance led to frequent administrative replacements. They rewrote their constitutions during Reconstruction, revised them after the end of Reconstruction, and altered them again following World War II, particularly during the reapportionment revolution of the 1960s.

The turnover in the office of governor has traditionally been high in the South because of constitutional limits on the terms of office and inadequate revenues to meet campaign promises once in office. Beginning in the 1970s, southern states revised or amended their constitutions to strengthen the institutional powers of the governor and permitted four year and consecutive terms. These changes are displayed in Table 9.1. Three states changed the length of the governor's term and all but Virginia allow for consecutive terms. Five states adopted new constitutions in the period between 1950 and 2000. Virtually every state grants the governor a line item veto.

Southern governors often came to office with unusual personal power to offset their limited institutional or constitutional responsibilities. They had exceptional control over their personal schedule, staff administrative jobs, road projects, purchasing, and public improvements. In time the formal powers of the gubernatorial office began to change as well. As four-year repeating terms became the norm, and the appointive power of the governor began to expand, most southern governors acquired the veto. These powers enabled them to negotiate on the budget even though they had limited ability to create it.

The formal powers granted by constitutions, statutes, and referenda were important in explaining executive leadership in the southern states, but the informal powers inherent in the culture counted for something as well. Most southern states retained a huge native-born population, and in the smaller southern states people often had a connection to politics at some personal level. Relationships were such that family ties to previous governors or state senators linked the government to people in informal ways. Take, for example, the memories of Cornelia Wallace, second wife of Governor George Wallace and niece of former Alabama governor Jim Folsom. "Uncle Jimmy ran his campaign out of his house or out of his car . . . the dining room was always full of campaign literature . . . [to] rural route box holders. One day he drank a glass of buttermilk with a family while he listened to their problems [and promised] to pave the dirt road in front of their house . . . after he won he appropriately named it Buttermilk Road."[22]

As the populations expanded the personal aspects of government gave way to

Table 9.1 Southern State Constitutions

State	Number of Constitutions	Effective Date of Most Recent	Governor's Terms				Line Item Veto
			1950	2000	Year Changed	Consecutive Terms	
Alabama	6	1901	4	4	N/A	2	Yes
Arkansas	5	1874	2	4	1984	2	Yes
Florida	6	1969	4	4	N/A	2	Yes
Georgia	10	1983	4	4	N/A	2	Yes
Louisiana	11	1975	4	4	N/A	2	Yes[a]
Mississippi	4	1890	4	4	N/A	2	Yes
North Carolina	3	1970	4	4	N/A	2	No
South Carolina	7	1896	4	4	N/A	2	Yes
Tennessee	3	1870	1	4	1954	2	Yes
Texas	5	1876	2	4	1974	No Limit	Yes
Virginia	6	1971	4	4	N/A	1	Yes

Source: Harold W. Stanley and Richard G. Niemi. *Vital Statistics on American Politics: 1900–2000.* Washington, D.C.: CQ Press, 2000. pp. 288–297; Thad Beyle, *State and Local Government.* Washington, D.C.: DQ Press, 2000, p. 212.

Note: a. For appropriations only.

the media of more polished communications. The recasting of state government took place across the nation in the 1960s and 1970s, and the South followed suit with the rest of the country. Governors made these reforms central issues when they campaigned for office, and their crusades were part of a national effort to strengthen the office of lieutenant governor, enact legislative reapportionment legislation, and reform the state tax structure. Jimmy Carter ran as a "New Democrat" who brought "zero-based budgeting" to Georgia state government. Gradually the chief executives of the various states were given authority to reorganize state agencies and streamline the departments they supervised.

A comparison of the effects of these changes is seen in Table 9.2, which compares the formal powers of the governor for each of the fifty states at two points in time, in 1971 and 2003. The rankings evaluated governors on four criteria: (1) tenure potential, meaning their ability to succeed themselves once in office, (2) appointment powers, (3) budget power, and (4) veto power.[23] The rankings show a mixed record of success for the southern states in this period. The states of Texas and Georgia appear to have changed the most, positively for the former and negatively for the latter. North Carolina, Mississippi, and South Carolina remain mired at the bottom of the rankings and most southern states are in the second half of the list. The evidence shows that the southern states reformed their constitutions, along with the rest of the country. In the end, thirty years of change may have streamlined the office, but the changes didn't significantly alter the power of the southern governor relative to his or her peers in the rest of the country.

If the powers of the gubernatorial office remain minimal, how do southern governors survive, and even prosper? The answer appears to be in their use of the informal aspects of the office. In the 1970s governors began to shift their attention from negotiating with the legislature to the recruitment of industry. In an earlier time, out-of-state trips were looked upon as a waste of taxpayer money, and the appearance of a governor in a neighboring state or a foreign country was cause for scandal. The emerging global economy changed the role of the governor from domestic politician to spokesman and recruiter of industry. In 2003 Governor Perry of Texas and Governor Huckabee of Arkansas, both Republicans, competed with one another over the location of a Toyota truck manufacturing plant for their respective states. Texas won.

The role of governor as economic recruiter is not one historically associated with the office. Prior to the New Deal, every southern state had laws on the books limiting what localities could do to attract external investment. For example, the agrarian tradition in Mississippi resulted in a 1936 "BAWI" (Balance Agriculture With Industry) program in the first statewide effort to recruit businesses to a southern state.

As governor of Tennessee in the late 1970s and 1980s, Lamar Alexander argued that "a governor's role was to see the state's most urgent needs, develop strategies to address them, and persuade at least half the people that he or she is right."[24] In his first term, Governor Alexander put his convictions to work and spent

Table 9.2   Ranking of States on the Formal Powers of the Governor

State Rank in 1971	State Rank in 2003
1. New York	1. New York
2. Illinois	2. Alaska
3. Hawaii	3. Maryland
4. Wyoming	4. New Jersey
5. Michigan	5. Connecticut
6. Minnesota	6. Illinois
7. New Jersey	7. Utah
8. Pennsylvania	8. West Virginia
9. California	9. Hawaii
10. Utah	10. Minnesota
11. Connecticut	11. Pennsylvania
12. Delaware	12. **Tennessee**
13. Colorado	13. Nebraska
14. Ohio	14. New Mexico
15. Massachusetts	15. Michigan
16. Missouri	16. North Dakota
17. **Tennessee**	17. Ohio
18. North Dakota	18. South Dakota
19. Nebraska	19. **Texas**
20. Maryland	20. Kansas
21. **Virginia**	21. Wisconsin
22. **Alabama**	22. Maine
23. Arizona	23. Montana
24. Washington	24. Wyoming
25. Alaska	25. Massachusetts
26. Idaho	26. **Virginia**
27. Kentucky	27. Oregon
28. Montana	28. Arizona
29. Wisconsin	29. California
30. **Louisiana**	30. Idaho
31. Oregon	31. Iowa
32. Iowa	32. Kentucky
33. West Virginia	33. **Florida**
34. Oklahoma	34. **Louisiana**
35. **Georgia**	35. Rhode Island
36. **Florida**	36. Washington
37. Nevada	37. Colorado
38. Vermont	38. Delaware
39. **Arkansas**	39. Indiana
40. Maine	40. Missouri
41. Kansas	41. Nevada
42. Rhode Island	42. **South Carolina**
43. New Mexico	43. **Alabama**
44. South Dakota	44. **Arkansas**
45. New Hampshire	45. **Mississippi**
46. **North Carolina**	46. New Hampshire
47. Indiana	47. Oklahoma
48. **Mississippi**	48. **Georgia**
49. **Texas**	49. Vermont
50. **South Carolina**	50. **North Carolina**

Source: Sarah McCally Morehouse, *State Politics, Parties and Policy.* New York: Holt, Rhinehart and Winston, 1981, pp. 493–495; Sarah McCally Morehouse and Malcolm Jewell, *State Politics, Parties and Policy.* 2d ed. Lanham, Md.: Rowman & Littlefield, 2003, pp. 174–175.

time traveling abroad to showcase the merits of the Volunteer State. His efforts were rewarded in 1980 when Nissan motors announced it would build a plant south of Nashville that would ultimately employ over 5,000 people, and serve as a magnet to bring collateral industry to the middle Tennessee area. Economic success led to political success, and Governor Alexander won a second term in office. His early economic accomplishments became political capital that he successfully used to push through educational reform as a Republican governor in a state where Democrats dominated the legislature.

The true measure of any governor and administration is how well he or she actually performs the various roles for which they are individually responsible. The principal role of the chief executive is to set the tone and define the values of the state. In this regard several southern governors had noteworthy accomplishments: Carter on race in Georgia, Alexander and Clinton on private sector growth, and George W. Bush in education and the privatization of social services in Texas. The expanding economy of the 1990s allowed governors to expand their reforms and add services to the states.

State Legislatures

While governors may have attracted more attention, the office of state legislator most embodied the stereotype of a southern politician. The protection of local interests was paramount there. In a confidential memorandum to V. O. Key written in 1947, Alexander Heard tells how an illiterate character, named "Tom" here, from Clayton, Georgia, won election to the state senate. The man ran for, and habitually lost, every election race he entered, be it for sheriff, county clerk, or mayor. People sometimes threw a token vote his way, but since he couldn't read it didn't matter. But everybody in town loved him. Big and rangy, with a penchant for wide-brimmed Stetsons and hoedown music, he had been a bailiff at the courthouse for as long as anyone could remember.

In 1946, just before the Democratic primary, some county veterans got together and decided to back Tom for the state senate:

> Why not? They reasoned. We've sent all the best people to the Legislature. We've sent lawyers and doctors and schoolteachers and bankers and farmers. And what have they ever done for us? Absolutely nothing! Every one of them has gone to Atlanta, put his hand in the till and lined his pocket. So he is illiterate. He can't do worse than the people we've sent before.[25]

So the people of the county, accustomed to getting nothing from their government, decided to make it official. Of course the man won, and to quote the interview, "And sure enough, he did not do worse than his predecessors."[26]

For most of its history, and well into the twentieth century, state legislatures in the South were the repository of local characters, and local power by courthouse

---

Vignette 9.2　"Mr. Speaker," Thomas B. Murphy (1924–)

Thomas B. Murphy was the epitome of a country lawyer, a legislator, and the most powerful Democrat in Georgia politics. For forty-two years Tom Murphy represented counties that were once textile mill villages. For twenty-eight years he ruled the Georgia house of representatives with an iron gavel as speaker.

In 2002 the suburbanization of Atlanta caught up with Tom Murphy, and he lost by 505 votes to an upstart Republican. Murphy was a World War II Navy veteran, first elected to the legislature in 1960, and rose to become speaker fourteen years later. In the 1970s and 1980s he went toe-to-toe with governors, lieutenant governors, and Republicans. From his capitol office Murphy watched as former legislators Zell Miller, George Busbee, Joe Frank Harris, and Roy Barnes won the governorship. Each one had to deal with Tom Murphy.

Murphy assumed office when the county-unit system of Georgia politics was coming to an end. Under the county-unit rule all of Georgia's 159 counties were equally represented in the legislature regardless of population. Under the "one person, one vote" rule in the 1960s, metro Atlanta came to dominate legislative redistricting. Even though Murphy fought to fund major projects in Atlanta, his attention was never far from the rural areas of his childhood and heart. Many chairmanships in his tenure went to rural Democrats, and he regularly arranged for Republican incumbents to face one another as a minority-party punishment.

In 2002 Murphy campaigned on his record, wearing his trademark Stetson hat and handing out pencils fashioned with two erasers to look like his speaker's gavel. "Keep the gavel in the 18th," was his motto, but newer residents and younger voters in new subdivisions failed to appreciate his contributions.

In the end Tom Murphy was a victim of the very system of redistricting he used to punish his political opponents. The exurban reach of Atlanta, and the once-a-decade legislative redistricting, led to the elimination of the state's most powerful Democrat. He lost his seat on the same night that Georgia elected a Republican governor for the first time since Reconstruction.

---

politicians. A good legislator could prove his worth by defending the interests of his home county from new legislation and by getting state revenues for public works. This pervasive localism narrowed the perspective of the state administration to the distribution of favors statewide, often to the neglect of urban areas.

The power of governing politicians was most convincingly demonstrated through road-building programs. Even in hard times, state highway departments were ideal venues to distribute local favors for legislators. The state highway commission oversaw the spending of millions of dollars each year, and southern capitals usually had numerous mansions owned by highway contractors. In a single legislative year the road-building industry touched deposit holders, contractors, engineers, cement manufacturers, supervisors, and laborers. Thousands of jobs were at stake with these contracts as the most visible expression of government largesse.

Huey Long was a master at using road-building money to put together his notorious Louisiana political machine. Parishes in the state were pocked with inlets, waterways, and bayous that defied highway construction. The governor had complete control of all road building, so the delegates from one rural parish journeyed to Baton Rouge to talk to the governor about getting the first paved highway in their community. Long agreed to build the road, but stipulated that there was to be no organized opposition to his candidate for the state supreme court in the approaching election. The delegation returned home to beseech all local politicians with a newspaper ad reading: "We want that highway; don't keep us down in the mud."[27]

The local orientation of most Southerners meant they evaluated state government by the visibility of state programs in their county. Political relationships were dominated by the "courthouse rings" that linked locals to the state capital. No courthouse clique in any rural county ever existed as a formal political organization; rather it was a small group of men who ruled by virtue of their long residence, social prominence, and business ties. They exerted influence through personal relationships.

The state legislature in the first half of the twentieth century was the repository of these local elites. The focus of legislation was to accommodate the economic and cultural values of the home communities. The "county-unit" system of representation in Georgia, and the Byrd machine in Virginia, both used local ties to rural elites for support. Until midcentury the poll tax, literacy test, and other voter qualifications assured white domination, and exclusion of the uneducated, black, and poor from the ballot box.

The pervasive localism led to legislatures that were unrepresentative, malapportioned, and dominated by rural interests. They did not meet often or address major problems in the state; instead they lacked clerical staff and professional assistance. Urban areas were ignored in pending legislation. As a group, legislators were poorly paid and at the mercy of special interests.

All this changed in the 1970s. The reapportionment revolution was precipitated by the Supreme Court decisions of *Baker v. Carr* (1962) and *Reynolds v. Sims* (1964). "The decade from about 1965 to 1975 can appropriately be termed the period of 'the rise of the legislatures.'"[28] Legislatures were apportioned equitably, terms were lengthened, and pay improved. The body, as an institution, became better staffed and began to address serious problems of infrastructure, tax policy, and welfare reform. The purpose of all the reorganization was to increase governmental accountability and efficiency by making the body a more professional organization.

Legislative reform provoked new criticism, that of legislators becoming "professional politicians" at the expense of their fellow citizens. As legislatures grew more professional they attracted a new generation of politicians, those willing to devote most of their time to the job at the state level away from their home district. The legislators increased their own salaries to compensate for the greater commitment. The "rural bumpkin" lawyer connected to the courthouse crowd was replaced by a commuting professional, who left responsibilities as a lawyer, pharmacist, accountant, or owner of a small business for duties in the legislature.

A study of the professionalism of state legislatures divided them into three categories: professional, hybrid, and citizen. Professional legislatures met almost year round, and their members were full-time employees. California legislators are paid $100,000 per year. Citizen legislatures, by contrast, are in session for briefer periods of time, members are not full-time, and salaries are lower and staffs smaller. In the mid-1990s rankings, two southern states (Georgia and Arkansas) were listed as citizen or amateur legislatures, while the rest were classified as hybrid, and no southern state was listed as professional.[29]

The suspicion of power, characteristic of the traditional political culture, remains strong in the South. Southerners believe, and quote, the old adage: "no man sleeps well when the legislature is in session." Southern legislatures in the national states had to become more professional to accommodate the varied populations and complex issues that accompanied economic development within their boundaries. Legislators were expected to serve in public office for reasons other than salary. The pay in southern states tends to be low, with Alabama's $10 per day for the 105 calendar-day regular session being at the bottom. National states like Texas, with a salary of $7,200, plus a per diem when in session, and Florida, with a salary of $27,900, with travel and a per diem, are typical.[30]

The effects of partisanship in state legislatures was shown earlier in Chapter 6. Because the Democratic Party has played such a significant role in southern politics, any discussion of partisanship has to begin with the loyalty Southerners have for the party of Jefferson, Jackson, and Roosevelt. During the last decade of the twentieth century the nation's state legislatures became more competitive bodies at election time. The Republican upsurge of the 1990s left the nation's legislatures almost equally divided: 51.5 percent Democratic, to 49.5 percent Republican.

The analysis in Chapter 6 shows that the Republican allegiance trickled down to the legislature from presidential races. Most states were two-party competitive at the state level by 2002, but North Carolina, Alabama, Arkansas, and Mississippi retained a modified one-party allegiance to the Democrats at the statehouse level. Since state legislatures are organized along party lines the emergence of two-party competition has led to divided government: meaning that one party controls the governorship and the other controls one or both legislative chambers. A study of the patterns of unified and divided government in the United States from 1979–2000 found all the southern states classified as, "usually unified Democratic or divided with a Republican governor."[31] Most southern states had unified Democratic governments until the late 1980s and 1990s.

Southern states have traditionally lagged behind the rest of the country when it came to adopting new policies. A 1969 study of eighty-eight program innovations found that larger, wealthier states adopted programs faster than smaller and poorer states.[32] The rapid urbanization and in-migration of residents into southern states forced them to adapt. State leaders took to looking at nearby states for ideas and solutions to policy problems. Georgia became a leader in the South with its economic and development plans and adoption of the lottery to cover budgetary short-falls.

Political competition helped stimulate the adoption of new programs. When political parties compete for office they advance a number of new ideas, and once in office they know that in the next election they will be held responsible for their promises. In southern states many governors sought to make a mark in education or economic development as an accomplishment on which to campaign. Politically competitive states have been shown to be more innovative.[33]

Turnover in office also leads to more policy change. A new governor, or a different party in control of the legislature, allows new ideas to surface. Legislators are more active during these changes and experts outside of government often seize these opportunities to press their case for change. As southern states became more competitive politically, they became more innovative.

The contemporary picture of southern party division is shown in Table 9.3, which reveals the balance of power in the house and senate of each southern state in 2001. Democrats are a majority in every state but three (Florida, Virginia, and South Carolina), but their margin of leadership is shrinking. Competition has come to these races where once there was none. Republicans held only 10 percent of these seats in 1960; today they average nearly 45 percent across the South.[34]

Table 9.3   Party Allegiance in Southern Legislatures, 2001

	Senate		House		Total	
	D	R	D	R	D	R
Georgia	57%	43%	59%	41%	58%	42%
Florida	38%	62%	36%	64%	37%	63%
Virginia	45%	55%	35%	65%	38%	62%
Texas	50%	50%	52%	48%	51%	49%
North Carolina	70%	30%	52%	48%	51%	49%
Tennessee	55%	45%	58%	42%	57%	43%
Alabama	69%	31%	63%	47%	65%	35%
Arkansas	77%	23%	70%	30%	72%	28%
South Carolina	46%	54%	42%	58%	44%	56%
Mississippi	65%	35%	72%	28%	70%	30%
Lousiana	64%	36%	68%	32%	66%	34%
N=	264	192	726	591	990	783
Totals	58%	42%	55%	45%	56%	44%

Source: Council of Governments, *The Book of the States.* Lexington: University of Kentucky Press, 2004.

Two-party competition may be the most important issue explaining legislative effectiveness or ineffectiveness. Party organization extends to the legislative committees, the chairs of which are members of the majority party, and the proportion of majority and minority members on each committee is roughly the same as the proportion of the whole chamber. Partisan competitiveness means that the minority party can occasionally pick up a stray Democrat or two, and win as the split in the legislature approaches even.

At the turn of the century southern legislatures considered a number of issues such as educational policy, transportation, growth management, and welfare reform. By 2002 these issues paled in comparison to the issue of budget deficits. After seven straight years of tax cuts, the mild national recession left forty of the fifty states with deficits. The terrorist attacks of September 11, 2001, pushed security issues to the top of the legislative agenda. Suddenly legislators had to deal with bioterrorism, the response of the public health system to terrorist threats, antidotes, vaccines, and antibiotics in crisis. Added expenses came from tightened security around state capitols, legislative office buildings, metal detectors, and x-ray machines. All these requirements of government came in a time of shrinking tax revenues.

The legislatures also faced criticism and public controversy in the process of redrawing district lines for themselves, and members of the US Congress. Part of the party realignment in state legislatures was a result of black majority districts drawn in the 1990s. Most of these decisions cost Democrats dearly in the decade. Between 1992 and 1998 Democrats in Alabama lost three US House seats, four state senate seats, and ten state house seats. The dispute over black congressional districts in Georgia led to three appeals to the US Supreme Court in the same time period. No state had a harder time reapportioning its congressional districts than North Carolina, which has an African American population evenly spread across numerous counties. From 1989 to 1999 Louisiana held congressional elections under four different maps.

The future of southern politics rests in the reapportionment of state legislatures after the 2000 census. The growth patterns of the suburbs are tending to favor Republicans. In Alabama nine of the ten fastest growing state house districts are held by Republicans. Georgia has the fastest-growing boom districts in the exurban counties of metro Atlanta, and in Florida, Democrats could not add to their number of seats for fifteen years from 1982 to 1998.

The closeness of party representation and growth of more professional legislatures gave rise in the 1990s to the term limits movement and use of the initiative. As more legislators became career politicians, they had to raise more money, much of which came from interest groups to which they had become politically indebted. The call by citizen groups was for legislative reform that imposed limitations on the number of terms that members could serve. Florida adopted a term limits law in 1992 that took effect in 2000, and Louisiana adopted like legislation in 1995 that takes effect in 2007. In Arkansas the term limits apply separately to the state house and senate. Adopted in 1992, they took effect in 1998 in the house and 2002 in the senate. These were the only three southern states to adopt this legislation. In its formal and informal effects, the term limits movement worked to benefit the Republican Party in the South, since it disproportionately impacted incumbent Democrats. Three states (Arkansas, Florida, and Louisiana) adopted term limit laws, but all southern states were influenced by the rhetoric of citizen legislators and lawmaking accountability. Nationwide the term limits movement ran out of steam by 2000, with about one-third of the state legislatures across the country so limited.

The constitutional initiative by petition allows individuals or groups to draft proposed state constitutional amendments or state laws if they can collect enough signatures supporting the proposal. A proposal subsequently appears on the ballot to be adopted or defeated by the voters. About half the states in the United States, but only three in the southern states, have the initiative. The measure grew out of the Reform Movement of the early 1900s, and has been most extensively used in California. The three southern states that have constitutional amendment by initiative are: Arkansas, Florida, and Mississippi. The number of signatures required on an initiative petition varies from 8 percent of the total votes cast in the last presidential election in Florida to 12 percent of the total votes for governor of Mississippi. For the most part the initiative has been a neglected part of legislative reform in the southern states.

Summary

The color of southern politics and politicians remains, but it has been refined by television and moderated by economic improvement. Today governors are expected to lead and manage state government, and legislators take a pragmatic approach to budgets and lawmaking. Together they have produced a new breed of state government officials who are highly educated and professionally trained. In the 1980s and 1990s the increasing complexity of state bureaucracies meant meeting the challenge of performing their tasks in the face of financial restrictions. Southern states worked to "reinvent" government by privatizing functions and abandoning public regulation in favor of market competition. State governments in the South are much more representative, professional, and policy oriented than they were fifty years ago.

From time to time symbolic issues, especially those evocative of traditional southern values, such as the flying of the Confederate flag above public buildings and honoring Confederate soldiers, or social issues, such as gambling, prayer in schools, and limiting abortions, enter and dominate the public agenda. Often the agenda of social conservatives must contend with a demand for economic progress. Many state officials in the South are busy reforming public education, attracting higher wage industries, providing job opportunities for welfare workers, balancing economic development and environmental concerns, and in general taking a pragmatic approach to government within the context of the limited role demanded by economic conservatives. The South today is marked by change and continuity in political culture, economic structure, social configuration, and government and political leadership. The interactive relationships between the values of the past and forces of modernization or progress have redefined the fault lines for partisan politics.

Notes

1. George E Sims, *The Little Man's Big Friend: James E. Folsom in Alabama Politics, 1945–1956.* Tuscaloosa: University of Alabama Press, 1985, p. 46.

2. Stephen Lasher, *George Wallace: American Populist.* New York: Addison, Wesley Publishing Co., 1994, p. 102.

3. T. Harry Williams, *Huey Long.* New York: Alfred A. Knopf, 1969, p. 214.

4. Stephen Lasher, *George Wallace: American Populist,* p. 361.

5. Robert A. Caro, *The Years of Lyndon Johnson: Means of Ascent.* New York: Alfred A. Knopf, 1990, p. 219.

6. Hugh David Graham, "Demagogues," in Charles Regan Wilson and William Ferris (eds.), *Encyclopedia of Southern Culture.* Chapel Hill: University of North Carolina Press, 1989, p. 1163.

7. Carl M. Logue and Howard Dorgan, *The Oratory of Southern Demagogues.* Baton Rouge: Louisiana State University Press, 1981, p. 144.

8. Allan A. Michie, *Dixie Demagogues.* New York: Vanguard Press, 1939, p. 269.

9. Francis Butler Simkins and Charles Pierce Roland, *A History of the South.* New York: Alfred A Knopf, 1972, p. 43.

10. Walter Edgar, *A History of South Carolina.* Columbia: University of South Carolina Press, 1993.

11. Dewey W. Grantham, *Southern Progressivism: The Reconciliation of Progress and Tradition.* Knoxville: University of Tennessee Press, 1983, p. xvi.

12. T. Harry Williams, *Huey Long,* pp. 124–136.

13 . Ibid., p. 304.

14. Larry Sabato, *Goodbye to Good-time Charlie.* 2d ed. Washington, D.C.: Congressional Quarterly Press, 1983, p. 1.

15. Robert A. Caro, *The Years of Lyndon Johnson,* pp. 698–703.

16. George E. Sims, *The Little Man's Big Friend,* p. 90.

17. *New Yorker,* June 4, 1960.

18. David Boaz, "Pardon Abuse: Déjà Vu," *Cato Institute.* www.cato.org., March 7, 2001.

19. Southern Politics Collection, "Alabama," Vanderbilt University, Special Collections.

20. George E. Sims, *The Little Man's Big Friend,* p. 221.

21. Virginia Gray, Russell L. Hanson, and Herbert Jacob (eds.), *Politics in the American States.* 7th ed. Washington, D.C.: Congressional Quarterly Press, 1999, p. 224.

22. Cornelia Wallace, *C'Nelia.* New York: A.J. Holman Company, 1976, pp. 129–131.

23. Sarah McCally Morehouse, *State Politics and Policy.* New York: Holt, Rinehart and Winston, 1981, Appendix Two, pp. 493–495; Sarah McCally Morehouse and Malcolm

Jewell, *State Politics and Policy.* 2d ed. Lanham, Md.: Rowman & Littlefield, 2003, pp. 174–175.

24. Virginia Gray and Herbert Jacob, *Politics in the American States: A Comparative Analysis.* 6th ed. Washington, D.C.: Congressional Quarterly Press, 1996, p. 238.

25. Southern Politics Collection, "Georgia," Vanderbilt University, Special Collections.

26. Ibid.

27. Southern Politics Collection, "Louisiana," Vanderbilt University, Special Collections.

28. Alan Rosenthal, "The Legislature: Unraveling of Institutional Fabric," in Carl Van Horn (ed.), *The State of the States.* Washington, D.C.: Congressional Quarterly Press, 1996, p. 108.

29. Sarah McCally Morehouse and Malcolm E. Jewell, *State Politics, Parties and Policy*, p. 213.

30. Council of State Governments, *The Book of the States, 2002.* Lexington, Ky.: The Council of State Governments, 2002, pp. 86–87.

31. Sarah McCally Morehouse and Malcolm Jewell, *State Politics, Parties and Policy*, p. 211.

32. Jack L. Walker, "The Diffusion of Innovations Among the American States," *American Political Science Review* 63 (September 1969), pp. 880–899.

33. Virginia Gray and David Lowry, "The Corporatist Foundations of State Industrial Policy." *Social Science Quarterly* 71 (1990), pp. 3–24.

34. Council of State Governments, *Book of the States, 2002,* p. 61.

10

The South and the Nation

Southern life is a subset of US life. The task of explaining the South in the context of the social history of the rest of the nation is an ever-present one for any book on the region. The argument here is that the job is best done by understanding subcultural influence within a political system. In other words, Southerners have different expectations about institutions and values, and they are best understood in contrast to the rest of country. Variations in opinion and influence are especially common in the federated structure of the United States.

The reliance on voting data and economic statistics in earlier chapters relegates some aspects of the political culture concerned with history, patriotism, and the role of women and the home, to the edge of the analysis. "In the age of social science," wrote southern agrarian Allen Tate in 1959, "the term 'image' is not clear, and this, I suppose, is due to the disappearance, in such an age, of the deep relation between man and a local habitation."[1] This chapter discusses some aspects of life that are not easily measured, but remain significant in the general scheme of social and political life in the South. These cultural legacies can, and have had, implications for national policy.

The traditionalistic political culture of the region found unique expressions in many aspects of the society. Richard Weaver described the legacy of participation this way: "The South possesses an inheritance which it has imperfectly understood and little used."[2] The "imperfectly understood" part of the tradition is seen in the allegiance to the unfurled Confederate flag as an excuse for racial hatred, the belief that one-party politics is best precisely *because* it limits participation, and the acceptance of rural poverty as a kind of virtue. A part of the populace believes the South is poor and good, and that it should stay that way. Beneath this expression is a deeper ideal, one that repeatedly surfaces in any political controversy. The South has historically been concerned about the dominant cultural presuppositions of American life, and particularly the relationship of newer values to the native region. The one southern wish is to maintain an identity and avoid becoming "modern." Provincialism is seen as a brake on the national trends of political centralization and the imposition of alien beliefs.

The South has a "little used" testament as well. This strain is apparent in the abundant resources, both natural and human, that populate the region. Sunbelt growth and affluence capitalized on these native resources and produced a successful business and professional middle class that was uneasy with its new status. Countless Southerners identified with a character like Charlie Crocker, the protagonist in Tom Wolfe's *A Man in Full*, who looks down on the towers and trees of Atlanta from his airplane and declares: "I did that! That's my handiwork! I'm one of the giants who built this city! I'm a star!"[3] At the same time Charlie's good-ole-boy real estate empire, with his sprawling south Georgia plantation, a mansion in the best part of town, a half-empty skyscraper named for him, hordes of servants, a fleet of jets, and a free-spending trophy wife, have left him terribly vulnerable to spiritual bankruptcy. The newly prosperous are often the most insecure.

The imperfect and the neglected traditions, acting together, make the South what it is today; a region distinct from the rest of the country and the differences are seen in select vignettes. The language of politics, an orientation to political symbols, and the expectations people have about the role of government in their lives are all cultural at base. These unique elements are apparent in parts of daily life that are often taken for granted. Throughout this book, the emphasis has been on the traditional values of religion, family life, and history that are important influences on social and political life.

Year after year the South remains a mutineer to the uniformity of US culture. "The unreconstructed Southerners have done their part to keep it Balkan."[4] Southern exceptionalism began with the role the region played in the American Revolution, the founding of the US Republic, the dramatic consequences of the Civil War, the Lost Cause, and the legacy of poverty that followed the military defeat. "Southerners know history has happened . . . because Southern history has been compounded of tragedy and many of the elements of that tragedy are still apparent today."[5] The twentieth century brought economic improvement, but the classifications "South" and "non-South" came to characterize a host of statistics summarizing US life. A persistent difference abides in the region. In time, the socioeconomic legacy was added to the historical one to define a separate region.

Being southern was not just geographic, it was also how people came together with ties of loyalty and identification to define themselves. *Southern Living* magazine, writes John Shelton Reed, "implies month after month that there is such a thing as Southern living, that it is different and (by plain implication) better."[6] The concern of some natives is that in the face of postwar progress, the South came perilously close to losing its identity. In shopping mall traffic outside a southern city a bumper sticker on the window of a pickup reads: "I am the proud descendent of a brave Confederate soldier." The truck owner was holding to a part of the past that people in other regions of the country have forgotten, and they have no similar bumper stickers declaring their genealogy to a Union soldier. In this chapter the original list of six southern distinctives is expanded to include some not-so-apparent aspects of life in the southern culture. Collectively their influence on politics may be as abiding as the earlier ones.

The first, and most publicly visible, regional influence is the long-standing legacy of representation in the US Congress. In the US House and Senate, Southerners have traditionally supervised important committees and controlled the flow of legislation. Tenure in office was valued in a part of the country that depended on the federal government for help in times of trouble. A second legacy is the heritage of military service, a tradition that dates from the Civil War, and found a recent expression in the armed forces of the Middle East conflicts. Plaques in county courthouses memorialize locals who paid the ultimate sacrifice for their country. Pickens County, South Carolina, to take just one example, has had more Congressional Medal of Honor winners than any other county in the nation. In Lexington, Virginia, and Charleston, South Carolina, a Veterans Day parade brings out a full corps of cadets from a state university with a one-hundred-sixty-year-old tradition of duty, honor, and country.

In the years after World War II the region underwent dramatic changes in race relations, the economy, and its political institutions. But the third influence, the "War" as it is called, remains as an enduring legacy. The war is the Civil War, and the memory abides in storytelling of how people in one section of the country used the power of the federal government to oppress those in another part of the nation. In other regions the Confederate flag is a museum relic, like the Union Jack or the Spanish flags of the conquistadors. But in South Carolina, to take one example among several, the southern battle flag flew over the state capitol for forty years in a visible display of defiance to federal mandates. The conflict over the flag's removal stirred historical memories that many thought were dead, and cost a sitting governor his job in a bid for reelection. The Sons of Confederate Veterans marched to the statehouse lawn to protest any change in the status of the flag, and its continued display caused the NAACP to call for a boycott of the state. Why, after one hundred and forty years, are the words of a Civil War journalist about Columbia, South Carolina—and the South—still appropriate? "In no other city that I have visited has hostility seemed to me so bitter."[7]

A fourth distinct legacy of the South is the role of women in the politically and religiously conservative region. The South has a history of being resistant to changes in family life. In opposing the equal rights movement of the 1970s, southern women registered their opposition to the social forces gripping the rest of the country. Divisions between male and female roles have historically defined family responsibilities in the South. A debutante ball in Mobile, Savannah, or Jackson has trappings of social respectability unimaginable in other cities. The role of women in the domestic heritage of the South remains strong and insulates a culture that esteems feminine charms, upholds traditional values, and disdains homosexuality.

The absorption of Dixie into the mainstream of America was planned by executives in gleaming glass office parks beside suburban shopping malls. Thirty years ago, John Edgerton wrote that divisions along the lines of race and class, an obsession with growth and consumption, urbanization, and a steady erosion of place and community would make the South like the rest of America. "The dominant trends are unmistakable," he wrote, "[but] the idea that change is a threat to be resisted is too deeply rooted in the Southern mind."[8] The alteration of southern life was inconsistent. A uniformity of fast food outlets and shopping malls only papered over the differences between the region and the rest of the country. Politics in the South owes much to the legends and myths about its past, many of which find expression in contemporary life that separate it from the national consciousness.

The Congressional Legacy

The protection of distinctive southern interests with the weapons of the national government has a legacy that predates the Civil War. The region needed safety for slavery from forces in the West and North, and the regional defense depended on legislative maneuvers in the US Congress. John C. Calhoun, of South Carolina, developed the political theory of "nullification" as a technique to protect southern minority rights in Congress. For decades Southerners used Calhoun's arguments to block the designs of abolitionists and free thinkers outside the region. The southern devotion to regional protection was pragmatic. In 1860, southern delegates walked out of the Democratic convention demanding federal protection of slavery; one hundred years later they wanted recognition of states' rights.

Southerners saw legislatures as conservative bastions of power and procedure useful in stopping institutional change. Kentucky congressman Henry Clay developed remarkable skills of parliamentary maneuvering to protect his slave state. No matter how loud the demand for racial justice or the abolition of slavery, the South could work methodically in committee with a deaf ear to the noise. Clay served six terms as Speaker of the US House. He put together the Missouri Compromise of 1820, and his ideas guided the Compromise of 1850. Clay was a master of legislative statecraft and knew how to use the House rules to force agreement.

Calhoun and Clay became cultural icons, and inspired a host of southern imitators with followers like: John Nance "Cactus Jack" Garner, Sam Rayburn, Lyndon Johnson, Richard Russell, Strom Thurmond, Newt Gingrich, and Tom DeLay. These southern legislators rose to unusual heights because of their knowledge of legislative procedure and natural powers of persuasion. The perennial minority status of the South led to the expectation that it would be protected by its elected politicians in Washington. The talent Southerners had in abundance was their skill of using position to help the home region.

The complexity of the rules in the House, and the even more obtuse ones in the Senate, conspired to shield southern leaders from public accountability. Southern

---

Vignette 10.1 Tom DeLay (1947–)

Tom DeLay served as the House majority leader in the 108th Congress, and epitomizes the rise to power of a conservative, suburban, Republican leader.

DeLay is a native Texan, from the Rio Grande in the historic town of Laredo. His father worked in the oil and gas industry and, as a child, the future congressman lived in South America. These experiences were formative in his political experience, and influenced his subsequent career. The family lived through revolutions and political violence, the effects of which galvanized DeLay's convictions about politics.

After starting his education at Baylor University, DeLay graduated from the University of Houston in 1970 with a degree in biology. Shortly afterward he opened Albo Pest Control and became a successful businessman. The experience of operating a small business convinced DeLay that the major impediments to successful business were excessive taxes and government regulation. In 1978 he seized upon an opportunity to change what he saw as the onerous burdens of intrusive government.

In a Fort Bend County Republican Committee meeting, a party official suggested DeLay run for an open Texas house seat. He won his first race and served in the legislature until 1984. When Reagan began his second term, DeLay emerged from a five-candidate congressional primary with 52 percent of the vote, and then won the general election with 65 percent. Tom DeLay has been elected by similar margins in general elections ever since.

In Washington DeLay showed a talent for attention to detail and vote counting that impressed his colleagues. The trait served him well in 1994 when he anticipated a

Republican surge to the majority by contributing $2 million to Republican candidates. As a result he won the whip job and became a part of the new GOP leadership. Over the years DeLay built a formidable organization to manage victories with razor-thin majorities. He won the nickname "The Hammer," for his ability to forge majorities on the floor in the face of hostile Democrats and Republicans who are prone to defect.

Tom DeLay has cultivated the image of a hard-nosed partisan who wields power without apology and to a specific end. When Newt Gingrich resigned in November of 1998, it was DeLay who helped promote Dennis Hastert to the Speaker's chair. The legacy of hard-nosed politics came back to haunt DeLay in 2005 when he was indicted by an Austin prosecutor for mishandling campaign funds. The Washington persona he cultivated was that of a bargainer who used his vote-counting ability to make minimum concessions to amass a majority. Like leaders before him, including the legendary Sam Rayburn, DeLay expects members to support the leadership on procedural votes. He rewards and punishes members of the GOP on the basis of their loyalty. As majority leader, DeLay had control of the legislative agenda and the levers of Republican power in the nation's most partisan legislative body.

In 2002 Tom DeLay emerged as a loud voice of support for Israel, and a critic of Yasser Arafat. Tom and Christine DeLay have a daughter, and share a deep interest in foster care.

His indictment in October 2005 for using corporate contributions in political campaigns forced DeLay to step aside as GOP House majority leader.

---

domination of the legislature began early, in December of 1846, when the Senate instituted a new way of selecting committee chairs. The ranking of members for selection as chair was based on their experience and length of service on the committee. Seniority favored the South, where the new procedure, explained a senator at the time, "operated to give to Senators from slaveholding states the chairmanship of every single committee that controls the public business of this Government."[9] Things were little different in the Reconstruction period following the Civil War. Southern one-party politics produced long careers in Congress for elected representatives who rarely faced opposition once they won election. In the early decades of the twentieth century southern power increased in the face of party competition in other states.

House Republicans revolted against their leader in 1910, and the fall of Speaker Joe Cannon was a result that benefited the South. The outcome of this insurgency was a committee system much more independent of the Speaker. The committees now enjoyed fixed jurisdiction over a particular policy no matter how the Speaker felt about the issue. Seniority on a committee, defined as the number of years served continuously, would determine the ascent to leadership regardless of the member's relationship with the Speaker. The overall effect of the revolt was to make committee chairs more powerful, and reward seniority.

Since southern politicians had little or no chance of winning national office, they invested themselves in mastering the rules of parliamentary procedure, seniority, and legislative precedent in Congress. Southern leaders knew what the rules covered, what was not covered, and how to use the difference to get what they wanted. They were consulted by their colleagues and asked how to "work something out." A regional specialty of legislators was their willingness to oblige the request of their colleagues for compromise; they knew how to cut deals and how to get something done. The arrangement forged a bond, and the coalition of southern power expanded when favors were called in. One-party politics and the seniority system combined to boost Southerners to party leadership positions and places on major congressional committees.

The extent of this power is seen in Table 10.1, which summarizes fifty years of southern representation on important committees. The table shows when Southerners chaired congressional committees, regardless of party. In the US House of Representatives a Southerner has chaired the Appropriations Committee every year since 1965, or 70 percent of the time covered in the table. The House Ways and Means Committee has been led by Southerners over half the time. Southerners dominated the Armed Services committees, in both the House and the Senate, with the result that billions of dollars were channeled to their home states.

The Senate became the special lair of southern power, and the power of the South there went beyond numbers. The political longevity of southern politicians, along with support from sympathetic midwestern conservatives and their ability to act in concert, gave Southerners a huge advantage over other factions in Congress. Originally the power was in the hands of southern Democrats, but after 1980, and especially after 1994, it switched to conservative southern Republicans.

The power and position of the South was everywhere evident in the region's opposition to civil rights legislation, an issue that occupied the national agenda for

Table 10.1 Southern Chairmanship of Major Congressional Committees, 1949–2002

Congress	1949–1950	1951–1952	1953–1954	1955–1956	1957–1958	1959–1960	1961–1962	1963–1964	1965–1966	1967–1968	1969–1970	1971–1972	1973–1974	1975–1976	1977–1978	1979–1980	1981–1982	1983–1984	1985–1986	1987–1988	1989–1990	1991–1992	1993–1994	1995–1996	1997–1998	1999–2000	2001–2002
	81	82	83	84	85	86	87	88	89	90	91	92	93	94	95	96	97	98	99	100	101	102	103	104	105	106	107
House Committees																											
Appropriations		•		•	•	•	•	•	•	•	•	•	•		•	•	•	•	•	•	•	•	•	•	•	•	•
Ways & Means		•		•	•	•	•	•	•	•	•	•	•					•	•	•	•			•	•	•	•
Rules												•									•						
Judiciary			•	•	•	•	•	•	•	•	•	•	•							•	•	•	•	•	•	•	
Armed Services	•	•																									
Senate Committees																											
Appropriations		•		•		•	•		•	•	•	•	•	•	•								•				•
Foreign Relations		•		•		•	•		•	•	•	•	•	•	•				•	•							
Judiciary				•		•	•		•	•																	
Armed Services				•	•	•	•													•	•						
Finance	•	•											•		•	•	•	•		•	•	•		•	•	•	•

Source: Congressional Quarterly and US Statistical Abstracts for various years.

two decades in the 1950s and 1960s. Especially in the US Senate, where the filibuster rule was sacrosanct, the power of southern legislators was unmatched. Their position was initially strengthened in 1946, when many northern representatives and senators of equal seniority went down in defeat at the hands of the Republicans. Southern Democrats renewed their alliances with midwestern Republican conservatives. Together they erected a barricade against civil rights legislation.

The South was led by Richard Russell, chairman of the Armed Services Committee, and the respected leader of the Senate's inner circle. Russell's knowledge of the Senate rules, the power of his personality, and his seniority combined to enable him to keep threatening legislation at bay. "It has not escaped the notice of other senators," wrote columnist Meg Greenfield in the *Washington Post* at the time, "that Russell, like the Lord, has the power to both give and take away."[10]

To pundits in the balcony, it seemed like the South could not lose, but lose it did. First, in 1948, President Truman integrated the armed services by executive order when he failed to get legislation through Congress. Second, in 1957 and 1960, the southern bloc lost when two civil rights acts passed the Congress in defiance of southern power. Both of these acts dealt with voting rights for blacks, but southern senators successfully stripped enforcement provisions authorizing the Department of Justice to initiate suits from the legislation. Later, the same group removed authorization of a presidential committee to investigate discrimination from the 1960 act. Yet even with these successes, the handwriting was on the wall for both white supremacy and regional resistance.

Southern supporters of segregation approached the Democratic Convention of 1960 with trepidation. Their worst fears were realized when the delegates dismissed their regional concerns, and wrote a strong civil rights plank into the party platform. In the subsequent election, Kennedy's Catholicism was suspect in the Protestant South, but Richard Nixon offered native voters no choice on the issue of racial integration. The Republican position was even more explicit than Kennedy's. Southern reservations were calmed when Democrats selected Lyndon Johnson as the party's vice presidential nominee. In 1960 Nixon carried only three southern states: Virginia, Tennessee, and Florida. By holding the bulk of the South, Kennedy won the presidency by the narrowest of margins.

Once in office President Kennedy appointed many blacks to high positions, and inaugurated a number of lawsuits to force the desegregation of southern schools. The legal strategy meant that the president could bypass the southern roadblock in Congress. Elementary and secondary schools across the South succumbed to the federal pressure, as did institutions of higher learning. The violent confrontations of the civil rights movement during the 1960s only increased the calls for more federal legislation, a chorus that culminated in another civil rights act. The legislation proposed by Kennedy, and later championed by Lyndon Johnson, prohibited discrimination in hotels, restaurants, public schools, libraries, and hospitals.

Most southern congressmen fought the legislation at every turn. Regional opposition to federal intervention, judicial mandates, and meddling bureaucrats became a mantra at election time. Richard Russell, assisted by James O. Eastland of Mississippi and Sam Ervin of North Carolina, used every maneuver in the book to kill or weaken the legislation. The acrimony and debate in the US Senate lasted for three months. Finally, the Senate adopted cloture to end debate and broke the southern bloc to pass the most significant civil rights bill in the nation's history. President Johnson signed the bill into law on July 2, 1964.

Passage of the 1964 civil rights bill ended the resistance of southern legislators and brought them face-to-face with the inevitable. Delaware senator Joe Biden recounted this lost legacy of southern power in his eulogy for Senator Strom Thurmond in 2003. Biden recalled his first weeks as a freshman senator in 1972 when he paid a courtesy call on the senior members. John Stennis, the venerable veteran from Mississippi, greeted his new colleague sitting at the end of a long table. After opening pleasantries the senior senator asked why Biden had run for office, and received a two-word answer: civil rights. "And as soon as I [said it]," Biden recalled, "I could feel the beads of perspiration pop out of my head and get that funny feeling. . . . And he looked at me and nodded his head saying, 'Good, good,' and that was the end of the conversation."

Eighteen years later, when Stennis was leaving the Senate, this time in a wheelchair because his leg had been amputated to prevent the spread of cancer, Biden paid a return visit. The Delaware senator was looking at office space, because his seniority now allowed him the take Stennis's office. "He looked at me as if it were yesterday," said Biden, "and asked me if I remembered the first conversation." The passage of time had dulled the younger man's memory, but not so with the retiring senator. "And [Stennis] ran his hand back and forth across that mahogany table in a loving way and asked, 'Do you see this table?'" The Mississippian did not wait for an answer, but explained, "This table was the flagship of the Confederacy . . . we sat here, most of us from the Deep South . . . and we planned the demise of the civil rights movement."

Biden knew about the legislation of the 1950s and 1960s, but he had never heard Stennis talk about them before. As the older man ran his hands over the table he said, "now it's time that this table go from the possession of a man against civil rights, to a man for civil rights." The gigantic mahogany table had been the desk of Richard Russell and was the platform upon which the "Southern Manifesto" was signed. "One more thing, Joe," said John Stennis, "the civil rights movement did more for the white man than the black man." With his hand on the table, the senator who served forty-two years in the US Senate fighting against civil rights said, "It freed my soul, it freed my soul."[11]

The civil rights movement had the unexpected effect of enriching the power of the South in Congress. Southerners continued to send representatives to Washington in the face of federal desegregation remedies. They inevitably gained seniority and worked the levers of institutional power to favor their home districts. Deeply ingrained in the southern psyche was a respect for tradition, and nowhere was tradition more a fact of day-to-day life than in the US Congress, especially in the US Senate. "As Constitutional Convention delegate James Wilson of Pennsylvania put it, the framers belied 'that the least numerous body was the fittest for deliberation.'"[12]

The protracted civil rights struggle in Congress taught the South that an intense minority committed to the defense of an ideal—no matter how unpopular or controversial—could prevail through obstruction and procedure. Ultimately the South lost the crusade for limiting civil rights, but the battles southern legislators fought showed them that there was victory in delay, obfuscation, and knowledge of parliamentary procedure. The ability to defeat legislative intent became a hallmark of southern representation, especially in the Senate. Jesse Helms, the former senator from North Carolina, used his seniority and knowledge of Senate rules to frustrate a host of Clinton administration initiatives and appointments before his retirement in 2002. Senator Robert Byrd of West Virginia is the latest in a long line of Southerners who is an expert on the rules and history of that august body.

The Military Tradition

"The idea of a southern military tradition is a prominent, but not universally accepted, theme in the historiography of the South."[13] The original claim by commentators was that the geography, the frontier, the legacy of warfare in the defense of slavery, and the cultural ideas of honor and martial glory made the South unique. Alexis de Tocqueville said the Southerner was "passionately fond of hunting and war," and for a time the main heroes of the South were nearly all soldiers. Southerners rushed to join the military for the War of 1812, and the Mexican War (1846), in contrast to a more tepid response, and even civil disobedience, in northern states.

At the time of the Civil War the military ethos was even more marked. Secession gripped every state except Florida, and all either supported a military college or extended aid to one. These schools provided expertise and officers to the Confederate cause. Virginia Military Institute had more than four hundred officers in the US military at the time of the Civil War.[14] The relationship between southern arms and southern politics was inevitable. The South lost the war because it ran low on troops, but the enthusiasm of the soldiers who remained was fierce even in defeat.

After Reconstruction, volunteer military units proliferated in the region. W. J. Cash wrote in *The Mind of the South* that in 1898 young Southerners rushed to don blue uniforms for the Spanish-American War. A military career was one of the few means of escaping the poverty and despair of the postwar South. Applications for the military academies were such that in 1910, 93 percent of US Army generals were southern.[15]

During the Civil War, Congress passed the Morrill Land Grant Act, to provide federal land grants for state agricultural and mechanical colleges that were required to furnish military instruction. All across the defeated and impoverished South, "aggie" schools revived the military school tradition that had previously furnished troops for the Confederate cause. Each southern state established a land grant school to provide military training: Arkansas (1871), Auburn and Virginia Tech (1872), Mississippi State (1878), Georgia Tech (1885), North Carolina State and Clemson (1889), and Louisiana State and Texas A&M (1871), which by World War II furnished more regular army officers than West Point. In addition, some older state universities offered military instruction when the Reserve Officer Training Corps Acts of 1916 and 1920 extended it to schools other than land grant colleges.

For some in the South the opportunity to go to college was only possible because of the ROTC program. At Clemson University in South Carolina, for example, thousands of young men enrolled in the all-male college to take a mechanical engineering or agriculture degree paid for with an ROTC commitment. The early lore of the college is replete with tales of freshmen hazing; the freshmen were called "Rats" because their head was shaved the first week of school. One graduate opined, when the university dedicated a memorial to the original vision of the school, that "ROTC was the only way a poor boy in South Carolina could get a college education."

Despite controversy, the ROTC program survived two world wars, scrutiny from academics and the professional military, violent opposition from a small but dedicated group of students on campus, and the end of the draft. While controversial elsewhere, ROTC units remained popular on the campuses of southern colleges and universities. In the post-Vietnam era active ROTC units were "disproportionately southern and midwestern, while the disestablishment units were mostly eastern."[16] Table 10.2 shows the gain and loss of ROTC units in this period. While every other region in the country lost ROTC units, the South expanded its offerings during this contentious time.

At the end of the twentieth century southern universities continued their allegiance to ROTC programs and military service. The military legacy at schools like Texas A&M, Virginia Tech, Clemson, and Auburn is evident on campus every Thursday afternoon when formations of officer candidates are in uniform across campus. The commissioning of second lieutenants is a ceremony that occurs at the same time as graduation at these universities, and is an occasion for public recognition before parents and friends.

The South's reputation for military service went beyond the officer corps. The defeat of the Civil War won endorsement of the Lost Cause in an earlier century, and in the twentieth century military service gained vitality with each new conflict. The enthusiasm for military service came from the job security, upward mobility, and public support accorded officers. In World War II, the contributions of Southerners were similarly impressive. Dramatic battles like Pearl Harbor, the

Table 10.2   Net Gain or Loss of ROTC Units, 1968–1974

Region	Total Units 1968	Total Units 1974
East	123	93
Midwest	115	112
West	88	80
South	147	180

Source: Michael S. Neiberg, *Making Citizen-Soldiers: ROTC and the Ideology of American Military Service.* Cambridge, Mass.: Harvard University Press, 2000, p. 172.

Bataan Death March, D-Day, the Battle of the Bulge, and Iwo Jima were felt more in the South because of the disproportionate number of natives in the services. "When the Korean War broke out, 46 percent of the American military elite had southern affiliations, although the South's population was only 27 percent of the country's total."[17]

The postwar years witnessed a dramatic expansion in US military responsibilities around the world. The South overcame a deep suspicion of federal funds to enthusiastically embrace military bases and an increase in defense expenditures. Southern congressmen and senators used their seniority to steer Pentagon funds to their home states. Military service was seen as a respectable way to defend the United States from communism and at the same rime raise a family in the economical and friendly confines of the South. Even in the base closings after the Cold War ended in 1990, the region seemed to suffer less than other parts of the country.

Table 10.3 shows the military and civilian defense personnel from the nation and the South in 2002. The region has around 30 percent of the nation's population, but supplies over 45 percent of the country's military enlistments. The effect of this presence is dramatic in homes and military communities across the South. Military personnel are a unique citizenry in that they are transient, economic windfalls for local people who benefit from their presence, many of whom have relatives living in the South. In addition, the effects of foreign wars on local communities are a source of regional news stories, and the effects of family loss and separation are regular features on the state media outlets. For example, Tennessee has one of the smallest personnel figures in Table 10.3. But the metropolitan area of Nashville is the same media market as Ft. Campbell, Kentucky, home of the 101st Airborne. From 1990 to 2004 the base generated an avalanche of human interest stories on the personal effects of US foreign policy on military families. Such coverage has the collateral effect of reinforcing sympathy for military solutions and conservative policies.

Table 10.3   Civilian and Military Defense Personnel by State, 2002

State	Total Personnel	Percentage of Total US Personnel
Georgia	95,559	5.7
Florida	89,959	5.0
Virginia	167,970	10.0
Texas	152,338	9.1
North Carolina	110,740	6.6
Tennessee	5,496	0.9
Alabama	31,828	1.9
Arkansas	8,541	0.5
South Carolina	47,313	2.8
Mississippi	23,294	1.4
Louisiana	23,981	1.4
Total South	757,019	45.3
Non-South	916,086	54.7
Total	1,673,105	100.0

Source: Department of Defense Directorate for Information Operations and Reports, "DOD Military and Civilian Personnel by State," http://web1.whs.osd.mil/mmid/M02/fy03/M02_2003_Personnel.pdf.

More than 20,000 Pentagon employees are in Virginia, with key installations at the naval base in Norfolk, and the Marine headquarters in Quantico. These are located close to the Army's big base in neighboring Fort Bragg, North Carolina. The suburbs of Washington, D.C., are stocked with military and defense personnel. The Army has important installations in Fort Benning, Georgia, and Fort Hood, Texas. In peacetime nearly one-quarter of the entire Marine Corps, 43,000 in all, trains at the sprawling base at Camp Lejeune, North Carolina. Florida is home to the Central Command, the Special Operations Command, and Elgin Air Force Base. "During the past 15 years, the percentage of recruits from the Northeast and north central regions has decreased with a corresponding increase in the percentage of recruits from the South."[18] War may be hell, but in the South there is a special appreciation of both it, and the warriors.

The political importance of military service and allegiance to military personnel in southern cities is seen in the way the South supported both the Gulf War of 1991 and the Iraq War of 2003. Gallup poll results in the Gulf War conflict showed that 72 percent of the southern populace supported President George Bush's policies in Kuwait.[19] After the conflict was over, the same number favored immediate military action against Iraq.[20] When the time for war against Sadaam Hussein came in 2003, a Zogby Interaction poll found that the South had the highest number of people supporting the United States against Iraq.[21] While antiwar rallies flourished in cities like Boston, New York, and San Francisco, the South had patriotic parades in support of the troops. In both conflicts the region led the nation in backing the administration's war policy.

It should come as no surprise that the first casualty of the Iraq War was "a Mississippi native who grew up in a military family and graduated from the Citadel, the South Carolina military academy."[22] Marine 2nd Lieutenant Therrel Childers, thirty, was a member of the Junior ROTC in high school, and enlisted as soon as he graduated in 1990. The commanding officer of the operations in Iraq had a similar pedigree. General Tommy Franks graduated from Robert E. Lee High School in Midland, Texas, just ahead of First Lady Laura Bush. He entered the University of Texas for a time, then departed for military colleges and a career that culminated in working for his classmate's husband. Childers and Franks are typical of thousands of natives of the South who believe that a military commitment is as much a part of growing up as a high school or college degree. When war is over, Southerners mourn the fallen and welcome home the survivors, in disproportionate numbers compared to the rest of the country.

The final legacy of the military may be the most surprising: full integration of the races. One recruiter commented in 2003 that of the 2,000 active duty enlistments in South Carolina, western North Carolina, and part of Georgia, the battalion was almost evenly divided racially. Military conflict has done something Congress, the president, and the courts could never do: bring reconciliation between black and white in the crucible of war.

The Confederate Flag Controversy

In March of 2003 former president Jimmy Carter, who was awarded that year's Nobel Peace Prize for his diplomatic efforts, was handed another challenging assignment. After mediating disputes between Arab and Jew, liberal and conservative, and Democrat and Republican, Carter had to tackle the controversy over whether his home state of Georgia should enlarge the Confederate emblem on its state flag. More than one hundred forty years after the Civil War began, display of the Confederate battle flag remains as divisive a political issue today as it once was in conflict.

Rebel flags became front-page news all across the South in the 1990s, and into the next century. Civil rights groups worked to discredit a symbol they associated with slavery and racism. Their campaign provoked a response from white "heritage defenders" who said the battle flag was a relic handed down by heroic ancestors. As the twenty-first century opened, the Confederate flag remained the most visible symbol of the unfinished Civil War, and an issue more contentious than taxes, lotteries, or immigration in several southern states.

The so-called rebel flag is a well-known oblong red banner on which the blue cross of St. Andrews is displayed along with thirteen white five-pointed stars. Pro-flag groups invoke the powerful themes of defiance, state sovereignty, and the death of heroes as justification for displaying a symbol imaginatively soaked in blood and revered for generations. The flag itself is a modification of the original square one designed by P. G. T. Bureaugard for his troops. The "stars and bars" became the official flag of the Confederate states and it gradually became an informal symbol of resistance to federal authority and defiance of societal norms. It was widely popular in the 1950s as an emblem of dissatisfaction with the Supreme Court desegregation decision and the perceived intrusion of the federal government into southern affairs.

The "heritage" groups across the South adopted the flag, along with Confederate reenactors and sympathetic whites, in a statement to commemorate the southern legacy of defiance and allegiance to regional values. For some, the flag was a symbol of racial antipathy, for others a historical memory, and for some it represented a fighting spirit. At one time its most conventional use was to rally football teams at games on Saturday afternoons. In the tense years of racial conflict in the 1960s the University of Georgia ceased playing the song "Dixie" and waving the Confederate flag. This cessation was an irony given that fully two-thirds of the state flag was a rendering of the Confederate banner.

The flag's latter-day association with racial controversy had more to do with a change in its relationship with society, than any change in its inherent meaning. When the fight for civil rights was joined, the flag became a symbol of belligerence and the memory of an order under attack by the federal government. Each southern state faced the controversy in a different way.

In the 1990s, Alabama lowered its Confederate symbol and placed it beside the capital's monument to the Civil War dead. Alabama's state flag was less ostentatious than the rebel banner flown by heritage groups, but it dated from the same war experience and echoed the crossed bars of defiance. Virtually every county seat in the South has a Confederate memorial on the county square and many displayed the discredited banner with that memorial. Parades in the South often feature Confederate reenactors as invited participants.

Mississippi is the only southern state to have adopted Confederate emblems into its state flag before the controversy of the civil rights movement. The Mississippi flag was approved in 1894. Nearly one hundred years later, in 1983, three black cheerleaders refused to carry the state flag emblazoned with the rebel banner at college football games, and some students opposed the playing of "Dixie" at games. In the 1990s, Mississippi, along with South Carolina and Georgia, provided the nation with a political spectacle unmatched since the civil rights struggles of the 1960s.

The Mississippi controversy was resolved on April 17, 2001, when voters chose to retain the 1894 state flag that included a representation of the Confederate battle flag rather than replace it with a design recommended by a commission appointed by the governor and other state officials. The vote came at a time that left Mississippi as the only state honoring the battle flag in this way. The issue was decided by a public vote, and passed by nearly a two-to-one margin. The referendum drew more voters than a 1999 statewide election for governor, lieutenant governor, and other state officials. Research after the referendum found that the vote was explained less by race, than education, since "white voters most supportive of the 1894 flag tended to reside in the . . . rural white counties."[23]

The conflict over public display of the Confederate battle flag in South Carolina began in a familiar place, the statehouse, which still bore brass markings from the cannonballs General William T. Sherman fired on the building in 1865. One hundred years after the firing on Ft. Sumter the state legislature decreed that the red and blue battle flag, identical to the one carried by rebel armies, fly above the capitol dome. At the time the justification for the decision was to commemorate the state's Confederate dead, but it was also a blatant challenge to the burgeoning civil rights movement. From 1962 until 1994 the flag was at various times an embarrassment, a historical legacy, and a source of head-shaking curiosity, more than a symbol of controversy. But in 1994, a group of business and professional leaders brought a lawsuit challenging the legality of its public display. "We need economic development," said one of the plaintiffs.[24] The group declared that the banner over the capitol was an embarrassment when it came to the recruitment of new industry. The state legislature tried, and failed, to resolve the controversy.

The issue festered until October of 1996. In that month Governor David Beasley, who ran as a staunch flag supporter, changed his mind after a morning prayer and Bible study. The born-again decision came because Beasley believed the flag had become a symbol of strife. "The plowshare has been turned into a sword," he said. Not everyone shared his conviction. Conservatives accused Beasley of bowing to the "scourge of political correctness," and said they did not care that hate groups used the banner, they wanted it to continue in public display.[25] The state house of representatives called for a statewide referendum, ducking a floor vote on the measure. The issue reached a climax in the gubernatorial election of 1998, when Beasley lost his bid for reelection in part because of his flip-flop on the flag issue.

The new governor from the opposite political party found the going no easier. In November of 1999 hundreds of men paraded in Charleston dressed in gray uniforms along with women in black widows' dresses to rebury the remains of twenty-two Confederate sailors whose resting place had mistakenly been covered over. Newspapers across the country were intrigued by the story of a disagreement thought long dead. Television coverage invariably showed Confederate reenactors extolling the virtues of law, honor, and love of country that they attributed to the banner. The NAACP reacted to this publicity, and other public displays of support for the rebel flag, by calling for a statewide boycott to end tourism in the state.

In countless closed-door talks and public statements a compromise appeared, and then disappeared. Huge demonstrations by both sides served to poison the debate. One state senator from Charleston called the NAACP the "National

Association for Retarded People," and the black opponents linked flag supporters to the Ku Klux Klan. A Republican legislator, sitting under a painting of Robert E. Lee and Stonewall Jackson, found a parallel with the term limits, balanced budgets, and tax limits of the GOP's "Contract with America." "Our ancestors were a little off with their timing, but their rebellion against the federal government is finally seeing fruition."[26]

The attempt by state leaders to portray South Carolina as a good vacation and business place was being undermined by a debate over the legislature's inability to remove the Confederate flag from the statehouse dome. Finally, in May of 2000, the legislature agreed to a compromise and the flag was removed from above the statehouse to a flagpole adjacent to a Confederate soldier's memorial near the front of the capitol. The compromise pleased no one. The NAACP continued a tourism boycott, and the Confederate defenders complained about the gravity of the historical insult.

A study conducted after the controversy concluded that groups favoring removal of the flag successfully expanded the scope of the conflict, while opponents experienced cascading defections.[27] In the end the, the Confederate flag was more visible in front of the capitol that it ever was above the dome, and the NAACP continued to insist that black athletes not come to South Carolina to participate in intercollegiate activities.

Some wrote off the South Carolina dispute as the erratic behavior by eccentric personalities in a state with a history of recalcitrance. No sooner was the ink dry on the flag compromise in the Palmetto State, than the same issue flared in next-door Georgia. In 2001 Governor Roy Barnes, a Democrat, led a successful effort to change Georgia's state flag, which then prominently featured the Confederate battle cross. The new flag put the state seal on a largely blue background and shrank the rebel symbol to a small box at the bottom of the flag. The next year Barnes, who had a strong record on education and taxes, suffered a stunning upset in his bid for reelection. For the first time since Reconstruction, the Peach State would not have a Democrat in the governor's mansion, and the new governor promised a referendum for a new flag design.

No sooner had Sonny Perdue moved into the governor's mansion, than he faced a lobbying effort by the Sons of Confederate Veterans and the Heritage Preservation Association to put the issue on the ballot. At the gubernatorial inauguration, airplanes circled the state capitol towing banners that read: "Let Us Vote," and "You Promised."[28] A poll by the *Atlanta Journal Constitution* newspaper found that 50 percent of the respondents thought the Confederate battle flag was more a symbol of "heritage and history," than a reminder of "oppression and racial division."[29] The final flag compromise in 2004 was red, white, and blue with historical arches and the words, "In God We Trust" in gold letters.

The Almighty was in evidence on April 17, 2004, when the remains of eight crewmen from the Confederate submarine *CSS H. L. Hunley* were buried with full military honors in Magnolia Cemetery in Charleston, South Carolina. Rebel flags and butternut uniforms were the order of the day. The event attracted 50,000 visitors and live television coverage. The *Hunley* was sunk on February 17, 1864, after leaving Sullivan's Island and sinking the *USS Housatonic*, a Union blockade ship. The 140th anniversary of the event was billed as "the last Confederate Funeral," and garnered international attention and interest.

The controversies over the Confederate battle flag and the *Hunley* funeral, as symbols of the Civil War, say something about the stubborn legacies of region and culture in the contemporary South. The flag became a concentrated symbol of ascendant conservatism, distrust of government, and hostility to "political correctness." For some, race plays no part in their allegiance to the flag, and for others prejudice is dominant. The Confederate flag has become a flashpoint of controversy with two opposite visions of regional history and future politics. At stake in the controversy is the ability of states to set their regional agenda and determine how the nation's most self-conscious region will remember itself.

Southern Womanhood

From the colonial period to the present, the work and place of women has helped define the South as a distinct region. An examination of the behavior of women in Columbia, South Carolina, in 1865 found that their fierce defense of the city was rooted in their native concept of female honor and a woman's relationship to the Confederate cause.[30] The myth of a Scarlett O'Hara ideal persists, of native women who were iron-willed and strong but operated with velvet-glove smoothness. The real-life residents were much more complex and diverse than the flirtatious southern belles and formidable steel magnolias portrayed in fiction and film. But it is undeniable that they were still more constrained by law, religion, and custom—not to mention race—than women in other parts of the country. They were slower to question the premise that women should be subordinate to men, and they were in a place where for most of its history only white men enjoyed the privileges of citizenship.

Gender differences in the South were a part of life from the beginning. In most of the original colonies, the family laws were English, which meant that marriage was monogamous and indissoluble. In Virginia until 1794 marriage services were performed by Anglican clergymen. In Spanish Florida and in the formerly French territory of Louisiana, Catholic bishops presided at weddings. Marriage was esteemed as a sacred and solemn obligation to God and the community at large.

The grace and hospitality of southern white women held that they were sexually pure, pious, deferential, and content with their place in society. Most southern women were willing perpetuators of this system. Whether through public pressure or by choice, they had little desire to speak in public or embrace humanitarian reform movements that were popular in the North. Campaigns such as advocacy for the blind, the insane, the criminal, and the uneducated were linked to movements like Transcendentalism, Unitarianism, prohibition, and abolition in the public mind. Outside the South these movements involved large numbers of women, but that was never the case in the South.

Black women enjoyed no respite from the weight of antebellum work on the land. In addition to their own homes and families, they managed the kitchen, children, and domestic needs of their white masters. They worked in the homes, in the barns, and in the fields at harvest time. The difficulties of life for a black female slave were compounded by the likelihood of a move and subsequent separation from her own family.

Upper- and middle-class white women rarely worked outside the home; instead they supervised the needs of the estate and tended the children. Housework was performed by slaves or indentured servants. Most women had limited education and tended to associate with other women in similar social situations. They repudiated reform movements on religious grounds and devoted themselves to otherworldly practices.

The Civil War disrupted this ideal environment, and Confederate women assumed the burden of providing needed items for their men at the front. They nursed the sick and improvised at home, doing without and sharing necessities with neighbors. Some fled the Yankee invaders, while other faced the consequences with supreme courage. When the Appomattox surrender ended the war, physical destruction and parched land faced pessimistic families.

One year after General Joseph E. Johnston surrendered the last Confederate field army, southern women began organizing to care for soldier graves. Memorial associations appeared all across the South, where they more than atoned for their previous inactivity in the antebellum years. They picked days like the "South's All Soul's Day," or Robert E. Lee's and Jefferson Davis's birthdays to commemorate the dead. The societies worked to save historic homes, preserve battlefields and graveyards, as well as remember the past.

A paradox of the Civil War is that it served to liberate southern women from traditional rules. Before 1860, women in most parts of the country couldn't run a business, unless they were widowed or let a man manage their property.[31] Activities during the war led to women taking jobs as clerks, nurses, factory workers, and assistants in businesses. While women in the region never embraced the suffragette movement with the enthusiasm of their northern counterparts, their abilities in the home and farm became legendary.

Most women in the South still saw their lives as being satisfied in religious activities. Baptist, Methodist, and Presbyterian women all developed missionary societies. When men assumed leadership in the church, women joined the ladies auxiliary. The failure of people with dramatically different religious orientations to migrate to the South in the postwar years led to the institutional reinforcement of the traditional family structure. Local civic and social functions were a reflection of the patriarchal nature of all southern institutions.

Urban and commercial development came slower to the South, so opportunities for female employment were less. Many women left the farm to be employed in newly built cotton mills. Female mill workers, and their children, became the region's first industrial workers to provide wages to supplement the farm life. "I was eleven years old when I went to work in the mill," recalled Bertha Miller of Thomasville, North Carolina, "they learnt me to knit."[32] Even with these jobs, the differences between North and South were stark. "In 1910, 83 percent of southern female work was in agriculture and domestic service, compared to 33 percent in the North."[33] In the twentieth century domesticity remained the chief obligation of a southern wife or daughter.

Women's suffrage received a dull reception in the South. The early women's suffrage movement was a northern phenomenon. Southerners were not associated with its rise, nor was there any significant suffrage activity in the region until about 1913.[34] Nine of the ten states that failed to ratify the Nineteenth Amendment were in the South, although Arkansas, Tennessee, and Texas had partial women's suffrage provisions in their state laws. The right to vote was seen as part of a general reform movement that might culminate in racial integration, so women's suffrage was restricted. Only the dreaded fear of federal intervention brought full citizenship to women in 1920.

The suffrage movement revealed some of the unique handicaps feminist crusades would have in the South. First, the past brought a unique legacy of its own, that of being southern with the full weight of southern history, mythology, and legend. Second, the region had an enduring image of the "belle" or "lady"—a fragile, dewy, femme fatale who was flirtatious, but sexually innocent. Third, the haunting legacy of race applied directly to black women, but it was also relevant to white females.[35] These traditions made any crusade for gender equality doubly difficult.

Perhaps the most striking characteristic of Southerners in the early decades of the twentieth century was the social distinctions in small town southern life. Although upper-class women often went to college, after graduation they worked in domestic pursuits or joined women's clubs. The South persisted with an outdated chivalric code that had one set of morals for women, and another for men. Good manners and good taste persisted even if money was not there to support the perceived lifestyle.

The status of women in the South changed more by evolution, than by any sudden transformation, in the postwar years. Both the world wars disturbed the South's economic, social, and moral isolation, and had a demonstrable impact on family life. In some cities women went to work, and, after World War II, men went to college. Employment opportunities were plentiful, and for the first time since before the Civil War, any native in the South who wanted a job was able to find one.

Employment opportunities for black women were not nearly as lucrative as for whites; many went to work as "domestics." The early morning bus stops in major southern cities were crowded with black women making the commute to white neighborhoods where they performed the same tasks of cook, caregiver to children, and nurse that once characterized the lives of their enslaved grandmothers. In many white homes, black women arrived at sunup to prepare breakfast and stayed until the male breadwinner came home in the afternoon. One view of their lives was well chronicled in the movie, *Driving Miss Daisy*, where black workers were suspected of theft, criticized for disloyalty, and treated as second-class members of the household. An opposite picture appears in Harper Lee's book, *To Kill a Mockingbird*, where conflict between children and the family cook is described as, "epic and one-sided. . . . Calpurnia always won mainly because Atticus always took her side. . . . I had felt her tyrannical presence as long as I could remember."[36] The stories chronicle a social reality in the South that is often ignored—the lives of black and white were intertwined. In the 1955 Montgomery Bus Boycott, the absence of black women workers in white homes effectively brought the city political establishment to its knees.

Once in the workforce, women were willing to consider other occupations, but these considerations occurred more slowly in the South than elsewhere in the country. Allegiance to family, faith, community, and patriarchy were stronger in the region. Table 4.6 in Chapter 4 shows that over three-quarters of the southern population is native to the region. Families tended to remain in the same region for longer periods of time, which meant that southern families had more extensive kinship and social ties.

The abiding resistance to change by native southern women was shown in the 1970s, when they played a prominent role in the defeat of the Equal Rights Amendment (ERA). In the years before 1972 there appeared to be support for feminist goals in public opinion polls across the nation, and even across the South. All the southern states created commissions on the status of women, and Texas and Virginia added equal rights amendments to their constitutions. When Congress voted overwhelmingly in 1972 to submit the amendment to the states, two southern senators (Sam Ervin of North Carolina and John Stennis of Mississippi) voted against it, along with nine regional congressmen.

The opposition was led by Midwesterner Phyllis Schlafly and her Eagle Forum, along with the National Committee to Stop ERA. They used a number of arguments, but the ones that resonated in the South were religious at their base. Opponents declared that women were most fulfilled through marriage and motherhood and that the feminist reforms would diminish these roles and weaken the traditional family. The message resonated well in the South, where the whole concept of sexual equality flew in the face of ingrained biblical teaching. In a movement that would prefigure the Christian Coalition in the next decade, conservative church activists organized against the ERA.

Initial polls showing support for the amendment declined as the arguments of the loosely coordinated opponents took root and public opinion began to change.

Vignette 10.2   Elizabeth Dole (1936–)

Elizabeth Dole was born in Salisbury, North Carolina, and today serves as US senator for the state of her birth. Her numerous positions and honors are examples of success by a southern native who is as gracious as she is ambitious.

The daughter of a wholesale florist, Elizabeth Hanford graduated from Duke University, took a masters degree in education at Harvard, and taught school in Boston. In 1962 she entered Harvard Law School and upon graduation worked in Washington. She changed her registration from Democrat to Independent in 1969, and married Senator Bob Dole in 1975. When Dole ran for vice president with Gerald Ford in 1976, Elizabeth Dole campaigned at his side.

When Ronald Reagan won the White House in 1980, she worked in the Public Liaison Office and in 1983 was appointed secretary of transportation. Later she served in President George H.W. Bush's administration as secretary of labor. Bill Clinton's election to the White House ended her appointed office, but in 1992 Elizabeth Dole had already left the administration to serve as president of the American Red Cross. For eight years she was a highly visible and effective spokesperson for the charity. In January of 1999, she launched a campaign for the presidential office, which she subsequently closed down to endorse George W. Bush.

In every job she's had in Washington, Elizabeth Dole has earned a reputation as a hard-working perfectionist without a sharp ideological edge. She is put off by the term "feminist," but at the same time has a reputation of talking about equal rights and equal opportunities for women and minorities. For many women in the South, she epitomizes the best of the regional tradition: gracious, smart, determined, and successful without being offensive.

When senior North Carolina senator Jesse Helms announced he would not run in August of 2001, Elizabeth Dole moved back to her mother's house in Salisbury and announced for office. She made the shrewd decision to campaign in every one of North Carolina's one hundred counties where she was greeted as an American celebrity with almost unlimited star power appeal.

"Liddy" Dole won the Republican primary with 80 percent of the vote. In the general election she faced Erskine Bowles, a former Clinton administration chief of staff and the son of a prominent North Carolina family. The race was expensive and hard fought, attracting national attention. On Election Day Dole won a convincing 54 percent to 46 percent decision. Her wins in two of the three largest media markets offset Democratic strengths in Durham and Chapel Hill.

The opposition was strongest in state legislatures. Even when governors like Jim Hunt of North Carolina, Reuben Askew of Florida, and James B. Edwards of South Carolina endorsed ratification, the more conservative legislators remained defiant. Supporters of the ERA succeeded in carrying endorsement in the North Carolina and Florida house, only to fail in the senate. When supporters searched for the final votes to secure ratification, one advocate declared that "a handful of willful and mischievous men" in the southern states of Florida, North Carolina, and South Carolina ultimately sealed the fate of the ERA.

The campaign for the constitutional amendment highlighted the image of the southern woman, a stereotype of feminine mystique that was organized around youth, physical attractiveness, sensuality, and a command of the social graces. Two researchers defined six characteristics of southern women based on participant observation and interviews with subjects. Their findings encapsulate the myth of southern womanhood that persists in the South, and was opposite the ideal presented by feminists. The first trait was "never forget your status lest others forget theirs," meaning that social differences are inevitable and are expressed in the attraction women have to organizations, sororities, and clubs as a way of keeping social boundaries. Second, "honor the 'natural' distinctions between men and women." The reliance on traditional sex roles in the South is a way women defer to men and expect social considerations in return. Third, "don't be a slut." The classical southern female ideal emphasized sexual chastity, but the same myth said women should be endlessly flirtatious and physically provocative. Fourth, "remain loyal to the southern tradition." Southern women were gracious and kept alive the memories of localism and loyalty to religious ideals expressed in social courtesies. Fifth, "you can never be too rich or too thin." Southern women expected conspicuous consumption as a birthright, and cultivated appropriate dress, looks, demeanor, and social rituals to go with their place in life. Sixth, "pretty is as pretty does." A southern woman expected confirmation of her appearance and manners in public, and expected men of whatever age to acknowledge her gender.[37]

In the end it was the political culture, not the legislators, that ended the ERA. Opponents successfully appealed to the native social and religious conservatism and the aversion the South historically has to the expansion of federal power. North Carolina senator Sam Ervin wrote a minority report on the effects of the ERA adoption that was widely circulated among the opponents. It argued that the amendment would mandate sexual integration of prisons and restrooms, and compel the military to draft women for combat. Opponents declared that passage of the constitutional amendment would mean that US women would no longer be supported by their husbands, and would have to go to work and leave their children in state-run childcare facilities. All these anxieties, real or imagined, flew in the face of the traditional values Southerners had for women.

Arguments for the protection of southern womanhood, coupled with fear of expanded federal power, proved a compelling case in the South. The region was still chafing over the Supreme Court decision on school prayer and integration; busing was a controversial policy across the region, and parents of school-age children resented programs like mandatory sex education programs in the public schools. The ERA controversy ignited the "Pro-Family" movement that ultimately became a significant part of the Christian Right. Opponents saw the ERA as part of a larger feminist effort to federally fund childcare facilities, promote gay rights, expand abortion practices, and limit the practice of the Christian faithful. The ERA birthed the Eagle Forum, Conservative Caucus, National Right to Life, the Mormon Club, and a host of related groups intent on limiting federal power.

Feminist supporters of the ERA gained an extension for ratification from a deadline in 1977 to one in 1982, but the delay made no difference since no state ratified the legislation in the interim. To add insult to injury, Tennessee voted to rescind its earlier endorsement. None of this mattered; by 1980 the family groups succeeded in persuading the Republican Party to place an antiabortion plank in the platform and for all practical purposes feminism was dead in one major political party. Opponents of the ERA claimed credit for Ronald Reagan's decisive victory over Jimmy Carter. The former Georgia governor's enthusiastic endorsement of the ERA was one reason why he was unsuccessful in his reelection bid.

The ERA campaign resulted in a resurgence of antifeminism and social conservatism, and the results influenced electoral politics across the nation. This legacy of the conflict is shown in Table 10.4, which ranks the states by the percentage of women serving in the state legislature. Ten of the eleven southern states are below the national average, and two—Alabama and South Carolina—are at the bottom of the list.[38]

The patterns in the table confirm that southern women have been less successful than women elsewhere when it came to winning electoral office. A study of Florida legislators in 1986 found that women representatives differed markedly among themselves as to their ideology and voting record.[39] Their presence has changed the tone and tenor of debate, but not altered the major political agenda. While many poll respondents say that women's equality is valued in the region, there is some conflict between image and reality.

In the highly acclaimed 1991 movie, *Fried Green Tomatoes,* a middle-aged housewife living in suburban Alabama is transformed from a timid housewife into a self-assured working woman. While there is some basis for the change, surveys have repeatedly shown that Southerners hold more conservative values about women in politics and employed women. A 1988 study found that Southerners were more likely to think that women should take care of their homes and leave the running of the country to men, are less likely to say they would vote for a woman for president, and less likely to say that women were emotionally suited for politics.[40] A 1995 study came to similar conclusions: "our analyses indicate that southern attitudes are the most traditional when the topic is women in politics," even though the differences between the South and other regions of the country are moderating.[41]

An examination of gender roles from county elections in eight southern states found that women were able to routinely win election to process-oriented offices, like county clerk, but were unable to move up the electoral ladder into the more competitive arena of high-profile statewide and federal leadership offices.[42]

A pattern of resistance to national trends is seen in another emotional political issue: homosexual rights. Historically the South has undergone more momentous change than the rest of the country, but most of the modifications have been imposed from the outside. Native Southerners have a chivalrous and sentimental tie to marriage and divorce, and an opposition to gay rights. Homosexual activists have not emerged as successful participants in mainstream southern politics. "The

Table 10.4   Women Legislators in the United States, 2005

State	Total Members	Women Legislators	Percent Women
1. Delaware	62	21	33.9
2. Maryland	188	63	33.5
3. Washington	147	49	33.3
4. Nevada	63	21	33.3
5. Vermont	180	60	33.3
6. Arizona	90	30	33.3
7. Colorado	100	33	33.0
8. Kansas	165	53	32.1
9. New Mexico	112	35	31.3
10. California	120	37	30.8
11. New Hampshire	424	128	30.2
12. Minnesota	201	60	29.9
13. Connecticut	187	54	28.9
14. Oregon	90	26	28.9
15. Illinois	177	49	27.7
16. Idaho	105	29	27.6
17. Hawaii	76	20	26.3
18. Wisconsin	132	34	25.8
19. Massachusetts	200	49	24.5
20. Nebraska	49	12	24.5
21. Maine	186	45	24.2
22. Montana	150	36	24.0
23. **Florida**	160	37	23.1
24. New York	212	49	23.1
25. **North Carolina**	170	38	22.4
26. Missouri	197	43	21.8
27. Michigan	148	30	20.3
28. Utah	104	21	20.2
29. Iowa	150	24	20.0
30. Ohio	132	26	19.7
31. **Texas**	181	35	19.3
32. Alaska	60	11	18.3
33. **Georgia**	236	43	18.2
34. **Tennessee**	132	23	17.4
35. North Dakota	141	24	17.0
36. **Louisiana**	144	24	16.7
37. **Arkansas**	135	22	16.3
38. Indiana	150	24	16.0
39. Rhode Island	113	18	15.9
40. New Jersey	120	19	15.8
41. West Virginia	134	21	15.7
42. Oklahoma	149	22	14.8
43. Wyoming	90	13	14.4
44. South Dakota	105	15	14.3
45. **Virginia**	140	19	13.6
46. Pennsylvania	253	33	13.0
47. **Mississippi**	174	22	12.6
48. Kentucky	138	17	12.3
49. **Alabama**	140	14	10.0
50. **South Carolina**	170	15	8.8

Source: Center for American Woman and Politics (CAWP), and the National Center on State Legislatures (NCSL), December 2002.

Note: National Average = 22.4 percent; Southern Average = 16.2 percent; Non-South Average = 24.2 percent.

change in virtually all areas is consistently below the amount of change that is occurring in the rest of the country." The movement from the shadows of society to leadership on issues like hate crime legislation has not been a characteristic of the southern subculture.[43]

Until 1995 the law in every US state defined marriage to be between a man and a woman. By 2003 thirty-seven states, including *every* one in the South, adopted laws that specifically prohibited same-sex marriages, defining marriage as unions of couples of the opposite sex. In 1996 President Bill Clinton signed the Defense of Marriage Act (DOMA) that prohibits same-sex marriages. The law forbade couples from receiving federal marriage benefits and allowed states to ignore same-sex marriages that may be sanctioned in other states.

Southern states were enthusiastic supporters of DOMA. The states duplicated the federal language and specifically declared that marriages between individuals of the same gender were not binding in the South. In 2004 Southerners passed state constitutional bans on same-sex marriage by large margins: Arkansas, 75 percent; Georgia, 77 percent; and Mississippi, 86 percent.

Summary

The South that V. O. Key described limped into the twentieth century, and at mid-century was still a poor, racially separate society suffering under one-party rule and existing in a labor-intensive, agricultural environment. Legislative rule, military allegiance, Confederate ideals, and traditional roles for women seemed more appropriate for that age. After all, self-serving white elites had kept the South out of the mainstream of US life for decades.

It was widely believed that urban-industrial development would quickly eradicate a host of regional ills. Henry Grady, the visionary editor of the *Atlanta Constitution*, proclaimed in 1889 that when capital and technology were added to the natural endowments of the South, spectacular new communities would spring up in the piedmont landscape. In large measure the vision of Grady has been realized. Today six-lane highways circle modern cities, there is no racial separation by law, and the nation elects southern presidents. Yet this development has not obliterated the southern legacy. Southern legislators still acquire power, only now it is on the Republican, not the Democratic, side of the aisle. Southerners still seek military careers where they have gained national recognition for their service. They retain a more traditional view of family and home life. Finally, at least among whites, there is a longing to keep vestiges of the past—and that includes the Confederate flag—flying over the new affluence.

The controversy of retaining such southern distinctives as the battle flag was seen in the Democratic Party presidential debate of 2003. When Vermont governor Howard Dean said a goal of the Democratic Party should be to "get southern whites with Confederate flags flying on their pickups," to vote for the party nominee, the other candidates roundly criticized him. The symbol of southern defiance remains as controversial today as it was one hundred and forty years ago.

The distinctiveness of legislative rule, military allegiance, traditional family life, and Confederate valor remain, but they are watered down. Despite its changing nature the southern subculture persists. Place is still an important value in the South, and while the region is more urbanized today than anytime in the past, its soul remains in the small town values that once characterized life there. Being southern is still more a state of mind than anything else. The values of religion, social and family relations, past myths, and self-image endure.

Notes

1. Allen Tate, "The Profession of Letters in the South," in *The Collected Essays of Alan Tate.* Vanderbilt Library, Private Collection, 1959.

2. Richard M. Weaver, *The Southern Tradition at Bay: A History of Postbellum Thought.* Washington, D.C.: Regnery Gateway, 1968, p. 372.

3. Tom Wolfe, *A Man in Full.* New York: Farrar, Straus Giroux, 1998, p. 63.

4. Donald Davidson, "Still Rebels, Still Yankees," in Thomas Daniel Young, Floyd Watkins, and Richamond Croom Beatty (eds.), *The Literature of the South.* New York: Scott, Foresman and Co., 1968, p. 739.

5. T. Harry Williams, *Romance and Realism in Southern Politics.* Athens: University of Georgia Press, 1961, p. 3.

6. John Shelton Reed, *My Tears Spoiled My Aim.* Columbia: University of Missouri Press, 1993, p. 23.

7. Tony Horowitz, *Confederates in the Attic: Dispatches from the Unfinished Civil War.* New York: Vintage Books, 1999, p. 76.

8. John Edgerton, *The Americanization of Dixie.* New York: Harper & Row, 1974, pp. xv, 5.

9. Alvin Josephy Jr., *The Congress of the United Stated.* New York: McGraw-Hill, 1975, p. 206.

10. Cited in Robert A. Caro, *The Years of Lyndon Johnson: Master of the Senate.* New York: Alfred A. Knopf, 2002, p. 201.

11. Senator Joe Biden, "Eulogy for Strom Thurmond," July 1, 2003.

12. Fred R. Harris, *Deadlock or Decision.* New York: Oxford University Press, 1993, p. 15.

13. Rod Andrew, *Long Gray Lines: The Southern Military School Tradition, 1839–1915.* Chapel Hill: University of North Carolina Press, 2001, p. 3.

14. John Hawkins Napier III, "Military Schools," in Charles Reagan Wilson and William Ferris (eds.), *The Encyclopedia of Southern Culture.* Chapel Hill: University of North Carolina Press, 1989, p. 258.

15. John Hawkins Napier III, "Military Traditions," in *The Encyclopedia of Southern Culture*, p. 642.

16. Michael S. Neiberg, *Making Citizen-Soldiers: ROTC and the Ideology of American Military Service.* Cambridge, Mass.: Harvard University Press, 2000, p. 172.

17. John Hawkins Napier III, "Military Traditions," in *The Encyclopedia of Southern Culture*, p. 642.

18. "Military Tradition Among Southerners Is Continuing in War Careers in Services," *Winston-Salem Journal*, March 28, 2003.

19. Gallup poll, April 11, 1991.

20. Ibid., July 26, 1992.

21. *The Atlanta Journal-Constitution*, August 24, 2003.

22. "Military Smaller, Smarter, Older for War in Iraq," *Charleston Post and Courier*, March 30, 2003.

23. Douglas G. Feig, "Explaining the Mississippi Flag Vote," a paper presented at the Citadel Symposium on Southern Politics, March 4–5, 2004, Charleston, South Carolina.

24. "S.C. High Court Hears Debate Over Confederate Battle Flag," *Charlotte Observer*, November 16, 1994.

25. "The Flag and the Fury," *US News and World Report*, March 10, 1997.

26. Tony Horowitz, *Confederates in the Attic*. New York: Vintage Books, 1999, p. 77.

27. Laura R. Woliver, Angela Ledford, and Chris Dolan, "The South Carolina Confederate Flag: The Politics of Race and Citizenship," *Politics and Society* 29 (2001), pp. 708–730.

28. "Georgia's New Governor Is Pressed to Make Good on His Pledge About the Flag," *New York Times*, January 21, 2003.

29. Ibid.

30. Jacqueline G. Campbell, "The Most Diabolical Act of All the Barbarous War: Soldiers, Civilians, and the Burning of Columbia, February, 1865," *American Nineteenth Century History* 3 (Fall 2002), pp. 53–72.

31. Tony Horowitz, *Confederates*, p. 268.

32. Victoria Byerly, *Hard Times Cotton Mill Girls*. Ithaca, N.Y.: Cornell University Press, 1986, p. 48.

33. Mary Frederickson, "Working Women," in *The Encyclopedia of Southern Culture*, p. 1568.

34. Kenneth R. Johnson, "Kate Gordon and the Woman-Suffrage Movement in the South," *Journal of Southern History* 38, no. 3 (1972), pp. 365–392.

35. Margaret Ripley Wolfe, "The View from Atlanta: Southern Women and the Future," in Joe P. Dunn and Howard L. Preston (eds.), *The Future South: A Historical Perspective for the Twenty-First Century*. Urbana: University of Illinois Press, 1991, p. 127.

36. Harper Lee, *To Kill a Mockingbird*. New York: Harper & Row, 1960, p. 6.

37. John Lynxwiter and Michele Wilson, "The Code of the New Southern Belle," in Caroline Matheny Dillman, *Southern Women*. New York: Hemisphere Publishing, 1988, pp. 113–125.

38. Cindy Simon Rosenthal, *When Women Lead: Integrative Leadership in State Legislatures*. New York: Oxford University Press, 1998.

39. Joanne V. Hawks and Mary Carolyn Ellis, "Creating a Different Pattern: Florida's Women Legislators, 1928–1986," *Florida Historical Quarterly* 65 (July 1987), p. 83.

40. Jeanne S. Hurlbert, "The Southern Region: A Test of the Hypothesis of Cultural Distinctiveness," *Sociological Quarterly* 30 (1988), pp. 245–266.

41. Tom L. Rice and Diane L. Coates, "Gender Role Attitudes in the Southern United States," *Gender & Society* 9 (1995), pp. 744–756.

42. David Lublin and Sarah E. Brewer, "The Continuing Dominance of Traditional Gender Roles in Southern Elections," *Social Science Quarterly* 84 (June 2003), pp. 379–396.

43. Hastings Wyman, "Gay Liberation Comes to Dixie—Slowly," *Southern Review of Politics* 23 (2002), pp. 167–192.

11

The South and the Future

More than any other region of the country, the South is anxious about its future. Writers, who once focused on the region's tumbled-down poverty and poor education, now stand before gleaming skyscrapers in cities where the prospects for tomorrow never seemed brighter. The South isn't what it was, but no one is very sure of what it is becoming either. The concern of some is that the "persistent and significant differences," to quote Gabriel Almond and Sidney Verba, of the southern subculture will disappear and the region will become a cultural colony to the rest of the nation.[1] Other observers agree with the comment of John Shelton Reed, one of the wittiest commentators of this change: "Every time I look at Atlanta I see what a quarter million Confederate soldiers died to prevent."[2]

Because so much of the history of the South has been in opposition to the values of the rest of the nation, the prospect of joining the larger whole strikes many residents as something inevitable, while for others it is a tragedy of monumental proportions. John Edgerton compared the South of the 1970s with the segregated, rural region of thirty years earlier and concluded that, "the South is just about over as a separate and distinct place."[3] Certainly in the area of racial attitudes there has been a dramatic turnaround. In 1942 virtually all whites in the South said black and white children should attend separate schools, by 1970 only 16 percent opposed school desegregation, and by 1980 only 5 percent were in opposition. The latter figure was the same as for white parents nationally. "A regional difference of great importance only yesterday seems to have disappeared almost completely."[4]

Did the lifting of racial discrimination, the movement of new industry to the region, the attraction of foreign investment, unprecedented urbanization, and wealth beyond imagination transform the subculture of the South to the point where it is no longer distinct? The South remains a unique subculture even though it is no longer a colony in the more prosperous nation. The predominantly rural and small-town residential South is gone, along with a concentration in agriculture, and low-

415

level industrial occupations. In income per person it has nearly caught the rest of the nation, despite having practiced slavery and segregation into the modern era. It has a high crime and imprisonment rate, yet practices the death penalty with impunity. The region is among the most religious in the world, and Southerners are more likely than others to join voluntary associations. Yet, it has one of the lowest ratios of voter participation in the country, and in many ways is almost an undemocratic democracy.

Persistent regional differences remain in attitudes and beliefs. When asked where they would like to live, Southerners' preference for their own region has been evident since the early days of survey research. Southerners are more likely to own guns and oppose the regulation of firearms. An enduring legacy of church attendance at Protestant services continues, in spite of general cultural secularization. Non-Southerners moving into the region are coming to share the attitudes of the South.[5]

The South's unique origins produced a distinctive value system and unusual politics that survived the onslaught of change. Today the geography is urban, but the countryside still attracts tourists, retirees, and outsiders, who have had their own influence on the culture. The legacy of economic underachievement has been drowned in an ocean of financial prosperity and the new racial mix in some southern cities is sometimes more diverse than any other region of the country. Blacks are prominent in local and county politics, and in some places returning as in-migrants back to the South. The religious effect is now housed in suburban megachurches with Internet and television influence in subdivision homes. The one-party Democratic political legacy is steadily being eroded by Republican influence, and in some places outright GOP domination. The political culture of the South now favors executive leadership and legislative innovation at the state level. The predictions of future prosperity are such that the region will never again be an inferior stepchild in the US family. It rejoined the country in the last quarter of the twentieth century, and by 2000 was leading the political parade in a headlong rush to make up for lost time.

Virtually every decade, from the late nineteenth to the mid-twentieth, heralded the birth of the New South. The most distinctive need was always economic. This was the legacy that concerned Thomas Wolfe when he wrote about the natives saying, "there was in all of them something ruined, lost, or broken—some precious and irretrievable quality which had gone out of them and which they could never get back again."[6] But they did get it back: and when they did the concern was that the South lost as many virtues as vices in the final exchange. In the new golden prosperity the region remains the most conservative part of the country, still drenched in religion and still carrying a grudge.

John Shelton Reed presented convincing evidence in the 1980s that southern-ness has not disappeared, and is guarded most jealously by upwardly mobile residents who live in the new suburbs.[7] More recent scholarship, in surveys taken from

1990 to 2001, still found a remarkable 70 percent of respondents who considered themselves to be Southerners.[8] It is in private schools that flourish next to huge churches with an allegiance to traditional family values and the Republican Party that new Southerners prosper. The civil communities of Marietta, Georgia, and Brentwood, Tennessee, and Plano, Texas, are breeding grounds of a new regional individualism, where residents are optimistic about the future and see government as the only cloud on their horizon. It was in these places that resolutions were passed against abortion, in favor of the Gulf War, and condemning the "gay lifestyle" as incompatible with community standards.

In the last chapter of a book on southern politics it is fitting to ask what effect all this change has had on the six elements of the political culture identified earlier. By definition, a political subculture mandates distinctive constituent elements, but the previous chapters have chronicled how much these traits have changed. What does the ascendancy of the South mean for its future?

"Everything about the Americans," wrote Alexis de Tocqueville, "is extraordinary, but what is more extraordinary still is the soil that supports them."[9] The **geography** of the South is of course unchanged, but it now contains a new demography. While the metropolitan areas flourish along interstate highways with their suburbs and shopping malls, there are rural areas floundering in abject poverty. The differences are stark between rustic counties with a high black population, minimal education opportunities in small towns without industry, and the gleaming city suburbs. An examination of nineteen Alabama counties in the Black Belt showed that "almost everyone is poorer, unhealthier, less well-educated, and with worse jobs than those in the rest of the state."[10] Half the counties have double the state's unemployment, the median income is more than $10,000 less, and life expectancy nearly two years shorter. These rural areas face a difficult prospect. Their populations are dependent, skewed toward the elderly, and offer little attraction for outside investment or appeals to entrepreneurs.

Historically, the fate of rural areas has been inextricably linked to the fate of neighboring cities. The galloping economy has created a considerable imbalance within metropolitan regions. There are high-skilled, white-collar suburban employees opposite poorly educated, low-skilled workers with little hope of upward mobility. In the South, this dichotomy is exacerbated by race, with inner-city blacks and Hispanics unable to travel to the metropolitan periphery where there is a demand for low-skilled workers. Like many cities, the Sunbelt growth of the southern economy ignored mass transit in favor of interstate highways.

Depending on their location, some rural areas have begun to blossom as retirement communities. As the huge cohort of postwar babies age, they are looking for inexpensive locations to live out their "golden years." The southern appeal of natural beauty, sunshine, and location make downstate rural counties close to cities, lakes, and the ocean very appealing. In virtually all of Florida, low-country South Carolina, downstate Georgia, Mississippi, and Alabama, and central Texas retirees have moved into communities where they vote in huge numbers. These are towns that have no problem with traffic jams or an overtaxed infrastructure.

The persistent imbalance between central city and the metropolitan fringe is also an environmental concern. As the cities expanded across the southern landscape, they brought air and water pollution issues to the political agenda. Growth management, the destruction of farmland, and the obliteration of historic structures are now central issues in southern cities. The states of Georgia and Florida are cooperating to create statewide development plans, but they face criticism from advocates of economic expansion.

The new context of southern politics requires southern leaders to work in tandem with business, universities, and citizen groups to collectively accommodate postindustrial development. The South now has suburb-to-suburb immigration patterns that have altered the demography, tax rates, governmental structures, and family life of communities. Overwhelmingly white suburban and out-town communities have schools that are the envy of the state. They stand in sharp contrast to crumbling inner-city schools and rural districts. The division is especially evident in separate city and county school systems in cities like Atlanta, Nashville, Charlotte, and the Dallas–Fort Worth region.

The **agrarian heritage** and the **legacy of economic underachievement** in the South have gone the way of the steamboat on the Mississippi and the cowboy of the Old West. Today the residents of metropolitan areas in Atlanta, Houston, Charlotte, and Nashville are Southerners basking in the glow of economic accomplishment. The cities are pistons in the engine of an international, knowledge-based, service economy. Pockets of poverty remain, and the deprivations for Mississippi's blacks in the Mississippi Delta, and Latinos in the lower Rio Grande River are real. Even so, the poorest of the traditional southern states has improved relative to their wealthier neighbors and the nation as whole.

The 1970 *Fortune* magazine listing of the two hundred largest corporations found only nine with a southern address. In 2003 forty-three of the top two hundred *Fortune* companies were located in the South, including Wal-Mart, number one on the list. Sam Walton opened his first store in 1962, and the headquarters of his empire remains in Bentonville, Arkansas. Wal-Mart has revenues of over $220 billion, with profits of $7 billion, and over one million employees. An examination of the state locations of the *Fortune 500* companies on the 2002 list shows that the eleven southern states had 28.5 percent of the national business revenues. Table 11.1 shows the ranking of the *Fortune 500* companies within the states.

The table shows that every southern state had at least one *Fortune 500* company within its borders.[11] Their presence means the South has reached a level of economic achievement that was unimaginable to the grandfathers of present native residents. The growth of some of the companies on the list, like Wal-Mart in Arkansas, Home Depot in Atlanta, and Dell Computer in Austin, made early investors overnight millionaires. Five southern cities: Houston, Atlanta, Charlotte,

Table 11.1   *Fortune 500* Companies Ranked Within States, 2002

States	Number of *Fortune 500* Companies
1. California	56
2. New York	51
3. **Texas**	46
4. Illinois	36
5. Ohio	28
6. Pennsylvania	26
7. Michigan	22
8. New Jersey	21
9. Minnesota	16
10. **Virginia**	16
11. **Georgia**	14
12. **North Carolina**	14
13. Connecticut	13
14. Massachusetts	13
15. Missouri	12
16. **Florida**	11
17. Washington	11
18. Wisconsin	11
19. **Alabama**	7
20. Maryland	7
21. **Tennessee**	7
22. Colorado	6
23. Oklahoma	6
24. **Arkansas**	5
25. Indiana	5
26. Kentucky	5
27. Nebraska	5
28. Arizona	4
29. Idaho	4
30. Nevada	4
31. Delaware	3
32. District of Columbia	2
33. Iowa	2
34. Kansas	2
35. Oregon	2
36. Rhode Island	2
37. **Louisiana**	1
38. **Mississippi**	1
39. **South Carolina**	1
40. South Dakota	1
41. Utah	1

Source: Fortune magazine, April 15, 2002, vol. 145, no. 8, p. F32.

Birmingham, and Dallas, were home to at least six *Fortune 500* companies, and join a select list in that only sixteen such cities were so recognized. The pace and reach of the development of these southern companies is one of the more remarkable facts of life in the history of US socioeconomic development.

More has been written about **race relations** in the South than on any other subject in its history. This is as it should be, because no topic is as important or central to politics in the region as race. But history is no prediction of the future, and the distinctive features of past black and white relations—violence, legal segregation, sharecropping, and one-party rule—are only in history books. While many native blacks left the region, it still contains a large and concentrated African American population within its boundaries.

The first, and most important, future racial legacy is likely to be the role the southern black electorate plays in political elections. This population is increasingly concentrated in urban areas and votes Democratic. The downtown areas of Atlanta, Georgia; Arlington, Virginia; Dallas and Houston, Texas; Memphis, Tennessee; and New Orleans, Louisiana, are places where the size and cohesion of the black vote can determine the outcome of statewide elections. For years conservatives in the Republican Party have complained that black followers are more conservative than their leaders, but in the foreseeable future it is unlikely that they will give up their allegiance to the Democrats.[12]

Political power by black Southerners has led to more appointed and elected positions held by African Americans at all levels of government. In some cases the proportion of elected black representatives is the same as that of the population. While African Americans have not fully utilized their potential in every southern state, their turnout and participation can be decisive in close races. Doug Wilder won a statewide race in Virginia, and Andrew Young ran a serious, but unsuccessful, biracial campaign in Georgia. Together they established a pattern and set a standard for black politicians who follow in their wake.

The major legacy of race relations in the South may have nothing to do with the historic black-white division. In two states—Texas and Florida—Hispanics are the major ethnic group that can swing elections. The sizable populations in these two national states are important, because virtually every southern state is swelling with an influx of new legal, and illegal, immigrants. The future of racial politics in the South is less about black and white relations than it is about these two traditional groups in a mix with Hispanics and Asians.

An abiding legacy is the **religious culture** that is endemic to southern life. The expansion of biblical Christianity in the region is likely to remain a feature of the subculture for decades to come. Churches today, in the South and nationwide, are megabusiness concerns, where pastors often act as chief executives and use business tactics to expand their churches. The Potter's House in Dallas, Texas, has over 18,000 members, a record label, a daily talk radio show, a prison satellite network, and a television show that reaches thousands with any given broadcast. Today five of the ten largest Protestant megachurches are in the South.

The megachurch phenomenon is a feature of southern urbanization, where worshippers number over 3,500 with a $5 million church budget. The faithful are reached through a combination of radio, television, and sponsored conferences. Nationwide over 750 churches qualify for the megachurch label, and they proliferate in the surrounding suburbs of cities like Dallas, Houston, Atlanta, and in the metropolitan areas of Florida.[13] Many of the new megachurches were not started until 1980, and their expressed purpose seems to be to defend Christian orthodoxy against the threats of modernity in the hope of preserving Christian civilization in the United States. In addition to these large churches, there are literally thousands of smaller ones that number anywhere from a few hundred to several thousand members. Collectively the churches give the region a distinct character.

When Jimmy Carter won the presidency in 1976, *Time* magazine estimated that of the 32 million Protestants in the South, over 20 million were evangelicals.[14] Today that number may have swollen by half again of what it was thirty years ago, and the evangelicals are now fixtures in the southern political—and Republican—landscape. The Religious Right is well integrated into the South's GOP. While more traditional Republicans were originally uncomfortable with this influence, they have learned to accommodate it with the widening prospect of victory.[15] White, conservative, evangelical Christian voters are a permanent aspect of southern politics, but white Southerners held conservative views on homosexuality, national defense, and the family long before the Moral Majority was ever organized. The churchgoing South takes very public positions on social issues, especially education issues, challenging the teaching of evolution in public schools, and controversial books in the library, and advocating public prayer on public school campuses. The southern states were among the first to outlaw partial birth abortion and adopt defense of marriage statutes.

While other characteristics of southern life are likely to attenuate, this one is most likely to expand. The 1973 *Roe v. Wade* decision that legalized abortion had the collateral effect of spurring a new wave of Christian fundamentalism. In the 1990s this effect was felt on foreign policy issues. Franklin Graham, son of Billy Graham, called Islam "a wicked religion."[16] The former president of the Southern Baptist Convention labeled the prophet Mohammad, "a demon-possessed pedophile."[17] In the last quarter-century Christian evangelicalism nationwide experienced a revival. "Every 5 years since 1965, while more liberal Protestant denominations suffered a near 5 percent decline in membership, evangelical churches won converts at a rate of 8 percent."[18]

Harper Lee captured a part of southern life when she wrote in *To Kill a Mockingbird* that, "In Maycomb, grown men stood outside in the front yard for only two reasons: death and politics."[19] In the rural South political power was once rooted in courthouse assemblies that informally handled power in the **one-party South**. No more. Today single-party domination is returning, but it is with Republican loyalty at the presidential and statewide level, and an uneven pattern of dual-party competition below.

The region began to change in the decade before the 1980 presidential election. During this time areas outside the South moved into the Democratic Party with a result that it had a base in liberal areas of the country. At the same time, the more conservative South marched steadily into the open arms of the Republican Party. Previously the liberal inclinations of the Democrats were tempered by the conservative "Solid South" allegiance, and the conservative tendencies of the Republicans were moderated by its Yankee northeastern base. As each political party shed its restraining geographical element, the nation's politics became more polarized. The 1980 presidential election showed this new alignment in stark detail, as Ronald Reagan captured the conservative South and Midwest.

After Reagan's 1980 triumph, the diversity of the two parties declined, reducing internal conflicts and making for a more unified party ideology and electorate. The growth of independent voters was a reflection of this change, since nonaligned voters wanted something from each party. "The economic change in the South has created many more affluent districts, and these districts strongly support Republicans."[20] National politics has become more partisan because now the conservative South is aligned with the party of a like ideology.

The GOP captured the South in the 2000 presidential election based on a foundation of support laid in the Reagan victory twenty years earlier. Republicans dominated every southern state classified here as "national," with the possible exception of Georgia, in the 1990s. The trend continued in the 2002 midterm election, with Republican victories for the US Senate and gubernatorial office in the lone holdout of Georgia. Now even the Peach State was a part of the green grass Republican majority in the South. Both the emergent states of North Carolina and Tennessee had a historic mountain base from which the GOP could expand in the 1990s. In the Deep South traditional states, only Arkansas and Louisiana kept their Democratic allegiance intact, the rest gravitated to the Republican Party.

Today the party system of the United States looks very much like the party map of a European country, with geography allied to ideology. The Midwest and South are conservative and Republican, while the West and Northeast are liberal and Democratic. The nation is beset with sharp ideological differences between a Republican Party of order representing the economic haves, and a Democratic Party of change representing the have nots.

Politicians in the South have gone from being pariahs to being presidents, and the legacy of political leadership and legislative control has been transformed. The region had a history of legislative domination, but most states strengthened their executive offices in the 1990s. The reform movement increased gubernatorial terms from two years to four, and allowed governors to seek reelection. The reduced turnover led to governors like Jimmy Carter, Bill Clinton, and George W. Bush compiling records of accomplishment that led to their election to the White House.

In spite of these changes, the office of governor in southern states is not as strong as it is in many other parts of the country. The institutional powers of appointment, budgetary decisionmaking, and legislative oversight in the southern governor's office are not impressive, but the informal accomplishments of some occupants are far reaching. Mike Huckabee and Bill Clinton in Arkansas, Lamar Alexander in Tennessee, Jim Hunt in North Carolina, Jeb Bush in Florida, and George W. Bush in Texas all overcame the formal limitations of the gubernatorial office with the force of their personality. Governors in office have been able to develop closer relationships with the legislature and with voters through television, allowing their personal power to become a springboard to national office.

The governors of two populous states—Texas and Florida—are in the national political spotlight. They have great influence in national political conventions with their state delegations, and in Congress with their congressional delegations. The national press covers them closely, giving their state activities national attention.

Southern governors have used their time in office to work on economic development in their states. The recruitment of industry, especially foreign companies, has become a factor in stated accomplishments and reelection possibilities. The conservative, nonunion culture of the South served as a breeding ground for industry to transfer from other areas of the country. It is also a seedbed for domestic companies to flourish, be they fast food franchises, home improvement warehouses, or general merchandising. Elected officials in the South are regularly charged to protect this halcyon business environment from excessive taxation and regulation.

Legislative offices in the South have become friendlier to blacks, but women have not had the success there that has become a feature of their participation nationwide. The lawmaking bodies are likely to keep their "amateur" (that is, low-paid) designation, business-related orientation, and low-tax mentality. A recent study found that, "Lawyers are quite prominent in some southern legislatures, constituting at least 20 percent in Florida, Louisiana, Texas, South Carolina, Virginia, and Mississippi."[21]

* * *

When Flannery O'Connor received the Georgia Writers' Association Scroll for her novel, *The Violent Bear It Away*, she told a story about a female friend from Wisconsin who moved to Atlanta and was sold a house in the suburbs. The man who sold it to her was from Massachusetts, and when he recommended the property he said, "You'll like the neighborhood. There's not a Southerner for two miles." O'Connor surmised that whatever else could be said about natives of the region, "At least we can be identified when we do occur."[22] The character of the region has been revealed in its manners, history, and culture.

The earliest explanation for southern distinctiveness was the climate. In 1778 a South Carolina assemblyman, William Henry Drayton, spoke in opposition to the Articles of Confederation because he believed them to be a threat to the plantation economy.[23] For all of its history the region was a conscientious objector to the rest of the country. The climate-determined, agricultural South has forever disappeared, to be replaced by a tradition-rich culture that keeps alive a kaleidoscope of mythical images and stereotypes from the past.

Novelist James Dickey wrote that now, "there are huge corporations in Jericho," and one of them, "makes a soft drink men have died for."[24] The South today is bigger than Coca-Cola of course, but it has become "Americanized" by affluence, education, and the conditions of modern life. Yet, even in the face of all this modification, parts of it refuse to change. Traditional values underlie southern exceptionalism and remain to influence US behavior in the twenty-first century.

Profound transformations in the South since the 1960s have led some to again sound the region's death knell. In a *Time* magazine article in 1990, Hodding Carter III, a former Mississippi newspaper editor, declared, "the South as South, a living, ever regenerating mythic land of distinctive personality, is no more."[25] The same conclusion was reached by two researchers in 2003 who declared, in the fall issue of *Southern Cultures*, that survey research was showing that "identification as a Southerner has clearly suffered a modest decline since 1991."[26] Unsaid in the surveys is the remarkable consistency of people who live in the region wishing to stay in the region.

No single attribute, or collection of conditions, can explain the continuing allegiance of the population to a separate South. The six cultural tenets discussed here in detail provide a fuller explanation, but in the final analysis it may be that the idea of the South is stronger than any empirical explanation of change. The rest of the nation has lived with this difference for two centuries, and in the future it will have to continue to regard some aspects of southern exceptionalism as more or less permanent. The South's stress on its past, its individualism, religiosity, small-government conservatism, and intense patriotism are likely to remain.

H. L. Mencken castigated the region as the "Sahara of the Bozart," a place without quality, taste, or culture. In Mencken's day the finer qualities of refinement were in the elite parlors of the Northeast. Today no such restricted view of culture dominates US life. The South always had a culture; it just wasn't one that Mencken would appreciate. The place may have been rural, poor, and despised, but beneath the Sunday School assemblies and county courthouse politicians, flourished a vibrant social community that is now more mainstream in America. It is this traditional culture that adapted to the tide of modernity, while still keeping its values intact.

The South may not be what is pictured in glossy photographs of *Southern Living* sentimentality, a land of verdant wooded trails, affluence, and an ease of life, as a model for the rest of the country to envy, but it is certainly identifiable when it does occur. The pressure of assimilation is very strong in US life, but it has not obliterated the fundamental tenets of southern culture. The pasteurized television culture can rub off the edges of any regional distinctiveness, but a number of cultural elements, from styles of clothing to food eaten to predominant political attitudes, are likely to remain. Southerners seem intent on keeping as much of their history and traditions alive as possible. As Robert Penn Warren wrote, "Home is a state of mind, a proper relation to the world."[27]

Notes

1. Gabriel Almond and Sidney Verba, *The Civic Culture*. Boston: Little, Brown, 1963, p. 16.

2. Tony Horowitz, *Confederates in the Attic*. New York: Vintage Press, 1999, p. 238.

3. John Edgerton, *The Americanization of Dixie: The Southernization of America*. New York: Harper's Magazine Press, 1973, p. xxi.

4. John Shelton Reed, *The Enduring South: Subcultural Persistence in Mass Society*. Chapel Hill: University of North Carolina Press, 1986, p. 92.

5. Ibid., pp. 100–102.

6. Thomas Wolfe, "Of Time and the River," *Scribner's Magazine*, 1934.

7. John Shelton Reed, *Southerners: The Social Psychology of Sectionalism*. Chapel Hill: University of North Carolina Press, 1983.

8. Larry J. Griffin and Ashley B. Thompson, "Enough About the Disappearing South: What About the Disappearing Southerner?" *Southern Cultures* 9, no. 3 (Fall 2003), pp. 51–67.

9. Alexis De Tocqueville, *Democracy in America*. Chicago: University of Chicago Press, 2000, p. 265.

10. "Life After Cotton," *The Economist*, August 30, 2003, p. 21.

11. The 2002 list was before the bankruptcy of WorldCom and Enron.

12. "Who's Out of Touch?" *The New Republic*, November 4, 1985, p. 15.

13. "Megachurches, Megabusinesses," *Forbes*, September 17, 2003.

14. Evangelicals accept the Bible as literal truth and believe in a "born-again" conversion experience. "A Born-Again Faith," *Time*, September 28, 1976.

15. Mark Caleb Smith, "With Friends Like This: The Religious Right, the Republican Party and the Politics of the American South." PhD dissertation, University of Georgia, 2002.

16. *New York Times,* August 15, 2002.

17. *Washington Post,* June 20, 2002.

18. "From Revival Tent to Mainstream," *US News and World Report*, December 19, 1988.

19. Harper Lee, *To Kill a Mockingbird*. New York: Harper & Row, 1960, p. 145.

20. Jeffrey M. Stonecash, Mark D. Brewer, and Mack D. Mariani, *Diverging Parties*. Boulder, Colo.: Westview Press, 2003, p. 96.

21. Virginia Gray, Russell L. Hanson, and Herbert Jacob (eds.), *Politics in the American States: A Comparative Analysis*. 7th ed. Washington, D.C.: Congressional Quarterly Press, 1999, p. 165.

22. Flannery O'Connor, *Mystery and Manners*. New York: Farrar, Straus and Giroux, 1957, pp. 28–29.

23. Walter Edgar, *South Carolina: A History*. Columbia: University of South Carolina Press, 1998, p. 37.

24. Hubert Shuptrine and James Dickey, *Jericho: The South Beheld*. Birmingham, Ala.: Oxmoor House, 1974, p. 73.

25. Hodding Carter III, "The End of the South," *Time*, August 6, 1990.

26. Larry J. Griffin and Ashley B. Thompson, "Are Southerners a Dying Breed?"

27. Robert Penn Warren, quoted in a flyer for the Tennessee Literary Festival, October 9–11, 1986, Nashville, Tennessee.

Selected Bibliography

Abernathy, Ralph David. *And the Walls Came Tumbling Down*. New York: Harper & Row, 1989.

. Agee, James. *A Death in the Family*. New York: Grosset and Dunlap, 1957.

Agee, James, and Walker Evans. *Let Us Now Praise Famous Men*. New York: Ballentine Books, 1939.

Almond, Gabriel A. "Comparative Political Systems." *Journal of Politics* 18 (1956).

Almond, Gabriel A., and G. Bingham Powell. *Comparative Politics: A Developmental Approach*. Boston: Little, Brown, 1966.

Almond, Gabriel A., and G. Bingham Powell. *Comparative Politics Today*. 6th ed. New York: Longman, 1996.

Almond, Gabriel A., and Sidney Verba. *The Civic Culture*. Princeton, N.J.: Princeton University Press, 1963.

American Political Science Review 52 (1954).

——— 62 (December 1968).

——— 63 (September 1969).

——— 20 (August 1976).

American Review of Politics 24 (Spring 2003).

Angelou, Maya. *I Know Why the Caged Bird Sings*. New York: Random House, 1969.

Applebome, Peter. *Dixie Rising: How the South Is Shaping American Values, Politics and Culture*. New York: Times Books, 1996.

Aristotle. *The Politics*. New York: Vintage Press, 1969.

Associated Press, November 4, 1998.

Atlanta Journal and Constitution. July 10, 1992.

Bailey, Stephen K. *Congress in the Seventies*. 2d ed. New York: St. Martin's Press, 1970.

Barker, Lucius J., Mack H. Jones, and Katherine Tate. *African Americans and the American Political System*. Upper Saddle River, N.J.: Prentice Hall, 1999.

Barone, Michael. *The Almanac of American Politics*. Washington, D.C.: National Journal, 1972–2004.

Barry, John M. *Rising Tide: The Great Mississippi Flood of 1972 and How It Changed America*. New York: Simon and Schuster, 1998.

Bartley, Numan V. *The Rise of Massive Resistance*. Baton Rouge: Louisiana State University Press, 1969.

Bass, Jack, and Walter DeVries. *The Transformation of Southern Politics*. New York: New American Library, 1976.

Belknap, Michael. *Federal Law and Southern Order*. Athens: University of Georgia Press, 1987.

Berkin, Carol, et al. *Making America: A History of the United States*. Boston: Houghton Mifflin, 1995.

Bernstein, Robert A., and Jim Seroka. "Alabama's Tax Reform: What Went Wrong and Why?" Paper presented at the biennial Citadel Symposium on Southern Politics, Charleston, S.C., March 2004.

Billingsley, Andrew. *Mighty Like a River*. New York: Oxford University Press, 1999.

Billington, *Westward Expansion*: *A History of the American Frontier*. New York: Macmillan, 1967.

Birmingham News, May 19, 2003.

Black, Earl, and Merle Black. *Politics and Society in the South*. Cambridge, Mass.: Harvard University Press, 1987.

———— *The Rise of Southern Republicans*. Cambridge, Mass.: Belknap Press of Harvard University Press, 2002.

———— *The Vital South*. Cambridge, Mass.: Harvard University Press, 1987.

Bradley, Martin B., Norman M. Green Jr., Dale E. Jones, et al. *Churches and Church Membership in the United States, 1990*. Atlanta: Glenmary Research Center, 1991.

Bragg, Rick. *All Over but the Southin'*. New York: Vintage Books, 1997.

Branch, Taylor. *Parting the Waters: America in the King Years*. New York: Simon and Schuster, 1988.

Brinkley, David. *Washington Goes to War*. New York: Alfred A. Knopf, 1988.

Brown, Claude. *Manchild in the Promised Land*. New York: Macmillan, 1965.

Bruce, Steve. *Conservative Protestant Politics*. New York: Oxford University Press, 1998.

———— *The Rise and Fall of the Christian Right*. New York: Clarendon Press, Oxford, 1961.

Bullock, Charles S. III, and M.V. Hood III. "Tracing the Evolution of Hispanic Political Emergence in the Deep South." Paper presented at the biennial Citadel Symposium on Southern Politics, Charleston, S.C., March 2004.

Bullock, Charles S., and Mark J. Rozell. *The New Politics of the Old South: An Introduction to Southern Politics*. 2d ed. Lanham, Md.: Rowman & Littlefield, 2003.

Burnham, Walter Dean. *Critical Election and the Mainsprings of American Politics*. New York: Norton, 1970.

Cameron, William, and Walter Dean Burnham (eds.). *The American Party Systems: Stages of Political Development*. New York: Oxford University Press, 1967.

Campaigns and Elections. September, 1994.

Capers, Gerald A. *The Biography of a River Town*. Memphis, Tenn.: Gerald Capers, 1966.

Carmines, Edward G., and James A. Stimson. *Issue Evolution: Race and the Transformation of American Politics*. Princeton, N.J.: Princeton University Press, 1989.

Caro, Robert A. *The Years of Lyndon Johnson: Master of the Senate*. New York: Alfred A. Knopf, 2002.

Carson, Clayborne. *In Struggle: SNCC and the Black Awakening of the 1960s*. Cambridge, Mass.: Harvard University Press, 1969.

Carter, Hodding III. "The End of the South." *Time*, August 6, 1990.

Carter, Jimmy. *Why Not the Best?* Nashville, Tenn.: Broadman Press, 1975.

Carter, Luther F., and David S. Mann. *Government in the Palmetto State*. Columbia: University of South Carolina Press, 1983.

Cash, W.J. *The Mind of the South*. New York: Alfred A. Knopf, 1941.

Catton, Bruce. *Never Call Retreat.* New York: Doubleday, 1965.

———— *The Coming Fury.* New York: Doubleday, 1961.

Chronicle of Higher Education. June 6, 2003.

Chubb, Jerome M., William H. Flanigan, and Nancy H. Zingale. *Partisan Realignment: Voters, Parties and Government in American History.* Beverly Hills, Calif.: Sage, 1980.

Coleman, Kenneth (ed.). *A History of Georgia.* Athens: University of Georgia Press, 1991.

Conroy, Pat. *My Losing Season.* New York: Doubleday, 2002.

———— *The Prince of Tides.* Boston: Houghlin Mifflin, 1986.

Contosta, David R., and Robert Muccigrosso. *America in the Twentieth Century: Coming of Age.* New York: Harper & Row, 1988.

Cooper, Christopher, and H. Gibbs Knott. "Defining Dixie: Seeking a Better Measure of the Modern Political South." Paper presented at the biennial Citadel Symposium on Southern Politics, Charleston, S.C., March 2004.

Corrigan, Matthew. "Consequences of Partisan Realignment in the South." Paper presented at the biennial Citadel Symposium on Southern Politics, Charleston, S.C., March 2004.

Council of State Governments. *Book of the States, 2002.* Lexington, Ky.: The Council of State Governments, 2002.

Crisswell, Robert. *The Book of Southern Wisdom,* Nashville, Tenn.: Papermill Press, 1990.

Cromartie, Michael. "Religious Conservatives in American Politics: 1980–2000." The Witherspoon Fellowship Lectures, Family Research Council. March 16, 2001.

Dabney, Virginius. *Virginia: The New Dominion.* Garden City, N.Y.: Doubleday, 1971.

Daniell, Rosemary. *Fatal Flowers.* New York: Holt, Rinehart and Winston, 1980.

Davidson, Chandler, and Bernard Grofman (eds.). *Quiet Revolution in the South.* Princeton, N.J.: Princeton University Press, 1994.

Dent, Harry. *The Prodigal South Returns to Power.* New York: John Wiley and Sons, 1978.

De Tocqueville, Alexis. *Democracy in America.* Chicago: University of Chicago Press, 2000.

Devine, Donald J. The *Political Culture of the United States.* Boston: Little, Brown, 1972.

Dewey, Donald O. *Union and Liberty: A Documentary History of American Constitutionalism.* New York: McGraw-Hill, 1969.

Dickey, James. *Jericho: The South Beheld.* Birmingham, Ala.: Oxmoor Press, 1989.

Dougar, Michael B. *Arkansas Odyssey.* Little Rock: Rose Publishing, 1994.

Douglass, Frederick. *Narrative of the Life of Frederick Douglass.* New York: Oxford University Press, 1963.

Down, Anthony. *An Economic Model of Democracy.* New York: Harper & Row, 1957.

Dunn, Charles W. (ed.). *Religion and American Politics.* Washington, D.C.: CQ Press, 1989.

Economist. August 30, 2003, January 25, 2003, August 14, 2004.

Edgar, Walter. *South Carolina, A History.* Columbia: University of South Carolina Press, 1993.

Edgerton, John. *The Americanization of Dixie: The Southernization of America.* New York: Harper's Magazine Press, 1973.

Edwards, George C. III. *Presidential Approval.* Baltimore: Johns Hopkins University Press, 1990.

Elazar, Daniel J. *American Federalism: A View from the States.* 3rd ed. New York: Harper & Row, 1984.

———— *The Metropolitan Frontier and American Politics.* New Brunswick: Transaction Publishers, 2003.

Faulkner, William. *The Faulkner Reader.* New York: Random House, 1942.

Fehrenback, T.R. *Lone Star: A History of Texas and Texans.* New York: Macmillan, 1995.

Fiorina, Morris. *Retrospective Voting in American National Elections.* New Haven: Yale University Press, 1981.

Fischer, David Hackett. *Albion's Seed: Four British Folkways in America.* New York: Oxford University Press, 1989.

Forbes, September 17, 2003.

Franklin, John Hope, and Alfred A. Moss Jr. (eds.). *From Slavery to Freedom: A History of African-Americans.* New York: McGraw-Hill, 1994.

Freeman, Criswell (ed.). *The Book of Southern Wisdom.* Nashville, Tenn.: Walnut Grove Press, 1994.

Foote, Shelby. *The Civil War: A Narrative.* New York: Random House, 1958.

Frech, Mary L, and William F. Swindler (eds.). *Chronology and Documentary Handbook of the State of Florida.* Dobbs Ferry, N.Y.: Oceana Publications, 1973.

Fulks, Bryan. *Black Struggle.* New York: Laurel-Leaf Library, 1969.

Gainsborough, Juliet. *Fenced Off: The Suburbanization of American Politics.* Washington, D.C.: Georgetown University Press, 2001.

Gaquin, Deidre A., and Katherine A. DeBrandt (eds.). *Education Statistics.* Lanham, Md.: Bernan Press, 2000.

Garrow, David J. *Bearing the Cross: Martin Luther King, Jr.* New York: Vintage Books, 1988.

Gayle v. Browder, 352, US 903 (1956).

Geertz, Clifford. *The Interpretation of Culture.* New York: Basic Books, 1973.

Giles, Janice Holt. *Forty Acres and No Mule.* New York: Houghton Mifflin, 1952.

Glaser, James M. *Race, Campaign Politics, and Realignment in the South.* New Haven, Conn.: Yale University Press, 1996.

Glusker, Irwin (ed.). *A Southern Album: Recollections of Some People and Places and Times Gone By.* New York: A&W Visual Library.

Gould, Lewis L. *Grand Old Party: A History of the Republicans.* New York: Random House, 2003.

Grantham, Dewey W. *Southern Progressivism: The Reconciliation of Progress and Tradition.* Knoxville: University of Tennessee Press, 1983.

————. *The South and Modern America: A Region at Odds.* New York: HarperCollins, 1994.

Gray, Virginia, Herbert Jacob, and Robert B. Albritton (eds.). *Politics in the American States.* Glenview, Ill.: Scott Foresman/Little, Brown, 1990.

Gray, Virginia, Russell L. Hanson, and Herbert Jacob (eds.). *Politics in the American States: A Comparative Analysis.* 7th ed. Washington, D.C.: Congressional Quarterly Press, 1999.

Greenville News. October 26, 2002.

Grifffin, Larry J., and Ashley B. Thompson. "Are Southerners a Dying Breed?" *Southern Cultures* 9 (Fall 2003).

Grubbs, Donald H. *Cry from the Cotton.* Chapel Hill: University of North Carolina Press, 1971.

Hadley, Charles D., and Larry Bowman (eds.). *Southern State Party Organizations and Activists.* Westport, Conn.: Praeger, 1995.

Harlan, Louis R. (ed.). *The Booker T. Washington Papers.* Vol. 3. Urbana: University of Illinois Press, 1974.

Harris, Frederick C. *Something Within: Religion in African-American Political Activism.* New York: Oxford University Press, 1999.

Hart, D.G. *Defending the Faith: J. Gresham Machen and the Crisis of Conservative*

Protestantism in Modern America. Grand Rapids, Mich.: Presbyterian & Reformed, 1994.

Hartman, D.B., and Donald C. Bacon. *Rayburn: A Biography*. Austin: Texas Monthly Press, 1987.

Havard, William C. (ed.). *The Changing Politics of the South*. Baton Rouge: Louisiana State University Press, 1972.

Hirsch, E.D. Jr. *Cultural Literacy*. Boston: Houghton Mifflin, 1987.

Henry, O. (William Sidney Porter). "Laws and Order." *Everybody's Magazine*, September 1910.

Holt, Thomas C. *Encyclopedia of Southern Culture*. Chapel Hill: University of North Carolina Press, 1989.

Horowitz, Tony. *Confederates in the Attic*. New York: Vintage Books, 1999.

Howard, Donald S. *The WPA and Federal Relief Policy*. New York: Da Capo Press, 1973.

Hunter, James D. *Culture Wars: The Struggle to Define America*. New York: HarperCollins, 1991.

Jacob, Herbert, and Kenneth N. Vines (eds.). *Politics in the American States*. Boston: Little, Brown, 1965.

Jones, Suzanne W. (ed.). *Growing Up in the South: An Anthology of Modern Southern Literature*. New York: Signet Classics of Penguin Books.

Journal of Black Studies 33 (2003).

Journal of Politics 17 (1955).

——— 36 (1974).

——— 50 (1988).

——— 65 (2003).

Judis, John B., and Ruy Teixeira. *The Emerging Democratic Majority*. New York: Scribner, 2002.

Kantrowitz, Stephen. *Ben Tillman: And the Reconstruction of White Supremacy*. Chapel Hill: University of North Carolina Press, 2000.

Keith, Bruce E., David B. Magleby, Candice J. Nelson, Elizabeth Orr, Mark C. Westyle, and Raymond Wolfinger. *The Myth of the Independent Voter*. Berkeley: University of California Press, 1992.

Key, V.O. *Southern Politics in State and Nation*. 2d ed. Knoxville: University of Tennessee Press, 1977.

Kincaid, John (ed.). *Political Culture, Public Policy, and the American States*. Philadelphia: Institute for Study of Human Issues, 1982.

King, Coretta Scott. *My Life with Martin Luther King, Jr*. New York: Holt, Rinehart & Winston, 1972.

King, Martin Luther Sr., with Clayton Riley. *Daddy King*. New York: Warner Books, 1979.

Kluger, Richard. *Simple Justice: The History of* Brown v. Board of Education *and Black America's Struggle for Equality*. New York: Alfred A. Knopf, 1976.

Knuckley, Jonathan. "The Structure of Party Competitiveness in the South: The Case of Florida." Paper presented at the biennial Citadel Symposium on Southern Politics, Charleston, S.C., March 2004.

Kousser, J. Morgan. *Colorblind Injustice: Minority Voting Rights and the Undoing of the Second Reconstruction*. Chapel Hill: University of North Carolina Press, 1999.

Krane, Dale, and Stephen D. Shaffer. *Mississippi Government and Politics: Modernizers and Traditionalists*. Lincoln: University of Nebraska Press, 1992.

Kroeber, Alfred A., and Clyde Kluckohn. *Culture: A Critical Review of Concepts and Definitions*. New York: Vintage Books, 1963.

Ladd, Everett Carl Jr., and Charles Hadley. *Transformations of the American Party System*. New York: W.W. Norton, 1975.

Lander, Ernest Jr. *South Carolina*. Northbridge, Calif.: Windsor Publications, Inc., 1988.

Larson, Edward J. *Summer for the Gods*. New York: Basic Books, 1997.

Lasher, Stephen. *George Wallace: American Populist*. New York: Addison, Wesley Publishing, 1994.

Lawson, Steven F. *Black Ballots*. New York: Columbia University Press, 1976.

Lee, Harper. *To Kill a Mockingbird*. New York: Warner Books, 1960.

Lefler, Hugh Talmage, and Albert Ray Newsome. *North Carolina: The History of a Southern State*. Chapel Hill: University of North Carolina Press, 1963.

Legge, David, and Lyman A. Kellstedt. *Rediscovering the Religious Factor in American Politics*. Armonk, N.Y.: M.E. Sharpe, 1993.

Levy, Michael B. (ed.). *Political Thought in America: An Anthology*. 2d ed. Prospect Heights, Ill.: Waveland Press, 1992.

Lindsey, William, and Mark Silk. *Religion and Public Life in the Southern Crossroads: Showdown States*. Walnut Creek, Calif.: AltaMira Press, 2005.

Little Rock Democrat-Gazette. June 2, 1991.

Logue, Carl M., and Howard Dorgan. *The Oratory of Southern Demogogues*. Baton Rouge: Louisiana State University Press, 1981.

Longfield, Bradley J. *The Presbyterian Controversy*. New York: Oxford University Press, 1991.

Lyman, Robert Hunt (ed.). *The World Almanac and Book of Facts for 1933*. New York: New York World Telegram, 1933.

Machiavelli. *The Prince*. New York: Viking Press, 1978.

MacManus, Susan A. "Demographic Shifts: The Old South Morphs Into the New." Paper presented at the biennial Citadel Symposium on Southern Politics, Charleston, S.C., March 2004.

Manchester, William. *The Glory and the Dream*. New York: Bantam Books, 1974.

Maraniss, David. *First in His Class: A Biography of Bill Clinton*. New York: Simon & Schuster, 1995.

Marsden, George M. *Fundamentalism and American Culture*. New York: Oxford University Press, 1980.

Martin, William. *With God on Our Side: The Rise of the Religious Right in America*. New York: Broadway Books, 1996.

Marty, Martin E. *Pilgrims in Their Own Land*. New York: Penguin, 1986.

Mathews, Donald C. *Religion in the Old South*. Chicago: University of Chicago Press, 1977.

Mayhew, David R. *Electoral Realignments: A Critique of an American Genre*. New Haven, Conn.: Yale University Press, 2002.

Mays, Benjamin E., and Joseph W. Nicholson. *The Negro's Church*. New York: Arno Press, 1933.

McGill, Ralph. *The South and the Southerner*. Boston: Little, Brown, 1959.

McMurtry, Larry. *In a Narrow Grave: Essays on Texas*. New York: Simon and Schuster, 1968.

Michie, Allan A. *Dixie Demogogues*. New York: Vanguard Press, 1939.

Midwest Journal of Political Science 15 (November 1971).

Miller, Zell. *A National Party No More: The Conscience of a Conservative Democrat*. Macon, Ga.: Stroud & Hall, 2003.

Mitchell, Brodus. *The Rise of the Cotton Mills in the South*. Baltimore: Johns Hopkins University Press, 1921.

Mitchell, Margaret. *Gone With the Wind.* New York: Macmillan, 1936.

Mobile Register. November 4, 1985.

Money Magazine. October 2001.

Morehouse, Sarah McCally, and Malcolm E. Jewell. *State Politics, Parties and Policy.* 2d ed. Lanham, Md.: Rowman & Littlefield, 2003.

Morris, Willie. *North Toward Home.* New York: Dell Publishing, 1967.

National Association of Colored People (NAACP). "Thirty Years of Lynching in the United States." Privately printed, 1967.

Neuhaus, Richard John, and Michael Cromartie (eds.). *Piety and Politics: Evangelicals and Fundamentalists Confront the World.* Washington, D.C.: Ethics and Public Policy Center, 1987.

Neustadt, Richard E. *Presidential Power.* New York: John Wiley & Sons, 1960.

Neumann, Sigmund (ed.). *Modern Political Parties: Approaches to Comparative Politics.* Chicago: University of Chicago Press, 1956.

New Republic. November 4, 1985.

New Yorker. May 28, 1960, June 4, 1960, June 11, 1960.

Niemi, Richard G. (ed.). *The Politics of Future Citizens.* San Fransisco: Jossey-Bass, 1974.

Oates, Stephen B. *Let the Trumpet Sound.* New York: Harper & Row, 1982.

O'Connor, Flannery. *Mystery and Manners.* New York: Farrar, Strauss and Giroux, 1961.

Olasky, Marvin. *Compassionate Conservatism.* New York: Free Press, 2000.

———— *The Tragedy of American Compassion.* Washington, D.C.: Regnery Gateway, 1992.

Olson, Laura, and Sue Crawford (eds.). *Christian Clergy in American Politics.* Baltimore: Johns Hopkins University Press, 2001.

Parker, Joseph B. (ed.) *Politics in Mississippi.* Salem, Wis.: Sheffield Publishing Co., 1993.

Parsons, Talcott. *The Social System.* New York: Free Press, 1951.

Polity 2, no. 1 (Fall 1969).

Pollack, Norman (ed.). *The Populist Mind.* New York: Bobbs-Merrill, 1967.

Potter, David M. *The South and the Concurrent Majority.* Baton Rouge: Louisiana State University Press, 1972.

Pride, Richard A., and J. David Woodard. *The Burden of Busing.* Knoxville: University of Tennessee Press, 1985.

Raines, Howell. *My Soul Is Rested.* New York: Putnam, 1977.

Ransom, Roger, and Richard Sutch. *One Kind of Freedom.* New York: Cambridge University Press, 1977.

Reagan, Charles W. *Baptized in Blood: The Religion of the Lost Cause, 1865–1920.* Athens: University of Georgia Press, 1980.

Reagan, Charles W., and William Ferris (eds.). *The Encyclopedia of Southern Culture.* Chapel Hill: University of North Carolina Press, 1989.

Reed, John Shelton. *The Enduring South: Subcultural Persistence in Mass Society.* Chapel Hill: University of North Carolina Press, 1986.

———— *Southerners: The Social Psychology of Sectionalism.* Chapel Hill: University of North Carolina Press, 1983.

Reed, Ralph. *Active Faith: How Christians Are Changing the Soul of American Politics.* New York: Free Press, 1996.

Robertson, Ben. *Red Hills and Cotton.* Columbia: University of South Carolina Press, 1942.

Rodgers, Marion Elizabeth (ed.). *Mencken and Sara: A Life in Letters.* New York: McGraw-Hill, 1987.

Rosenbaum, Walter A. *Political Culture.* New York: Praeger. 1975.

Sabato, Larry. *Goodbye to Good-time Charlie.* 2d ed. Washington, D.C.: Congressional Quarterly Press, 1983.

Sale, Kirkpatrick. *Power Shift: The Rise of the Southern Rim and Its Challenge to the Eastern Establishment.* New York: Random House, 1976.

Sams, Ferroll. *Run with the Horsemen.* New York: Viking Penguin, 1982.

———— *The Whisper of the River.* New York: Viking Penguin, 1984.

Scammon, Richard M., and Ben J. Wattenberg. *The Real Majority.* New York: Coward, McGann and Geoghpean, Inc., 1971.

Schaeffer, Francis A. *A Christian Manifesto.* Westchester, Ill.: Crossway Books, 1981.

Schattschneider, E.E. *The Semisovereign People: A Realist's View of Democracy.* New York: Holt, Rinehart and Winston, 1960.

Sernett, Milton C. (ed.). *African American Religious History.* Durham, N.C.: Duke University Press, 1999.

Shaara, Michael. *The Killer Angels.* New York: Random House, 1974.

Shuptrine, Hubert, and James Dickey. *Jericho: The South Beheld.* Birmingham, Ala.: Oxmoor House, 1974.

Simkins, Francis B., and Charles P. Roland. *A History of the South.* New York: Alfred A. Knopf, 1947.

Sims, George E. The *Little Man's Big Friend: James E. Folsom in Alabama Politics, 1945–1956.* Tuscaloosa: University of Alabama Press, 1985.

Smith, Mark Caleb. "With Friends Like This: The Religious Right, the Republican Party and the Politics of the American South." PhD Dissertation, University of Georgia, 2002.

Smith, Oran. *The Rise of Baptist Republicanism.* New York: New York University Press, 1997.

Snider, William D. *Helms and Hunt: The North Carolina Senate Race, 1984.* Chapel Hill: University of North Carolina Press, 1985.

Social Science Quarterly 71, 1990.

Sorenson, Theodore C. *Kennedy.* New York: Harper & Row, 1995.

Southern Politics Collection, Vanderbilt University.

Stacks, John F. *Watershed: The Campaign for the Presidency, 1980.* New York: New York Times Books, 1981.

Stonecash, Jeffrey M. *Class and Party in American Politics.* Boulder, Colo.: Westview Press, 2000.

Stonecash, Jeffrey M., Mark D. Brewer, and Mack D. Mariani. *Diverging Parties.* Boulder, Colo.: Westview Press, 2003.

Sundquist, James L. *Dynamics of the Party System: Alignment and Realignment of Political Parties in the United States.* Washington, D.C.: Brookings Institution, 1973.

Talon News. August 22, 2003.

Time Magazine. September 28, 1976.

Tindall, George B. *The Emergence of the New South: 1913–1945.* Baton Rouge: Louisiana University Press, 1967.

———— *South Carolina Negroes: 1877–1900.* Columbia: University of South Carolina Press, 1952.

Tolson, Jay. *Pilgrim in the Ruins: A Life of Walker Percy.* Chapel Hill: University of North Carolina Press, 1994.

Twelve Southerners. *I'll Take My Stand: The South and the Agrarian Tradition.* New York: Peter Smith, 1951.

University of California Regent v. Bakke, 438, US 265 (1978).

U.S. News and World Report, December 19, 1988.

Van Horn, Carl (ed.). *The State of the States*. Washington, D.C.: Congressional Quarterly Press, 1996.

Wald, Kenneth D. *Religion and Politics in the United States*. 2d ed. Washington, D.C.: Congressional Quarterly, 1992.

Wald, Kenneth D., and Ted G. Jelen. "Religion and Political Socialization in Context: A Regional Comparison of the Political Attitudes of American Jews." Paper presented at the biennial Citadel Symposium on Southern Politics, Charleston, S.C., March 2004.

Wallace, Cornelia. *C'Nelia*. New York: A.J. Holman Company, 1976.

Warren, Robert Penn. *All the King's Men*. New York: Harcourt, Brace and Jovanovich, 1946.

Watkins, T.H. *The Great Depression*. Boston: Little, Brown, 1993.

Weaver, Richard. *The Southern Tradition at Bay*. Washington, D.C.: Regnery, 1989.

Wheat, Leonard F., and William H. Crown. *State Per-Capita Change Since 1950*. Westport, Conn.: Greenwood Press, 1995.

Wicker, Tom. *JFK and LBJ*. Baltimore: Penguin Books, 1968.

Wilcox, Clyde. *Onward Christian Soldiers: The Religious Right in American Politics*. Boulder, Colo.: Westview Press, 1996.

Williams, T. Harry. *Huey Long*. New York: Alfred A. Knopf, 1969.

——— *Romance and Realism in Southern Politics*. Athens: University of Georgia Press, 1961.

Wills, Garry. *Under God: Religion and American Politics*. New York: Simon and Schuster, 1990.

Wilmore, Gayraud S., and James H. Cone. *Black Theology: A Documentary History, 1966–1979*. New York: Orbis Books, 1979.

Wilson, Charles Reagan, and William Ferris (eds.). *Encyclopedia of Southern Culture*. Chapel Hill: University of North Carolina Press, 1989.

Wolfe, Thomas. *"Of Time and the River."* New York: Charles Scribner's Sons, 1934.

Woodson, C.G. *The History of the Negro Church*. Washington, D.C.: Associated Publishers, 1921.

Woodward, C. Vann. *The Burden of Southern History*. Baton Rouge: Louisiana State University Press, 1960.

——— *Origins of the New South: 1877–1913*. Baton Rouge: Louisiana State University Press, 1951.

——— *Tom Watson: Agrarian Rebel*. New York: Oxford University Press, 1938.

Wooten, James. *Dasher: The Roots and Rising of Jimmy Carter*. New York: Warner Books, 1979.

Wright, Gavin. *Old South, New South: Revolutions in the Southern Economy Since the Civil War*. New York: Basic Books, 1986.

Wright, Lawrence. *In the New World: Growing Up with America*. New York: Alfred A. Knopf, 1988.

www.cato.org.

www.pewtrusts.com/campaigndisclosure.

www.sbc.net.

Young, Thomas D., Floyd C. Watkins, and Richmond C. Beatty (eds.). *The Literature of the South*. Atlanta: Scott, Foresman and Co., 1968.

Index

About the Book

In this comprehensive new text, J. David Woodard integrates the best features of a state-by-state focus on politics in the southern states with a thematic overview of the region's social, economic, and political life.

Notably, the text:

- Profiles significant figures and events from the real world of politics
- Highlights vital dimensions of political culture (e.g., race, religion, and partisanship)
- Navigates essential historical context
- Underscores the region's growing role in national politics
- Incorporates up-to-date coverage of ongoing controversies and trends
- Suggests a well-defined organizational structure for courses

Treating subjects as diverse as the Confederate flag dispute, the role of women in society, and the region's military traditions, *The New Southern Politics* is an innovative and readable introduction designed to engage students and scholars alike.

J. David Woodard is Strom Thurmond Professor of Government at Clemson University. His publications include *The Conservative Tradition in America* (with Charles Dunn).